APPLIED TECH

fo

Golden Key
Educational Publishing

Paul Enright

Acknowledgements

Paul Enright and Golden Key would like to thank the following people for their assistance in the publication of this book:

The Enright family
Paul McCarthy and his technology students, Loreto Secondary School, Balbriggan
Pat Boylan, Gerry Leavy and Colin Daly, Skerries Community College
Eugene Osborne, Stephen Leader and John Knox
David, Aisling, Isabel, Leo and Des Cooke.

Exam questions are reproduced with the permission of the State Examinations Commission.

Picture credits

Photographs are the copyright of Dreamstime.com or as listed in Appendix 1.

Golden Key

56 Holmpatrick
Skerries
Co. Dublin

Tel. 01 849 0598

www.goldenkey.ie
info@goldenkey.ie

ISBN - 13: 978-1- 9998293-2-2

Published by Golden Key Educational Publishing, 2020.
Second edition

Design by: Acrobat Design, Skerries, Co. Dublin.

Printed in Ireland by Printrun Ltd, Ballymount, Dublin 12.

Contents

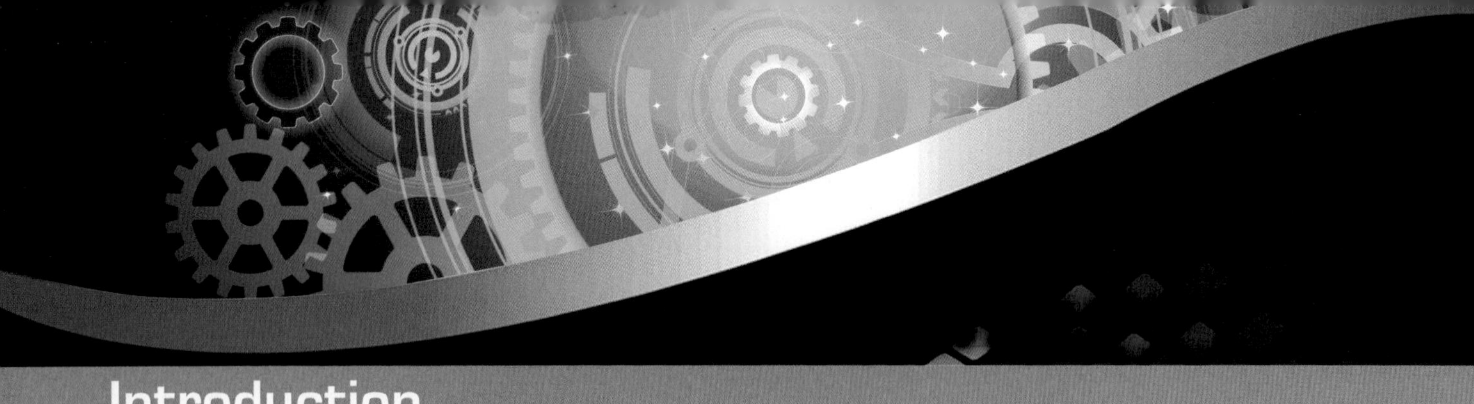

Introduction

Welcome to Junior Cycle Applied Technology. This is a practical book that will help you to understand technology, build your own technology projects, and to do well in your examinations and Classroom-Based Assessments (CBAs).

The diagram below shows how the chapters are related, and how you can progress through the book. Early chapters develop your knowledge and skills in areas such as materials, mechanisms and electronics. Later chapters, such as "Assembling projects" and "Design and manufacture" help you to bring these different skills together.

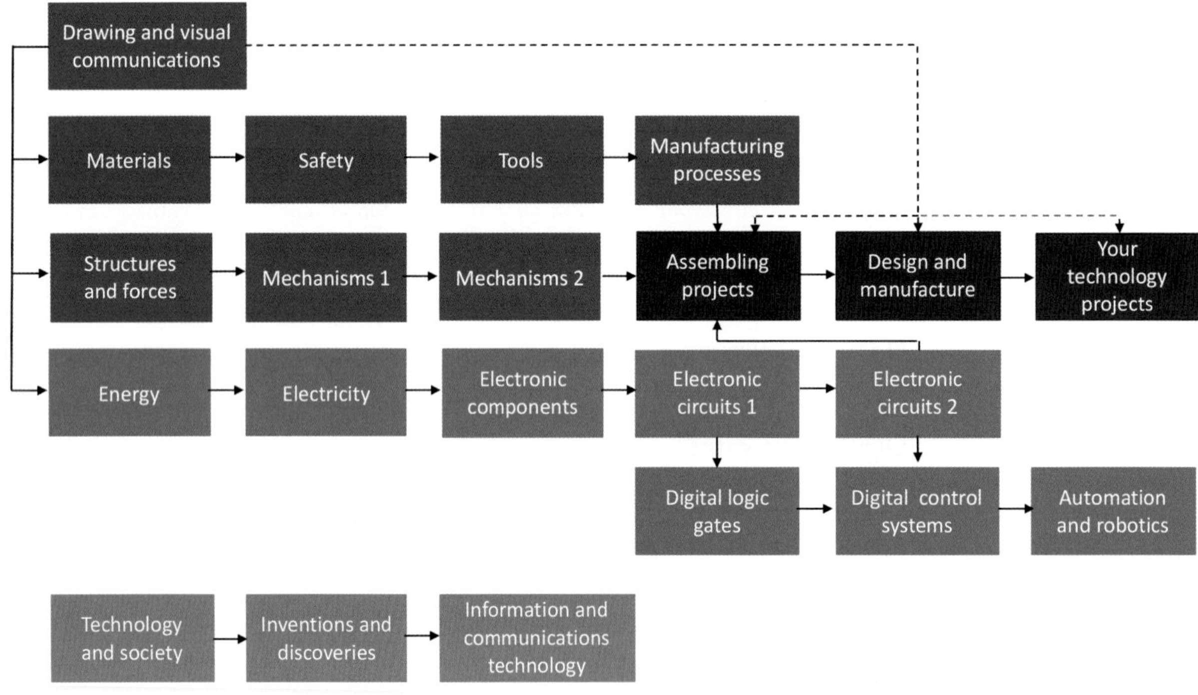

Key:	Strand 1 Principles and practices	Strand 2 Energy and control	Strand 3 Technology and society	The project process

CHAPTER 1

Drawing and visual communication

Introduction

Drawing is an important way of communicating about how products and designs should look, and how they should be made. This chapter explains different types of drawings, and gives you plenty of practice at producing them yourself. It also mentions other forms of visual communication such as logos, emblems, reports and graphs.

What you need to know for exams and projects

Drawing is a very important part of your skills for technology for Junior Cert. Drawing will help you with all your practical activities, projects, exams and with other chapters in this book. The skills required for exams and for projects are listed below.

For your examinations you must be able to:	For your projects you must be able to:
• Sketch developments, orthographic and isometric drawings. • Add dimensioning and rendering to drawings. • State the advantages of CAD, logos, reports, graphs, and icons.	• Create multiple design sketches. • Create detailed manufacturing drawings with dimensions. • Draw circuit diagrams/schematics. • Draw wiring diagrams.

Drawing techniques

This section provides a summary of drawing and visual communication techniques. Later sections help you to practice each technique.

A **2D object** has only two dimensions: height and width.

A **3D object** has three dimensions: height, width, and depth (distance away from you).

There is a basic problem when it comes to drawing objects. They have three dimensions but paper has only two dimensions. So how do we draw a 3D object on a 2D piece of paper? Luckily, there are several standard techniques for this. Drawings of 3D objects are often called projections because a 3D object is projected onto 2D paper.

Pictorial drawings

A pictorial drawing is any drawing where the object looks like it is in 3D, i.e. it appears to have depth, and the object is being viewed from a certain angle. The two main types of pictorial drawings are perspective and isometric, which are described below.

Perspective drawings

In perspective drawings, the depth of 3D objects is shown by converging lines. There are two types of perspective drawings, single-point perspective and two-point perspective.

In single-point perspective, the depth lines converge at one vanishing point (VP) whereas in two-point perspective the depth lines converge at two vanishing points.

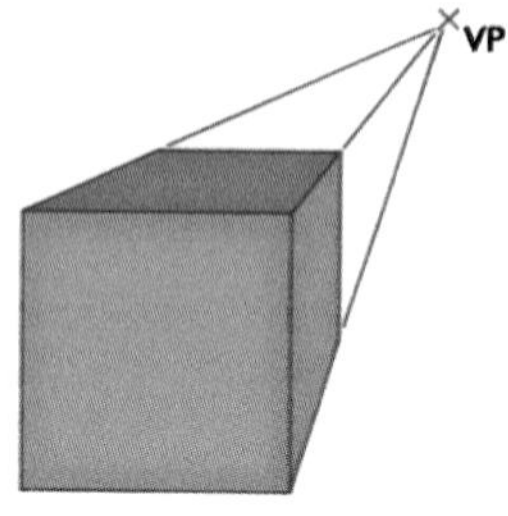

Single-point perspective

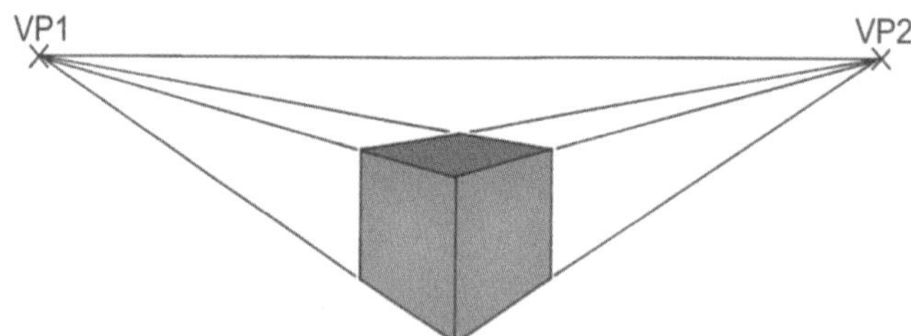

Two-point perspective

Isometric drawings

In an isometric drawing, vertical lines on the object remain vertical, but all horizontal lines on the object are drawn at 30° to the horizontal.

In contrast to perspective drawings, the depth lines are parallel and do not converge at a vanishing point. Isometric drawings are not as realistic as perspective drawings, but they are easier to draw because the depth lines are parallel. You can use isometric grid paper as a template.

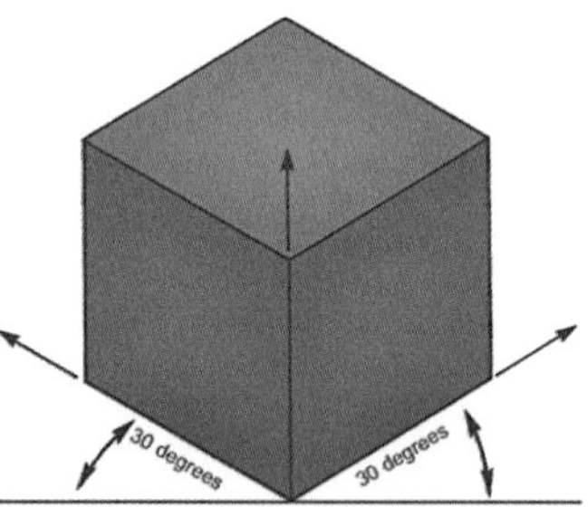

Isometric drawing

Exploded views

Exploded views are also called assembly drawings. This type of pictorial drawing shows you how to assemble items. It shows objects a distance apart so that you can see how they are designed to fit together.

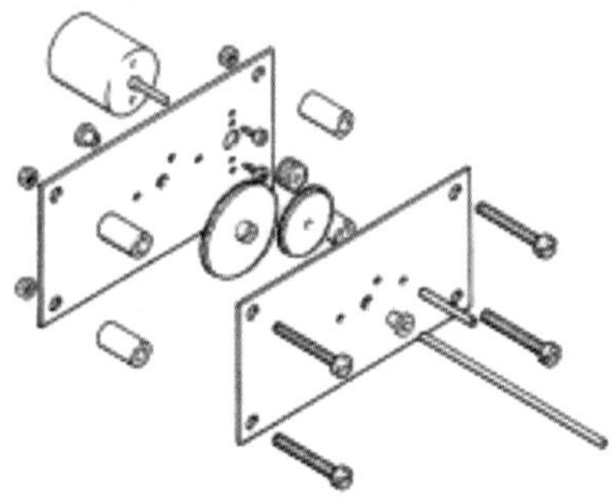

Exploded view

Cutaway drawings

A cutaway drawing shows part of the casing or other components cut away, as if they were not there, so that you can see other components inside. Cutaway drawings are often used by students to show hidden workings in models, as in the drawing shown.

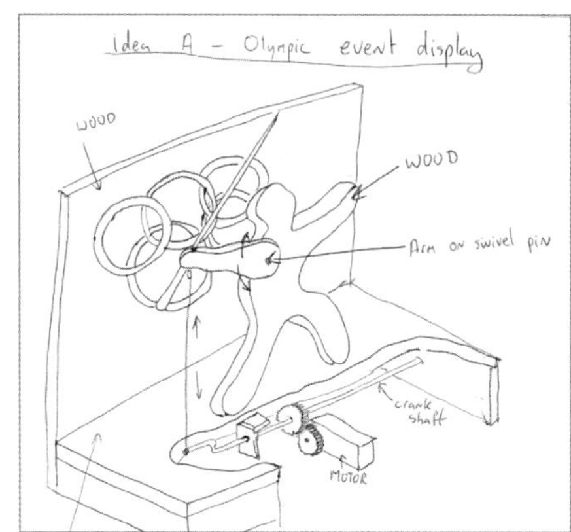

Dotted or dashed lines can be used to show where the original edge of the object was, before it was drawn as cut away.

Orthographic drawings

Orthographic drawing is a technique for representing 3D objects by making two or more 2D drawings of the object, with each one taken from a different angle/viewpoint. Orthographic drawings usually consist of one or more side views, called elevations, and/or a top view, called a plan.

Elevation

An elevation is a 2D drawing of the object, drawn as if you were looking at it from one side. You may need two elevation drawings to provide enough information, e.g. one from the front and one from the side (at 90° to each other).

Plan

A plan is a 2D drawing of the object as if you were looking down at it from above.

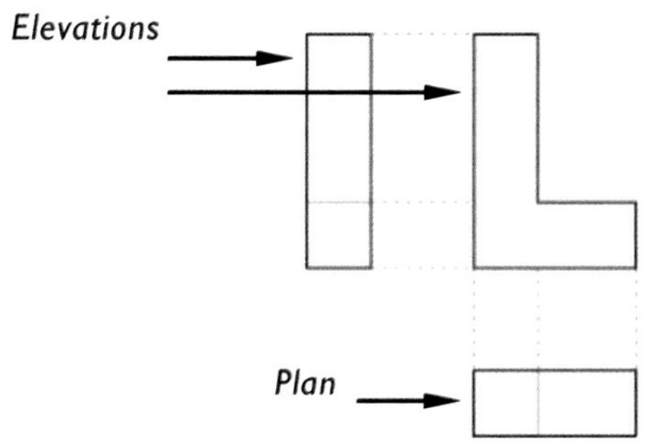

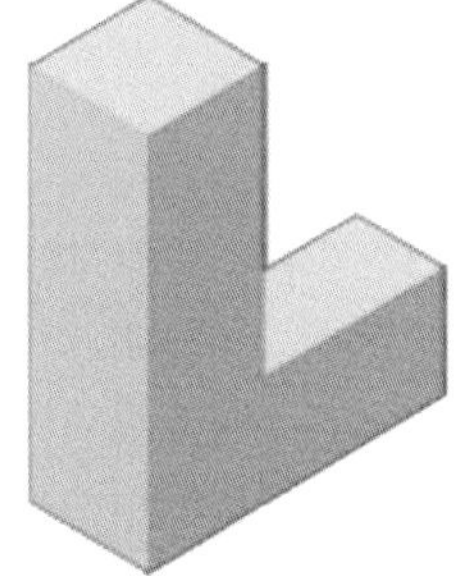

Two elevation views and a plan view of the object shown on the right

Hand-drawn sketches

Sketches are drawn freehand, without using a ruler. They can be pictorial drawings or 2D drawings.

Development drawing

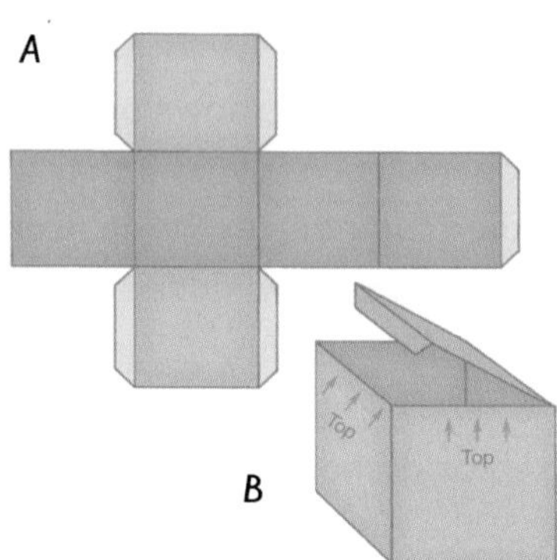

A development is a type of drawing that shows how a 2D shape can be folded up to make a 3D shape. In the picture, diagram A is the development of diagram B, i.e. you can make B by folding up A.

Take apart a cereal box carefully (where it is glued) to see how this is done.

Rendering

Rendering is a collection of techniques for shading, colouring, adding shadows, and drawing patterns on surfaces to make them look more realistic and three dimensional, such as in the sketch of a magnifying glass.

Dimensioning

Dimensioning is the correct way to indicate size measurements on drawings. Each measurement should be shown using an arrow. The value and units should be written beside the arrow.

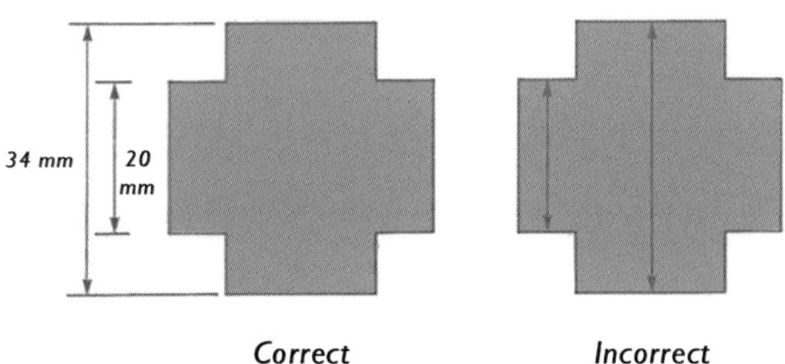

Correct *Incorrect*

Designing a car using a CAD system

CAD

CAD (computer-aided design) software is used to design objects on a computer. It can produce very detailed and high quality 2D and 3D drawings, with rendering and dimensions.

CAD drawings can be used by manufacturing software to control the machines that make those objects.

Advantages and disadvantages of CAD

Drawings are easy to store digitally, easier to change than paper, and easy to transmit to others. However, the computers and software are more expensive than paper.

Electrical diagrams

Electrical diagrams show how electronic components are connected. There are two main types: circuit diagrams (or schematics) and wiring diagrams.

Circuit or schematic diagrams

Circuit diagrams use symbols to show how electronic components are connected in an electric circuit.

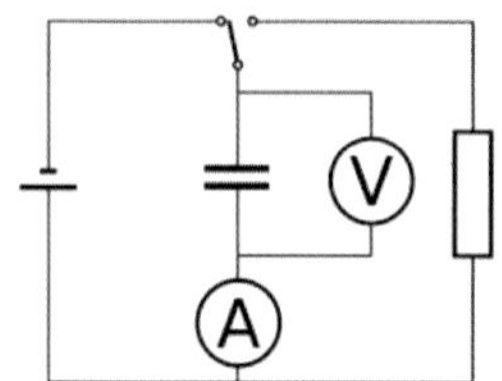

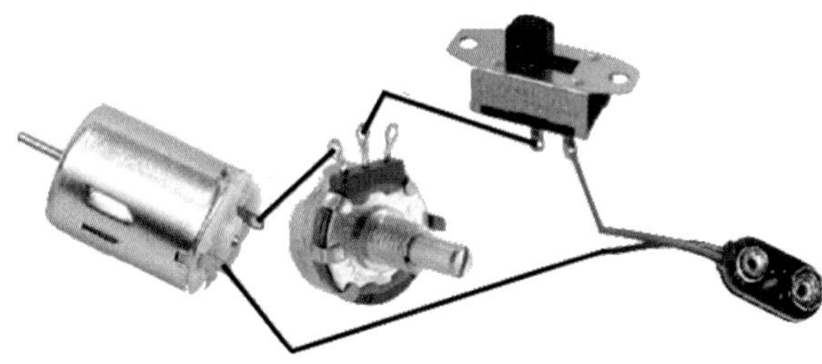

Wiring diagrams

Wiring diagrams show how the physical components of a circuit are wired together.

Other types of visual communication

Logos, emblems, icons

Logos or emblems are symbols that represent an organisation. Logos generally represent a company or product and serve a commercial purpose. Emblems usually relate to a non-commercial organisation or idea, e.g. the Olympic Games. Companies use logos to create an instantly recognizable brand.

Emblem of the Olympic Games

Icons are symbols used on computer screens to represent a certain function. The advantage of icons is that they take up little space and are internationally recognized.

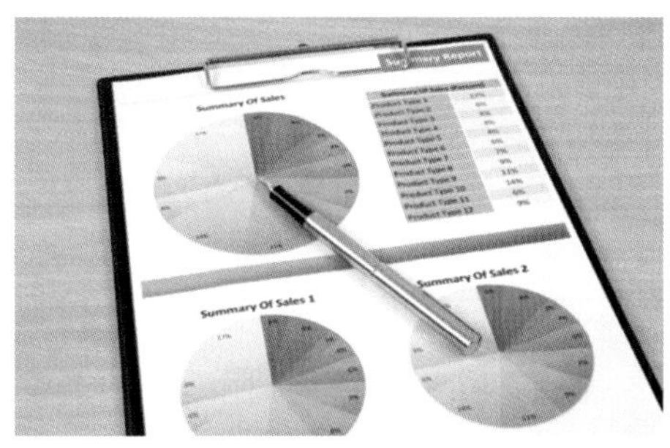

Business report

Reports and presentations

Most forms of technical communication are compiled into reports or multimedia presentations. Reports usually contain lots of drawings, graphs and photos as well as text.

Multi-media presentations are designed to be projected on large screens and often have video and audio playback as well as graphs and photos, and small amounts of large-sized text so that they can be viewed from a distance.

Graphs and charts

Graphs are a highly effective way of summarising data in a visual way. Most people find graphs much easier to understand than numbers on their own.

There are a number of different types, such as line graphs (shown), bar charts and pie charts.

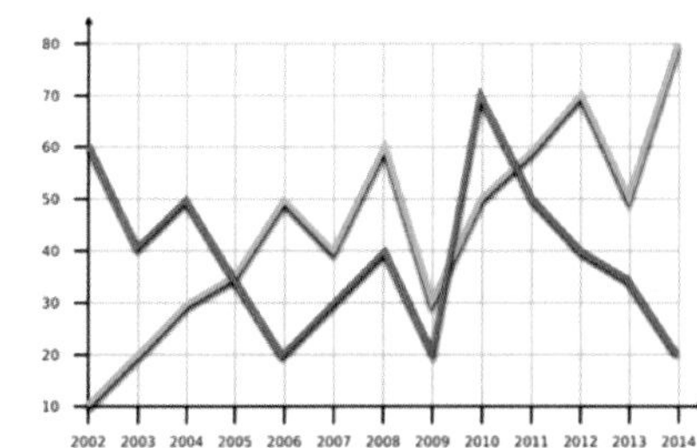

Photos and images

Photos and images convey meaning, improve visual layout and give a professional look to communications.

Test yourself

1. Name the type of projection shown.

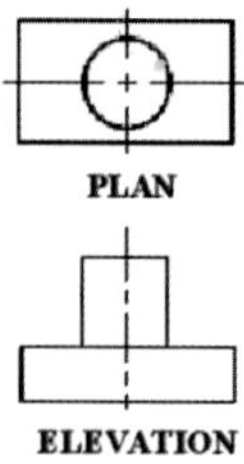

2. What does perspective mean?
3. What are the two common types of perspective drawings?
4. What is meant by a development?
5. What is meant by rendering?
6. The four drawings on the right provide different views of the same object:
   (i) What is the name of the view at X?
   (ii) What type of drawing is shown on the bottom left?

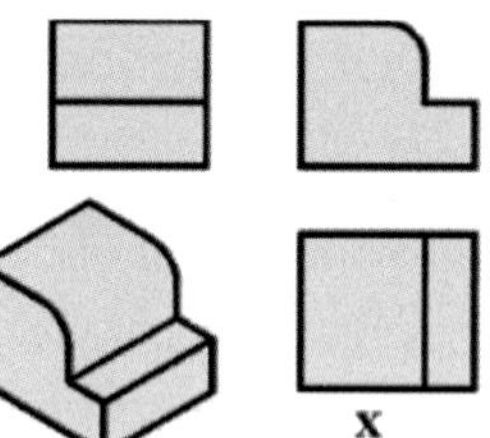

7. Identify each of the drawings below as one of the following types:
   (i) Exploded view.
   (ii) Elevation.
   (iii) Plan view.
   (iv) Pictorial view.
   (v) Development.
   (vi) Perspective projection.
   (vii) Isometric projection.

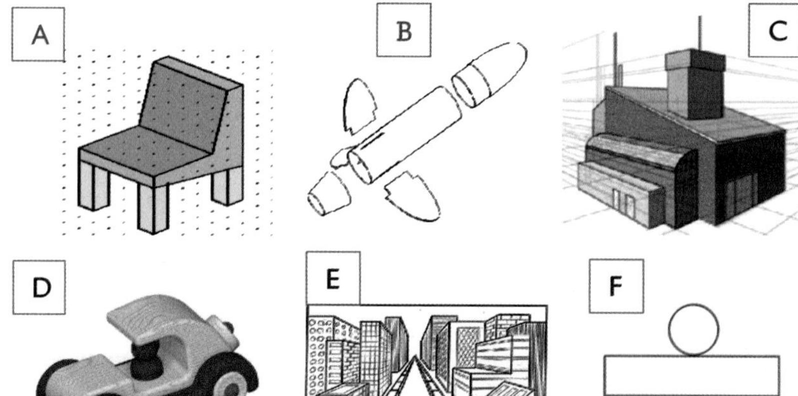

8. What is the difference between a circuit diagram and a wiring diagram?
9. What does CAD mean? State two advantages and one disadvantage of CAD drawings.
10. Why do companies use logos?
11. What is meant by dimensioning?
12. Name two types of graphs or charts.
13. Why are cutaway drawings useful?
14. Which of the shapes A, B or C shown opposite is a rotation of shape X?

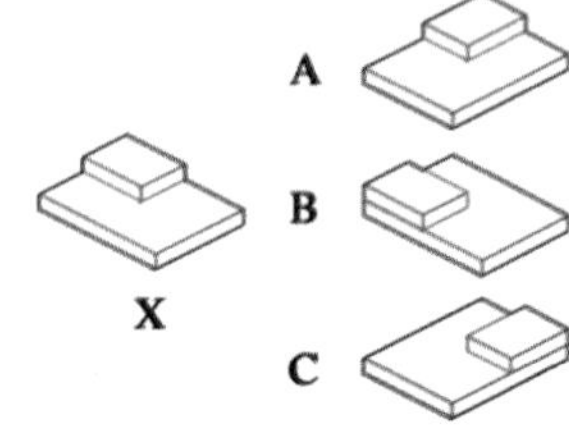

Drawing equipment

Before you start to practice drawing, you will need to have the following equipment:

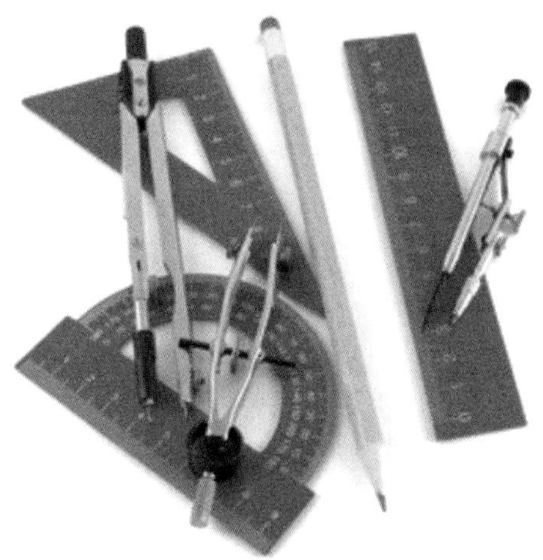

- A4 or A3 sheets of paper.
- Pencils (a selection from 3B to 3H).
- Some coloured pencils.
- Ruler, eraser, sharpener.
- Compass for circles, stencils for ellipses.
- Protractor for measuring angles.
- Set squares: 45° and 30°/60°.
- Drawing board and T-square.
- Isometric paper (you will find some at the back of this book).

Practising drawing basic shapes and viewpoints

Carry out the activities below to get used to drawing basic shapes, and to get used to the idea of seeing things from different viewpoints. This is useful before you go on to more complex shapes. The 3D drawings requested here do not need to be isometric or perspective drawings, just pictorial sketches.

Activities

Using a ruler:

1. Draw a number of parallel lines.
2. Draw another set of parallel lines on the same page at 90° to the first set of parallel lines.
3. Draw a number of different sized rectangles on the same page.
4. Draw a number of different-sized circles on the same page.

You can do the following as freehand sketches, or using a ruler:

5. Draw a cube when seen from the top only (plan).
6. Draw a cube when seen from the side only (elevation).
7. Draw a cube when looking downwards at it from a slight angle, with a top corner closest to you.
8. Draw an isometric diagram of a cube.
9. Draw a 2-point perspective diagram of a cube.
10. Draw a cylinder (e.g. a tin can) when seen from the side only. What shape is it?
11. Draw a cylinder when seen from the top only. What shape is it?
12. Draw a cylinder when seen from an angle.
13. Draw a cone shape when seen from the side only (elevation). What shape is it?
14. Draw a cone shape when seen from the top only (plan). What shape is it?

Activities

15. Draw a cone shape when seen from an angle looking down at it.
16. Choose a simple solid object around you. It could be a pencil, an eraser, a block of wood. Position it at different angles to you and draw what you see. Draw the edges that you can see, and the angles they are at.
17. Decide which of the developments shown below (A, B, C or D) will fold up to make the die shown. Now make the cubic die, of side 5cm, from paper or cardboard.

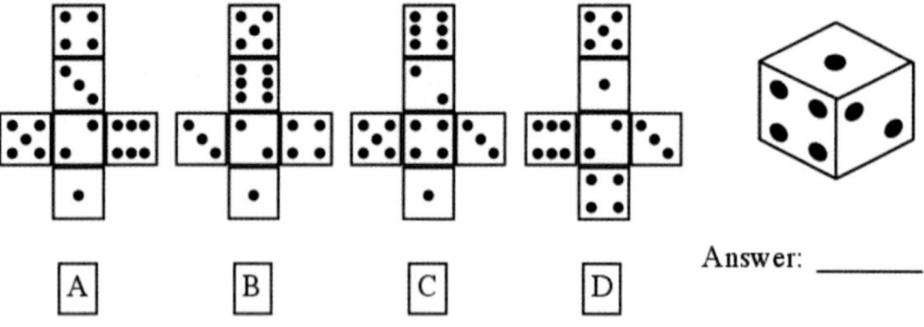

Answer: _______

Practising dimensioning

The following techniques are used for dimensioning. Dimensions are assumed to be in millimetres (mm).

Dimensioning straight lines

When dimensioning straight lines:

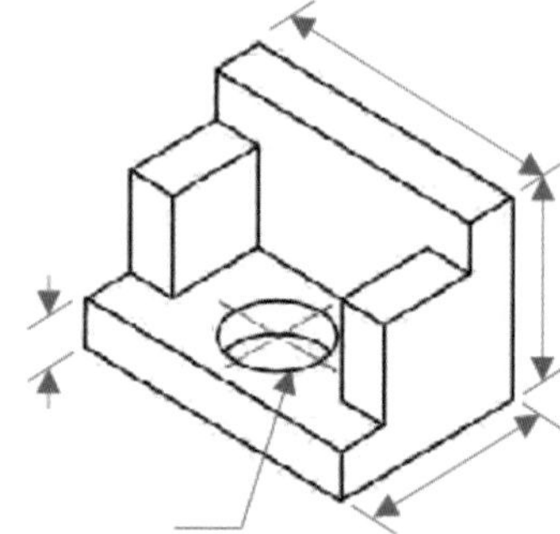

- Use a double-headed arrow to indicate length.
- Place the arrow outside the object, not on it.
- Extend out lines from the ends of the object (as shown) to show what distance the arrow refers to.
- If the drawing is isometric (like the example shown), extend the lines out on the isometric grid at 30° (same as the object lines).
- Write in the value and units of each dimension beside each arrow. (Not shown in example.)

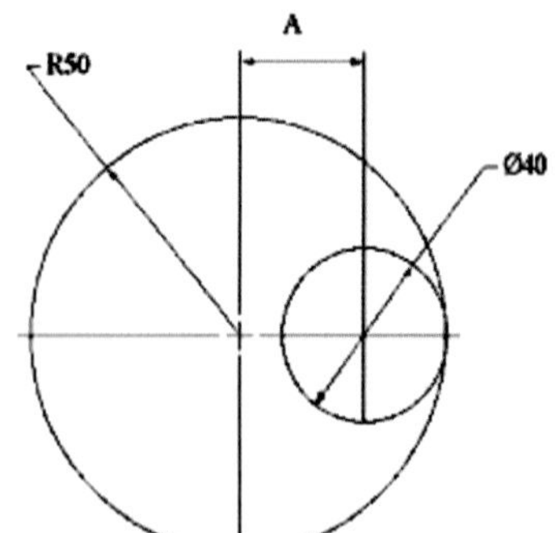

Dimensioning circles, spheres or arcs

Circles and arcs (part of a circle) are dimensioned by writing down the value of the length of the radius or the diameter of the circle. For circles:

- Draw in the radius or diameter of the circle, as a double-headed arrow.
- Extend the arrow line outwards and write in the length of the radius or diameter at the end.
- Use the symbol R for radius and the symbol ∅ for the diameter.

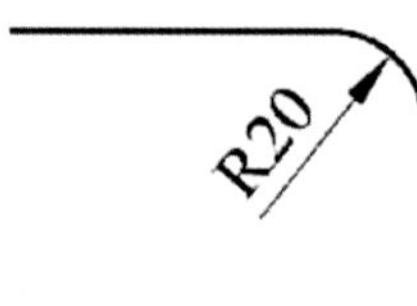

When dimensioning arcs, do not draw in the radius, just point to the arc with the arrow and indicate the radius value.

Activities

Use a fine pencil for these activities.

1. Using the diagrams of the basic shapes you made in the previous activities, add in dimensions for each side. You can make up the values. Show the dimensions of the circle part of the cylinder and the cone. Show the dimensions on the 3D drawings as well as on the 2D drawings.

2. Draw in two dimensions on the diagram shown.

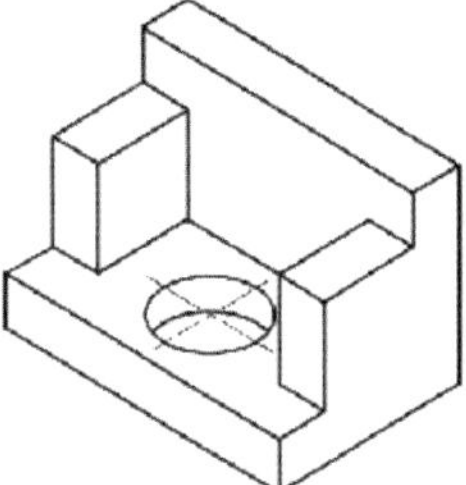

Test yourself

1. Calculate the dimensions A and B on the diagram shown on the right.

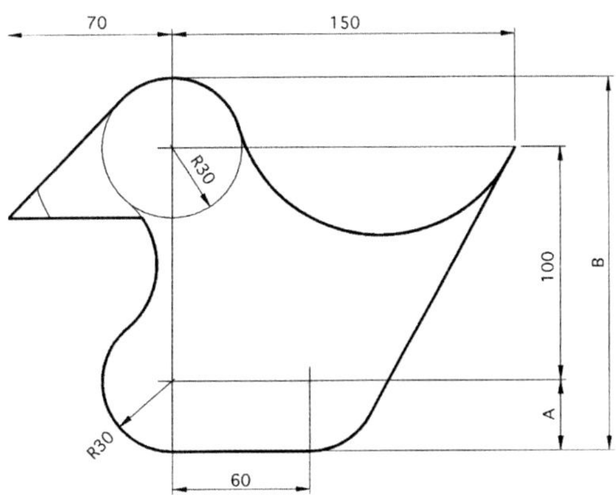

2. What is the diameter of the large circle shown?

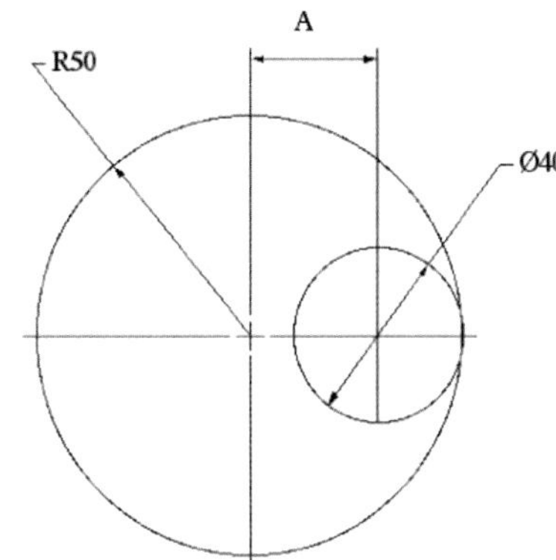

Practising rendering

The following techniques are used for rendering.

Shading

Shading shows the effect of adding an imaginary source of light, and light and dark sides, to make the object look more realistic. In the example shown, the light is coming from the left.

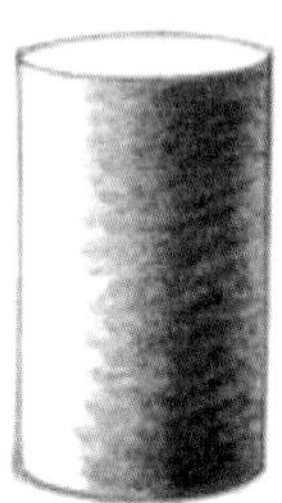

When shading:

- Pick a place or an angle from where imaginary light would be shining on the object.
- Darken the sides of the object that would not be lit up directly by the imaginary light.
- Use a very soft pencil (e.g. 2B or 3B) to shade.

Adding shadows

Adding shadows can add more realism to an already-shaded diagram, by adding a shadow to the surface on which the object is resting. When adding shadows:

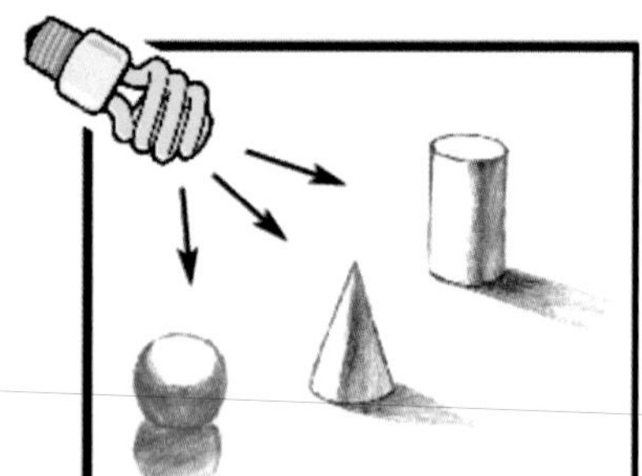

- Use the same location for the imaginary light as when adding shading.
- Extend out the imaginary rays of light beyond the edges of the object.
- Shade in the area inside the imaginary rays on the surface that the object is resting on.
- Blur the edges of the shadow.

Colouring

Colouring makes a drawing more attractive, distinguishes different parts, and can make it look more realistic.

- If you are shading, do the shading first, then the colouring.
- Choose colours close to those in real life.
- Do not use too many colours.

It may not be necessary to colour in the background.

Texturing

Texturing techniques are used to indicate the type of material used, e.g. wood or plastic.

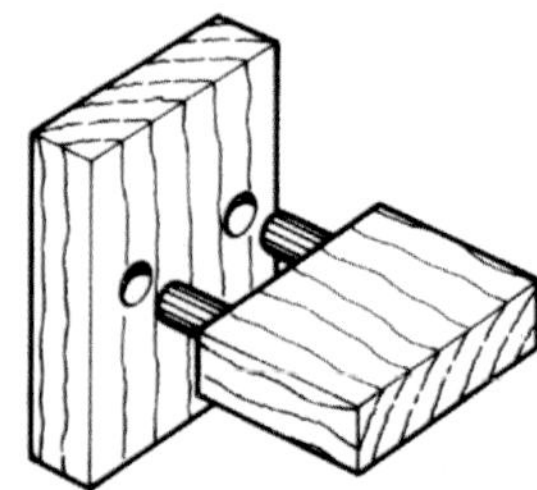

Texturing to indicate wood

When texturing to show that an object is made from wood, draw light wavy patterns on the surface to indicate grain.

Texturing to indicate plastic, glass and metal

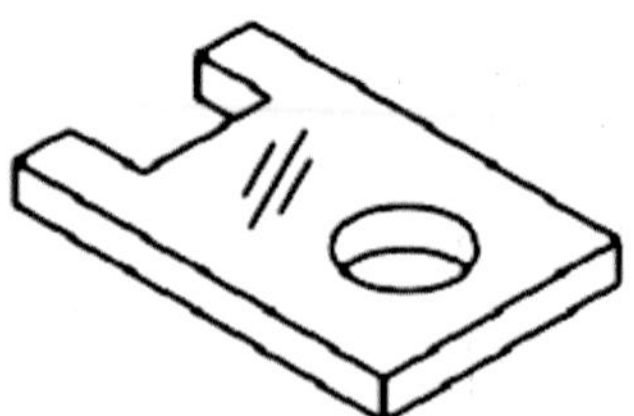

Draw two or three parallel lines on the surface to indicate the material is flat, shiny and reflective, e.g. acrylic. This technique is also useful for indicating glass or metal.

Hatching

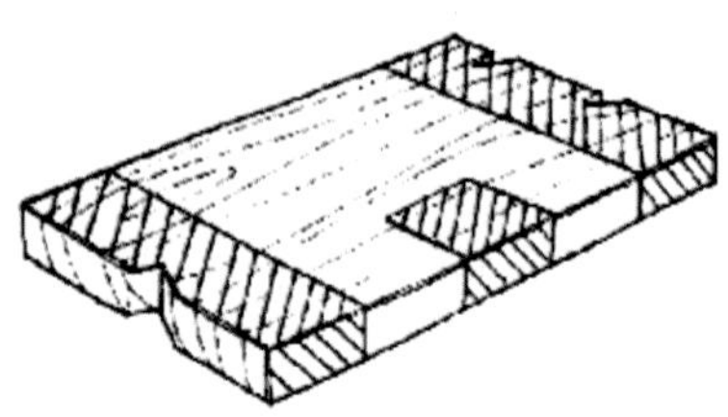

Shading by drawing parallel, angled lines that are close together is called hatching. Hatching is often used to indicate waste material. When a drawing shows how to cut a piece of material, the pieces to be cut away (the waste pieces) can be indicated with hatched lines.

Worked example: Apply shading and shadow

Past exam question

Apply shading to the sketch to suggest a light source in the position shown.

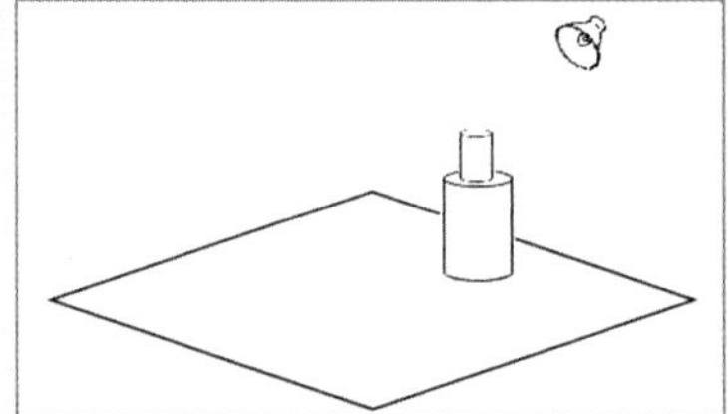

Valid answer

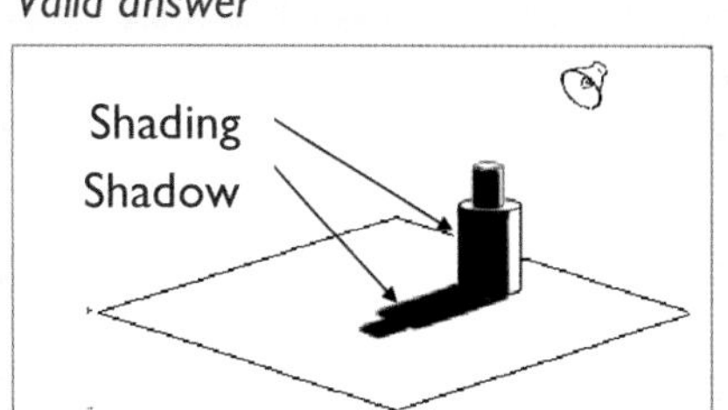

Worked example: Apply shading and shadow

Past exam question

Use two rendering techniques on the graphic shown to suggest a sphere.

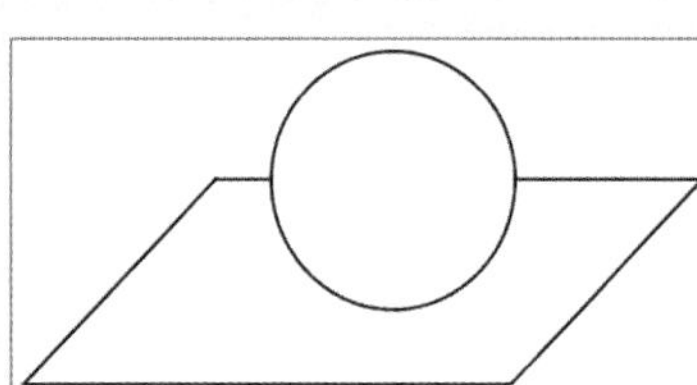

Valid answer

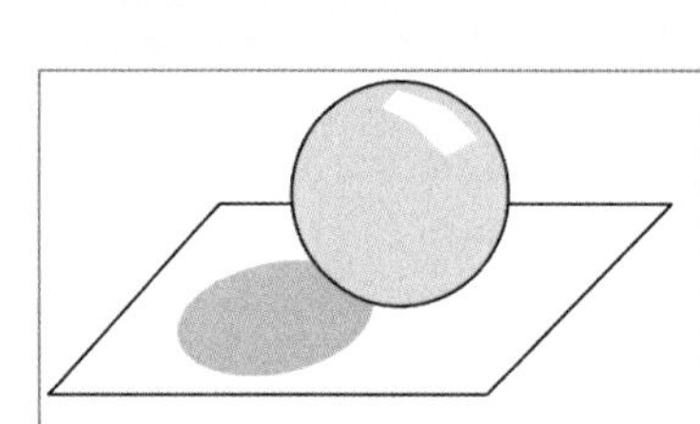

Worked example: Rendering/cutaway

Past exam question

State two pieces of information communicated by the sketch.

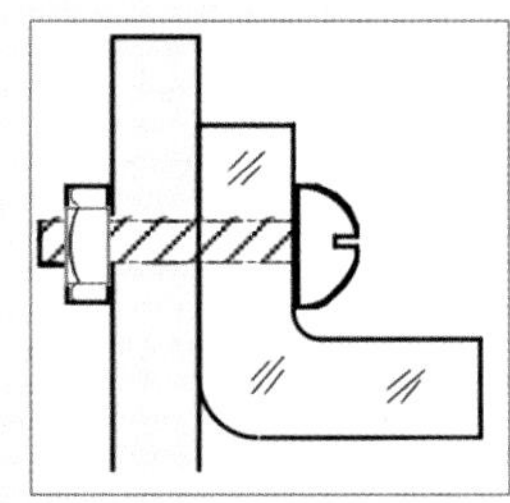

Valid answers

- The right hand object is made of metal or plastic.
- The screw goes through a hole in both pieces of material to join with the nut on the other side.

Test yourself

1. What material is this shape made from?

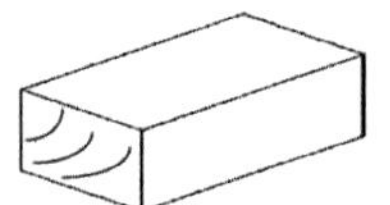

2. Use two rendering techniques on the image below to suggest a light source at X.

Activities

1. Place a small rectangular block of wood in front of you. Notice which parts are lighter and darker. Move the block around, closer to the light, twist it around, to see how the light and dark patterns change. Draw what you see, shading in. Is there a shadow?
2. Using the 3D drawings of the cube, cylinder and cone that you drew in the previous activities, draw in a light source in one corner of the drawing, and shade in the darker side(s) of the object. Some parts of the object may be darker than others.
3. On the above drawings, add in a shadow, as if the object was resting on the ground.
4. Repeat activities 2 and 3 with the light source in a different position on the drawings.
5. With the above drawings, indicate that the cube is made from acrylic, and the cylinder is made from wood.
6. Add some colour to the above drawings.
7. Draw a ball without any shading. What shape do you get? Is it easy to tell that it is a ball?
8. Try to indicate that the ball is three dimensional by adding shading.
9. Place a real ball in front of you. Notice which parts of the ball are lighter and darker than others. Draw what you see.

Past exam questions

1. Apply shading to the sketch to suggest a light source at X.

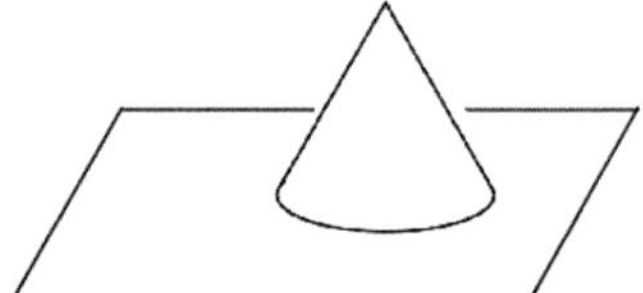

2. Use two rendering techniques on the sketch shown to suggest a light source at X.

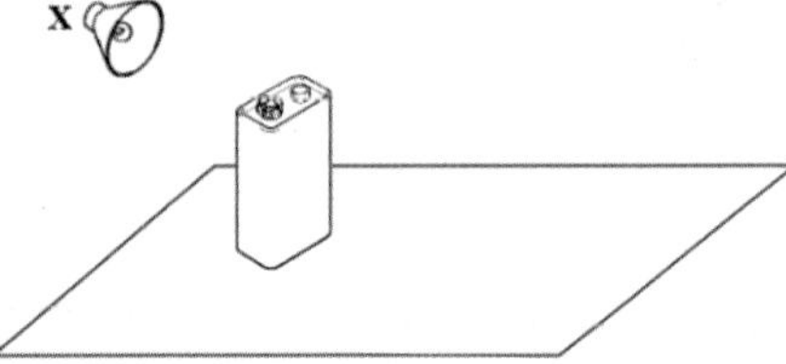

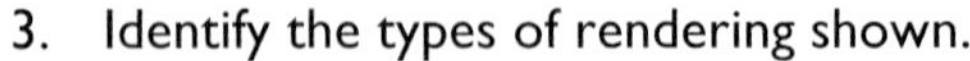

3. Identify the types of rendering shown.

4. Use two rendering techniques on the image below to suggest a light source at X.

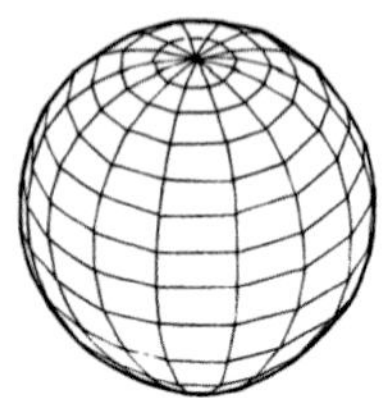

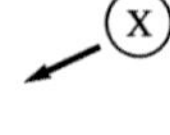

Practising drawing with perspective

Worked example: Find the vanishing points

Past exam question

Indicate the location of the two vanishing points for the perspective drawing shown on the right.

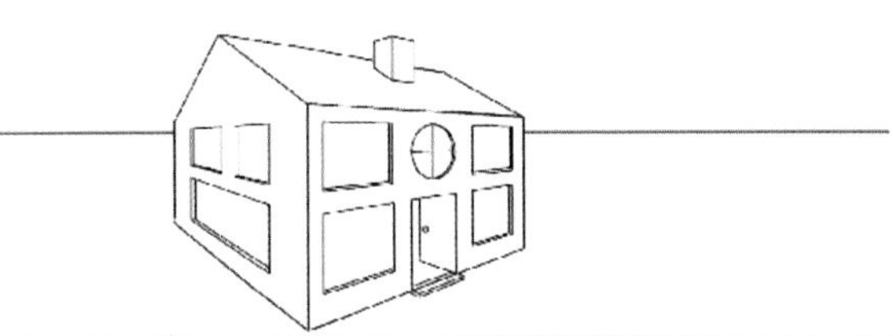

Answer

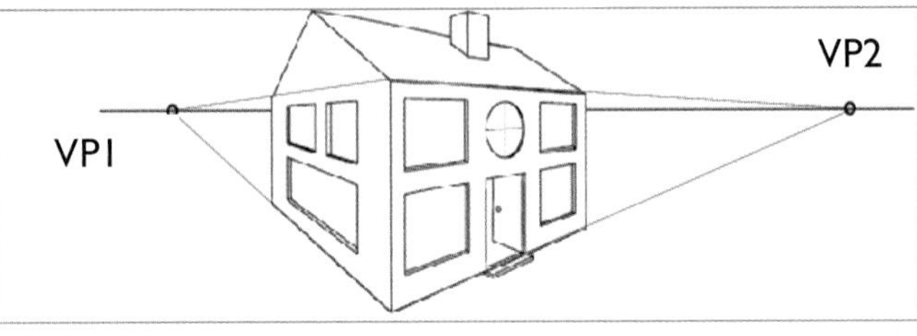

Method: continue the "horizontal" lines of the house back (on both sides) until they converge.

Past exam questions

1. Locate the second vanishing point VP2 and complete the perspective of Box 2.
2. Indicate clearly how to locate the vanishing points in the sketch shown.

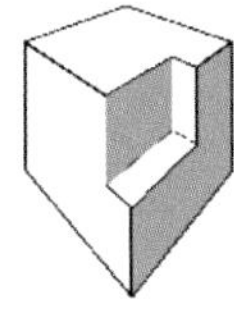

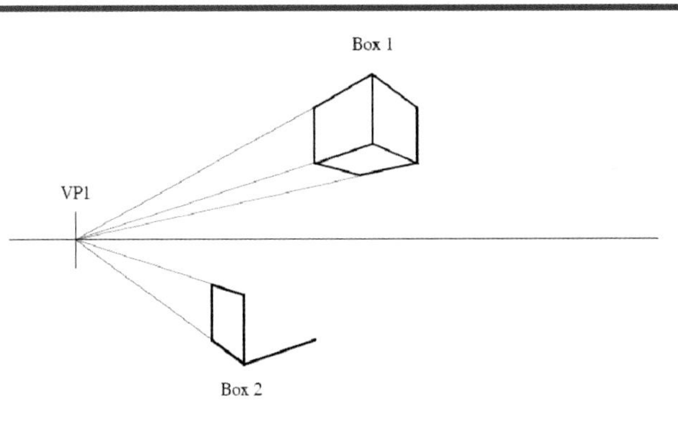

Practising developments

When drawing developments, use dashed lines to show the location of bend lines.

Test yourself

1. What shape does this development make? Make a 3D sketch of it.

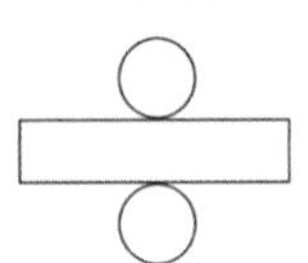

2. What shape does this development make? Make a 3D sketch of it.

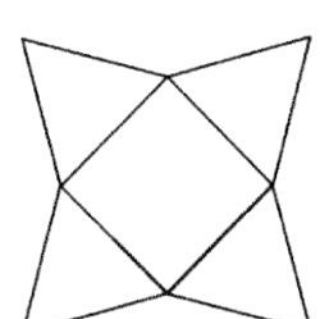

Worked example: Development of mobile phone holder

Past exam question

The graphic shows a design for a mobile phone holder.
Draw a well-proportioned freehand sketch of the development of part A, indicating all fold lines.

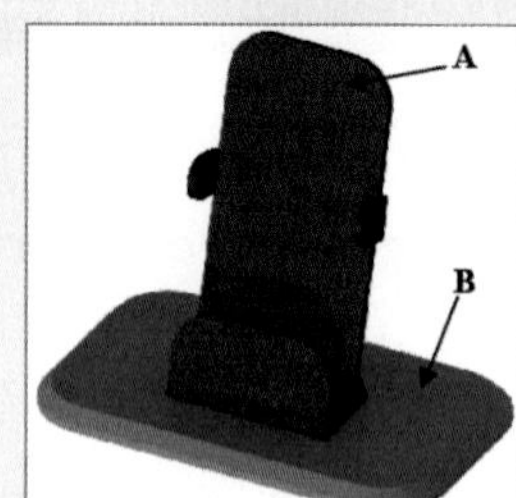

Valid answer

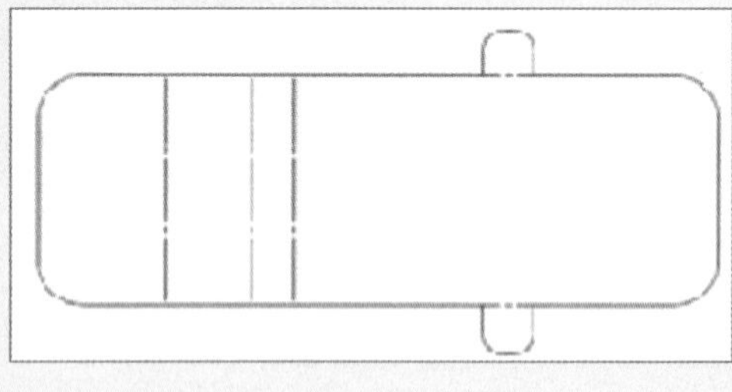

Worked example: Development of a magazine rack

Past exam question

Complete the development of the magazine holder shown.

Valid answer

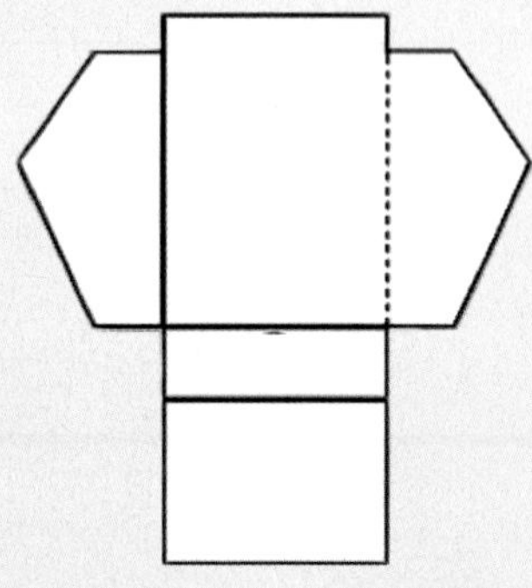

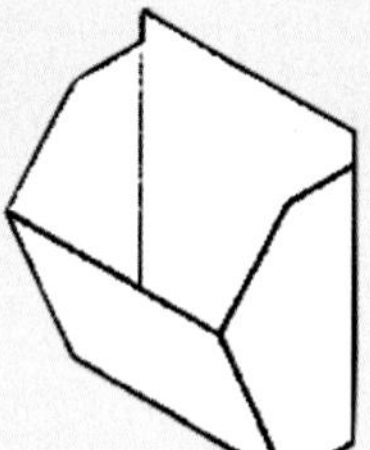

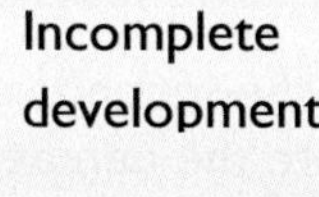
Incomplete development

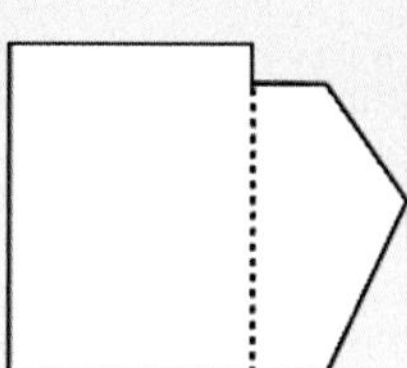

Past exam questions

1. Draw the development of the box shown, on grid paper.

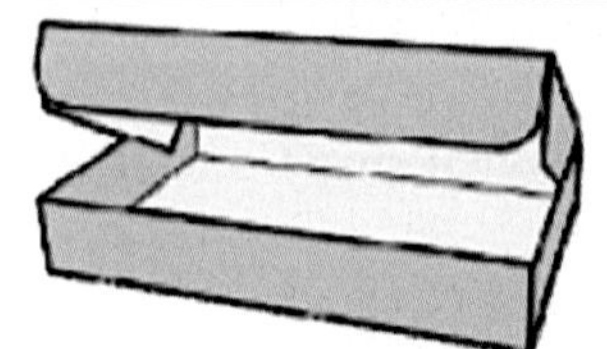

2. Make a 3D sketch of the object formed by this development.

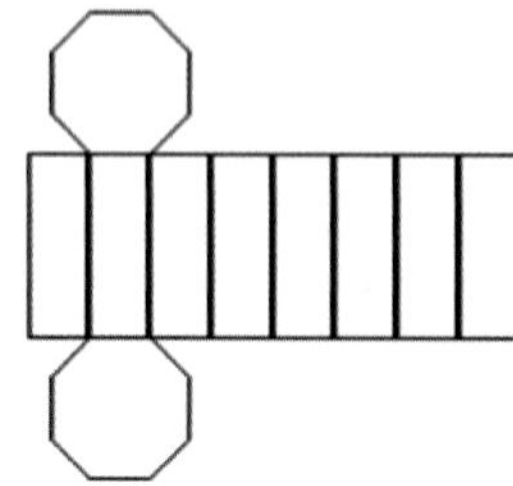

Past exam questions

3. Draw the development of the hexagonal container shown.

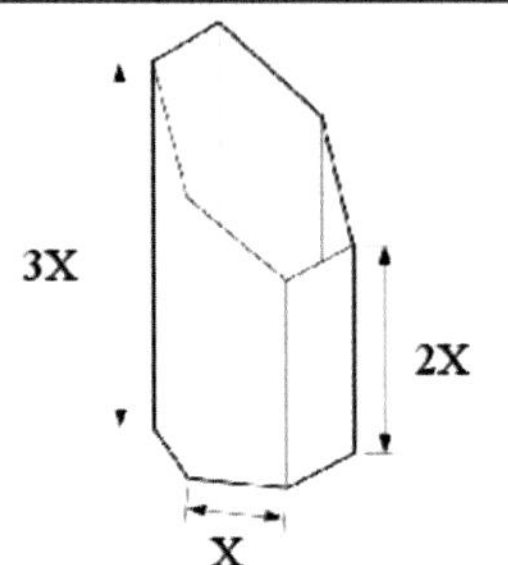

Practising orthographic projections

Test yourself

1. Name the projections of the radio shown at A, B and C.

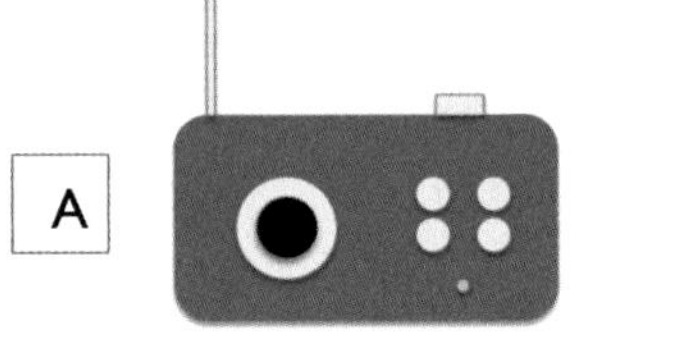

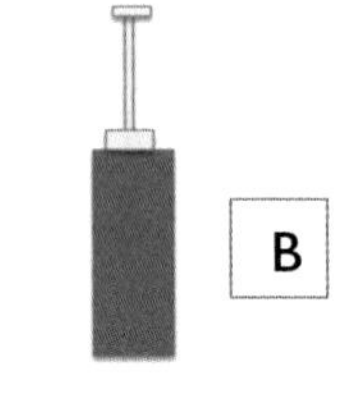

C

2. Draw the elevation of the object shown when viewed from the direction of arrow A.

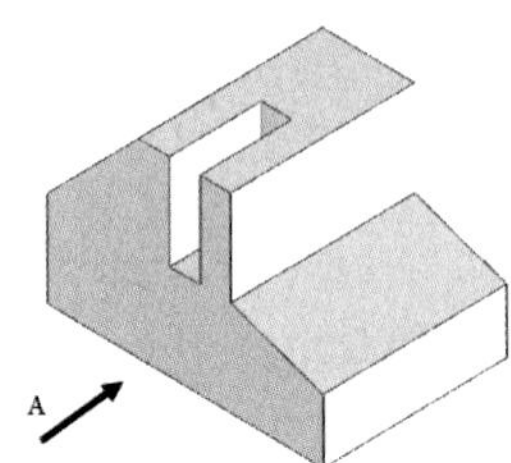

Worked example: Elevation, plan and development of skip

Past exam question

Complete the elevation, plan and development of the skip shown.

Valid answers

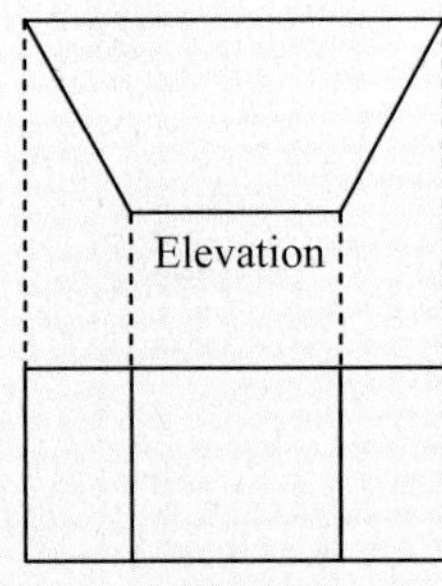

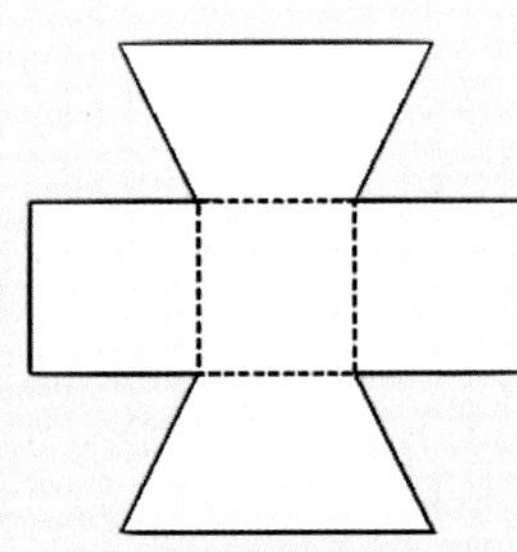

Worked example: Plan and elevation of toy plane

Past exam question

The sketch shows a design for a toy plane.
Make well-proportioned sketches of the following views:

- An elevation in the direction of arrow X.
- A plan in the direction of arrow Y.

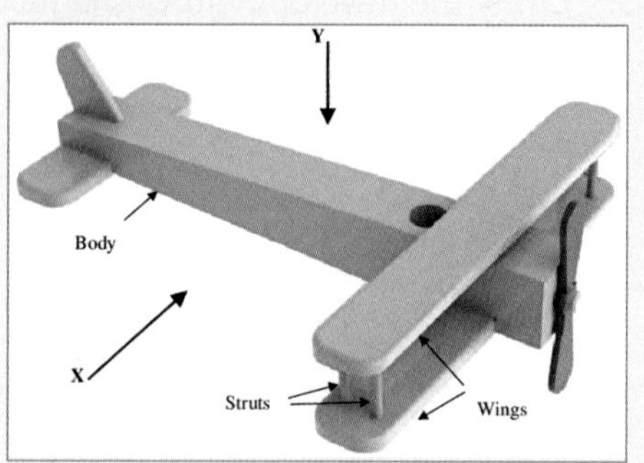

Valid answers

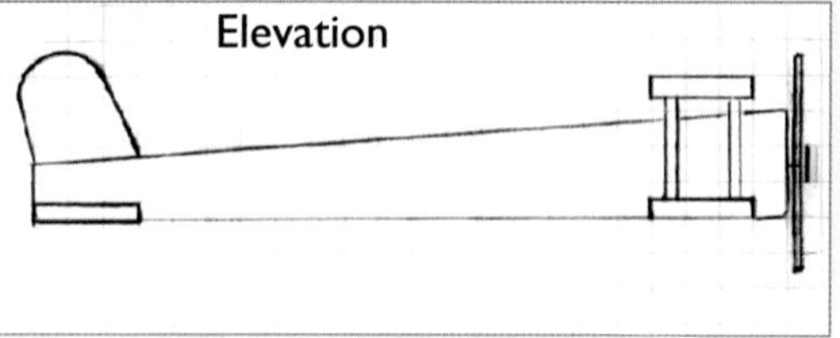

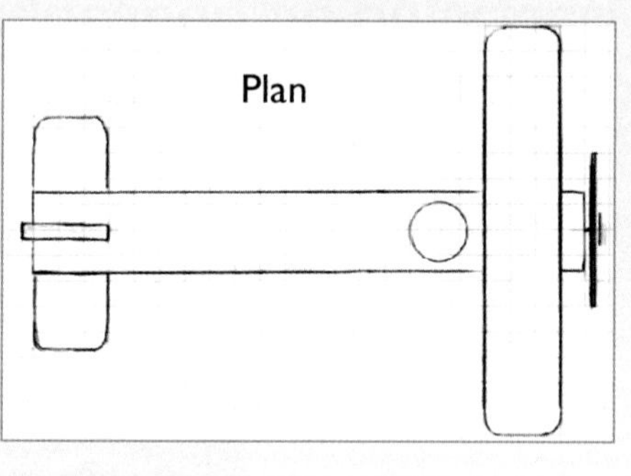

Worked example: Draw an elevation from an isometric

Past exam question

An isometric view of an object is shown. On the grid, complete the front elevation of the object when viewed in the direction of arrow A.

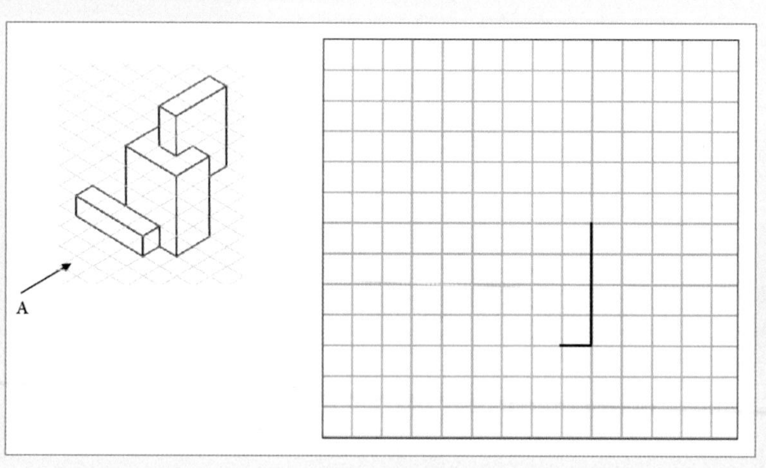

Valid answer

A completed elevation is shown.

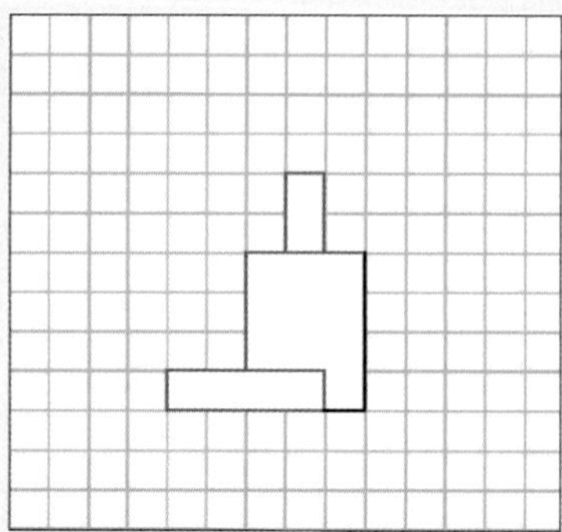

Past exam questions

1. Draw an end view of the toast rack in the direction of arrow X.

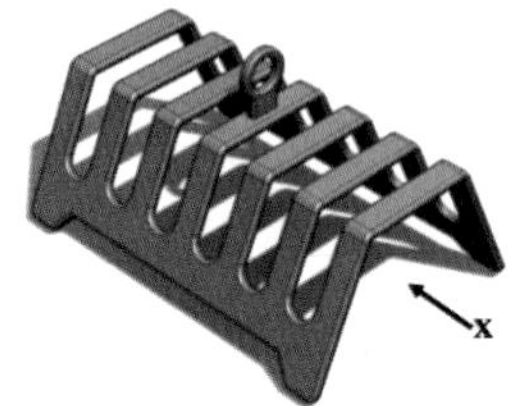

2. Complete the plan view of the part shown.

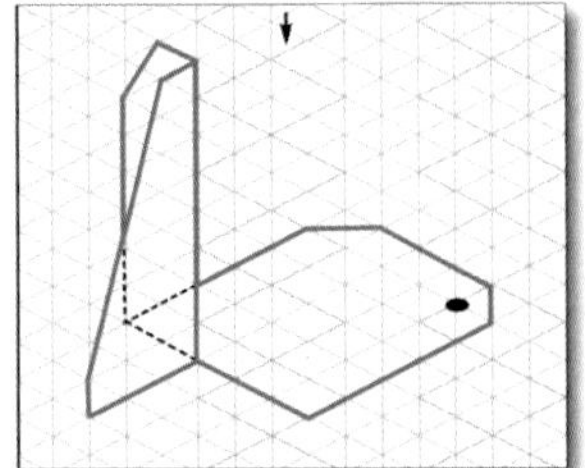

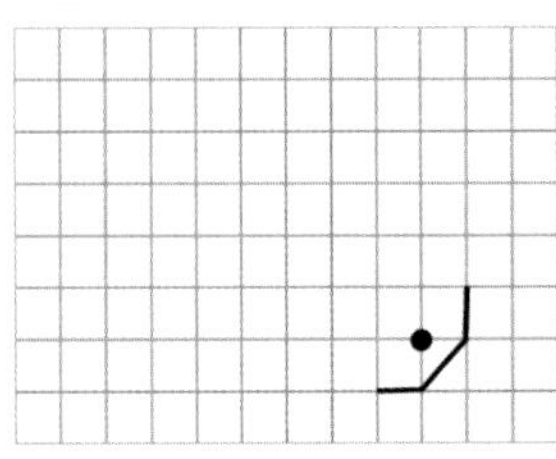

3. Make a well-proportioned sketch of two principal orthographic views of each of the following.

4. Draw the end view of the part shown.

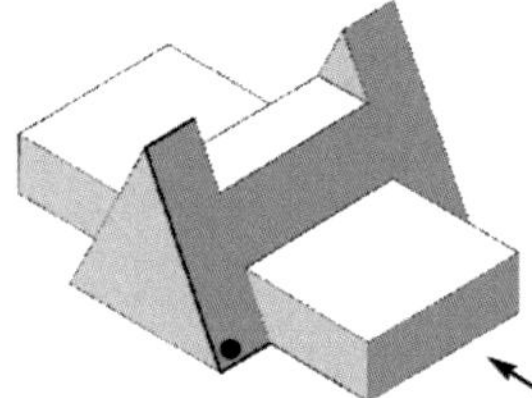

5. The graphic shows a toy car. Make well-proportioned sketches of the following views:
   - An elevation in the direction of arrow X.
   - An end view in the direction of arrow Y.

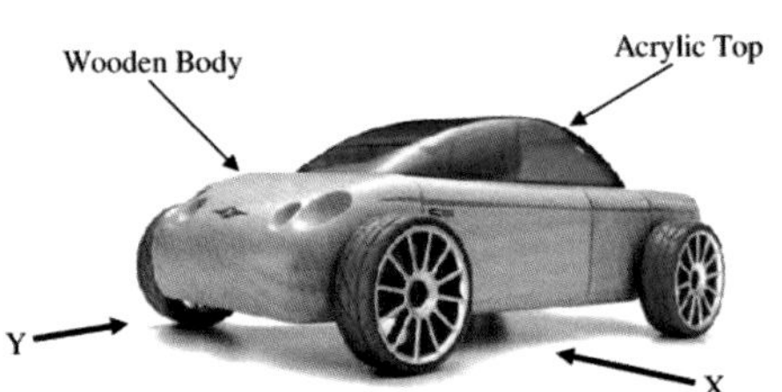

6. Make a well-proportioned sketch of three principal orthographic views of the laptop shown.

7. Sketch an elevation of the buggy when viewed in the direction indicated by arrow A.

A

Practising isometric drawing

Activities

1. Copy the isometric view shown here, on to your own isometric grid paper.

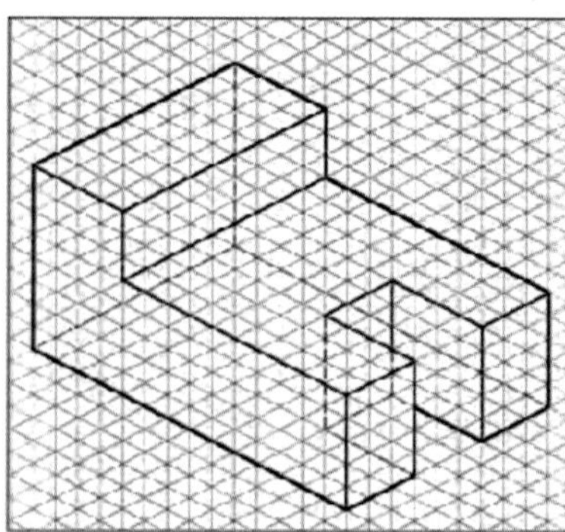

Converting orthographic to isometric

Worked example: Orthographic to isometric

Past exam question

The sketch on the right shows a student design, in plan, elevation and end view, for a laser pen display pack. The pack is manufactured from paper board and holds 12 laser pens.

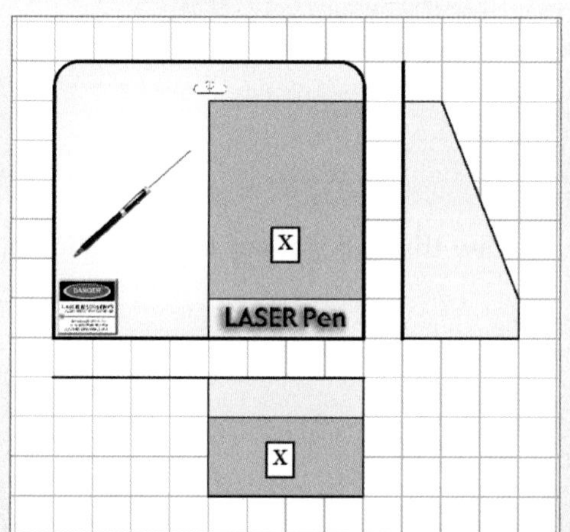

Sketch a well-proportioned isometric view of the display pack on isometric grid paper.

Valid answer

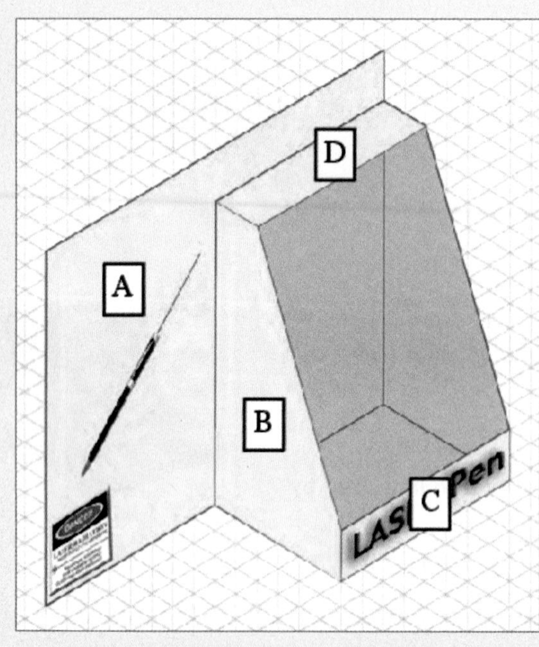

Worked example: Orthographic to isometric

Past exam question

An orthographic projection of a table is shown on the right.
Draw the isometric sketch of the table.

Valid answer

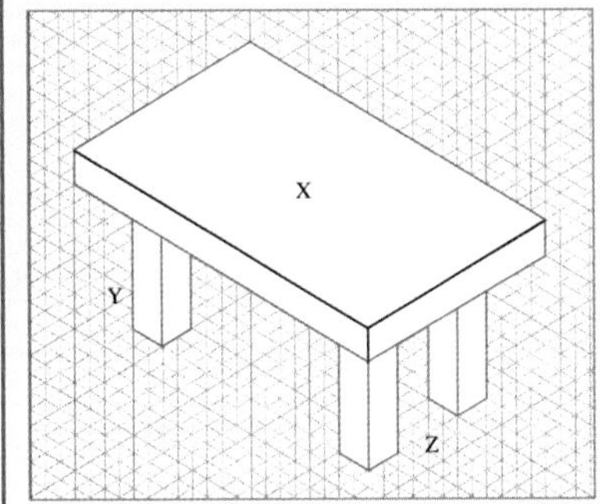

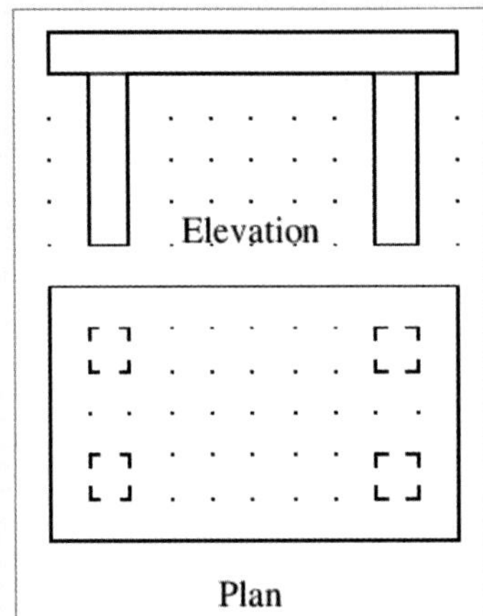

Past exam questions

1. The sketch shows a plan, elevation and end view of a student design for a child's toy. Sketch a well-proportioned isometric view of the toy on isometric grid paper. The wheels can be omitted from the sketch. Include three overall dimensions on your sketch.

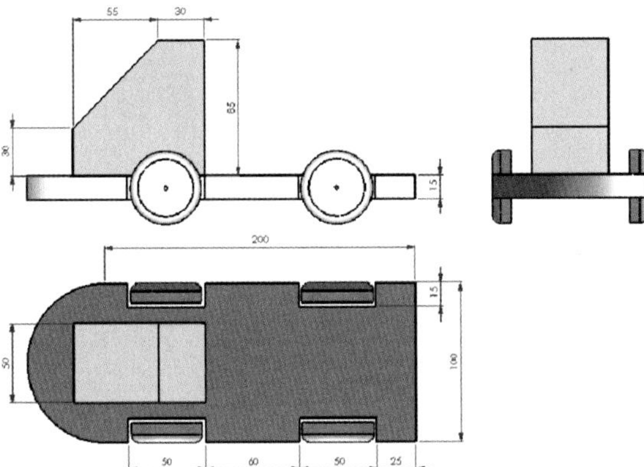

2. Complete the isometric sketch of the component shown.

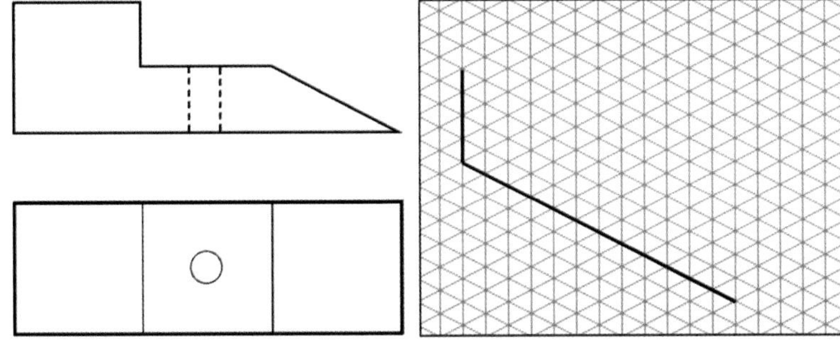

Past exam questions

3. An orthographic projection of a table is shown. Complete the isometric sketch of the table on isometric grid paper.

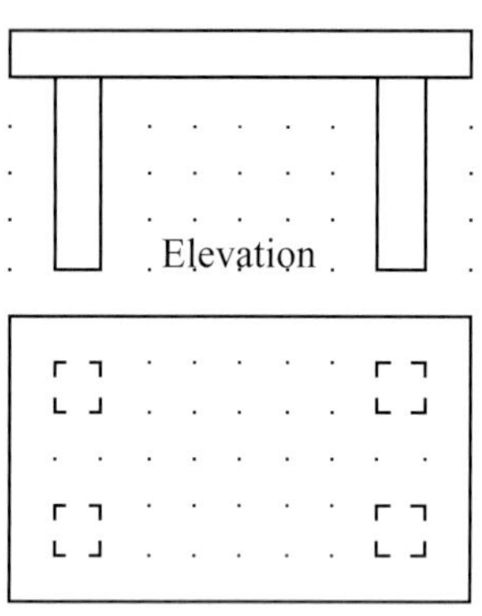

Plan

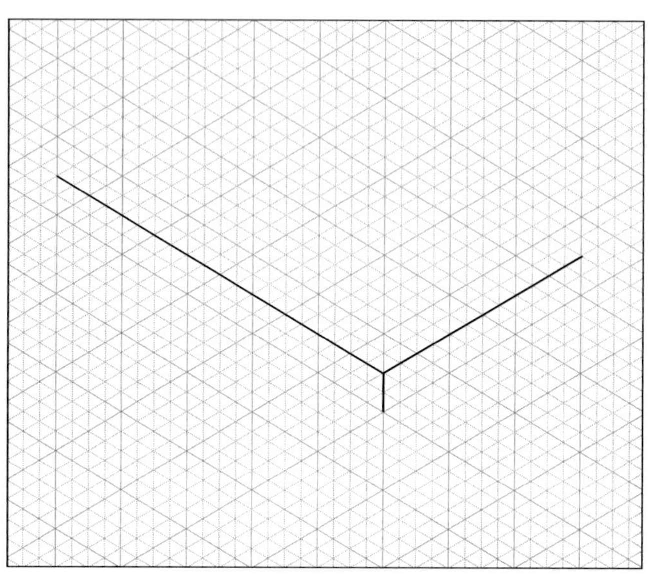

Logos and emblems

Google

Some well-known logos and one emblem are shown above. What does the emblem of the harp represent?

When designing a logo/emblem for a product or an organisation, your design should be:

- Relevant to the product or organisation.
- As simple as possible.
- Colourful.
- Easy to recognise or read, even from a distance.

Activities

1. Download and play a logo identification game. Test your knowledge of well-known logos.
2. Airboats are used in search and rescue missions on water throughout the world. Make a sketch of your design for a logo for such a search and rescue airboat.

Past exam questions

1. A company producing solar panels requires a logo to be etched onto a tinted display panel. Make a sketch of your design for this logo.

2. A 3D graphic of a popular game is shown. Make a sketch of one of the side supports and draw a suitable logo on it to represent the product.

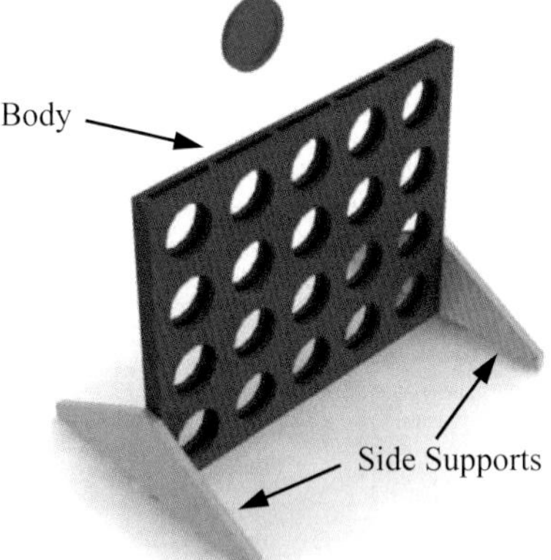

3. Many manufactured products have a logo on them or on their packaging. List two reasons why companies use logos.

2 CHAPTER

Materials

Introduction

This chapter describes the materials that you will need to know about for your examinations. It also covers the materials that you will use in your practical activities and projects. After this chapter, you will go on to learn about safety, tools, and how to make objects from these materials. The types of materials covered in this chapter are: wood, plastics, metals, ceramics, composites and smart materials.

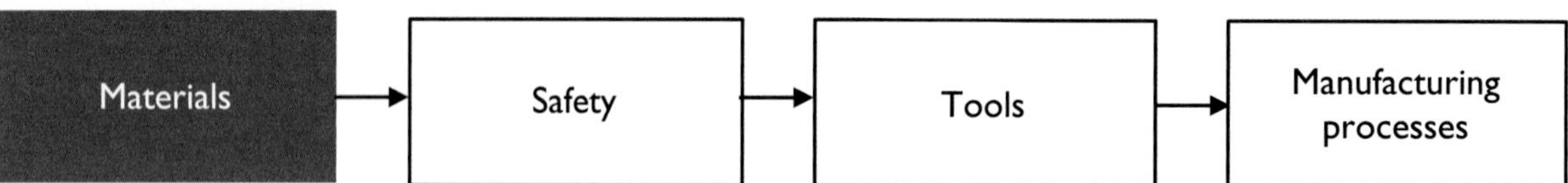

Types of material

Materials are either natural or synthetic. By natural we mean that the material exists in nature or is made directly from materials that exist in nature, e.g. wood. By synthetic we mean that the material does not exist in nature but is man made, e.g. plastic.

The main material types covered in this chapter are briefly described below.

Cutting wood, a natural material

Material type	Description
Wood	Natural material made from the trunks and branches of trees.
Plastic	Synthetic materials made from chemicals extracted from oil, coal and gas.
Metal	Natural hard shiny materials, often extracted from rocks by smelting (melting metal).
Fabric	Soft material made by weaving thin fibres together. Fibres can be natural (e.g. cotton, wool) or synthetic (nylon, polyester).
Ceramics	Materials that are made from clay and heated by sun or an oven until they are hard.
Composites	Materials that consist of one or more materials layered or bonded together. Not the same as an alloy.
Smart	Materials whose properties change in reaction to the environment.
Alloy	A metal formed by mixing two or more metals together. This results in a new metal that is usually stronger and more useful than the metals that it was made from.

Properties of materials

Different materials have different properties. It is the properties of a material that makes it suitable for a particular use. The table below explains the meaning of some common properties of materials.

Property	Extent to which a material ...
Conductivity	Conducts heat or electricity.
Insulation	Retains heat or electricity.
Biodegradability	Can be broken down by living organisms.
Malleability	Can be beaten or stretched out in all directions without breaking.
Elasticity	Can be deformed and will return to its original shape.
Ductility	Can be stretched out into a wire.
Hardness	Resists a dent or scratch.
Strength	Resists a constant force without breaking or bending.

Wood

Wood is a natural material that is widely used in furniture and the building industry. It is visually attractive and is easy to shape with tools. Wood is also called timber. There are three main categories of wood: hardwood, softwood and manufactured wood.

Hardwood

Hardwood comes from broad-leaved deciduous trees, i.e. trees that lose their leaves in winter.

Hardwoods are hard and durable, and look attractive. They are expensive because hardwood trees are becoming scarce. Some hardwood trees only grow in tropical areas. Hardwood trees take a long time to grow, and so take a long time to replace after they have been cut down. Common hardwoods are shown below.

Common hardwoods	
Oak Light brown colour, strong, hard, tough. Widely used in high quality furniture and wooden floors. 	**Beech** White to pinkish-brown colour with a close grain. Hard and tough. Has no odour or taste. Used in toys, chopping boards, tool handles and furniture. 
Balsa Very light hardwood. Easy to work with. Suitable for projects where lightness of weight is essential, e.g. model aircraft. 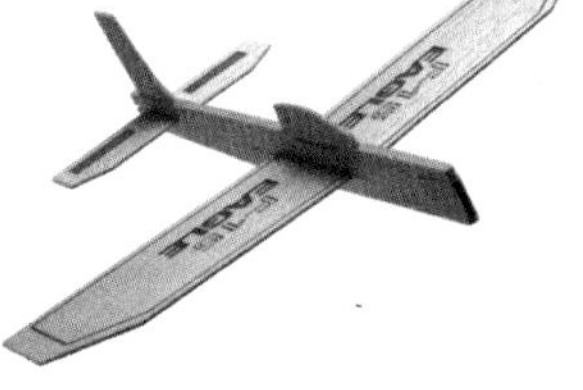	**Ash** Creamy-brown colour. Light, tough, flexible, resistant to shocks. Used for hurleys, hockey sticks and other sports equipment. 

Softwoods

Softwood comes from evergreen coniferous trees, i.e. trees that have cones and keep their leaves in winter. Softwood is cheaper than hardwood because softwood trees are much more plentiful and grow relatively quickly. Many softwood forests are sustainable. This means trees are only cut down when new trees are grown to replace them.

Softwoods are easy to cut and work with. There are many different types of softwood. Sometimes they are just called the generic name "pine". Two of the most common softwoods available in Ireland are shown below. Other softwoods are cedar, spruce, fir and larch.

Common softwoods	
Red deal Comes from the Scots pine tree. Widely used in the building industry. Not grown in Ireland. 	**White deal** Comes from the Sitka spruce and Norway spruce trees. Very light. Widely grown in Ireland. Used in the building trade, budget furniture, and to make manufactured boards. 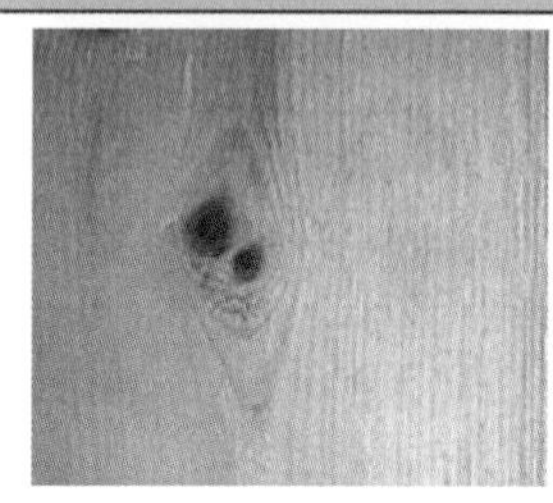

Manufactured wood

Also called engineered wood, manufactured wood is made by glueing layers or small pieces of wood together. Manufactured wood is cheap because small pieces and sawdust can be used. Manufactured woods have the advantage that they can be made into large sheets, they stay straight, and they have no knots. Most manufactured woods have no grain, so they do not look well unless painted.

Manufactured wood	
Plywood Made by glueing thin layers of wood at right angles to each other. Very strong and rigid. 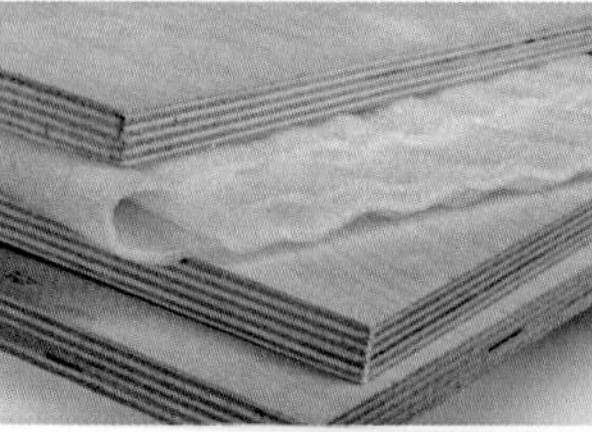	**Chipboard** Made from small wood chips and glue. 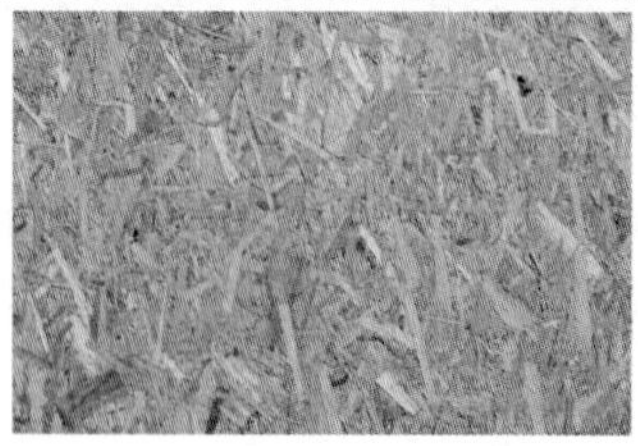
MDF (Medium density fibreboard) Made from fine particles of wood (sawdust), compressed and glued together. Very strong and easy to work with, can be hazardous to cut and sand. Easily damaged by water. 	**Laminated/ veneered boards** To improve the appearance of manufactured wood, a thin sheet of real wood is glued on to the outside of chipboard or MDF. Most furniture and kitchen cupboards are made this way. Unlike other manufactured wood, grain is visible on the veneer. 

Wood for technology projects

Pine, red deal, plywood and MDF are all suitable woods for technology projects. It is important to use dust control/suction systems if you are using MDF, and to wear face masks.

Advantages and disadvantages of different wood types

When choosing a type of wood for a project, consider the advantages and disadvantages listed below.

Type of wood	Advantages	Disadvantages
Hardwood	• Attractive appearance • Hard-wearing	• Expensive • Comes from unsustainable forests • Not available in sheets
Softwood	• Cheap • Easy to work with • Attractive appearance	• Can twist and bend • Not available in sheets • Not weather-resistant
Manufactured wood	• Large sheets • Cheap • No knots/defects • Good for painting	• Poor appearance unless veneered or painted • MDF hazardous to cut because of fine dust

Plastics

Plastics are synthetic materials usually derived from oil and gas using industrial processes. Compared to other materials, they have many advantages, and some disadvantages, as listed below.

Advantages of plastics	Disadvantages of plastics
• Cheap • Easy to mould to any shape • Can be made in different colours • Light • Hard-wearing • Waterproof • Safe, non-toxic • Do not corrode • Hygienic, wash well • Good insulators of electricity and heat • Suitable for mass-production • Some plastics are recyclable	• Not biodegradable • Can cause a lot of damage to the environment when discarded • Less visually attractive than wood

Types of plastics

Plastics belong to one of two main categories: thermoplastics and thermosetting plastics.

Thermoplastics can be re-heated, re-moulded and re-shaped many times, which means that they are recyclable. Examples include acrylic, polyethylene, PET, PVC or polystyrene.

Thermoplastics can be softened by heat and re-moulded many times.

PVC pipe fitting

Bakelite phone

Once set, thermosetting plastics cannot be melted and re-shaped again. They are difficult to recycle. Examples include bakelite, melamine and synthetic rubber.

Thermosetting plastics can be softened by heat and moulded only once.

Plastics for technology projects

Suitable plastics for technology projects include acrylic, PVC, HIPS (high impact polystyrene) and ABS (see next page). These plastics can be shaped using a vacuum former, bent using a strip heater, cut and drilled. HIPS is the easiest to use in a vacuum former.

Acrylic, shown on the left, has a smooth finish, is visually attractive, and is available in both clear and coloured sheets. It has the disadvantage that it can easily crack.

Each sheet comes wrapped in a protective paper sheet to prevent scratches and to allow marking out on the surface.

Properties of plastics

Different plastics have different properties. It is important to be aware of these when you are selecting materials for technology projects. Some plastics are more suitable than others for projects and some are not suitable at all.

The following table lists the more common plastics, their properties, uses and points related to using them for technology projects.

Name of plastic	Properties	Uses	Technology project points
Acrylic	• Hard, smooth, can crack	• Car lights • Safety glasses	• Shape with a vacuum former • Bend with a strip heater • HIPS is easiest to vacuum form • Use acrylic for a high quality finish and as an alternative to glass
HIPS	• Not brittle • Low cost	• Casings • Toys	
ABS	• Shock resistant • Gloss finish	• Toys • Brakes in cars	
PVC	• Flexible	• Pipes • Windows • Bank cards	
Polythene, PET	• Easy to clean • Hygienic	• Bottles • Food containers	• Not easy to vacuum form
Expanded polystyrene (styrofoam, aeroboard)	• Very light • Good insulation	• Packaging	• Can be shaped with a hot wire cutter
Polypropylene	• Light • Tough • Resistant to wear	• Chairs • Ropes • Fasteners	• Not suitable
Nylon	• Slippy • Elastic • Hard wearing	• Clothes, • Fishing lines	• Use for gears
Polyurethane foam	• Flexible • Light	• Stuffing in furniture	• Not suitable
Synthetic rubber	• Elastic • Waterproof • Good insulation	• Wheels • Wetsuits	• Use for project wheels or rubber feet
Bakelite, melamine	• Heat resistant • Good electrical insulation	• Kitchen worktops • Saucepan handles	• Not suitable
Plastics made from cornstarch	• Not strong • Biodegradable	• Eco-friendly bin bags	• Not suitable

Metals

Ferrous and non-ferrous

Metals are strong, shiny materials. Most of them are extracted from the earth by mining. Unlike wood and plastics, they are good conductors of heat and electricity. Because they are much stronger, they are more difficult to cut, drill, and bend than wood or plastics.

Metals are divided into two categories: ferrous and non-ferrous.

Ferrous metals contain iron and are attracted to magnets. Ferrous metals will rust unless their surface is coated with another material.

Examples of ferrous metals include cast iron, mild steel, carbon steel, stainless steel and galvanised steel.

Rusty steel rods

Ferrous metals contain iron and are attracted to magnets.

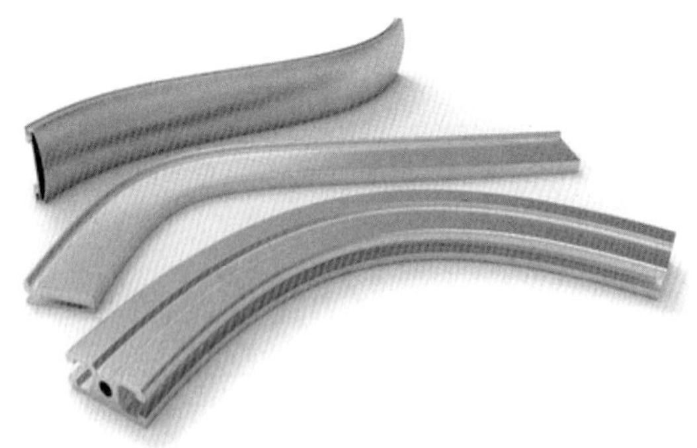

Curved aluminium sections

Non-ferrous materials contain no iron. They are not attracted to magnets. They react less with water than ferrous metals. Many react with oxygen to form a coating that protects the underlying metal, unlike rust.

Examples of non-ferrous metals include aluminium, copper, gold, silver, lead and zinc.

Non-ferrous metals do not contain iron and are not attracted to magnets.

Alloys

An alloy consists of one or more metals mixed together. Mixing metals together can result in a material that has more useful properties than either of its components.

For example stainless steel is an alloy of iron and chromium. It does not rust, resists stains and is easy to clean. It is a popular choice for cutlery and catering equipment. Other examples of alloys include brass, bronze and solder.

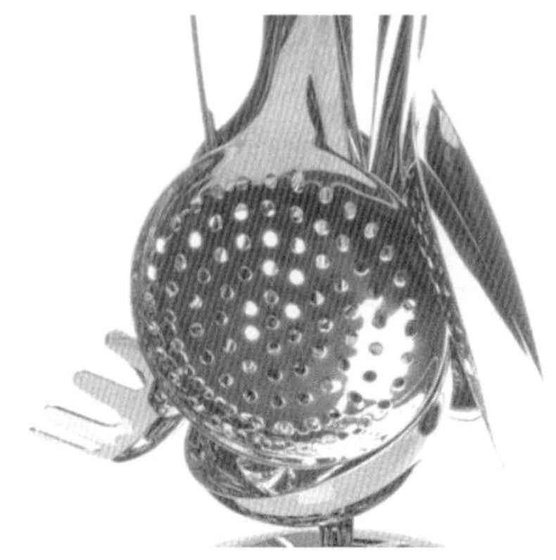

Metals for technology projects

There are many applications of metal in technology projects. These include metal tubing or rods to construct a frame, sheet metal for a platform or surface, steel fixtures and fittings, copper wire, and solder.

Properties of metals

As with other materials, the choice of metal for a given purpose depends on its properties. The table lists common types of metal, their properties, uses and points related to using them for technology projects.

Name of metal	Properties	Uses	Technology project points
Steel (Alloy of iron and carbon)	• Strong • Cheap	• Cars • Bridges • Buildings	• Suitable for axles and brackets
Stainless steel (Alloy of iron and chromium)	• Shiny • Does not rust • Resists stains	• Cutlery • Sinks	• Not suitable
Galvanised steel (Steel with a thin coating of zinc)	• Does not rust	• Gates • Roofs	• Not suitable
Aluminium	• Light • Does not rust	• Planes • Cars • Cans	• Can be bent, cut, or drilled
Copper	• Attractive appearance • Conducts	• Electrical wires • Hot water cylinders • Saucepans	• Can be bent, cut, or drilled
Bronze (Alloy of tin and copper)	• Hard • Attractive appearance	• Sculptures	• Not suitable
Brass (Alloy of copper and zinc)	• Attractive appearance • Does not rust • Tough	• Hinges • Plumbing • Screws	• Not suitable
Solder (Alloy of tin and lead)	• Melts at low temperatures	• To join electronic components	• Use for making circuits
Silver and gold	• Attractive appearance. • Soft	• Jewellery • Electrical contacts	• Not suitable
Tungsten	• Strong • High melting point	• Light bulbs	• Not suitable
Titanium, magnesium alloys	• Light • Strong • Expensive	• Aircraft • Cars • High quality bicycles	• Not suitable

Fabrics

Fabrics are sheets of material woven from many separate threads or fibres. They are soft and flexible. The fibres can be either natural or synthetic.

Natural fibres come from plants or animals and synthetic fibres are made from plastics. The table below gives examples, uses, advantages and disadvantages of both types of fibre.

	Natural fibres	Synthetic fibres
Examples	Cotton, wool, linen, silk	Nylon, polyester, acrylic
Uses	Clothes, furniture, curtains	Waterproof clothes, sails, tents, umbrellas, ropes
Advantages	Warm, attractive, breathable	Strong, hard-wearing, waterproof, no need to iron
Disadvantages	Retain water, are not very strong	Do not allow air and moisture through

Natural fibres come from animals or plants.

Synthetic fibres are made from plastics.

Nylon umbrella

Most fabrics nowadays are a combination of natural and synthetic fibres, e.g. 80% cotton, 20% nylon. Such combinations provide the warmth and attractive appearance of natural fibres, and the strength of synthetic fibres. Have a look at the labels on your clothes.

Ceramics

Natural ceramics are made from clay, sand or finely-ground stones mixed with water, moulded into shape, and fired in an oven to a high temperature. Ceramics are hard and have a very high resistance to heat, are good insulators, but are also brittle.

Examples include bricks, plates, pottery, vases and tiles. Glass is also a type of ceramic, as it is made from sand.

Synthetic ceramics have also been developed in order to be able to withstand extremely high levels of friction and heat. Examples include tungsten carbide, which is used in cutting tools, and special tiles used on the outside of the space shuttle, which have to withstand very high temperatures.

Ceramics are not very useful for your technology projects because they cannot be shaped further after they are made.

Composites

Composites are made by bonding or layering materials together, to make a new material that is stronger and that has more useful properties than the original materials.

Composite	Description	Uses
Paper, cardboard	• Lots of wood fibres bonded together • Cardboard can be corrugated for strength	• Writing paper • Packaging
Plywood	• Thin layers of wood glued together • Increases strength and rigidity	• Construction • Projects
Concrete	• Mixture of rocks, sand, cement, and steel	• Construction
Reinforced concrete	• Concrete reinforced with steel bars	• Construction
Fibreglass /GRP (glass-reinforced plastic)	• Plastic reinforced with fibres of glass • Light and strong • Can be moulded	• Boats • Fishing rods • Attic insulation
Carbon fibre	• Plastic reinforced with fibres of carbon • Light and strong • Can be moulded	• High quality bicycles • Cars • Sports gear
Kevlar fibre	• Strong • Flexible • High impact resistance	• Bullet-proof vests • Tennis rackets • Sails
Gore-tex	• Waterproof synthetic fabric that is also breathable (allows air and vapour through)	• Outdoor sports clothes • Sports shoes

Smart materials

Smart materials change their properties in response to the environment, or have extraordinary properties. Different categories of smart materials and their uses are described in the table below.

Photochromic sports sunglasses

Material type	Description	Uses
Polymorph	• When heated to 62° in water, it forms a soft plastic that can be moulded by hand • Cools to form a hard plastic	• Technology projects
Piezo-electric	• Generates an electric charge when pressed	• Cigarette lighters • Microphones
Photochromic	• Changes colour depending on the light level	• Sunglasses
Thermochromic	• Changes colour when temperature changes	• Thermometers
Shape memory alloy	• Super elastic, returns to programmed shape	• Flexible eyeglasses

Worked example 1: Advantages of plastic

Question

An injection-moulded plastic toolbox made in a factory is shown.

List three advantages of using plastic to make this toolbox.

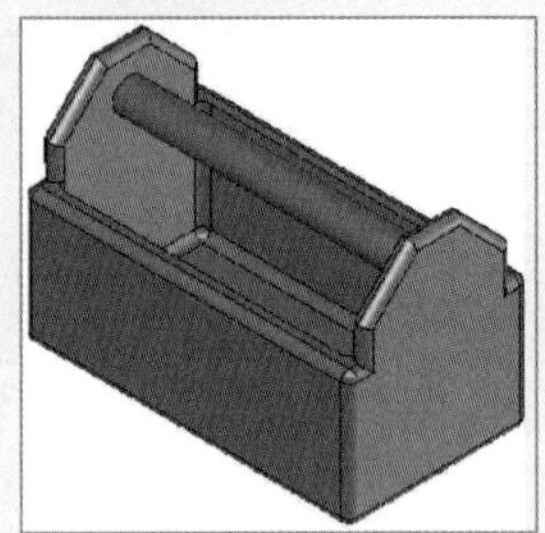

Valid answers

a) Plastic can be mass-produced cheaply, with very little waste.
b) It is easy to produce safe round edges using a plastic mould.
c) Plastic has an attractive colourful finish.
d) Plastic is light, which makes it easy to carry.

Worked example 2: Suitable materials for schoolbag

Past exam question

The schoolbag shown is manufactured from a variety of materials. For each labelled part, name a suitable material and suggest a property that makes the material suitable for this use.

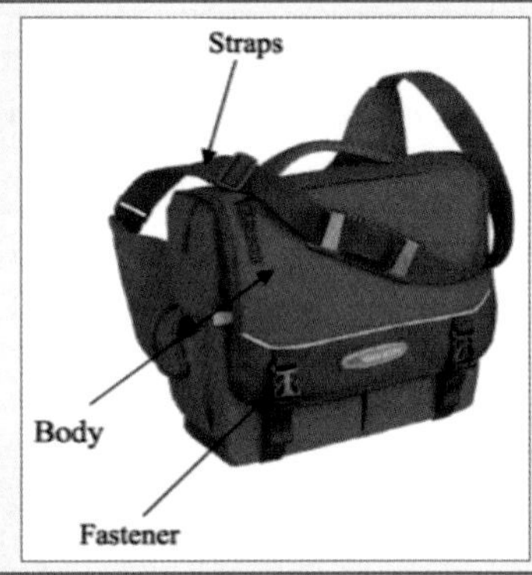

Valid answers

Straps: Nylon because it is strong, flexible and hard-wearing.

Body: Nylon fabric because it is strong, light and waterproof.

Fastener: Polypropylene because it is bend and wear resistant.

Worked example 3: Advantages of manufactured board

Past exam question

State two reasons why manufactured board is more widely used than native timber in furniture manufacture.

Valid answers

Manufactured board is cheap, has no defects or knots, rigid, and is available in large sheets.

Worked example 4: Suitable materials for a boat

Past exam question

List some materials the the boat shown could be made from. Refer to the sail, hull and mast in your answer.

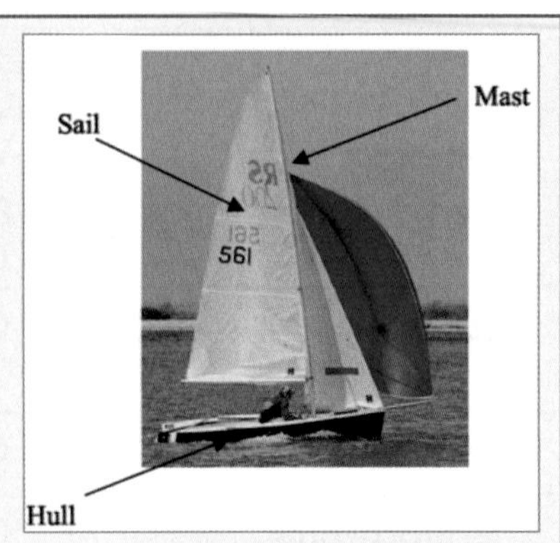

Valid answers (two options provided for each)

Mast: (a) Carbon fibre is light, strong and flexible.

(b) Aluminium is lightweight, strong and cheaper than carbon fibre.

Sail: (a) Nylon fabric is light and cheap.

(b) Kevlar is light, extremely strong and tear resistant.

Hull: (a) Fibreglass is light, strong and cheaper than carbon fibre.

(b) Plywood is cheaper than composites and lighter than steel.

Activities

1. Look around your technology room. Try to name the specific types of wood that you see, the specific types of plastic, and the specific types of metal.
2. Look at the labels on your clothes. List three natural materials and five synthetic materials that you find.
3. Find and name one item in your home that is made from each of the following categories: (a) hardwood, (b) softwood, (c) a laminate or veneer, (d) thermosetting plastic, (e) cotton, (f) polyester, (g) nylon, (h) steel, (i) stainless steel, (j) brass.

Test yourself

1. What is a synthetic material?
2. Which would you say is stronger: metal or plastic?
3. Which material would you say is the easiest to shape (with tools): wood, plastic, metal, or ceramics?
4. Why are clothes made out of fabric?
5. Name a type of material that can conduct electricity.
6. Name two types of material that could be damaged by water.
7. Name two types of material that are good insulators.
8. What uses could wood and plastic have in a school technology project?
9. Why are composites and smart materials not usually used in school technology projects?
10. What is a good material to use in a vacuum forming machine?
11. What material other than glass would be suitable to make something transparent (see-through)?
12. What material is the filament in a light bulb made from?
13. Tick the appropriate column to indicate whether the wood is a hardwood, softwood or a manufactured board:

Name	Hard wood	Softwood	Manufactured wood
Pine			
Beech			
Ash			
Oak			
Red Deal			
Plywood			

14. Tick the appropriate column to indicate whether the metal is ferrous or an alloy (or both):

Metal	Ferrous	Alloy
Aluminium		
Steel		
Iron		
Solder		
Brass		

Past exam questions

1. Give two reasons why copper is a good choice of material for this night-light holder. State two common uses of copper in the home.

2. Suggest one natural and a synthetic material used in the manufacture of bicycles, stating where each is used.

3. Give two reasons why new materials had to be developed in order to manufacture the first space shuttle.
4. Suggest a lightweight material suitable for the body of a yacht (boat). Name two properties of fabrics that make them suitable for use as sails on boats.
5. Name a suitable material to make the body of the hair straightener shown, and state one reason for using that material.

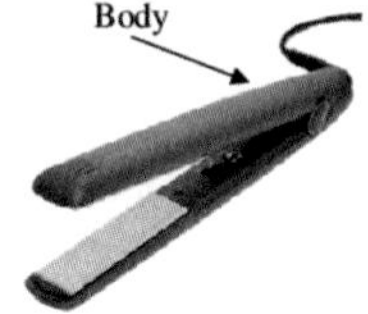

6. Explain the terms "MDF" and "Veneer".
7. Explain the term "biodegradable" and name one common biodegradable household material.
8. Explain the term "alloy". What is the process of coating steel to prevent rusting called?
9. Why is carbon fibre a popular choice for fast bicycles and wind turbines?
10. State the purpose of the covering material on the acrylic sheet shown.
11. Explain the term "thermoplastic" and explain why plastics are used for electrical appliances. Give one advantage and one disadvantage of using plastics in manufacturing.

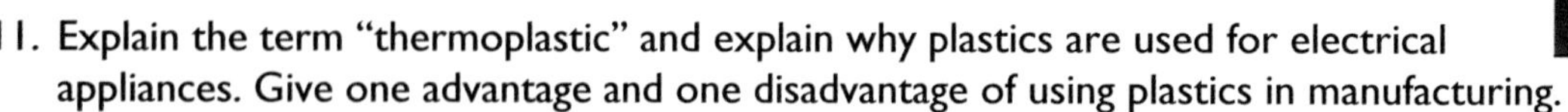

12. Suggest one natural and one synthetic material suitable for raingear.

13. Tennis rackets were traditionally made from wood. Give three reasons why this is no longer the case, and suggest one material that is more suitable.
14. Name a suitable material to make the shape shown.

15. Name a plastic suitable for the wheel centres on the child's toy car shown.

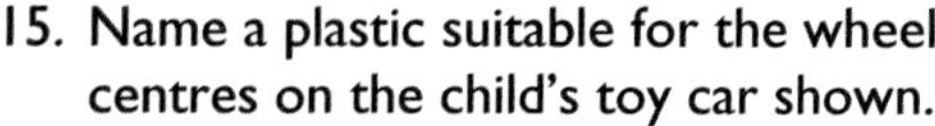

16. Name some suitable materials for the body of the car shown.

CHAPTER 3

Safety

Introduction

This chapter covers safety in the technology room. It should be read before the "Tools" and "Manufacturing processes" chapters. Designing safe products is covered in the "Design and manufacture" chapter.

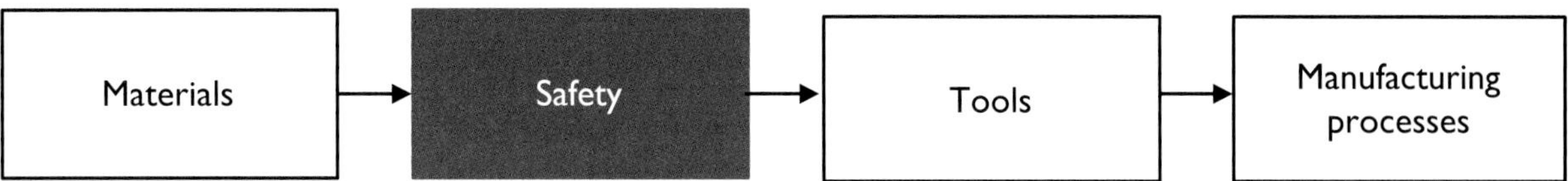

This chapter also provides safety questions from previous Junior Cycle exams, with some worked examples.

You will find that some tools and processes are mentioned here that may be unfamiliar to you. This is done to keep safety information in one place. When you move on to the "Tools" and "Manufacturing processes" chapters, your teacher will show you the safety rules for each tool and process again. After you have studied these chapters and have more experience, come back to this chapter and answer the safety questions again.

Why bother with safety rules? What could happen?

If you do not implement the safety rules in the technology room, you are at risk of serious injury to your:

- Eyes.
- Hands.
- Body.
- Hearing.
- Breathing.

It is important to study this chapter before using any tools in the technology room.

Keep asking yourself the following questions:

- Is this safe?
- Did I carry out the safety checks first?
- What could go wrong here?
- How can I make this safer?

Safety rules for the technology room

General conduct

While in the technology room, observe the following general rules:

- Do not enter the technology room unless the teacher is present.
- Obey the teacher's instructions at all times.
- Do not use tools without asking the teacher first.
- Pay attention at the tool and process demonstrations.
- Do not run around.
- Do not eat or drink.
- Do not approach, touch or interfere in any way with someone who is using a tool.
- Do not help anyone to use a tool. Tools are strictly for one person only.
- Do not talk to someone while they are using a tool.
- When you are using a tool, ensure you have sufficient room and are not close to another person.
- Report any accidents, breakages, spillages or sparks to your teacher immediately.
- Alert your teacher if you think something might not be safe, even if nothing dangerous has happened.
- If you are at all unsure about how to use a tool, do not use it. Ask your teacher to show you.

Clothing and hair

Follow these rules to avoid risks related to clothing and hair:

- Do not wear loose clothing.
- Wear a work apron over your clothes.
- Remove loose jewellery, e.g. necklaces, and store safely.
- Tie up long hair.

General procedures when working

Follow these procedures to stay safe when working:

- Store bags, clothes, your work and your tools and materials in the areas designated by your teacher.
- Clean and tidy up your work area as you go along.
- Do not leave tools and waste materials lying around.
- Brush off all dust and small items from your desk or work area with a brush, not with your hand.
- Do not leave tools or materials overhanging the desk.
- Turn off all electrical equipment unless it is in use.
- Never open up an electrical device powered by electricity.
- Never attempt to fix a mains electrical device.
- Keep all bench vices closed and the handles vertical.

Common safety equipment

The table below lists common items of safety equipment, indicating when you need to wear each one.

Safety equipment	Picture	You need to wear these
Safety glasses/visor		When drilling, chiseling, or whenever there is a risk of any loose pieces flying off.
Ear defenders		When using loud machinery, e.g. pillar/bench drill, band saw, scroll saw
Safety gloves		When handling or standing close to something hot, e.g. strip heater, hot glue guns
Dust mask		When cutting wood or plastic
Fume mask		When working with strong fumes and sprays, e.g. epoxy glues, spray paint, oil-based paints, or oil-based varnishes

Safety when handling materials

Sheet metal

When working with sheet metal:

- Wear protective gloves. Metal edges can be extremely sharp and dangerous, even before cutting.
- Wear protective safety glasses to prevent any shards getting into eyes.
- File away any rough edges after cutting or drilling. Do not leave rough pieces of metal lying around.

Wood

When working with wood:

- Watch out for splinters. Wear protective gloves when handling rough wood.
- Avoid knots. Mark out your pieces so you never have to cut, drill, nail, screw, plane or chisel into knots. Knots can be a safety hazard because they are extremely hard, and resistant to tools.

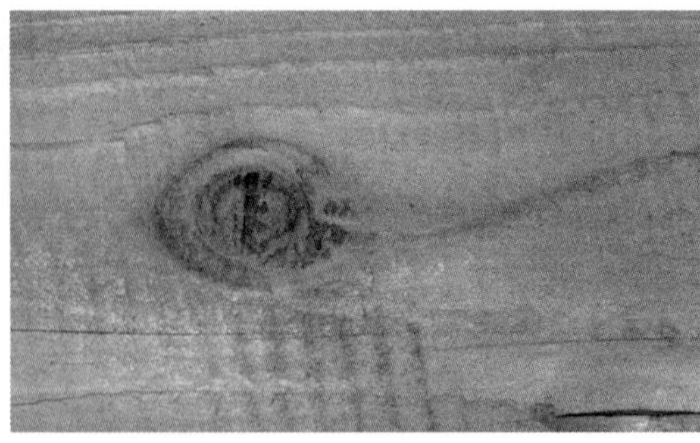

Knot on wood panel

Holding and clamping

This is a most important safety step. Many accidents happen, not because of tools, but because the material was not secured properly. The material can fly off and cause serious injury.

- If you are using a hand-held tool like a saw, drill or chisel, make sure you secure the material in a bench vice first (see right).
- If you are using a fixed electric drill (like a pillar drill), make sure to use clamps (as shown below) to secure the material.

Avoid working in any situation where, if anything slipped, you could injure yourself or others.

Before starting to use any tool

Never start to use a tool or switch on an electric tool, unless you:

- Know that it is the right tool for the job.
- Have been instructed on how to use the tool.
- Have been given permission by the teacher to use the tool.
- Have secured/clamped the material that you are working on first.
- Have taken any specific safety precautions for that tool or process.
- Know exactly what is going to happen when you turn it on/use it.
- Know exactly how to turn it off and where the emergency STOP button is.

Additional safety precautions for tools and processes

Tool/process	Picture	Extra safety steps needed
Hand saws (tenon saw, coping saw)		• Secure the material in a bench vice.
Electric hand saws (jigsaw)		• Secure the material in a bench vice. • Ensure the correct blade is fitted. • Wear safety glasses. • Make sure the electric cable is secured. • Keep the exposed blade away from people, and ensure the saw is unplugged when not in use. • Wear a dust mask if cutting a large piece of wood or MDF.
Electric fixed saws (scroll saw, band saw)		• Do not use for small items. • Ensure the correct blade is fitted. • Ensure the blade guard is down. • Wear safety glasses. • Wear ear protection if noisy. • Wear a face mask if cutting MDF. • Hold the material firmly. • Keep hands far away from blades. • Make sure no one is near you. • Do not take your eye off it. • Turn off the saw when finished sawing.
Hand drills (incl. cordless electric)		• Secure the material in a bench vice. • Unplug before fitting new drill bit. • Ensure the correct bit is fitted. • Remove the chuck key. • For metals, ensure the location is marked with a punch. • Drill a pilot hole first for larger diameter holes. • Use a low speed for large diameter holes and for plastics.
Electric fixed drills (pillar or bench drills)		• Secure the material with clamps. • Unplug before fitting new drill bit. • Ensure the correct bit is fitted. • Remove the chuck key. • Ensure the drill guard is down. • Wear safety glasses • For metals, ensure location is marked with a punch. • Drill a pilot hole first for larger diameter holes. • Use a low speed for large diameter holes and for plastics.

Tool/process	Picture	Extra safety steps needed
Sanding (hand sanding and electric)		• Wear a dust mask. • Ensure built-in suction systems are turned on before use. • Sweep up immediately after use.
Chiselling		• Secure the material in a bench vice. • Keeps hands away from blades. • Wear safety glasses. • Chisel away from you.
Hot wire cutter		• Keep hands and face away from hot wire. • Do not use for small items. • Wear safety gloves.
Vacuum forming		• Wait until plastic has cooled before removing it. • Wear safety gloves.
Strip heater		• Turn off when not using. • Use safety gloves when placing the plastic on top and removing it.
Soldering		• Keep the soldering iron in its holder when not in use. • Never leave the hot tip down on the bench or elsewhere. • Do not touch the hot tip. • Do not solder directly under your nose/mouth. • Place the hot tip only on the metal components to be soldered. • Do not overheat the metal components. • Turn off when not using. • Work in a well-ventilated area.
Painting, varnishing, staining, oiling		• Wear protective clothing. • Use water-based products where possible. • Wear a face mask if spray painting. • Ensure there is ventilation if using oil-based products.
Hot glue gun		• Do not place your hands anywhere near where the glue is being applied.

Tool/process	Picture	Extra safety steps needed
Using glue		• Ensure there is adequate ventilation in the room. • Wear a face mask when using epoxy glues. • Be very careful not to get Super Glue on your skin. • Never rub your eyes. • Solvent cements should be kept locked away by teachers.

Safety symbols

You need to understand the meaning of the following safety symbols.

Emergency stop	Emergency exit	Emergency meeting point	Wear safety glasses	Wear ear protection	Wear face mask

Fire hazard/ flammable	Fire extinguisher	Danger of electrocution	Toxic substance	Toxic substance	Keep guard on saw

Worked examples: Safety features and precautions when drilling

Past exam question

Identify two safety feature on the drill shown.

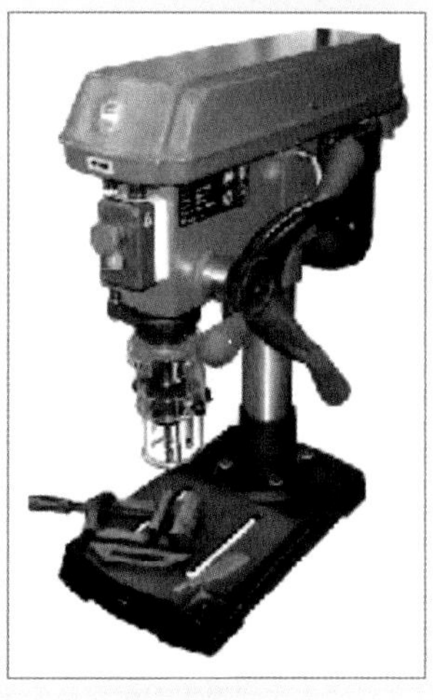

Valid answers

- Emergency stop button
- Drill guard
- Clamps for work piece

Past exam question

Identify two safety precautions taken by the student when drilling the work shown.

Valid answers

- Safety visor
- Apron
- Work piece clamped
- Drill guard down

Past exam questions

1. Safety is very important in the technology workshop. List four safety precautions that must be observed in your day-to-day work in the technology room.

2. State two hazards associated with using the jig saw shown.

3. State two safety precautions that should be observed when using a jig saw.

4. List two safety precautions you should take when working with sheet copper.

5. State the meaning of each of the symbols below.

6. State two safety precautions that must be observed when using the power tool shown.

Orbital sander

7. State two safety precautions that must be observed when using a soldering iron/soldering electronic components.

8. State two precautions that should be taken to prevent an acrylic sheet from shattering when drilling a hole in the sheet. *(You will need to study the "Manufacturing processes" chapter before you can answer this.)*

CHAPTER 4

Tools

Introduction

This chapter provides an overview of the tools that are commonly available in school technology rooms, and it provides a selection of exam questions in relation to those tools. This chapter does not provide instructions or processes for how to use these tools to make objects from different materials. This is covered in the next chapter, "Manufacturing processes". You should read this chapter after the "Materials" and "Safety" chapters.

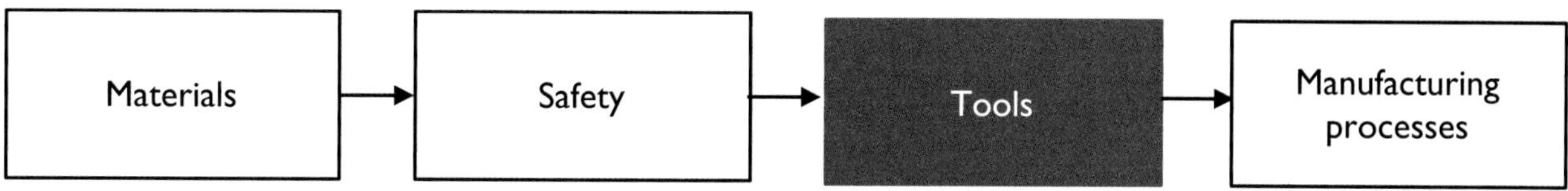

Format of this chapter

Tools are grouped by the type of action or process that they are used for, e.g. drilling, cutting, etc. Both hand tools and electrical power tools are included.

Tools are presented in tables. The right-most column in the table indicates what type of materials the tool can be used with. The material types are colour-coded: red-brown for wood, green for plastic, blue for metal, black for others. Some tools work with only one type of material. Other tools will work with many types of materials.

Measuring and marking out tools

Measuring and marking out are the first essential steps of any practical task. Measuring and marking out means drawing lines or points on the object that you are working on, so that you can accurately cut, drill, shape or join at those points.

If you do not measure and mark out accurately, you will experience difficulties later, and you may have to start again.

Tool	Picture	Description and usage	Materials
Tape measure		Used for measuring long or short distances. The thin metal measuring strip rolls out and back into the housing via a spring mechanism. This creates a space-saving device. The tape can be locked in any position.	• Wood • Plastic • Metal
Steel rule		Used for measuring short distances. It is resistant to damage.	• Wood • Plastic • Metal
Calipers		Used to accurately measure the distance between opposite sides of an object, e.g. an inside calipers can accurately measure the inside diameter of a hollow tube. An outside calipers can measure the outside diameter of a tube.	• Wood • Plastic • Metal
Scriber		Has a very sharp point that is used to mark out thin lines on metal work surfaces. Creates lines that are easy to see, and can't be rubbed off.	• Metal
Spring dividers		Two sharp points, held apart by a spring, with an adjustable distance between them. Use to mark out distances, or to scribe out a circle, by fixing one leg and pivoting the other.	• Wood • Plastic • Metal
Punch		Centre punches and dot punches have sharp points on one end. They are hit with a hammer to make small dent in a piece of metal, to provide a guide for drilling. A nail punch is used to drive the head of a nail further into the wood. This gives a more attractive finish.	• Wood • Metal
Sliding bevel		Used to set a desired angle for marking out. Can also be used to measure an angle in one location, and mark out that same angle in another place or on another piece of material.	• Wood • Plastic • Metal

Tool	Picture	Description and usage	Materials
Try square		Used to mark out right angles (90°). Also used to check whether existing angles are square, i.e. that lines are at 90° to each other.	• Wood • Plastic • Metal
Marking (mortise) gauge		A tool used to mark out lines on wood or metal, which are parallel to an edge. Often used to mark out a joint to be made in wood.	• Wood • Metal
Marking knife		Used with a ruler or straight edge, to cut fine, accurate lines in the material before further cutting or chiseling.	• Wood • Leather

Holding tools

In order to work on materials accurately and safely it is essential to hold the materials securely in a fixed position. Holding tools are essential for this purpose. Serious accidents can occur if materials are not held properly. Large machine tools (see later) often have holding tools built in to them.

Name	Picture	Description and usage	Materials
Pliers		Used to grip small objects between metal fingers, which have flat (usually serrated) surfaces. Operates like a scissors. Applies more force to hold an object than you could with your hands, and is safer. Not useful or safe for holding objects for cutting or drilling.	• Wood • Plastic • Metal
Vice		A vice holds an item between two strong metal jaws that are closed together using a screw mechanism (see "Mechanisms 2"). It exerts a large force and is self-locking. A bench vice attaches to a workbench. A hand vice does not attach to a bench and can be used anywhere. Because a vice can exert a great force on an object, you may need to protect the surface of the object with spare pieces of wood on either side, or use special fibre grips.	• Wood • Plastic • Metal

Name	Picture	Description and usage	Materials
Clamp		Similar to a vice. Often used to hold two pieces together while glue sets.	• Wood • Plastic • Metal
Bench stop		A piece of wood or metal fixed to the top of a workbench. This allows you to put your pieces of material up against it so that it won't move in that direction while you are working on it. Only stops motion in one direction.	• Wood • Plastic • Metal
Bench hook		An "S"-shaped piece of wood placed over the side of a workbench, which makes a temporary bench stop.	• Wood • Plastic • Metal

Cutting tools

Cutting is one of the first steps in shaping many materials. Make sure your materials are marked out and held securely before cutting (see above). After cutting, rough edges will need smoothing (see later).

Name	Picture	Description and usage	Materials
Snips		Very sharp scissors for cutting thin metal strips, or wire.	• Metal
Side cutters/ wire cutters		Used to cut wire. Acts as a lever to transfer a large cutting force to the sharp jaws.	• Metal
Pincers		Used to cut wire. Also useful for removing nails from wood.	• Metal
Wire stripper		Used to remove the plastic insulation from electrical wires.	• Plastic

Name	Picture	Description and usage	Materials
Tenon saw		Used to cut wood in straight lines. The metal bar on top of the blade stops the blade from bending, so helping to cut a straight line.	• Wood
Coping saw		Used to cut wood and plastic in curved lines. The angle of the blade relative to the frame can be changed.	• Wood • Plastic
Hacksaw		Used to cut metal and plastic. The blade has small and closely-set teeth. A hacksaw is not suitable for cutting wood because the wood clogs up the teeth. Also available in a smaller (junior hacksaw) version.	• Metal • Plastic
Jigsaw		A hand-held electric saw with a reciprocating (moving back and forth) narrow blade enabling it to cut curved or straight lines. Difficult to cut long straight lines with a jigsaw because it is hand-held. A jigsaw is hazardous because it has an exposed blade, an electric wire that could be cut accidentally by the blade, and because it can generate a lot of dust and wood particles.	• Wood • Plastic
Electric fretsaw/ scroll saw		An electric saw for cutting curved or straight lines in wood, plastic, or metal. The saw remains fixed in one place, and the material to be cut is pushed around the blade to make the cut. The blade moves up and down in a reciprocating motion. Different materials require different blades. Contains a guard and is a hazardous machine.	• Wood • Plastic • Metal
Band saw		An electric saw for cutting straight lines or curves in wood, plastic or metal. The blade only moves in one direction. Provides a high quality cut. Different materials require different blades. Contains a blade guard and is a hazardous machine.	• Wood • Plastic • Metal

Drilling tools

The tools below are used for making holes in different materials. Make sure the material is securely held before drilling.

Tool	Picture	Description and usage	Materials
Bradawl		A sharp point used to make a pilot (guide) hole in soft wood before drilling a larger hole, or before screwing. You just push and twist the bradawl back and forth to make the hole.	• Wood
Hand drill/ brace drill		Turning the handle at the side turns the drill bit. Different drill bits are used for different materials.	• Wood • Plastic • Metal
Cordless electric drill		Electric drill with a rechargeable battery. Very convenient as it has no cable, and allows for drilling in tight spaces. A disadvantage is its short battery life and the need to recharge it frequently. With the speed turned down, these drills can be used as electric screwdrivers. They can drill different materials using different drill bits.	• Wood • Plastic • Metal
Bench drill/ pillar drill		Large fixed electric drills designed to make drilling accurate holes easy. A bench drill is fixed to the top of a workbench. A pillar drill is fixed to the floor. The material to be drilled is lined up under the drill bit, and secured with clamps, and the lever is pulled down to bring the drill bit down on to the material.	• Wood • Plastic • Metal
Chuck		The chuck is the part of the drill that holds the drill bit. To change drill bits, use a chuck key to turn the chuck to release the drill bit, hold the new drill bit in place, and tighten the chuck again on the new drill bit.	• Wood • Plastic • Metal
Drill bit		A drill bit is a metal cylinder with a screw thread in it that cuts a hole in the material when twisted by a drill. Choose a drill bit that matches the size of the hole that you want to drill, and the material that you want to drill.	• Wood • Plastic • Metal

Tool	Picture	Description and usage	Materials
Counter-sink bit		A countersink drill bit is used to make a shallow conical hole so that when you screw in a screw, the head of the screw fits down into the conical hole, and the screw doesn't stick out over the top of the material. This is called countersinking. It gives a neat finish.	• Wood • Plastic • Metal
Spade bit, Forstner bit		The spade bit is used to drill a larger diameter hole in wood. Use a low drill speed. The Forstner bit is similar and is used to drill holes that don't go the whole way through the material, and have a flat bottom.	• Wood

Shaping tools

Shaping means removing pieces from materials so that they take the form that you want. The tools in this section are used for shaping materials once they have been initially cut to the right size using cutting tools.

Tool	Picture	Description and usage	Materials
Hot wire cutter		When turned on, the wire gets hot, and will shave pieces off easy-melt plastics, such as expanded polystyrene, aeroboard, aerofoam and foam. Often used to shape plastic packaging materials to safely transport breakable items.	• Plastic
Chisel		Has a sharp blade at one end, and is hit on the other end with a hammer or a mallet. Used to cut away small pieces out of wood. Used for making slots, notches, recesses and mortises, and cutting into awkward corners.	• Wood
Plane		A sharp angled blade is pushed across the piece of wood with two hands, to slice off very thin layers. Removes more wood than can be removed by sandpaper or files. Not suitable for MDF.	• Wood
Lathe		Lathes are used to make objects that are circular in cross-section, such as round table legs, lamps, bowls and toys. A piece of wood is held and spun rapidly in the lathe, and a cutting blade is brought over to the material to pare away the waste material. This is called wood turning.	• Wood • Plastic • Metal

Tool	Picture	Description and usage	Materials
Laser cutter		Laser cutters use a high-energy laser beam to burn through different materials. They give a very accurate and high-quality finish. They can be programmed to produce different patterns (computer-aided manufacturing - CAM). They are becoming cheaper and more popular in schools.	• Wood • Plastic • Metal
Router		A router is a power tool used to make grooves in materials. It is like a drill with special router bits. Router bits can be changed to suit the type of groove required, and to suit different materials. Routers can be controlled by computers.	• Wood • Plastic • Metal

Bending tools

The tools below are used to bend different materials in a controlled way, to get an even and accurate bend.

Tool	Picture	Description and usage	Materials
Strip heater		A strip heater has a heating element along its length. It is designed to heat plastics along a line so they can be bent along that line into the desired shape. Strip heaters will work with thermoplastics, such as polythene and acrylic.	• Plastic
Bench vice		Metal can be bent by inserting it into a vice and hitting a piece of protective wood or metal (with a mallet or hammer), which in turn bends the metal. This is useful for school projects.	• Metal
Bending machine		For more industrial use, special bending machines are used to bend large or small metal sheets accurately.	• Metal

Forming tools

Forming means changing the shape of something without removing pieces of it. Forming is suitable for materials that can be softened or melted, such as thermoplastics and metals, which then form into the new shape when they cool.

Tool	Picture	Description and usage	Materials
Vacuum former	*Source of heat* *Plastic sheet* *Mould* *Vacuum pump*	A vacuum-forming machine is used to shape thermoplastics such as polythene and acrylic. It works by heating up a sheet of plastic to soften it, and then the sheet is sucked (using a vacuum) on to a wooden or metal mould, so that the plastic takes the shape of the mould. Only thin sheets of plastic can be used because otherwise they won't bend well around the mould.	• Plastic
Moulding		Moulding can be used to form plastics and metals into different shapes. First you need a metal mould in the shape of the item. Hot liquid plastics or metals are poured or injected into the mould and allowed to set.	• Plastic • Metal • Ceramic

Joining tools

The tools below are used to join materials together.

Name	Picture	Description and usage	Materials
Nails and staples		A metal spike with a small head, driven into wood with a hammer, and used to join two pieces of wood together. Staples are U-shaped nails that can be used to hold items close to wood, e.g. cables, or to act as a hook.	• Wood
Hammer		Used to beat nails in to wood, or used with chisels. Has a heavy and strong metal head. A claw hammer has a lever device on the other side of the hammering head, which can be used to prise nails out of wood.	• Wood

Name	Picture	Description and usage	Materials
Screw		A metal fastener with a screw thread on the outside, twisted into objects to hold them together. There are many different kinds of screws, e.g. a wood screw, which pulls itself into wood as it is twisted with a screwdriver and a self-tapping screw, which can tap its own hole as it is driven into the material. Screws can have different types of heads depending on the effect you want, e.g. a countersunk head sits into a conical hole.	• Wood • Plastic • Metal
Screw-driver		A tool used to twist screws. The head of the screwdriver has a special shape to fit in to the head of the screw. The different shapes are: • Slotted: a straight edge fits into a single straight groove in the screw head. • Pozidrive: a cross-shape fits in to a matching shape in the screw head. • Phillips: a different cross shape, fits in a matching shape in the screw head.	• Wood • Plastic • Metal
Nut		A nut screws on to a bolt to fasten parts together. When rotation or vibration may loosen a nut, a lock nut/locking nut can be used. This is a second nut that is tightened against the first nut.	• Wood • Plastic • Metal
Bolt		Used with a nut to fasten objects together. Passed through a hole drilled in the objects. Looks like a screw, but it doesn't have a sharp point, and it doesn't screw into the material itself, it only screws into a nut. The bolt usually has the same shaped head as the nut, or it may have a slot in it for a screwdriver.	• Wood • Plastic • Metal
Washer		A washer is a wide ring of metal or rubber. It is often used between the nut (and/or bolt) and the material, in order to protect the material and to provide a wider flat surface for the nut and bolt to pull the pieces together.	• Wood • Plastic • Metal

Name	Picture	Description and usage	Materials
Wrench/ spanner		A metal tool that grips on to a nut or a bolt to turn it. Acts as a lever (see "Mechanisms 1") and can apply great force. Wrenches come in different types and sizes to match different-sized nuts and bolts: • Open wrench (left side of spanner in picture). • Ring spanner (right side of spanner in picture). • Combination wrench (seen in picture – contains an open and a ring side). • Adjustable wrench: the size of the opening can be adjusted, so that one wrench can fit many different sized nuts and bolts.	• Wood • Plastic • Metal
Taps and dies		A tap and a die are used to create screw threads in metal objects. A tap (shown on the bottom) is twisted into a hole to create a screw thread inside the hole. A die is twisted around the outside of a metal bar to make a thread on it. These tools are very useful when making axles for projects. If you create a thread on the end of the axle, you can screw a nut on to it to hold on the wheels.	• Metal
Pop rivet gun		Used to join objects together using rivets. A manual pop rivet gun is shown. You can also get electric and pneumatic pop rivet guns.	• Wood • Plastic • Metal
Pop rivets		Pop rivets are aluminium fasteners. They are designed to be inserted through holes in both objects. A pop rivet gun pulls the rivet from one side so that it makes a secure fastening.	• Wood • Plastic • Metal
Wood glue		Used to glue wood to wood. Wood glue is slow-setting so you need to hold the pieces together in a vice or clamp until the glue sets. PVA is a common type of wood glue.	• Wood

Name	Picture	Description and usage	Materials
Plastic glue		Liquid solvent cement, such as Tensol cement, is very good for joining plastics such as acrylic. Pieces must be clamped together for 24 hours. Adequate ventilation is essential when using these glues.	• Plastic
Hot glue gun		A hot glue gun can be used to glue plastics and other materials together. The glue is made from thermoplastic, which is inserted into the back of the gun (in pellets), heated by the gun, and drips out of the nozzle when the trigger is pressed. When the plastic glue cools, it sets and bonds the items together. Not as strong as Tensol cement.	• Wood • Plastic • Metal
Super Glue		Super Glue is an extremely quick-setting adhesive. It is best used on non-absorbent surfaces like plastics and ceramics. It is not good for wood as it soaks into it. It doesn't bond well to metals. It is a dangerous substance and can stick your fingers together in seconds.	• Plastic • Ceramic
Soldering iron		A soldering iron is used to join two pieces of metal together using solder. Solder is a soft metal alloy made from tin and lead, and comes in rolls of soft thick wire. The tip of the soldering iron gets hot when turned on and melts the solder onto the joining point. See "Electronic circuits".	• Metal
De-soldering pump		Used to suck away molten solder so that objects previously soldered can be separated. See "Electronic circuits".	• Metal

Smoothing tools

The tools below are used to create a smooth surface on materials. Cutting, drilling and shaping can create rough edges. Smoothing is essential to create a good surface finish so that the material looks good, and also so that the material can be treated with different surfaces finishes, such as paint.

Tool	Picture	Description and usage	Materials
Sandpaper		Strong paper coated with a layer of sand or other abrasive material. Used to scrub the surface of the material to make it smooth. Comes in different types and grades (roughness). Fine sandpaper (with smaller particles on it) is used to achieve a smooth finish. Fine sandpapers are suitable for plastic and metal. A wet-and-dry sandpaper is suitable for metal.	• Wood • Plastic • Metal
Sanding machine/ Belt sander		An electric machine that has a rotating belt of sandpaper. It is much easier to use this than to sand by hand. You will need different types and grades of sandpaper for different materials and finishes.	• Wood • Plastic • Metal
File		A file is a tool with a handle and a metal serrated surface, used to smooth and shape materials. Files come in various shapes (e.g. flat, round), and grades (roughness).	• Wood • Plastic • Metal

Surface finishes and tools

Surface coatings:

- Provide an attractive finish on materials.
- Protect the material from damage from the environment (e.g. rain water, grease).
- Allow the materials to be more easily cleaned.
- Provide a more hygienic surface.

Plastic does not necessarily need a protective coating as it is already resistant to water and stains, and can be manufactured in a variety of colours. The choice of surface finish is important on all items, especially on children's toys as the surfaces need to be smooth and non-toxic.

The table below shows common surface coatings and the tools that are used to apply them.

Name	Picture	Description and usage	Materials
Paintbrush		Used to apply most surface coatings .The brush holds the liquid coating in between its bristles, and releases it as you brush. The flexible brush allows coatings to be applied to different shapes and into corners.	• Wood • Metal

Name	Picture	Description and usage	Materials
Roller and tray		Used to apply surface coatings to large areas quickly. Cannot coat small, rough, or hard-to-access surfaces well.	• Wood • Metal
Spray gun, or spray can		Used to apply surface coatings in an even way, especially to complicated shapes. A special spray area is required and safety equipment is needed for breathing.	• Wood • Metal
Oil		Oils such as tung oil, danish oil, and linseed oil, can provide an attractive finish to natural wood that has grain, especially hardwoods. Soaks into, slightly darkens, and protects the wood, allowing the grain to be seen.	• Wood • Metal
Paint		Provides an attractive appearance, protection from wetness, stains, grease, and makes the surfaces more hygienic and easier to clean. Reduces the chance of wood splitting. Paints can be oil-based, or water-based. Water-based paints are more environmentally-friendly and are easier to use.	• Wood • Metal
Stains		Stains change the colour of wood while still leaving the grain visible. Can provide weather protection.	• Wood
Varnish		Varnish provides a clear tough surface on wood. Provides protection against moisture. Can be oil-based or water-based. Water-based varnishes are more environmentally friendly and brushes can be easily washed with water.	• Wood
Plastic coating		Applies a plastic coating to metal. Protects the surface of metal, changes its appearance and feel. Also makes it electrically resistant. One way of plastic coating metal is to dip hot metal into plastic powder. The plastic melts and adheres to the metal.	• Metal

Name	Picture	Description and usage	Materials
Electro-plating		Applies a very thin coat of a different metal over the original metal. Uses electricity to attract the coating metal particles out of a solution and on to the material to be coated. Applying a very thin coat of zinc on to steel is called galvanizing. This stops steel from rusting.	• Metal

CAM and CAD

Many of the large tools mentioned in this chapter, such as lathes, routers and laser cutting machines, can be controlled by a computer. Two terms associated with this are CAD and CAM.

A CAD (computer-aided design) package is a piece of software that allows you to draw your designs on a computer.

Examples of CAD software are SolidWorks and AutoCAD.

Engineer using a CAD system to design a component

CAD stands for computer-aided design

CAM (computer-aided manufacturing) is the process of controlling machines by computer. CAM computers and software use the information in the CAD drawings to tell the machines what to do.

CAM stands for computer-aided manufacturing

Worked example: Threading a rod

Past exam question
Name a tool that could be used to cut the thread shown at x at the end of the brass rod.

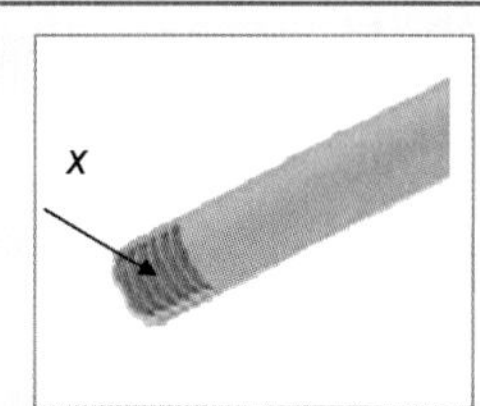

Valid answer
A tool that can be used to cut a thread on the rod is a die.

Activities

1. Walk carefully around your technology room, under the guidance of your teacher. Make a list of as many tools as you can from this chapter.
2. Draw a high quality sketch of each type of hand saw that you find.
3. Find a mould for a vacuum former. See if you can find the small holes drilled in it.
4. Find out what tools your technology room doesn't have, e.g. you may not have a router, lathe or laser cutter. Find videos of these on YouTube so that you can see how they work.

Test yourself

1. Name each of the tools shown below, and give a use for each.

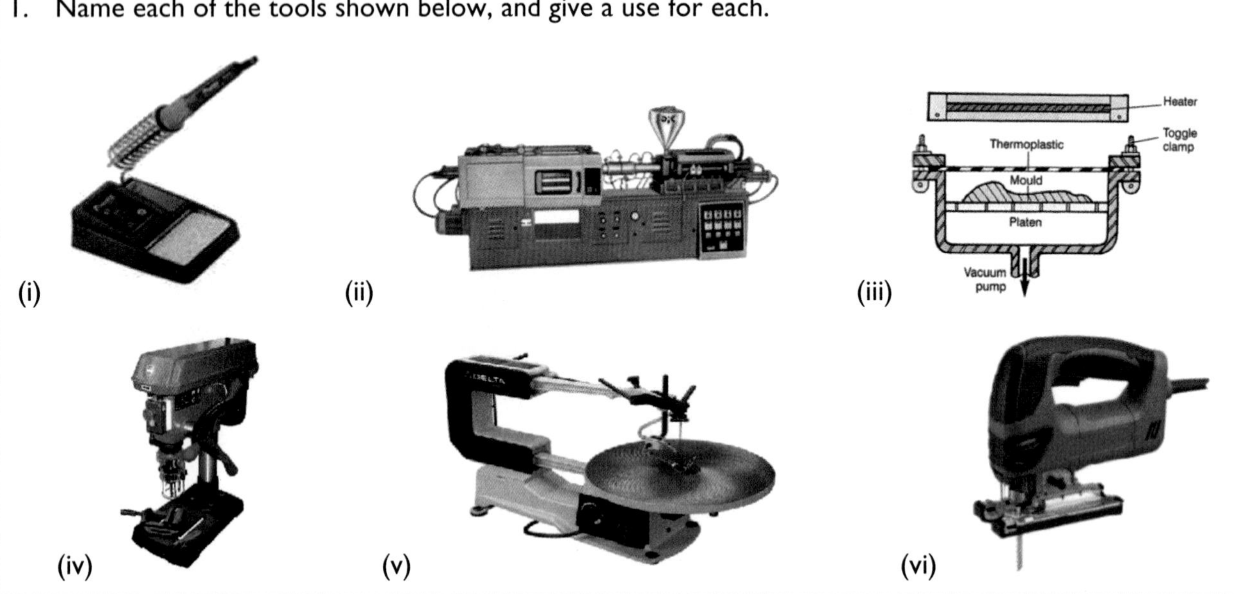

Past exam questions

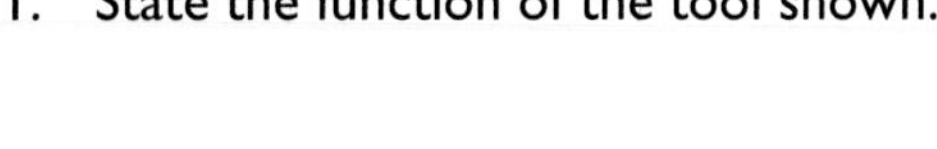

1. State the function of the tool shown.

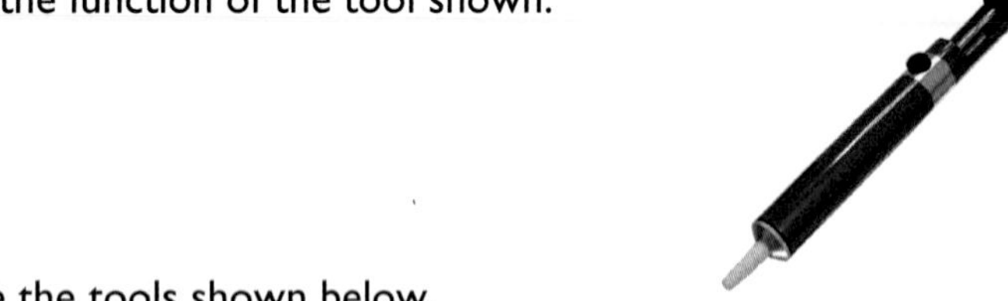

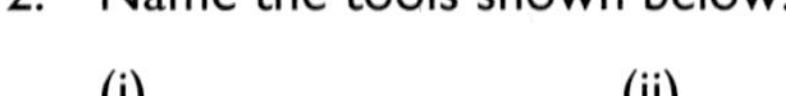

2. Name the tools shown below.

(i) (ii) (iii) (iv)

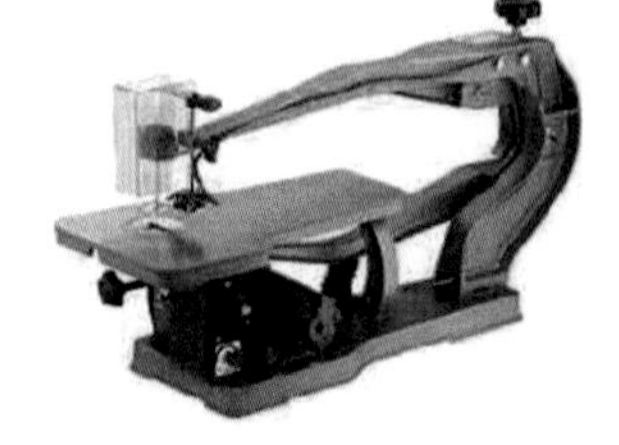

Past exam questions

3. The tool shown uses a thermoplastic adhesive. Name the tool shown and explain the term thermoplastic.

4. Name the tool on the right and state what it is used for.

5. Name a suitable material for cutting with (i) a tenon saw and (ii) a hacksaw.

6. Name the tools labeled X and Y.

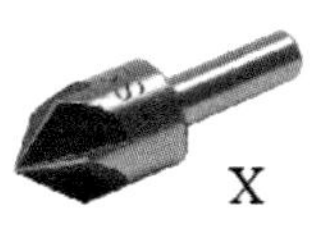

7. Name the piece of equipment used to bend acrylic into the shape shown.

8. Name the two metals used to manufacture solder.

9. State one advantage and one disadvantage of using the type of drill shown.

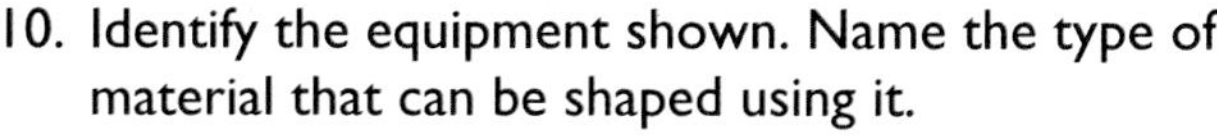

10. Identify the equipment shown. Name the type of material that can be shaped using it.

11. State the purpose of the tool Y shown.

12. Name the tool shown and give a use for it.

5 CHAPTER

Manufacturing processes

Introduction

This chapter explains how to make objects from wood, plastic and metal. It describes the processes that are required to manufacture objects from those materials. These processes include: measuring, marking out, cutting, drilling, shaping, forming, surface finishing and joining. The details of these processes are different depending on the type of material being used.

There are separate sections covering the manufacturing processes for each material. Each section:

- Explains the processes for the relevant material.
- Provides activities.
- Provides worked examples and past exam questions.

This chapter uses the tools and materials that were introduced in the "Tools" and "Materials" chapters, so it is important to read those chapters first.

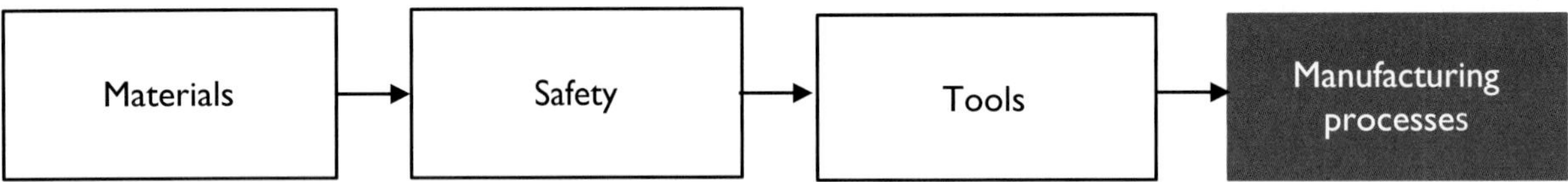

When you have studied this chapter, and the "Mechanisms" and "Electronic circuits" chapters, you can then go on to the "Assembling projects" chapter.

The descriptions here describe processes that can be carried out in school technology rooms, rather than in factories.

Note on answering examination questions

If an exam question asks you for processes or steps, your answers should use terms like measuring, marking out, cutting, drilling, shaping, and finishing.

If a question asks for tools and processes, you can use phrases such as "using a tenon saw, cut the…", "drill using a pillar drill with the correct size wood bit inserted", "smooth using sandpaper", "finish by applying paint with a paintbrush".

If you are asked to describe how to make a particular object, provide steps that are a little more specific to that object. For example: mark out and cut the main body piece using tool X, mark out and cut the slot in the body using tool Y, mark out and cut the back panel using tool Y, attach the back panel to the body using screws, smooth all surfaces and apply two coats of paint, etc.

Manufacturing with wood

This section looks at manufacturing processes for wooden objects.

Measuring and marking out wood

- Measure out the distances you need on the wood using a rule or tape measure, and mark out the line with a pencil.
- Use a try square to mark out any right angles.
- Use a compass to mark out any circles.
- Use a marking gauge to mark out any lines that are parallel to and close to an edge.
- Check your marked out lines or points again before you cut or drill.

Cutting wood

Wood can be cut using hand saws such as a tenon saw and a coping saw, or electric/power saws such as a jigsaw, scroll saw or band saw, as long as they have a blade suitable for wood inserted.

Blades for wood have large teeth, and lots of space between the teeth. The band saw will give the best cut, but it is not suitable for very small items as it is too dangerous to have your hands close to the blade.

Tenon saw	Coping saw	Jigsaw	Scroll saw	Band saw
Use for straight lines and smaller cuts.	Use for curved lines on small items.	Use for curved or straight lines on larger items.	Use for curved or straight lines on larger items.	Use for straight or curved lines on larger items. Best quality.

Process

The process of cutting wood includes the following steps:

- Mark out the lines to be cut (see "Measuring and marking out" above).
- If you are cutting a curved shape, use a coping saw, jigsaw, scroll saw or band saw.
- When using hand tools such as tenon saws, coping saws or jigsaws, hold the piece of wood securely in a bench vice.
- With electric saws such as jigsaws, scroll saws or band saws, make sure the right type of blade for wood is inserted and that the blade is inserted the right way round. Ensure the blade guard is down, then turn on the saw.
- Cut along the lines that you have marked out previously.
- If you are cutting straight lines using the band saw, cut parallel to the edge, using a spacer.

- If you are using a coping saw to cut curved shapes, you many need to change the angle of the blade a few times. This can be done by squeezing in the metal holder so that the blade becomes loose, and rotating the blade. Your teacher will show you how to do this.
- When you get close to the end of the cut, slow down and hold the side of the wood that is about to be cut off. Otherwise the last piece of wood can break off under its weight, and you get an uneven cut.
- When you have cut out the piece, smooth the surfaces (see "Smoothing wood" below).

Drilling wood

The tools below can be used to drill holes in wood.

Bradawl	Hand drill	Electric drill	Bench or pillar drill	Drill bits
Used to start the hole first.	Useful for smaller items held in a vice.	Useful for smaller items held in a vice.	The best quality	Choose and fit the correct size wood bit.

Process

The process of drilling wood includes the following steps:

- Choose the drill bit to match your desired diameter hole. Make sure you use a wood drill bit.
- Measure and mark out your desired holes with a pencil.
- Use a bradawl to create a pilot hole in the wood.
- If you are drilling hardwood, drill a small diameter pilot hole first.
- Ensure the material is held securely in a vice for hand drilling, or secured with clamps on the pillar/bench drill.
- Insert the drill into the drill chuck and tighten the chuck.
- If you are only drilling to a certain depth (not the whole way through the material), set the depth stop on the pillar drill, or place a depth stop or a piece of tape on the drill bit at the desired distance.
- For a good surface finish, drill into the material with the good side facing up. You will get more burred edges when the drill comes out at the other side of the material.
- With hand drills, try to keep the drill bit straight as you can, and apply downward pressure.
- With a bench or pillar drill, make sure the drill guard is down and lower the drill bit on to the wood using the lever.
- If you want to countersink the head of a screw in the hole, change the drill bit to a countersink bit, and drill a small conical depression, the size of the screw head, at the top of the hole.
- After drilling, smooth out burred edges with a round file.

Shaping wood

Shaping means removing pieces of wood so that the wood takes up the shape that you want.

You can use a coping saw to cut away the shape that you want to create. Other tools that can be used for shaping wood are a chisel, plane, router, lathe and laser cutter.

Chisel	Plane	Router	Lathe	Laser cutter
Used on softwoods to chip out shapes and make joints. Hit with hammer or mallet.	Used on softwoods to create flat surfaces. Not good on manufactured boards.	Used for cutting grooves or hollow shapes in wood.	Used to make circular profile shapes such as lamp holders and table legs. Wood is turned at high speed against a movable cutting blade.	Used for cutting different patterns into wood.

Note on planing

Planes are best used along the grain of the wood. If planing on an end grain (where the grain is perpendicular to you), clamp a piece of waste wood to the edges to prevent the edge from breaking off. Also plane from the edge in, not outwards towards the edge.

Creating cut-outs in wood

This consists of removing material from the inside of a sheet or block of wood, leaving the outside edges intact.

To create a cut-out in a sheet of wood

- Mark out the shape you want to cut out of the sheet.
- Drill holes at the corners of the shape that you want to cut out. Stay inside the marking lines.
- Insert the blade of a coping saw through a hole, and tighten the blade back on to the frame.
- Cut out the shape using the coping saw. You may have to cut out several pieces depending on the shape that you need.
- Use sandpaper to smooth the internal edges of the shape (see below).

To create a hollow space in a block of wood

Here the aim is to create a hollow space with a bottom on it (not cutting the whole way through the material). You can use a chisel, a hand-held router, or a drill with a wide Forstner bit (which creates a flat bottom). First mark out the top of the shape you want to cut out.

Then using a chisel:

- Use a chisel to chop down around the edges of the shape to be cut out.
- Use the chisel to keep chopping small pieces out from the block.
- Keep chopping down with the chisel at the edges to keep the edges straight.
- Use sandpaper to smooth the internal edges of the shape.

Method 1, using a drill with a Forstner bit:
- Drill a series of holes beside each other to the same depth so that you remove most of the material.
- Finish off the shape with a chisel, and sand smooth with sandpaper.

Method 2, using a router:
- Set the depth of the router.
- Move the router over the shape to be cut out to remove the material.
- Finish off the corners with a chisel if required, and smooth with sandpaper.

Smoothing wood

The following tools and processes can be used to smooth wooden surfaces.

Sandpaper	Electric sander	File
Wrap sandpaper around a block of wood or a special-purpose sanding block. Use rough sandpaper first to remove most material, and then use fine sandpaper to get a smooth finish.	Useful for large pieces and straight surfaces. Ensure you wear a face mask to protect you from dust.	Useful for getting into corners and smoothing out right angle shapes for joints.

Joining wood

The section below explains common ways of joining wooden pieces to other wooden pieces. Joining wood to other materials and to mechanical and electrical components is covered in the "Assembling Projects" chapter.

Nailing

This method is most suitable when you want to attach a thin piece of wood to a thicker piece, for example to attach a thin back panel to a thicker wooden frame:

- Nail from the thin side.
- Choose the right size nails and hammer.
- Do not nail too chose to the edge of the wood.
- Position the nails evenly across the area to be nailed.
- Do not position nails close together or the wood may split.

For a more attractive finish, use a nail punch to push the heads of the nails slightly below the surface of the wood. If you are painting, you can fill the little nail depression with filler or plastic wood, and paint over it, giving a smooth finish where you can't see the nails.

For an even stronger join, apply wood glue to the surfaces to be joined before you nail them together. The nails will clamp the pieces together while the glue sets.

Screwing

Screws provide a stronger connection than nails. They also have the advantage that they can easily be unscrewed. The disadvantage of screws is that they require more time and work than nails.

First choose a wood screw of the correct length for the pieces to be joined. Screws are more easily used when you are joining a thin piece of wood to a thicker one (screw from the thin side to the thick side). If the outside piece of wood is thick, drill a hole in the outside piece first, so that the screw passes through more easily. Make a guide hole in the other piece with a bradawl. To create a really neat result, drill a countersink hole on the outside hole, so that the head of the countersink screws sits into the countersink hole.

For an even stronger join, apply wood glue to the surfaces to be joined before you screw them together. The screws clamp the pieces together while the glue sets.

Glueing

Use wood glue (often called PVA glue) to glue wooden parts together. Apply glue to both sides to be joined, and spread out evenly. Note that the parts must be tightly pressed and held together for 24 hours before the glue fully sets. This means you must place the parts in a vice or use clamps. You can also nail or screw the parts together.

Joints

A joint is the way in which two surfaces of wood make contact with each other.

The simplest type of wood joint is called a butt joint where the end of one piece is simply placed up against the face of the other piece. A butt joint can be weak if it is just glued, so it often needs to be nailed or screwed as well. Another way to strengthen a butt joint is to glue another piece of wood to the inside corner.

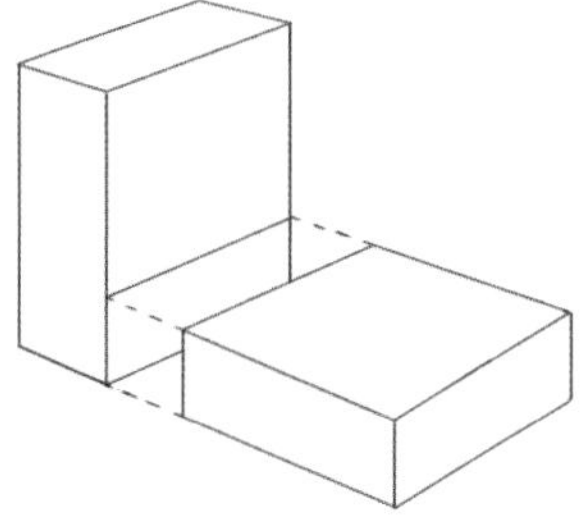

Butt joint

Other strong joints between wooden pieces are shown below. Each of these joints is shaped first, and then the pieces are glued and clamped together until the glue sets.

Dowel joint

To make a dowel joint, partial holes are drilled in the surfaces to be joined, and dowels (small wooden cylinders) are inserted into the holes with glue.

This forms a strong and very neat joint, which is often used for assembling furniture.

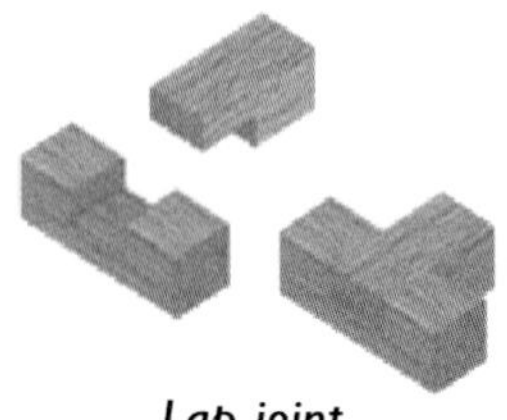

Lap joint

In a lap joint, half of the thickness of each piece is cut away using a saw and chisel, and the pieces slot over each other. This joint is used in cabinet making.

When making a halving joint, half of the thickness of each piece is cut away using a saw and chisel, and the pieces slot into each other. This type of joint is very useful for building frames.

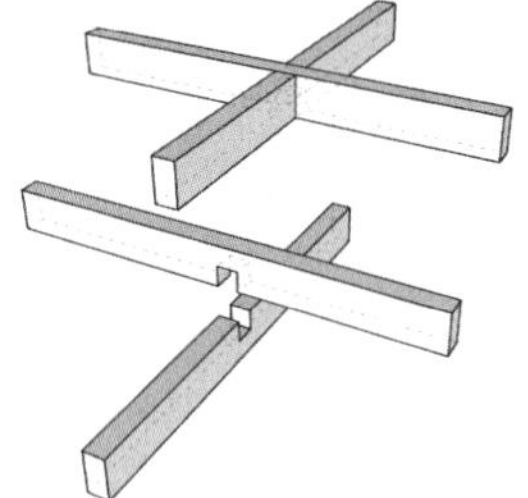

Halving joint

Dovetail joint

A dovetail joint is a complex but extremely strong joint. It is used in high quality furniture, e.g. drawers. The pieces that interlock have angled sides (like a dove's tail) so that they cannot pull apart.

Finishing wood

Oil, paint, stains and varnishes provide good surface finishes for wood. The type of treatment depends on the type of wood and whether you want to allow the natural grain of the wood to show through.

The general process is as follows:

- Apply several coats.
- For best results, use an undercoat or primer coat before painting.
- Apply with a brush, apart from oils, which can best be applied with a clean cloth.
- Between coats, smooth out with a very fine sandpaper.
- Use water-based paints and varnishes: they have low odour, dry fast, and brushes can be washed out with water.
- For a more hard-wearing finish, apply varnish over stains when dry.

Suitable finishes for different types of wood are shown below.

Wood type	Suitable finishes
MDF, HDF, chipboard	Paint
Softwoods, plywood	Paint, stains, varnishes
Hardwoods	Oils (danish oil, tung oil, linseed oil), stains, varnishes

Activities

1. Make the following regular shapes from wood: (a) rectangle, (b) square, (c) triangle, (d) circle. Give each piece a smooth surface finish. Use different woods for each piece, e.g. softwood, manufactured board and hardwood.
2. Make irregular shapes from softwood or manufactured board, e.g. the shape of a fish or a bird. Drill holes for eyes. Create a smooth surface finish.
3. Create a large rectangular or circular cut-out in a sheet of wood (e.g. plywood or hardboard).
4. Hollow out a rectangular space inside a thick block of wood.
5. Create a wooden mould for the hull of a boat, see example opposite. You will use this in the next section to manufacture a plastic hull using a vacuum-former machine.
6. Practice nailing and screwing pieces of wood together. Try this with different sizes and types of wood.
7. Make a butt joint and glue the parts together. Make another butt joint and use both glue and screws.
8. Make a lap joint. Glue and clamp together.

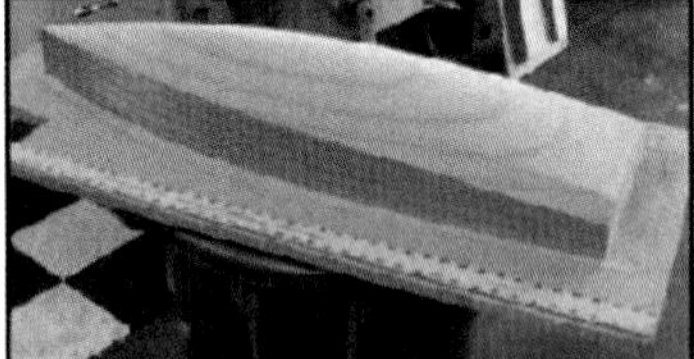

Key points

1. For cutting wood, use a tenon saw, coping saw, jigsaw, scroll saw or band saw.
2. For drilling wood, use hand or electric drills. Select wood drill bits of the right size.
3. Use a coping saw, chisels, planes, or files to create desired shapes. Use lathes to create circular pieces. Use routers to create grooves.
4. Join wood together using nails, screws, glue, or a combination. To make a better, stronger and more attractive join, shape the wood to make a "joint", e.g. a dowel joint or a lap joint.
5. Smooth wooden surfaces using sandpaper, electric sanders and files.
6. Finish the surface using oil, paint, stain, or varnish. Use oil, stain and/or varnish when you would like to see the grain of the wood afterwards.

Test yourself

1. Before cutting a piece of wood with a hand saw, what do you need to do with the wood first?
2. Before drilling a hole in a piece of wood, what should you do with the drill first?
3. Which would give a stronger connection: nails or screws?
4. What type of glue should be used for joining wood?
5. How would you make a curved shape from wood?
6. How would you cut out the pieces required to make a halving joint?
7. What advantages have screws over nails?
8. How would you go about screwing two pieces of thick wood together? What should you do first?

Worked example: Manufacture a wooden body

Past exam question

The graphic shows a design for a toy plane. The body of the plane is to be made from 30 mm x 30 mm red deal. Describe the steps to make the body of the plane.

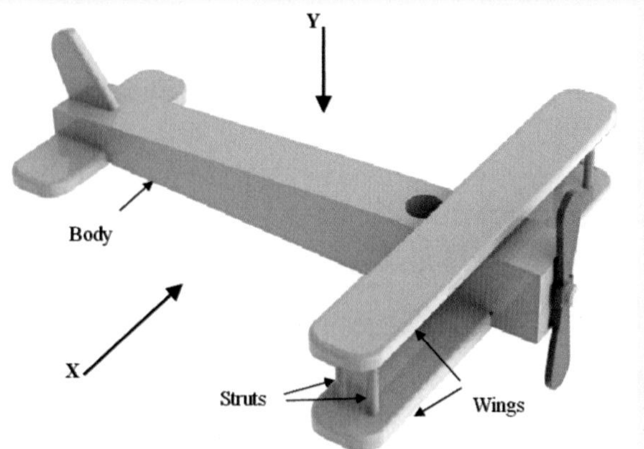

Valid answers

- Mark out and cut the 30 mm x 30 mm piece to the length of the body, using a band saw.
- Mark out the angle to be cut from the bottom of the body piece, and cut with a band saw. Smooth edges with sandpaper.
- Mark out the hole for the cockpit. Hold the body piece in a bench vice and drill out the hole using a hand drill and a wide spade bit. Do not drill the whole way through.

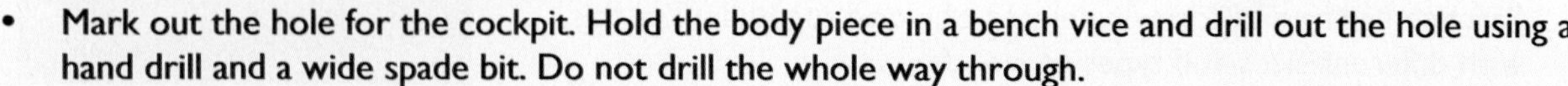

- Mark out and cut out the horizontal and vertical tail fins from a thin piece of red deal using a coping saw and a bench vice to hold. Sand smooth.
- Mark out and cut out the bottom slot for the horizontal tail fin out of the body piece, using a tenon saw, holding the body piece in a bench vice.
- Mark out and cut out a slot for the vertical tail fin using a tenon saw to cut the edges and a thin chisel to remove the waste material. Alternatively use a router to make a groove for the tail fin.
- Apply wood glue to the tail fins and body piece slots, and hold in position using G-clamps until the glue sets.

Past exam questions

1. Name the type of joint shown and provide one advantage of this type of joint.
2. The graphic below shows a rotating display unit. Suggest a suitable material for the rotating disc, and three processes that would be used to make it.

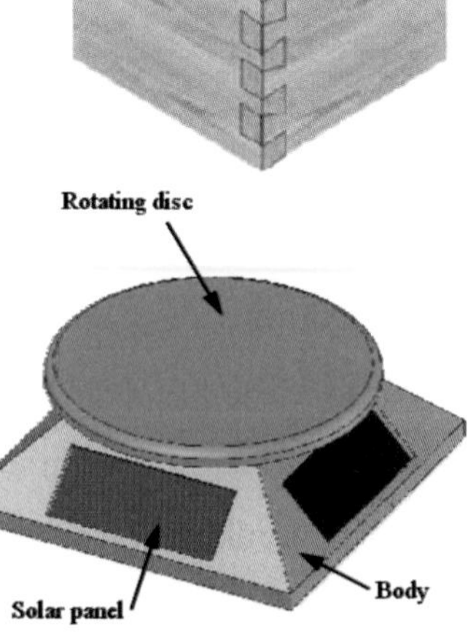

3. A hollow space is required under the body of the car to hold a battery, motor and gearbox. Describe how this space could be formed.

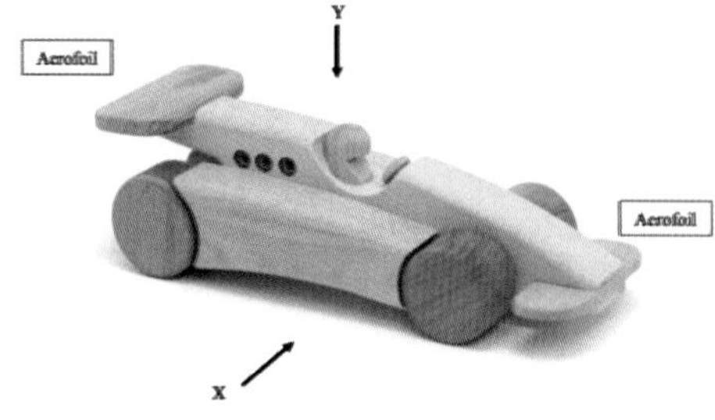

Past exam questions

4. Suggest two ways of joining the giraffe-shaped side panel to the rocker piece at the bottom.

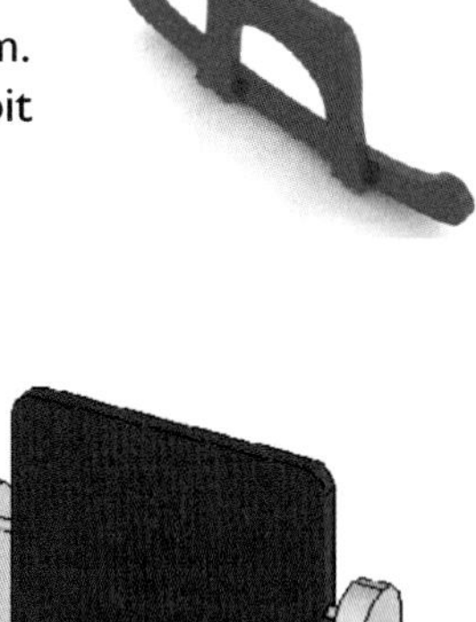

5. Eight holes need to be drilled in the wooden base shown, to a depth of 20mm. Explain how you would ensure that the drill bit does not drill deeper than 20 mm for these holes.

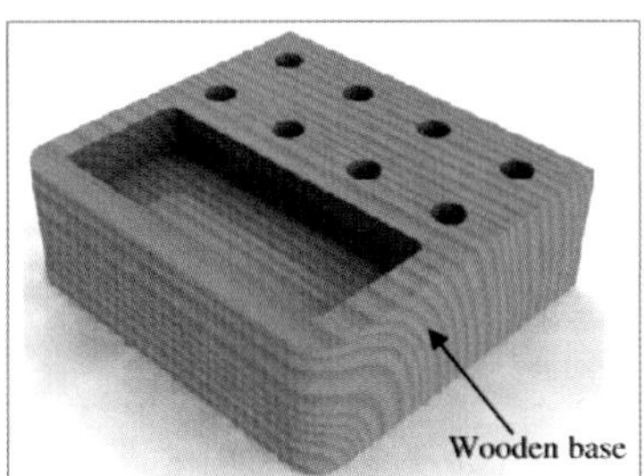

6. A model of a rotating advertising sign is shown. The base and upright are to be made from hardwood. How would you join the uprights to the base?

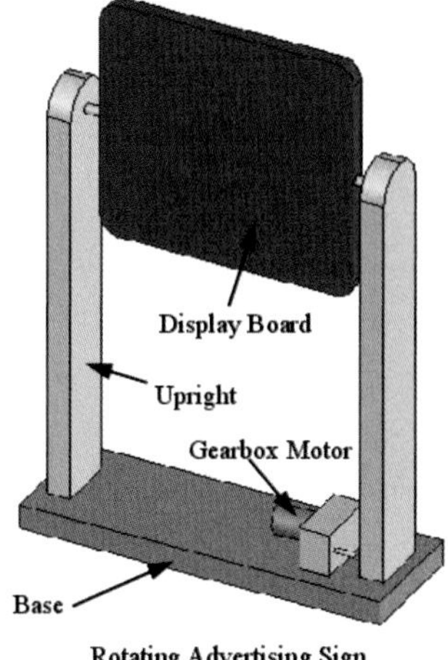

Rotating Advertising Sign

Manufacturing with plastics

This sections looks at manufacturing processes for plastics. Some processes are similar to those for wood, in these cases, only the differences are mentioned.

Marking out on plastics

Use a felt-tip permanent marker, a china-graph pencil, or a marking scribe to mark out plastics. Acrylic sheets come with a thin protective paper or plastic film on them, so you can mark out on that.

Cutting plastics

Use a hacksaw for hand-cutting plastics. This is because the blade for cutting plastics must have very small (fine) teeth, with many teeth positioned close together (close-set). You can also use a jigsaw, scroll saw or band saw to cut plastics, but you must have a fine close-set blade inserted. A band saw gives a clean cut, as the blade moves in one direction only. If you have a speed setting on the saw use a low speed, because high speeds can melt the plastic.

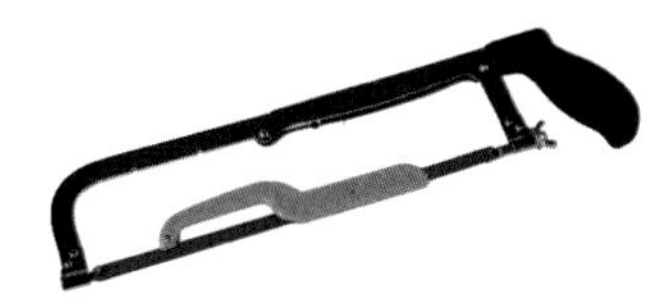

Acrylic tends to break easily so when cutting it use the following process:

- Use a band saw. There is less chance of the acrylic breaking as the blade only moves in one direction.
- When clamping acrylic in a vice, use protective pieces of wood on either side.

Drilling plastic

When drilling plastics of all types including acrylic:

- Use a drill bit designed for plastic.
- Use low speeds on the drill.

To drill acrylic:

- Place a protective piece of waste wood underneath to prevent the acrylic cracking when the drill bit gets through to the other side.
- Drill a small diameter pilot hole first. Then drill your final hole using the pilot hole as a guide.

Forming plastic using a vacuum former

This process is shown on the right. It can be used to create a moulded piece of thermoplastic (such as acrylic or polythene or HIPS). A thin piece of plastic is softened and forms the shape of a mould underneath.

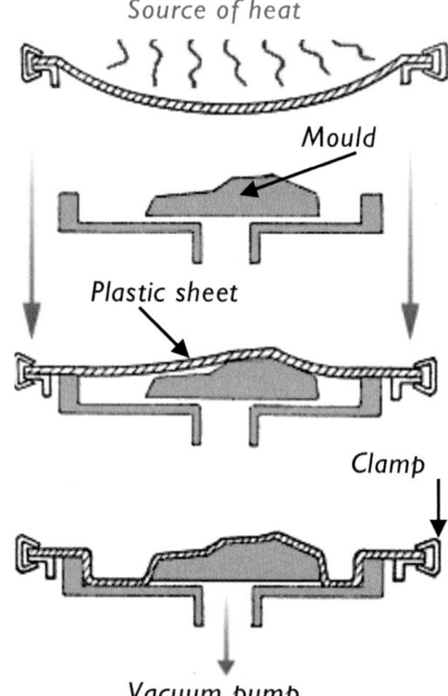

- Buy or make a mould from wood, in the shape that you need. (See previous "Activities" section.) The vertical sides of the mould should be less than 90° to allow for easy removal of the shaped plastic.
- Ensure holes are drilled in the mould so that the plastic is sucked on to the mould evenly, and so that it is easier to remove the finished item from the mould.
- Clamp a thin sheet of plastic above the mould.
- Turn on the heater. The plastic slowly becomes flexible.
- Turn off the heater. Usually the machine will indicate the right time to do this.
- Use the lever to lift the mould upwards under the plastic until it locks in place.
- Turn on the vacuum pump. The air is sucked out and the plastic sheet bends around the mould.
- Turn the pump off.
- Remove the plastic when cooled.
- Trim off excess material using a hacksaw or snips as required and smooth out the edges with a file.

Bending plastic using a strip heater

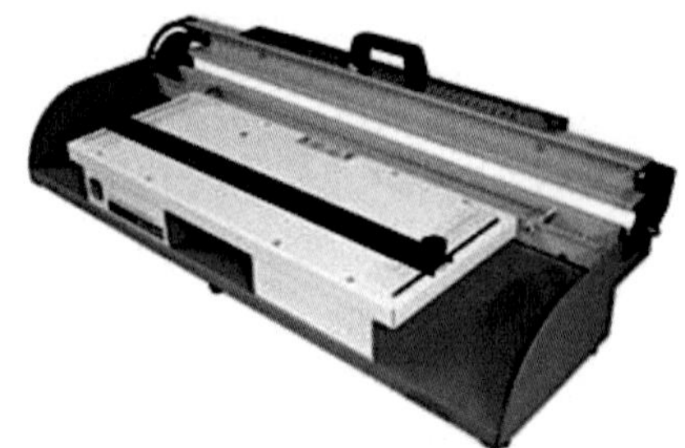

Thermoplastics such as acrylic can be bent along a line using a strip heater. Wear protective gloves.

You will need some pieces of wood to make a former, which you can use to bend the acrylic into the exact angle that you want. For example, if you want to bend the sheet by 90°, you can use two pieces of wood fixed together at an angle of 90°, allowing you to bend or push the sheet in to that angle.

Cut the sheet of acrylic to the right size before you bend it.

When using the strip heater, follow these steps:

- Take off the protective coating on the acrylic.
- Mark the line on the piece of acrylic using a china-graph pencil or marker.
- Turn on the heater.
- Place the acrylic on the strip heater so that the marked-out line is directly over the heating element.
- Close the safety guard.
- Turn over the sheet every 30 seconds or so, to that it heats it evenly on both sides of the line.
- When the acrylic gets soft at the line, take it off the heater, and push it into or over the wooden former using another piece of wood, and keep it there until it cools and takes the shape of the former. It should only take about 2 minutes to cool.
- If you are carrying out more than one bend in the material wait until each bend has fully cooled and set before carrying out the next bend.
- Turn off the heater.

Smoothing plastic

Rough edges on plastic can be smoothed using a file. Use cross-filing first, i.e. push the file away from you across the edge or at a slight angle, to remove most of the material. Finish off with draw filing, i.e. hold the file sideways and push and pull the file along the edge, to get a finer finish.

Surface finishes for plastic

Plastic already has a smooth, and hard-wearing finish and doesn't need any further surface finishes applied. It can be painted, but will need a special primer applied before paint will adhere to it correctly.

Joining plastics

Plastic can be joined by a number of different types of glue including liquid solvent cement (slow-setting, strong), hot glue gun (fast-setting, not as strong), epoxy glue or super glue (fast-setting, strong).

Plastic pieces can also be drilled and held together with nuts and bolts, or pop rivets, but these are not very attractive-looking joining solutions for plastic.

Worked example: Manufacture an acrylic shape

Past exam question

The graphic shows a student's unfinished design for an A4 document stand. The stand is to be manufactured from a single sheet of 3 mm acrylic. Explain the steps required to manufacture the stand from the acrylic sheet.

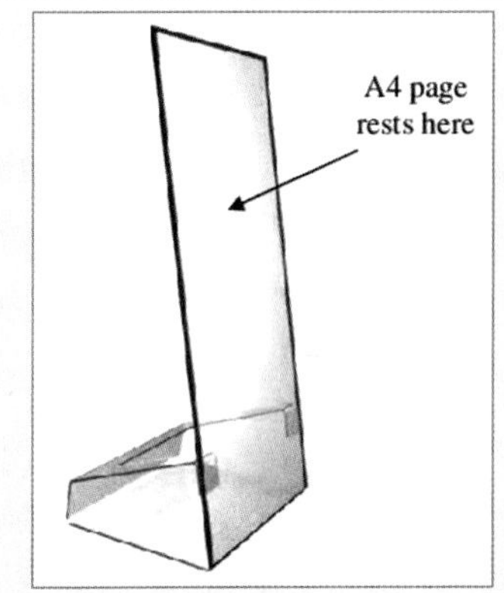

Valid answers

- Measure and mark out the required shape.
- Cut out the shape using a hacksaw or pillar or scroll drill.
- Smooth all edges using a file.
- Use a strip heater to make the four bends required, making one at a time.

Activities

1. Cut out the following shapes from plastic: (a) rectangle, (d) circle, (c) fish. Give them smooth finishes.
2. Create a moulded plastic hull for a boat. Use the wooden boat mould that you created in the previous "Activities" section. What machine will you use to mould the plastic?
3. Practice drilling holes in different plastics, including acrylic.
4. Bend a sheet of acrylic along a single line to an angle of 60°. What machine will you use? How will you ensure the angle is 60°?
5. Join another piece of plastic to the sheet of acrylic that you bent above. What will you use?

Key points

1. Cut plastics with a hacksaw or if using electric tools, a jigsaw, scroll saw or band saw. Make sure a fine tooth blade is fitted and use a low cutting speed.
2. Drill plastics with a suitable drill bit and use a low drill speed.
3. When drilling acrylic, place waste wood under the sheet, and drill a pilot hole first.
4. You can form thermoplastics like acrylic or HIPS into shapes using a vacuum former. Make a wooden mould and ensure there are holes in the mould.
5. You can bend thermoplastics such as acrylic using a strip heater to heat along the bend line.
6. Smooth plastics using a file.
7. Join plastics using liquid solvent cement, a hot glue gun, epoxy glue or super glue.

Test yourself

1. What kind of blade do you need for cutting plastic?
2. How can you bend plastic along a line?
3. How could you mould plastic into different shapes?
4. What is the best way to drill a hole in acrylic?

Past exam questions

1. Why is it necessary to drill small vent holes in a vacuum forming mould?
2. When drilling acrylic, why is it important to:
   (a) drill a pilot hole?
   (b) place a piece of waste wood under the acrylic?

Past exam questions

3. A student intends to manufacture a toy airboat with a flat hull based on the design shown. Describe the steps required to manufacture the hull of the boat from a suitable material.

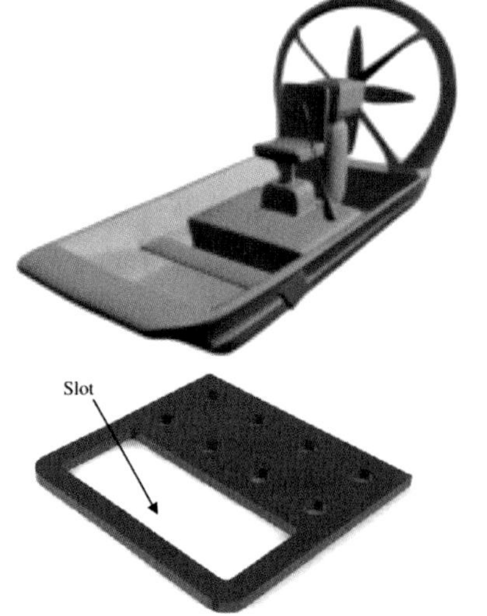

4. The shape of a slot removed from the plastic top surface of desk tidy below is rectangular with the corners rounded. To make the slot, a drill, scroll saw and file where used. Explain how the tools listed were used to do this.

Working with metals

Marking out metal

Use a scriber to mark out cut lines on metals.

Cutting metal

Metals need a fine blade with lots of closely-set teeth, so use a hacksaw, or a jigsaw, scroll saw or pillar saw with a fine blade attached.

Drilling metal

When drilling metal:

- Mark out the location of the hole with a centre punch.
- Use any type of drill.
- Ensure the metal is clamped before drilling.
- Use a metal drill bit.
- Smooth out roughness around the hole with a small round file.

Bending metal

A piece of metal can be bent by placing it in a bench vice between two waste pieces of wood to protect it (note that the image does not show these pieces of wood). The material is marked where it is to be bent, and clamped along the bend line. A third piece of wood is then placed next to the bend line. Hitting this with a hammer or a mallet bends the metal along the bend line over the end of the vice.

In industry, special bending machines are used.

Smoothing metal

Use a file to create a smooth surface on metal. Use cross-filing to begin with and then use draw-filing to finish off.

Finishing metal

Some metals have an attractive finish without any coating such as bronze, copper or aluminium. Metals can be painted, but you should apply a metal primer coat first.

Joining metal

Glueing

Metals can be glued together. Two-part epoxy glues are the best. When glueing metals:

- Mix the two parts of the glue together on a spare piece of material with a wooden spatula.
- Apply the glue to both parts with the spatula.
- Clamp the pieces together and allow the glue to set. This usually takes 24 hours.

Nuts and bolts

Nuts and bolts give a very solid join to metal pieces.

- Choose an appropriate size nut and bolt for the pieces to be joined.
- Choose a drill bit size that is slightly larger than the bolt diameter.
- Drill holes through the objects to be joined.
- Place the pieces to be joined against each other and line up the joining holes.
- Push the bolts through the holes and tighten the nuts on the other side, using a wrench.
- Use a washer inside the nut for a better join.
- If the object you are joining will be vibrating or moving, use a second nut to lock against the first one, to prevent the nut becoming loose over time.

Advantages of nuts and bolts	Disadvantages of nuts and bolts
• Form a strong join. • Inexpensive. • Can be disassembled.	• Can look unattractive if they are visible on the outside. • Require drilling holes in the pieces to be joined. • Need access to both sides of the material.

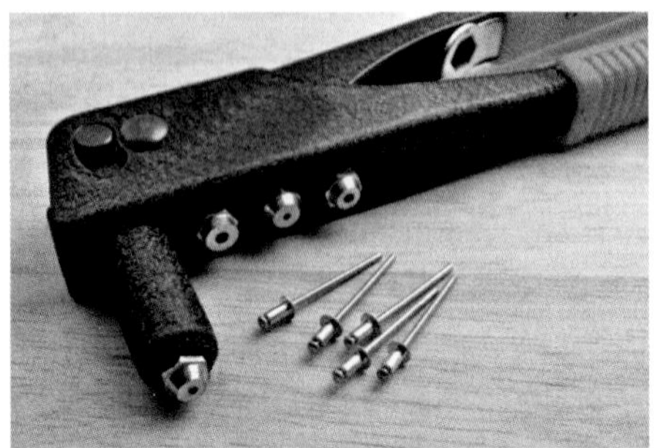
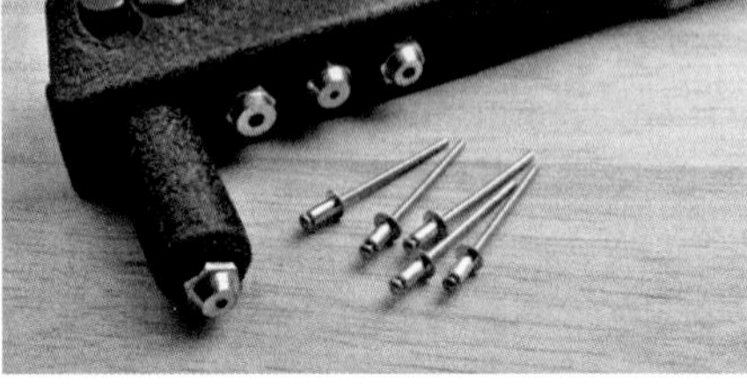

Pop rivets

Metal objects can also be attached to each other using a pop rivet gun and pop rivets.

The process for pop riveting is as follows:

- Choose a pop rivet type and size that is appropriate for the pieces to be joined.
- Choose a metal drill bit with a diameter slightly larger than the diameter of the body of the pop rivet.
- Drill holes through both pieces to be joined, and line up the holes opposite each other.
- Push the pop rivet into the hole, so that the collar/head of the rivet is against the material.
- Put the pop rivet gun down over the long narrow piece that is sticking out of the rivet.
- With a manual pop rivet gun, squeeze the handles several times. With an electric rivet gun, pull the trigger once.

The gun pulls the far side of the rivet inwards and causes it to bulge outwards over the hole on the other side. When there is sufficient tension, the outside piece of the rivet that is being pulled by the gun, will automatically break off. The rivet now holds the parts together.

Advantages of pop rivets	Disadvantages of pop rivets
• Can look better than bolts and nuts. • Fast to assemble if you have an electric pop rivet gun. • Only requires access to one side of the material. • Inexpensive.	• Cannot be disassembled. • Must be cut or drilled off. • Require drilling holes in the pieces to be joined.

Soldering

Soldering is used to join metals together. It is most often used to connect electrical wires and other electronic components to each other. It creates a join that conducts electricity because solder is made from metal (tin and lead). Because it is mostly used for joining electronic components, this process is described in detail in the "Electronic components" chapter.

Creating movable joints

A movable joint is one where two parts are held close together but are still able to move relative to each other. A common example is where one part must to be able to rotate or pivot around the other. This can be done using bolts and nuts, or pop rivets, provided that they are not tightened fully. These methods are suitable for metal, plastic and wooden parts.

Make a movable joint using a bolt and nuts	Make a movable joint using a pop rivet
• Drill the same size hole in both parts. • Insert the bolt. Use a washer on both the nut and bolt sides. • Do not tighten the nut fully. Leave a little space between it and the washer/material. • Put on a second nut and tighten it against the first nut. • You could also glue the first nut to the desired position.	• Drill the same size hole in both parts. • Place a piece of stiff paper or thin cardboard between the parts. • Attach a pop rivet in the normal way. • Tear off the sheet of paper/cardboard. This creates a little space between the parts and allows them to pivot around the rivet.

Depending on the type of movement you require, a linkage, axle, or hinge may be a better choice.

Worked example: Manufacture a metal shape

Past exam question

Describe how the night light holder shown could be bent into shape.

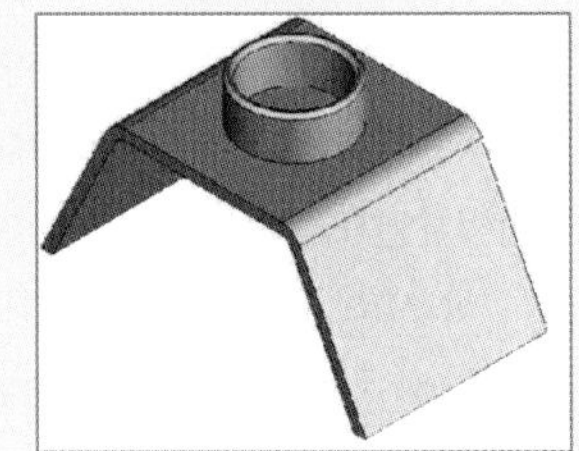

Valid answers

Insert the metal sheet in to a bench vice, and tighten the vice. With a mallet, hit a piece of protective wood on the metal, which in turn bends the metal.

A special metal bending machine could also be used.

Activities

1. Cut out a rectangular shape from a sheet of metal and create smooth edges.
2. Drill a number of holes in a sheet of metal.
3. Join two pieces of metal with small nuts and bolts.
4. Create a movable joint between two pieces of metal using a pop rivet.
5. Bend a sheet of metal to 60°.

Key points

1. Mark out cut lines on metal with a scriber.
2. Mark out drill points on metal using a centre or dot punch with a hammer.
3. Bend metal in a bench vice using protective pieces of wood and a hammer or mallet.
4. Smooth metal with a file.
5. Join metals with epoxy glue, nuts and bolts, pop rivets, or soldering.
6. If painting metal, apply a primer coat first.

Test yourself

1. Why is a centre punch useful when drilling metal?
2. What type of hand saw would you use to cut metal?
3. Name three methods of joining metal.
4. Define a movable joint and explain how to make one.
5. State two advantages and disadvantages of using nuts and bolts to join metals.
6. State two advantages and disadvantages of using pop rivets to join metals.

Past exam questions

1. A (metal) lamp post is shown on the right. Parts C and D must be fixed together using a suitable joining method. Suggest a method and describe three steps in carrying out this process.

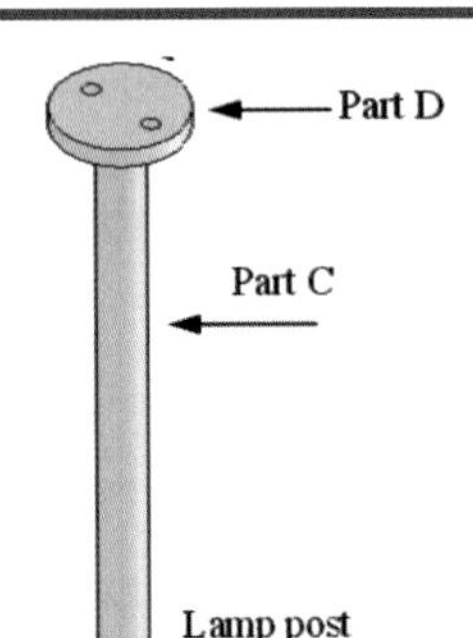

2. The sketch below shows a design for a pizza cutter, in elevation and isometric view. Choosing a named metal, describe the steps necessary to shape the material into the handle design shown. All dimensions are in mm.

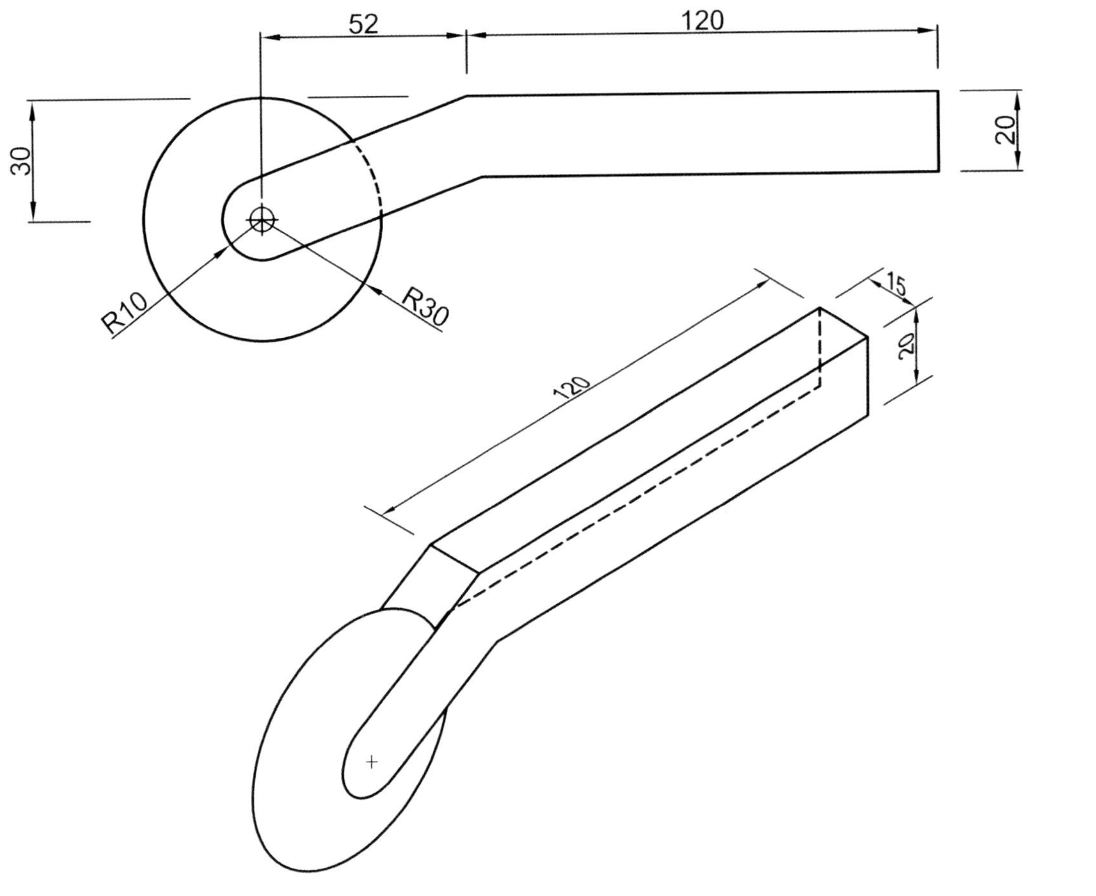

Structures and forces

Structures and forces

This chapter is about the forces that act on structures, and how to design structures so that they can withstand those forces.

The Shard, London

What is a force?

A force is a push or pull that can cause something to move. Forces are measured in newtons (N).

What is a structure?

A structure is any object that is made in a particular shape using particular materials. It may have many parts, like a building, or it may be a shape made in one piece, such as a plastic container.

Where do forces on structures come from?

- Gravity - whenever structures are designed to hold up heavy loads, such as cars or people, the weight of those objects results in forces on those structures.
- The structure itself - the weight of the structure itself creates forces within the structure. Different parts of the structure will experience different types of forces.
- The environment - wind, waves and earthquakes can exert large forces on structures.
- Moving parts - if a structure contains moving parts, the movement of the parts will create forces on the structure.

Why is it important to understand forces on structures?

If a structure is not designed to withstand the forces acting on it, the structure can fail and break. This can be catastrophic if the structure is a building or a bridge.

What determines how strong a structure is?

The strength of a structure depends on:

- **The material** that the structure is made from.
- **The shape** of the structure.
- **The type of force** acting on the structure.

Types of forces on structures

Compression

Image	Description	Examples
	The object is being squashed together. Two opposite forces are pushing against the object. A material that can withstand this type of force has high compressive strength, e.g. concrete.	• Columns supporting a building (gravity pushing down, the ground resisting) • Legs on a table • Rafters supporting a roof • Struts used in a structure (see later)

Tension

Image	Description	Examples
	The object is being stretched. An object that can withstand this kind of force has high tensile strength. A material that can withstand this type of force has high tensile strength, e.g. steel wire.	• Steel cables supporting a bridge • Strings on a guitar • Strings on a tennis racket • Spokes on a bicycle wheel • Chain on a bicycle • Ropes and stays on masts, tent poles, flag poles • Ties used in a structure (see later)

Torsion

Image	Description	Examples
X	The object is being subjected to a twisting force, called a torsion force.	• Axles of cars and all machines • Twisted elastic bands • Twisting a Rubik's Cube • Opening the lid of a jar

Shear

Image	Description	Examples
	Two forces are pushing on the object from opposite sides. The two forces are not lined up directly against each other, but are slightly separated. This causes a sliding or shearing force in the material, which can break it.	• Paper being cut by a scissors

Bending

Image	Description	Examples
	A bending force is a combination of compression and tension. In the example beam shown on the left: • The lower half of the beam is stretched, and is in tension. • The upper half is squashed, and is in compression. • In between (along the dotted line), there is neither compression nor tension.	• A shelf, with a bracket at either end, supporting an object in the middle • A bench, with a support at either end, supporting a person sitting on it

Forces in structures with multiple parts

Parts of a structure are often called members. It can sometimes be difficult to tell which members in a structure are under compression and which are under tension. Some examples are provided below.

Worked example 1: Forces on a triangular structure

Question

The triangular structure opposite is made from three metal bars joined to each other. The base of the triangle is resting on the ground. A downwards force is applied to the top of the triangle. What forces are on three bars of the triangle?

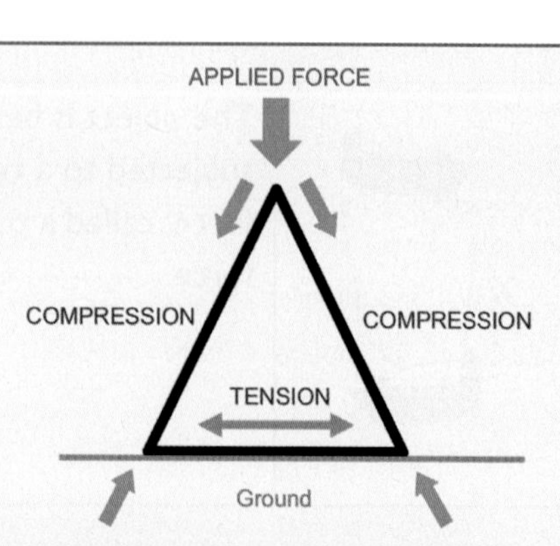

Solution

- The two sides of the triangle are in compression. This is because the applied force is pressing downwards but the ground is not moving (is pressing back).
- The bottom of the triangle is in tension. This is because the force applied on the top is pushing the two sides bars of the triangle out to the sides, and so the bottom bar is stretched.

Worked example 2: Forces on a rectangular structure

Question A

A rectangular structure is made from four bars of metal. A force is applied to the middle of the top bar as shown in the diagram.

What forces are on the members of the structure?

APPLIED FORCE
BENDING
COMPRESSION
COMPRESSION
NO FORCE
Ground

Solution

- The top bar is under a bending force. This is because the two sides of the top bar are supported, but not the middle.
- The two sides of the rectangle are in compression. The downward force that is applied to the middle of the top bar is transferred across to the two side bars via the top bar.
- All of the applied force is directed downwards, so the bottom bar it is not in tension or compression horizontally along its length.

Question B

A diagonal bar is attached to the rectangular structure, as shown. What effect does this have on the forces on the structure?

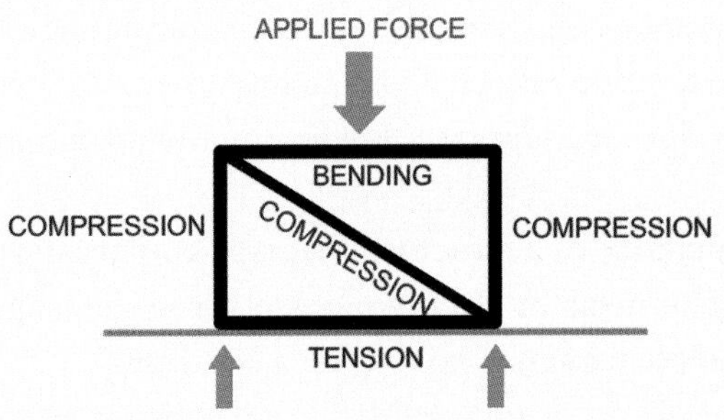

Solution

- Neither the left nor the right side of the diagonal bar can move (because they are fixed to the side bars), so the diagonal bar is under compression from the downward force.
- The diagonal bar is pushing against the bottom right hand corner, so it is stretching the bottom bar out to the right, and so the bottom bar is in tension.
- There are no other changes to the types of forces in the structure - the top bar is still bending, and the bars on the sides are still under compression.

However, there is less compression on the two side bars because some of the applied force has been diverted to the diagonal bar and the bottom bar. So we can say the structure is stronger as a result of adding the diagonal bar. Adding a diagonal bar is a form of triangulation – used to make structures stronger. Triangulation is discussed later in the chapter.

Worked example 3: A bicycle wheel

Question

What are the forces acting on the spokes of a bicycle wheel?

Solution

When the wheel is made, the spokes are tightened between the hub (centre) and the rim (outside) of the wheel, so the spokes are in tension, just like the strings of a tennis racket.

Worked example 4: Sitting on a bicycle

Question

What happens when you sit on a bicycle? Why don't the thin bottom spokes just bend and crumple under your weight?

Solution

When you sit on a bicycle, you don't bend the bottom spokes because you are hanging from the top spokes. The top spokes can support your weight because wire is very strong in tension - it won't break.

The bottom spokes cannot take your weight because the thin wires would just crumple under compression. Note also that on a bicycle wheel, the spokes are angled in a criss-cross fashion. This is an example of triangulation (see later), which makes the wheels stronger.

Ties and struts

A member of a structure that is in tension is called a tie. A tie helps to prevent two objects from pulling apart and separating. Ties are usually thin, for example stays holding up the mast on a yacht.

A member of a structure that is in compression is called a strut. A strut helps to stop two objects from moving closer together, for example, columns holding up a building.

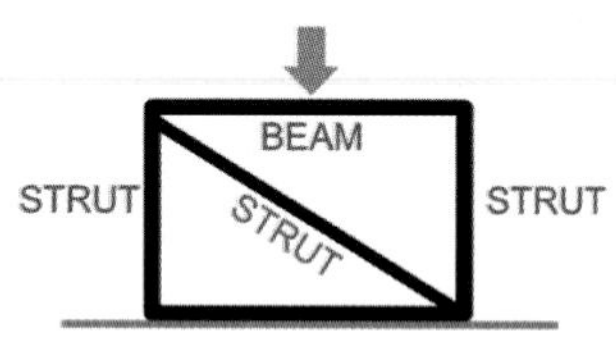

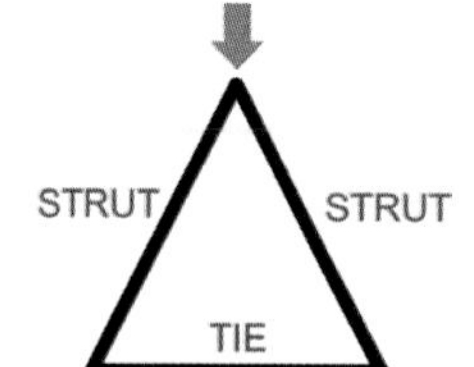

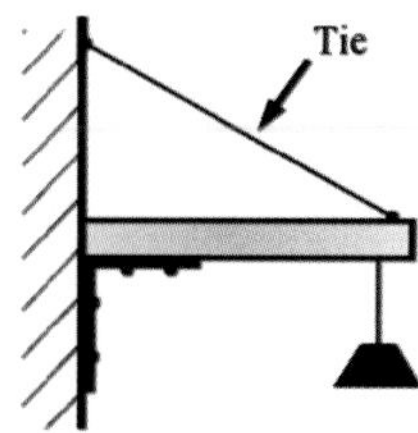

A **tie** is any member of a structure that is in tension.

A **strut** is any member of a structure that is in compression.

Tension or compression?

When working out whether a member of a structure is in tension or compression, ask yourself this: if the member were to suddenly break, which way would the pieces move?

- If the pieces would move towards each other, the member is under compression.
- If the pieces would move away from each other, the member is under tension.

Past exam questions

1. The downward force produced by a house acting on the ground is:
   - Shear?
   - Torsion?
   - Compression?

2. The force applied when twisting a Rubik's cube is called:
   - Compression?
   - Torsion?
   - Bending?

3. Name the forces operating at X (spoke cables) and at Y (frame legs) in the structure shown.

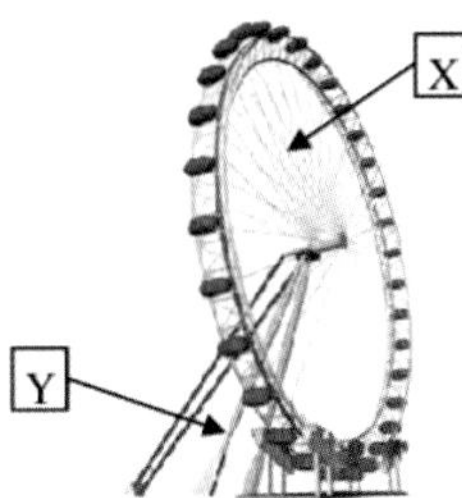

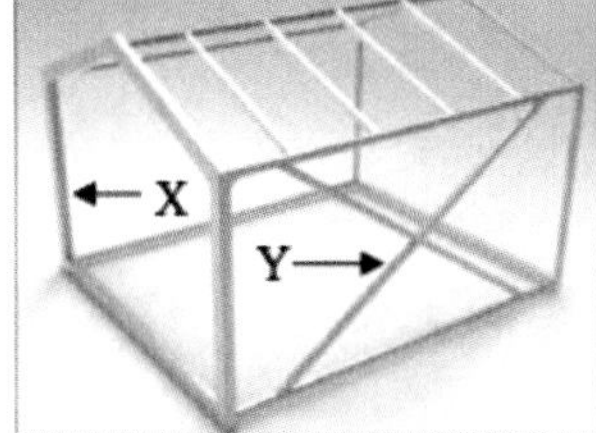

4. Name the forces acting on the members labeled X and Y.

5. Guitar strings are in:
   - Torsion?
   - Compression?
   - Tension?

6. The tie is in:
   - Shear?
   - Tension?
   - Compression?

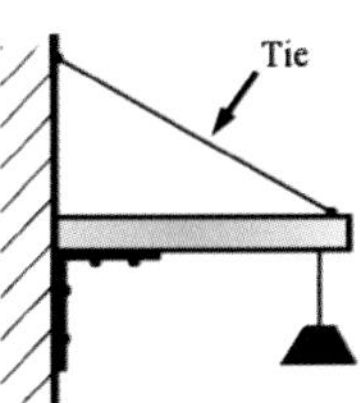

Past exam questions

7. The spokes in the wheels of a bicycle make them strong and lightweight. Name the force acting on the spokes of a bicycle wheel.

8. Sail cloth must be strong in:

   - Compression?
   - Tension?
   - Both of the above?

9. The strings in a tennis racket are in:
   - Compression?
   - Tension?
   - Torsion?

10. The force on the bar shown is:
    - Torsion?
    - Bending?
    - Compression?

11. What is a tension force? Identify two parts of this bicycle that are in tension.

12. Name the forces acting at X and at Y on the swing shown.

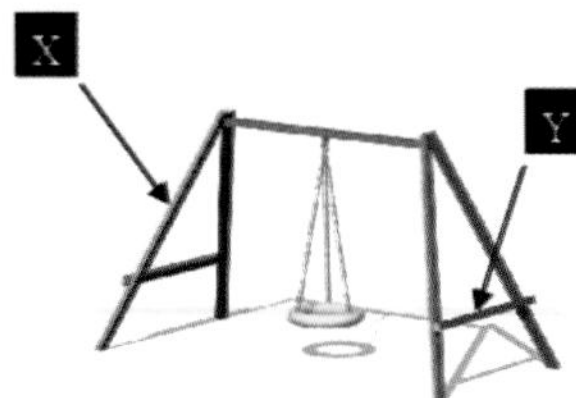

13. Name the forces operating at X and at Y in the bending beam shown.

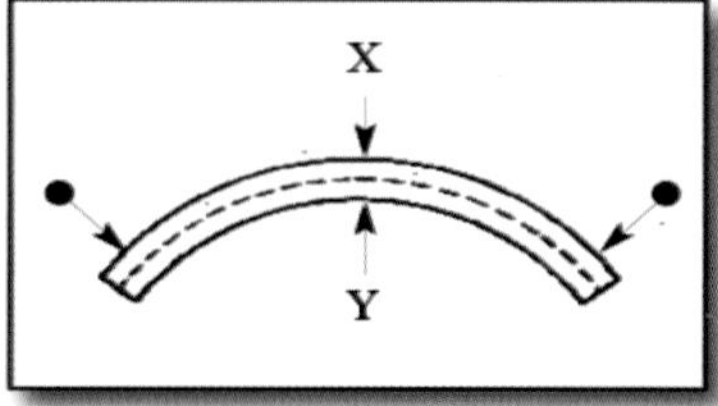

14. Shown is a toy plane, which uses a rubber band. The force in the rubber band is:
    - Compression?
    - Tension?
    - Bending?

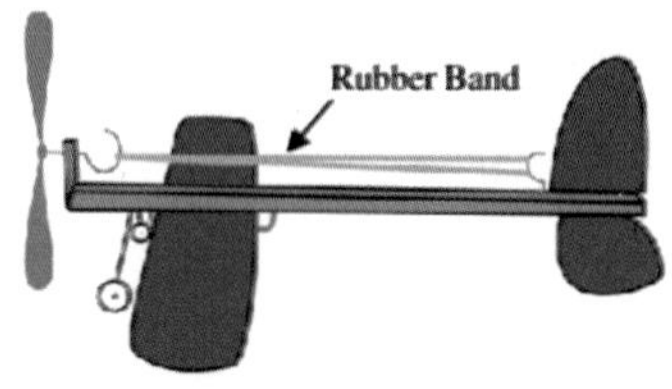

Past exam questions

15. Name the forces operating at A, B and C.

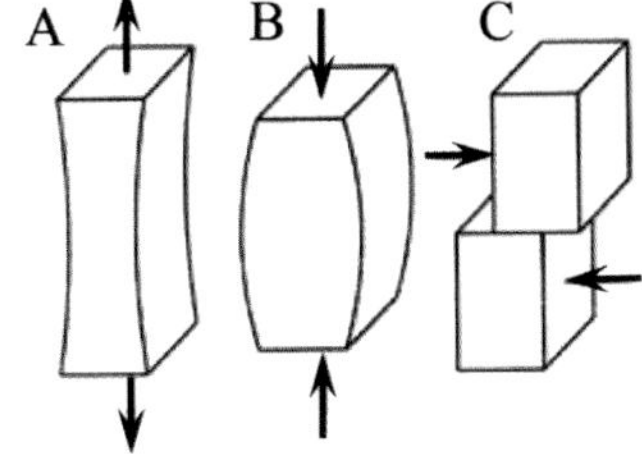

16. The sketch shows a land yacht. Name the main force acting on the non-rigid stay "X".

17. Name the forces operating at X and at Y as shown.

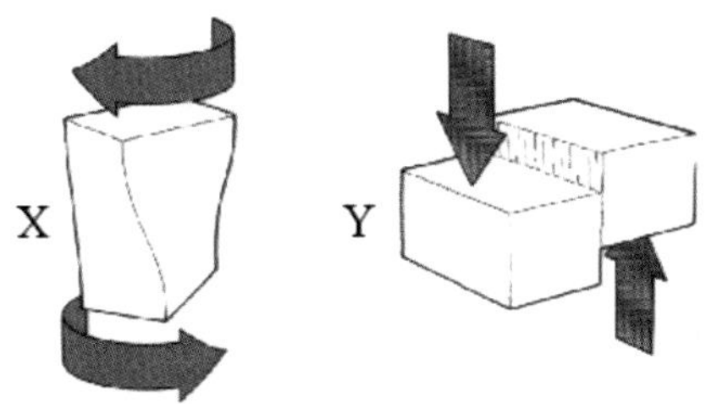

Stability of structures

When a structure is stable, it is resistant to falling over. The more sideways force it can withstand without falling over, the more stable it is.

Which of these objects is the most stable, and which is the least?

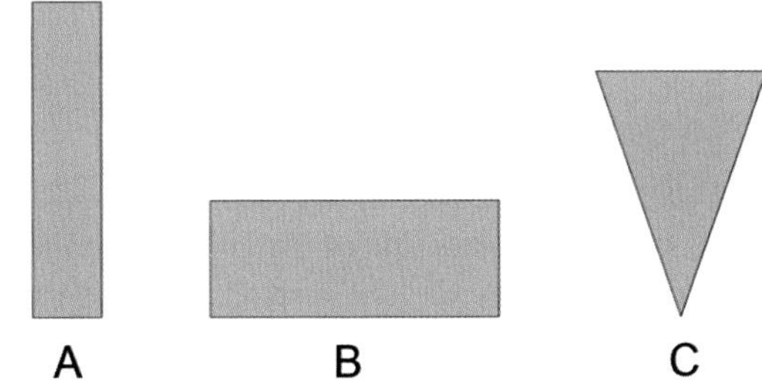

Why is object B more stable than object A, and why is object C completely unstable? The answer has to do with centre of gravity.

Centre of gravity

The centre of gravity of an object is the point at which all of its weight seems to be concentrated, as if the whole object was just one point. An object can be balanced on its centre of gravity.

The **centre of gravity** of an object is the point at which all of its weight seems to be concentrated.

Stability and centre of gravity

The stability of an object is determined by: (a) how high the centre of gravity is (shown in red dots below) and (b) how far its centre of gravity is from the edge of its base (shown by the blue arrows).

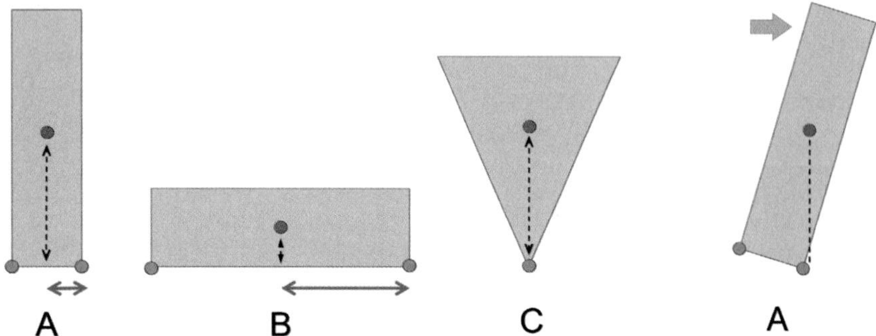

- Object A has a high centre of gravity and a narrow base, so it is not very stable.
- Object B has a low centre of gravity and a wide base, so it is very stable.
- Object C has a centre of gravity directly over its only support point, so it is unstable.

The diagram above on the right shows how far you can tilt object A before it will fall. An object will fall when a vertical line drawn down from its centre of gravity lies outside its base. You don't have to tilt object A very far for the line from its centre of gravity to lie outside its base. It would take a much greater force and distance to achieve the same thing with object B. With object C, it would be practically impossible to keep the line from its centre of gravity inside its base, so it falls over easily.

Racing cars have a very low centre of gravity and wide-set wheels. This makes them very stable, and hard to flip over when turning corners at high speeds. Compare the centre of gravity of a racing car to that of a double-decker bus.

Activities

Try to find the centre of gravity of some common (and light) objects by balancing them on your finger, for example a ruler. Try to find an object that is heavier at one end (like a golf club), and see where it balances.

Can you balance a set square or a try square on your finger? Why not? This is because its centre of gravity is actually outside the object, in the air.

Strengthening structures

This section provides a number of techniques for making structures stronger.

Strengthening by bending and corrugating

If you have a flat piece of material, you can make it much stronger by bending it. If you bend it back and forth repeatedly, you have what is called a corrugated sheet.

Corrugated sheets are much stronger than flat sheets because you have effectively made the material thicker at the bent sections. If you were to make the material itself to that thickness, it would be too heavy and expensive.

Corrugated metal sheets are widely used to make roofs. Corrugation allows us to make strong and light cardboard boxes from very weak paper. Two flat paper sheets are glued on to either side of a corrugated paper sheet. This stops the corrugated paper sheet in the middle from folding flat.

Activities

Take a piece of stiff cardboard and corrugate it. Can you support objects on top of it? (You'll probably have to make right angle bends so that they don't flatten out too easily.)

Strengthening using shell structures

Using the same principle as strengthening by bending, objects that are moulded in non-flat shapes are stronger. These types of structures are known as **shell structures**. This process is widely used with plastics because they are easily moulded.

A good example is a plastic toy brick. These are hollow and light (saving material), but extremely strong. Another example of a shell structure is an egg box.

Strengthening structures using struts and ties

Here is an example of using struts and ties to strengthen a structure. How would you strengthen a wooden flagpole to prevent it being blown over by the wind? The diagram on the left shows wire cables tightened around the flagpole, and the diagram on the right shown wooden pieces attached to the flagpole. Note that the wires can only strengthen the structure when stretched (when used as ties in tension). The wooden pieces can work as struts or ties, depending on where the force is coming from.

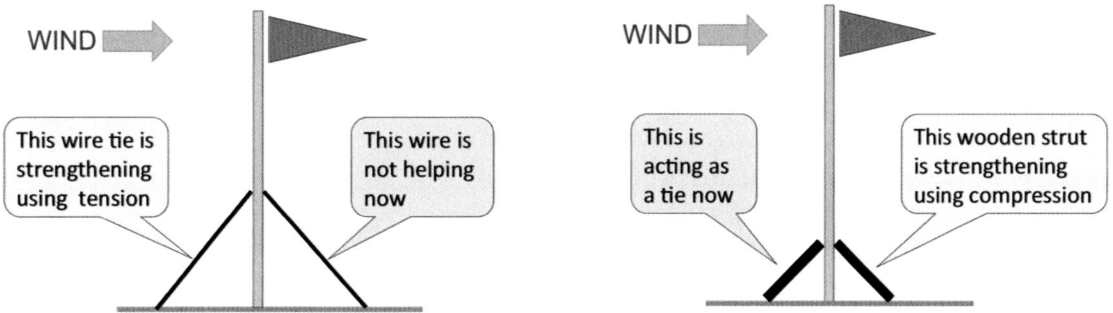

Test yourself

How would you hold up the Leaning Tower of Pisa? Where would you place a strut? Where would you place a tie?

Beams

Beams are used to bridge a gap between two structures and to support a weight. They are usually made from wood, stone or metal. Beams are used over window and door openings to support the walls above. Beams are also used as a support to hang things from, such as pulleys. A beam is the simplest type of bridge.

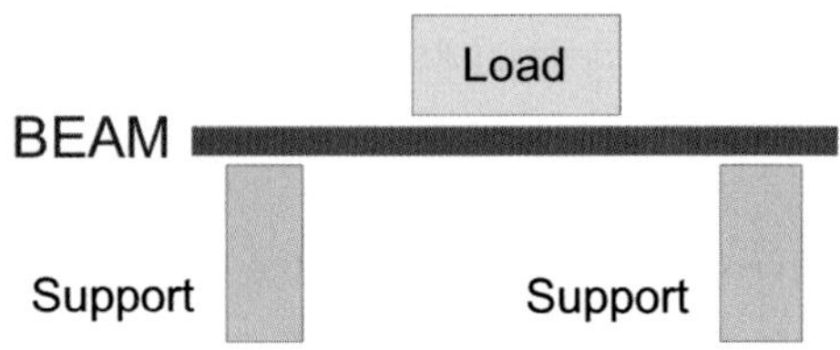

Beams need to be very strong because they are subject to strong bending forces from the loads they have to support. Beams can be made strong by making them:

- From strong materials like steel.
- As thick as possible.
- In certain shapes (see below).

Beam shapes

Instead of using a large amount of material to make a beam, which would be expensive and heavy, we can make beams in certain shapes that are still very strong. This is using the "strengthening by bending" principle that we saw earlier.

Common shapes for beams are shown below. These shapes are shown in cross-section. A cross-section is the shape you would see if you looked at the beam from the end on, or if you cut through it. These beams are typically made from steel, and they are widely used in the construction of buildings.

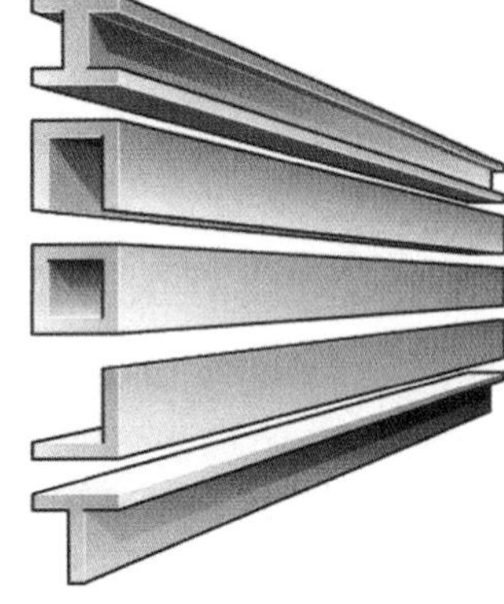

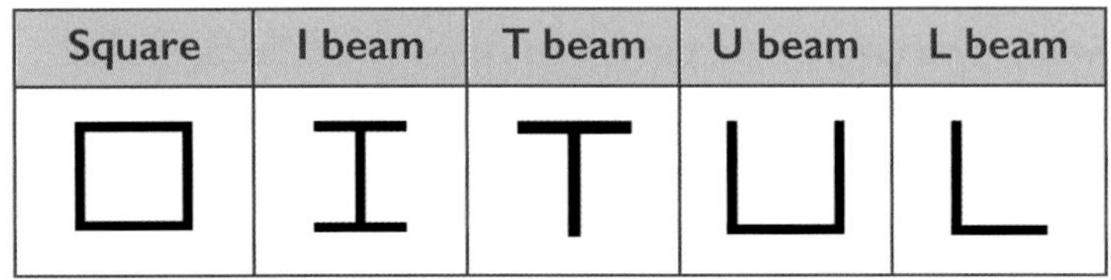

Square	I beam	T beam	U beam	L beam
□	I	T	U	L

Arches

An arch is a curved beam that can support a great weight because of its shape. When you press down on an arch, it doesn't bend - it only compresses. Many materials like concrete, brick, stone and metal are extremely strong in compression, so they are suitable to make arches from.

An arch also diverts the downward pressure to its side supports, which are usually stronger than it is.

Arches are very successful at what they do. This is why they have been used for thousands of years to build structures such as bridges and churches.

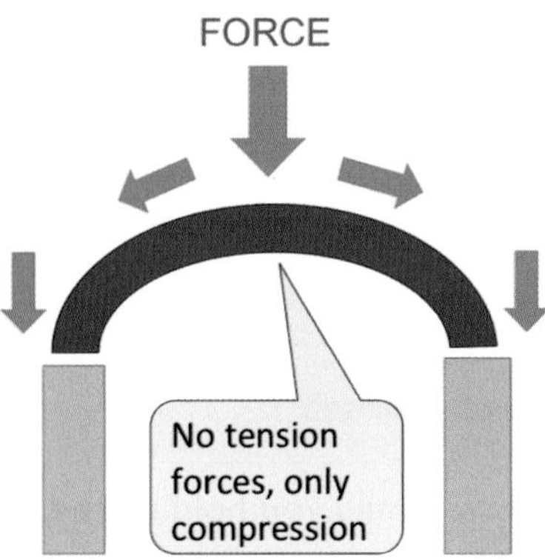

Worked example 5: Strengthening beams and a gantry crane

Past exam question

The graphic shows a design for a working model of a lightweight gantry crane. The crane will allow small loads to be lifted and moved around a workshop.

(a) Sketch two possible cross sections for beam A to support a vertical load. Your design must ensure the beam is lightweight and will resist bending.

(b) Copy the crane design shown and sketch clearly additional members to (i) further support beam A and (ii) increase the stability of the crane.

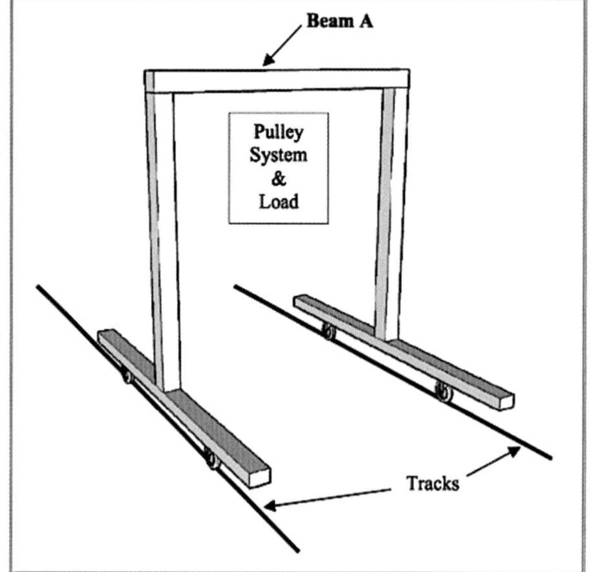

Solution

(a) Two possible cross sections for beam A that will be lightweight and resist bending are shown below.

(b) (i) The struts shown in pink will further support beam A.

(ii) The struts shown in blue will increase the stability of the crane.

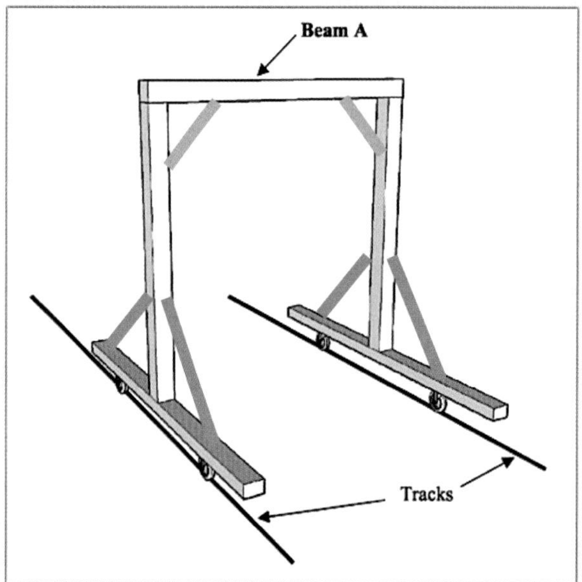

Triangulation

Triangulation is a very important way of strengthening structures. A common problem that triangulation solves is described below.

Worked example 6: Basic triangulation

Problem

On the left is a square structure made from four metal bars, bolted together at the corners. The corner joins are the weak spots. If there is pressure on the square, it may buckle out of shape, as shown on the right.

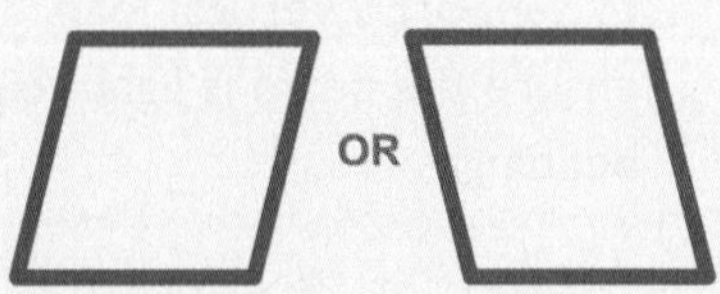

Solution

The solution is to brace the square with another metal bar across the diagonal, as shown. This prevents the square from buckling, because if it tried to do so, it would have to compress or stretch the entire diagonal metal bar, which is difficult to do.

It doesn't matter which diagonal you choose, because the metal bar will work in both compression and tension. If you only had thin metal wire to strengthen the square, you would have to stretch it across both diagonals, because the wire will only work in tension.

In the example above, we made the structure much stronger by replacing one square with two triangles. The triangle is a very strong structure. Notice the number of triangles in the crane structure shown on the right. Cranes need to be strong, so lots of triangles are needed.

Another example of using triangles for strength is in bicycle frames.

Worked example 7: Triangulation of more complex shapes

Question

How would you make the structure on the right more rigid?

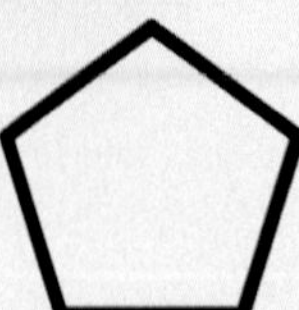

Solution

If you added one cross-member, the structure would look like this:

This still has a weak section on the bottom that could buckle.

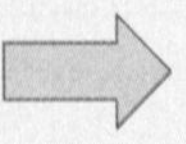

You need to keep adding cross-members until all you have left are triangles:

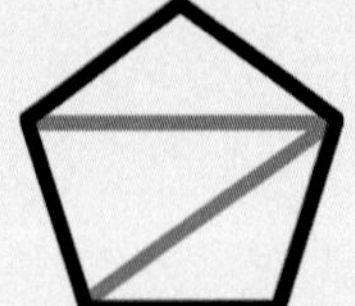

This shape is very strong.

Frame structures

Frames allow you to make large structures that are light and strong. With a frame structure, multiple pieces (members) are joined together to form a "skeleton". A frame structure may or may not have flat sheets on the outside.

Modern office buildings and timber-framed houses are made by making a frame first, and then attaching the walls and windows to the frame. Both the building and the crane shown on the right are examples of frame structures.

If you make a frame in 3D, i.e. not just a flat frame, it becomes very strong. If you use triangulation in your frame, it becomes even stronger. Some more examples of frame structure are shown below.

Examples of frame structures		
A natural example  Webs are extremely strong and flexible structures for their weight.	*A pyramid frame*  Triangulation in 3D.	*A famous triangulated tower* 
Box frame 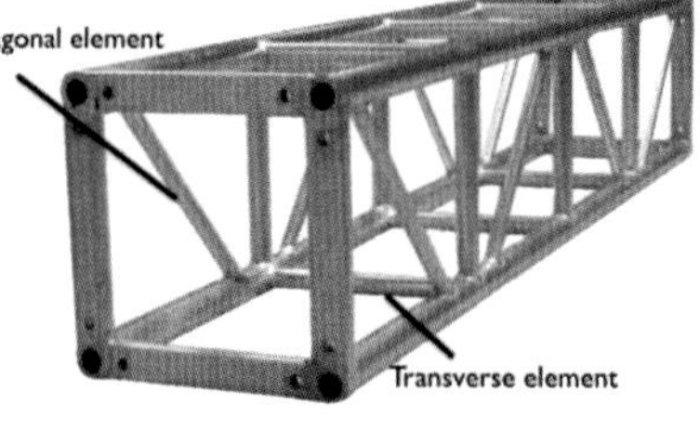 This is like the frame structure seen in a crane. It has members at 90° in all 3D directions (width, height and depth), and it also has diagonal members for triangulation and strength.	*Geodesic frame*  A geodesic frame is a hemisphere-shaped dome frame made from triangles. Material (e.g. glass) can be spanned across each flat triangular section.	*Electricity pylon* 

Bridges

Different bridge designs demonstrate many of the structural techniques we have seen in this chapter.

Strutural techniques used in bridges	
Arch bridge  A concrete arch takes the load under compression. As the arch is not fully under the level of the walkway, a combination of struts and ties is used to connect the walkway to the arch.	*Cable-stayed bridge*  The roadway is suspended from a concrete strut using high-tension metal cables (ties). This works because concrete is resistant to compression and steel wire is resistant to tension.
Arch suspension bridge  The bridge above demonstrates the use of multiple structural techniques in one bridge. The arch is made from a triangulated metal frame structure, and the arch takes the weight of the roadway, which is suspended from the arch using metal cables. In a suspension bridge the cables are vertical, while in a cable-stayed bridge the cables run directly back to the strut at an angle.	

Key points

1. The main types of forces on structures are:
   - Compression (squashing).
   - Tension (stretching).
   - Torsion (twisting).
   - Shear (sliding).
   - Bending (combination of compression and tension).
2. Examples of structural elements under tension are: guitar strings, tennis racket strings, bicycle spokes, cable ties on flagpoles, and masts.
3. Examples of structural elements in compression are: table legs, building columns, and arches.
4. A low centre of gravity gives you a stable structure.
5. You can make flat sheets stronger by bending or corrugating them.
6. Shells are strong structures because they are moulded in single-piece shapes that are not flat.
7. Struts are elements of a structure that are in compression.
8. Ties are elements of a structure that are in tension.
9. You can strengthen structures by adding ties and/or struts.
10. You can strengthen structures by triangulation, i.e. adding cross-members to make triangles.
11. Bicycle frames are example of triangulation.
12. Beams span a gap, are supported at both ends and are subject to bending forces.
13. Beams can be made lighter and use less material by making them in square, I, T, U, or L cross-sections.
14. You can make structures light and strong by making them as frame structures.
15. Examples of frame structures are electricity pylons, cranes, and timber-framed houses.

Activities

1. Make a square or rectangular frame using four lengths of stiff paper or cardboard, and some pins. Notice how wobbly it is. Now attach a diagonal piece and see how it improves it.
2. Make a simple beam bridge using a ruler laid across two small blocks of wood. Feel the ruler bending when you press it. Turn the ruler on its edge. Can you bend it along its edge?
3. Notice the shape and design of bridges when you are passing them. Are they straight beams, do they use arches, are they suspension bridges?
4. Notice electricity pylons when you are passing by them. Do they contain triangles?
5. Look at some cardboard boxes. Can you see the corrugated paper?
6. If you are making a project in the technology room, consider making a frame structure first, and then attaching the base and sides to the frame. Think about using struts to make your design more stable.

Past exam questions

1. To make a bicycle frame stronger, designers make use of:
   - Triangulation?
   - Surface finishing?
   - Parallelogram shapes?

2. This basin is an example of a:
   - Shell structure?
   - Frame structure?
   - Shell and frame structure?

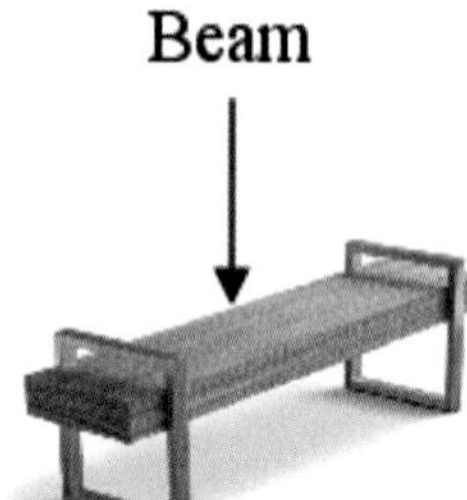

3. The solid beam shown can be replaced by a lower cost beam containing less material. Sketch cross sections of two suitable replacement beams.

4. Shown is a geodesic dome. A geodesic dome is a:
   - Frame structure?
   - Shell structure?

5. Draw in the least number of bars to make each framework rigid.

Framework 1

Framework 2

Framework 3

6. A bicycle frame uses triangles (triangulation) to make it rigid. Name and sketch in 2D, two other structures that use triangles to make them rigid.

7. The sketch shows a bridge distorting under the force shown. Sketch the location of two struts that will prevent the bridge from distorting.

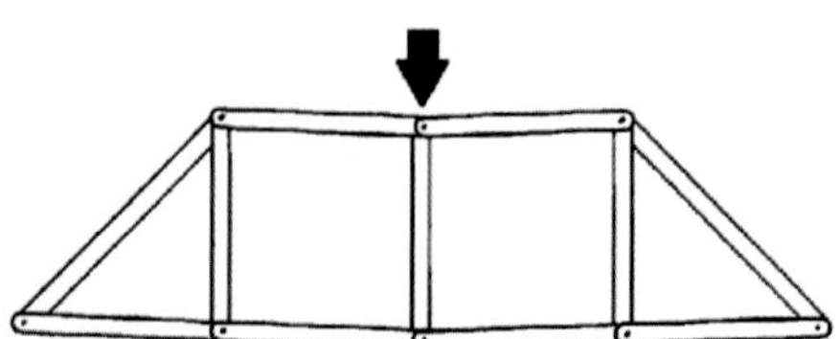

8. This structural framework model is a:
   - Prism?
   - Pyramid?
   - Cone?

Past exam questions

9. The uprights, platform and base of a model bridge structure are shown. Cables are to be attached to the bridge to make it stronger.

   Using a pencil, sketch the cables needed to strengthen the bridge.

10. What kind of a bridge is shown below?

    - An arch bridge?
    - A beam bridge?
    - A suspension bridge?

11. Name the structural feature that makes the tower-crane both strong and lightweight.

12. Identify the two types of structure used in the egg box at "X" and in the dome at "Y".

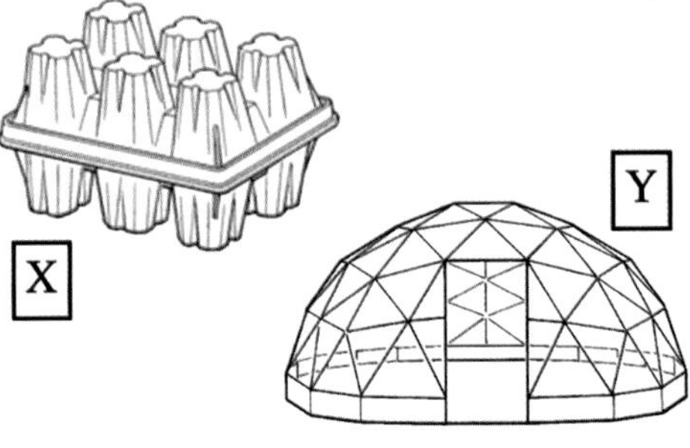

7 CHAPTER

Mechanisms 1

What are mechanisms?

Mechanisms are devices that transform an input motion or force into an output motion or force. The mechanisms covered in this chapter are levers, linkages, springs, cams and cranks. Gears, pulleys, chain and belt drives and other mechanisms are covered in "Mechanisms 2".

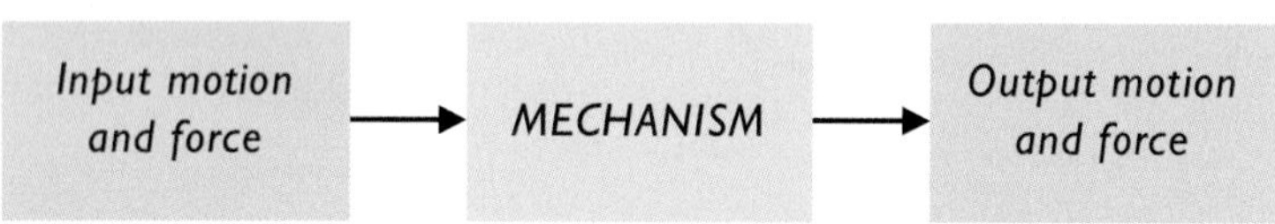

Complex mechanisms inside a watch

All machines are made up of simple mechanisms. We don't always see mechanisms because they are sometimes hidden inside outer casings.

A **mechanism** is a device that converts an input motion and force, into an output motion and force.

Example of a mechanism

The picture on the left shows a mechanism called a pruning scissors. The pruning scissors is used to transform a relatively small input force exerted by the hand into a large enough output force to cut the branch off the bush.

Understanding mechanisms

Mechanisms are essential for Leaving Cert projects, come up in exam questions, and are tricky to understand. For these reasons it is important to spend plenty of time on this topic. The following tips may help you:

- Practice lots of answers and calculations yourself using the "Test yourself" and "Past exam questions" sections.
- Build and play with real mechanisms in the technology room.
- Watch videos or animated images of each mechanism operating.
- Use mechanisms in your technology projects.
- Review the summary table at the end of the "Mechanisms 2" chapter.

What are the different types of motion?

Because mechanisms work with motion, we first need to learn about the different types of motion.

Type of motion	Meaning	Symbol	Example
Linear	Moving in a straight line	→	A train running along a straight track
Rotary	Turning, moving around in a circle	↷	A wheel turning
Reciprocating	Moving back and forth in a straight line	↔	Sawing a piece of wood
Oscillating	Swinging from side to side in an arc	↶↷	A pendulum swinging in a clock

Test yourself

1. What type of motion is the entire train undergoing?
2. What type of motion are the train wheels undergoing?
3. What type of motion are the bars / cranks connected to the wheels experiencing?

4. What types of motion do you think might be happening in the picture on the right?

5. Does a jigsaw blade oscillate, reciprocate or rotate?

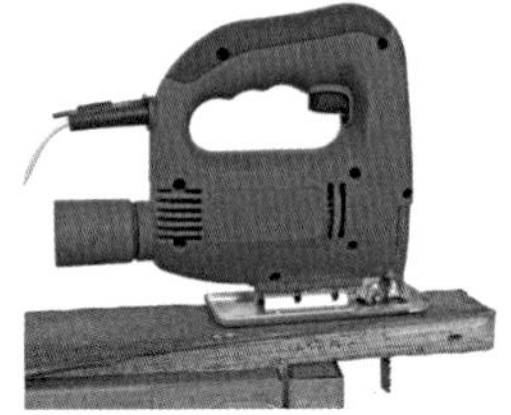

Past exam questions

1. What type of motion do the outer spheres in Newton's Cradle carry out?
2. A moving swing is an example of what type of motion?
3. The blade of a scroll saw moves up and down. Is this rotary motion, oscillating motion, or reciprocating motion?

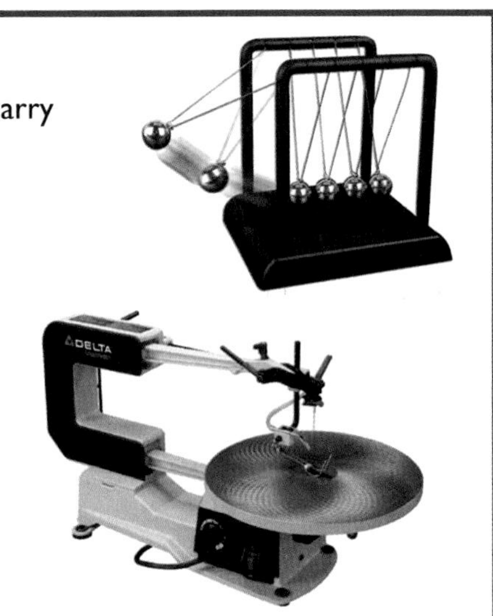

Levers

A lever is a rigid bar that pivots around a fulcrum or fixed point.

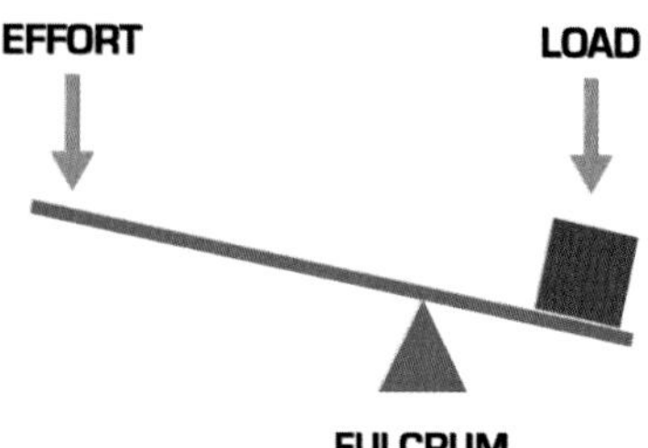

The fulcrum is the point around which the lever turns. The load is the output force. The effort is the input force that you apply to move the load.

Load and effort are forces and are measured in newtons (N).

> A **lever** is a rigid bar that pivots around a fulcrum.

Mechanical advantage

Mechanical advantage means that a heavy load can be moved using a smaller effort. Mechanical advantage is calculated using the formula below. Both effort and load are forces and are measured in newtons.

$$\textbf{Mechanical advantage} = \frac{\text{load (force in newtons)}}{\text{effort (force in newtons)}}$$

From the formula, we see that mechanical advantage is the ratio of two forces. Therefore it has no units - it is just a number.

Uses of levers

Levers are used to make certain jobs easier such as:

- Lifting heavy loads, using mechanical advantage.
- Moving objects at a distance.
- Applying strong cutting or pinching forces.

Example of mechanical advantage

A wheelbarrow is a type of lever. If a 200 N load can be moved in the wheelbarrow with an effort of 100 N, the mechanical advantage of the lever is 2.

Test yourself

1. If a 200 N load can be moved with an effort of 50 N, what is the mechanical advantage?
2. If it takes 200 N to move a load of 200 N, what is the mechanical advantage?
3. If it takes an effort of 400 N to move a load of 200 N, what is the mechanical advantage?

How does a lever create mechanical advantage?

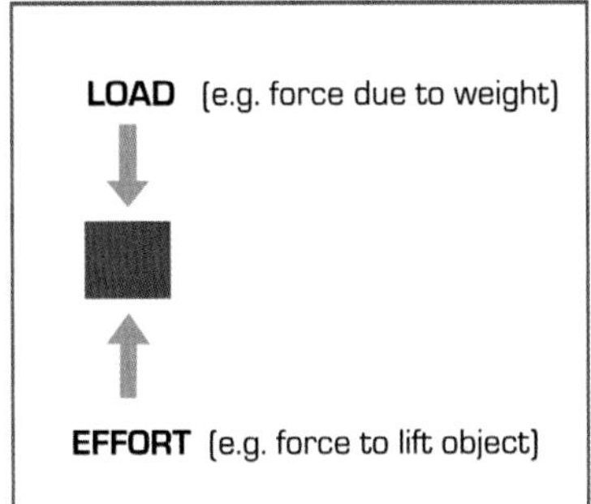

Normally to move an object, the effort force must be larger than the load force (see left). So how does a lever move a large load force with a smaller effort force?

The answer lies in the fact that a lever creates a moment, also known as a turning effect, or turning force.

Moments

A lever creates a moment, or turning effect, when it pivots around a fulcrum (see right).

The greater the distance from the fulcrum that the force is applied, the greater is its turning effect, i.e. its moment.

This is shown in the diagram on the right.

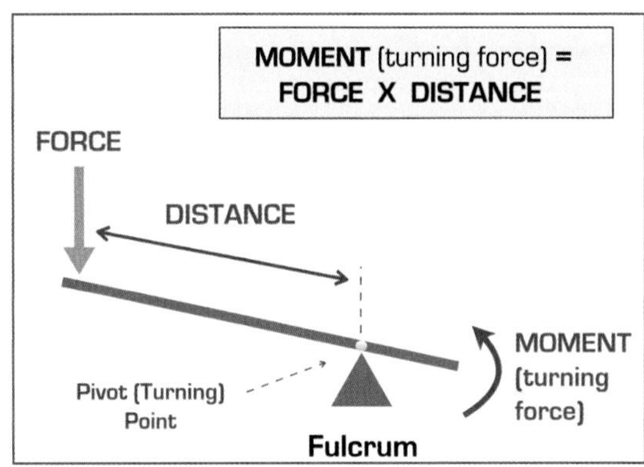

The moment of a force is equal to the magnitude of the force, multiplied by the distance from the fulcrum to where the force is applied. It is measured in newton metres, (Nm).

Moment = force × distance (Nm)

A balanced lever

Moments explain why two different weights can be balanced on a lever. When a lever is balanced, it is said to be in equilibrium.

The diagram below shows a force of 100 N on the left of the fulcrum, and a force of 200 N on the right. They can be balanced if the 100 N force acts at twice the distance from the fulcrum as the 200 N force.

Calculations

Moment = force × distance

Moment on the effort side = 100 N × 2 m = 200 Nm

Moment on the load side = 200 N × 1 m = 200 Nm

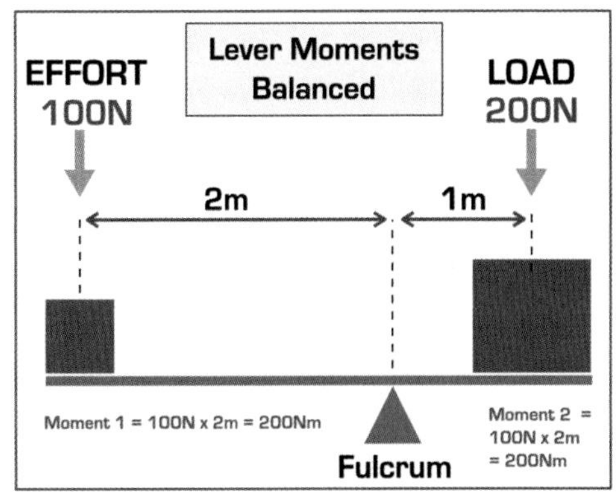

Since the magnitudes of the moments on the two sides are the same, they cancel each other out, and the lever doesn't move. This means that a smaller weight on one side can balance a greater weight on the other. Try it out.

Law of the lever

As we have seen, with a balanced lever:

Force × distance on the effort side = force × distance on the load side

Moment on left side = moment on right side

This formula is known as the law of the lever and it can be used to carry out many useful calculations with levers.

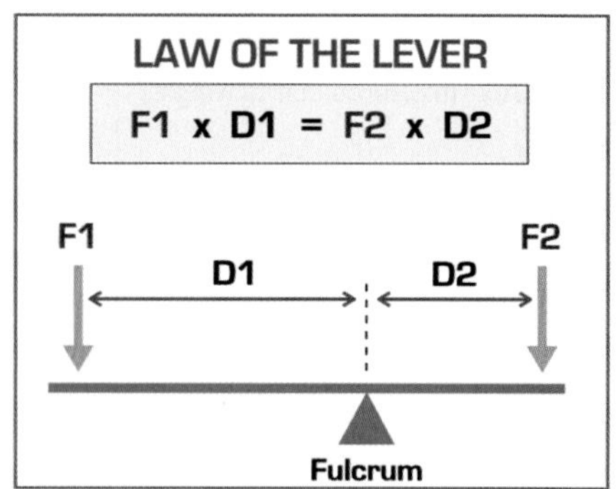

Law of the lever

Effort force × distance of effort to fulcrum = load force × distance of load to fulcrum

Uses of law of the lever

The law of the lever allows us to do many useful things, such as calculate the:

- Effort needed to lift a certain load.
- Load we could lift with a given effort.
- Distance at which we would need to apply a certain effort in order to lift a certain load.

Worked example 1: Calculate lever effort and mechanical advantage

Question (A)

What effort is required to balance the load shown?

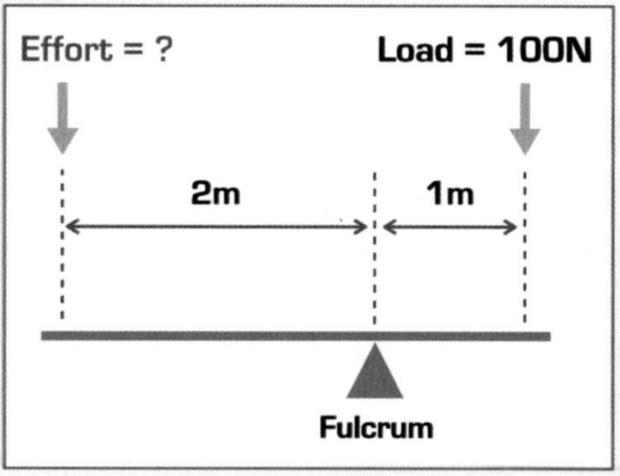

Solution by reasoning

The effort, F(effort), is applied at twice the distance from the fulcrum than the load, so the effort required, F(effort), will be half of the load force, i.e. (half of 100 N) 50 N.

Solution by applying the law of the lever formula

$$\text{F(effort)} \times 2\text{ m} = 100\text{ N} \times 1\text{ m} = 100\text{ Nm}$$

$$\text{F(effort)} = \frac{100\text{ Nm}}{2\text{ m}} = 50\text{ N} = \text{ effort required}$$

Question (B)

What is the mechanical advantage of the system?

Solution

$$\text{Mechanical advantage} = \frac{\text{load}}{\text{effort}} = \frac{100\text{ N}}{50\text{ N}} = 2$$

The mechanical advantage can also be calculated from the ratio of the distances:

$$\text{Mechanical advantage} = \frac{\text{distance from effort to fulcrum}}{\text{distance from load to fulcrum}} = \frac{2\text{ m}}{1\text{ m}} = 2$$

Worked example 2: Calculate lever load and mechanical advantage

Question (A)

What load can be supported by the lever shown?

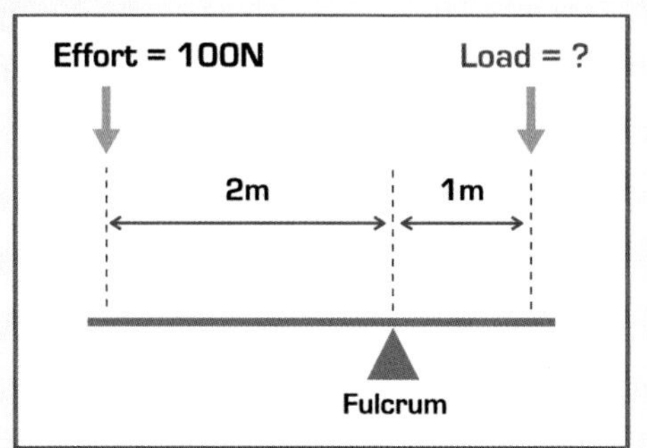

Solution by reasoning

The load, F(load), is applied at half the distance from fulcrum compared to that of the effort, so the load will be equal to twice the effort, i.e. 200 N.

Solution by applying the law of the lever formula

$$\text{F(load)} \times 1\text{ m} = 100\text{ N} \times 2\text{ m} = 200\text{ Nm}$$

$$\text{F(load)} = \frac{200\text{ Nm}}{1\text{ m}} = 200\text{ N}$$

Question (B)

What is the mechanical advantage of the system?

Solution

$$\text{Mechanical advantage} = \frac{\text{load}}{\text{effort}} = \frac{200\text{ N}}{100\text{ N}} = 2$$

Worked example 3: Calculate distance from fulcrum and mechanical advantage

Question (A)

In the lever arrangement shown, at what distance will a 200 N load have to be placed from the fulcrum, in order to be supported by a force of 100 N applied at 1 metre from the fulcrum?

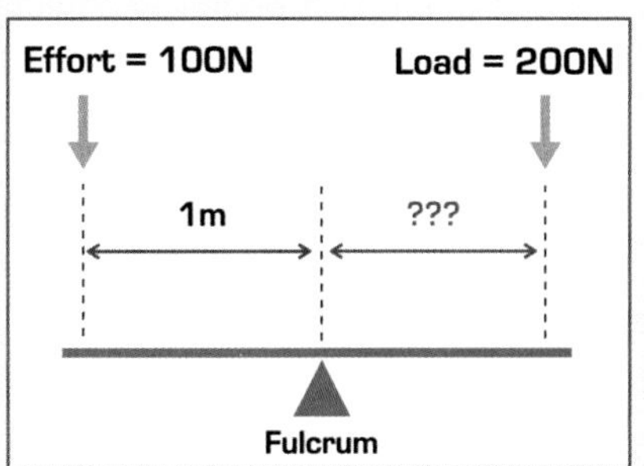

Solution by reasoning

The load force F(load), is twice the effort force, so the load distance must be half the effort distance, i.e. 0.5 metres.

Solution by applying the law of the lever formula

$$100\text{ N} \times 1\text{ m} = 200\text{ N} \times \text{D(load)} = 100\text{ Nm}$$

$$\text{D(load)} = \frac{100\text{ Nm}}{200\text{ N}} = 0.5\text{ m}$$

Question (B)

What is the mechanical advantage of the system?

Solution

$$\text{Mechanical advantage} = \frac{\text{load}}{\text{effort}} = \frac{200\text{ N}}{100\text{ N}} = 2$$

Or by using the ratio of the distances:

$$\text{Mechanical advantage} = \frac{\text{distance from effort to fulcrum}}{\text{distance from load to fulcrum}} = \frac{1\text{ m}}{0.5\text{ m}} = 2$$

Test yourself

1. What effort is required to support the load shown on the right? What is the mechanical advantage?

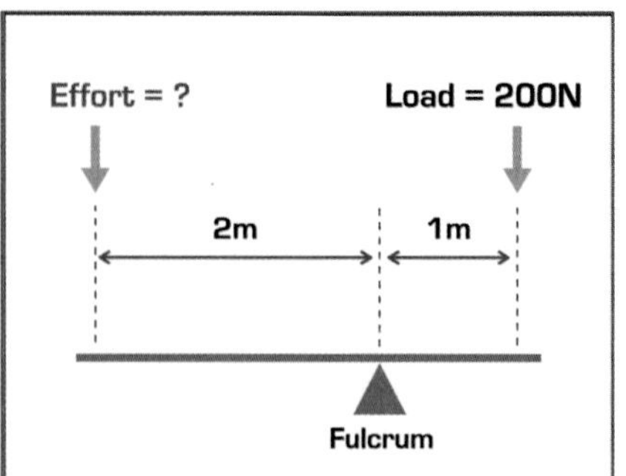

2. What load can be supported by the lever on the right? What is the mechanical advantage?

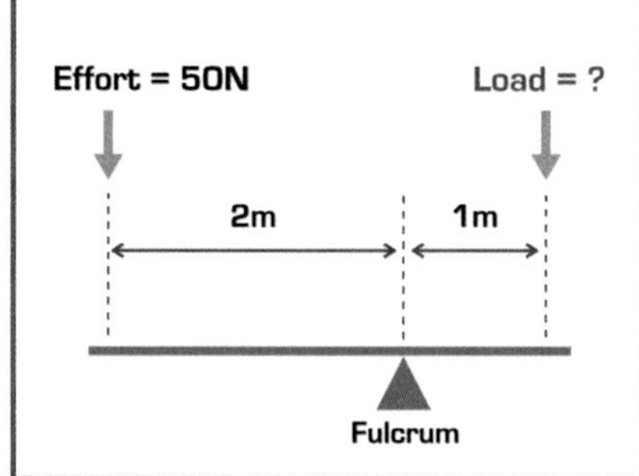

3. What effort is required to support the load on the right? What is the mechanical advantage?

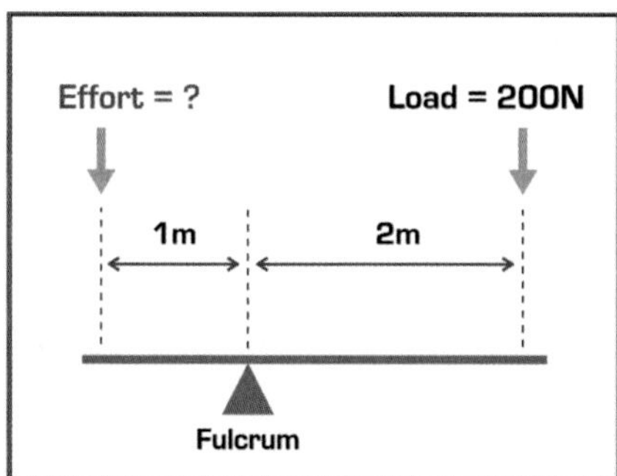

4. In the system on the right, at what distance from the fulcrum would the effort need to be applied, in order to support the load? What is the mechanical advantage?

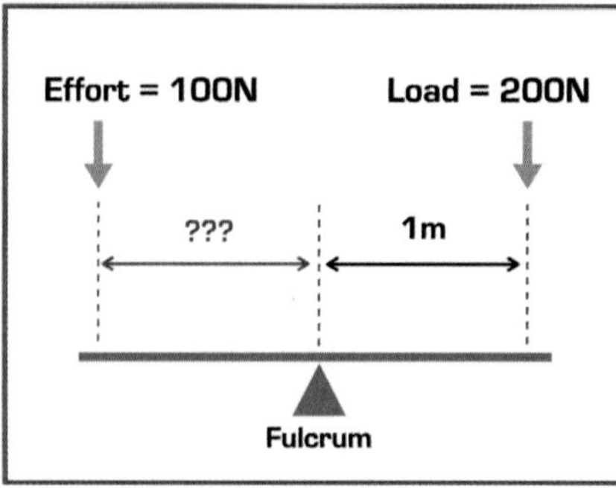

Lever classes

There are three classes of levers, depending on where the fulcrum, effort and load are situated with respect to each other.

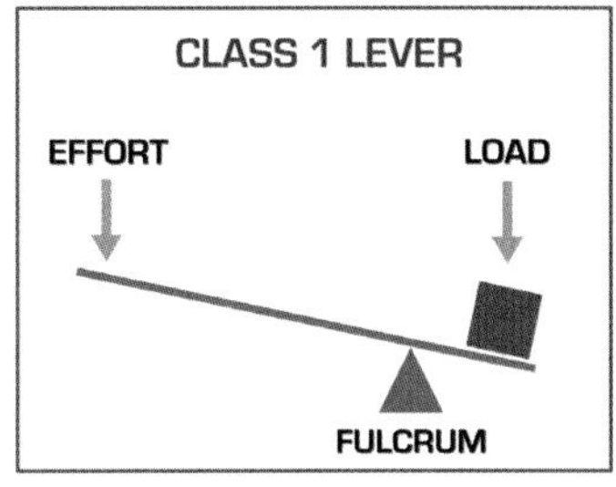

***F**ulcrum in the middle*

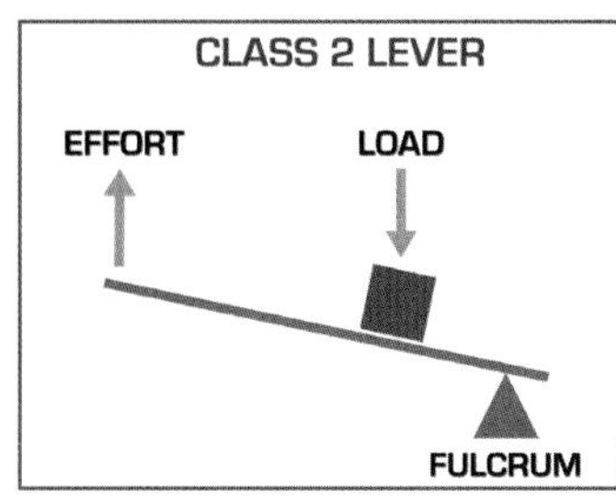

***L**oad in the middle*

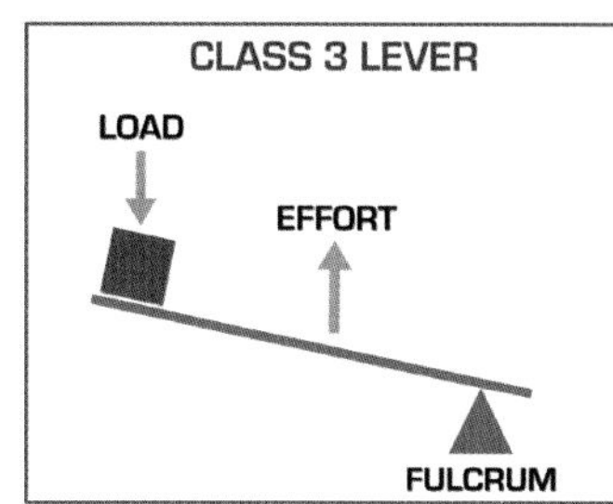

***E**ffort in the middle*

An easy way to remember what's in the middle for each of the class 1, 2 and 3 levers, is to remember the first letter of each word: **F**ulcrum, **L**oad, and **E**ffort – **FLE**.

Uses of the different classes of lever

Class	Middle element	Main uses	Examples
Class 1	Fulcrum	**Mechanical advantage** (i.e. to apply a greater force to the load, than is applied to the effort)	Claw hammer (when removing nails; it is a class 3 lever when hammering in nails), scissors, crowbar, see-saw
Class 2	Load	**Mechanical advantage** (i.e. to apply a greater force to the load, than is applied to the effort)	Wheelbarrow, bottle opener, nutcracker, garlic press, brake pedal
Class 3	Effort	**To amplify motion** (i.e. to move the load a greater distance than the effort moves)	Tongs, tweezers, fishing rod, shovel, robot arms, hammer

Mechanical advantage of different lever classes

Class 1 can provide mechanical advantage, but only if the distance from the effort to the fulcrum is greater than the distance from the load to the fulcrum.

Class 2 always provides mechanical advantage, because the load is always closer to the fulcrum than the effort. Class 2 will provide greater mechanical advantage than class1 for the same length of lever. This is because the distance from the effort to the fulcrum is always greater than the distance from the load to the fulcrum. This explains why nutcrackers are designed the way they are.

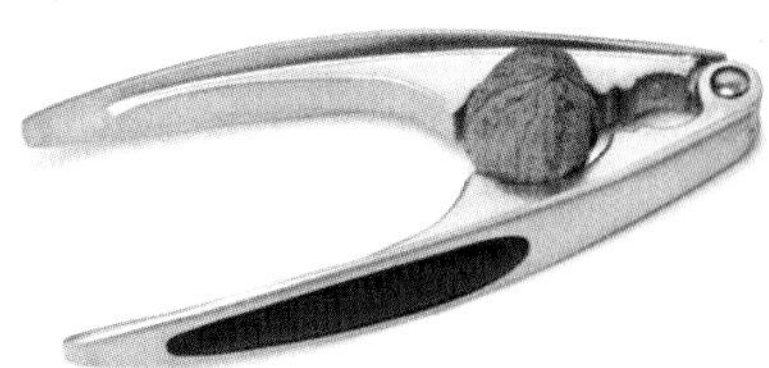

Class 3 cannot provide mechanical advantage, because the load is always further from the fulcrum than the effort.

Test yourself

1. Identify the class of lever being used in each of the pictures shown below.

2. When does a claw hammer function as (a) a class 1 lever and (b) a class 3 lever?

3. For each lever, identify where the effort is being applied, where the load is, and where the fulcrum is.

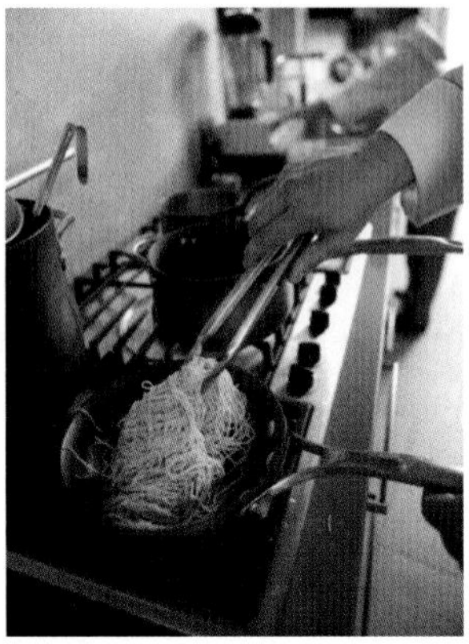

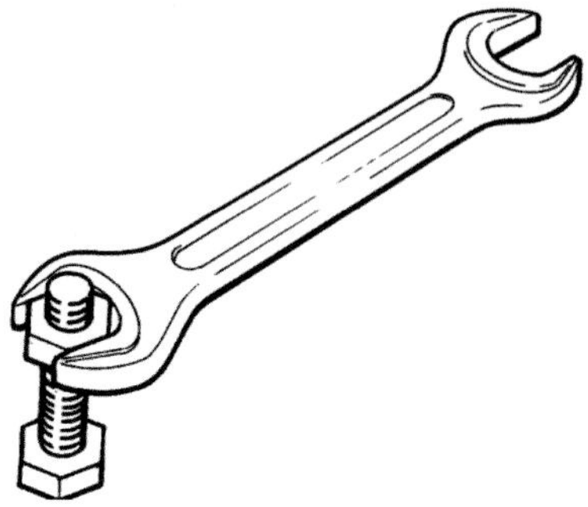

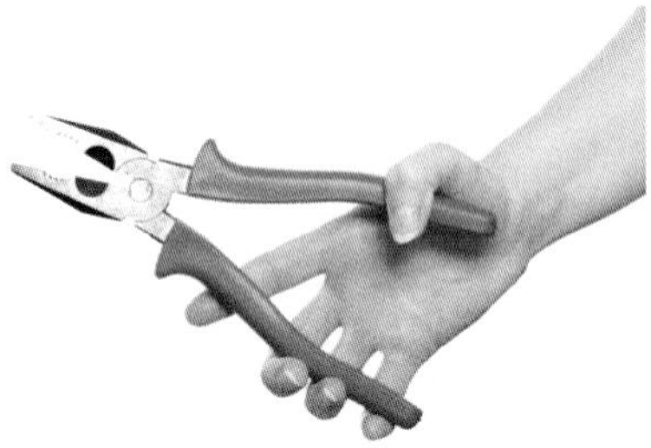

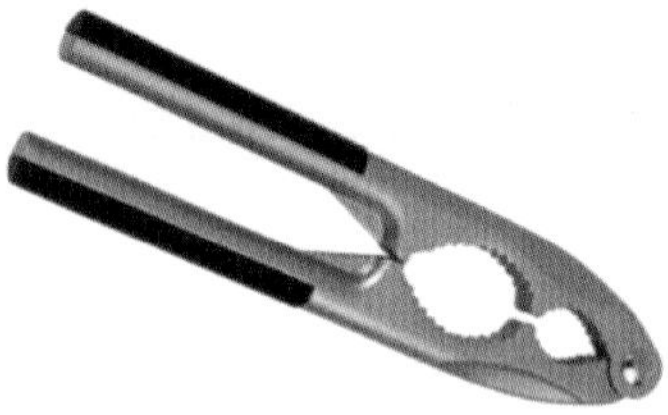

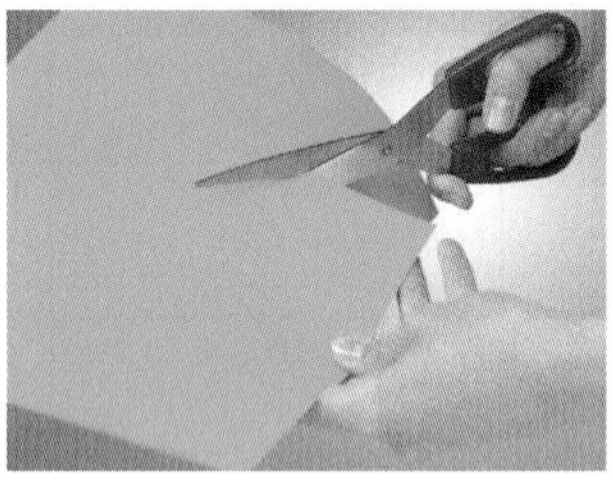

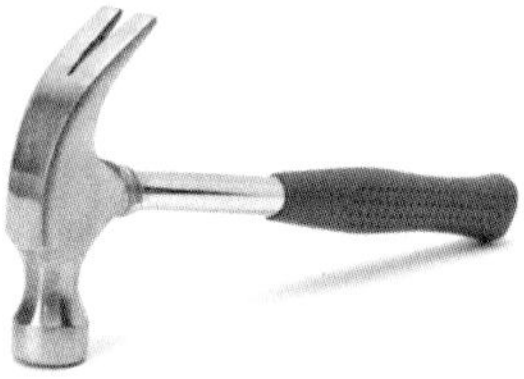

4. With regard to the foot-pump, does the arrow point to the:
   - Effort?
   - Fulcrum?
   - Load?

Calculating forces for class 2 and 3 levers

The law of the lever applies to all classes of lever. Previous worked examples have shown calculations for class 1 levers. The following worked examples show how you can calculate forces and mechanical advantage for class 2 and class 3 levers.

Worked example 4: Calculate effort and mechanical advantage in a class 2 lever

Question (A)

What effort is required to support the load shown?

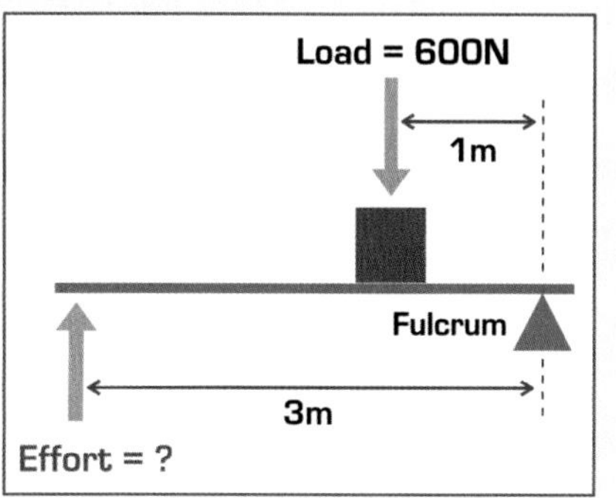

Solution by reasoning

The effort is applied at three times the distance from the fulcrum than that of the load, so the effort required will be one third of the load force, i.e. 600 N/3 = 200 N.

Solution by applying the law of the lever formula

$$\text{F(effort)} \times 3\text{m} = 600\text{ N} \times 1\text{ m} = 600\text{ Nm}$$

$$\text{F(effort)} = \frac{600\text{ Nm}}{3\text{ m}} = 200\text{ N}$$

Question (B)

What is the mechanical advantage of the above system?

Solution

$$\text{Mechanical advantage} = \frac{\text{load}}{\text{effort}} = \frac{600\text{ N}}{200\text{ N}} = 3$$

Or by using the ratio of the distances:

$$\text{Mechanical advantage} = \frac{\text{distance from effort to fulcrum}}{\text{distance from load to fulcrum}} = \frac{3\text{ m}}{1\text{ m}} = 3$$

Worked example 5: Calculate effort and mechanical advantage in a class 3 lever

Question (A)

What effort is required to support the load shown?

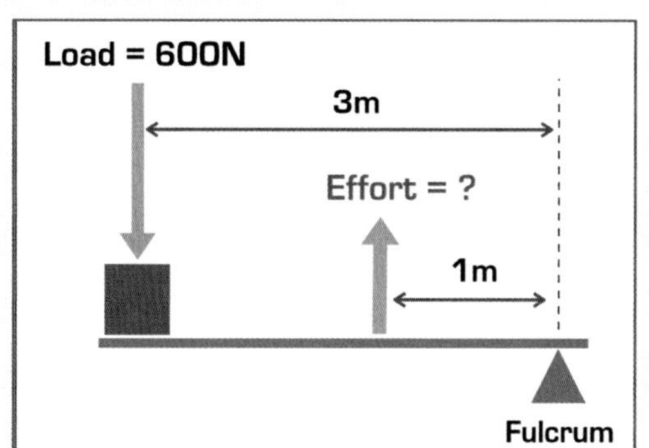

Solution by reasoning

The effort is applied at one third of the distance from the fulcrum than that of the load, so the effort required will be three times the load force, i.e. 600 N x 3 = 1800 N.

Solution by applying the law of the lever formula

$$\text{F(effort)} \times 1\text{ m} = 600\text{ N} \times 3\text{ m} = 1800\text{ Nm}$$

$$\text{F(effort)} = \frac{1800\text{ Nm}}{1\text{ m}} = 1800\text{ N}$$

Question (B)

What is the mechanical advantage of the system?

Solution

$$\text{Mechanical advantage} = \frac{\text{load}}{\text{effort}} = \frac{600\text{ N}}{1800\text{ N}} = \frac{1}{3}$$

This is a **mechanical disadvantage.** Using the ratio of the distances:

$$\text{Mechanical advantage} = \frac{\text{distance from effort to fulcrum}}{\text{distance from load to fulcrum}} = \frac{1\text{ m}}{3\text{ m}} = \frac{1}{3}$$

Velocity ratio of a lever

The velocity ratio of a lever is the distance travelled by the effort divided by the distance travelled by the load.

$$\textbf{Velocity ratio (of a lever)} = \frac{\textbf{distance travelled by effort}}{\textbf{distance travelled by load}}$$

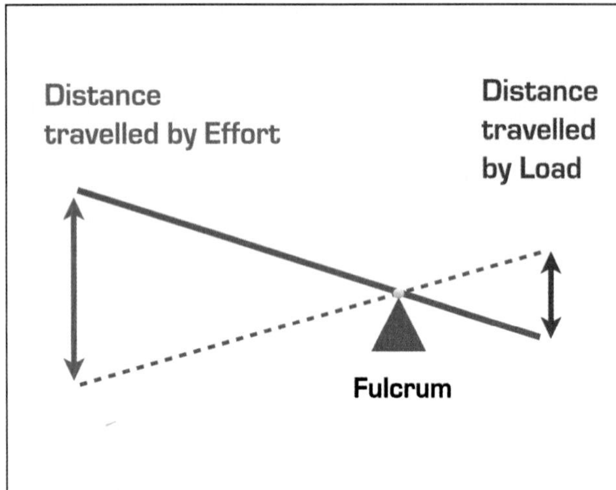

For example, if the effort travels 20 cm, and the load travels 10 cm, the velocity ratio is 2. If the effort travels 10 cm, and the load travels 40 cm, the velocity ratio is ¼, or 0.25.

Class 1 levers - the velocity ratio can be greater than, equal to, or less than, one.

Class 2 levers - the velocity ratio is always greater than one.

Class 3 levers - the velocity ratio is always less than one.

Worked example 6: Calculate velocity ratio

Question

What is the velocity ratio of the lever shown?

Solution

$$\text{Velocity ratio} = \frac{\text{distance travelled by effort}}{\text{distance travelled by load}} = \frac{2\text{ m}}{1\text{ m}} = 2$$

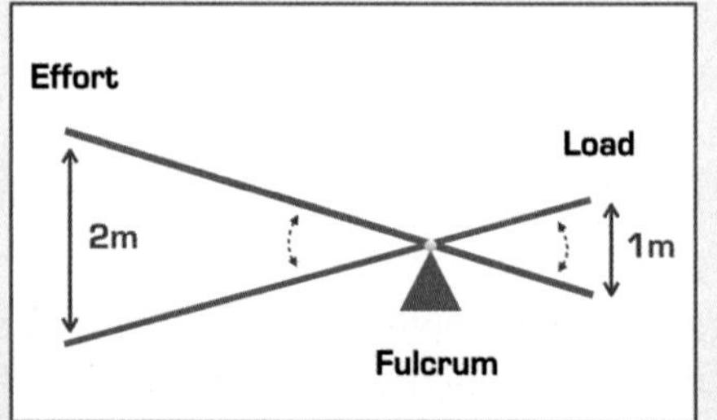

Activities

1. Open the lid of a paint can, using a screwdriver. Do you see the lever action working?
2. Use a scissors to cut some paper. There is a lever action working here too – do you see it?
3. Look around the technology room. How many examples of levers can you find? How do they make the job easier?
4. Make a lever yourself by placing a ruler flat on your desk and letting a small part of the ruler hang over the edge of the desk. Hold the outside edge of the ruler and move it down gently, pivoting the ruler on the edge of the desk. Feel how hard it is to press down and tilt up the rest of the ruler when only small portion of the ruler is hanging over the desk. The ruler feels heavier. Why is this?
5. Make a simple lever using technology room materials and equipment. How would you make the fulcrum?
6. Experiment with balancing different weights at different distances on either side of the fulcrum.

Activities

(Note that the lever may be difficult to balance because the moments (turning effects) will never be exactly equal, but you can get close).

7. Try to find a see-saw where you sit closer or further back from the fulcrum. See where a smaller student can balance a larger adult.

Test yourself

1. In the lever on the right, how far would you need to move the effort in order to move the load by 1 cm?

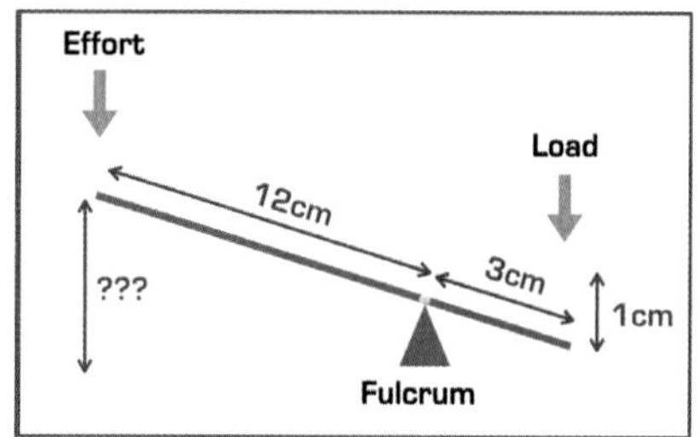

2. A lever has a velocity ratio of 3. How far would you need to move the effort in order to move the load by 3 cm?

Key points

1. A lever is a rigid bar that pivots around a fulcrum.
2. Class 1, 2 and 3 Levers have these elements in the middle respectively: (1) fulcrum (2) load (3) effort.
3. Class 1 levers only provide mechanical advantage if the distance from the effort to the fulcrum is greater than the distance of the load to the fulcrum.
4. Class 2 levers always provide mechanical advantage.
5. Class 3 levers do not provide mechanical advantage but can amplify motion.
6. Mechanical advantage = $\frac{\text{load}}{\text{effort}}$
7. The law of the lever: F1 × D1 = F2 × D2. Use this to calculate forces and distances.
8. Velocity ratio = $\frac{\text{distance travelled by effort}}{\text{distance travelled by load}}$

Past exam questions

1. When the beam shown is in equilibrium (balanced), the mass at X is: (a) 15 kg, (b) 30 kg or (c) 10 kg?

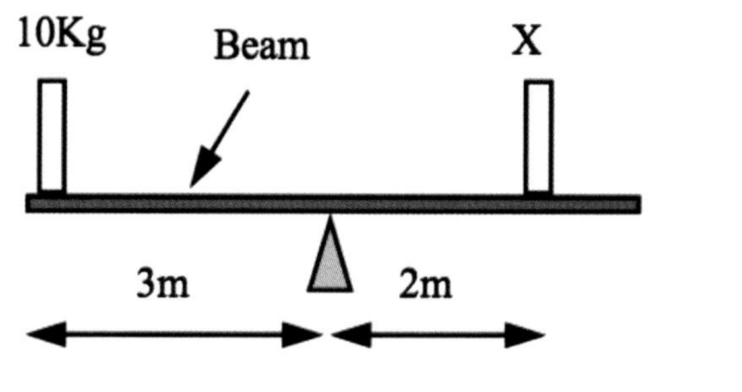

Past exam questions

2. On the nutcracker picture shown, indicate clearly the location of the Load (**L**), Effort (**E**) and Fulcrum (**F**)

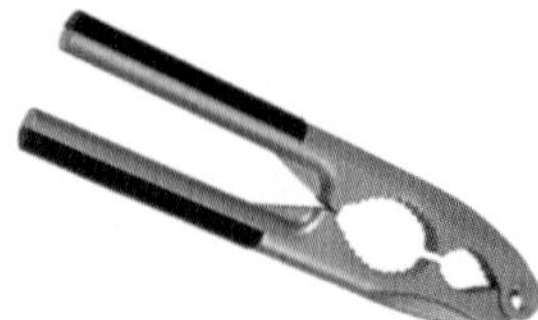

3. Two lever diagrams are shown below. For diagram 1, calculate the **load** force and for diagram 2 calculate the **effort** force.

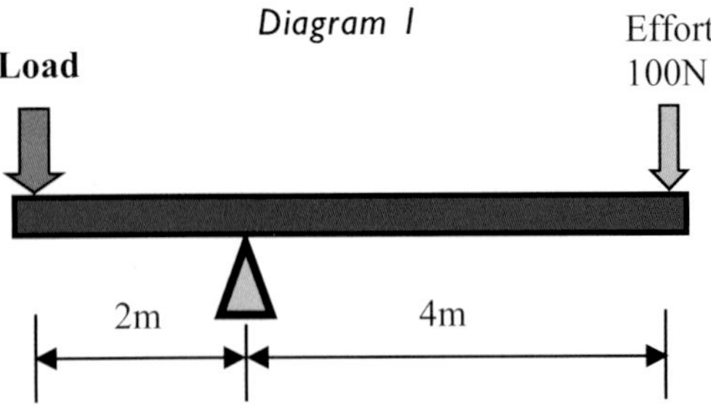

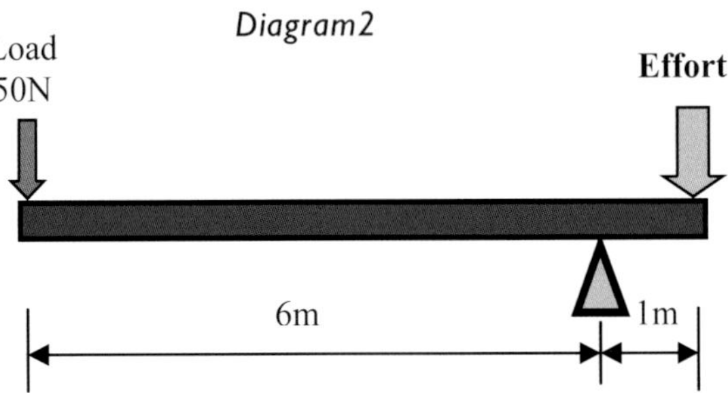

4. An image of a mountain bike is shown. Name **two** parts of the bike that use a lever mechanism.

5. Calculate the mechanical advantage (MA) available in the nutcracker shown.

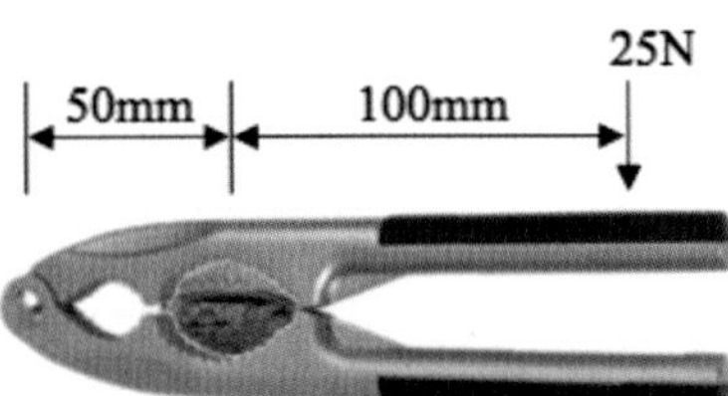

6. For the wheelbarrow on the right, the effort force is: (1) greater than the load; (2) equal to the load, or (3) less than the load?

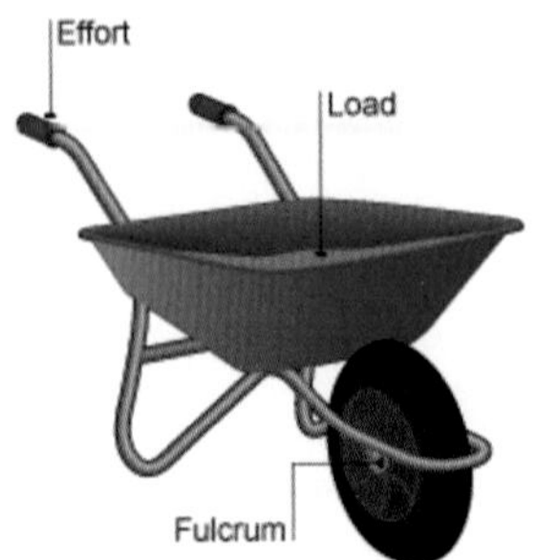

7. Calculate the force required at X, on the spanner shown, to produce a turning force (moment) of 15 Nm.

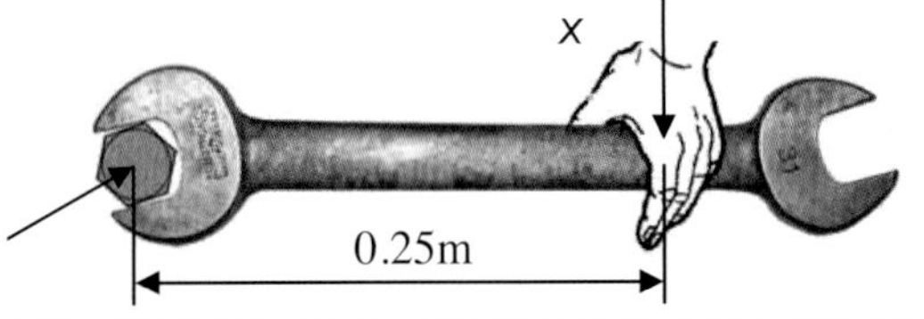

Linkages

A **linkage** is a set of levers connected together to direct movement in a desired direction.

The most common types of linkage are described below.

Reverse motion linkage

The picture shows a reverse motion linkage. Pushing the top bar to the right causes the bottom bar to move to the left. Pulling the top bar to the left pushes the bottom bar out to the right. This is because the lever in the middle rotates around its pivot point (fulcrum) and changes the direction of motion.

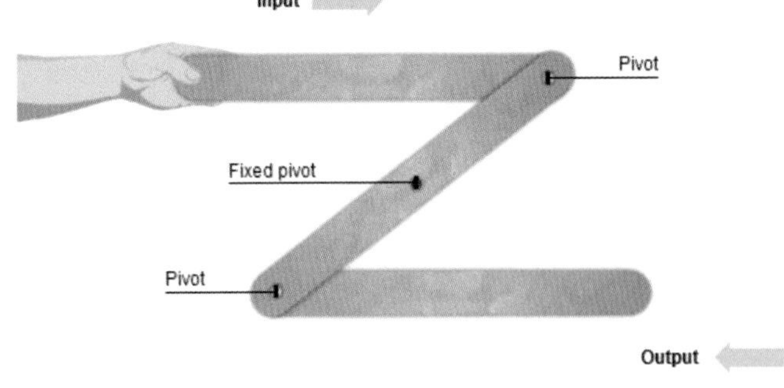

As with any lever, if the fulcrum is not in the centre, the input and output will move at different speeds (i.e. there will be a velocity ratio and a mechanical advantage).

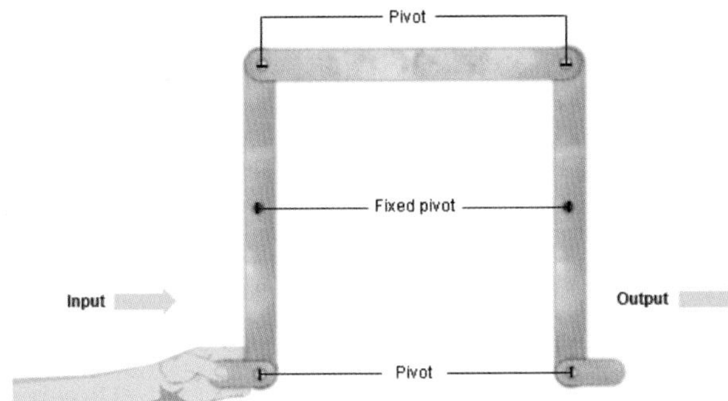

Push-pull linkage

The picture on the left shows a push-pull linkage. It translates the input motion into output motion in the same direction. This is because there are two levers involved, each of which reverses the direction of motion.

Parallel motion linkage

A parallel motion linkage ensures that motion occurs in parallel between two sides. It consists of a pivoted parallelogram shape, to ensure that opposite sides stay parallel.

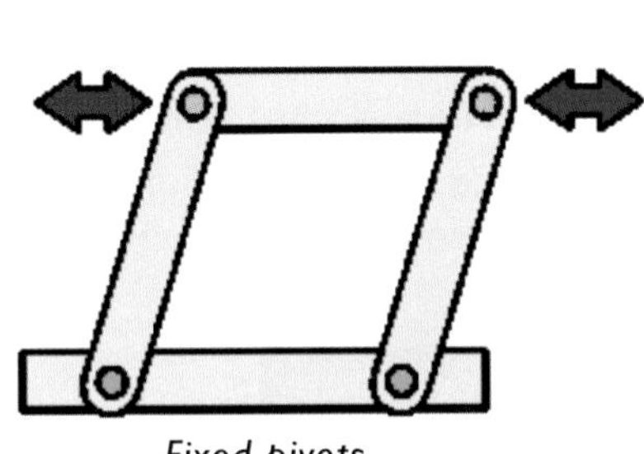

For example, in the toolbox shown, the linkages allow the drawers of the toolbox to be lifted over to each side, allowing access to the inside of the box, while keeping the drawers flat so that the contents do not spill.

Scissors linkage

An everyday example of a scissors linkage is shown on the right. The base of the mirror stays parallel to the wall as the mirror extends in and out at 90° and the linkage bars remain parallel to each other.

The scissors linkage is used in situations where you want something to extend and then completely retract, leaving no part of the mechanism extended. Other examples of this type of linkage include a scissors lift and lazy tongs.

Bell crank linkage

A bell crank linkage is used to change the direction of motion, usually through 90°. Bell cranks are often used with cables or rods attached to the input and output.

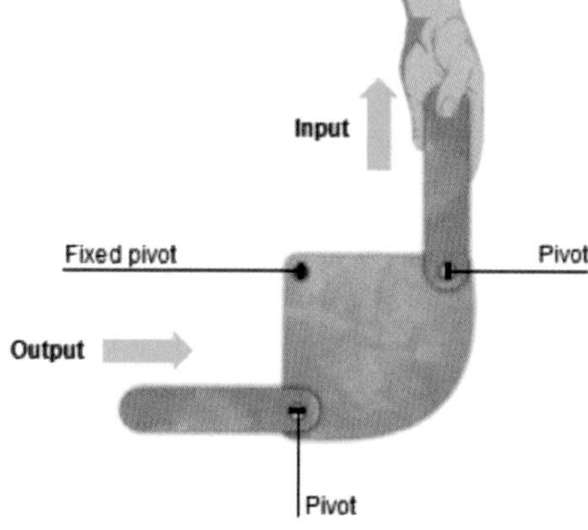

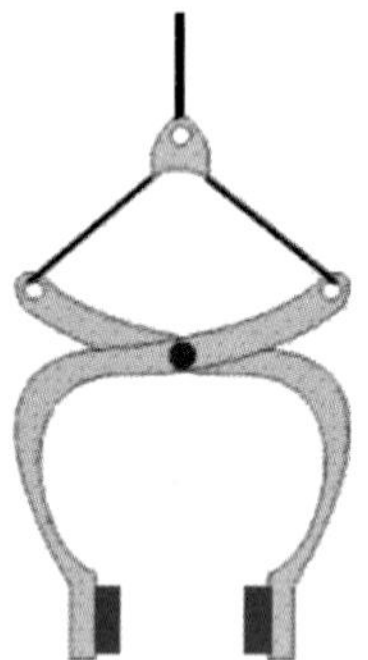

A common example of a bell crank linkage is a bicycle brake.

The cyclist pulls the brake lever, which pulls the brake wire, which pulls the bell crank upwards so that the two top sections are pulled towards each other. This causes the bottom sections with the brake blocks to move closer to each other. The brake blocks then push against the wheel and cause a braking effect.

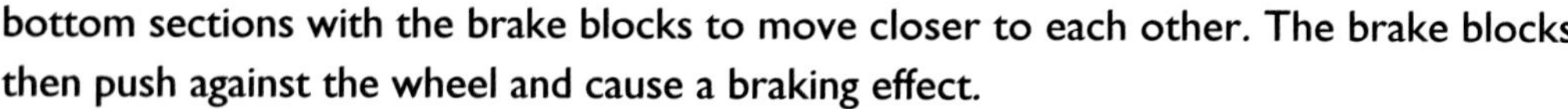

Activities

1. Make each of the linkages using cardboard and tacks. Test them out and see them working.
2. Use linkages in your projects. Think about using connecting pieces and levers as ways to transmit motion from one place to another in your projects.
3. Take a look at a bell crank mechanism on bicycle brakes. Pull the brakes and see the effect.
4. Fold up a clothes horse, wheelchair or child's pushchair. Identify the linkages used to do this and notice how the motion is transmitted.

Key points

1. A linkage is a set of levers designed to translate motion in a certain direction.
2. The most common types of linkages are reverse-motion, push-pull, parallel, bell crank and scissors.
3. A bell crank changes the direction of linear motion, usually by 90°.

Test yourself

1. If you wanted to translate motion by 90°, what type of linkages could you use?
2. Why do you think a scissors linkage is called a scissors linkage?
3. What kind of linkage is used to fold and unfold an ironing board?

Past exam questions

1. The mechanism on the side of the toolbox shown is an example of (1) rack and pinion, (2) parallel linkage, or (3) simple gear train?

2. Bicycle brakes change a (1) push into a pull, (2) push into a push, or (3) pull into a push?

Springs

Springs are elastic devices, which means that they can be bent, compressed, twisted or stretched out of shape, and then they spring back to their original shape when the altering force is removed.

Springs are used in other mechanisms to return the mechanism to its original state once the load or effort is removed. The most common type of spring is made from a coil of metal, as shown on the right, and is called a coil spring.

A flat piece of metal or plastic is another shape for a spring. Flat metal springs are often used as clips, e.g. for holding backing card onto picture frames.

Types of springs

Compression springs

Compression springs are used with a compression load. The spring is compressed to a smaller size by the load force, and returns to its normal size when the force is removed.

Compression springs are used in car suspension systems such as the one on the right, mattresses, and mechanical weighing scales.

Tension springs

Tension springs are used with a tension force, i.e. a stretching force. The spring is stretched out/elongated by the load force, and returns to its normal size when the force is removed.

Tension springs are used in trampolines, door handles, and mechanical weighing scales.

Torsion springs

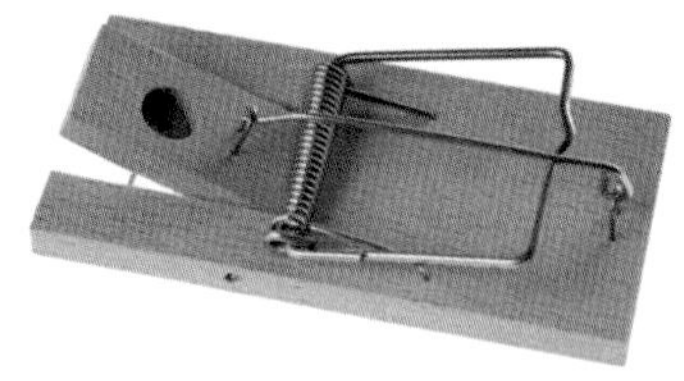

Torsion springs are used with a twisting load force. The spring is twisted/rotated with the load, and returns to its normal shape once the load force is removed.

Torsion springs are used in old fashioned mousetraps.

Note that a metal coil spring can function as a compression, tension or torsion spring, depending on how it is used.

Cams and cranks

The mechanisms in this section convert rotary motion to reciprocating or oscillating motion and vice versa.

Cam-and-follower

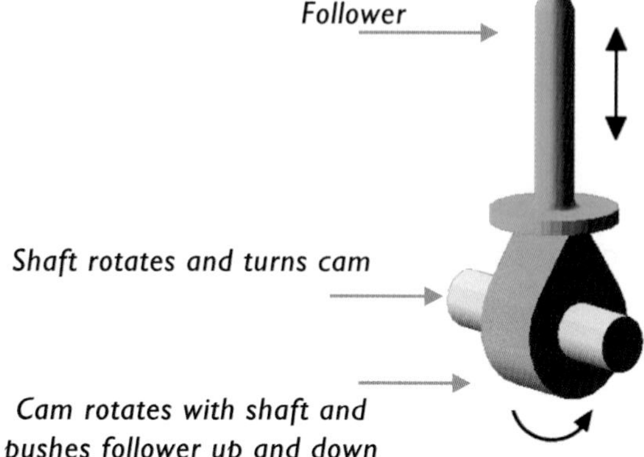

A cam is a non-circular object attached to a rotating axle, designed to make sliding contact with another object, called a follower, to cause that piece to move up and down or from side to side in a reciprocating motion. The shape of the cam determines how the follower moves.

In the image shown, the follower rests on the edge of the turning cam and is free to move up and down. It is prevented from moving from side to side by a guide (not in the picture).

A camshaft consists of a number of cams connected to the same axle. Each cam will activate its own follower. A camshaft connects one place of rotary motion to a number of places of reciprocating motion.

A car engine camshaft, such as the one on the left, raises and lowers the engine valves to let petrol and air into the engine, in time with the revolution of the pistons.

Cams and followers are very useful for creating up and down motion in technology projects.

Cranks

A crank is a bar attached at right angles to an axle. It is used to change reciprocating motion into rotary motion, and vice versa.

A manual crank is used to convert the reciprocating motion of your elbow (via your connecting forearm and hand) into the rotary motion of an axle, e.g. as shown in the coffee grinder. The crank operates like a lever, i.e. the further the crank handle is from the axle (the fulcrum), the less effort it takes to turn the axle.

An example of a crank operating the other way round (i.e. converting rotary motion to reciprocating motion) is given in the "crank-and-slider" mechanism overleaf.

Uses of crank handles and cranks

Crank handles are used in pencil sharpeners, door handles, car jacks and winches. Cranks are also used in crankshafts, crank-and-slider mechanisms and peg-and-slot mechanisms.

Crankshafts

A crankshaft consists of a number of cranks connected to the same axle. It connects two or more places of reciprocating motion to one place of rotary motion.

Uses of crankshafts

Uses of crankshafts include:

- **Car engine crankshaft** (see right). This converts the up and down motion of the pistons into the rotary motion of the crankshaft, which eventually turns the wheels.
- **Bicycle pedals or toy car pedals,** which convert the , movement of your knees into the rotary motion of the wheels.

Crank-and-slider

The crank-and-slider mechanism converts rotary motion into reciprocating motion and vice versa.

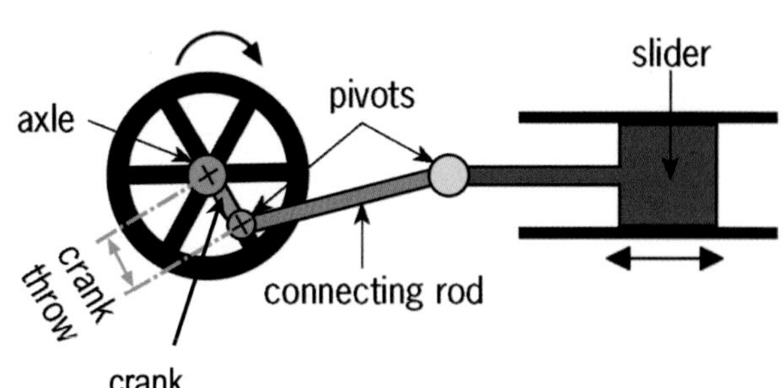

In the example shown, the crank (in blue) is attached to the axle and connects to the slider via a connecting rod. There is a pivot between the crank and the connecting rod, and a pivot between the connecting rod and the slider.

As the wheel turns, the crank alternately pushes and pulls the slider in and out, in reciprocating motion. The distance between the centre of the axle and the rod is called the crank throw.

The crank-and-slider is a useful mechanism for technology projects to create a reciprocating motion from the rotary motion of a motor.

The crank-and-slider mechanism is found in car engines where the reciprocating motion of the piston is converted into the rotary motion of the engine.

Peg-and-slot

The peg-and-slot converts rotary motion into oscillating motion. The slot part can be pivoted at the top or the bottom.

As the wheel rotates, the peg travels up and down in the slot itself, and causes the slot part to swing or wave from side to side.

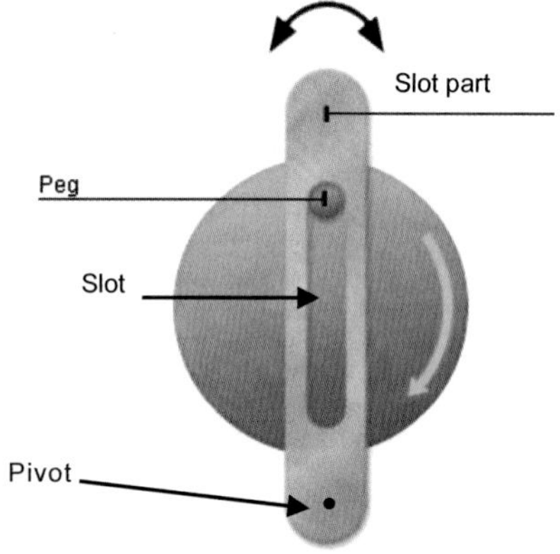

Activities

1. Look at videos or animated graphics of the above mechanisms working.
2. Look at previously built projects in the technology room and see what mechanisms are used in them.
3. Build your own cam-and-follower and crank-and-slider mechanisms in the technology room.

Test yourself

1. What types of mechanisms could you connect to a motor to make something go up and down?
2. What mechanism could you connect to a motor to make something swing from side to side?

Past exam questions

1. Name and sketch a suitable mechanism that will produce any one of the movements shown, when the toy train moves.

2. Name the parts labeled X and Y of the mechanism shown on the right.

   Does the part labeled X rise slowly and fall quickly, or rise quickly and fall slowly?

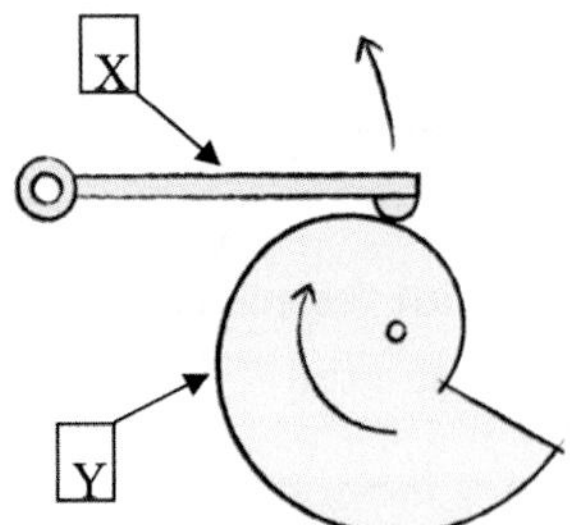

3. A crank handle is used to turn the mechanism on the right (for tensioning the net on a tennis court).
   a) Name two other devices/mechanisms that use a crank handle.
   b) Suggest one change that could be made to the crank to make it easier to turn.

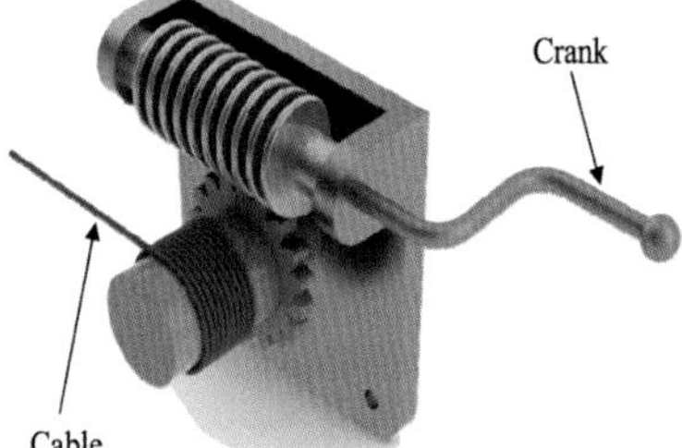

4. An engine crankshaft and piston shown is an example of a:

   (a) crank-and-slider,
   (b) bevel gear system,
   (c) chain and sprocket?

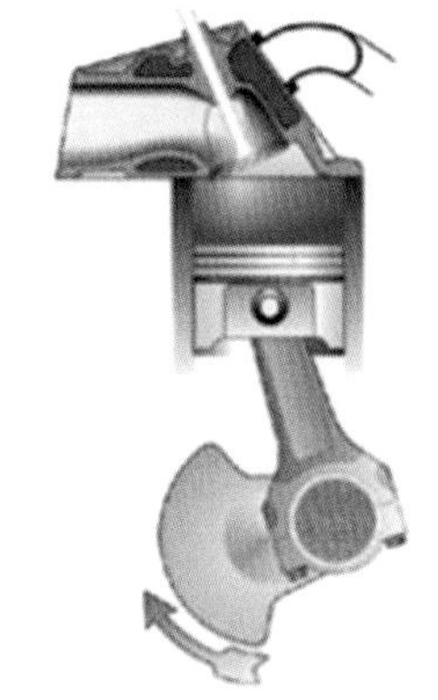

5. Name the mechanisms shown at X and Y.

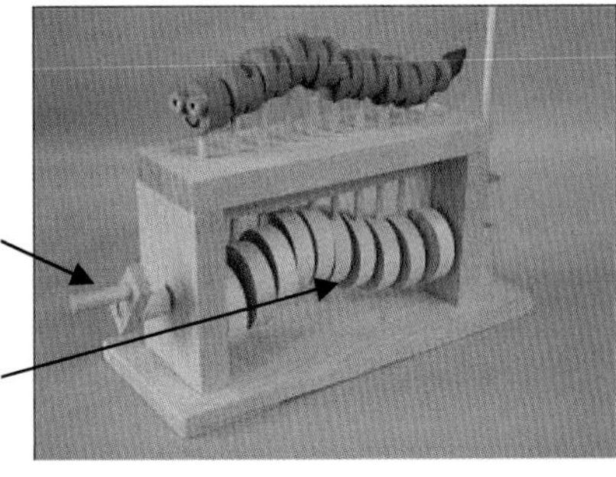

Mechanisms 2

This chapter covers gears, chain and belt drives, pulleys, the wheel and axle, and the screw mechanism. Other mechanisms are dealt with in "Mechanisms 1". This chapter also includes a section on friction.

Gears

Gears are wheels with teeth. They rotate on a central shaft or rod, called an axle. Gears are used to:

- Transmit rotary motion from one place to another.
- Change the speed of rotation.
- Change the direction of rotation.
- Change the angle of rotation.
- Transmit force from one place to another.
- Change the torque (the turning effect of a force – explained later in this chapter).

Gears are wheels with teeth, which engage with each other to transmit force and rotary motion.

Driver and driven gears

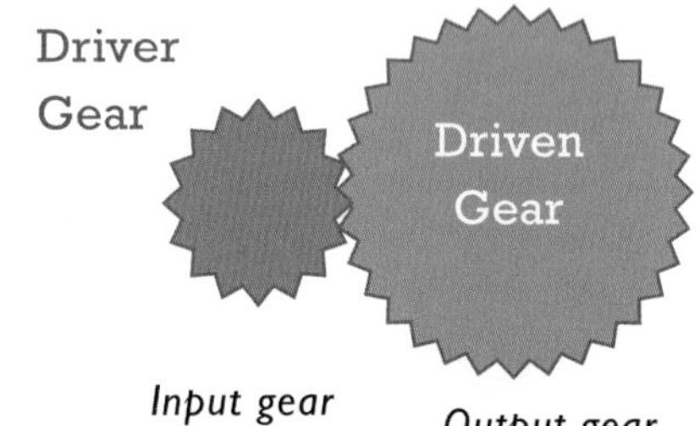

Input gear *Output gear*

In any system of gears, the gear to which the input force is applied is called the driver gear, or input gear. In technology projects, the driver gear is often turned using a small electric motor. The driver gear can also be turned by hand, e.g. by using a crank (see "Mechanisms 1").

The driver gear turns the driven gear, or output gear. If there are more than two gears in a sequence (see "gear train" later), the driven gear is always the final gear that is being turned.

Speed of rotation and gear ratio

When the teeth of two gears are meshed together, turning one gear will turn the other in the opposite direction.

The gears shown in the image are called spur gears. The teeth are straight on the edge of the wheel, i.e. parallel to the wheel's axis.

Smaller gear turns faster

If the two gears are the same size, they will turn at the same speed. If the two gears are different sizes, the smaller gear will turn faster than the larger gear.

The smaller gear turns faster than the larger gear because the gears are joined to each other at their circumferences (outside surfaces). The smaller gear has a smaller circumference than the larger gear, and so the smaller gear must turn more times to match the larger circumference of the larger gear. This can be expressed by the following equation:

$$\frac{\text{Speed of driver gear}}{\text{Speed of driven gear}} = \frac{\text{circumference of driven gear}}{\text{circumference of driver gear}}$$

This means that the ratio of the speed of the driver gear to the speed of the driven gear is the same as the ratio of the circumference of the driven gear to the circumference of the driver gear. An easy way to measure the circumference is to count the number of teeth on each gear. This allows us to calculate the ratio of the two speeds easily:

$$\frac{\text{Speed of driver gear}}{\text{Speed of driven gear}} = \frac{\text{circumference of driven gear}}{\text{circumference of driver gear}} = \frac{\text{number of teeth of driven gear}}{\text{number of teeth of driver gear}}$$

This ratio is called the gear ratio (also known as the speed ratio or velocity ratio).

$$\textbf{Gear ratio} = \frac{\text{speed of driver gear}}{\text{speed of driven gear}} = \frac{\text{number of teeth on driven gear (output gear)}}{\text{number of teeth on driver gear (input gear)}}$$

Example

If the driven (output) gear has 40 teeth, and the driver (input) gear has 10 teeth, then

$$\text{Gear ratio} = \frac{\text{number of teeth on driven gear}}{\text{number of teeth on driver gear}} = \frac{40}{10} = 4$$

This means that the driver gear rotates four times for every one rotation of the driven gear.

Gear speeds

Gears are used to change speed of rotation. Rotation speeds are measured in RPM (revolutions per minute). For example, a typical speed of rotation of a car engine would be 3,000 RPM. This means the engine makes 3,000 rotations every minute.

You can calculate the relative speed of the input and output gears directly from the gear ratio, using the formula below.

$$\textbf{Speed of driven (output) gear} = \frac{\text{speed of driver gear}}{\text{gear ratio}}$$

For example, if the speed of the driver (input) gear is 100 RPM, and the gear ratio is 2, then the speed of the driven (output) gear is 100 RPM divided by 2 = 50 RPM.

Worked example 1: Calculate gear ratios and gear speeds

Question (A)

What is the gear ratio of the gears shown?

Solution

$$\text{Gear ratio} = \frac{\text{number of teeth on driven gear}}{\text{number of teeth on driver gear}} = \frac{30}{15} = 2$$

Question (B)

If the speed of the driver (input) gear is 100 RPM, what is the speed of the driven (output) gear?

Solution by applying formula

$$\text{Speed of driven gear} = \frac{\text{speed of driver gear}}{\text{gear ratio}} = \frac{100\text{ RPM}}{2} = 50\text{ RPM}$$

Solution by reasoning

The smaller gear always rotates faster than the larger gear. If the gear ratio is 2, the smaller driver gear must be rotating twice as fast as the larger driven gear. So if the driver gear is rotating at 100 RPM, the driven gear must be rotating at 50 RPM.

Worked example 2: Calculate gear ratios and gear speeds

Question (A)

What is the gear ratio of the gears shown?

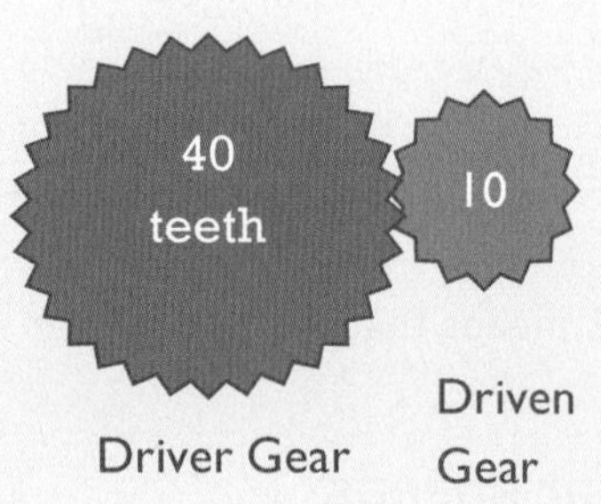

Solution

$$\text{Gear ratio} = \frac{\text{number of teeth on driven gear}}{\text{number of teeth on driver gear}} = \frac{10}{40} = \frac{1}{4} = 0.25$$

Question (B)

If the driver gear (input) speed is 100 RPM, what is the driven gear (output) speed?

Solution by applying formula

$$\text{Speed of driven gear} = \frac{\text{speed of driver gear}}{\text{gear ratio}} = \frac{100\text{ RPM}}{0.25} = 400\text{ RPM}$$

Solution by reasoning

The smaller gear always rotates faster than the larger gear. If the gear ratio is 0.25, i.e. ¼, the smaller driven gear will rotate four times as fast as the larger driver gear.

So if the driver gear rotates at 100 RPM, then the driven gear will rotate at 400 RPM.

Test yourself

For each of the gear systems shown below, write down the gear ratio and the speed of the driven gear, i.e. the output speed.

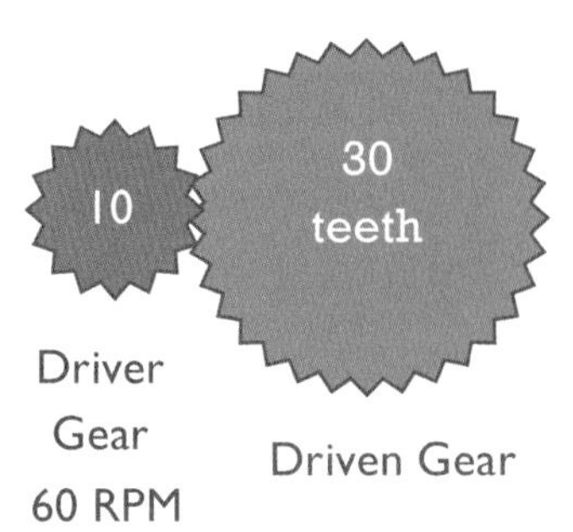

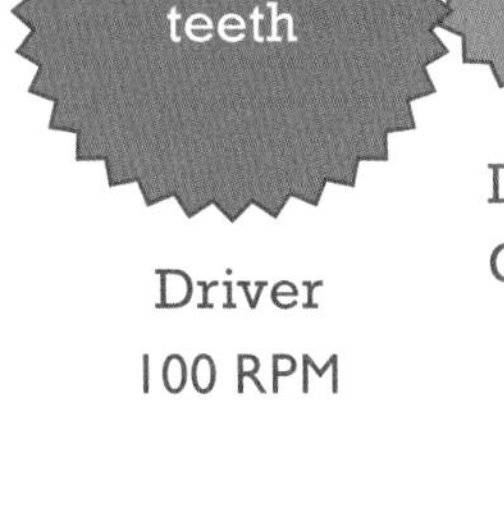

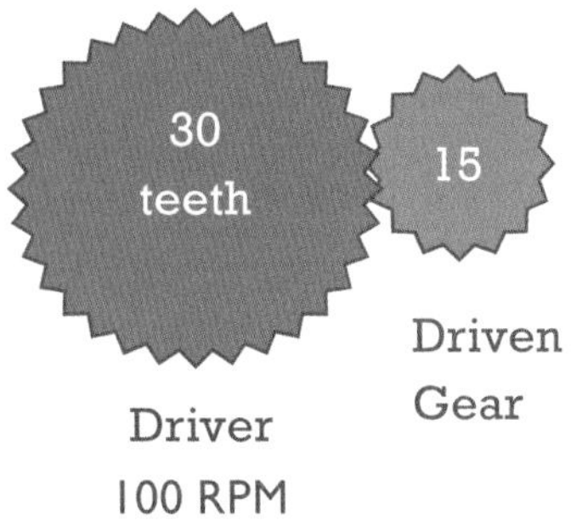

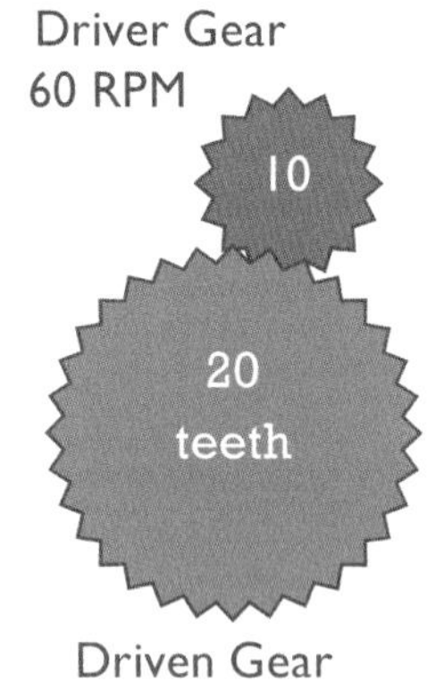

Gear ratio =
Output speed =

Gear ratio =
Output speed =

Gear ratio =
Output speed =

Gears and torque

In "Mechanisms 1" we saw that a lever creates a moment when it pivots around a fulcrum. The greater the distance from the fulcrum at which the force is applied, the greater is its turning effect, or moment.

Similarly, in gears, a turning effect is created when the gear rotates around its axis. In this case, the turning effect (also referred to as turning force) is called torque.

The greater the radius at which the force is applied, the greater is the torque (τ).

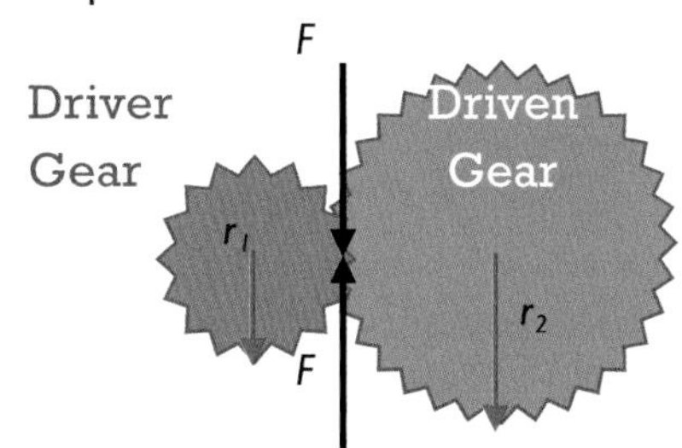

Torque = force × radius (Nm)

In the diagram on the right:

Torque of driver gear $\tau_1 = F \times r_1$

Torque of driven gear $\tau_2 = F \times r_2$

The driven gear has a greater radius than the driver gear, which means that it has a greater torque. Greater torque means a greater ability to turn or lift heavy objects.

Example

In the diagram on the right, the driven gear has twice the radius of the driver gear and so has twice the torque.

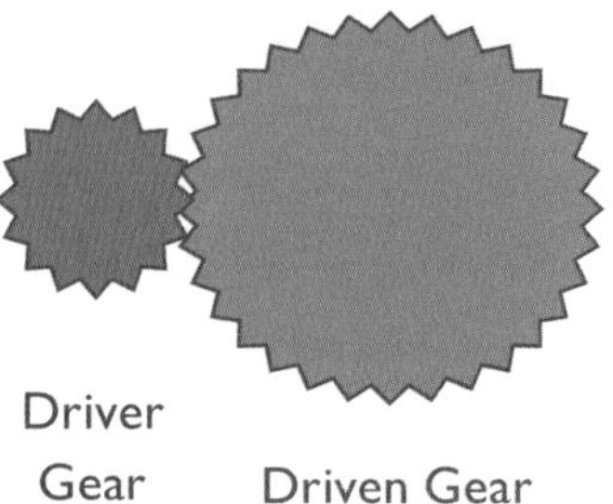

Gears and mechanical advantage

Since gears can be used to change an input torque to a greater output torque, a gear system provides mechanical advantage.

The mechanical advantage of a gear system is defined as the ratio of the output torque to the input torque.

$$\text{Mechanical advantage} = \frac{\text{output torque (Nm)}}{\text{input torque (Nm)}}$$

We know that this is equivalent to the ratio of the radius of the driven (output) gear to the radius of the driver (input) gear.

$$\text{Mechanical advantage} = \frac{\text{radius of driven gear (m)}}{\text{radius of driver gear (m)}}$$

Since the radius of a gear is directly proportional to its circumference,

$$\text{Mechanical advantage} = \frac{\text{circumference of driven gear (m)}}{\text{circumference of driver gear (m)}}$$

As mentioned earlier, an easy way to measure the circumference is to count the number of teeth on each gear, which means that

$$\text{Mechanical advantage} = \frac{\text{circumference of driven gear (m)}}{\text{circumference of driver gear (m)}} = \frac{\text{number of teeth on driven gear}}{\text{number of teeth on driver gear}} = \text{gear ratio}$$

Earlier in this chapter the gear ratio is defined as the ratio of the number of teeth on the driven gear to the number of teeth on the driver gear. This means that the mechanical advantage of a gear system is equal to its gear ratio.

Mechanical advantage (of a gear system) = gear ratio

Example – linking gear ratio, gear speed, torque and mechanical advantage

If we have a gear system with a gear ratio of 2 (i.e. the output gear is twice the size of the input gear), the speed of the output gear will be halved with respect to the input gear. However, the torque available to turn things with the output gear will be doubled. So the mechanical advantage is 2. This arrangement provides an output torque twice as great as the input torque (but we have to turn the input gear twice as often as the output gear).

Summary

In a system of two gears of different sizes, the larger gear has more torque than the smaller gear but it rotates more slowly.

Step-up and step-down gears

When gears are used to increase speed they are called step-up gears and when they are used to reduce speed, they are called step-down gears.

Uses of step-down gears in technology projects

Small electric motors are often used in technology projects. We may want to use the motor to turn or lift something quite slowly, e.g. a gate, barrier or winch.

However, electric motors turn very quickly, and small electric motors cannot exert much torque.

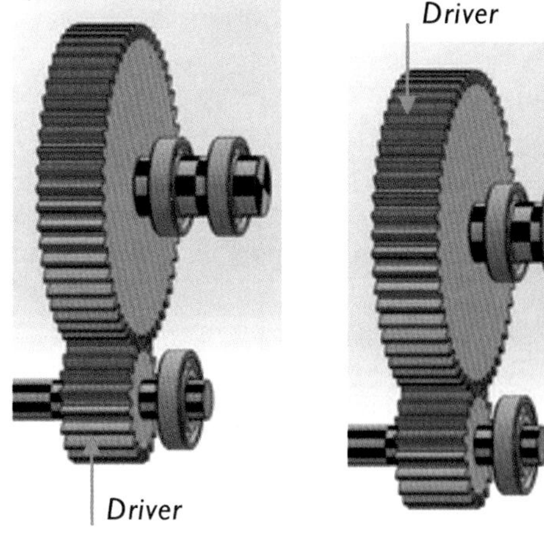

Step-down gears *Step-up gears*

This problem can be solved by using a system of step-down gears on the output of the motor to:

- Reduce the speed of rotation.
- Increase the torque of the output gear so it can turn or lift heavy objects.

Gear trains and idler gears

A gear train is an arrangement of two or more gears connected together as shown below.

Gears in between the driver gear and the driven gear are called idler gears.

Idler gears have no effect on the gear ratio (hence the name). It doesn't matter how many idler gears you have in between the driver and the driven gear, it is only the number of teeth on the driver (first) gear and on the driven (last) gear that determines the overall gear ratio.

Driver Gear
Idler Gear
Driven Gear

A gear train

This is because both sides of the idler gears are moving at the same speed. They just connect the other gears together (and change the direction of rotation each time).

Idler gears are used to:

- Change the direction of rotation. Every time you insert an idler gear, you reverse the direction of rotation.
- Connect gears together to cause the rotation of the driven gear to occur at a different place to that of the driver gear.

Test yourself

1. Will the driven (output) gear rotate in the same direction as the driver (input) gear?

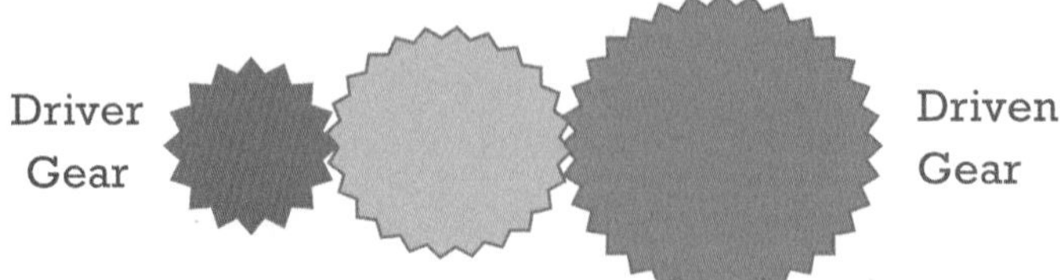

2. Will the driven (output) gear rotate in the same direction as the driver (input) gear?

3. What it the gear ratio of this gear train?

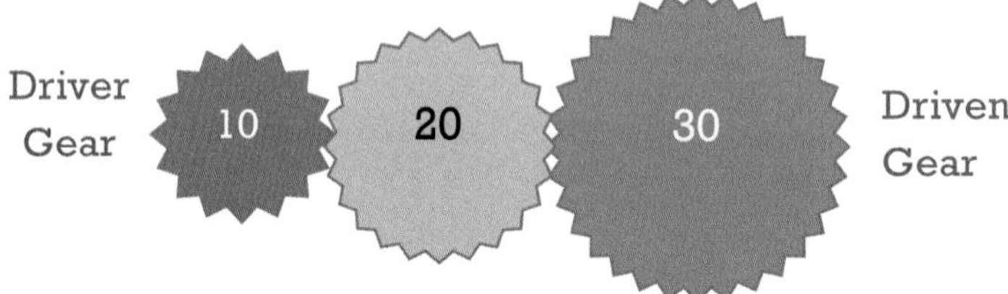

4. What it the gear ratio of this gear train? What is its mechanical advantage?

Compound gears

A compound gear is composed of two or more gears of different sizes fixed next to each other on the same axle, so that they rotate at the same speed.

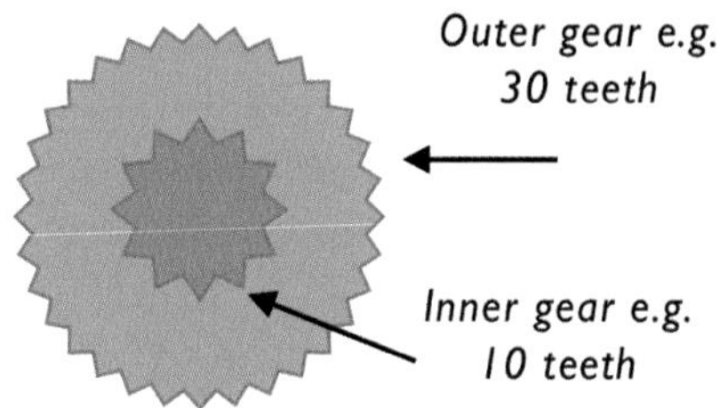

A compound gear is extremely useful because it can be used to multiply the gear ratio.

How is a compound gear used?

With a compound gear, we get two gear ratios because there are two different-sized gears. The gear ratio on the driver gear side is called the input gear ratio and that on the driven gear side is called the output gear ratio.

These two ratios are multiplied together to give the total gear ratio.

Total gear ratio for a compound gear = input gear ratio × output gear ratio

In technology projects, compound gears are often used with small electric motors to give a reduced output speed and a corresponding increase in output torque.

Example

The diagram shows a typical example of how a compound gear is used. The driver (input) gear turns the larger outer gear of the compound gear, and the smaller inner gear of the compound gear turns the final driven (output) gear.

In this example, it takes 3 turns of the input driver gear to make one turn of the outer gear of the compound gear. But it takes 3 turns of the inner gear of the compound gear to make 1 turn of the final output gear.

So in total, it takes 9 turns of the input driver gear to make 1 turn of the output driven gear.

Driver Gear

Compound Gear

Final Driven Gear

10 30 10 30

Total gear ratio = *Input gear ratio = 30/10 = 3* X *Output gear ratio = 30/10 = 3* = 9

Worked example 3: Calculate gear ratio of a compound gear train

Question (A)

What is the gear ratio of the gear train shown?

Solution by applying the formulae

$$\text{Input gear ratio} = \frac{\text{number of teeth on driven small compound gear}}{\text{number of teeth on driver gear}} = \frac{10}{20} = \frac{1}{2} = 0.5$$

$$\text{Output gear ratio} = \frac{\text{number of teeth on final driven gear}}{\text{number of teeth on large compound gear}} = \frac{10}{40} = \frac{1}{4} = 0.25$$

$$\text{Total gear ratio} = \text{input gear ratio} \times \text{output gear ratio} = 0.5 \times 0.25 = 0.125$$

Or alternatively

$$\text{Total gear ratio} = \text{input gear ratio} \times \text{output gear ratio} = \frac{1}{2} \times \frac{1}{4} = \frac{1}{8}$$

Solution by reasoning

- The compound gear turns twice as fast as the driver gear (gear ratio of 1/2).
- The final driven gear turns four times as fast as the compound gear (gear ration of 1/4).
- Therefore the final driven gear turns eight times as fast as the input driver gear (gear ratio of 1/8).

Test yourself

1. What is the total gear ratio of the compound gear train shown below?
2. If the input speed is 1200 RPM, what is the output speed?

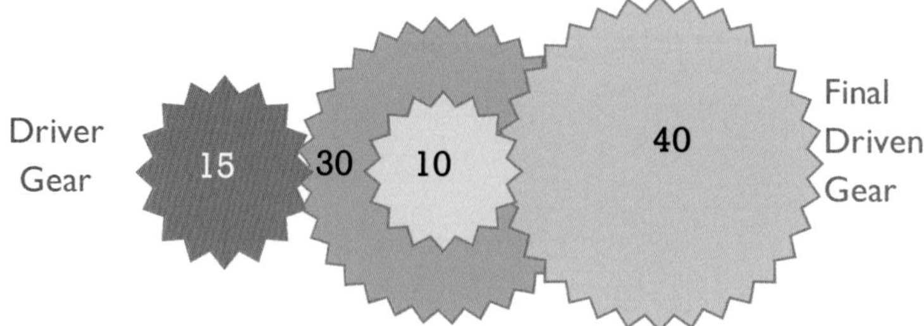

Bevel gears

A bevel gear changes the angle of rotation by 90°. The teeth on bevel gears are angled so that the gears mesh at 90° rather than straight-on (as is the case in spur gears).

A **bevel gear** changes the angle of rotation by 90°.

A common use of bevel gears is in the hand drill shown below.

The handle turns the large bevel gear via a hand crank (see cranks).

The large bevel gear turns the small bevel gear, which is at right angles to it. The small gear turns the drill bit.

Notice the high speed conversion - one turn of the handle will turn the drill bit perhaps 7 or 8 times depending on the gear ratio.

Rack and pinion

A rack and pinion gear mechanism changes rotary motion to linear motion (and vice versa).

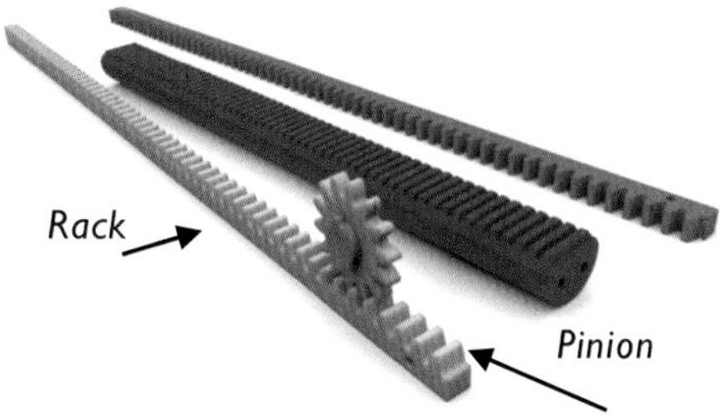

Uses of rack and pinion

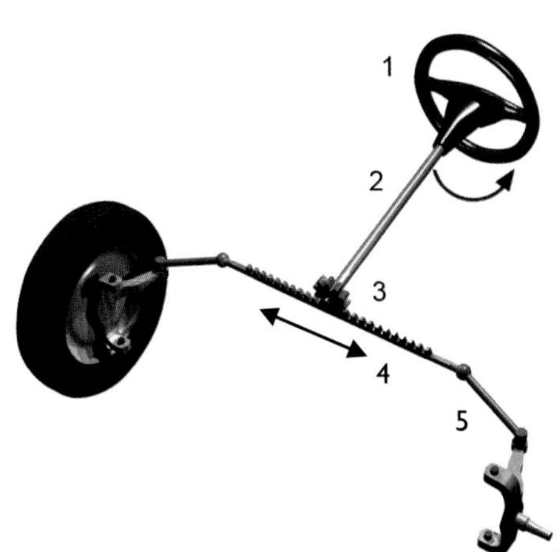

The most common use of a rack and pinion is in car steering systems, such as the one on the left. The steering wheel (1) turns the steering column (2), which turns the pinion (3). The pinion (3) moves the rack (4) from side-to-side to turn the car wheels via a linkage (5). Note that the pinion is a spur gear.

Rack and pinion mechanisms are used in stair lifts and in rack railways to climb steep hills. They are also useful in technology projects for opening and closing gates etc., using an electric motor.

A **rack and pinion gear** mechanism changes rotary motion to linear motion (and vice versa).

Worm gears/worm drives

A worm gear (or worm drive) mechanism is a set of two gears composed of a threaded shaft called a worm, and a large gear wheel called a worm wheel. Unlike other gears, the axle of the worm is at 90° to the axle of the worm wheel. The worm is the driver gear and the worm wheel is the driven gear.

This mechanism changes the direction of motion through 90°.

For each revolution of the worm, the worm wheel moves forward by only one tooth.

The worm wheel has slightly angled teeth to mesh with the screw thread of the worm.

Advantages of worm gears

Worm gears provide some significant advantages over other types of gear mechanisms:

- **Very high gear ratios** - this is very useful for reducing speed and increasing torque of the worm wheel.
- **Locking** - when the worm stops, it locks the worm wheel in place. This is very useful when the worm wheel is supporting a heavy load, because the load can't move the worm wheel.
- **Take up less space** – this is useful when space is limited.

Uses of worm drives

Worm drives are very often used directly on the output of motors, and in winches as shown below.

Worm drive connected to output of small motor

Winch with heavy duty worm drive and motor

Another use of worm gears is in guitar string tuning pegs, as shown on the right.

The worm prevents the tuning wheel slipping back under the high tension of the strings, which are wrapped around the axle connected to the worm wheel.

The worm gear on the left is part of a mechanism used to drive car windscreen wipers.

Gear ratio of worm drives

Normally a gear ratio is calculated as follows:

$$\text{Gear ratio} = \frac{\text{number of teeth on driven gear}}{\text{number of teeth on driver gear}}$$

But, in the case of a worm drive, how many teeth does the worm have?

With each rotation of the worm, the worm wheel turns by only one tooth. So the effective number of teeth on the worm is one. This leads us to the formula below.

Gear ratio (of a worm drive) = number of teeth on the worm wheel

This explains why worm drives have such high gear ratios, e.g. if there are 60 teeth on the worm wheel, the gear ratio of the worm drive is 60. This is very difficult to achieve with normal spur gears or even with compound gears.

Worked example 4: Worm drives and time to move through a certain angle

Past exam question

The sketches show two mechanisms to operate a robot claw.

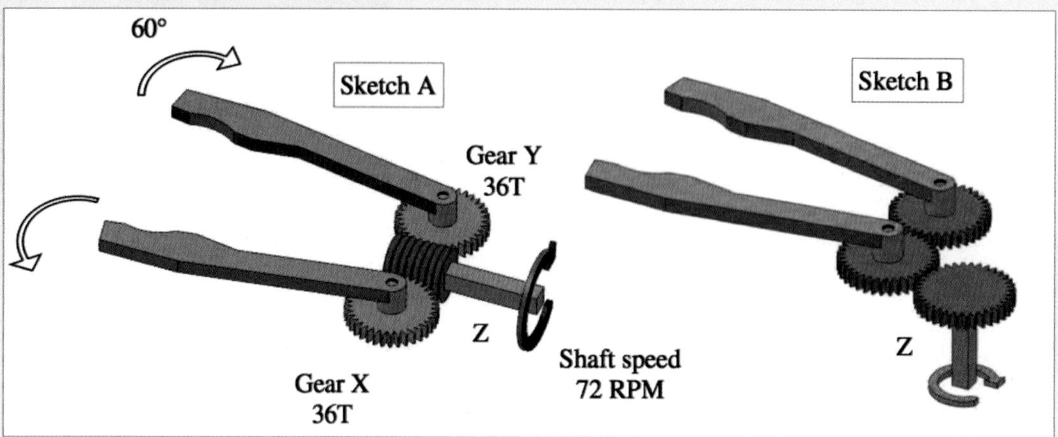

(i) Name the gear mechanism shown in Sketch A.

(ii) State two advantages of using the mechanism in Sketch A, over the mechanism in Sketch B, to operate a robot claw.

(iii) Using the information in Sketch A, calculate the time taken for the arms of the claw to rotate through 60°.

Solutions

(i) The mechanism shown in Sketch A is called a worm drive. It consists of a worm and a worm wheel.

(ii) Advantages of using the worm drive shown in Sketch A, over the spur gear mechanism in Sketch B, are as follows:

a) The worm drive reduces speed and increases torque in the robot claw.

b) The worm drive locks the robot claw in place and prevents it from moving when there is no turning force applied to the worm.

(iii) The time taken for the arms to rotate through 60° in Sketch A can be calculated as follows.

We want to move the arm/worm wheel by 60°. There are 36 teeth on the worm wheel, which covers 360°. So we would need to move the worm wheel by 6 teeth to move the arm by 60°.

We know that one rotation of a worm turns the worm wheel by one tooth. So we will need 6 rotations of the worm to move the arm by 60°.

We know the input shaft/worm rotates 72 times in a minute (60 seconds). But we only want to rotate 6 times, so the time taken for that would be 60 seconds x 6/72 = 60/12 = 5 seconds.

Worked example 5: Worm drives and time to move a certain distance

Past exam question

The sketch shows a mechanism to lock and unlock a door.

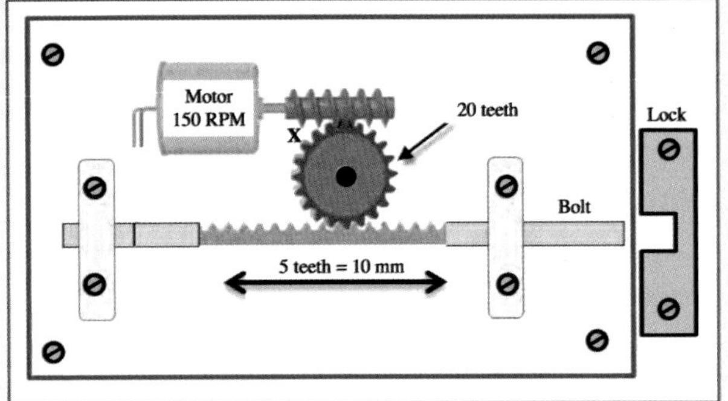

(i) Name the mechanism shown at X. State one advantage of using this mechanism in a lock.

(ii) The mechanism at X changes the direction of motion through 90°. Name and sketch another mechanism, which also achieves this change.

(iii) Using the information in the sketch above, calculate the length of time for which the motor must run to move the bolt a distance of 30 mm.

Solutions

(i) The mechanism at X is a worm drive. It consists of a worm and a worm wheel.

(ii) Another mechanism that changes the direction of motion through 90° is a bevel gear.

(iii) The time taken to move the bolt 30 mm be calculated as follows:

We are told that 5 teeth covers 10 mm, so we will need to move 15 teeth to cover 30 mm.

We know that a worm wheel moves by 1 tooth for every full rotation of the worm/motor.
We know what the motor rotates 150 times a minute, which will move 150 teeth per minute.

But we only want to move 15 teeth, so

$$\text{Time required} = 1 \text{ minute} \times \frac{15}{150} = \frac{1 \text{ minute}}{10} = 6 \text{ seconds}$$

Ratchet and pawl

A ratchet and pawl mechanism such as that shown, allows rotary motion in one direction only. As the ratchet wheel (1) turns, the pawl (2) is raised and drops in behind each "tooth" of the ratchet, preventing the ratchet from rotating the other way.

The pawl can be lifted to release the ratchet mechanism.

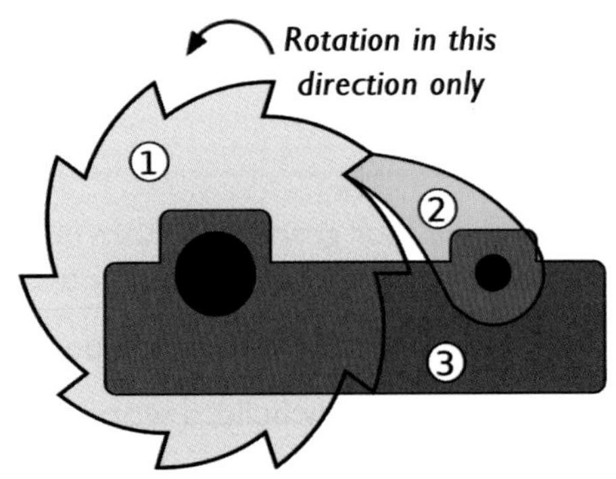

1 = ratchet; 2 = pawl; 3 = base

Uses of ratchet and pawl

Ratchet and pawl mechanisms may be found in:

- **Turnstiles,** to prevent them from turning backwards.
- **Bicycles,** to allow the rear wheel to free wheel when the cyclist is not pedalling.
- **Winches,** to prevent the cable from slipping back.
- **Ratchet spanners,** so you don't have to take the spanner off the nut for each rotation.

Winch with ratchet (pawl not visible)

A **ratchet and pawl mechanism** allows rotary motion in one direction only.

Using construction kits

Experimenting with construction kits, such as Meccano, will help you to develop your understanding of how mechanisms work.

These kits contain many components designed to work with each other, e.g. wheels, axles, gears, pulleys, belts, crank handles, winches, motors and battery packs.

Construction kits also include structural members that can be screwed together, made into levers, linkages, screwed on to metal or wooden bodies, etc.

Activities

1. Make a spur gear mechanism in the technology room with different-sized gears. Insert one and two idler gears in between and note the difference.
2. Turn, or ideally build, a compound gear mechanism. Notice the high gear ratio.
3. Turn, or ideally build, a worm drive. Try to turn the worm wheel.
4. Use Meccano or a similar construction kit to build something containing one or more of the mechanisms described so far in this chapter.

Key points

1. The driver gear is the input gear.
2. The driven gear is the output gear.
3. Gear ratio = $\frac{\text{number of teeth on driven gear}}{\text{number of teeth on driver gear}}$
4. Speed of driven gear = $\frac{\text{speed of driver gear}}{\text{gear ratio}}$
5. A gear train is a sequence of connected gears.
6. Gears in a gear train between the driver and driven gears are called idler gears.
7. Idler gears are used to reverse the direction of rotation.
8. Idler gears have no effect on the gear ratio.
9. A compound gear is composed of two differently-sized gears fixed next to each other on the same axle.
10. Compound gears change the gear ratio.
11. Compound gears can create large gear ratios.
12. To calculate the total gear ratio with a compound gear, calculate the gear ratio on the input side, and the gear ratio on the output side, and multiply them together.
13. A worm drive consists of a worm and a worm wheel.
14. A worm drive changes the direction of motion through 90°.
15. The gear ratio of a worm drive = number of teeth in the driven gear.
16. A worm drive has a very high gear ratio.
17. A high gear ratio means the speed reduces, and the torque increases.
18. A worm drive is locking, i.e. the worm wheel cannot turn the worm.
19. Worm drives are useful where a heavy load must be lifted and held, because the worm drive provides increased torque to move the load, and it locks to prevents the load from moving the driver gear.
20. Gears that mesh straight-on are called spur gears.
21. A bevel gear has angled gears, which change the angle of rotation by 90°. They are used in hand drills.
22. A rack and pinion changes the rotary motion of the pinion gear into the linear motion of the rack. Typical uses are in car steering systems, rack/mountain railways, stairs lifts, and fork lifts.
23. A ratchet can only rotate in one direction. The pawl prevents it from turning the other way. Ratchet and pawl mechanisms are used in turnstiles and bicycle wheels.

Past exam questions

1. Name the gear below labelled X and state its function.

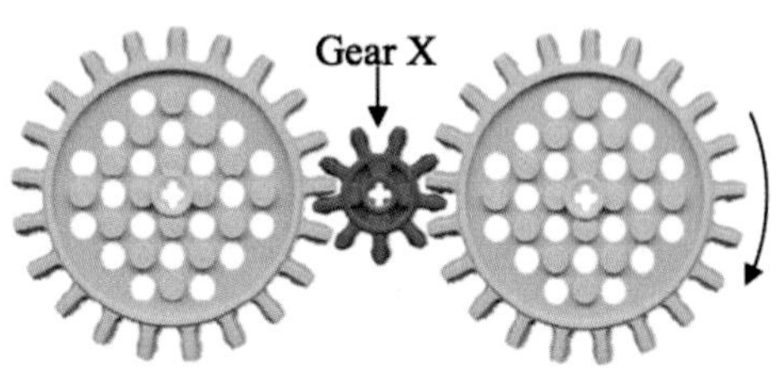

2. Name the mechanism at X.

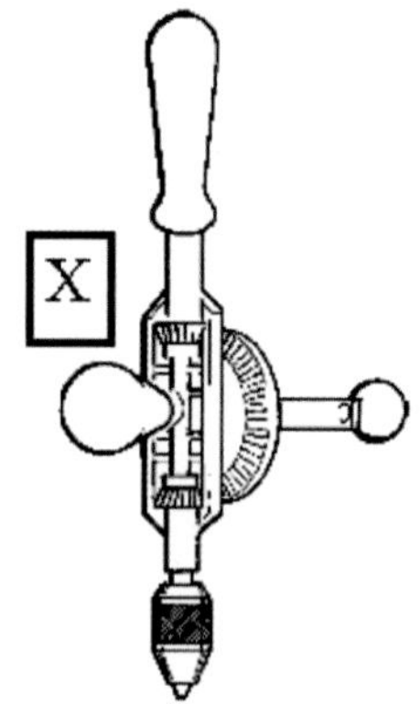

3. What is the name of the gear at A?

4. Calculate the output speed of the gear train shown opposite. The driver input speed (left-most gear) is 18 RPM.

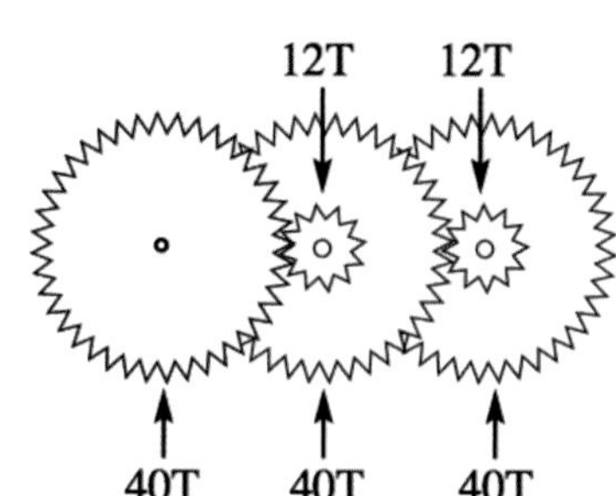

5. What type of mechanism is connected to the motor at X?

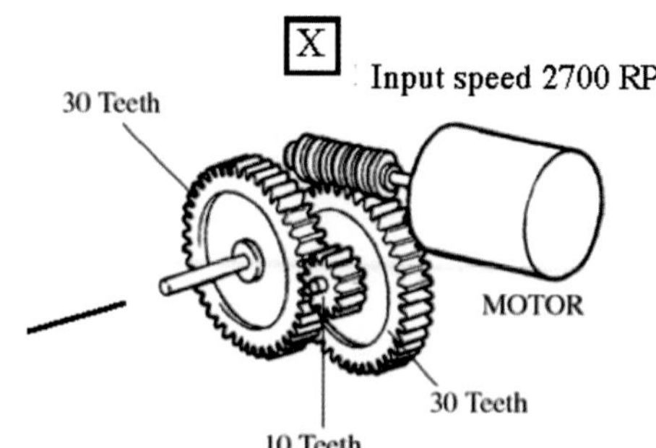

6. Name the mechanism shown and state the function of part X.

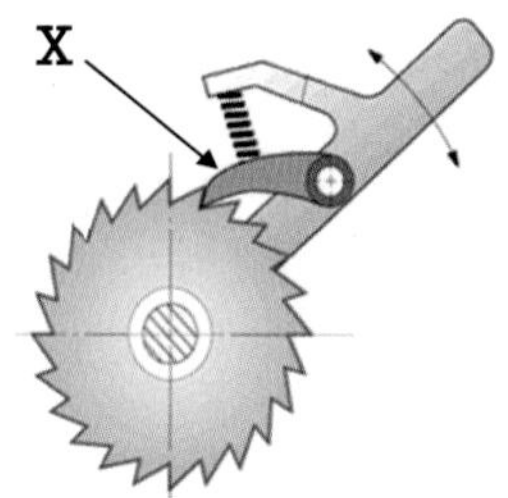

Past exam questions

7. Calculate the speed of gear Z if gear X is rotating at 120 RPM.

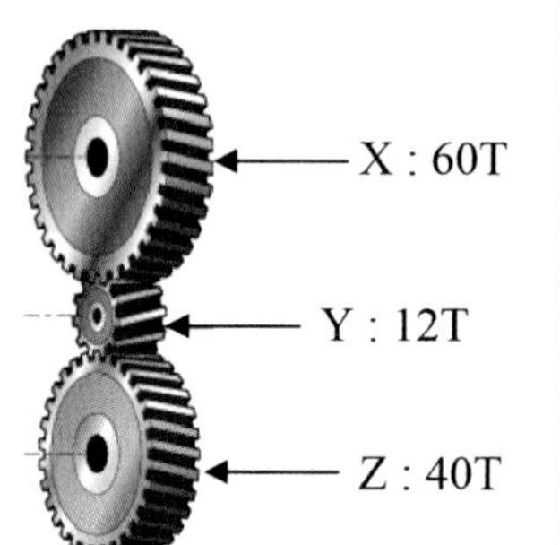

8. Name the mechanism attached to the motor shown at X. State two advantages of this mechanism.

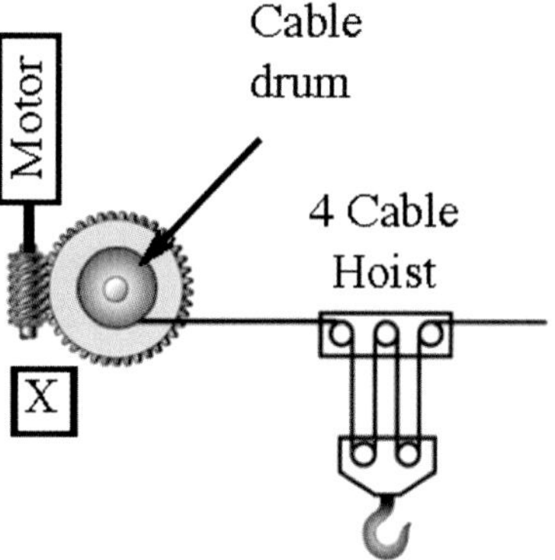

9. In the gear system shown below, if shaft A turns at 5 RPM, calculate the speed of shaft B.

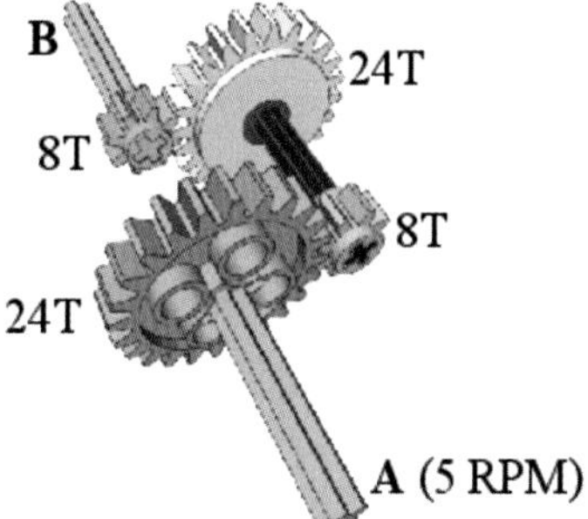

10. The free-wheel (free hub) on the back-wheel of a bicycle, shown on the right, uses a ratchet mechanism. Name two other everyday devices that use a ratchet mechanism.

11. In the gear train shown below, gear A has 15 teeth, gear B has 30 teeth and gear C has 30 teeth. Calculate the rotary speed of gear C if the driver gear is rotating at 80 RPM.

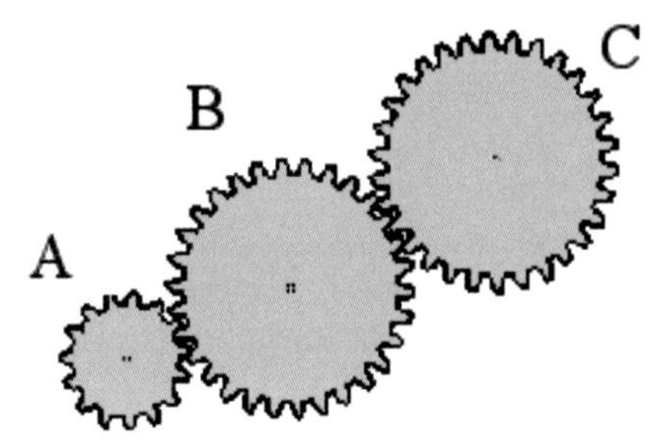

Chain and belt drives

Chain drives and belt drives are similar to gears, in that they connect wheels of different sizes together. However the wheels do not mesh together, instead they are connected to each other using a chain or a belt.

Chain and belt drives have a driver wheel and a driven wheel. Turning the driver wheel causes the driven wheel to rotate, via the chain or belt. If the two wheels are different sizes, chain and belt drives will change the output speed of rotation and the output torque.

Chain and sprocket

In a chain and sprocket mechanism, the toothed wheels, called sprockets, are connected via a loop of metal chain. Each sprocket has a set of teeth, which fit into the links of the chain.

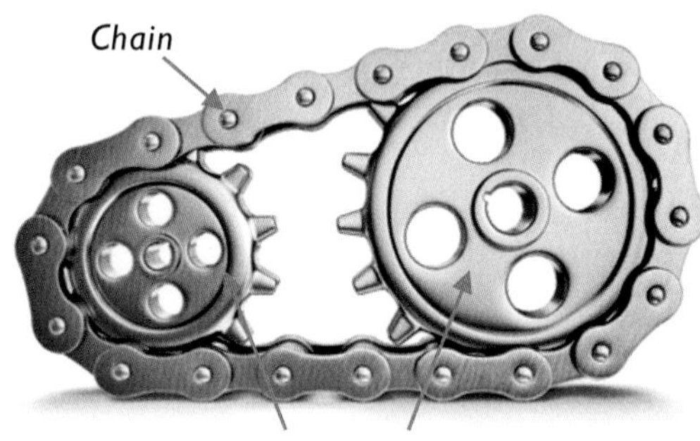

Chain and sprocket mechanisms are very strong, do not slip easily, but need to be lubricated with oil or grease to reduce friction and prevent sticking.

Uses of chain and sprocket

Chain and sprocket mechanisms can be found in:

- Bicycles, where a chain is used to connect the rear wheel to the pedals.
- Cars, where a chain, called a timing chain, is used to connect the crankshaft to the camshaft, (see "Mechanisms 1").

Belt drives

In this mechanism, shown below, the wheels are connected using a belt. The belt is in the shape of a loop, usually made from rubber.

A belt and pulley system being driven by a motor

The wheels are called pulleys. They have a groove along their edge to keep the belt in place.

A belt drive operates more quietly than a chain drive, but the belt must be kept tensioned tightly against the pulley wheels or it may slip.

Belts are not good for high force applications (e.g. lifting heavy loads) as the belts may slip against the pulley wheels.

Toothed belt

In a toothed belt system, seen here on the right, the belt has teeth on its underside, which mesh with teeth on the wheels.

Toothed belts have better grip than flat belts, and so are less likely to slip.

Toothed belts are commonly used as timing belts, e.g. in sewing machines, inkjet printers and to drive the camshafts in a car engine.

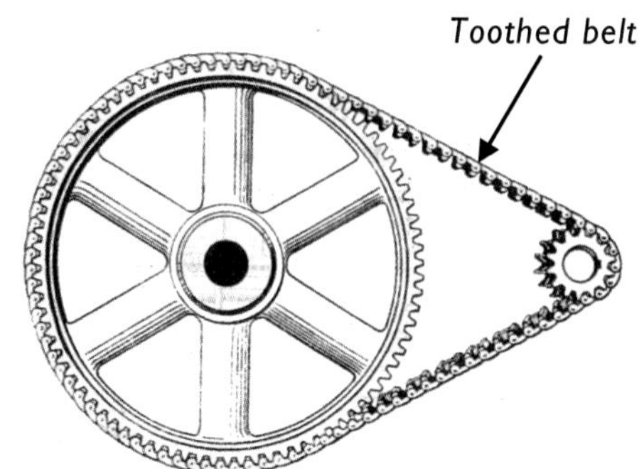

A toothed belt system

Chains versus belts - advantages and disadvantages

The advantages and disadvantages of chain drives versus belt drives and vice versa are summarised below.

	Advantages	Disadvantages
Chain drive	• Non-slip • Stronger • More durable • Suitable for high output torque	• Noisier than belts • Needs oil for lubrication (can get stuck or rust otherwise)
Belt drive	• Quieter • Lighter • Cheaper • Doesn't require lubrication	• Can slip (toothed belts have lower chance of slipping) • Not suitable for high output torque

Worked example 6: Chain drives

Past exam question

(i) This rowing machine uses a chain drive. Give two reasons for using a chain drive for this purpose.

(ii) Name two other machines that use a chain drive.

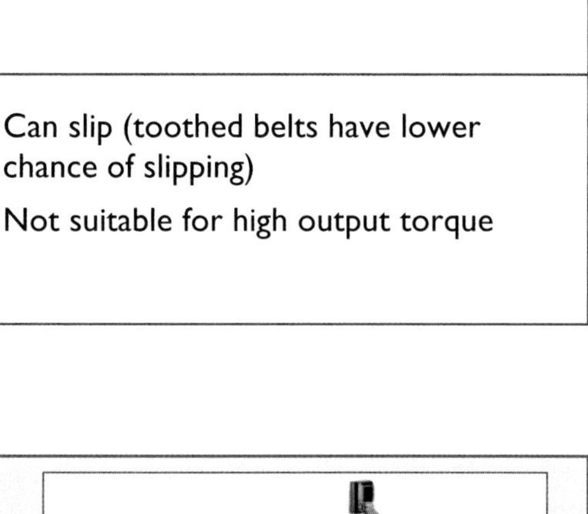

Solutions

(i) Reasons for using a chain drive in the rowing machine are:

a) A chain drive will not slip easily, whereas a belt drive may - considering the rowing machine will be subjected to a strong pulling force.

b) A chain drive is made from metal and so will be strong and durable. The metal chain will withstand the force of being repeatedly pulled by the rower, better than the rubber material typically used in a belt drive.

c) A chain is flexible and will accommodate different heights and sizes of rower, as opposed to using a non-flexible mechanism such as a rack and pinion system.

(ii) Two other machines that use chain drives are (a) a bicycle, (b) a car (in the timing chain).

Worked example 7: Chain and belt drives

Past exam question

State two reasons why a pulley and toothed belt is used instead of a gear and chain on an inkjet printer.

Solutions

A toothed belt is: (1) lighter, (2) cheaper, (3) less noisy, and (4) doesn't require lubrication. The toothed belt is also (5) easier to replace and change than a chain drive. (6) A chain drive is not needed as a large torque is not required, and a belt is unlikely to slip.

Chain and belt drive rotation speeds

The speeds for chain and belt drives are calculated in a similar way to gears. Remember that speeds of rotation are measured in RPM (revolutions per minute).

Velocity ratio

The velocity ratio is equal to the speed of the input wheel divided by the speed of the output wheel. It is dependent on the circumference of the wheels. It can be calculated using the following formulae.

$$\textbf{Velocity ratio for belt and pulley} = \frac{\text{speed of driver (input) gear}}{\text{speed of driven (output) gear}} = \frac{\text{diameter of driven (output) wheel}}{\text{diameter of driver (input) wheel}}$$

$$\textbf{Velocity ratio for chain drives and toothed belts} = \frac{\text{number of teeth on driven (output) wheel}}{\text{number of teeth on driver (input) wheel}}$$

Output speeds

Once you know the velocity ratio, you can calculate the speeds of the output wheel as follows:

$$\textbf{Speed of driven } \text{(output)} \textbf{ wheel} = \frac{\text{speed of driver (input) wheel}}{\text{velocity ratio}}$$

When calculating speeds, remember the larger wheel always turns more slowly than the smaller wheel, so your calculations must result in a smaller RPM (revolutions per minute) for the larger wheel.

Worked example 8: Calculate speed of driven pulley

Past exam question

Calculate the speed of the driven pulley from the information given. (The symbol ϕ stands for diameter.)

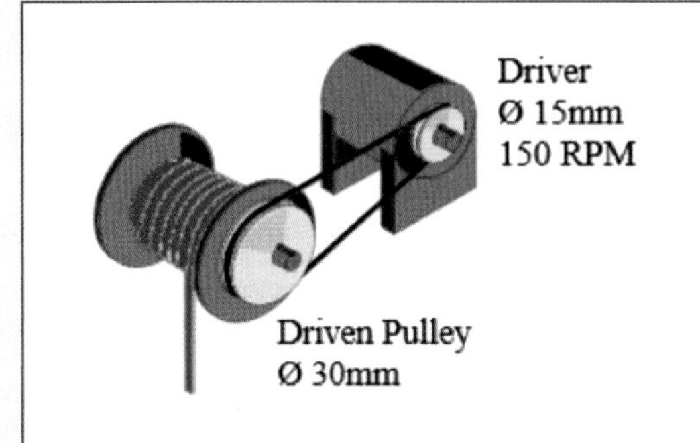

Solution using reasoning

The driven pulley is twice as large as the driver, its circumference is twice as large, so it will be rotating at half the speed of the driver pulley. So speed of driven pulley = 75 RPM.

Solution by applying formulae

$$\text{Velocity ratio for belt and pulley} = \frac{\text{diameter of driven (output) wheel}}{\text{diameter of driver (input) wheel}} = \frac{30\text{ mm}}{15\text{ mm}} = 2$$

$$\text{Speed of driven pulley} = \frac{\text{speed of driver pulley}}{\text{velocity ratio}} = \frac{150\text{ RPM}}{2} = 75\text{ RPM}$$

Worked example 9: Calculate speed of driven sprocket

Past exam question

Calculate the speed of the driven sprocket if the driver is rotating at 20 RPM.

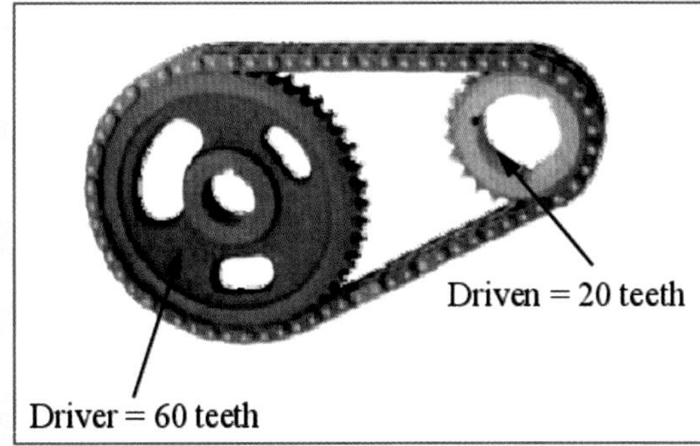

Solution using reasoning

The driven sprocket is three times as small as the driver, so it will be rotating at three times the speed of the driver. So speed of driven sprocket = 3 x 20 RPM = 60 RPM.

Solution by applying formulae

$$\text{Velocity ratio for chain drive} = \frac{\text{number of teeth on driven (output) wheel}}{\text{number of teeth on driver (input) wheel}} = \frac{20}{60} = \frac{1}{3}$$

$$\text{Speed of driven sprocket} = \frac{\text{speed of driver sprocket}}{\text{velocity ratio}} = \frac{20\text{ RPM}}{(\frac{1}{3})} = 20\text{ RPM} \times 3 = 60\text{ RPM}$$

Activities

Make a small pulley and belt drive in the technology room. Attach a motor to the driver pulley. You will need to strongly secure the motor and the axles of the driver pulley and the driven pulley.

Key points

1. Chain drives are strong, good for heavy loads, do not slip, but require lubrication.
2. Belt drives are light, cheap, make less noise, but can slip under heavy loads.
3. The speeds for chain and belt drives are calculated in a similar way to gears.
4. The larger wheel turns more slowly than the smaller one.

Test yourself

1. Why is a chain drive used on a bicycle, as opposed to a belt drive?
2. What are the disadvantages of a chain drive?
3. If you were trying to lift a heavy weight, would you use a belt and pulley, or a chain and sprocket?
4. If the driver wheel is larger than the driven wheel, which wheel turns faster?
5. If the driver pulley is 20 mm in diameter and rotating at 100 RPM, and the driven pulley is 40 mm in diameter, what is the speed of the driven pulley?
6. If the driving sprocket has 48 teeth and its speed is 24 RPM, and the driven sprocket has 16 teeth, how fast is the driven sprocket rotating?

Past exam questions

1. State two advantages of the pulley and belt system shown, over a chain and sprocket system.

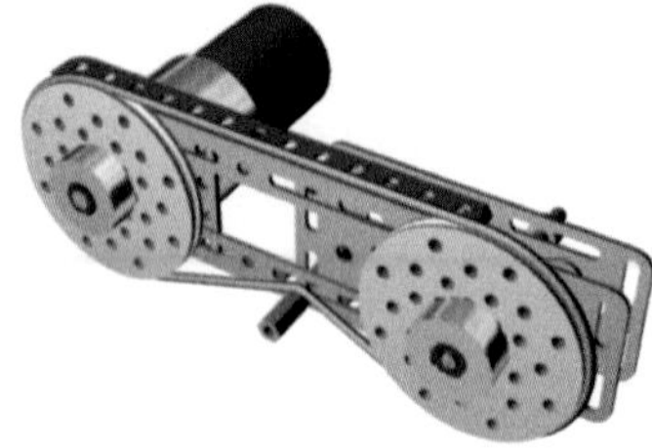

2. In the diagram shown, calculate the speed of the driven sprocket if the driver is rotating at 20 RPM.

Past exam questions

3. State two reasons why a chain is used in preference to a belt in a forklift hoist.

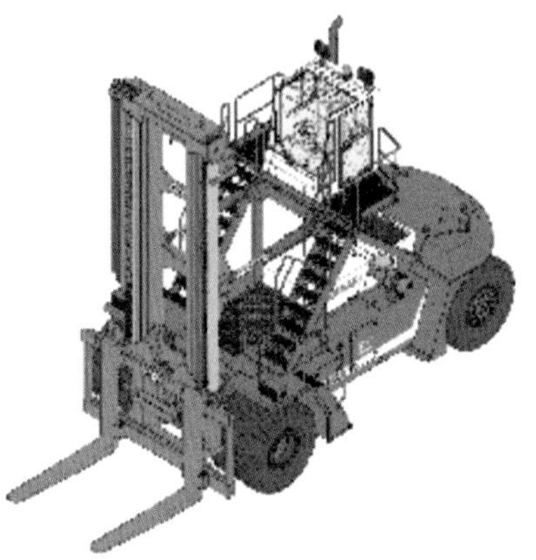

4. If the motor shaft shown turns at 90 RPM, calculate the speed of rotation of the pulley shaft.

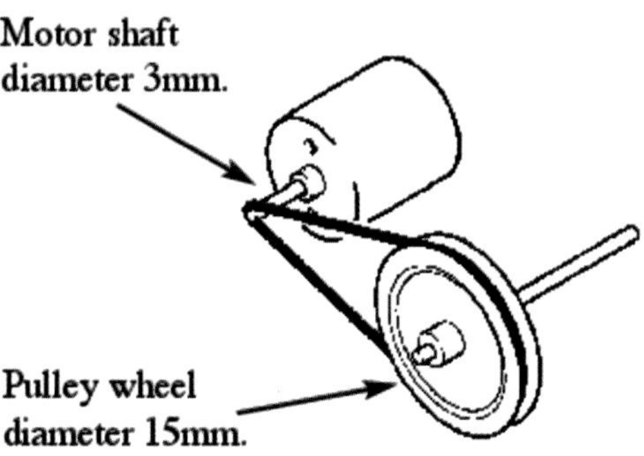

5. When in use, a pulley drive was found to slip. Suggest two methods of overcoming this problem.

6. A buggy is propelled using a motor and a pulley drive shown on the right. The motor is rotating at 400 RPM. If the driver pulley has a diameter or 2 cm and driven pulley has a diameter of 8 cm, calculate the speed of the driven pulley.

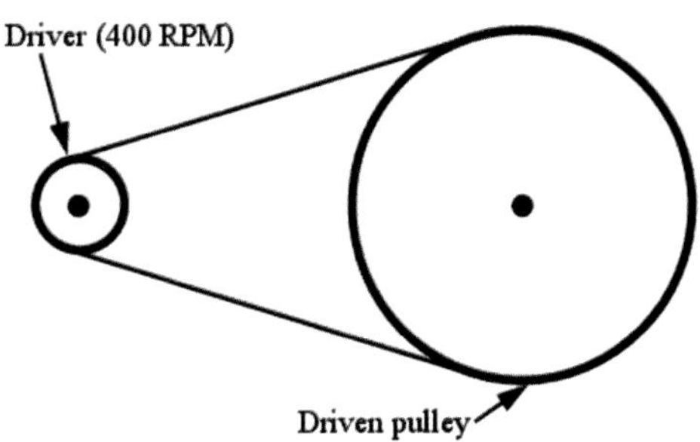

7. In the diagram shown, is the slowest rotating pulley A, B, or C?

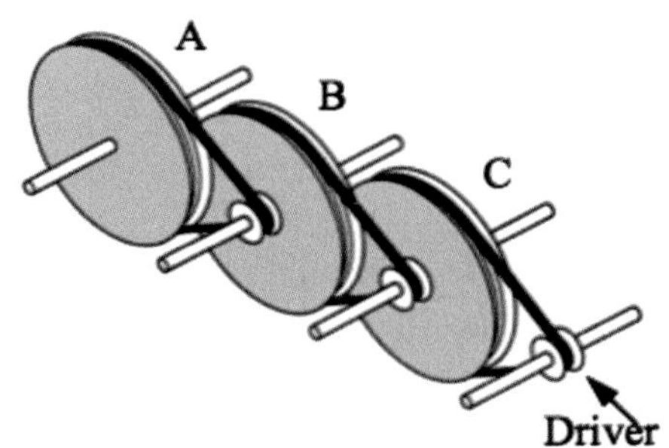

Pulley systems

A pulley wheel is a wheel with a groove in the rim to hold a rope, cable or belt.

We have seen pulley wheels in use already in the belt and pulley mechanism in the previous section. This was where two pulley wheels were used with a continuous loop or belt.

This section looks at pulley systems, which consist of arrangements of pulley wheels with ropes or cables designed to lift weights or move loads, by using mechanical advantage.

A **pulley wheel** is a wheel with a groove in the rim to hold a rope, cable or belt.

A **pulley system** is an arrangement of one or more pulley wheels and ropes or cables, designed to lift weights or move loads, using mechanical advantage.

Remember that the mechanical advantage of a mechanism is the ratio of the output force to the input force.

Mechanical advantage is calculated by the formula:

$$\text{Mechanical advantage} = \frac{\text{load (force in newtons)}}{\text{effort (force in newtons)}}$$

Pulley system used to distribute chicken feed

Single fixed pulley

The simplest pulley system has one pulley wheel attached to a fixed axle. The rope is fixed to the load. In order to raise the load by a given amount on one side of the pulley, the user must pull the rope down by the same distance on the other side.

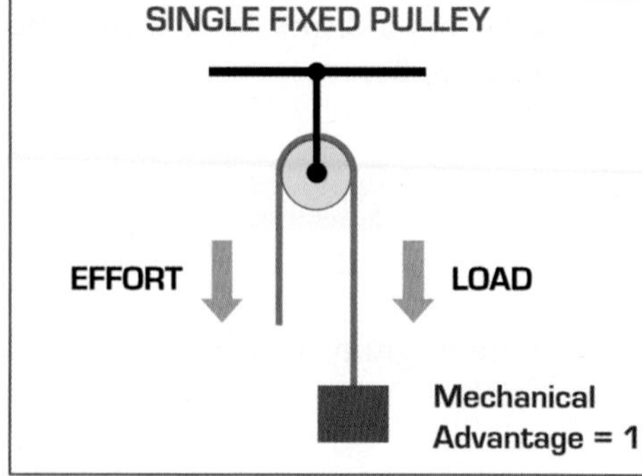

The pulley only changes the direction of the pulling force. There is no mechanical advantage. The forces are equal on both sides.

$$\text{Mechanical advantage} = \frac{\text{load}}{\text{effort}} = 1$$

However, single fixed pulleys are still very useful because it is easier and much safer for a person to lift a heavy weight by pulling down on a rope, than it is to try to lift the heavy weight directly.

Mechanical advantage of a single fixed pulley $= 1$

Single movable pulley

In a single movable pulley, the pulley wheel is attached to the load and the end of the rope is fixed. This causes the weight, i.e. force, of the load to be shared between the two ropes.

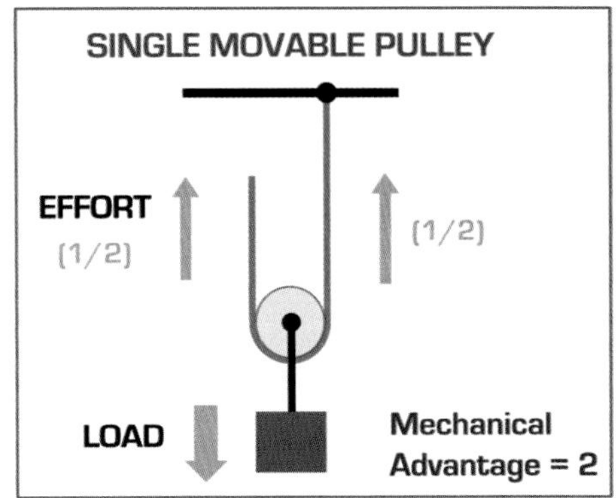

It only takes half the force to hold up the load on the effort side, because the fixed point is also sharing the load and in effect holding up the other half. So now we have a mechanical advantage of 2. We can hold up a given force (weight) with only half that force.

Notice that if you lift up the effort side of the rope by 1 m, the load will only rise up by 0.5 m. This is because the rope is doubled over, around the pulley wheel, and has to travel 0.5 m on both sides.

So we see, just like in the case of the lever, there is a trade-off between distance and force. We can lift a load with an effort equal to only half of the load, but we have to apply the effort over twice the distance.

Mechanical advantage of a single movable pulley = 2

One fixed and one movable pulley

What is the mechanical advantage of the pulley system shown on the right? Is it twice as much because we have twice the number of pulleys?

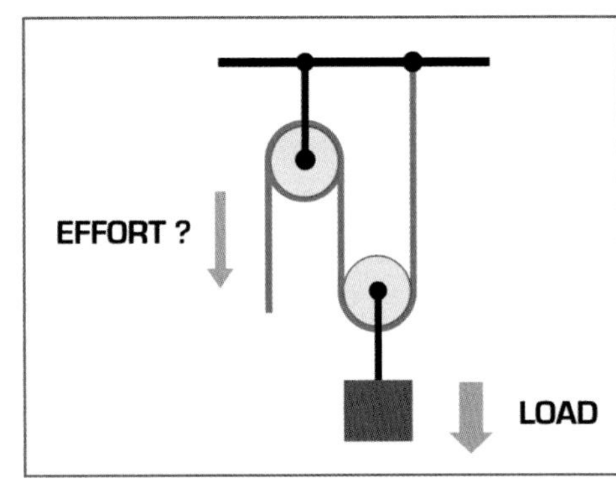

We can see from the diagram below that this pulley system is a combination of a single fixed pulley system (on the left) and a single movable pulley system on the right. We know the fixed pulley system doesn't have any mechanical advantage (it just changes the direction of pulling), so the total mechanical advantage for this system is 2.

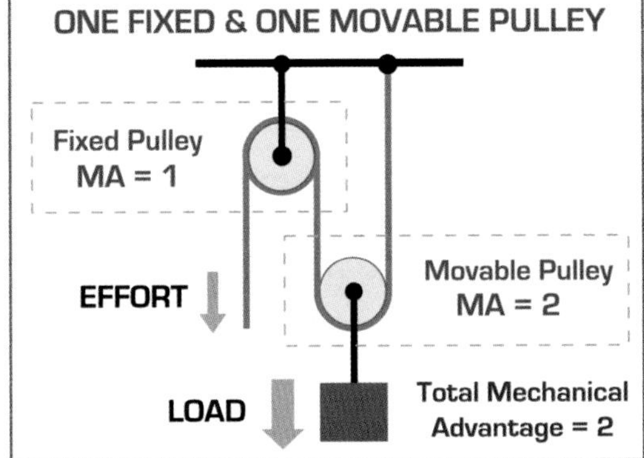

So again, in this case, you can lift a given weight with half the effort, but you'll have to pull the rope twice as far.

Note the advantage of this pulley system is that the operator can pull down on the effort side (rope). This is much easier and safer for the operator, than having to pull the rope **up**, as is the case with the single movable pulley system above.

Mechanical advantage of one fixed and one movable pulley = 2

This type of system is used so often, it has another name and a handy shape, called a block and tackle, shown here on the right.

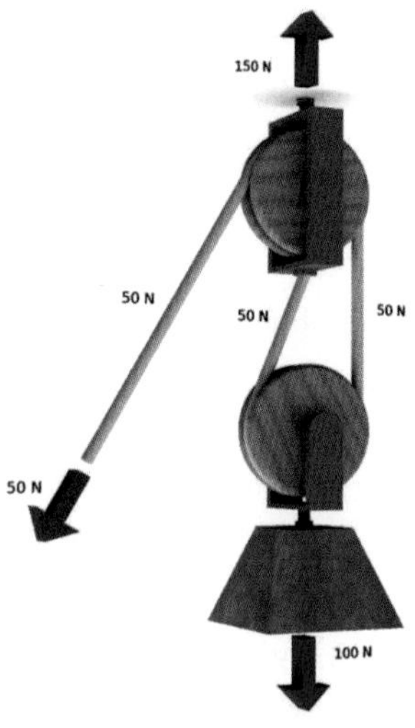

Block and tackle

Example

In the pulley system shown, the load is 100 N and the effort is 50 N. What is the mechanical advantage?

$$\text{Mechanical advantage} = \frac{\text{load (force in newtons)}}{\text{effort (force in newtons)}} = \frac{100\ \text{N}}{50\ \text{N}} = 2$$

Distances moved

For the single movable pulley system, and the one fixed and one single movable pulley system, the rope on the effort side will travel twice the distance that the load moves. In general, the distance travelled by the effort side, is given by the formula below. (This is the same formula for the lever).

Distance moved by effort = distance moved by load × mechanical advantage

A four-cable hoist

More complex pulley systems can be created to provide greater mechanical advantages. A common system called a four-cable hoist is show here.

The cable is fixed on the right. The load is a weight suspended from the hook. This load is shared/divided among four cables, so the mechanical advantage is 4. To raise the load by 10 cm, the motor will have to pull in the cable by 40 cm. However, it only needs ¼ of the force to do so.

The mechanical advantage is further increased by the worm drive powering the cable drum (see gears, previous section).

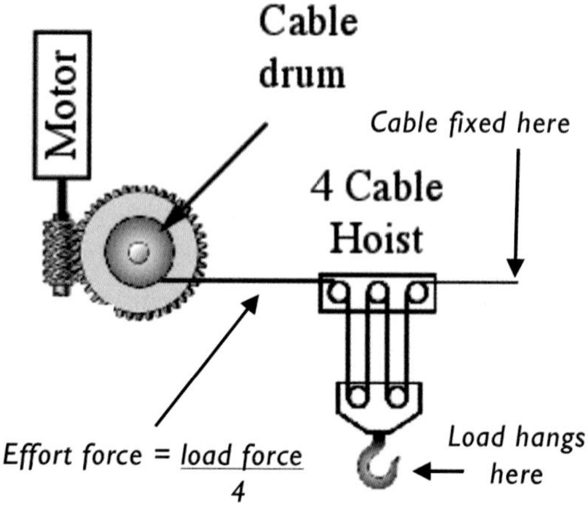

Another advantage of the 4-cable hoist is that the entire pulley mechanism can be moved horizontally on a gantry (bridge shaped frame for supporting cranes) without changing the height of the load.

This type of mechanism is used in dockyards to load and unload containers from container ships.

Worked example 10: Calculate effort and force for a pulley system

Past exam question

The pulley system shown lifts a load of 30 N a height of 0.5 m.
Calculate (i) the effort force and (ii) the distance moved, X.

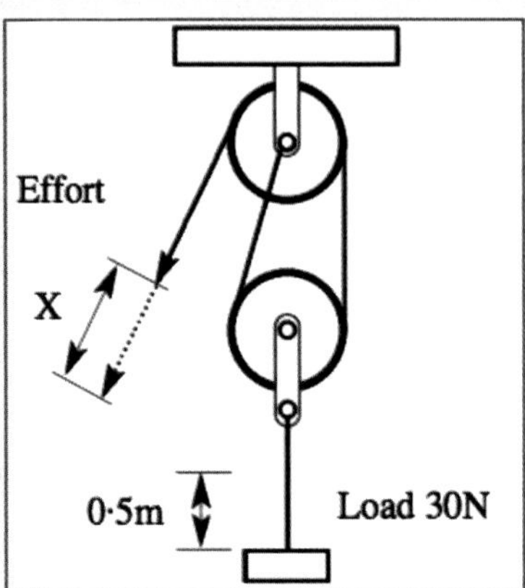

Solution using reasoning

This pulley system has one movable pulley and one fixed pulley, so its mechanical advantage is 2.

(i) If the mechanical advantage is 2, by definition this means that the effort required is half the load. Therefore effort = 30 N/2 = 15 N.

(ii) If the mechanical advantage is 2, then the effort distance must be twice the load distance = 2 x 0.5 m = 1 m.

Solution by applying formulae

This pulley system has one movable pulley and one fixed pulley, so its mechanical advantage is 2.

(i) Calculate effort force:

$$\text{mechanical advantage} = \frac{\text{load}}{\text{effort}} = 2$$

$$\text{load} = 2 \times \text{effort}$$

$$\text{effort} = \frac{\text{load}}{2} = \frac{30\text{ N}}{2} = 15\text{ N}$$

(ii) Calculate distance moved by load, X:

$$\text{Distance moved by effort} = \text{distance moved by load} \times \text{mechanical advantage} = 0.5\text{ m} \times 2 = 1\text{ m}$$

Activities

1. Build a single fixed pulley system in the technology room. Use or build a wooden frame or box. Use a u-shaped bracket to hold the axle of the pulley, and to attach the pulley to the underside of the frame or box.
2. Build a single movable pulley system. Use a u-shaped bracket to hold the axle of the pulley, and to attach a load to the pulley. Attach one end of the cable to a frame, box or table. Notice that to lift the load you have to move the other end of the cable twice as far, but it only feels half as heavy.

Key points

1. The mechanical advantage of a single fixed pulley is 1.
2. The mechanical advantage of a single movable pulley is 2.
3. The mechanical advantage of one fixed and one movable pulley is 2.
4. Force and distance calculations for pulleys are similar to levers and gears.

Past exam questions

1. In the pulley system shown, is the load force 0 N, 10 N, 20 N or 30 N?

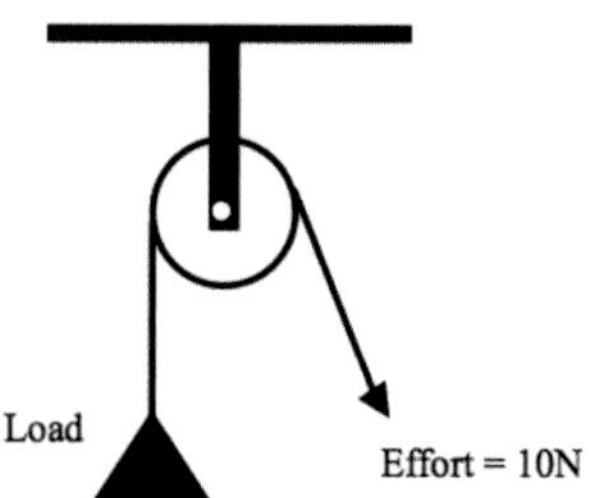

2. Calculate the mechanical advantage of the pulley system shown.

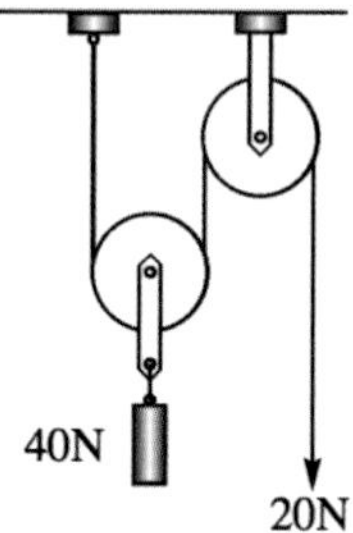

3. Calculate the force required to lift the load shown.

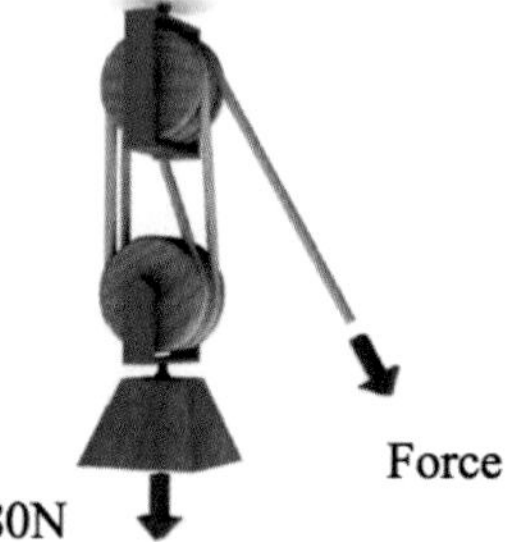

4. State two advantages of using the four-cable hoist shown.

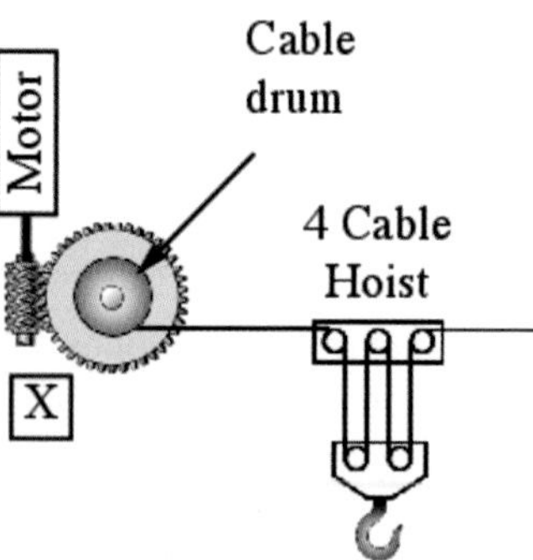

5. How much effort is required to lift the 12 N load shown? What is the distance X, by which the rope must be pulled, to lift the load by 2 m?

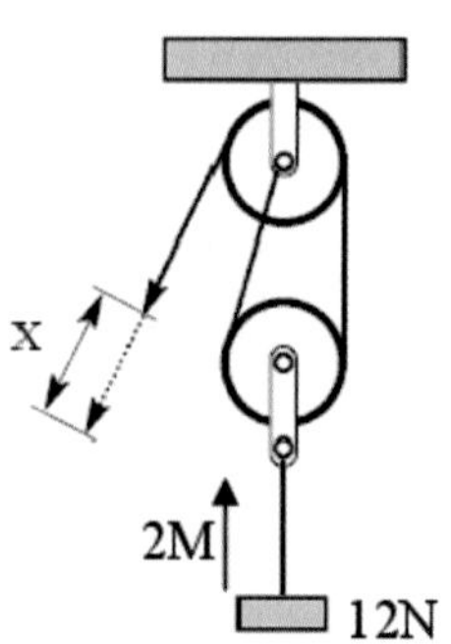

Other mechanisms

Wheel and axle

This mechanism consists of a wheel attached at its centre to an axle. The radius of the wheel is greater than that of the axle.

The wheel and the axle rotate together around the same axis, allowing a force to be transferred from one to the other. Effort can be applied either to the edge of the wheel or to the edge of the axle.

Effort applied to edge of wheel

In this case, the effort is applied at the edge of the wheel and transmitted to the load by the axle. Examples of this include a car steering wheel, door knob, tap and screwdriver.

Effort applied to edge of axle

Here the effort is applied at the edge of the axle and transmitted to the load by the wheel. Applications include the back wheel of a bicycle and a Ferris wheel.

Mechanical advantage of wheel and axle

Regardless of which way around the load and effort are applied, the mechanical advantage of a wheel and axle is calculated as follows:

$$\text{Mechanical advantage} = \frac{\text{load}}{\text{effort}}$$

Screw mechanism

A screw mechanism consists of an axle with grooves, called threads, around the outside. The threaded axle passes through a hole in another object, e.g. a nut. The hole has threads on the inside of the hole that mesh with the threads on the axle. The axle can be turned by a crank (as in the C clamp below) or by a motor.

The screw mechanism converts rotary motion to linear motion. It also converts torque (turning force) to a linear force. A small torque on the shaft can exert a large linear force on the load. The closer the threads of the screw are to each other, the greater is the mechanical advantage.

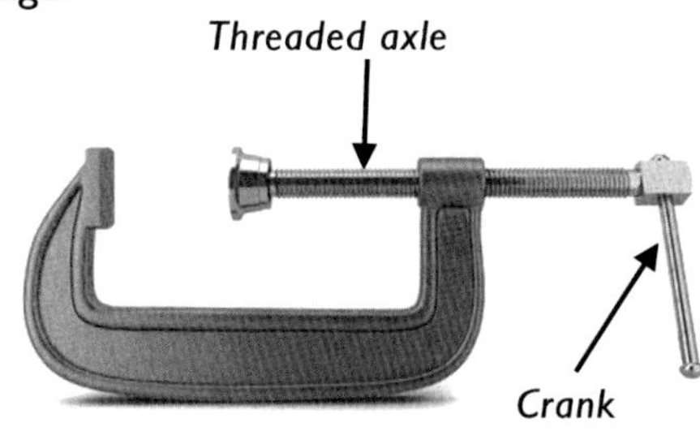

C clamp

The two main uses of a screw mechanism are for:

- Fastening or pressing objects together.
- Raising loads.

Common applications include:

- Threaded fasteners to join objects together, e.g. screw top container, or bolt and nut.
- Clamping or pressing tools, e.g. C clamp, bench vice, or screw press.
- Lifting equipment, e.g. car jack.

Friction and lubrication

Friction is important in mechanisms, and it needs to be considered when a mechanism is being designed. Sometimes we want lots of friction, sometimes we want as little as possible.

What is friction?

Friction is a force that slows down or prevents motion when two surfaces come in contact with each other. In other words, friction is an indication of how "slippy" something is. For example, we become very aware of friction when learning to skate on ice.

There is a lot less friction between the surface of the skates and the ice, than between the soles of our shoes and the ground. We have to adapt to this when learning to ice skate.

Low friction means that surfaces can slide past each other easily. High friction means that it can take a lot of force to get the objects to move against each other.

Materials with low friction	Materials with high friction
• Snow • Ice • Oil • Air	• Rubber • Velcro • Sandpaper

Materials like plastic, metal and wood have medium to low levels of friction, depending on how smooth the surface of the material is.

Friction is a force that slows down or prevents motion when two surfaces come in contact with each other.

Uses of friction

The table below lists situations where friction is useful and not useful.

When friction is useful	When friction is not useful
We want friction when we don't want things to move relative to each other, for example between: • Wheels and the road. • Brake pads and wheels. • A belt and a pulley wheel. • Our feet and the ground.	We don't want friction when we want parts to move easily relative to each other, such as: • Between a wheel and its axle. • Between a cam and a follower. • In a slider mechanism. • When gears are meshing together. • When chains and sprockets are meshing together.

Why is friction undesirable between moving parts?

If we have too much friction between moving parts, much of the energy of the mechanism gets wasted and is lost to the surroundings in the form of heat. Generating heat in this situation is not a good thing either as it can damage the mechanism or present a risk of fire or injury.

How can we reduce friction between moving parts?

Materials used to reduce friction are called lubricants, for example oil and grease.

Applying these to the moving parts of a mechanism, such as the gears shown, helps them to slide over one another more easily.

Oil and grease are good lubricants because they are "slippy", and they don't dry out too easily.

Using ball bearings greatly helps to reduce friction - see picture on the right.

The inner part is fixed, and the outer part slips around on the balls (like marbles). Or the outer part can be fixed and inner part moves. Ball bearings are used in all car and bicycle axles.

Other ways to reduce friction include:

- Using smooth surfaces.
- Using low-friction materials.
- Reducing the contact area between the surfaces (ball bearings use this principle – only a small part of the ball bearings touch the outer ring in the picture.)
- Reducing the weight or forces acting on the surfaces.

How can we increase friction?

Methods of increasing friction include:

- Using high-friction materials such as rubber.
- Increasing the contact area between the surfaces, e.g. using larger rubber feet, wider tyres.
- Using rough/irregular surfaces, e.g. tread patterns on shoes or on tyres, such as those shown on the bicycle tyres in the picture.
- Increasing the weight or forces acting on the surfaces, i.e. providing more contact pressure.

Activities

1. Rub your hands together hard for a while. What is heating them up? Spot the difference if you use soap suds between your hands.
2. Find an example of ball bearings in the technology room. See how freely they rotate.
3. In mechanisms that you build or use in the technology room, where there is a sliding contact - such as in a cam-and-follower, peg-and-slot, or crank-and-slider - apply some grease (e.g. Vaseline) between the sliding parts. Notice the difference and how much more easily they operate.

Key points

1. Friction is a force that slows down or prevents motion when two surfaces come in contact with each other.
2. Keep high levels of friction where you don't want to slip, e.g. by using rubber.
3. Reduce friction between moving parts with lubrication and ball bearings.

Test yourself

1. State two reasons why oil is used on the chain of a bicycle.
2. Give one reason for using ball bearings in a mechanism.
3. Name two materials that may be used to reduce friction between moving parts. What general name is given to these types of materials?

Past exam questions

1. State clearly, where on a bicycle, is it important to:

   (i) Maximise friction,

   (ii) Minimise friction.

2. The chain and sprocket is the main drive mechanism on a bicycle. Suggest one way to maintain the chain to keep it in good working order.

Summary of "Mechanisms 1 and 2"

Category	Type	Motion conversion	Formulae
Levers	Class I Class 2 Class 3	Linear to linear	Mechanical advantage $= \frac{\text{load}}{\text{effort}}$ Moment = force × distance (Nm) Moment on left side = moment on right side Velocity ratio $= \frac{\text{distance travelled by effort}}{\text{distance travelled by load}}$
Linkages	Reverse motion Push-pull Parallel Bell crank Scissors	Linear to linear	As for levers
Springs	Compression Tension Torsion	Linear to linear	
Cams and cranks	Manual crank	Reciprocating to rotary	Moment = force × distance (Nm)
	Crank-and-slider	Rotary to reciprocating, and vice versa	
	Cam-and-follower	Rotary to reciprocating	
	Peg-and-slot	Rotary to oscillating	
Gears	Spur gears	Rotary to rotary	Gear ratio $= \frac{\text{number of teeth on driven (output) gear}}{\text{number of teeth on driver (input) gear}}$ Torque = force × radius (Nm) Mechanical advantage $= \frac{\text{output torque (Nm)}}{\text{input torque (Nm)}}$ Mechanical advantage = gear ratio
	Idler gears	Rotary to rotary	
	Compound gears	Rotary to rotary	
	Bevel gears	Rotary to rotary with change of angle of rotation by 90°	

Category	Type	Motion conversion	Formulae
Gears	Worm drives	Rotary to rotary with change of angle of rotation by 90°	Number of teeth on the worm = 1 Gear ratio = number of teeth on the worm wheel
	Rack and pinion	Rotary to linear	
	Ratchet and pawl	Rotary to rotary one-way	
Chain and belt drives	Chain and sprocket Toothed belt	Rotary to rotary	$\text{Velocity ratio} = \frac{\text{number of teeth on driven wheel}}{\text{number of teeth on driver wheel}}$
	Belt and pulley	Rotary to rotary	$\text{Velocity ratio} = \frac{\text{diameter of driven (output) wheel}}{\text{diameter of driver (input) wheel}}$
Pulley systems	In general	Linear to linear	$\text{Mechanical advantage} = \frac{\text{load}}{\text{effort}}$ $\text{Velocity ratio} = \frac{\text{distance travelled by effort}}{\text{distance travelled by load}}$
	Single fixed pulley	Linear to linear	Mechanical advantage = 1
	Single movable pulley	Linear to linear	Mechanical advantage = 2
	One fixed plus one movable pulley	Linear to linear	Mechanical advantage = 2
	Four-cable hoist	Linear to linear	Mechanical advantage = 4
Wheel and axle	Effort at edge of wheel Effort at edge of axle	Rotary to rotary	$\text{Mechanical advantage} = \frac{\text{load}}{\text{effort}}$
Screw mechanism		Rotary to linear	

CHAPTER 9

Energy

Energy

This chapter explains what energy is and how it can be converted from one form to another. It describes different sources of energy, and the environmental impacts of energy consumption.

Light energy from a galaxy

What is energy?

Energy is the ability to do work - to cause something to happen. The universe is made up of energy in different forms. Energy cannot be created or destroyed - it can only be changed from one form to another.

Forms of energy

The main forms of energy are listed below.

Type of energy	Description
Kinetic energy	Kinetic energy is the energy something has because it is moving. The faster the object is moving, the more kinetic energy it has.
Heat (thermal) energy	Heat energy resides inside an object. It is caused by the vibrations of the atoms and molecules that make up the object. The faster the atoms and molecules vibrate, the hotter the object is.
Electrical energy	Electrical energy is created by electric charges. Electrical energy can be transported from one place to another place by electric current travelling through wires and other components.
Light energy	Light is a form of energy that we can see.
Sound energy	Sound energy is transported by vibrations in the air (and other materials), which we hear as sound.
Chemical energy	Chemical energy is stored inside the atoms and molecules of materials. When one material reacts with another, this chemical energy can be released and changed into another form of energy - such as heat, light or electrical energy.

Converting energy from one form to another

Energy conversions take place all around us. Our bodies convert chemical energy stored in food, into heat energy and kinetic energy (movement) via our muscles. Plants convert light energy into chemical energy, which is stored in sugars inside the plant. When we clap, we change kinetic energy into sound energy. Electrical devices commonly convert electrical energy to other forms, such as light, heat and movement.

The table below provides common examples of energy conversions. The components listed are described in more detail in the "Electronic components" and "Electronic circuits I" chapters. Note that more than one energy conversion may happen at the same time.

Name	Picture	Input energy	Output energy	Notes
Battery		Chemical	Electrical	Chemical reactions in the battery are converted into electrical energy, i.e. a voltage between the positive (+) and negative (-) terminals of the battery.
Bulb, LED		Electrical	Light	A bulb or LED converts input electrical energy (electric current) to light energy. However most of the electrical energy gets converted to heat energy.
Motor		Electrical	Kinetic	A motor converts input electrical energy (electric current) into kinetic energy (i.e. rotation of the shaft). Some of the input energy is converted to heat energy and sound energy.
Generator or dynamo		Kinetic	Electrical	A dynamo or generator does the opposite of a motor. It converts kinetic energy (i.e. rotation of the shaft) into electrical energy (current in the wire). Some of the motion is converted to heat energy because of the friction of the parts.
Speaker		Electrical	Sound	A speaker converts input electrical energy (electric current) into movement of the speaker (kinetic energy). The movement of the speaker causes the air to vibrate, which travels through the air as sound energy.
Buzzer		Electrical	Sound	A buzzer operates in the same way as the speaker above except it can only produce one sound.
Microphone		Sound	Electrical	A microphone operates like a reverse speaker. Sound energy vibrates a diaphragm inside the microphone, which generates an electrical current in the wires attached.
Solar cell		Light	Electrical	A solar cell converts light energy into electrical energy.

Energy losses and energy efficiency

As you may have noticed in the table above, energy is frequently converted into more than one type of output energy. This often occurs because of friction.

Friction generates heat energy

Friction is a force that resists something moving. For example, if you rub your hands tightly together, they do not slide easily past each other. If you continue to rub your hands together, your hands will get warm. This is an example of kinetic energy (rubbing your hands) being converted into heat energy by friction.

Another example of friction occurs in a motor or a dynamo. In a dynamo, some of the input kinetic energy (rotation) is converted into heat energy because of the friction of the mechanical parts rubbing off each other. Because of this, we are not able to convert all of the input kinetic energy into output electrical energy.

Bicycle dynamo

As an example, if 30% of the input kinetic energy were lost as heat energy, we would say that the dynamo was 70% efficient. We say that the heat energy is lost, because we cannot use it. The dynamo just warms the air around it and the heat disappears into the atmosphere.

Heat and light

Filament, CFL and LED bulbs

Heat and light energy are often generated together. For example, in a filament light bulb, 95% of the input electrical energy is used to heat up the filament inside the bulb, and only 5% of the electrical energy is converted into light energy.

Therefore a traditional light bulb is only 5% efficient. It requires a very large amount of electrical energy to produce sufficient light using a filament light bulb. For this reason, this type of light bulb is being phased out, and is being replaced by bulbs using LED (light-emitting diode) and CFL (compact fluorescent lamp) technologies, which are much more energy-efficient.

LEDs have overtaken CFLs in popularity because of the quality of the light, and because CFLs contain small amounts of mercury, which is hazardous and not environmentally friendly.

Measuring energy and power

Energy is measured in joules (J). Energy is measured in the same way for all forms of energy.

Power is the rate at which energy is being used, i.e. converted to another form. Power is measured in joules per second, which are called watts (W). One watt = one joule per second.

> **Energy** is measured in **joules (J)**.
> **Power** is measured in **watts** (W) (joules per second).

Because power = energy divided by time, energy = power multiplied by time. This means that energy can also be measured in watt-hours (Wh). This unit is used in your electricity bills.

Examples of everyday energy and power measurements

- Every second, a 60 W electric light bulb takes in 60 joules of electrical energy, and gives out 60 joules of light and heat energy.
- The output of electricity generating power stations is measured in megawatts (MW). 1 megawatt = 1 million watts.
- A 60 W light bulb, switched on for one hour, uses up 60 watt-hours (Wh) of electrical energy.
- On your electricity bill, you are charged for the number of kilowatt-hours you have used (1 kWh = 1000 Wh).

Energy conversions in electric circuits

There are often multiple energy conversions in one electric circuit.

In the example shown on the right, chemical energy in the battery is converted into electrical energy. The electrical energy is transported to the light bulb via the electric wires. The light bulb converts the electrical energy into light energy and heat energy.

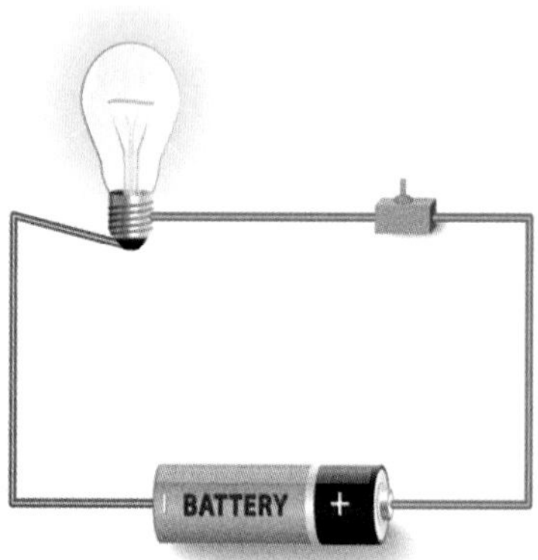

Worked example 1: Energy conversion in a motor

Past exam question
State two energy conversions taking place when an electric motor is running.

Solution

- Electrical energy is converted to kinetic energy.
- Kinetic energy is converted to heat (or sound) energy.

Worked example 2: Energy conversion in a generator

Past exam question
State two energy conversions taking place in the generator shown.

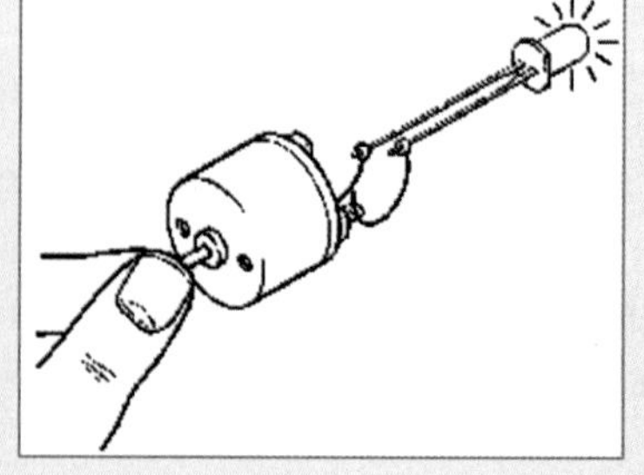

Solution

- Kinetic energy is converted to electrical energy.
- Electrical energy is converted to light energy.

Worked example 3: Energy conversion in a torch

Past exam question

Name two energy conversions that take place when the battery-operated torch shown is switched on.

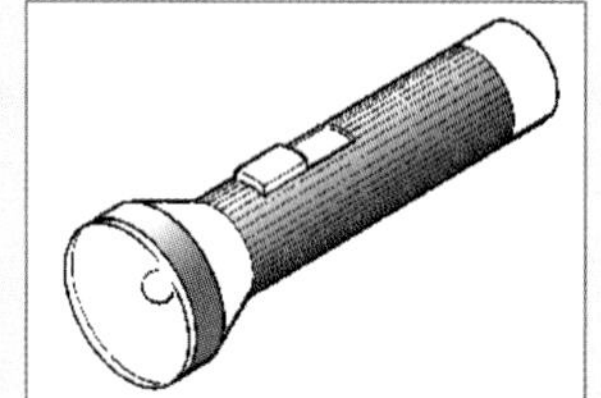

Solution

- Chemical energy is converted to electrical energy.
- Electrical energy is converted to light energy.

Past exam questions

1. The force that converts the kinetic energy of a car to heat energy in the brakes is called:
   - Bending?
   - Friction?
   - Tension?

2. Speakers:
   - Convert sound into electrical energy?
   - Convert electrical energy into sound?
   - Convert chemical energy into sound?

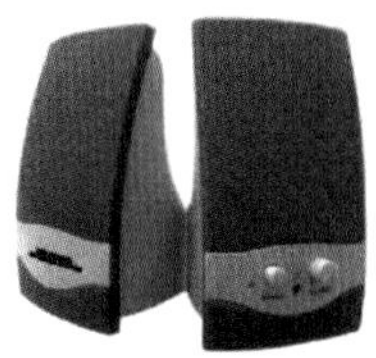

3. Name two energy conversions that take place when an electric current is applied to the motor shown.

4. Name two energy conversions taking place in the bicycle dynamo (generator) shown on the right.

5. A solar cell converts:
   - Light into electricity?
   - Electricity into light?
   - Sound into electricity?

6. For each of the four components shown on the right, state the type of energy conversion that takes place. In each case, state the input energy, and the output energy.

7. Complete the table below by stating the energy conversion for each device.

Device	Converts	To
Solar Cell	Light energy	Electrical energy
Microphone		
Motor		
Bulb		
Buzzer		

Sources of energy

Modern life requires large amounts of energy in order to allow to us travel from place to place, and to power our homes, schools, factories, businesses, and communications. Energy used by a country, an organisation, a product or a person is called energy consumption.

Energy usage and electricity usage

What is the difference between our energy usage and our electricity usage? Only a portion of our total energy comes from electricity. The rest of our energy comes from burning fuels like oil and gas directly in our cars and heating systems. As electricity doesn't exist in a usable form in nature, we have to generate it from another source of energy. The picture below shows how we use different energy sources: both directly as fuel, and indirectly to generate electricity.

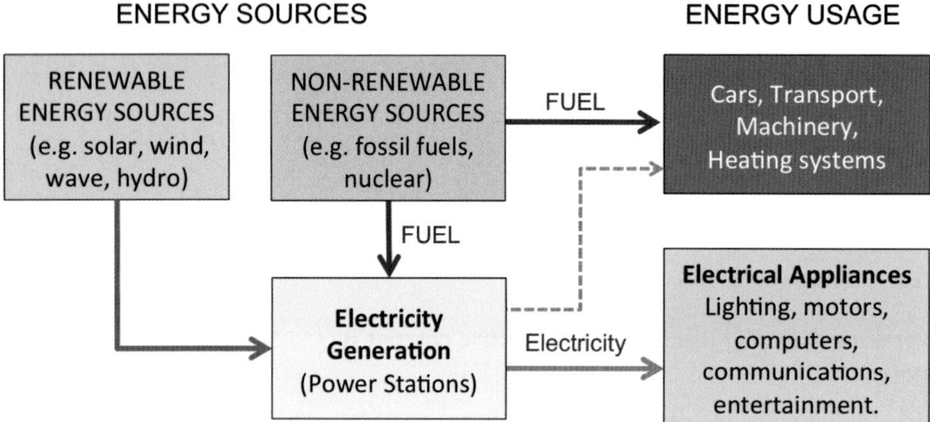

Although we have to generate it, electricity is an extremely useful form of energy, because it can be transported over long distances via wires, and can be used to power all kinds of useful devices. One disadvantage of electricity is that it is difficult to store.

Non-renewable and renewable sources of energy

Sources of energy are classified as non-renewable or renewable.

A **non-renewable** source of energy gets used up. It cannot be replaced.

A **renewable** source of energy does not get used up, or it can be replaced.

Non-renewable sources of energy

Fossil fuels

Non-renewable sources of energy include fuels such as oil, gas, coal and peat. These are known as fossil fuels because they have been created over very long periods of time in the ground. We burn fossil fuels in cars, transport and heating systems. We also burn fossil fuels in power stations to generate electricity.

Advantages of fossil fuels

- Fossil fuels provide a widely available and reliable source of energy. This is a major advantage for generating electricity, because the electricity supply can meet demand as required.

Disadvantages of fossil fuels

- Fossil fuels will run out.
- When the supply becomes scarce, the cost of the fuel will increase.
- Burning fossil fuels creates air pollution.
- Burning fossil fuels releases greenhouse gases into the atmosphere that contribute to global warming.

Nuclear power

Nuclear fuels such as uranium and plutonium are used in nuclear power plants to generate electricity. The nuclear reactions give off heat, which is used to boil water to create steam to turn the turbine generators.

Sellafield nuclear power station, Cumbria, UK

Advantages of nuclear power

- Nuclear power stations provide a reliable and constant source of electricity.
- Nuclear power can generate a huge amount of energy from tiny amounts of nuclear fuel.
- Nuclear material will not run out for a very long time.

Disadvantages of nuclear power

- Nuclear power stations generate highly toxic nuclear waste, which has to be disposed off deep at sea or deep inside mountains.
- If the nuclear power plant overheats and explodes, or is hit by a natural disaster such as an earthquake or tsunami, it will release highly dangerous (fatal) radioactivity into the atmosphere.

Renewable sources of energy

Wind

Wind turns turbines to generate electricity.

Advantages of wind power

- Wind is free.
- Wind will not run out.
- Wind does not pollute the atmosphere or generate any harmful gases.
- Wind turbines are relatively cheap to build.

Disadvantages of wind power

- Wind is not always present or constant. So the electricity supply from wind generators can be uneven and unreliable.
- Some people don't like the appearance of wind turbines in the landscape.

Wave and tidal power

Here, the movement of waves and tides move mechanisms to turn turbines to generate electricity.

Advantages of wave and tidal power

- Wave and tidal movements are free and will not run out.

Disadvantages of wave and tidal power

- It is very expensive to build far out to sea, and to get the electricity back to land.
- They are not as cost-effective as fossil fuel based power stations.

Hydroelectric

In hydroelectric power stations, a river is dammed and the pressure of the water flowing out of the dam is used to turn turbines to generate electricity.

Dam at hydroelectric power station

Advantages of hydroelectric energy

- Rivers are a renewable source of energy.

Disadvantages of hydroelectric energy

- Hydroelectric power stations are expensive to build.
- Supply of water is not always constant.
- Damage can be caused to the environment and communities by the changed water levels above and below the dam.
- There can be political problems or even war with other countries if the river crosses borders.

Solar

There are two types of solar generators. In one type, the sun heats water in lots of thin tubes. The hot water can be used to heat houses directly, or it be used to generate steam to turn turbines to generate electricity.

In the other type, light from the sun is converted to electricity using special devices called photovoltaic or solar cells.

Photovoltaic cells

Advantages of solar power

- The sun will continue to shine for several billion years.
- Solar energy causes no pollution.

Disadvantages of solar power

- Solar power only works during sunlight hours, so solar-generated electricity must be stored in large batteries for night-time use.
- Solar panels need to be large to collect enough sunlight.
- The power output from solar panels is relatively low.

Biomass and biofuels

This technology involves burning plant waste (biomass) to produce heat and electricity, or using plant material to manufacture biofuels such as bioethanol, which can be used in place of petrol in cars and machinery.

Rapeseed – a fuel crop and grown for food

Advantages of biomass and biofuels

- They are renewable as plants can be re-grown.

Disadvantages of biomass and biofuels

- Biofuels still pollute the atmosphere and contribute to global warming, because they are burned just like fossil fuels.

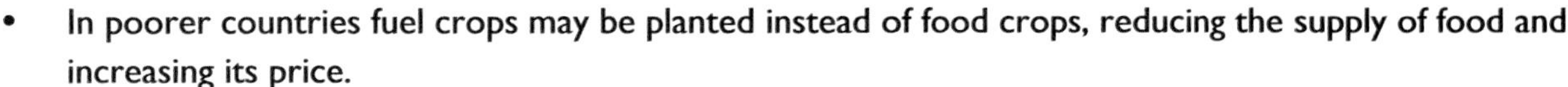

- In poorer countries fuel crops may be planted instead of food crops, reducing the supply of food and increasing its price.

Geothermal energy

The inside of the earth is hot. This technology involves drilling deep into the ground to use this heat to either heat homes directly, or to create steam to drive turbines to generate electricity.

Advantages of geothermal energy

- Renewable, not likely to run out.

Disadvantages of geothermal energy

- Can be expensive to explore and drill.
- To get enough power for a reasonable price, it use is limited to certain geographical locations where the earth's heat comes up to, or close to, the surface, e.g. parts of Iceland.

Human power

This includes walking, cycling, and using hand-powered dynamos to power simple devices.

Advantages of human power

Human power is:

- Free.
- Healthy.
- Non-polluting.

Disadvantages of human power

- Only low power is available.
- Can be very labour intensive.

Revision table for energy sources

Energy source	Renewable	Polluting	Examples	Advantages	Disadvantages
Fossil fuels	✖	✔	Petrol and diesel cars Coal, oil, peat and gas power stations	Widely available, cheap	Air pollution, global warming
Chemical	✖	✔	Batteries	Portable	Toxic waste
Biofuels	✔	✔	Biofuel cars Biofuel power stations	Renewable	Air pollution, global warming
Nuclear	✖	✔	Nuclear power stations	High power	Toxic waste, risk of accidents
Human power	✔	✖	Bicycles, dynamo-charged devices such as torches	Low cost	Low power
Solar	✔	✖	Solar house heating systems Solar garden lights, chargers	Renewable	Not constant, low power
Wind	✔	✖	Wind power stations House and factory turbines	Renewable	Not constant, impacts landscape
Waves	✔	✖	Wave power stations	Renewable, constant	Costly
Rivers	✔	✖	Hydroelectric power stations	Renewable	Costly, impacts environment
Geo-thermal	✔	✖	Geothermal heating for houses, electricity generation	Renewable	Only cost effective in some locations

Environmental impacts of high energy usage

Our requirement for large quantities of energy has a negative impact on our environment.

Burning fossil fuels causes a lot of damage. It releases polluting substances in to the atmosphere. It also releases lots of carbon dioxide and other greenhouse gases into the atmosphere. These gases are called greenhouse gases because they cause a "greenhouse effect" around the earth. They trap the heat of the sun and cause the earth to heat up.

Greenhouse gases are also called carbon dioxide emissions, carbon emissions, or just emissions.

Causing the earth to heat up creates climate change. Sea levels rise because ice sheets start to melt. Wind and sea patterns change. The weather changes, often creating storms, floods, and droughts. This can have harmful impacts on crops and food production.

A **carbon footprint** is the total amount of greenhouse gases generated by a person, a country, an organisation or a product.

Technologies that do less harm to the environment are often called **green technologies.**

An **eco-friendly** or **environmentally-friendly** product or solution is less damaging to the environment.

Examples of high energy usage

Burning fossil fuels in cars, buses, trains and planes is a primary cause of high energy usage and environmental damage. Two other areas that use large amounts of energy and cause environmental damage, are described below.

Generation of waste

Manufacturing and throwing away so many products damages the environment in several ways:

- The plastic and chemical waste generated causes pollution.
- Extra energy must be generated in order to manufacture new products.
- Wildlife can be poisoned or die by confusing plastic waste with food.

Production of food

It takes a great deal more energy, and more resources like land and water, to produce red meat than it does to produce other foods that have the same nutritional value.

Some foods can be produced with greater energy efficiency than others

What can we do to reduce the environmental impact of high energy use?

There are some basic steps that we can take to become more environmentally friendly and to reduce our carbon footprint.

Switch to renewable sources of energy

Ways to do this include:

- Power stations can switch to wind, solar and wave power.
- Public transport systems can switch to electric buses, trains and trams.
- Public lighting systems can use solar-powered lighting.
- People can switch to using electric cars.
- We can use solar-powered devices like garden lights and road signs.
- We can use dynamo-powered devices, such as torches.
- We can walk and cycle to work and school.

Use energy-efficient devices and materials

Ways to do this include:

- Use energy-efficient bulbs such as LEDs. These types of bulbs require less energy than incandescent (or filament) bulbs, and also last longer.
- Insulate our homes, and install double-glazed windows and doors. This means our homes lose less heat, which means that they need less energy to keep warm.
- Use modern heating boilers, which are 90% efficient.
- Use thermostats to control the temperature in each room.
- Use modern cars, which have smaller and more fuel-efficient engines.
- Use electric or hybrid cars. Most hybrid cars use an electric motor and a petrol or diesel-powered engine, and can switch between them.
- Use low-temperature washing powder, which saves energy on heating water.

Reduce energy consumption and waste

Ways to do this include:

- Turn off lights and devices when not in use.
- Use public transport and/or car pooling.
- Reduce air travel.
- Consider solar panels and/or a wind turbine for your house.
- Recycle products so that less energy is used in making new ones.
- Compost waste instead of sending it to landfill.
- Harvest rainwater.
- Buy local produce, to reduce the greenhouse gases caused by transporting food.
- Buy less red meat, to reduce the total energy required to produce food.
- Use rechargeable batteries.
- Use wood from sustainable forests.

Governments and the EU have set out targets to reduce greenhouse gas emissions and to combat global warming. The EU has implemented regulations on carbon dioxide emissions and regulations on waste. Countries not complying with these regulations are fined.

Worked example 4: Use of fossil fuels for travel

Past exam questions

1. The way in which we use fossil fuels for travel must change. Suggest three reasons for this.
2. Outline fuel sources other than fossil fuels which could be used to provide for the following:
   (i) Public and private transport.
   (ii) Electrical supply to industry and homes.

Valid answers

1. Three reasons to change the way we use fossil fuels for travel are:
   - We need to reduce air pollution caused by fossil fuels.
   - We need to stop global warming caused by greenhouses gas emissions from fossil fuels.
   - Fossil fuels will keep increasing in cost, and they will eventually run out.
2. (i) Alternative fuel sources for public and private transport include: electric trains, cars and buses, using electricity generated from renewable resources.
   (ii) Alternative fuel sources for electrical supply to industry and home include: wind, solar, hydroelectric, wave energy, biofuels, and nuclear.

Worked example 5: Use of LED bulbs

Past exam question

State two reasons why LED bulbs are recommended replacements for incandescent bulbs.

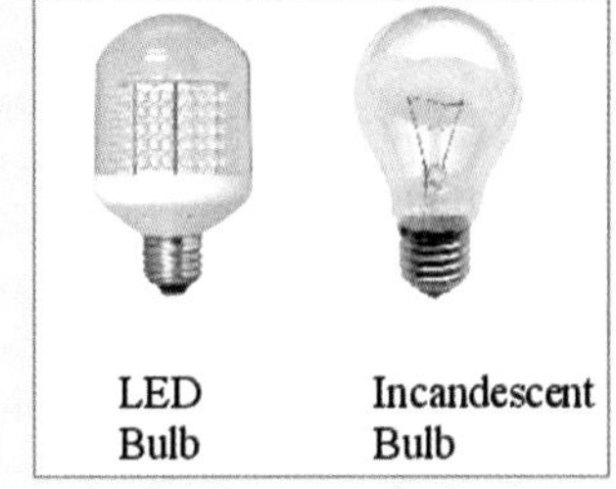

Valid answers

- LED bulbs use less energy than incandescent bulbs.
- LED bulbs last longer than incandescent bulbs.

Worked example 6: Carbon footprint of new cars

Past exam question

Modern car engines are engineered to have a lower "carbon footprint" than older car engines.
Explain what is meant by any three of the following terms: Carbon footprint, hybrid car, fuel crop, and electric car.

Valid answers

- The carbon footprint of a car is the total amount of greenhouse gases generated by producing the car, using the car, and disposing of the car.
- A hybrid car uses two or more power sources. Most hybrid cars use an electric motor and a petrol or diesel-powered engine, and can switch between them.
- A fuel crop is a plant such as rapeseed or sugar beet, which can be used to make biofuels to power cars and machinery.
- An electric car is powered by an electric motor and a rechargeable battery.

Worked example 7: Eco-friendly cars

Past exam question

Transportation is the largest single user of fossil fuels and a significant source of environmental pollution in developed countries. Modern hybrid cars are designed to use alternative energies and to be eco-friendly.

(i) Describe one way in which modern cars have reduced their dependence on fossil fuels.
(ii) Describe two ways in which modern cars can be eco-friendly.

Valid answers

- Modern cars have reduced their dependence on fossil fuels, because we now have electric cars, and bio-fuel cars, which do not burn fossil fuels.
- Modern cars are more environmentally friendly if they are (1) electric (no emissions), or (2) hybrid cars (reduced emissions). Also, modern petrol engines have reduced emissions.

Cars are also more environmentally friendly if their parts can be recycled when they are disposed of.

Key points

1. Energy cannot be created or destroyed; it can only be converted from one form to another.
2. The main forms of energy are kinetic (movement), heat, light, sound, electrical and chemical.
3. Energy is measured in joules (J) or watt-hours (Wh).
4. Power is measured in joules per second (J/s) or watts (W).
5. Non-renewable energy sources will run out. Renewable energy sources will not run out.
6. Non-renewable energy sources include fossil fuels (oil, coal, gas, peat) and nuclear fuel.
7. Renewable energy source include solar, wind, waves, biomass, rivers and geothermal.
8. Burning fossil fuels pollutes the atmosphere, releases greenhouse gases, and contributes to global warming.
9. Ways to combat global warming, reduce carbon footprint, and be more eco-friendly include:
   - Switching to renewable and non-polluting sources of energy.
   - Switching to electric-powered transport instead of petrol and diesel.
   - Using less energy.
   - Improving energy efficiency.
   - Recycling waste.

Activities

1. Write down three ways in which energy could be saved in your school.
2. Name three ways in which the government tries to encourage energy efficiency.
3. Using the Internet, try to find out the following about Ireland's use of energy:
   (i) What percentage of total energy used comes from burning fossil fuels?
   (ii) What percentage of total energy used comes from renewable sources?
   (iii) How much electrical power does the country need in total?
   (iv) How much does the country spend on importing (buying from abroad) fuel and energy?
   (v) What are the plans for the future?

Past exam questions

1. Filament light bulbs are gradually going out of production. Is this because:
    - They are too costly to make?
    - They waste a lot of electricity?
    - The materials are no longer available?

2. Give two common uses of solar cells.

3. This energy saving light bulb:
    - Has lower wattage than a standard light bulb?
    - Has higher wattage than a standard light bulb?
    - Has the same wattage than a standard light bulb?

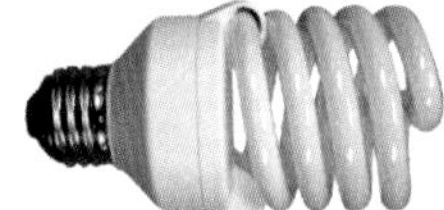

4. Which of the following is correct? Dynamo torches do not use:
    - Disposable batteries.
    - Electricity.
    - Energy.

5. Name one renewable and one non-renewable source of energy.

6. Electric cars are becoming more popular every year. Suggest two reasons for this.

7. Which of the following is correct? LEDs are now used in torches because they:
    - Use very little energy.
    - They look good.
    - They heat up.

8. Which of the following is correct? Solar phone chargers are devices that use:
    - Renewable energy.
    - Fossil fuels.
    - Geothermal energy.

9. Outline two reasons why we should be concerned about the use of our fossil fuels.

10. Outline two alternative energy sources available for energy production in Ireland.

11. State two reasons why it is important to invest in renewable energy.

12. Name two sources of renewable energy other than solar and wind power.

Past exam questions

13. State two ways in which we can reduce our "Carbon Footprint".

14. Give two reasons why public transport should be used in cities in place of cars.

15. List two environmentally-friendly methods of generating electricity. For each method, state one advantage and one disadvantage.

16. One of the more recent developments in car technology is the production of cars that run on compressed air.
    (i) Suggest two advantages of this type of technology.
    (ii) Name two other ways to power cars without using fossil fuels (diesel, petrol or gas).

17. State two ways in which modern motor cars have been made more energy efficient.

18. Describe one technological advance which has improved the energy efficiency of household equipment.

19. How can a house be made more energy efficient?

20. State two reasons why older household bulbs should be replaced with the type of bulb shown.

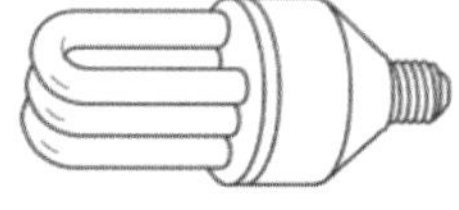
CFL bulb

21. The energy produced by devices such as solar cells is often referred to as:
    - Blue energy.
    - Green energy.
    - Red energy.

22. State two advantages of using LED lighting in public places.

CHAPTER 10

Electricity

Introduction

This is the first in a set of chapters covering electronics. In this chapter, you will learn about the basics of electricity.

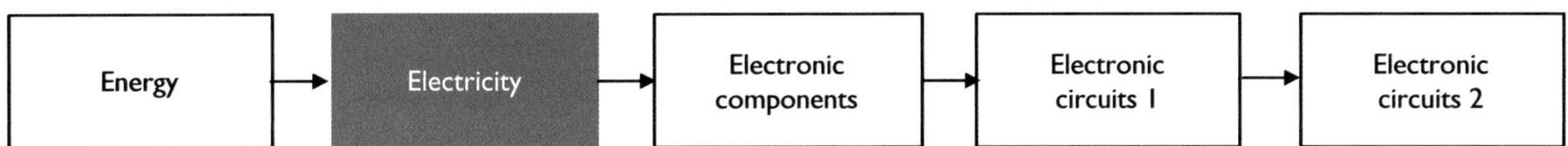

What is electricity?

We use electricity every day to provide lighting and heating for our homes, and to power domestic appliances like toasters and dishwashers.

Electric toaster

Electricity is a form of energy arising from the movement of electrons, which are tiny charged particles that reside inside every atom. Some materials, e.g. metals, allow electrons to move through them easily.

A flow of electrons from one place to another is called an **electric current**. The more electrons that flow, the greater the current there is. Electric current is measured in **amperes, also called amps (A)**.

> **Electric current** is the flow of electrons from one place to another.

Whenever there is more charge (i.e. more electrons) at one point compared to another point, we say there is a "potential difference" between those two points. Another name for potential difference is voltage, which is measured in volts (V).

The more potential difference (i.e. voltage) there is between two points, the more current will flow between them.

In the electric circuit shown, there is a potential difference between each end of the battery. This causes electric current to flow along the connecting wire and to light up the bulb, when the circuit is switched on.

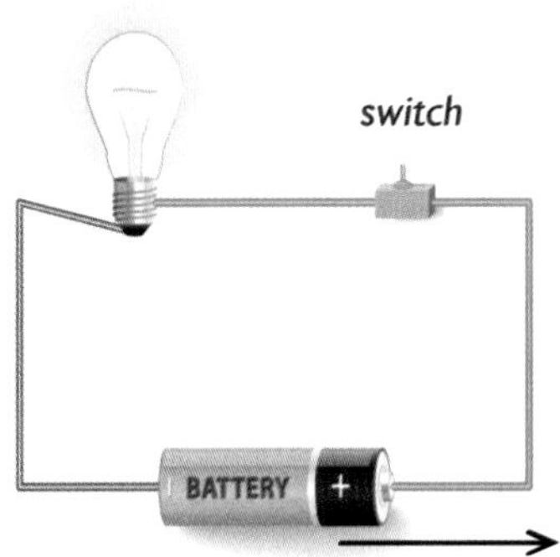

Direction of current

Electric current can only flow if there is a complete circuit from the power source, through the wires and back to the power source again.

A **voltage** between two points in a circuit causes electric current to flow from one point to the other.

Different materials have different resistances to the flow of electrons, or electric current. The higher the resistance of a material, the more it resists the flow of current. Resistance is measured in ohms (Ω).

Resistance is a measure of how much a material resists the flow of electric current.

Power is the amount of electrical energy being used up every second. It is calculated by multiplying the voltage by the current, and is measured in watts (W).

Power is the rate at which electrical energy is used up in an electrical circuit or device.

Conductors, insulators and semiconductors

Some materials, such as metals, allow electrons to pass through them very easily. They have very low resistance, and are called conductors.

A **conductor** conducts electric current easily.

Other materials, such as plastics and ceramics, do not permit electrons to pass through them easily. They have very high resistance, and are called insulators.

An **insulator** does not conduct electric current.

There is a class of materials called semiconductors that falls in between conductors and insulators. Semiconductors conduct electricity moderately well. Silicon is an example of a semiconductor.

Silicon is used to make electronic components like resistors, transistors and the integrated circuits or "chips" that power our phones, computers and the Internet.

Silicon chips on a control board

A **semiconductor** conducts electric current moderately well.

AC and DC

There are two main types of electricity: AC (alternating current), and DC (direct current).

AC is mains electricity, i.e. the type of electricity that comes in to your house. With AC, both voltage and current keep reversing direction. With mains electricity this happens at a rate of 50 times a second. It is much easier to transmit AC than DC across long distances.

With DC, the voltage remains constant, and the current flows in one direction only.

Units for measuring electricity

Property	Units of measurement	Symbol	Examples
Voltage	Volts	V	Mains electricity is 230 V AC. Small batteries are 1.5 V DC.
Current	Amps (short for amperes)	A, mA	(1 mA = 1/1000 A) Domestic appliances typically use from 1.5 to 13 A. For example the fuse inside a mains electrical plug for a washing machine is 13 A. A lamp requires a fuse of only 1.5 A. Electronic devices typically use less than 500 mA.
Resistance	Ohms	Ω, kΩ	(1 kΩ = 1000 Ω) Values of resistors used in electronic circuits range from about 100 Ω to 10 kΩ.
Power	Watts	W, kW	(1 kW = 1000 W) The power rating of an electrical appliance is the maximum power input that the equipment has been designed to use. Electric light bulbs are sold with different power ratings, for example 60 W, 40 W, or 10 W. The power rating of an electric kettle is usually 1.8 kW to 2 kW.

Where does our electricity come from?

Mains electricity

We get mains electricity from the electrical sockets in our home. Mains electricity is 230 volts AC. It is high voltage and it can kill you. It is powerful enough to drive large motors in domestic appliances, such as washing machines and vacuum cleaners.

Mains electricity is generated in large generating stations and it is carried into our homes using a network of high voltage wires.

Batteries

Batteries supply a very low DC voltage of just few volts, which is safe. Luckily, our electronic devices such as phones and laptops only require low DC voltages.

The voltage supplied by a battery is caused by a chemical reaction that takes place inside the battery. This chemical reaction eventually stops and the battery goes dead, i.e. it runs out of charge.

There are two main types of batteries: rechargeable, and non-rechargeable.

Rechargeable batteries can be recharged by a battery charger device, which takes current from the AC mains supply, and transfers it to the battery at a constant rate.

The battery stores the charge in chemical form, and can release it again later.

Power supplies

Power supplies convert high voltage mains AC into a low voltage DC suitable for powering electronic devices.

Examples of power supplies include the variable power supplies in the technology room. With these, you can choose the output DC voltage, e.g. 3, 6, 9 or 12 volts. Another example of a power supply is the charger for your phone. Your charger is really just a power supply providing a low DC voltage for your phone. The charging circuits for your phone battery are inside your phone.

Safety with electricity

Make sure that you follow these safety rules when working with electricity:

- Never open up devices that are powered by mains electricity.
- Never poke objects into mains sockets.
- Always switch off devices after use.

Generating electricity

Electricity can be generated in a number of ways. Most of these involve turning a turbine or generator. A generator is the reverse of an electric motor. If you rotate a set of coils of wire inside a large strong magnet, you will generate electric current in the wires. Many different methods can be used to turn generators, e.g. wind, water or steam.

Steam turbine

Electricity generating stations are often called power plants. Types of power plant include coal, oil, and gas based plants and those that use renewable energy sources such as solar, hydroelectric or wind. These are covered in more detail in the "Energy" chapter.

Activities

1. Look at the small power supplies that come with your phone or other devices. Identify the voltage that the power supplies generate and the current that they can supply.
2. Examine three electrical appliances and write down their power rating.

Key points

1. Electric current is the flow of electrons. It is measured in amps.
2. A voltage between two points in a circuit causes an electric current to flow between them. Voltage is measured in volts.
3. Resistance is a measure of how much a material blocks the flow of electric current. It is measured in ohms.
4. Power is the rate at which electrical energy is used up in a circuit or device. It is measured in watts.
5. The power rating of an electrical appliance is the maximum power input that the equipment has been designed to use.
6. Conductors allow electric current to flow through them easily. They have very low resistance.
7. Insulators block the flow of electric current through them. They have very high resistance.
8. Semiconductors allow current to flow them moderately well. They have medium resistance.
9. AC stands for alternating current.
10. DC stands for direct current.
11. Sources of electricity are mains (230 V AC), batteries and power supplies (low voltage DC).
12. Power supplies convert high voltage mains AC into a low voltage DC suitable for powering electronic devices.
13. Mains electricity is generated in power plants.

Test yourself

1. What is current? What units is it measured in?
2. What is voltage? What units is it measured in?
3. What is resistance? What units is it measured in?
4. What is power? What units is it measured in?
5. What does power rating mean?
6. What is a power supply?
7. What is (a) a conductor, (b) an insulator, (c) a semiconductor? Give an example of each.
8. What does AC stand for? Which way does the current flow with AC?
9. What is the voltage of (a) mains electricity, (b) a battery for a bicycle light?
10. State three safety rules that should be observed when working with electricity.
11. Name three ways that electricity can be generated.

11 CHAPTER

Electronic components

Introduction

This chapter introduces you to the electronic components that you will need to know about for your examinations, and for your projects. It provides a basic introduction to the operation of each component. The "Electronic circuits" chapters explain how these components work in circuits.

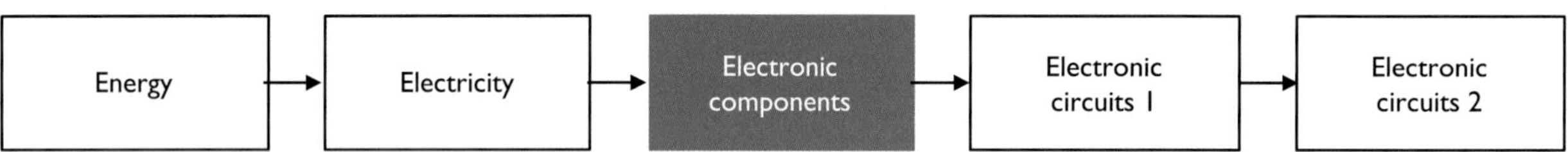

Power sources

The following components provide power to electronic circuits.

Component	Image	Symbol	Description and usage
Power supply		5V 0V	A power supply takes a mains AC voltage as its input and delivers a steady DC voltage at its output, for use in electronic circuits. You can sometimes choose the output voltage that you would like on the output, e.g. between 3 V, 5 V, 6 V, 9 V and 12 V.
Batteries	*9 V battery*   *1.5 V battery*	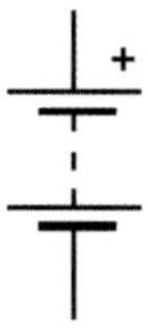 + 9V	Batteries come in various shapes and values. A 9 V battery and a 1.5 V battery are shown. AA and AAA are the most common sizes of 1.5 V batteries. Batteries need a battery connector to be used in circuits.
Battery connectors	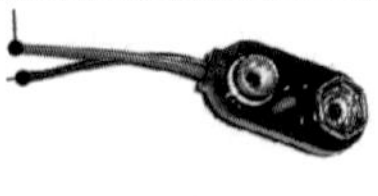 	N/A	The picture shows a battery connector for a 9 V battery (sometimes called a battery snap), and a holder/connector for four 1.5 V batteries.

Component	Image	Symbol	Description and usage
Fuse		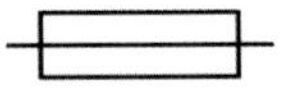	A fuse is a safety device designed to break when more than a certain amount of current flows through it, so that the current then stops. The picture shows a 13 A fuse inside a standard mains electricity plug.

Wires, cables and connectors

Examples of the most common types of wires, cables and connectors are shown below.

Component	Image	Symbol	Description and usage
Mains cable	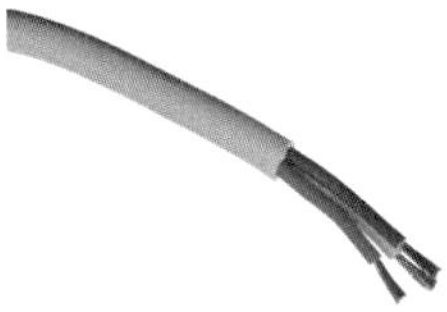	N/A	Has three separate wires inside, and each wire is separately insulated with plastic: • Brown wire = live. • Blue wire = neutral. • Green and yellow wire = earth (safety wire). You should not be working with mains cable because mains electricity is dangerous.
Single-strand connecting wire	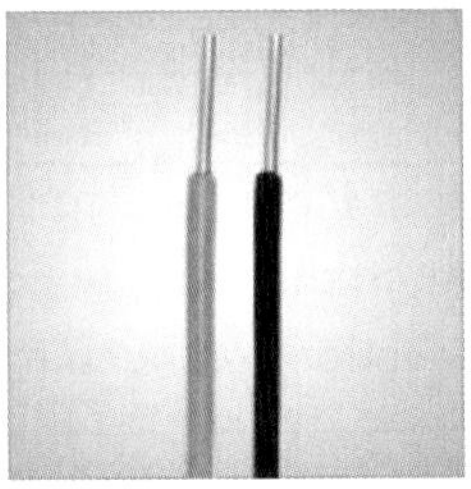	*Plain wire* *Wires crossed but not connected* 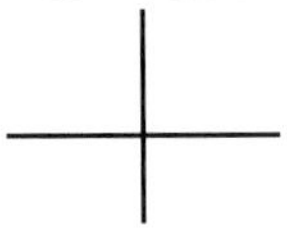 *Connected wire* 	Used to connect components like switches and battery holders to your electronic circuits. In circuit diagrams, a simple line is used to represent a wire. Wires are shown connected to each other using black dots where they meet.
Crocodile clips		N/A	Useful for connecting wires from the power supply in the technology room, to electronic circuits and technology projects. Can be attached and detached easily.
Audio connectors		N/A	Used for connecting audio equipment together, and for connecting electric musical instruments to amplifiers and speakers.

Component	Image	Symbol	Description and usage
Fibre optic cable		N/A	Used to conduct light, not electricity. Signals travel through them at the speed of light. These cables can transmit information over long distances.

Switches

A switch is inserted into a circuit to start or to stop current flowing, or to route current along different paths/wires. Switches work both mechanically and electrically.

Mechanical operation of a switch

Switches can be mechanically operated in several ways, e.g. by moving a lever, pushing a button, moving a slider, tilting the switch, and bringing a magnet close to it.

Electrical operation of a switch

The electrical operation of a switch is how the switch makes electrical connections on the inside. The table below explains terms commonly used when describing the electrical operation of a switch.

Term	Explanation
Connector/pin/terminal	These are the metal connection points on the switch on to which you attach your connecting wires.
Closed	If a switch is closed, it means that the switch inputs are connected to each other and current can flow between them. In this case, we can also say the switch is a closed circuit, or that the connection has been made.
Open	If a switch is open, it means that the corresponding switch inputs are not connected to each other, and no current can flow between them. In this case, we can also say the switch is an open circuit, or the connection has been broken.
Short circuit	Short circuit means that a connection operates as if a piece of wire was joining the two points.
Pole	A pole is a moving wire inside a switch that can move to a fixed wire (the throw) to make a closed circuit, or away from the fixed wire to make an open circuit.
Throw	A throw is a fixed contact point that the pole can connect to.

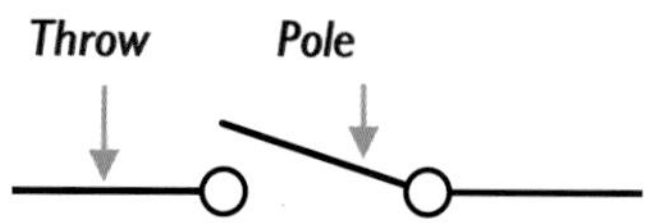

The most common types of electrical switches are shown in the following table, along with their electronic symbols.

Name of switch	Abbreviation	Symbol	Operation	No. of connections
Single Pole Single Throw	SPST		• One circuit • One current option (on or off)	2
Single Pole Double Throw	SPDT		• One circuit • Two possible current destinations	3
Double Pole Single Throw	DPST		• Two circuits • One switch position	4
Double Pole Double Throw	DPDT		• Two circuits • Two switch positions	6

Connecting to switches

In order to wire up a switch, you will need to know which pins/connectors are which, i.e. which connectors are the poles/inputs, and which connectors are the throws, i.e. the different possible outputs. This will usually be marked on the switch itself, if the switch has more than two connectors.

Note that you can wire up any type of switch to work as an SPST switch if you only connect two wires to it.

Switches - mechanical operation

The table below shows different ways in which switches can be activated mechanically.

Note that each type of mechanical switch can have different types of electrical switch on the inside, i.e. an SPST, SPDT, DPST, or DPDT. For example: if there are 2 input connectors on the switch, the switch will be an SPST; if there are 3 input connectors on the switch, it will be an SPDT; if there are 6, it will probably be a DPDT.

Component	Image	Symbol	Description and usage
Toggle switch			Operated by moving a lever up and down. The picture shows an SPST switch because there are only two connections to it. It is used as a simple on/off switch. Useful for technology projects.

Component	Image	Symbol	Description and usage
Slider switch			Operated by moving a slider mechanism. The picture shows three connections so this must be an SPDT switch. The middle connector will be the central (common) pole, and the two outside connectors will be the two throws, alternatively selected by the slider mechanism.
Rocker switch			Operated by a rocker mechanism. Most household light switches are of this type. The picture shown is an SPST (on/off) switch because there are only 2 connections to it.
Push-button switch		*Push-to-make* *Push-to-break*	SPST push-button switches come in two forms: • Push-to-make (PTM) - pushing the button causes the two input connections to be joined together inside the switch. • Push-to-break: (PTB) - the two input connections are normally connected inside the switch. Pushing the button causes them to be disconnected.
Reed switch			Is activated by a magnet. When the magnet is close by, it attracts the metal of the switch and activates it. An SPST reed switch is shown. Reed switches can be normally open or normally closed.
Float switch			Used to detect when the level of liquid reaches a certain point in a tank. The switch is fastened to the inside of the tank just above the desired liquid level. The piece at the bottom of the switch hangs down, and floats up as the liquid level rises. When the liquid rises to the correct level, it activates the switch, which can, for example turn off a pump.

<table>
<tr><th>Component</th><th>Image</th><th>Symbol</th><th>Description and usage</th></tr>
<tr><td>Limit switch</td><td></td><td>"Normally open" limit switch

"Normally closed" limit switch</td><td>Used to detect when a moving part has reached its desired end point. The moving part presses down on the lever and activates the switch, which is used to turn off the motor to prevent the part moving any further.

A limit switch has three connecting terminals: COM (common), NC (normally closed) and NO (normally open).
• NC operation - if you connect the wires to the COM and NC terminals, then the switch will be normally closed, i.e. it will act as a single piece of wire, for as long as the limit switch lever is not activated. When the lever is pressed, the switch will open and break the connection between the COM and NC terminals.
• NO operation- if you connect the wires to the COM and NO terminals, then the switch will be normally open, i.e. there will be no connection between the COM and NO terminals, for as long as the limit switch lever is not activated. When the lever is pressed, the switch will close and there will now be a connection between the COM and NO terminals.</td></tr>
<tr><td>Tilt switch</td><td></td><td>Closed

Open
Mercury ball</td><td>Used to detect when something is level or at a certain angle.

A tilt switch contains a piece of liquid mercury, which conducts electricity.

When the tilt switch is in the closed position (usually with connectors pointing downwards), the mercury makes contact with them and there is a closed circuit.

When the switch is tilted away from the closed position, the mercury ball rolls away, the connection is broken and there is an open circuit.</td></tr>
</table>

Component	Image	Symbol	Description and usage
Relay switch		*SPST relay* *SPDT relay*	Is an electrically operated switch. A current is passed through a coil, which creates a magnetic field, which pulls across the metal (ferrous) switch and makes or breaks the connection. When the current is removed, a spring returns the switch to its normal position. Note that different symbols may be used for the coil in relay switch symbols. The big advantage of a relay is that the circuit used to activate the switch is kept totally separate from the current that is switched by the relay. This means that a safe low voltage circuit can be used to turn on and off high currents and high voltages with no electrical connection between the two circuits.

Resistors

Component	Image	Symbol	Description and usage
Resistor			Limits the amount of current that can flow through it. Resistors are only made in certain values, which can be read using the colour bands marked on the resistor.
Variable resistors and potentio-meters (pots)		*Variable resistor* *Potentiometer* *Preset resistor* *Preset pot*	A variable resistor is a resistor where the resistance value can be changed by turning a knob. Variable resistors are created by connecting to the middle pin and one of the outside pins of a potentiometer or "pot". Pots and variable resistors are used in voltage divider circuits and are useful for controlling outputs such as volume, speed, brightness, temperature, etc. Preset resistors/pots are smaller, mounted on a PCB and can be turned with a screwdriver. They are typically used for one-time settings/ adjustments in a factory.

Resistor values and tolerances

Resistor values

The first three coloured bands on a resistor indicate its value in ohms. The first band represents the value of the first digit, the second band represents the second digit and the third band indicates the number of zeros. The colour codes are shown in the table.

Resistor values Colour codes	
Black	0
Brown	1
Red	2
Orange	3
Yellow	4
Green	5
Blue	6
Violet	7
Grey	8
White	9

For example in the resistor shown, the first band is brown (1), the second band is yellow (4) and the third band is red (2) so the value of the resistor is 1400 Ω or 1.4 kΩ. This is sometimes called a 1k4 resistor.

Resistor tolerances

Resistor tolerance values	
None	20%
Silver	10%
Gold	5%
Red	2%

The fourth band on the resistor tells us its tolerance, i.e. how accurate the resistor value is. The colour codes for tolerance are shown in the table.

Note that if the resistor has 5 bands, you still calculate the values the same way. The last (fifth) band will represent the tolerance, and the fourth band will represent the number of zeros.

Worked example: Reading resistor values

Question

(i) What is the value of the resistor shown?

(ii) What is the tolerance on this value?

Answers

(i) The value of the resitor can be calculated from the first three bands.

First band = brown = 1

Second band = black = 0

This means that the first two digits are 1 and 0.

Third band = red = 2

This means that there are two more zeros after the first two digits so the total value is 1000 Ω or 1 kΩ or1k0.

(ii) The tolerance of the resistor is indicated on the fourth band. The fourth band is gold which means that the tolerance is plus or minus 5%. This means that the measured value of the resistor will be 1000 Ω plus or minus 5% i.e. between 1050 Ω and 950 Ω.

Capacitors

Capacitors store electrical charge. Unlike batteries, they do not generate charge. They store the charge and release it later. Capacitors take a fixed time to charge up, and discharge. This means that they can be used as timers in circuits.

Capacitance is a measure of the amount of charge that a capacitor can store. It is measured in farads (F). Typical values of capacitors are in microfarads µF (millionths of a farad). The most common types of capacitor are described below.

Component	Image	Symbol	Description and usage
Electrolytic capacitor			These are polarised capacitors that are capable of holding a lot of charge. A polarised capacitor has a positive side and a negative side, and must be connected the right way round. The positive side is indicated by the longer leg, and the negative side has a bar mark next to it.
Non-electrolytic capacitor			These are non-polarised capacitors and can be connected either way round in a circuit. However, they cannot store as much charge as the electrolytic capacitors above.
Variable capacitor			In variable capacitors, the capacitance value can be varied by twisting a dial or knob. They are useful in adjustable timer devices.

Lighting

Component	Image	Symbol	Description and usage
Incandescent light bulb			Contains a tungsten wire (filament) inside a vacuum, which heats up and emits light. The power output of such bulbs is measured in watts (W). Common examples are 25 W, 40 W, 60 W and 100 W.
Low-energy light bulb			Use far less energy and power than incandescent bulbs, for the same light output. Typical values are 5 W, 7 W and 9 W. Low energy bulbs either contain gas or a number of LEDs (as shown).

Component	Image	Symbol	Description and usage
LED **(light-emitting diode)**			Produce light in an energy-efficient way and are small and inexpensive. They require only a low DC voltage. They are polarised components, i.e. they must be connected the right way around in a circuit. • The long leg is the anode (positive) side. • The short leg is the cathode (negative) side. It is next to the flat edge. This helps to identify the cathode when the LED has been soldered in to a circuit and both legs have been cut to the same size.
MES **(miniature edison screw) bulb**			This is a miniature incandescent bulb that can be used with a miniature socket in electronic circuits and projects. Sometimes used in torches and bicycle lamps.
Miniature edison screw socket		N/A	"Edison screw" is the name of one type of fitting for bulbs, i.e. how the bulbs fit in to their holders. Other types of bulb fittings are bayonet and GU10.

Sound

Component	Image	Symbol	Description and usage
Loudspeaker			A loudspeaker (or speaker for short) converts electrical signals into sound. They are used in radios, TVs, phones and computers.
Buzzer			A buzzer is a device that emits a fixed sound when activated by a certain voltage. They are used in alarms.

Sensors

Sensors are devices that convert a property in the real world, such as sound, heat or light, into an electric signal. The most commonly used sensors are described in the following table.

Component	Image	Symbol	Description and usage
LDR (light-dependent resistor)			The resistance of this device changes when light falls on it. Used in light detection circuits. • Resistance is high in darkness. • Resistance is low in the light.
Thermistor (temperature sensor)			This resistance of this device changes with heat. Used in heat/cold detection circuits. • Resistance is high in cold. • Resistance is low in heat.
Moisture probes		*or*	The resistance of this device changes with levels of moisture. • Resistance is high in dry conditions. • Resistance is low in wet conditions.
Proximity sensor		N/A	Detects the presence of an object without touching it. Used in automatic car parking sensors and automatic hoovers. Can use different technologies like infrared light, ultrasound, or electromagnetism to detect how far away an object is.
Microphone (sound detector)			Converts sound into electrical signals. Used so that speakers and performers can be heard, and to record voice and music.

Motors

Component	Image	Symbol	Description and usage
Motor		M	Converts electrical energy into kinetic energy (movement). A motor produces rotation on its output when a voltage is applied to its two input terminals. Large motors, such as those in domestic appliances, work from mains AC. Small motors (as shown) work from low DC voltage. These are extremely useful in technology projects.

Diodes and transistors

Diodes and transistors are semiconductors. Semiconductors are made out of materials like silicon. Transistors have enabled the creation of computers and the Internet. There are millions of transistors in your smartphone.

Component	Image	Symbol	Description and usage
Diode			A diode conducts current in one direction only - in the direction of the arrow shown in the symbol. The diode symbol may be printed on the physical diode. Diodes are made in the form of a thin cylinder that has a band or ring on one end. The band or ring indicates the negative (cathode) side of the diode. Diodes are used to convert AC into DC, and to protect circuits that use motors.
Transistor		*Collector* *Base* *Emitter*	Used to amplify current, or as an electronic switch. In digital chips, transistors are used as switches, and there can be millions of transistors in a single chip. A transistor has three connections: a base, an emitter and a collector. • If the voltage between the base and the emitter is less than 0.6 V, the transistor is off and no current flows between the collector and the emitter. • If the voltage between the base and the emitter rises to 0.6 V or greater, the transistor switches on, and current flows between collector and emitter, as if there were a short circuit between them. *Base* *Emitter* *Collector*

Integrated circuits

An integrated circuit (IC) is a complete electronic circuit that is built into a single solid piece of semiconductor material. This is housed in a plastic or ceramic casing, which has multiple output pins. There are many types of ICs and they are widely used in our computers, phones, cars and domestic appliances.

Component	Image	Symbol	Description and usage
Integrated circuit (IC/ chip)	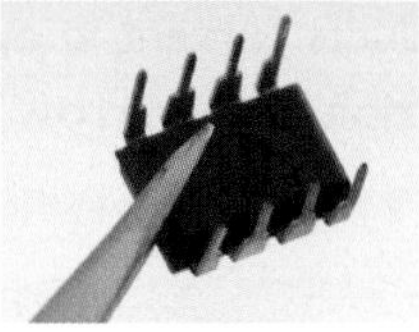 *8 pin IC*	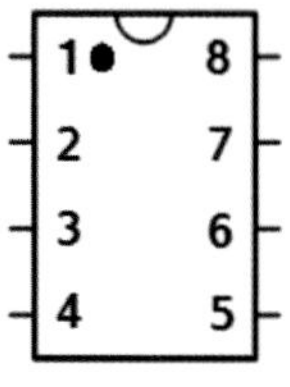 1 8 2 7 3 6 4 5	The numbering of the pins on a chip follows the following rules: • Pin 1 is indicated by a dot on the body or the position of the semicircle (or both). • Numbering is anti-clockwise.
555 timer IC	 NE555	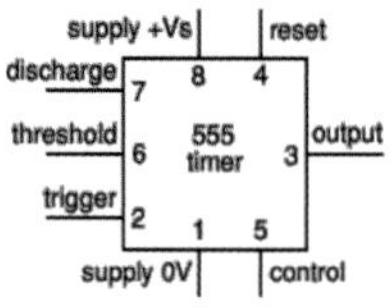 supply +Vs, reset, discharge 7, 8, 4, threshold 6, 555 timer, 3 output, trigger 2, 1, 5, supply 0V, control	Used in Junior Cert projects and exam questions.
IC/chip socket		N/A	ICs are usually inserted into chip sockets. The chip socket is first soldered on to the PCB (see below), and the chip is pushed in to the socket. The chip socket prevents damage to the IC from the heat of the soldering iron, and it also makes it easier to remove or replace the IC if it is faulty, or if other work needs to be carried out on the circuit/PCB.

Components for circuit building

A circuit consists of a number of components connected together to perform a useful function. A number of ways to support these components and to allow them to be connected together in circuits are shown below.

Component	Image	Description and usage
Breadboard	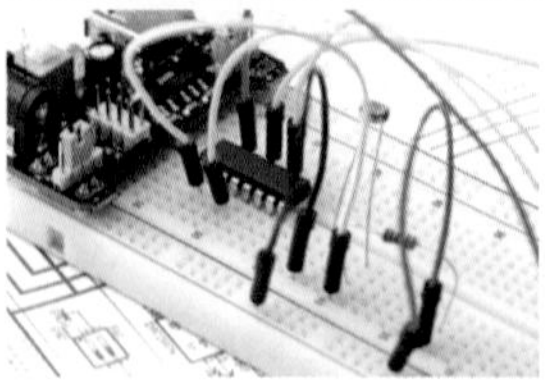	Used to make temporary circuits very quickly. No soldering is required and breadboards can be re-used many times. The legs/pins of the electronic components are pushed into holes in the breadboard. Connections are made between components because the rows and columns of holes are connected internally inside the breadboard.

Component	Image	Description and usage
Copper stripboard		Each row of holes in the stripboard is connected via separate copper strips at the back. The component legs are pushed though the holes and soldered to the copper strips. You can break the copper strip into sections if you want to use the same row to make more than one circuit on the same row. Stripboard makes better connections than breadboards but circuits take longer to make, and it is not easy to re-use.
PCB (printed circuit board)		A PCB is custom-made for one specific circuit. It has a set of holes and a set of custom-made copper connections at the back. The legs of the components are pushed through the holes and soldered to the copper strips. A PCB is the best solution for mass production, because it gives the best connections, and you can make the circuits very small. However the process is expensive and it takes a long time to make one. They cannot be re-used to make different circuits.

Tools for circuit building

You will need to use the following tools when building circuits.

Component	Image	Symbol	Description and usage
Side cutter/ snips		N/A	Used to cut wire and also to strip the plastic coating from electrical cable to expose the metal wire inside. The wire can then be soldered on to the desired connection.
Solder		N/A	Solder is used to join electronic components to wire or other components, or to join an electronic component to a PCB or stripboard. The solder is melted using a soldering iron.
Soldering iron		N/A	Used to heat up solder and the join between two electrical connectors. The solder melts and flows in around the joint, and then cools to create a really good electrical connection. You should always place the soldering iron back in its holder, turn off when not in use, use lots of ventilation and a face mask to avoid fumes.

Component	Image	Symbol	Description and usage
Multimeter		*Voltmeter* V *Ammeter* A *Ohmmeter* Ω	Can operate as a voltmeter, ammeter or an ohmmeter. • To measure voltage, place the cable probes on either side of the component(s) whose voltage you want to measure. • To measure current, put the meter in series with the current you want to measure, so that the current goes through the meter. Make a break in the circuit and insert the meter probes. • To measure resistance, turn off the power and place the probes on either side of the component. • To measure resistance with an ohmmeter, make sure that the component is not in a circuit, and place the probes on either side of the component.

Test yourself

1. Draw the electronic symbol for a battery.
2. Draw the electronic symbol for a bulb.
3. Draw the symbol for an SPST switch.
4. Draw the symbol for a push-to-make switch.
5. What is the name of the component whose symbol is shown? 
6. What is the value and tolerance of the resistor shown? 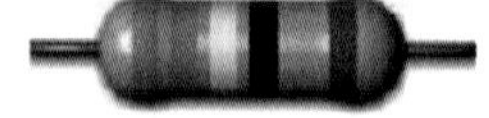
7. What is the name of the component whose symbol is shown below? What does it do?

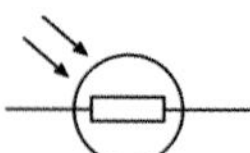

8. What does a capacitor do? What is the difference between an electrolytic capacitor and a non-electrolytic capacitor?
9. What does a diode do? Draw the electronic symbol for a diode.
10. What is a relay? What are the advantages of a relay?

Test yourself

11. What is the name of the component whose symbol is shown?

12. Draw the electronic symbol for an LED.

13. How do you identify the negative (cathode) side of a LED?

14. What does LDR stand for? What is it used for?

15. Draw the symbol for a DPDT switch.

16. What does LDR stand for? What is it used for?

17. Draw the symbol for a DPDT switch.

18. What is capacitance?

19. State the unit of capacitance.

20. State one advantage of using breadboard compared to stripboard to make circuits.

21. What are IC/chip sockets used for? State one benefit of using a chip socket. Where is pin 1 located on an IC?

22. Sketch the electronic symbols for the components shown.

Variable resistor

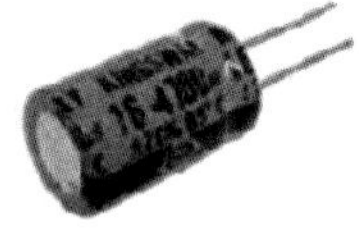

Capacitor

23. What is the name of the instrument shown? Name three things that can be done with it.

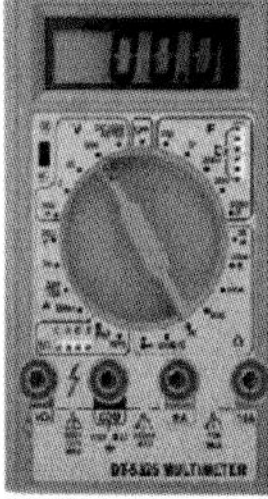

Past exam questions

1. Identify the base, emitter and collector on the transistor symbol shown.

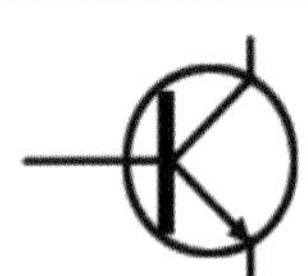

2. State two functions of a transistor in a circuit.

3. Provide the colour codes for a 330 Ω resistor, and a 2k2 resistor.

Past exam questions

4. Three electronic components are shown. Which of these components is used for light or dark sensing?

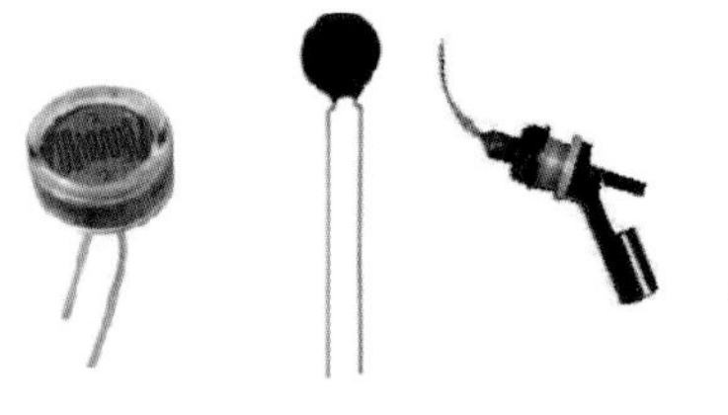

5. A capacitor is shown. Which of the following do capacitors store:
   (a) Sound energy?
   (b) Electric charge?
   (c) Chemical energy?

6. What does PCB stand for?

7. What property of a thermistor changes with a rise or fall in temperature? Sketch the electronic symbol for a thermistor.

8. Name the component shown. Name the legs labelled X and Y.

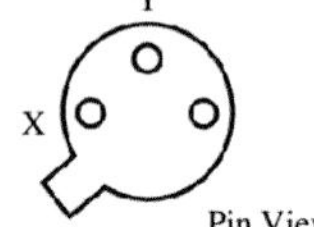

9. In electronics, which of the following does IC stand for:
   (a) Industrial chip?
   (b) Integrated circuit?
   (c) Internal circuit?

10. Explain why the use of a chip socket is recommended when soldering circuits.

11. Indicate clearly on the sketch the location of pins 4 and 8 on the chip shown.

12. The toggle switch shown is:
    (a) DPDT? (b) SPST? (c) SPDT?

13. (a) What is meant by the term LED? (b) List two uses of LEDs. (c) Explain how you would identify the cathode and anode of an LED. (d) State two advantages of using LED lighting in public places.

14. State two advantages of using a printed circuit board over copper stripboard to make circuits.

15. (a) What does LDR stand for? (b) What does the resistance of an LDR vary with?

16. The scientist Michael Faraday invented the electric motor. List four household devices that use an electric motor.

CHAPTER 12

Electronic circuits 1

Introduction

This chapter explains basic electronic circuits, and provides activities to help you build your own electronic circuits. These circuits will help you understand how electronic components work, and they will be useful for your technology projects. More complex circuits are provided in the "Electronic circuits 2" chapter.

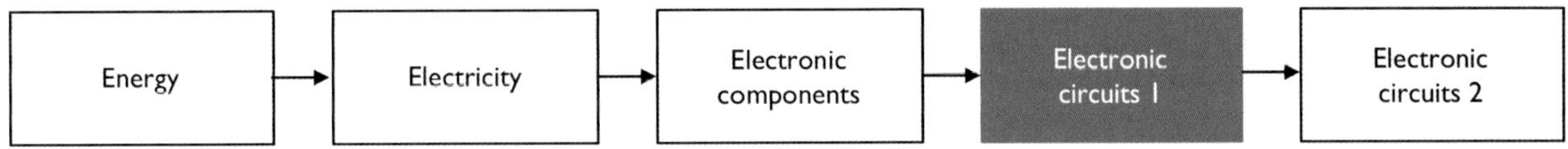

What is a circuit?

A circuit is a loop of electronic components through which current can flow. The word circuit means a circle. For current to flow, a circuit must have a source of voltage, such as a battery or a power supply.

A **circuit** is a loop of electronic components through which current can flow.

A basic circuit

A basic circuit consists of a battery and a resistor connected by wire. Current will follow from the positive terminal of the battery, through the resistor, and back in to the negative terminal of the battery.

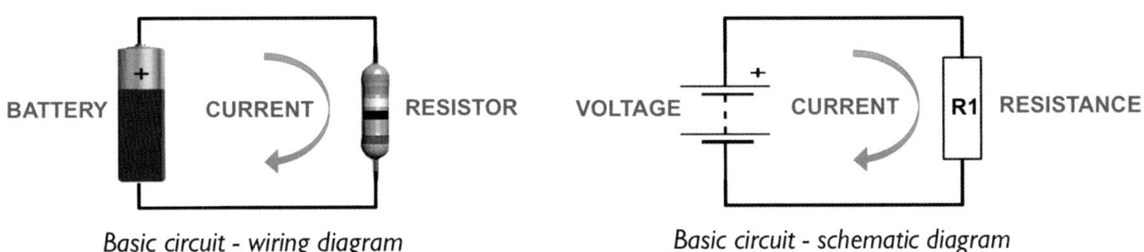

Basic circuit - wiring diagram

Basic circuit - schematic diagram

Circuit diagrams

Circuits are described using diagrams. There are two main types of diagram:

- **Wiring diagrams** – these show you how the physical components are wired together.
- **Schematic diagrams** – these show how the electronic symbols for the components are connected.

Note that if you are asked to sketch a circuit in an exam question, you need to draw a schematic diagram.

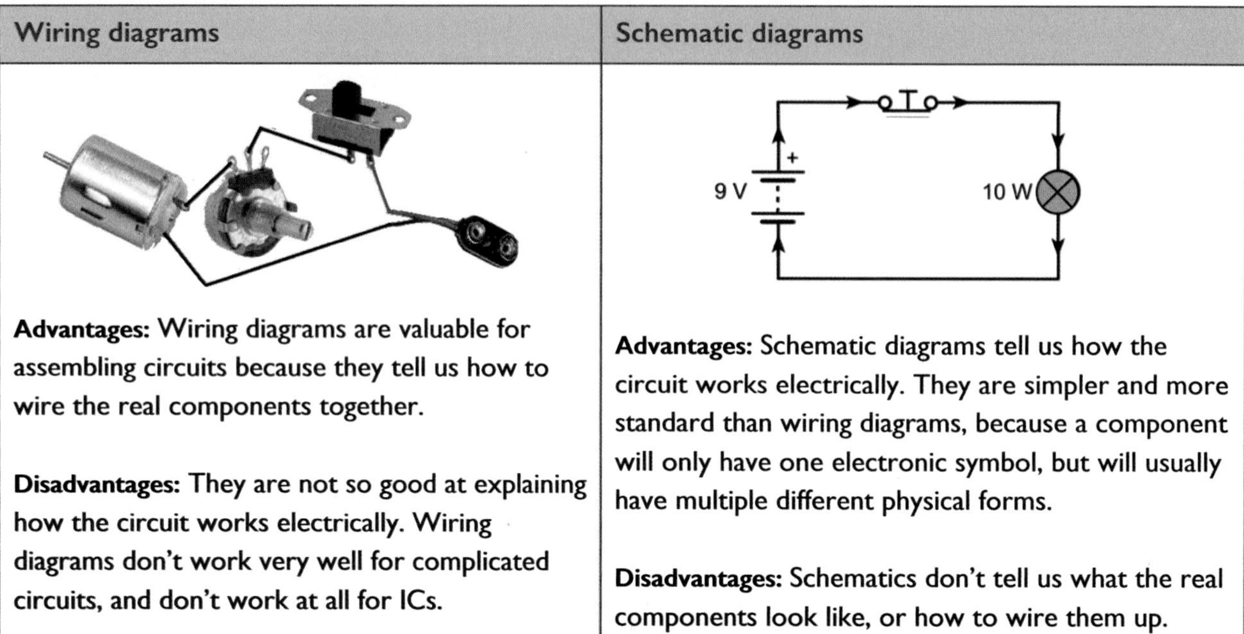

Wiring diagrams	Schematic diagrams
Advantages: Wiring diagrams are valuable for assembling circuits because they tell us how to wire the real components together. **Disadvantages:** They are not so good at explaining how the circuit works electrically. Wiring diagrams don't work very well for complicated circuits, and don't work at all for ICs.	9 V 10 W **Advantages:** Schematic diagrams tell us how the circuit works electrically. They are simpler and more standard than wiring diagrams, because a component will only have one electronic symbol, but will usually have multiple different physical forms. **Disadvantages:** Schematics don't tell us what the real components look like, or how to wire them up.

Sometimes you need both types of diagram, the schematic diagram to understand how it works, and the wiring diagram to tell you how to assemble it.

Connecting components

The table below contains common methods and terms used when connecting components in circuits.

Type	Descriptions
Closed circuit	If you have a closed circuit, you have an electrical connection between two points and current can flow.
Open circuit	If you have an open circuit, there is no electrical connection between two points and no current can flow.
In series	If two components are connected in series, they are connected end-to-end, and the same current flows through both components. *Components in series* Component 1 — Component 2 *Same current*
In parallel	If two components are connected in parallel, they are connected side by side to the same points. The current is divided between them. The voltage will always be the same across both components, because they are connected to the same points. *Components in parallel* Component 1 Component 2 *Same voltage*

Battery circuits

Batteries in series

When batteries (also called cells) are connected in series, their voltages are added up to get the total voltage across them. This is because voltage is measured as the total difference in voltage between two points.

When **batteries are connected in series**, their voltages are added up to get the total voltage.

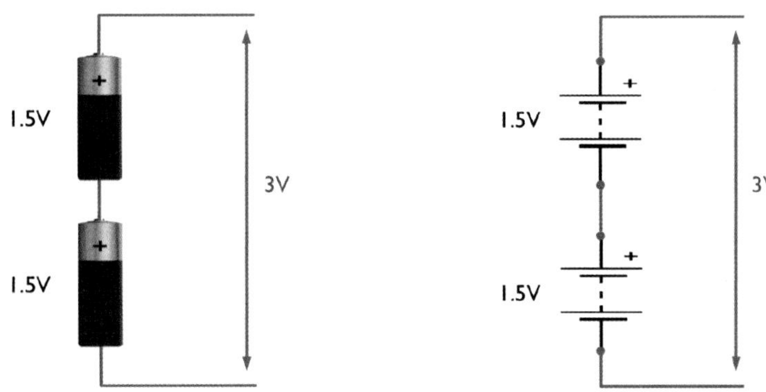

Note that the batteries must be connected the same way round, i.e. with the same polarity (the plus terminal on one battery must connect to the minus terminal of the other battery). A battery holder is often used to connect a number of 1.5 V batteries together in series to create a higher voltage.

Batteries in parallel

Batteries can also be connected in parallel in a circuit. In this case, the total voltage across them is equal to the voltage of one of the batteries.

When **batteries of the same voltage are connected in parallel,**
the total voltage is the same as the voltage of one single battery.

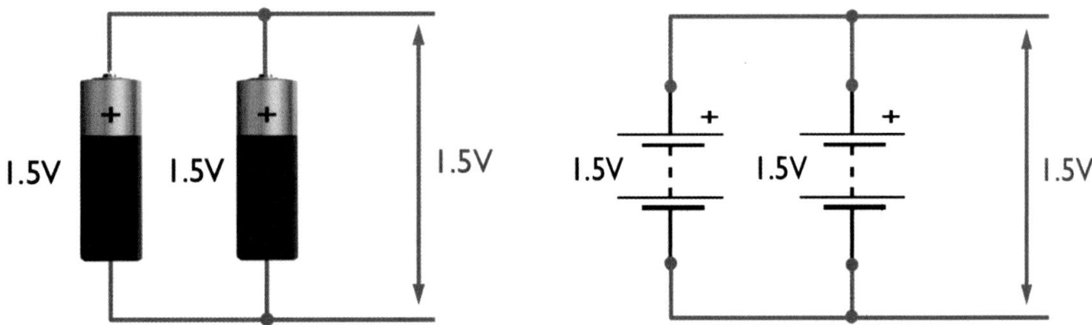

When batteries are connected in parallel, there is more current available, and they will last longer when compared to a single battery powering the same circuit.

Past exam questions

1. When the four 1.5 V batteries are placed in the battery holder, what will the total voltage of the batteries be?

2. State the total voltage supplied by four 1.5 V cells connected in parallel.

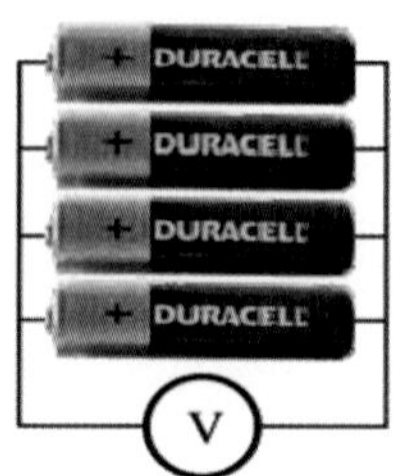

Bulb circuits

A bulb emits lights when current is passed through it. In your technology projects, you may use miniature bulbs and bulb holders like those shown here.

The circuit on the right shows a bulb and a switch connected in series with a battery. The arrows show the direction of the current. What kind of switch is used? What happens when you press the switch? This type of circuit is used to turn off the light in your fridge when the door is closed.

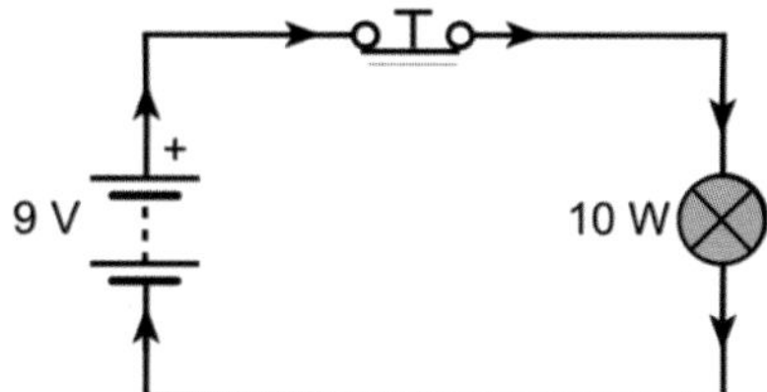

The circuit below shows two bulbs connected in parallel.

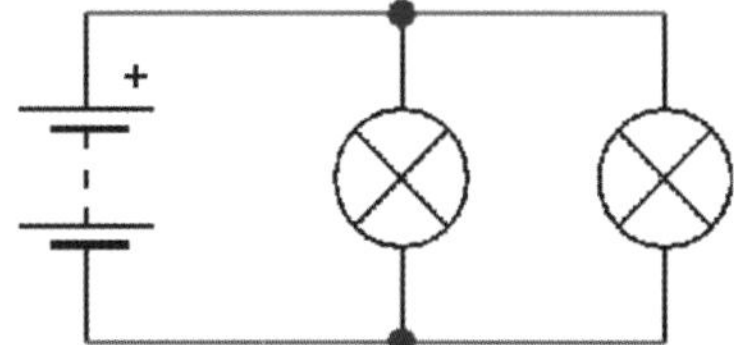

Equal current will flow in each bulb if their power rating is the same. Unlike LEDs, bulbs do not need a resistor in the circuit to limit the current.

Worked example 1: Create a wiring diagram for a bulb circuit

Past exam question

The two bulb holders, the switch and battery snap shown on the right are to be connected so that the bulbs are wired in parallel.

Valid answer

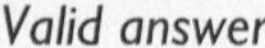

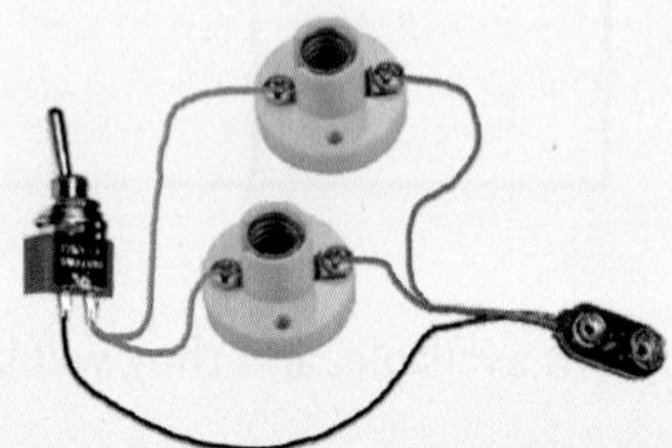

Worked example 2: Create a schematic diagram for a bulb circuit

Past exam question
Using appropriate symbols, sketch the electric circuit shown in the torch on the right.

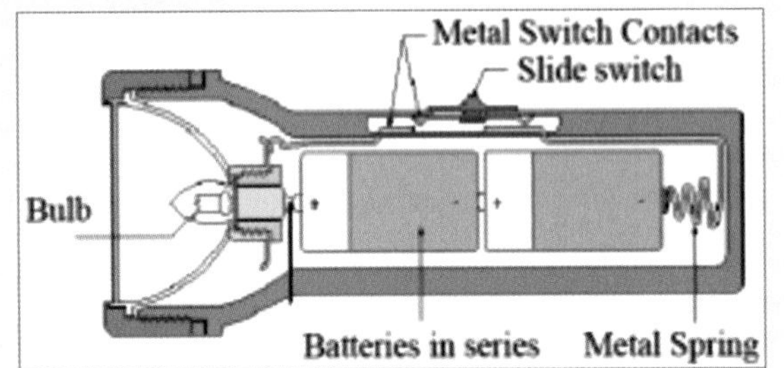

Valid answer
A torch is a circuit of one or more batteries connected in series with a SPST switch and a bulb.

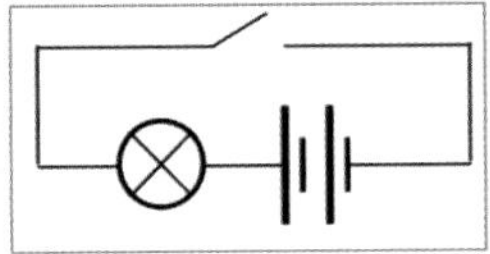

Past exam questions

1. Two bulbs are to be used to light up a display at night.
Draw the symbol for a bulb and show how both bulb holders can be connected in parallel.

Bulb symbol	Parallel connection
	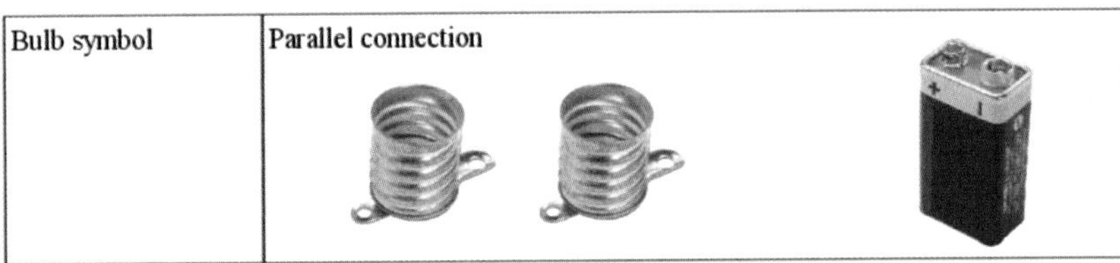

Ohm's law

Ohm's law describes the relationship between voltage (V), current (I) and resistance (R):

$$\text{Current} = \frac{\text{voltage}}{\text{resistance}}$$

To calculate	Equation
Resistance	$R = \frac{V}{I}$
Current	$I = \frac{V}{R}$
Voltage	$V = I \times R$

Ohm's law is used to calculate resistance, current and voltage in circuits. It tells us that the higher the resistance, the less current will flow across a given voltage. The table shows three versions of Ohm's law. You need to pick the relevant equation, depending on what you want to calculate.

When calculating using Ohm's law, make sure that your units of current are in amps, and your units of resistance are in ohms.

According to Ohm's Law, if you have a voltage of 1 volt across a resistance of 1 ohm, a current of 1 amp will flow. If you have a voltage of 2 volts across a resistance of 1 ohm, a current of 2 amps will flow. If you have a voltage of 1 volt across a resistance of 2 ohms, a current of 0.5 amps will flow.

Ohm's law

$$\text{Current} = \frac{\text{voltage}}{\text{resistance}}$$

Worked example 3: Calculate currents using Ohm's law

Question 1

A voltage of 6 V is connected across a 100 Ω resistor. What current flows through the resistor?

Answer

From Ohm's law:

$$\text{Current} = \frac{\text{voltage}}{\text{resistance}}$$

$$I = \frac{V}{R} = \frac{6\ V}{100\ \Omega} = 0.06\ A = 60\ mA$$

Question 2

A voltage of 10 V is connected across a resistor of value 5 kΩ. What current flows through the resistor?

Answer

From Ohm's law:

$$I = \frac{V}{R} = \frac{10\ V}{5000\ \Omega} = 0.002\ A = 2\ mA$$

(Note that kΩ are converted to Ω in the calculation.)

Worked example 4: Calculate resistances using Ohm's law

Question 1

A voltage of 10 V is connected across a resistor. A current of 0.5 A flows through the resistor. What is the value of the resistor?

Answer

From Ohm's law:

$$\text{Resistance} = \frac{\text{voltage}}{\text{current}}$$

$$R = \frac{V}{I} = \frac{10\ V}{0.5\ A} = 20\ \Omega$$

Question 2

A voltage of 10 V is connected across a resistor. A current of 20 mA flows through the resistor. What is the value of the resistor?

Answer

From Ohm's law:

$$\text{Resistance} = \frac{\text{voltage}}{\text{current}}$$

$$R = \frac{V}{I} = \frac{10\ V}{0.020\ A} = 500\ \Omega$$

(Note that mA are converted to A.)

Worked example 5: Calculate voltages using Ohm's law

Question 1

A current of 100 mA is flowing through a 100 Ω resistor. What is the voltage across the resistor?

Answer

From Ohm's law:

Voltage = current × resistance

$V = I \times R = 0.1\ A \times 100\ \Omega = 10\ V$

(Note that mA are converted to A.)

Question 2

A current of 2 mA is flowing through a 2 kΩ resistor. What is the voltage across the resistor?

Answer

From Ohm's law:

$V = I \times R = 0.002\ A \times 2000\ \Omega = 4\ V$

(Note that mA are converted to A and kΩ are converted to Ω in the calculation. This ensures that the answer is in volts.)

Voltage drops

We can see from Ohm's law and the above worked examples, that there is a voltage across every component that has current passing through it (assuming that the component has some resistance). This is called a voltage drop. Electrical wire has no resistance and so has no voltage drop across it.

Test yourself

1. What current flows if a 10 Ω resistor is connected to a 100 V power supply?
2. What resistance would be needed to cause a current of 5 mA to flow using a 5 V battery?
3. A 5 kΩ resistor has 2 mA running through it. What is the voltage drop across the resistor?
4. A 1 kΩ resistor is connected to a 1.5 V battery. What current flows in the resistor?
5. A 500 Ω resistor is connected to a 9 V battery. How much current flows?
6. A 3 V battery is connected to a resistor. We measure 100 mA flowing in the circuit. What is the value of the resistor?
7. A current of 10 mA is running through a resistor connected to a 5 V battery. What happens if the 5 V battery is replaced with a 10 V battery?
8. What current flows if a 100 Ω resistor is connected across a 3 V battery?
9. A current of 0.1 A is flowing through a 1 kΩ resistor. What is the voltage across the resistor?
10. A current of 5 mA is flowing through a resistor. What happens if the value of the resistor is doubled?
11. A 1 kΩ resistor is connected to a battery. There is 1mA flowing in the circuit. What is the voltage of the battery?

Measuring voltage, current and resistance

As well as calculating voltage, current and resistance using Ohm's Law, we can measure these directly in the circuit, to confirm that our calculations are correct.

To measure	Procedure
Current	• Connect an ammeter in series with the component. (A — Component 1)
Voltage	• Connect a voltmeter in parallel with the component. (V — Component 1)
Resistance	• Measure the voltage across the component (as above). • Measure the current flowing though the component (as above). • Calculate the resistance using Ohm's law. Why can't you use an ohmmeter to measure resistance? You can use an ohmmeter to measure resistance, but it is only reliable when the component is not in a circuit. (Ω — Component 1)

Worked example 6: Calculate resistance by measuring voltage and current

Past exam question

Indicate clearly on the circuit diagram shown, the correct location of:

(i) an ammeter 

(ii) a voltmeter 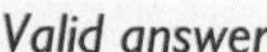

to measure the resistance of the bulb when lit.

Valid answer

The voltmeter is connected across (in parallel with) the bulb.
The ammeter is connected in series with the bulb.

The resistance of the bulb can be calculated using Ohm's Law:

$$\text{Resistance} = \frac{\text{measured voltage}}{\text{measured current}}$$

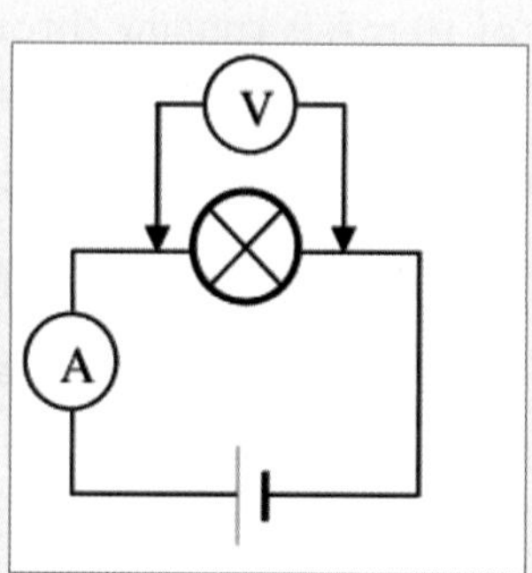

(Note that only the diagram needs to be shown in your answer.)

Test yourself

1. Why must an ammeter be placed in series with a component in order to measure the current that is flowing through that component?
2. Where must the probes of the meter be placed in order to measure the voltage across a component?
3. How would you measure voltage across two components?
4. A voltmeter measures 5 V across a component. An ammeter measures 1 A of current through the component. What is the resistance of the component?
5. A 1 kΩ resistor is connected across a 10 V power supply. How much current flows through the resistor?
6. What voltage is needed to get a current of 10 mA flowing in a 100 Ω resistor?
7. What are the advantages of a schematic diagram over a wiring diagram?
8. When would you use a wiring diagram?
9. What is the voltage of two 1.5 V batteries connected in parallel?
10. What is the voltage of two 1.5 V batteries in series?
11. Can you use a multimeter to measure current?
12. How can resistance be measured in a circuit?

Resistor circuits

Resistors in series

Resistors are connected in series when they are connected one after the other in a circuit. To find the total resistance of resistors connected in series, simply add up their individual resistances.

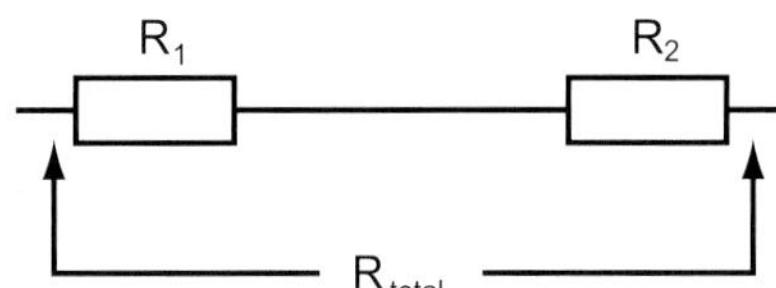

Resistors in series

$$R_{total} = R_1 + R_2 + \dots$$

Worked example 7: Calculate resistance of resistors in series

Past exam question

What is the total resistance of the resistors shown?

10 KΩ 10 KΩ

Solution

$R_{total} = R_1 + R_2 = 10\ k\Omega + 10\ k\Omega = 20\ k\Omega$

Resistors in parallel

When two resistors are connected in parallel, each resistor draws its own separate current. This means that there is more current flowing when you have two resistors in parallel, than when you just have one resistor.

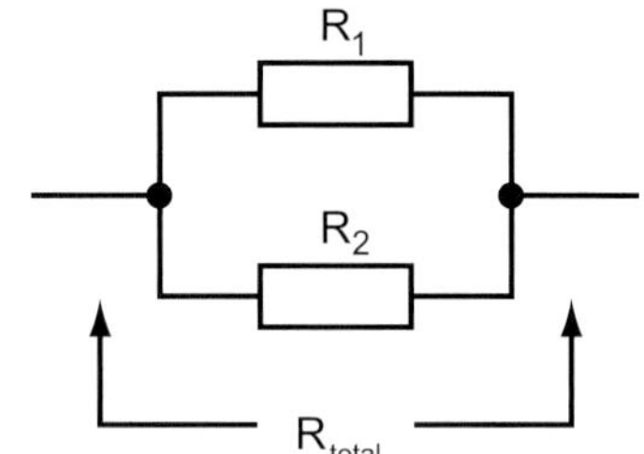

As there is more current flowing, the overall resistance of the two resistors in parallel must be lower than either resistor on its own.

The formula for calculating the total resistance of two resistors in parallel is given below. Use a calculator to calculate the value. Units used in the equation must all be the same.

Resistors in parallel

$$R_{total} = \frac{R_1 \times R_2}{R_1 + R_2}$$

Worked example 8: Calculate resistance of resistors in parallel

Past exam question
What is the total resistance of the resistors shown?

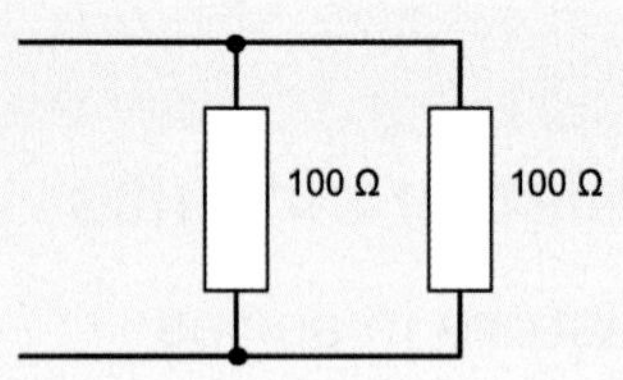

Solution by applying formula

$$R_{total} = \frac{R_1 \times R_2}{R_1 + R_2} = \frac{100\,\Omega \times 100\,\Omega}{100\,\Omega + 100\,\Omega} = \frac{10{,}000}{200} = 50\,\Omega$$

Solution by reasoning
As the resistors are the same, the current flowing into the combination of the two resistors will be twice what it would be if there were only one resistor. Therefore the resistance of the two resistors together must be half that of one resistor on its own.

Test yourself

1. What is the total resistance of a 1 kΩ resistor and a 300 Ω resistor in series?
2. What is the total resistance of the following resistors all connected in series? 100 Ω, 200 Ω, 300 Ω?
3. What is the total resistance of two 1 kΩ resistors connected in parallel?
4. What is the total resistance of four 1 kΩ resistors connected in parallel?

Past exam questions

1. Calculate the total resistance in this circuit.

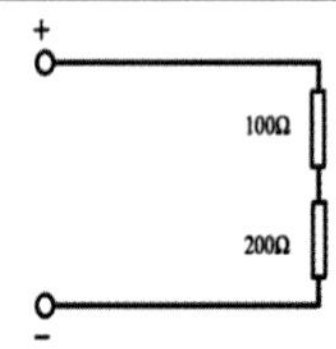

Potential divider circuits

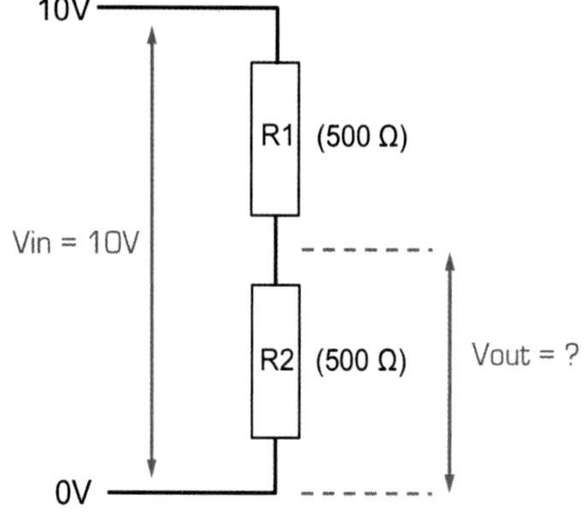

A potential divider circuit creates an output voltage that is lower than the voltage supplied by the power supply or battery, V_{in}. The circuit is composed of two resistors in series. This lower voltage, V_{out} is measured across the bottom resistor, as shown below.

We can use Ohm's law to calculate V_{out}, the voltage across R_2:

$$R_{total} = R_1 + R_2 = 500\ \Omega + 500\ \Omega = 1000\ \Omega$$

$$\text{Current} = \frac{\text{voltage}}{\text{resistance}} = \frac{V}{R_{total}} = \frac{10\text{ V}}{1000\ \Omega} = 0.01\text{ A}$$

$$V_{out} = \text{current} \times \text{resistance} = 0.01\text{ A} \times 500\ \Omega = 5\text{ V}$$

In this case, the output voltage is half the input voltage. This makes sense as there is 10 V across two equal-sized resistors.

Instead of using Ohm's Law, V_{out},, the voltage across R_2, can be calculated using the formula below. The voltage across R_2 depends on the ratio of R_2 to the total resistance ($R_1 + R_2$).

Output voltage of a potential divider circuit

$$V_{out} = V_{in} \times \frac{R_2}{R_1 + R_2}$$

We can check that this formula gives the same answer as Ohm's law for the circuit above.

$$V_{out} = V_{in} \times \frac{R_2}{R_1 + R_2} = 10\text{ V} \times \frac{500\ \Omega}{500\ \Omega + 500\ \Omega} = 10\text{ V} \times \frac{500\ \Omega}{1000\ \Omega} = 10\text{ V} \times \frac{1}{2} = 5\text{ V}$$

Worked example 9: Calculate the voltage from a potential divider

Past exam question

Calculate the voltage across resistor R2 in the circuit shown.

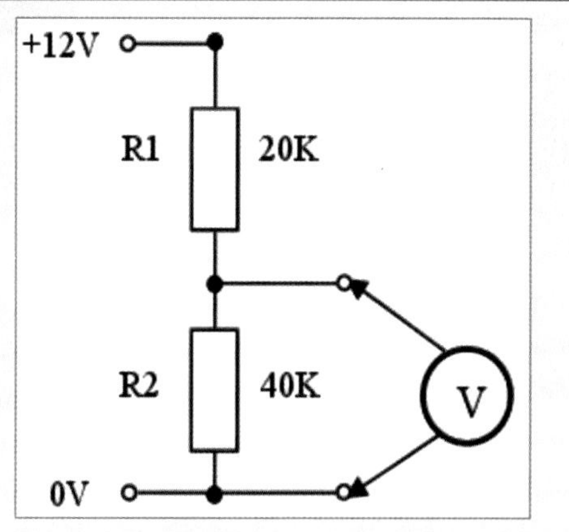

Solution

$$V_{out} = V_{in} \times \frac{R2}{R1 + R2} = 12\text{ V} \times \frac{40\text{ k}\Omega}{20\text{ k}\Omega + 40\text{ k}\Omega}$$

$$V_{out} = 12\text{ V} \times \frac{40}{60} = 12\text{ V} \times \frac{2}{3} = 8\text{ V}$$

Using a sensor resistor in a voltage divider

If we replace one of the fixed resistors in a voltage divider with a resistance that varies according to light or temperature, we will get an output voltage that varies with light or temperature.

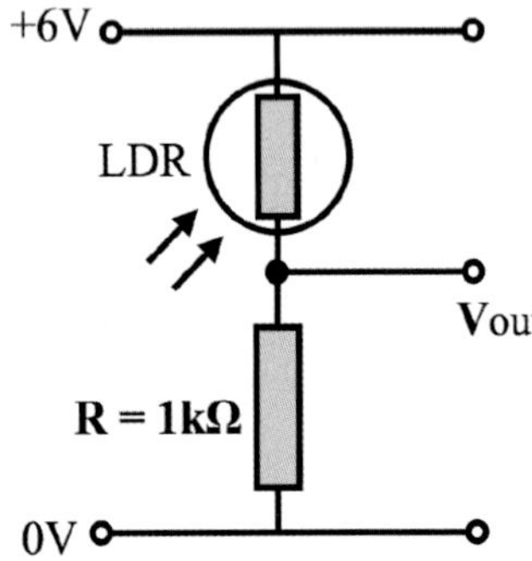

The circuit shown on the left will generate a high voltage when it is light, and a low voltage when it is dark.

If there is light, the resistance of the LDR will be low, and most of the resistance and corresponding voltage drop will be across the fixed resistor. Therefore V_{out}, the output voltage, will be high.

If it is dark, the resistance of the LDR will be very high, so most of the voltage drop will be across the LDR, and so V_{out} will be close to 0 V.

This type of circuit forms the basis for all the sensor circuits that are described in "Electronic circuits 2".

Using a potentiometer as a voltage divider

If we use a potentiometer instead of two fixed resistors, we will get a continually varying voltage (from 0 V to max input voltage) as we turn the knob of the potentiometer. This is because the resistance at the middle contact of the potentiometer can vary from minimum to maximum resistance. Note how the potentiometer is connected in the wiring diagram.

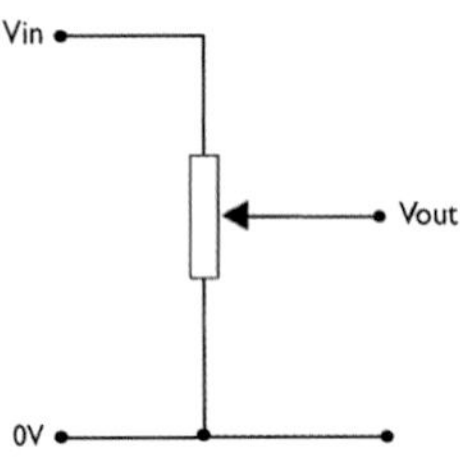

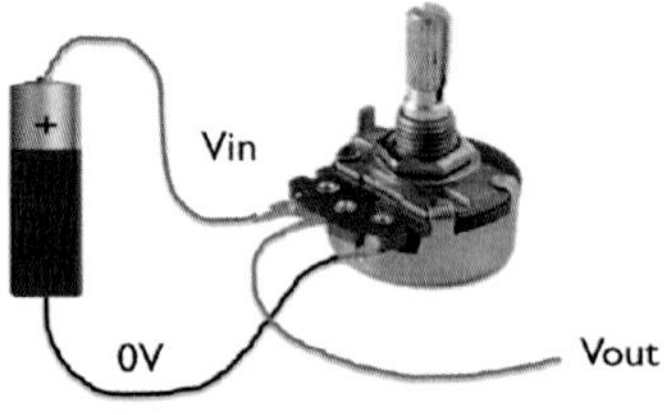

Using fixed resistors with variable resistors

Fixed resistors are often added on one, or both sides of a potentiometer or variable resistor in order to limit its effect. This may be done to prevent the current rising to unlimited levels if the resistance of the potentiometer is turned to zero.

Another reason for using fixed resistors in this way is to prevent the output voltage changing to 0 V or to V_{in}.

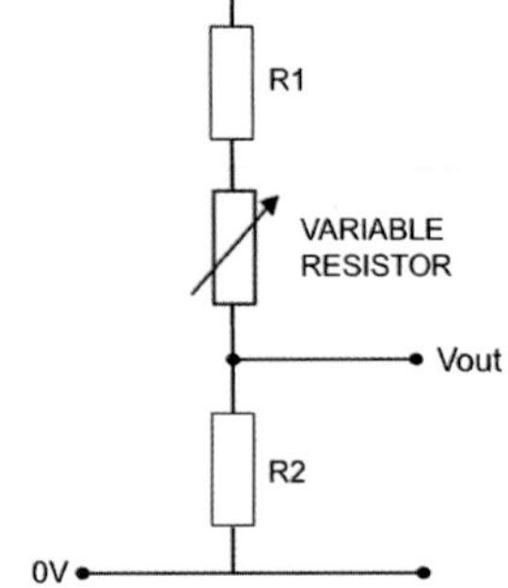

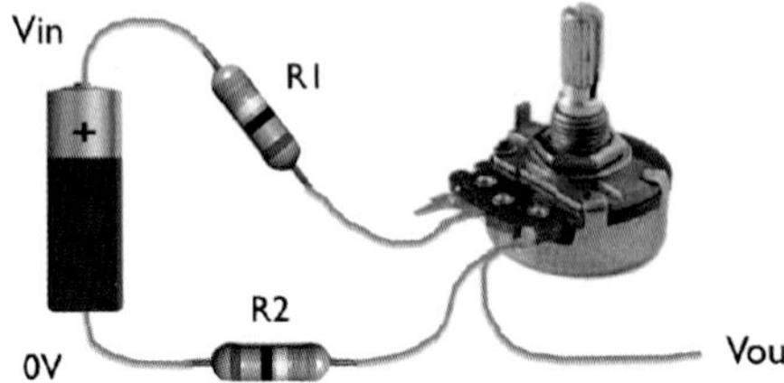

The circuit shown here is an example of this usage.

Note how the potentiometer is wired as a variable resistor (differently than above), by connecting the middle and outside contacts.

Test yourself

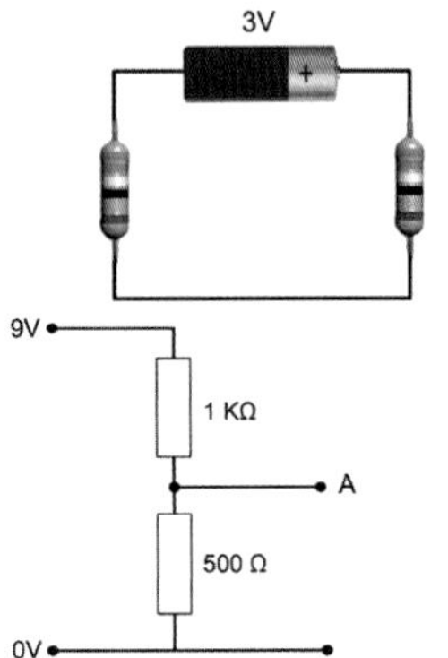

1. What is meant by a potential divider?
2. What is the voltage across the right hand resistor if both resistors have the same value?
3. How do you wire a potentiometer as a variable resistor?
4. In the circuit shown on the right, what is the voltage at point A?
5. How would you modify the circuit shown on the right to create an output voltage that varies with temperature?

Activities with resistors

The activities below will help you to understand more about resistors and potentiometers and how to use them in circuits. You will need the following equipment and components:

- A DC power supply, maximum 12 volts.
- A breadboard.
- A selection of resistors with values between 330 Ω and 33 kΩ.
- A multimeter with probes.
- Help and supervision from your teacher.

The diagram below shows how the rows and columns of a breadboard are connected.

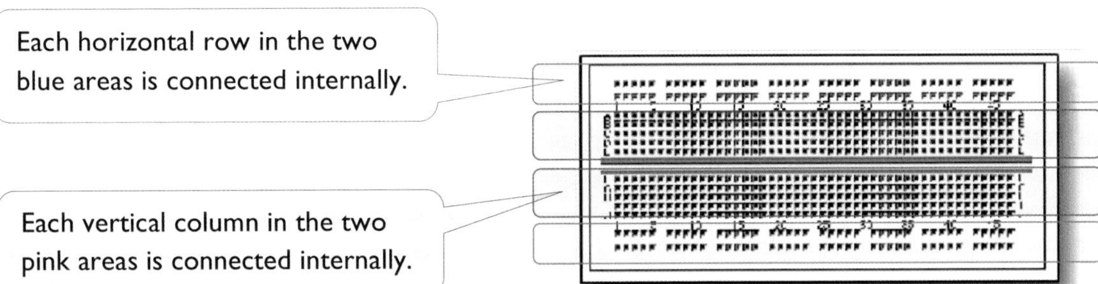

Activity 1: Measure the current through a resistor

To measure the current through a resistor:

- Connect the power supply leads across a resistor using crocodile clips.
- Set the multimeter to a current setting.
- Disconnect one of the crocodile clips from the resistor, and attach the multimeter in series with the resistor.
- Measure the current through the resistor. You may need to adjust the current range on the multimeter to get it to display the value.
- Read the value of the resistor using the colour code on the resistor. Calculate the current you should be getting through the resistor using Ohm's Law (I = V/R).
- Is the measured value close to the calculated value?
- If not, carry out the activity again with a resistor of higher or lower value.

Activity 2: Build a potential divider using two resistors

To build a potential divider using two resistors:

- Insert two resistors of the same value into a breadboard so that they are connected in series.
- Connect the power supply to the top and bottom leads of the set of two resistors.
- Set your multimeter to a voltage setting.
- Measure the voltage across one of the resistors.
- Is it half your power supply voltage?
- Do the experiment again with resistors of different values.
- Read the values of the resistors using the colour codes.
- Calculate the voltage you should be getting using the voltage divider formula.

Activity 3: Generate a variable voltage using a potentiometer

To generate a variable voltage using a potentiometer:

- Connect the power supply to the top and bottom contacts of a potentiometer.
- Set the multimeter to a voltage setting.
- Connect one of the multimeter probes to the middle contact of the potentiometer.
- Connect the other multimeter probe to one of outside contacts of the potentiometer.
- The multimeter should display a voltage somewhere in between 0 V and the voltage of the power supply.
- Twist the knob of the potentiometer and watch the measured voltage change.

LED circuits

LED stands for light-emitting diode. A simple LED circuit is shown below. Current from the battery flows through the LED and the resistor, and the LED lights up. The resistor is used to limit the current flowing through the LED. Current can only flow through a diode or LED in one direction.

The schematic diagram shows the current flowing through the LED from top to bottom, in the direction pointed by the triangle in the LED symbol.

The wiring diagram shows the positive side of the battery connected to the positive (anode) side of the LED, which is indicated by the long leg of the LED.

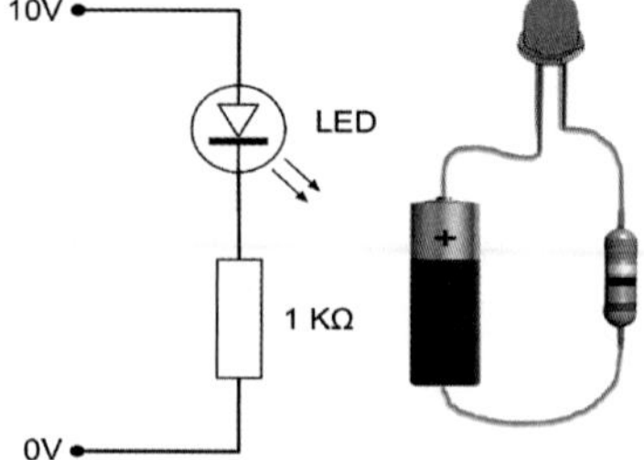

Current-limiting resistors

The LED circuit above illustrates one of the main reasons why resistors are used in circuits, i.e. to limit the current. Too much current will damage most electronic components, including LEDs. The resistor protects LEDs and other components by keeping the current at a level that they can withstand.

Without the resistor connected in series in the circuit above, a very large current would flow in the LED (because it has very low resistance in the forward direction) and this would damage it.

Calculating the resistor value required for an LED circuit

To calculate the value of the resistor we need in an LED circuit, we need the following information.

Information needed	Description
The level of current that can flow through the LED without damaging it	The maximum current that the LED can handle will be specified in the datasheet for the LED. This is called Imax. In an exam question, you will be told the required value of current, or you will be told the value of Imax.
The voltage drop across the LED	LEDs have a constant voltage drop of around 2 V across them when they are conducting current. This voltage is constant regardless of the amount of current flowing through the LED. This is contrary to Ohm's law, but LEDs don't follow Ohm's law because they are not resistors. Note that the LED voltage is sometimes called the forward voltage or V_f.

When we know the current we need, and the voltage drop across the LED, we can use Ohm's law to calculate the value of the resistor required to generate that amount of current, as follows:

$$\text{Value of resistor for LED circuit} = \frac{\text{power supply voltage} - \text{LED voltage}}{\text{desired LED current}}$$

$$\textbf{Value of resistor for LED circuit} = \frac{\text{power supply voltage} - \text{LED voltage}}{\text{desired LED current}}$$

Worked example 10: Calculate the value of the current-limiting resistor for an LED circuit

Past exam question

Using the information provided in the diagram, calculate the required value of R5.

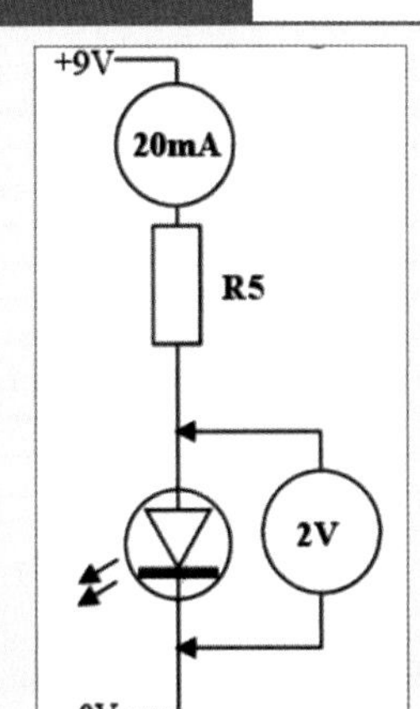

Solution by applying formula

$$R = \frac{(\text{power supply} - \text{LED voltage})}{\text{desired current}} = \frac{9\text{ V} - 2\text{ V}}{20\text{ mA}} = \frac{7\text{ V}}{0.02\text{ A}} = 3500\ \Omega$$

Using the table on the next page, the closest fixed resistor value is 3.6 kΩ.

Solution by reasoning

- **The diagram tells us that the current we need is 20 mA.**
- **The diagram tells us that the voltage drop across the LED is 2 V.**
- **The diagram tells us the voltage across the resistor and LED is 9 V.**
- **If there is 9 V across the LED and the resistor, and there is 2 V across the LED, there must be 7 V across the resistor (9 V – 2 V).**
- **Since we know the voltage across the resistor and the current through the resistor, we can calculate the value of the resistor using Ohm's law:**

$$R = \frac{V}{I} = \frac{7\text{ V}}{20\text{ mA}} = \frac{7\text{ V}}{0.02\text{ A}} = 3500\ \Omega = 3.5\text{ k}\Omega$$

Choosing the right fixed resistor

Resistors are only made in a certain values. Once we calculate the value of resistor that we need, it is very likely that a resistor of that exact value does not exist. Therefore we need to choose a fixed resistor with the closest value to the one we need.

Fixed resistors come in values where their first two digits can only have the values shown in the table.

Fixed resistor values
10, 11, 12, 15, 16, 18,
20, 22, 24, 27,
30, 33, 36, 39,
43, 47,
50, 56, 75, 82, 91

For example, if you needed a 1400 Ω resistor, the closest would be 1500 Ω. If you needed a 400 Ω resistor, the closest would be 390 Ω. If you needed a 4.5 kΩ resistor, the closest would be 4.3 kΩ or 4.7 kΩ.

Note that if you are asked to limit the current to a certain value, you must choose the closest resistor whose value is greater than your calculated value.

For example, if you calculated that you need 840 Ω for your current-limiting resistor, you must choose the 910 Ω resistor, because if you chose the (closer) 820 Ω resistor, the maximum current would be exceeded.

Note that in an exam question, if you need to choose a closest or best-fit resistor, you will be given a choice of resistor values.

Connecting LEDs in parallel

The circuit on the left below shows two LEDs connected in parallel. Each LED has its own current-limiting resistor. The circuit on the right shows two LEDs connected in parallel, with one resistor limiting the current for both LEDs. The value of the single resistor on the right is half that of the resistors on the left. This is to ensure that the current flowing through LED 1 and LED 2 is the same in both circuits.

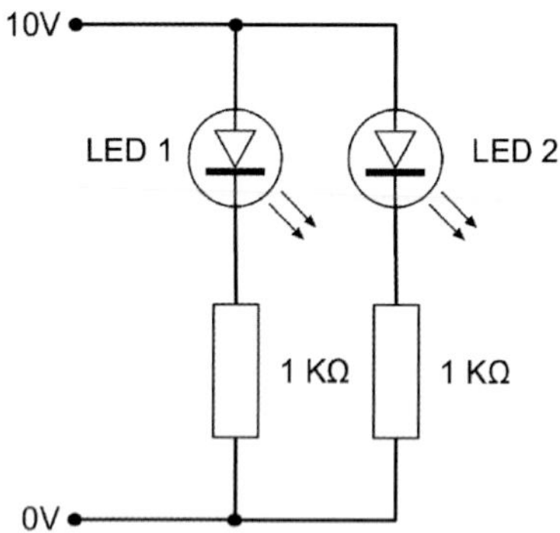

Two LEDs in parallel with individual resistors

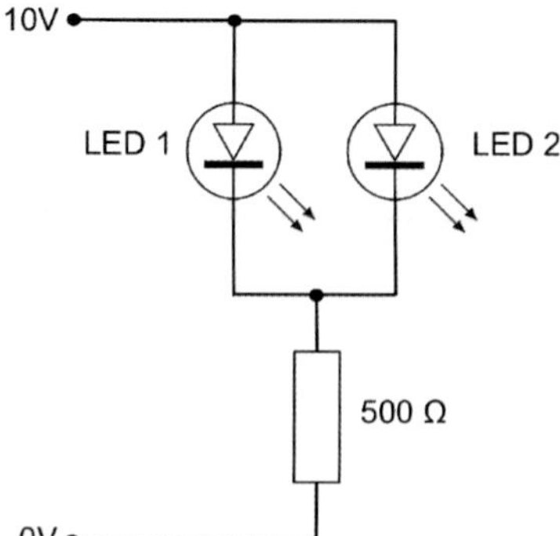

Two LEDs in parallel with a shared resistor

Connecting LEDs in series

LEDs can be connected in series. However, with LEDs in series, you may not be able to power them, because each LED requires approximately 2 V. For example, if you had a 5 V power supply, you could power two LEDs in series. However, you couldn't power three LEDs in series, as this would require 6 V.

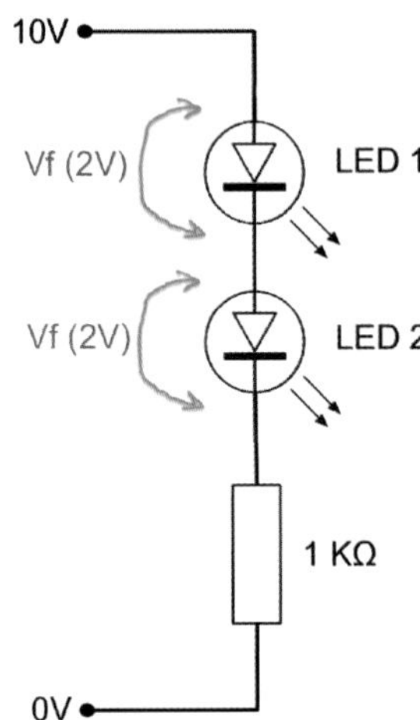

Note that when calculating the resistor value that you need for two LEDs in series, you will need to subtract two LED voltage drops (e.g. 2 x 2 V = 4 V) from the power supply voltage, before using Ohm's law.

LED pilot light with SPST switch

The diagram on the right shows an LED pilot light circuit.

A pilot light indicates that an electronic device is turned on. LEDs are commonly used as pilot lights.

As long as the on/off switch remains closed, the LED will remain lighting. When the on/off switch is opened (turned off), the LED will go out.

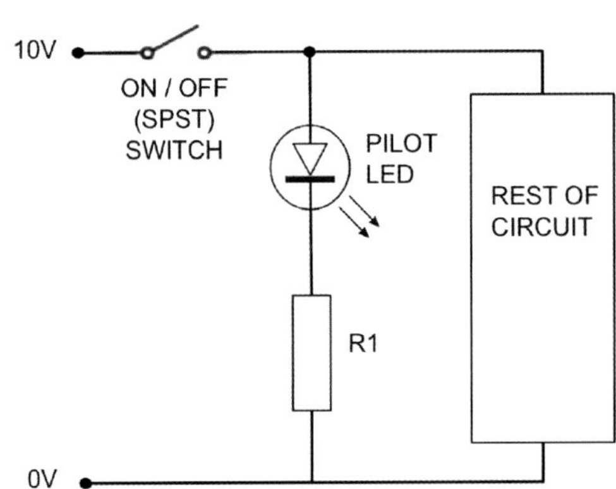

Two LEDs with an SPDT switch

This circuit below shows how an SPDT switch can be used to direct current to turn on one LED or the other.

You can build this circuit in the next Activities section.

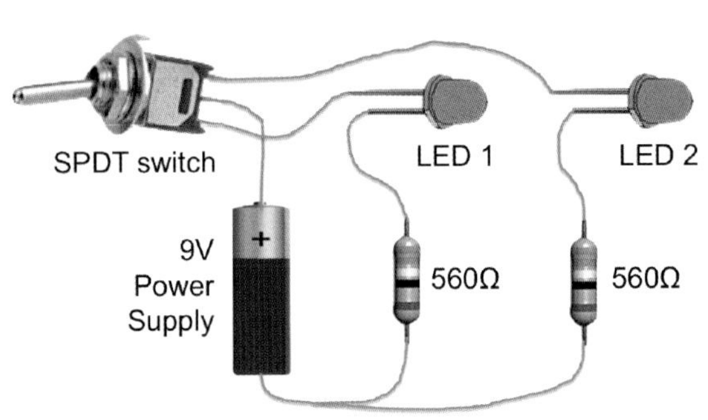

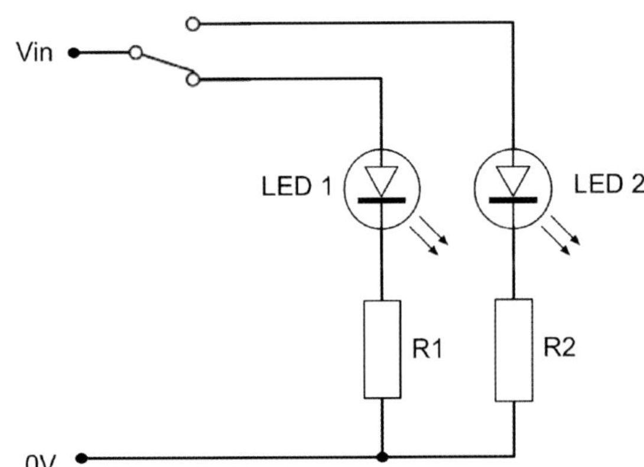

Worked example 11: Wire a switched series LED circuit

Past exam question
Two LEDs are used as lights for a buggy. The LEDs are wired in series. Connect the components shown to show how the LEDs and resistor would be connected in series to the battery snap and the switch.

Valid answer

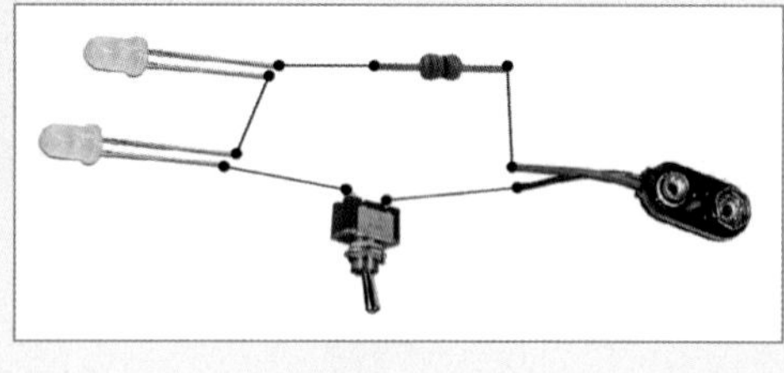

Activities with LEDs

The following activities help you to build the "Two LEDs and an SPDT switch" circuit shown on the previous page (using a power supply instead of a battery). There are three activities. Each activity adds another component to the circuit, until you have built the full circuit in Activity 3. Carrying out these activities helps you understand LED components and LED circuits, and will help you to build LED circuits into your technology projects.

You will need the following equipment and components to build this circuit:

- A DC power supply – set to 9 V.
- A breadboard.
- Two LEDs – preferably different colours.
- Two resistors of around 560 Ω each.
- One SPDT switch, e.g. a toggle switch.
- Some insulated wire and snips/wire stripper.
- A soldering iron and solder.
- Help and supervision from your teacher.

Safety when soldering

Before starting the activities below remember the following points about safety when soldering:

- Keep the soldering iron in its holder when not in use.
- Never leave the hot tip down on the bench or elsewhere.
- Do not touch the hot tip.
- Do not solder directly under your nose or mouth (because of fumes).
- Wear a fume guard mask.
- Do not overheat the metal components (heat for two seconds only).
- Turn off soldering iron when not in use.

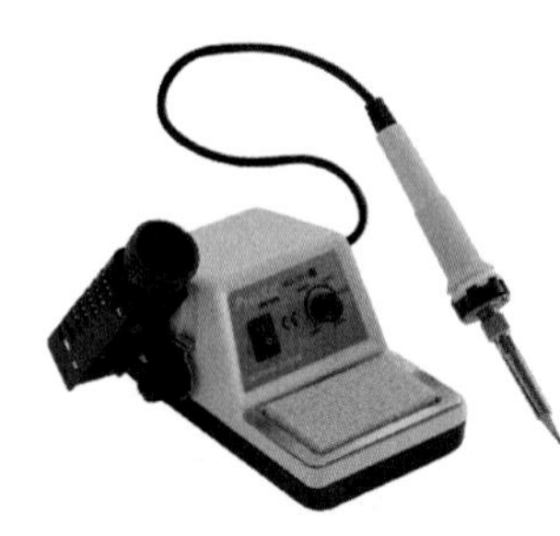

Activity 1: Build a circuit to light up one LED

To build a circuit that lights up one LED without a switch or soldering:

- Connect the negative side of a LED to one end of a 560 Ω resistor in a breadboard.
- Connect the negative of the power supply to the other end of the resistor.
- Connect the positive of the power supply to the positive side of the LED.
- The LED should light.
- Connect up the power supply the other way round. The LED will not light.

Activity 2: Add a switch to the LED circuit

To add a switch to the LED circuit above:

- Disconnect the positive end of the power supply from the circuit above.
- Strip three short pieces of wire.
- Solder the three pieces of wire to the three terminals of the SPDT switch.
- Using the breadboard, connect the wire from one of the outside terminals of the switch to the positive side of the LED.
- Connect the power supply back to the wire attached to the middle terminal of the SPDT switch.
- Operate the switch and watch the LED turn on and off.

Activity 3: Add another LED

To add another LED to the circuit above:

- Disconnect the positive side of the power supply from the circuit.
- Using the breadboard, connect up a second LED and resistor in parallel with your first LED and resistor.
- Make sure the bottom/negative ends of the two resistors are connected via the breadboard.
- Make sure the positive ends of the two LEDS are NOT connected via the breadboard.
- Using the breadboard, connect the wire from the other outside terminal of the SPDT switch to the positive side of the second LED.
- Connect the power supply back to the wire attached to the middle terminal of the SPDT switch.
- Operate the switch and turn on each LED in turn. Disconnect when finished.

Activity 4: Build a circuit using Circuit Wizard

Using the Circuit Wizard software (available in most schools), implement the above LED circuits on screen. The software will show you if the circuit works or not. It will also produce a wiring diagram or copper stripboard version of the circuit so that you can build it physically. This means that you can test your circuit before you build it.

Past exam questions

1. Use the symbols shown on the right to draw a diagram of a circuit that can be switched off and on and includes two LEDs that are connected in parallel.

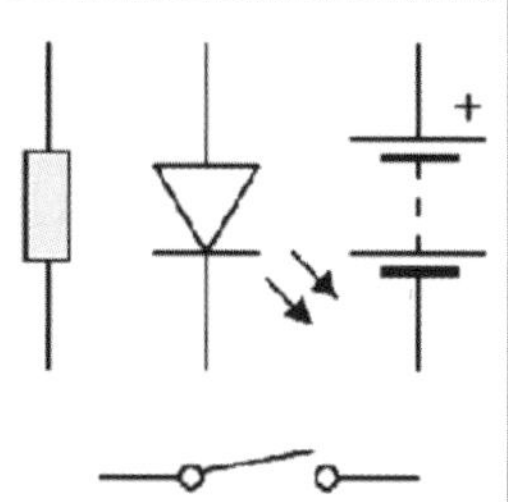

2. A student is required to manufacture a wall-mounted night light for a child's room based on the design shown. Sketch a suitable 9 V circuit diagram which will light a white LED in any four of the stars on the night light.

Motor circuits

This section describes a number of basic motor circuits. More complex motor circuits are described in "Electronic circuits 2".

Turning a motor on and off

The circuit on the right shows a simple motor circuit with an on/off (SPST) switch. The motor will rotate when the switch is closed.

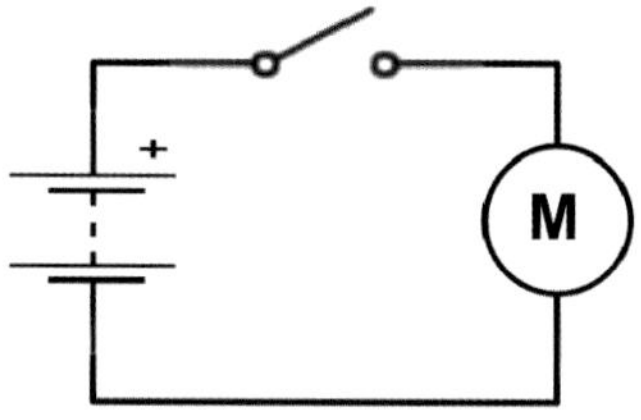

Controlling the speed of a motor with a variable resistor

You can control the speed of a motor by putting a variable resistor in series with the motor.

This reduces the current to the motor, and the speed of the motor.

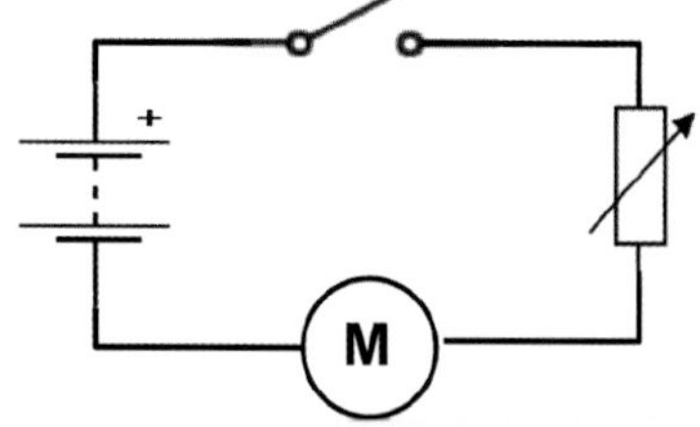

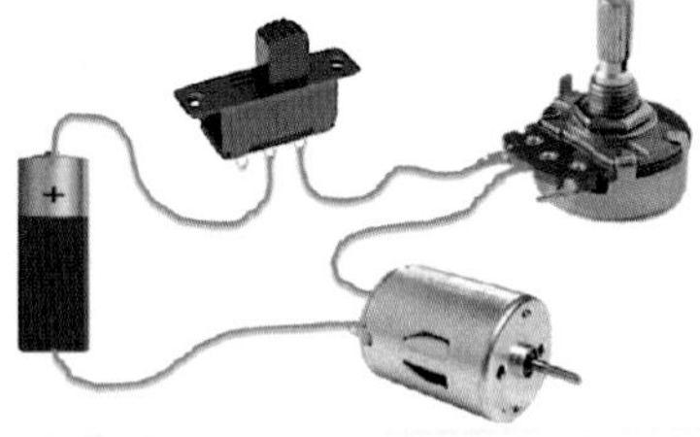

Reversing the direction of a motor using a DPDT switch

The circuit below shows you how use a double-pole, double-throw switch to change the direction of rotation of a motor. This circuit is important for exam questions and is useful in technology projects. It is explained on the following page.

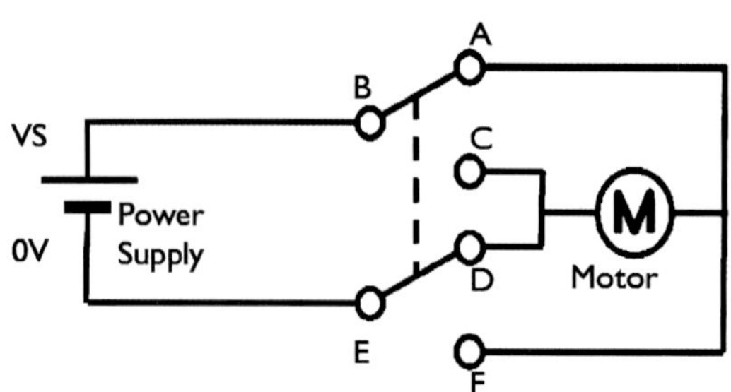

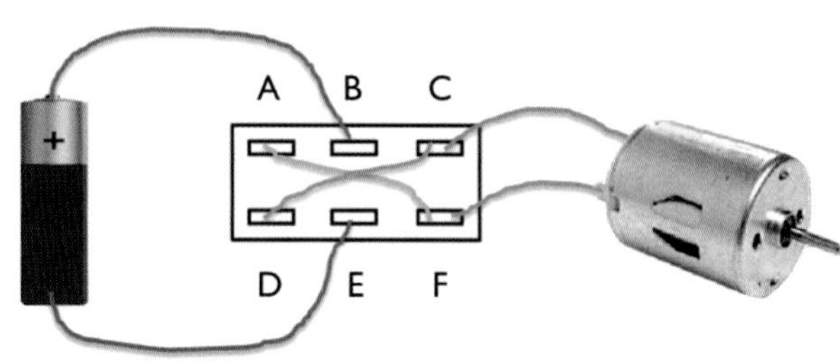

Explanation of the schematic diagram	Explanation of the wiring diagram
• When the switch is in the up position, current flows from B to A, through the motor and back to the power supply via D to E. This causes the motor to rotate in one direction. • When the switch is moved to the down position, the current flows from B to C, through the motor in the opposite direction than it did before and back to the power supply via F to E. This causes the motor to rotate in the opposite direction.	• The back of the DPDT switch, where you can see the six connections, is shown in the middle of the diagram. They are labelled the same way in both diagrams. • The switch operates like a slider: in one position it connects the middle two terminals to the left two terminals, and in the other position it connects the middle two terminals to the right two terminals.

Exercise: Study both of the diagrams on the previous page, understand them and see that they are showing the same thing.

Automatically stopping a motor using limit switches

In many technology applications and projects, a motor is used to move something, such as a door or gate. When the object gets to the end of its travel, the motor needs to be switched off. This can be done using limit switches, connected as shown in the diagrams below.

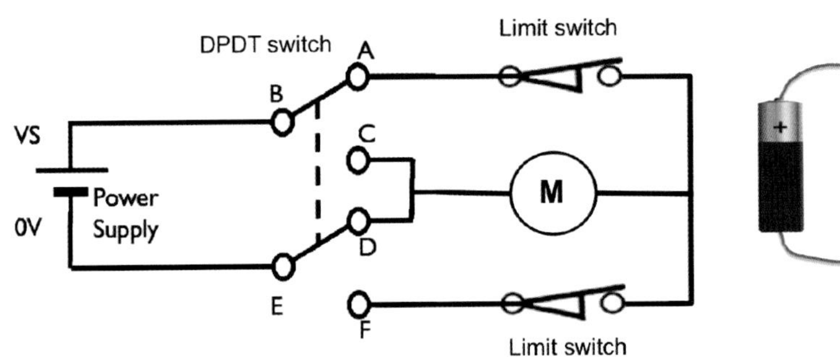

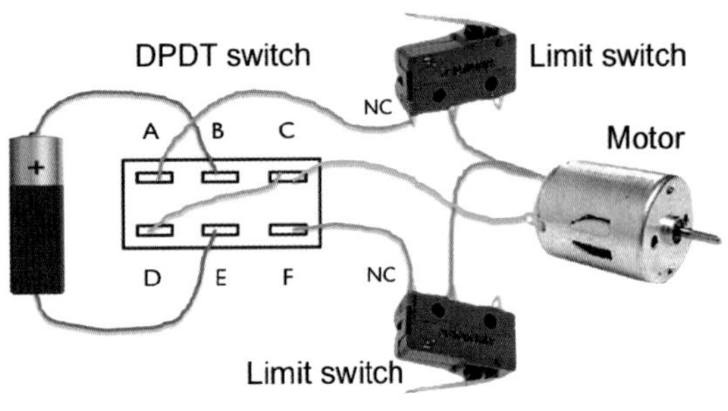

- The limit switch is placed so that when the object gets to the end of its travel, it pushes against the limit switch.
- This breaks the connection and the current and the motor stop.
- Next, the position of the DPDT switch is changed to reverse the direction of the motor.
- The object travels back the way it came (releasing the limit switch back to closed again).
- When it gets to the other end of its travel, the same thing happens again.
- The other limit switch is pressed, the connection is broken and the motor stops.

The limit switch is wired to the COM (common) and NC (normally-closed) connections, because we want the limit switch to be normally closed, and only open when it is pressed.

Activities with motors

Before carrying out the activity below you will need: a power supply, a small DC electric motor, a DPDT switch, two limit switches, some wire, a wire strippers, a soldering iron and solder, and teacher permission and assistance.

Activity: Build a reversible motor circuit with limit switches

To build the reversible motor circuit with limit switches shown in the previous section (using a power supply rather than a battery):

- If your school has the Circuit Wizard software, build and test the circuit using Circuit Wizard first.
- Strip and solder short lengths of wire on to the DPDT switch, limit switches and motor contacts as shown in the wiring diagram in the previous section. Include the wires to attach the power supply.
- Connect up the power supply. The motor should turn.
- Use the DPDT switch to reverse the rotation of the motor.
- Press on one of the limit switches. One of them will stop the motor (but it will start again when you release it).
- When you reverse the direction of the motor, it will be the other limit switch that stops the motor.
- Disconnect the power.

Past exam questions

1. A pictorial view of the components needed to drive a toy car is shown. Draw a circuit diagram for this system.

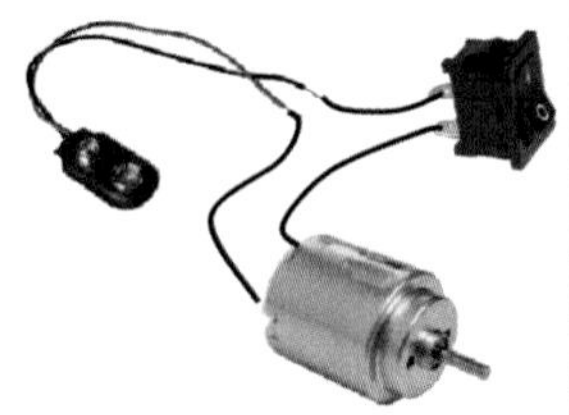

2. A number of symbols are shown. Select the correct symbols for a switch, battery and motor, and draw a circuit diagram for a motor circuit.

M

\+

3. A miniature motor is used to power a drive mechanism, and a variable resistor is used as a basic speed controller. Connect the components to show how this could be achieved.

Past exam questions

4. In a device, solar cells are used to power a motorised gearbox that in turn drives a rotating display. The gearbox, switch and one of the solar panels is shown below. Show how these components should be connected in order to power the motor.

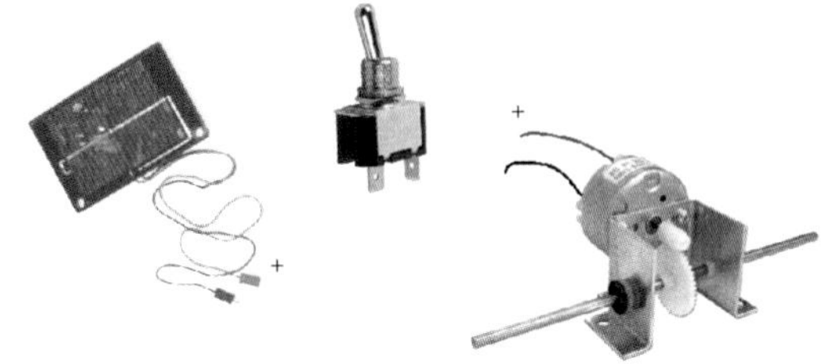

5. Using the symbols for the motor, DPDT switch and battery shown, indicate how the contacts on the switch should be wired to allow the motor to rotate clockwise or anticlockwise.

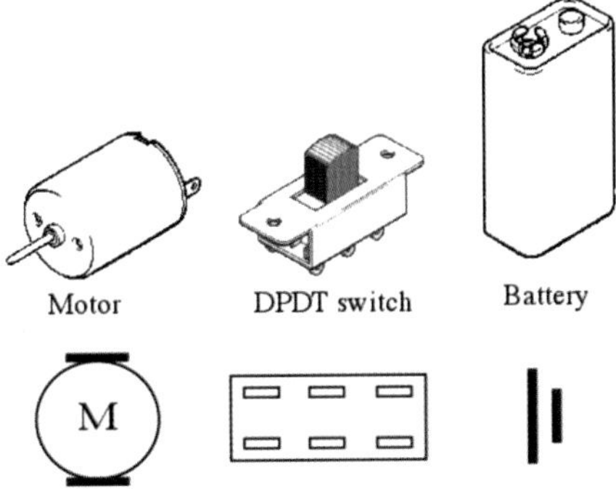

6. A door can be locked and unlocked, using a circuit constructed from the following components: a battery, a DPDT switch and a motor. Indicate how these components should be wired to allow the door to lock and unlock. Explain why limit switches should be used as part of the controlling circuit.

13 CHAPTER

Electronic circuits 2

Introduction

This chapter covers sensor circuits and timer circuits. It describes the use of transistors, diodes, relays and capacitors in those circuits. You will need to have studied "Electronic circuits 1" in order to understand this chapter.

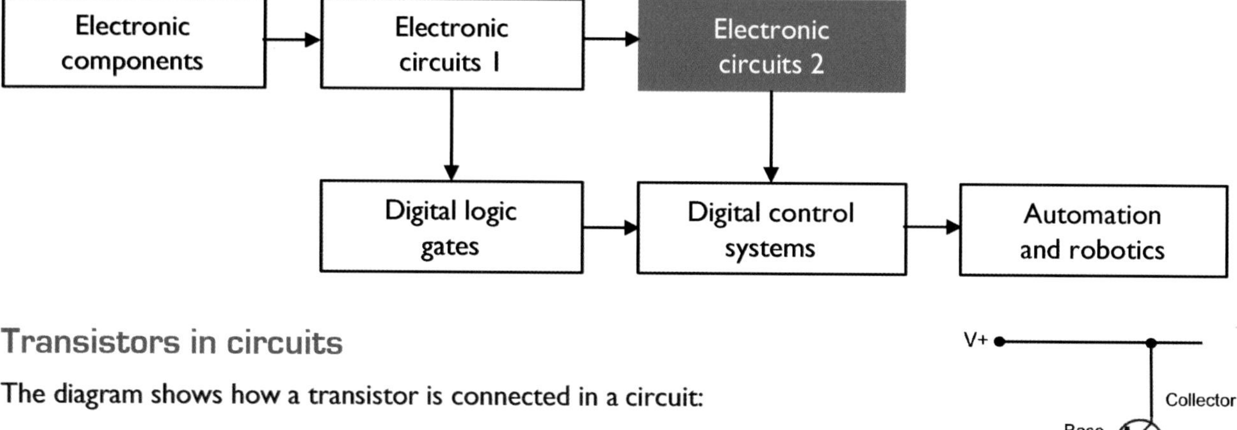

Transistors in circuits

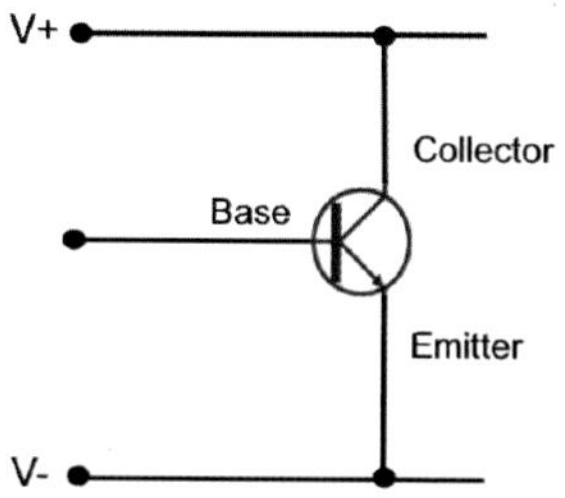

The diagram shows how a transistor is connected in a circuit:

- The emitter is connected to the negative (low) side of the power supply.
- The collector is connected to the positive (high) side of the power supply.
- The base is the controlling input, i.e. it determines what happens.

A transistor can be used as a current amplifier and as an electronic switch. The circuits in this chapter use the transistor as a switch. This means the transistor has two states: on and off.

> **Transistor off**
> A transistor is turned off, and no current flows between collector and emitter, when there is less than 0.6 volts between the base and the emitter.

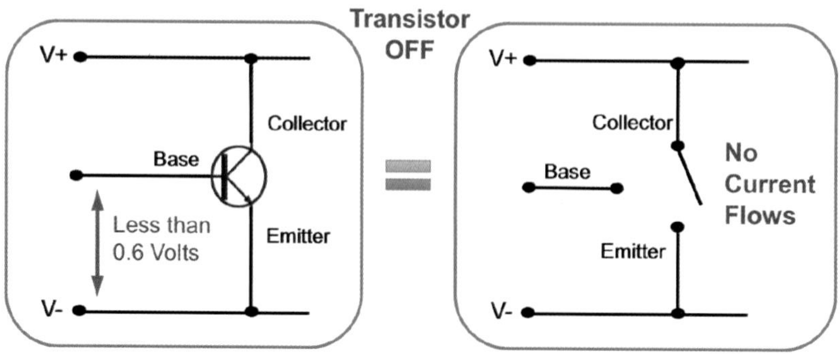

Transistor on

A transistor is turned on, and current flows between collector and emitter, when there is more than 0.6 volts between the base and the emitter.

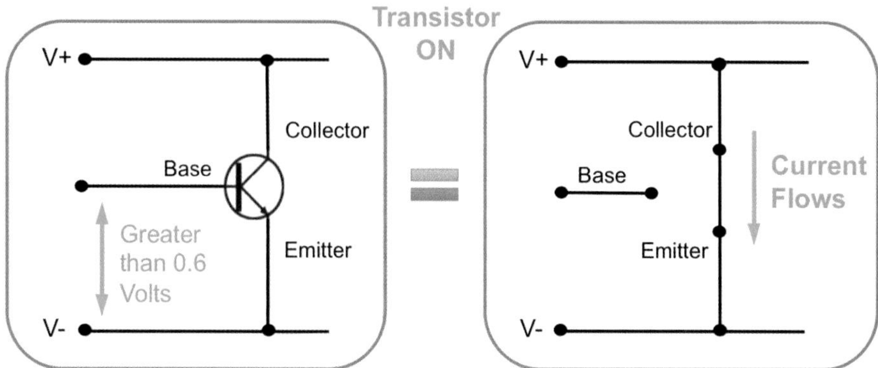

Benefit of using transistors

When a transistor is turned on, the base takes only a tiny amount of current. This means that we can cause a large amount of current to flow at the output, i.e. between the collector and the emitter, for the cost of only a small amount of current on the input, i.e. the base. Therefore the benefit of using a transistor is that the input itself doesn't have to supply the current to drive the output – the transistor does that.

In a real circuit, we can't allow a short circuit on the output, as it would burn out the transistor, so we need to add a resistor (or other load) to limit the current. This is explained below.

The basic transistor set-up circuit

The diagram below shows a common way to set up a transistor in a circuit. This transistor set-up is used for all the sensor circuits in this chapter.

- R1 and R2 form a potential divider (or voltage divider). This provides a voltage at point A to drive the base of the transistor.
- R3 limits the current going in to the base of the transistor from the voltage at point A.
- A resistor or other load is placed between the collector and the positive rail of the power supply.

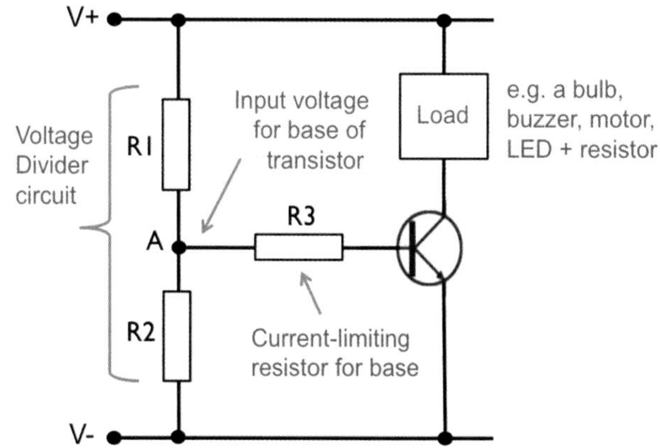

Using this basic set-up, we can use the transistor as a switch, by varying the voltage at point A. If we set a low voltage at A, the transistor will turn off and no current will flow through the load. If we set a high voltage at point A, the transistor will turn on and will conduct current through the load.

In circuit diagrams, the symbol used for the power supply can vary. It can be indicated as V+, Vs, Vcc, or as the actual voltage, e.g. 9 V. They all mean the same thing. Also sometimes 0 V is called "ground" or V-.

Sensor circuits

What is a sensor circuit?

A sensor circuit detects something changing in the real world, like temperature or water levels, and if the input exceeds a certain level, the sensor circuit causes something to happen on the output, such as turning on a light, buzzer, or making a motor move.

How do you make a sensor circuit?

A sensor circuit can be made using the basic transistor set-up circuit already described, and shown opposite, and by:

- Replacing one of the resistors in the voltage divider with a sensor component, e.g. LDR for light, thermistor for heat, or moisture probes for wetness.
- Choosing the type of output you want as the load, e.g. buzzer, motor, relay, or LED and resistor.

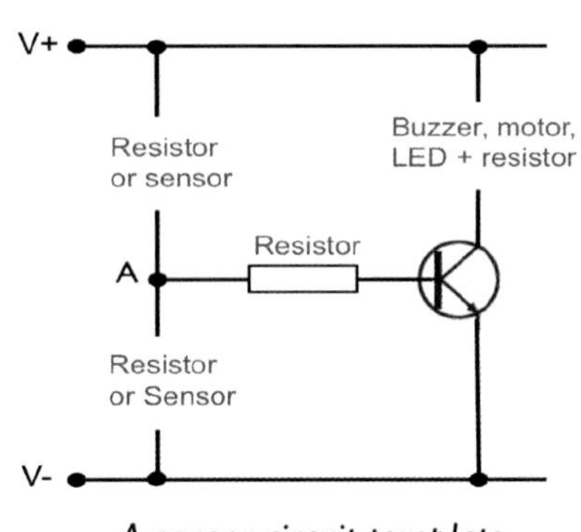

A sensor circuit template

The table below lists the main types of sensor circuits, the type of sensor used, and where it is placed in the voltage divider. Note that by swapping the position of the sensor and the resistor, you can change a darkness sensor into a light sensor, a heat sensor into a coldness sensor, and a wetness sensor into a dryness sensor.

Sensor circuit	Sensor component	Position in voltage divider
Light	**LDR** (high resistance in darkness)	Top
Darkness		Bottom
Heat	**Thermistor** (high resistance in cold conditions)	Top
Coldness		Bottom
Wetness	**Moisture probes** (high resistance in dry conditions)	Top
Dryness		Bottom

Darkness sensor circuit with an LED output

- In darkness, the LDR (R4) has high resistance, so the voltage will be high across the LDR. This turns on the transistor and current flows through the LED.
- R1 is the current-limiting resistor for the LED.
- In strong light, the resistance of the LDR will be very low, so the voltage across it will be too low to turn on the transistor. So the LED stays off.
- VR1 is a variable resistor. It is used to adjust the level of darkness at which the LDR will turn on the transistor, i.e. the amount of light or darkness needed.
- R3 makes sure that too much current doesn't flow through the LDR when VR1 is set to minimum.

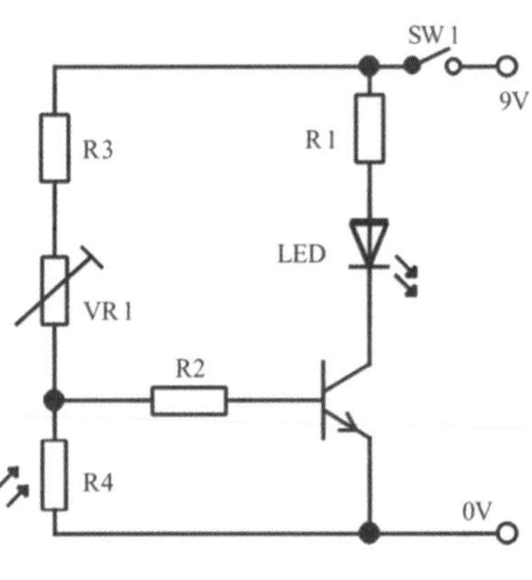

Darkess sensor circuit with a motor output

Worked example: Motorised night light

Past exam question

The graphic shows a motorised night light. The diagram shows an electronic circuit for the night light. The circuit will automatically turn on an LED and a motor to animate the figure in the design at night.

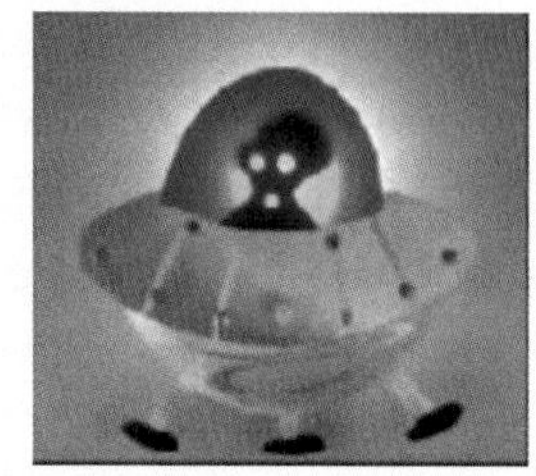

1. Explain the function of the fixed resistor R1 in the potential divider shown.
2. Explain the effect of swapping the positions of R1 and R2 in the circuit.
3. Explain the effect of swapping the positions of R2 and R3 in the circuit.
4. Explain the purpose of the fixed resistor R4 in the circuit.

Valid answers

1. The fixed resistor R1 prevents too much current flowing when R2 is set to a minimum, which could damage both R2 and R3.
2. Swapping the positions of R1 and R2 would have no effect. The combined resistance of the two would be the same.
3. Swapping the positions of R2 and R3 in the circuit would turn this darkness sensor into a light sensor, and the motor would run during the day.
4. The purpose of the fixed resistor R4 in the circuit is to limit the current flowing in to the base of the transistor, and to protect the transistor.

Diode across a motor

Note that the circuit above uses a reverse diode across the motor. This is done to prevent damage to the transistor when the motor stops. When current through a motor suddenly stops, the magnetic field in the motor tries to keep the current going. The diode allows the current to flow around until the magnetic field dies down. The current cannot flow through the transistor because it is off (open). If the diode is not there, a large voltage builds up which can damage the transistor.

The circuit also uses an LED pilot light to show that it is turned on.

Heat sensor with LED output

In the heat sensor circuit shown, note that the thermistor is at the top of the voltage divider.

- When the thermistor TH1 gets warm, its resistance decreases. This raises the voltage at the top of the present variable resistor VR1, which turns the transistor and the LED on.
- VR1 is used to adjust the level of heat needed in the thermistor to generate enough voltage across VR1 to turn on the transistor.

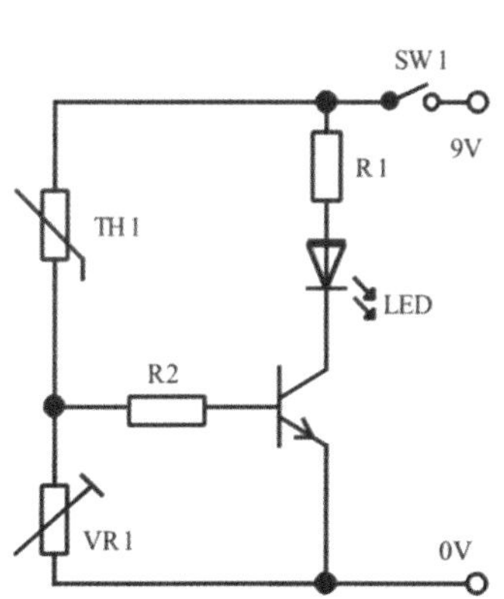

Heat sensor circuit with relay and motor output

The example below is from a previous Junior Cycle exam question, which uses a relay as an output.

Relays – how they work

A relay is an electrically operated switch. The diagram shows an SPDT (single-pole double-throw) relay. If you pass current through the coil on the left, it turns the coil into a magnet, which attracts the metal switch, pulling it over to make contact with the left hand contact/throw. If there is no current passing through the coil, the switch is kept connected to the right hand contact/pole via a spring mechanism.

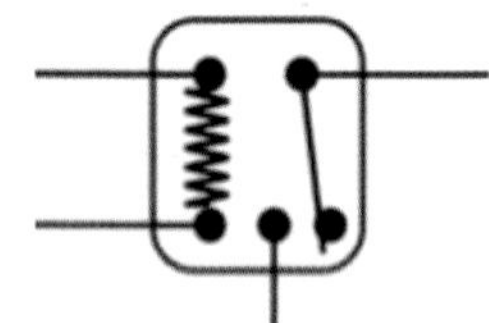

Advantages of a relay

Relays are used for safety reasons, to separate low-voltage circuits from high-voltage circuits. Using a relay, you can use a low-voltage circuit (e.g. powered by a battery) to switch on a high-voltage circuit (e.g. powered by mains electricity), without making any electrical connection between the circuits.

Worked example: Turn on a fan if the temperature is too high

Past exam question

The circuit shown is designed to automatically turn on a 12 V fan motor if high temperatures are detected by a sensing circuit.

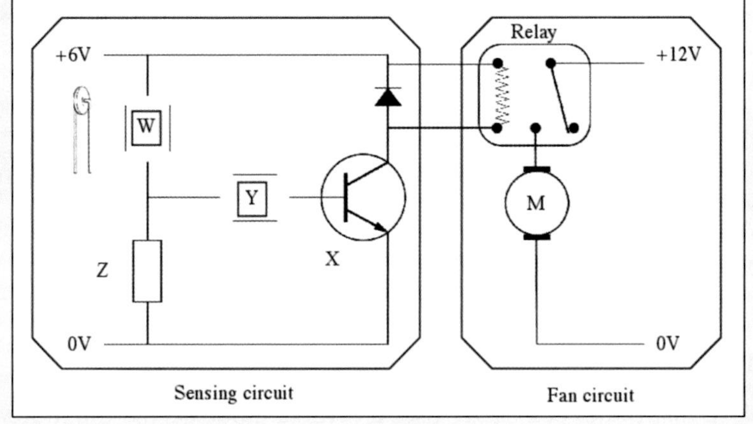

1. Sketch the electronic symbol for the thermistor W.
2. Explain the function of the transistor X in the circuit.
3. Name the missing component required at Y in the circuit.
4. Explain why a variable resistor is a recommended replacement for resistor Z.
5. Sketch a modification to the circuit to show the symbol and the most suitable location of an on/off switch for the sensing circuit.
6. Sketch a modification to the circuit to show the symbol and location of a green LED and a series resistor that will indicate that a working 6 V battery is connected to the sensing circuit.
7. Sketch a modification to the circuit to show the symbol and location of a red LED and a series resistor that will indicate that a high temperature has been detected by the sensing circuit.
8. What is the function of the series resistor in the LED circuit?

Valid answers

1. The symbol for the thermistor is shown at 'A' in the diagram below.
2. Transistor X is used as a current amplifier and as a switch. It allows a low current input to create a high output current.
3. The missing component at Y is a resistor. This is needed to limit the current to the base of the transistor.

Worked example: Turn on a fan if the temperature is too high

4. Using a variable resistor instead of fixed resistor Z would allow you to adjust the temperature at which the fan would come on.
5. The symbol for an on/off (SPST) switch would be added at location B.
6. The green pilot LED and resistor would be added after the on/off switch at location C.
7. The red LED and resistor could be added in two places. Either at location D, or in parallel with the relay and diode. (If you add the red LED at location D it affects the level at which the transistor turns on so you would have to adjust resistor Z to compensate.)
8. The function of the series resistor in the LED circuit is to limit the current through the LED.

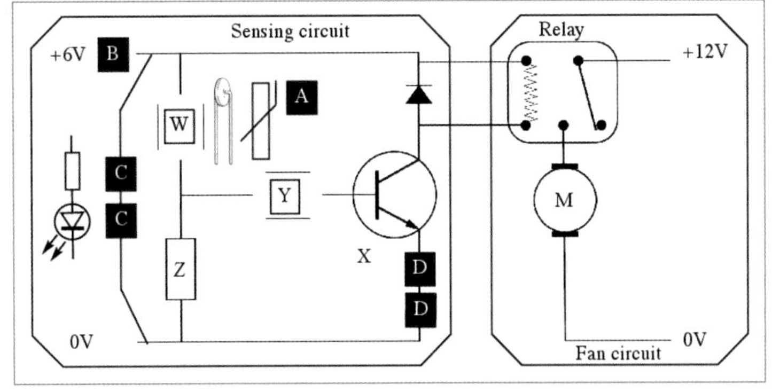

Wetness sensor circuit with an LED output

In wet conditions, the moisture probes have low resistance. This results in a high voltage across R3, turning on the transistor and the LED.

In dry conditions, the probes have high resistance, lowering the voltage across R3 and turning off the transistor and the LED.

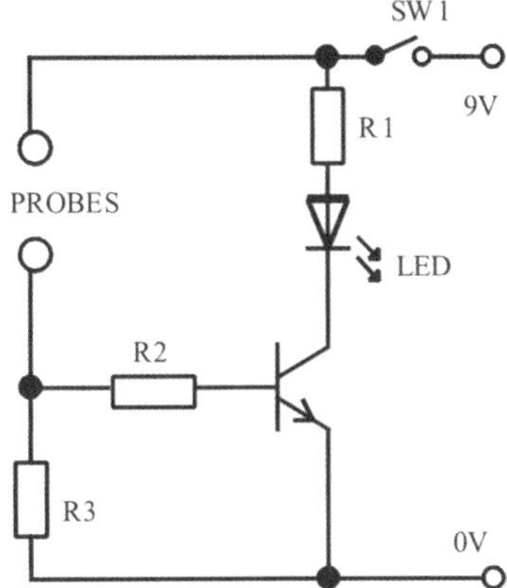

Wetness sensor circuit with a buzzer output

Worked example: A bathwater level sensor

Past exam question

An electronic circuit for a bathwater level sensor, and a housing for the completed device, are shown. The device will alert the user when the water level in a bath reaches a set height.

1. Identify the component at X.
2. Name and sketch the symbol for the additional component required at Z to prevent component X from damaging the transistor.
3. Explain why component U is required in the circuit.
4. Explain what is meant by a potential divider and outline why a potential divider is required.

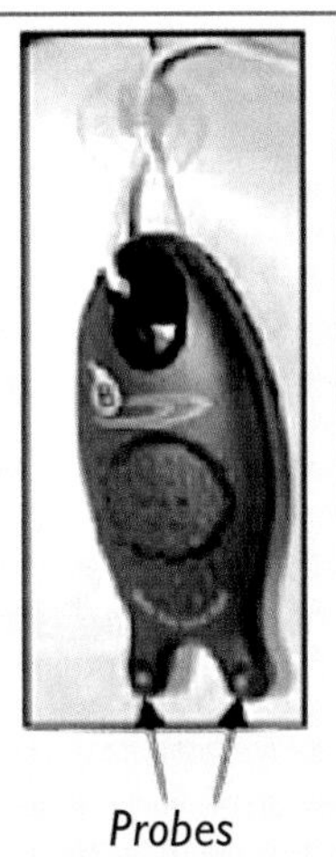
Probes

Worked example: A bathwater level sensor

Valid answers

1. The component at X is a buzzer.
2. The additional component at Z is a diode. Here is the symbol for a diode:

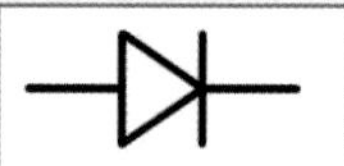

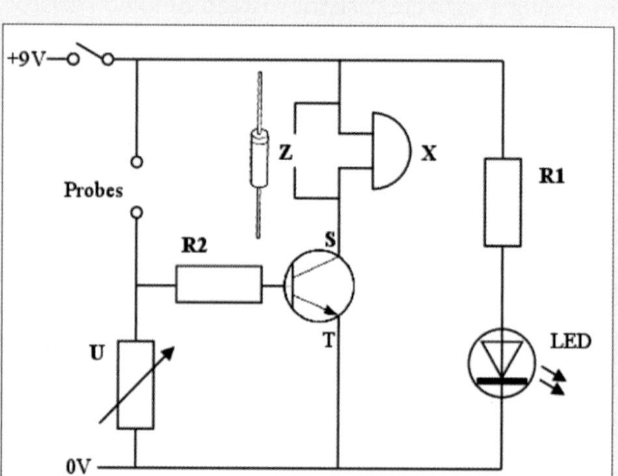

3. Component U is a variable resistor. This is used to adjust the sensitivity of the circuit, i.e. the level of wetness that will cause the buzzer to sound.
4. A potential divider is used to create a voltage in between the power supply voltage and 0 V.

   The potential divider is used in this circuit to turn the transistor on and off.

Activities: Build a darkness sensor with LED output

The circuit diagram for this activity is shown below.

- If you have Circuit Wizard software, create and test the circuit using the computer.
- Use a breadboard to assemble the components.
- Alternatively, you can buy specialised small sensor PCBs and assemble the circuit using those, by soldering in the components.
- Use the following values for the components.

Component	Value	Component	Value
R1	470 Ω	R4	LDR
R2	2.2 kΩ	LED	5 mm std
R3	1 kΩ	Transistor	BC108
VR1	47 kΩ	Switch	Toggle

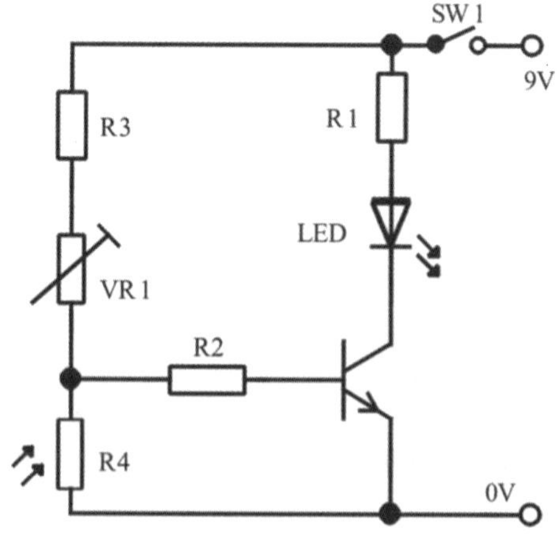

- Turn on the switch. The LED should not light.
- Cover the LDR with your finger to simulate darkness. The LED should light.
- If the LED does not light, try adjusting the sensitivity of the circuit using VR1.
- Double check all connections, and check that the LED and the power are connected the right way round.

Past exam questions

1. A company producing solar panels wishes to give a child's nightlight to each of its customers for advertising purposes. Two LEDs light up a display panel on which is placed a logo representing the company. An LDR is used in the control circuit of the nightlight. Explain the term LDR and suggest why it is needed.

2. The circuit shown below is designed to turn on a water pump if low water levels are detected in a fish tank.

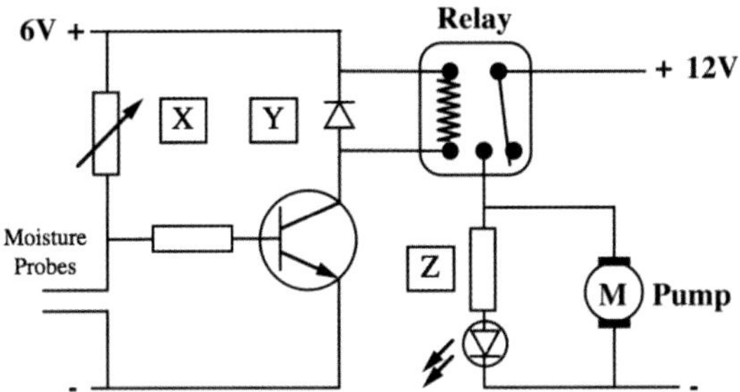

   a. Identify the component labelled "X" and state the function of this component in the circuit.
   b. Explain how the circuit would function if component "X" and the moisture probes were interchanged in the circuit.
   c. Identify the component labelled "Y" in the circuit.
   d. Label the emitter of the transistor in the above diagram.
   e. Name the type of relay shown in the circuit above and explain why a relay is required in the circuit.
   f. Calculate the required value for resistor "Z" from the following LED data: LED V_f = 2 V and LED I_{max} = 20 mA.

3. A student is required to manufacture a working model of a motorised car park barrier as shown in the diagram. The barrier will be opened by a security keycard. Explain why a DPDT relay and limit switches are recommended in the design.

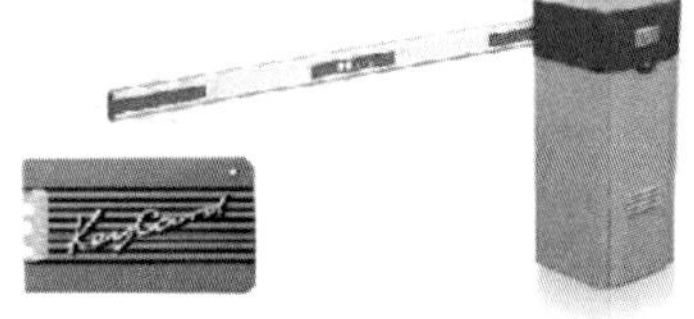

4. The components shown below are available to manufacture a water sensor as part of a flood warning system. Using these components, sketch a circuit diagram to include:
   - An on/off switch with an LED power on indicator.
   - A sensor circuit, which will activate the buzzer when rising water levels are detected.

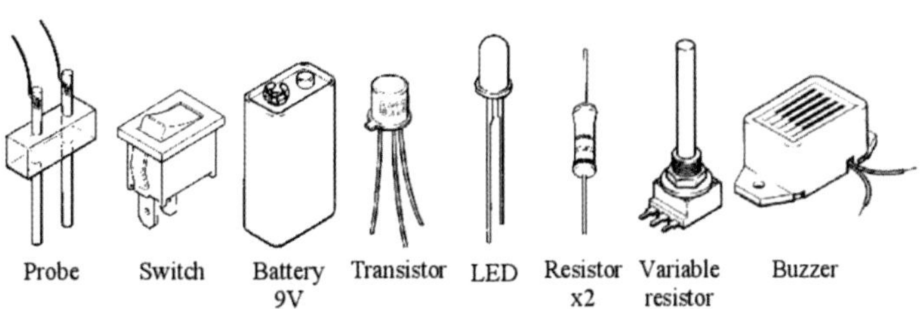

Timer circuits

A timer circuit is one where things happen after a certain time has elapsed. In timer circuits, capacitors are used to measure time, because they take a certain amount of time to charge up, and to discharge.

A basic transistor timer circuit

The circuit shown is the familiar transistor set-up circuit that we used for sensors. However the bottom resistor of the voltage divider has now been replaced with a capacitor. What happens?

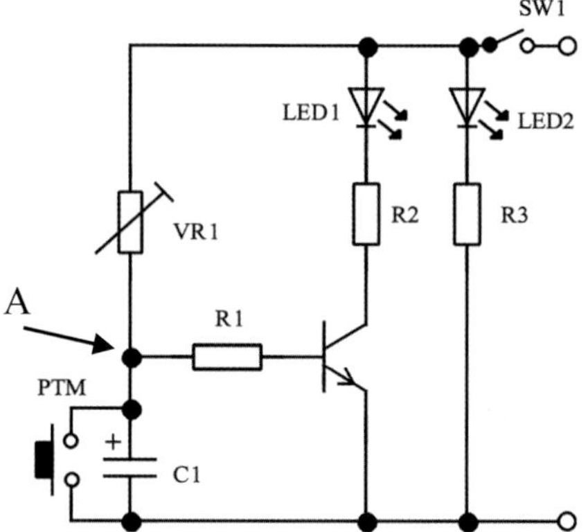

When the switch is closed, LED2 lights, but LED1 does not. After a while, LED1 lights. Why?

- When the switch is closed, the capacitor C1 starts charging up, via the current supplied through VR1. This means the voltage at point A, at the top of the capacitor, starts to rise.
- After a certain time the voltage reaches the required level to turn on the transistor, and LED1 lights.
- The voltage of the capacitor continues to rise until it is the same as the power supply, and fully charged. At this point no more current can flow in to the capacitor.
- If you press the switch PTM, the capacitor discharges quickly. All the charge in the capacitor escapes/ flows as current back to the power supply. The voltage at A goes back to 0 V again. This means that there is not enough voltage to keep the transistor turned on, and LED1 goes out.
- When you release the switch PTM, the cycle starts all over again: the capacitor starts to charge up, and LED1 will light again after a while, and will stay on until you press PTM again.

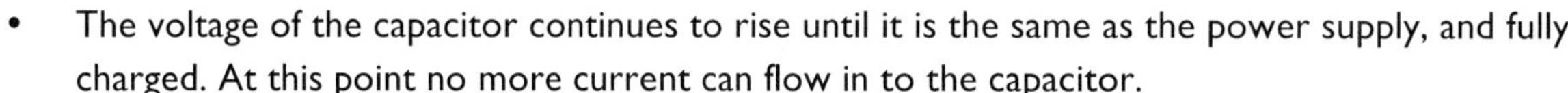

You can see the benefit of using the transistor in the above circuit – the base of the transistor only takes a tiny current so it doesn't affect the capacitor charging up.

Time for a capacitor to charge up

The length of time it takes a capacitor to charge up is dependent on the size of the capacitor, and the size of the resistor supplying the charging current. The larger the capacitor, the more charge it can take, and the longer it takes to charge up. Also, the larger the resistor, the less current is being supplied into the capacitor, and the longer it takes to charge up. So the combination of a large capacitor and a large resistance gives you the longest charge time.

An oscillator circuit

The following worked example shows an oscillator circuit which has appeared as a previous Junior Cert exam question. It uses two capacitors that take turns to charge up and to turn on and off two transistors and LEDs in turn. To explain how this circuit works in detail is beyond the scope of this book, and it is not necessary for you to understand how it works in detail. This example is included here to show you that you have the knowledge to answer questions on circuits like this.

The answers to the full exam questions often require knowledge from "Electronic circuits 1" and "Electronic components" as well as from this chapter.

Wetness sensor circuit with a buzzer output

Worked example: A flashing LED circuit

Past exam question

The diagram shows the component layout for a flashing LED circuit. (LED1 on, LED2 off, LED1 off, LED2 on)

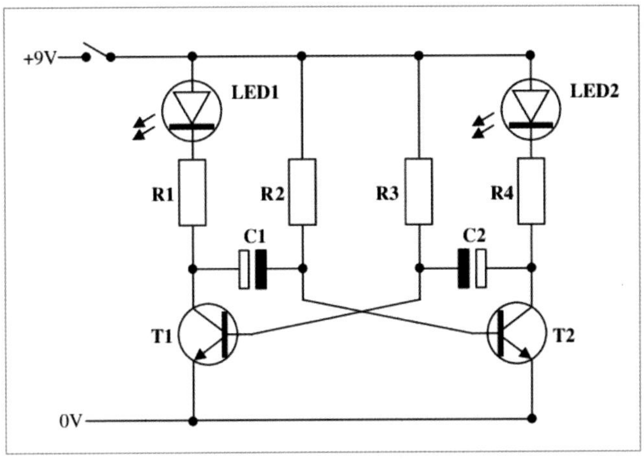

1. LED1 has the following values: V_f = 2 V and Imax = 0.02 A. Calculate the required value of R1 in the circuit.
2. The required value of resistor R2 is 47 kΩ. Use the resistor colour codes shown below to determine the colour bands of this resistor.
3. Identify the components shown at C1 and C2.
4. What unit is used to measure the value of C1 and C2?
5. What effect will increasing the value of these components have on the operation of the circuit?

Resistor Colour Codes	
Black	0
Brown	1
Red	2
Orange	3
Yellow	4
Green	5
Blue	6
Violet	7
Grey	8
White	9

Valid answers

1. The maximum current will flow in LED1 when transistor T1 is turned on. When a transistor is turned on, it acts like a short circuit (a wire). So it is as though the bottom of R1 is connected to 0 V. So the voltage across R1 is 9 V minus the 2 V across the LED. The max current is 0.02 A so we can work out the resistance needed using Ohm's Law.

$$R = \frac{(\text{power supply} - \text{LED voltage})}{\text{desired current}} = \frac{9\text{ V} - 2\text{ V}}{0.02\text{ A}} = \frac{7\text{ V}}{0.02\text{ A}} = 350\ \Omega$$

2. The colour bands of a 47 kΩ resistor are yellow (4), violet (7) and orange (three zeros).
3. C1 and C2 are capacitors.
4. Farads are the units used to measure the values of C1 and C2 (capacitance).
5. Increasing the value of C1 and C will increase the charging time, and therefore increase the time for "on" and "off" states, i.e. the LEDs will flash more slowly.

555 timer IC

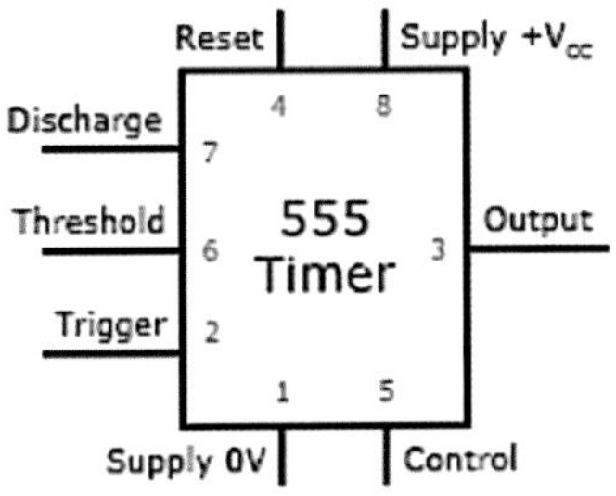

Due to the frequent need for timing circuits, manufacturers of ICs (integrated circuits) have developed a chip called a "555 timer", which is very widely used. The 555 chip can be connected in different ways to perform different timing functions. The schematic for the 555 is shown opposite.

It shows the three main inputs on the left, and the single output on the right.

Inputs and outputs of the 555 timer chip

The pinout (arrangement of the pins and their functions) of the 8-pin 555 timer IC is shown. The inputs to the chip (pins 2, 6 and 7) are analog. This means that they can be at any voltage between 0 V and the power supply voltage.

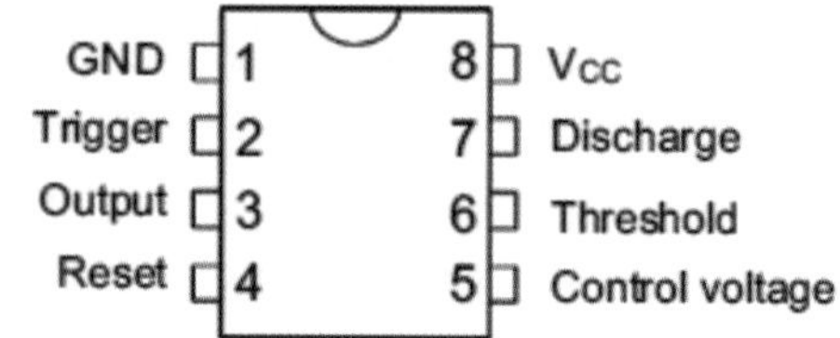

The output of the 555 timer chip (pin 3) is digital. This means that it that it can only be in one of two states: off (at 0 V) or on (at the power supply voltage).

We have seen this analog and digital behaviour already in the basic transistor circuits where the inputs vary in voltage (via sensors or capacitors), but the output is always either on or off.

Uses of the 555 timer chip

The 555 can be used to generate a single or delayed output signal when an input signal changes, or it can be used to generate a continuous on-and-off output (like the oscillator circuit we saw in the previous example).

Building a timer circuit using a 555 timer

"112 working circuits" is a set of electronic projects issued by stem.org.uk, which are suitable to be built by school students. The documentation for each circuit provides the schematic diagram, and explanation of the circuit, and the values of the components to use.

Activity: Build a timer circuit using a 555 timer

Choose one of the 555 timer circuits from "112 working circuits". If you have Circuit Wizard software, create and test the timer circuit using the computer, before you build the circuit physically using real components.

Answering exam questions on 555 timer circuits

It is beyond the scope of this book to explain how a 555 timer chip works in detail, and it is not necessary for you to understand this. 555 timers are usually connected in a standard set of ways, and the exam question will show you the entire circuit diagram and ask you a few questions about it. Your knowledge of the components and the concepts will be sufficient to answer the questions. Here are a few pointers to help you:

- The timing of the circuit is always determined by the capacitors and charging resistors that are connected to input pins 2, 6 and/or 7. To increase the time, increase the size (value) of the capacitor, and/or increase the value of the resistor that is charging the capacitor from the power supply.
- Ignore any capacitor that is connected to pin 5. This is only for the internal operation of the chip and has nothing to do with setting the timing.
- Pin 3 is the output, and can be connected to LEDs, bulbs, buzzers, motors, and relays, in similar circuits to the basic transistor circuit we used earlier. However, unlike the transistor circuit, the output of the 555 can also be used to push current out when it is high (V+), as well as take current in when it is low (0 V). This dual use is shown in the following worked examples.

Worked example: A time delay circuit using a 555 timer IC

Past exam question

The sketch shows an electronic circuit for a flashing LED circuit, to be mounted on the underside of a skateboard. (LED1 will flash, then LED2 will flash, then the sequence repeats.)

1. Using a sketch, explain how the pins 1 and 5 can be identified on the 555 IC.
2. The circuit requires an on/off switch. Indicate clearly where this switch should be placed in the circuit.
3. State two advantages to placing this circuit on a PCB instead of using copper strip board.

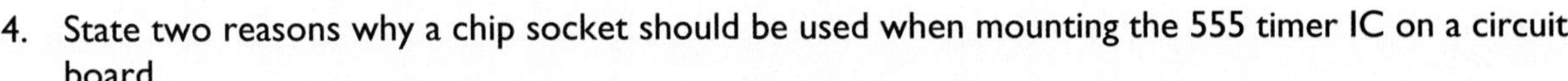

4. State two reasons why a chip socket should be used when mounting the 555 timer IC on a circuit board.
5. Blue LEDs will be used in this circuit. (Blue LED Vf = 3 V, Imax = 20 mA). Explain why protective resistors R3 are required for the LEDs.
6. Additional LEDs and resistors can be attached to the circuit in parallel with LED1 and LED2. Explain why these extra LEDs should be connected in parallel, and not in series.

Valid answers

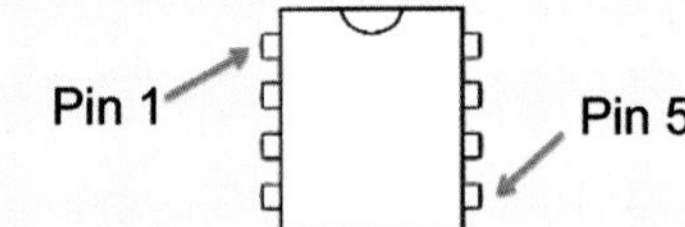

1. Pin 1 is to the left of the notch.
   Pins count anti-clockwise from pin 1.
2. The on/off switch should be placed in the top left of the circuit, between the power supply and all other components.
3. Advantages of placing this circuit on a PCB instead of using copper strip board:
   - It is faster to assemble the circuit on a pre-made PCB.
   - Errors are less likely to occur if the circuit is assembled on a pre-made PCB.
   - The circuit can fit in a smaller space using a pre-made PCB.
4. Reasons why a chip socket should be used when mounting the 555 timer IC on a circuit board:
   - It prevents damage to the IC that could be caused by soldering the IC in directly.
   - It is easy to insert and take out the IC. The IC can be replaced easily if necessary.
5. Protective resistors R3 are required for the LEDs, in order to protect them against too much current.
6. Extra LEDs should be connected in parallel with LED1 and LED2, because if they were connected in series, there would a total of 6 V lost across the two LEDs (2 x V_f), so there would be no voltage left to drive current through the LEDs.

Worked example: A time delay circuit to conserve water

Past exam question

In order to help conserve water use in a shower, the 555 timer circuit shown will be used to indicate that 4 minutes have passed. The timing circuit, when started by pushing the PTM switch, with turn on the green LED for 4 minutes and after that time will turn on the red LED.

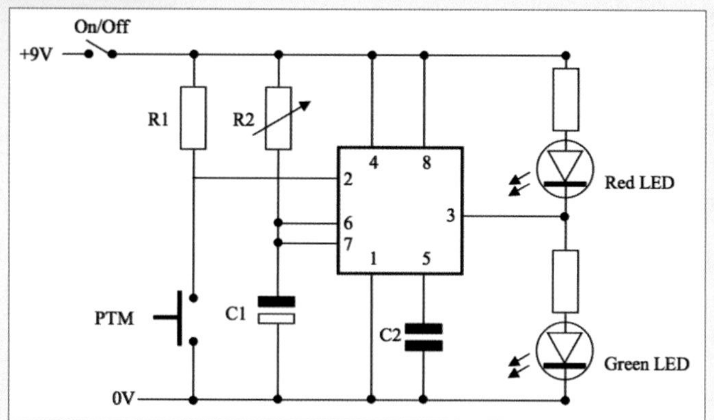

1. Explain the purpose of the notch on the 555 chip (see image below).
2. Explain why the use of a chip socket is recommended when soldering this circuit.
3. State two advantages of using a printed circuit board over copper stripboard to make this circuit.
4. Explain the difference between the on/off and PTM switches.
5. How could the 4 minute delay time be increased?
6. What change could be made to the circuit to produce a sound after the 4 minutes have passed?

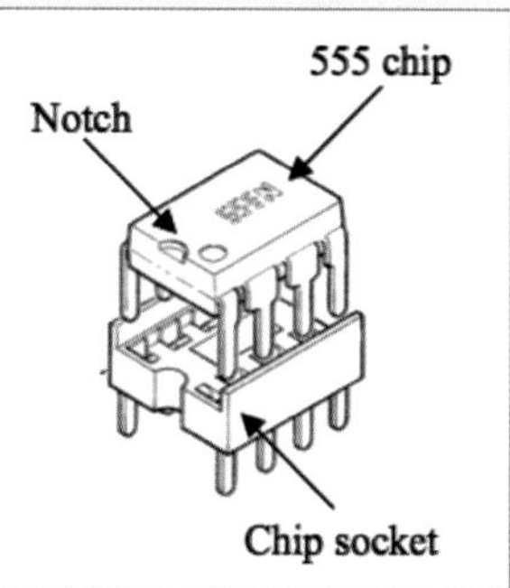

Valid answers

1. The purpose of the notch on the 555 chip is to indicate where pin 1 is.
2. A chip socket is recommended to prevent possible damage to the IC by soldering it in directly.
3. Advantages of using a printed circuit board over copper strip board to make this circuit:
   - It is faster to assemble the circuit on a pre-made PCB.
   - Errors are less likely to occur if the circuit is assembled on a pre-made PCB.
   - The circuit can fit in a smaller space using a pre-made PCB.
4. Difference between the on/off and PTM switches:
   - Once you set the on/off (SPST) switch to either the on or the off position, it will stay on or off, until you change it again.
   - The PTM is a push-to-make switch. When you push the button with your finger, it closes the connection. When you take your finger off the button, the button springs back and the connection is open again.
5. The 4 minute delay time could be increased by turning the variable resistor R2 so that it provides more resistance. If R2 was at maximum resistance, you could increase the delay time by using a larger value capacitor for C1.
6. The circuit could be changed to produce a sound after the 4 minutes have passed by attaching a buzzer in parallel with the red LED and resistor.

CHAPTER 14

Digital logic gates

Introduction

This chapter explains what logic gates are, what they do, and how to combine them to make digital circuits. It explains how to make sense of logic gates and digital circuits using ones and zeros.

You should complete the "Electronic circuits 1" chapter before starting this one.

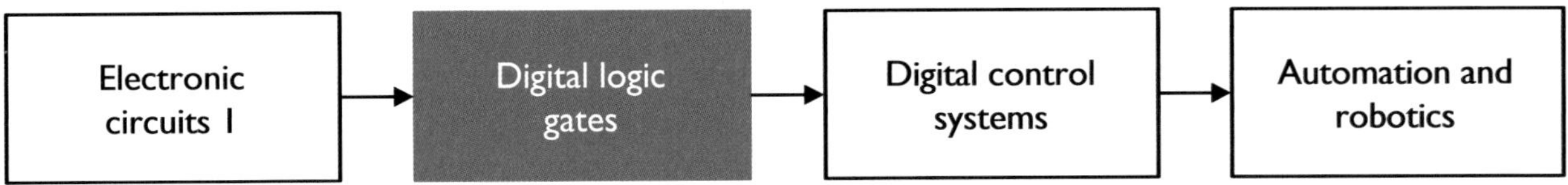

Logic gates as digital systems

Our lives are hugely influenced by digital systems such as computers, smartphones and the Internet. But what does the word "digital" mean?

In a digital device, all inputs and outputs and internal signals are either "on" or "off". There is no in-between state. For example, in a digital circuit powered by a 6 volt battery, 6 V would represent "on", and 0 V would represent "off". There are no values between 0 V and 6 V in the circuit.

Digital sound mixer

All parts in a digital circuit operate like switches and they are either "on" or "off".

Ones and zeros

An easier way of describing and working with digital systems is to say their values can only be "1" (one) or "0" (zero). Dealing only with ones and zeros also makes it easier to calculate outputs.

Digital systems and logic gates

The smallest, and most basic component of a digital system is called a logic gate. Digital systems are made up of many logic gates. The CPU (the main chip) that powers your computer or smartphone may contain hundreds of millions of logic gates.

Logic gates are called logic gates because they act like "gates" to control which input signals are allowed to get to the outputs. The word logic comes from the calculation system used for ones and zeros.

Logic gates and truth tables

A logic gate has one or two inputs, and one output. Because a logic gate is a digital device, its inputs and outputs are always ones or zeros. The operation of a logic gate is fully described using a truth table.

A truth table tells you what the value of the outputs will be for every possible combination of input values. The symbols and truth tables for each logic gate are shown below. A and B are inputs and Y is the output.

Name of gate	Symbol	Description	Truth table
NOT	A → NOT → Y	The output is the inverse (opposite) of the input: • If the input is a 1, the output is a 0. • If the input is a 0, the output is a 1.	A / Y: 0 / 1; 1 / 0
AND	A, B → AND → Y	The output is 1 when both A AND B are 1. It works like two switches in series. (+6 V, A, B, Q, 0 V)	A / B / Y: 0 / 0 / 0; 0 / 1 / 0; 1 / 0 / 0; 1 / 1 / 1
OR	A, B → OR → Y	The output is a 1 if either A OR B are 1. It works like two switches in parallel. (+6 V, A, B, Q, 0 V)	A / B / Y: 0 / 0 / 0; 0 / 1 / 1; 1 / 0 / 1; 1 / 1 / 1
NAND	A, B → NAND → Y	A NAND gate is an AND gate followed by a NOT gate. The output is 0 only if both inputs are 1.	A / B / Y: 0 / 0 / 1; 0 / 1 / 1; 1 / 0 / 1; 1 / 1 / 0
NOR	A, B → NOR → Y	A NOR gate is an OR gate followed by a NOT gate. The output is 0 if either input is 1.	A / B / Y: 0 / 0 / 1; 0 / 1 / 0; 1 / 0 / 0; 1 / 1 / 0

A truth table for a logic gate shows the value of the outputs for every possible combination of inputs.

Test yourself

1. What is a truth table? What does it tell you?
2. Which logic gate outputs a 1 only if its two inputs are 1?
3. What is the value of the output Y below?

4. What is the value of the output Y below?

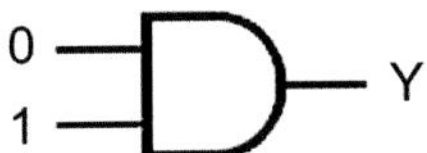

5. What is the value of the output Y below?

0
1
Y

6. What is the output of a NOR gate if one of the inputs is a 0 and the other is a 1?
7. If one of the inputs to an AND gate is a 0, what happens to the output if you change the other input?
8. What is the value of the output Y below?

1
1
Y

9. What is the value of the output Y below?

10. What is the value of the output Y below?

Combining logic gates

Logic gates become more useful when you put them together in combinations to make logic circuits. This is done by connecting the output of one gate to the input of another. The "Digital control systems" chapter provides lots of examples of connecting logic gates together to do practical things.

To work out the output when you have multiple logic gates connected together, start at the inputs and work your way through the gates from the first to the last. Calculate the outputs of each gate in turn, using the truth tables for each gate.

Calculating the output of a combination of logic gates

The examples below show how to calculate the output of a combination of logic gates. To make it easier to explain, intermediate outputs are labelled with an "X". Note that intermediate outputs are not usually labelled in examination questions, but you can label them yourself if it helps you.

Worked example 1: Calculate the output of a combination of logic gates

Question

What is the value of Y in the logic circuit shown?

1, 0 → X → Y

Solution

Using the truth table of the first OR gate, its output (X) must be 1, because one of the inputs to the OR gate is 1.

If X is 1, then the output of the NOT gate (Y) must be a 0.

This circuit is the same as a NOR gate.

Worked example 2: Calculate the output of a combination of logic gates

Question

What is the value of Y in the logic circuit shown?

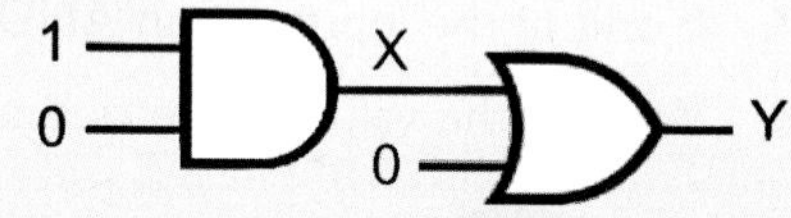

Solution

Using the truth table for the first (AND) gate, its output (X) must be 0 because only one of the inputs to the AND gate is 1.

The inputs to the second (OR) gate are now 0 and 0. Using the truth table for the OR gate, the output of the OR gate (Y) must be 0.

Truth tables for combinations of logic gates

If you are asked to provide or complete a truth table for a combination of logic gates, you will need to have or create a table with one column for each input and output. You can add intermediate outputs to the truth table also, to make the calculations easier. This is explained below.

Worked example 3: Truth table for a NAND gate with both inputs connected

Question

Provide a truth table for the logic circuit shown.

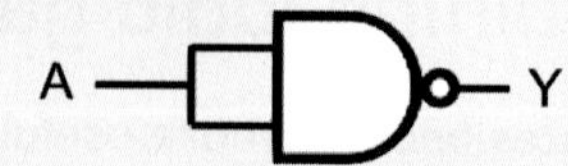

Solution

Although the gate is an NAND gate, both inputs are connected together, so it operates differently:

- When A is 0, both inputs to the NAND gate are 0, and so the output Y is 1.
- When A is 1, both inputs are 1, and so the output Y is 0.
- Here is the truth table:

A	Y
0	1
1	0

We can see from the truth table in the last example that a NAND gate with both inputs connected together, operates as a NOT gate. The same happens using a NOR gate.

NAND and NOR gates are often used as NOT gates. This is because individual ICs can contain many NAND or NOR gates. If some of these gates are not in use, they can be used as NOT gates. This avoids having to add another IC component into the circuit just to get a NOT gate.

Worked example 4: Truth table for multiple logic gates

Question

Provide a truth table for the logic circuit shown.

Solution

Step 1 – Draw a table with columns for all inputs (A, B, C), intermediate outputs (W, X) and output (Y). Fill in all the possible values for the inputs.

A	B	C	W	X	Y
0	0	0			
0	0	1			
0	1	0			
0	1	1			
1	0	0			
1	0	1			
1	1	0			
1	1	1			

Step 2 – Using the truth table for the OR gate, write in the values for W depending on the values of A and B.

A	B	C	W	X	Y
0	0	0	0		
0	0	1	0		
0	1	0	1		
0	1	1	1		
1	0	0	1		
1	0	1	1		
1	1	0	1		
1	1	1	1		

Step 3 – Using the truth table for the NOT gate, write in the values for X depending on the value of W.

A	B	C	W	X	Y
0	0	0	0	1	
0	0	1	0	1	
0	1	0	1	0	
0	1	1	1	0	
1	0	0	1	0	
1	0	1	1	0	
1	1	0	1	0	
1	1	1	1	0	

Step 4 – Using the truth table for the AND gate, write in the values for Y depending on the values of C and X.

A	B	C	W	X	Y
0	0	0	0	1	0
0	0	1	0	1	1
0	1	0	1	0	0
0	1	1	1	0	0
1	0	0	1	0	0
1	0	1	1	0	0
1	1	0	1	0	0
1	1	1	1	0	0

Worked example 4: Truth table for multiple logic gates

Step 5 – The final truth table should consist of the input columns A, B and C, and the output column Y.

You can delete the intermediate outputs W and X from the table.

A	B	C	W	X	Y
0	0	0	0	I	0
0	0	I	0	I	I
0	I	0	I	0	0
0	I	I	I	0	0
I	0	0	I	0	0
I	0	I	I	0	0
I	I	0	I	0	0
I	I	I	I	0	0

Step 6 – The final truth table. Notice that you can only turn the output on with one combination of inputs. Which combination of inputs does this?

A	B	C	Y
0	0	0	0
0	0	I	I
0	I	0	0
0	I	I	0
I	0	0	0
I	0	I	0
I	I	0	0
I	I	I	0

Making any logic circuit with NAND or NOR gates

We saw above that we can make a NOT gate using a NAND gate. In fact we can make any other logic gate (and therefore any logic circuit) using only NAND gates (or only using NOR gates).

Complete the truth table for the circuit below, and see if you can recognise what it represents.

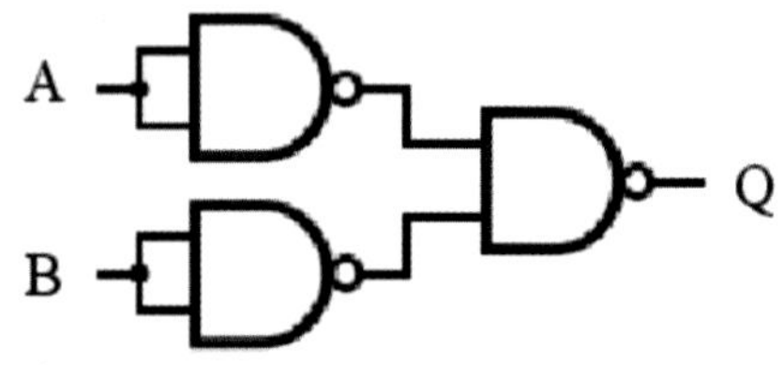

A	B	Q
0	0	
0	I	
I	0	
I	I	

Did you find that the above circuit has the same truth table as an OR gate? To make a NOR gate from NAND gates, just add another NOT gate (made from a NAND gate) to the end of the above circuit for an OR gate. How would you create an AND gate from two NAND gates?

Latches

Latches are a set of logic circuits that have "memory", i.e. their output can stay the same even if you take away or change the input. This is useful in lots of situations. For example, if a house alarm goes off because a burglar opened a window, it is important that the alarm continues to ring even if the burglar closes the window.

There are many types of latch circuits. The simplest one can be made with an OR gate, as shown. This works as follows:

- Input A and output Y are both 0 to start.
- If A goes to 1, then Y must go to 1 (because it is an OR gate).
- If A goes back to 0, Y will still stay at 1. This is because output Y is connected back to input B, and as long as one input to an OR gate is a 1, then the output will be a 1.

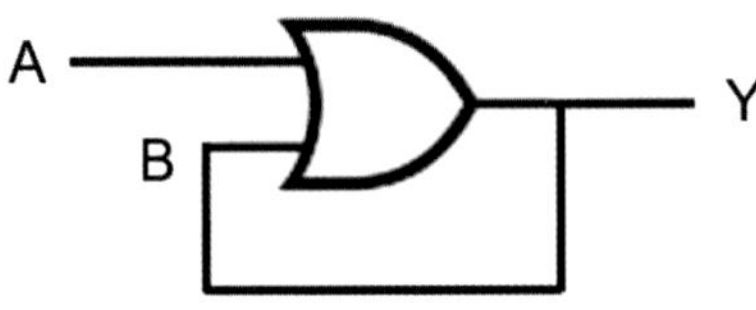

A latch made from an OR gate

Resetting the latch

When the latch circuit above has been triggered, i.e. by the input A going to 1, the output Y will stay at 1 forever (even if input A changes). How do we get the output back to 0 again, so we can re-use the circuit as a latch?

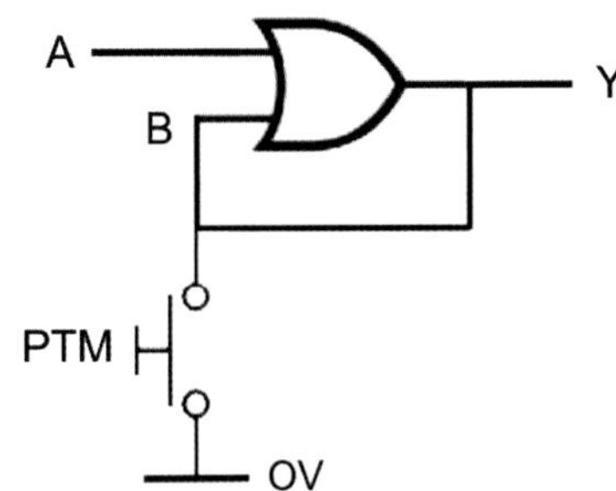

This can be done by using the modification opposite. If you press the PTM switch, it will make input B go to 0. Now both A and B are 0, so the output Y will be at 0 when you release the switch, and will remain at 0 until the latch is triggered again.

Packaging of logic gates

Logic gates are built using transistors, and are packaged inside ICs. The graphic opposite shows how four OR gates packaged inside a 14-pin IC chip are connected to the different pins (legs) of the chip.

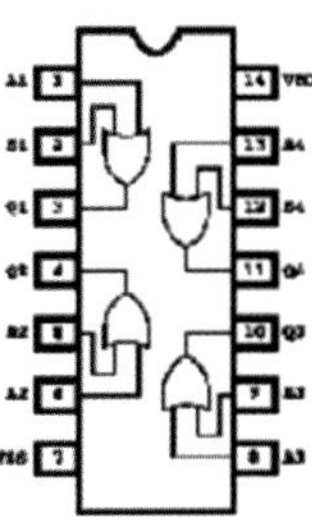

Key points

1. Digital systems work with 1s and 0s.
2. A NOT gate inverts its input, i.e. it converts a 1 into a 0, and a 0 into a 1.
3. The output of an AND gate is only 1 when both inputs are 1.
4. The output of a NAND gate is only 0 when both inputs are 1.
5. The output of an OR gate is a 1 when either input is a 1.
6. The output of a NOR gate is a 0 when either input is a 1.
7. A truth table has a column for every input and output. A truth table tells you the value of the outputs for every possible combination of input values.
8. To calculate the output of multiple logic gates connected together, calculate the output for each gate in turn, starting with the first gate. The output of one gate becomes the input for the next gate.
9. A latch remembers its output even when you take away or change its input. You can make a latch with an OR gate, by connecting the output of the OR gate back to one of its inputs.
10. You can make any logic gate using NAND gates or NOR gates.

Past exam questions

1. Which of these symbols is a NOT gate?

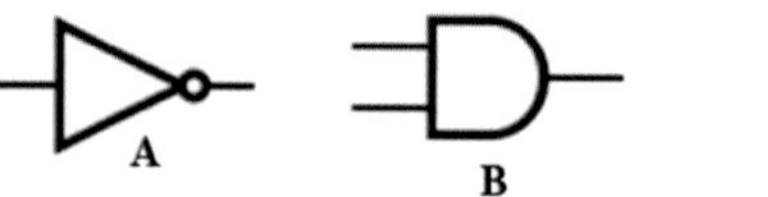

2. Name the logic gate represented by the symbol shown, and complete the truth table for that gate.

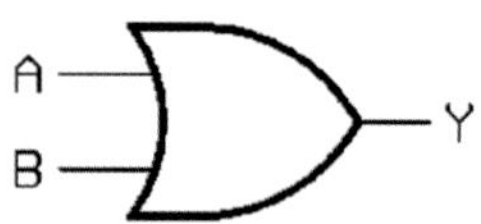

A	B	Y
1	1	
0	1	

3. Complete the truth table for the NAND logic gate shown.

A	Q
1	
0	

4. Complete the truth table for the logic gate shown.

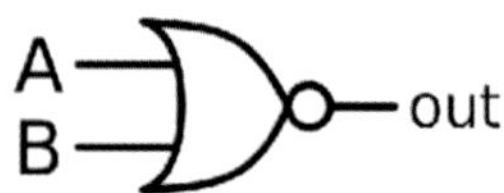

A	B	Out
1	1	
0	1	

5. Name the two gates required to produce a NAND gate.

6. The chip shown contains four logic gates. Complete the truth table for one gate.

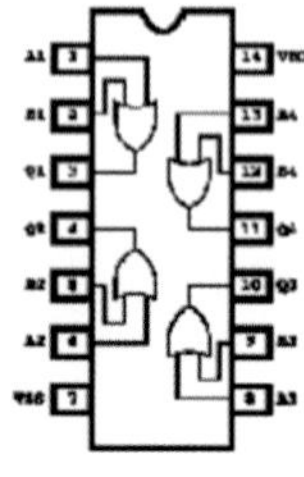

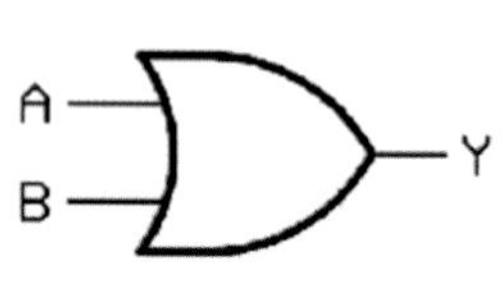

A	B	Y
1	1	
0	1	

7. Using a truth table, identify the logic gate produced when two NAND gates are combined as shown.

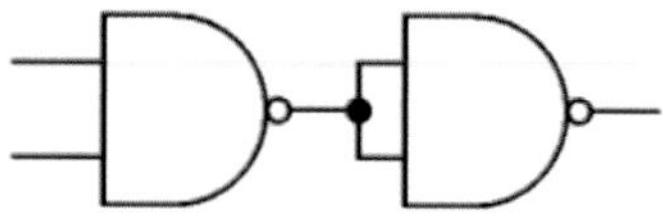

8. Identify the logic gate that will produce the truth table shown.

Input 1	Input 2	Output
1	1	0
1	0	1
0	1	1
0	0	1

9. A latched alarm is required to indicate that there is no oil in a tank. Explain how a latch alarm can be constructed from an OR logic gate.

Past exam questions

10. Using a truth table, determine the type of logic gate that has been constructed from the NAND gate arrangement shown.

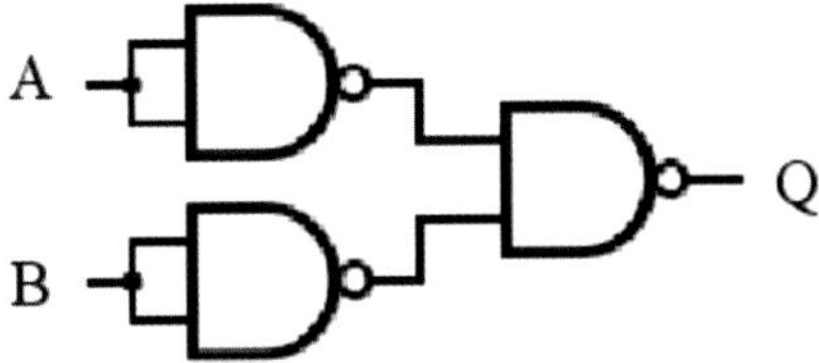

11. Complete the truth table for the NAND gate combination shown.

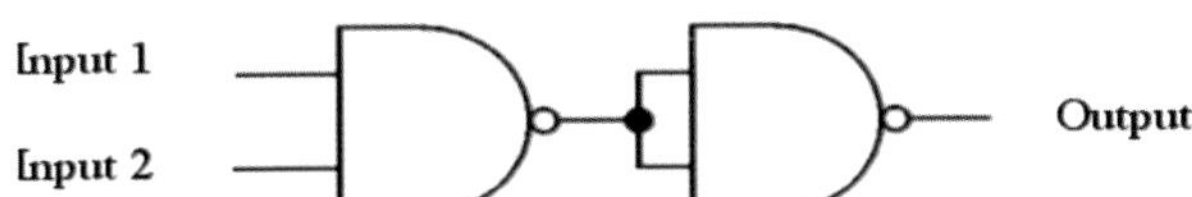

Input 1	Input 2	Output
1	1	
1	0	
0	1	
0	0	

12. Identify the logic states of the circuit at points X and Y.

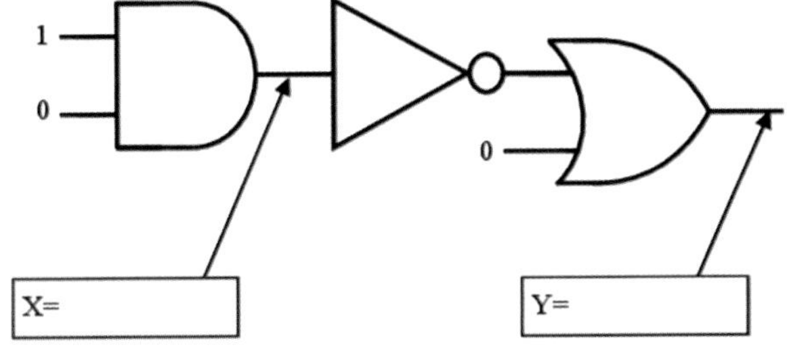

Digital control systems

Introduction

This chapter shows how digital circuits and logic gates can be used to control everyday devices and systems. Before studying this chapter, you should have completed the "Digital logic gates" chapter, and the "Electronic circuits 1" and "Electronic circuits 2" chapters.

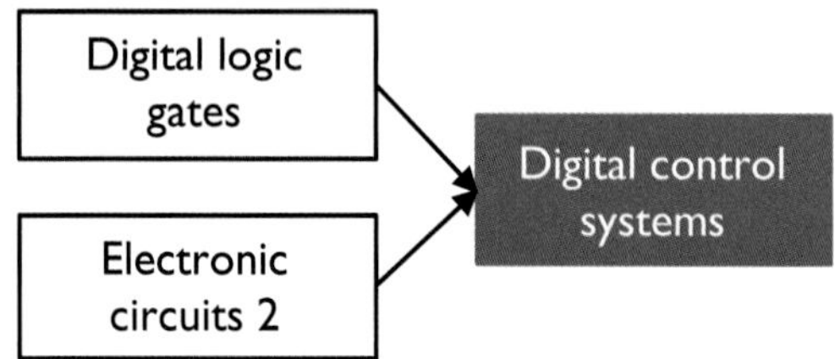

This chapter uses previous exam questions to explain digital control systems. Note that these exam questions usually ask questions based on more than one chapter. Including questions here that relate to other parts of the course provides a more realistic picture of the exam, and allows you to practice bringing your knowledge together from different chapters.

What is a digital control system?

Control systems are used in everyday devices such as washing machines, heating systems and cars.

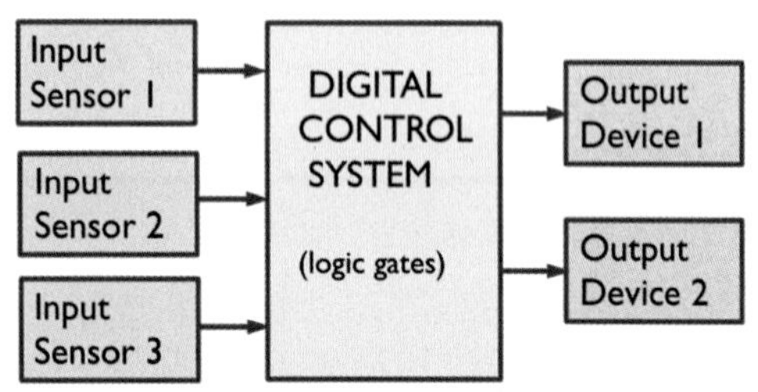

A digital control system takes inputs from its environment (often via switches and sensors) and uses that information to control output devices. The inputs and outputs to the system are digital signals. They are either "on" or "off" - 1s or 0s.

Logic gates inside the system control the outputs, depending on the values of the inputs.

Feedback loops and timers

The diagram opposite shows two other features often found in control systems. A feedback loop is where one or more outputs are "fed back" and used as inputs to the control system. This allows the system to measure and control the value of those outputs.

Some control systems use a timer on the outputs. This is useful where you want to do something for a specific period of time, for example to dispense coffee into a cup from a vending machine.

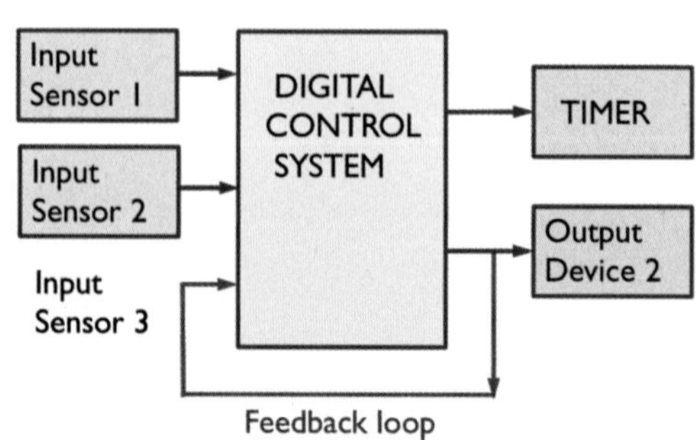

Examples of digital control systems

The following pages provide worked examples of digital control systems questions that have occurred in previous Junior Cycle exams. In order to explain things in detail, these worked examples provide more information in the answer sections than you will need to provide in your answers.

Calculating the outputs of a digital control system

The example below shows some logic gates inside a digital control system. There are 3 outputs, controlled by 2 inputs. You are asked to work out which outputs will be turned on by which input combinations. This can be done by filling out a truth table for each combination of input values, and calculating the outputs of the logic gates for each combination of inputs.

Worked example 1: Calculate traffic light outputs

Past exam question

A system diagram to control a set of traffic lights is shown. A coloured light will switch on if a "1" output is received from the system, and will switch off if a "0" output is received.

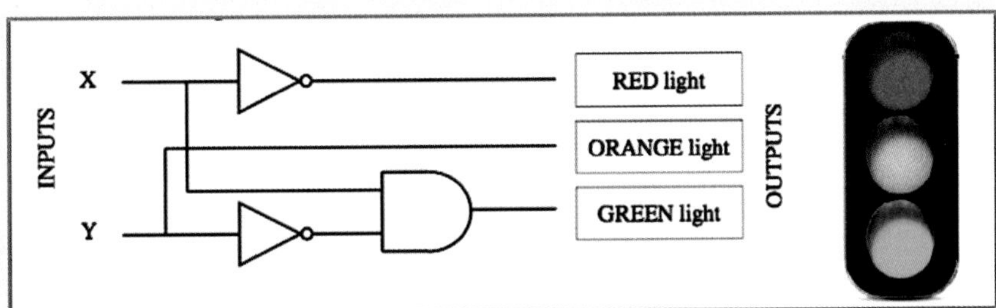

Complete the truth table below to indicate which lights will be switched on/off for each input shown.

X	Y	Red	Orange	Green
1	1			
1	0			
0	1			
0	0			

Solution

Truth table for the traffic light circuit:

- Because of the NOT gate, output "Red" will always be the inverse (opposite) of input X.
- Because output "Orange" is connected directly to input Y, it will always have the same value as Y.
- Because of the AND gate, output "Green" will only be 1 when X is 1 AND Y is 0.

X	Y	Red	Orange	Green
1	1	0	1	0
1	0	0	0	1
0	1	1	1	0
0	0	1	0	0

Looking at the truth table, we can see that:

- The orange light is turned on by the input combination X = 1, Y = 1.
- The green light is turned on by the input combination X = 1, Y = 0.
- The red and orange lights together are turned on by the input combination X = 0, Y = 1.
- The red light on its own is turned on by the input combination X = 0, Y = 0.

Selecting logic gates for a digital control system

In the worked example below, you are told how the system is supposed to work, but you have to work out which logic gates to use. Some tips for doing this are:

- Start with the outputs. For each output, find the sentence in the question that says when that output should be set, i.e. which combination of input values should result in that output being turned on.
- If you see the word "and" or "all" in the wording, you may need an AND gate.
- If you see the word "or" or "any" in the wording, you may need an OR gate.
- There may be implied "ands" and "ors" in the sentence. This occurs in the example below.
- Analyse any diagrams provided. This may provide additional information that is not provided in the text. You may see that an output is dependent on more inputs than is mentioned in the text.
- Make sure that you understand what a "1" or a "0" means for each input and output. You may need to invert some inputs or outputs using NOT gates in order to get the correct operation.

Worked example 2: Select logic gates for a vending machine control system

Past exam question

The system shown is used in a soft drinks dispensing machine. A soft drink is dispensed if the correct coin is inserted, the type of soft drink is selected and the drink chute contains a can.

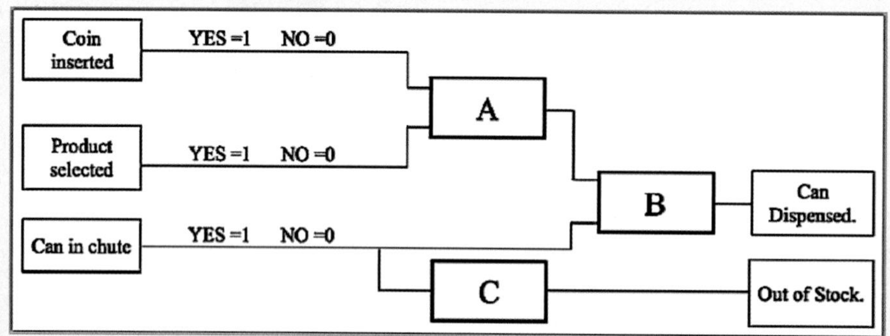

Question part (a)

(i) Identify the logic gates required at A, B and C.

(ii) Sketch and complete the truth tables for logic gates A and C.

Solution - part (a) (i)

First consider the first output "can dispensed". From reading the question carefully, we can see that a can is only allowed to be dispensed if all the following are true:

- A coin is inserted (coin inserted = 1)
- AND the product is selected (product selected = 1)
- AND there is a can in the chute. (can in chute = 1)

So the output "can dispensed" is an AND of all three inputs.

As we don't have an AND gate with three inputs, we can use two AND gates, and connect the output of the first AND gate to the input of the second AND gate.

So gates A and B are AND gates.

Worked example 2: Select logic gates for a vending machine control system

Next consider the second output "out of stock". We are not told anything about this output in the question text. However, we can see from the diagram that "out of stock" is dependent on the "can in chute" input only, via logic gate C. We can see that "out of stock" should be "1" when there are no more cans left in the chute, i.e. when the "can in chute" input = 0.

This means that the logic gate that we need for C is a NOT gate.

The full circuit that we need in our control system is shown. We can see that a can will only be dispensed if a coin is inserted, and a product is selected, and there is a can in the chute. Out of stock is true if there is no can in the chute.

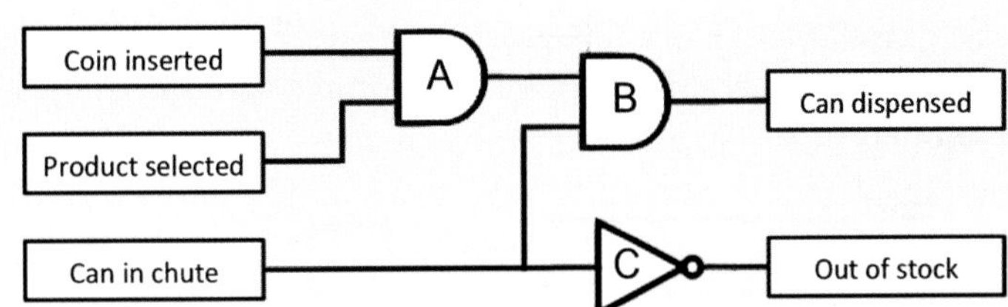

Solution - part (a) (ii)

Here are the truth tables for logic gates A and C.

Truth table for gate A (AND)

Input 1	Input 2	Output
1	1	1
1	0	0
0	1	0
0	0	0

Truth table for gate C (NOT)

Input	Output
1	0
0	1

Question part (b)

An additional system is required which will activate a refrigeration unit if any one of the chutes contains a can and a high temperature is detected.

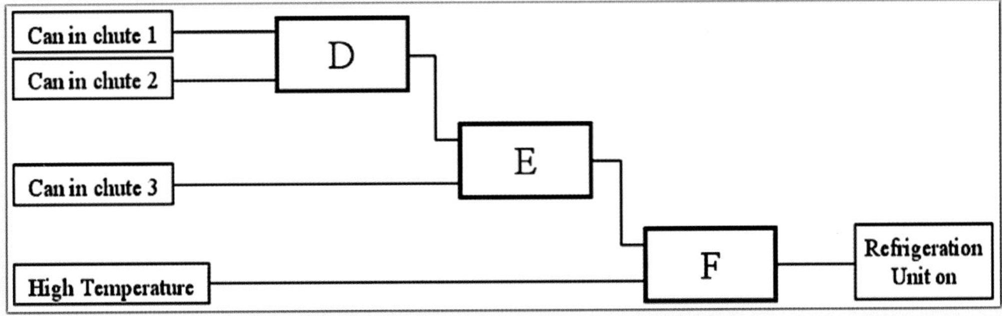

(i) Name the component that will detect a high temperature.

(ii) Identify the gates required at D, E and F.

(iii) Sketch a modification to this system that will turn on an "Out of order" light if all three chutes are empty.

Worked example 2: Select logic gates for a vending machine control system

Solution Part (b)

(i) A component that will detect high temperature is a thermistor.

(ii) The question tells us that the refrigeration unit should be activated if ANY of the chutes contains a can, AND a high temperature is detected. In other words: if there is a can in chute 1, OR there is a can in chute 2, OR there is a can in chute 3, AND there is a high temperature, the output to the refrigeration unit should be 1. So we need an OR function across the three chute inputs, and the output of that should be combined in an AND gate with the temperature input.

So gates D and E are OR gates, and gate F is an AND gate. This circuit is shown below. You can see that the refrigeration unit will turn on if a can is present in any chute, and there is a high temperature.

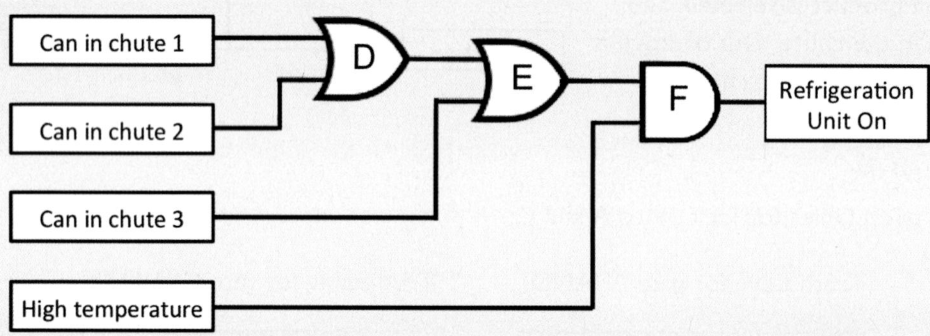

(iii) The question tells us that an "out of order" light should come on if ALL three chutes are empty. In other words: "out of order" should be 1 when "can in chute 1" is 0 AND "can in chute 2" = 0 AND "can in chute 3" = 0. So we know we are going to need an AND gate, but the output of an AND gate is only 1 when all the inputs are 1. But in our case, we need the output of the AND gate to be 1 when the inputs are all 0. This means we need to invert the inputs (change the 0s to a 1) before we send them to the AND gate. This is done using NOT gates.

The full logic circuit to turn on the "out of order" light is shown below. We can see that the light will turn on only if there are no cans in all of the chutes.

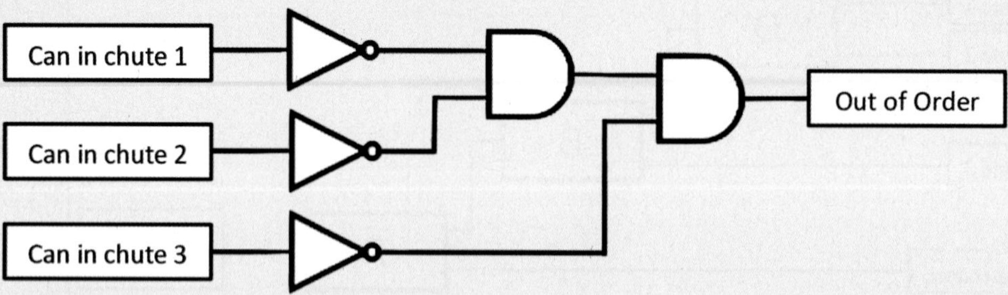

Worked example 3: Use of a latch in a digital control system

Past exam question

The system below is used to activate a flashing orange light if a fault develops. Name the special arrangement of the gate shown at X and explain why the PTB switch is used with this arrangement.

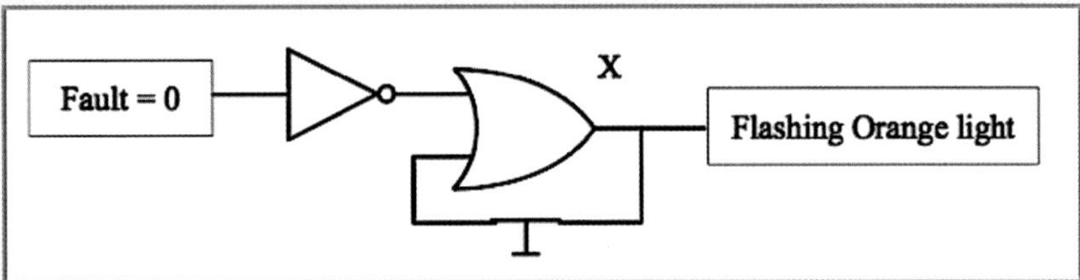

Valid answers

The circuit shown is a latch. The output of the OR gate is connected back to one of the inputs. This keeps the output of the OR gate at 1, even if the fault indication goes away.

The PTB (push-to-break) switch is used to reset the latch. Pressing the switch sends a 0 to the input of the OR gate. This causes the output of the OR gate, X, to go to 0, turning off the flashing orange light (if the fault is no longer present).

Worked example 4: Switches used as input to a digital control system

Past exam question

The relay, in the circuit shown, will only operate when a certain set of switches are closed. Indicate if the switches listed should be "open" or "closed" to activate the relay.

SWITCH	OPEN	CLOSED
A		
C		
E		
G		

+
2K2
A
B
C
D
E
F
G
H
Relay
10k
8 way DIP switch
-

Solution

In order to cause current to flow through the relay, the transistor must be turned on. In order to turn on the transistor, the base of the transistor must be raised to a high voltage. This can be done by closing switches A, C and F.

SWITCH	OPEN	CLOSED
A		Closed
C		Closed
E	Open	
G	Open	

This raises the voltage of the base of the transistor, because it is now connected to the positive power supply via the top resistor. (It creates a voltage divider circuit with the bottom resistor).

If any of the other switches (i.e. B, D, E, G, H) are closed, this connects the base of the transistor directly to ground/negative power supply, and so the transistor will be turned off. Switches B, D, E, G and H are wired in parallel, which is a logical OR arrangement of those switches.

(Note that switches A, C and F are wired in series, which is a logical AND combination of those switches.)

Worked example 5: Greenhouse control system

Past exam question

1. A control system is required to automatically control the temperature in a greenhouse. The system will automatically open the roof at high temperatures and close the roof at lower temperatures. At very low temperatures the system will turn on a heater. The system will only operate when a master switch is turned on.

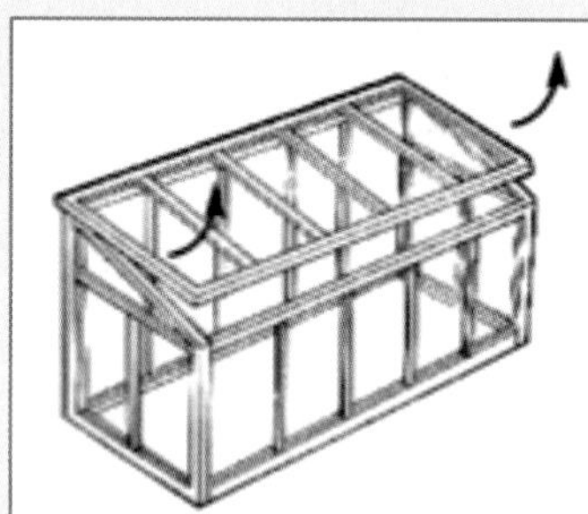

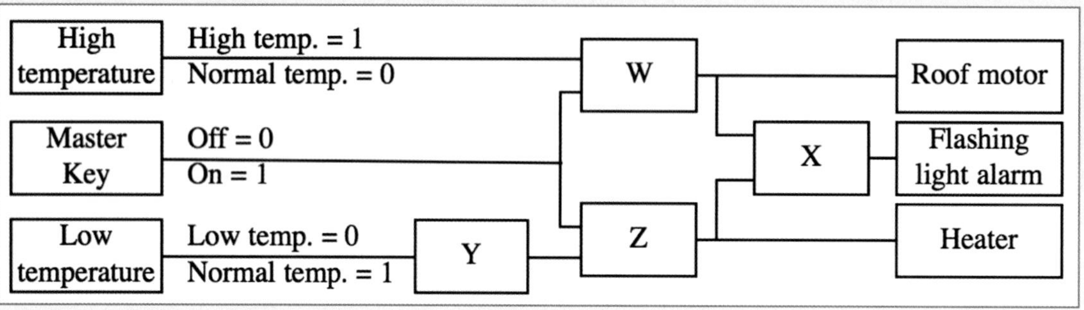

Part (a)

(i) Identify the logic gates required at W, X, Y and Z.

(ii) Sketch and complete a truth table for logic gates X and Y.

(iii) Two "limit switches" are required in the design of the roof opening mechanism. Explain why limit switches are required.

(iv) The control system requires a "latched" alarm system (flashing light) for the roof mechanism and for the heater. Explain the term latch and outline how a latch can be constructed from a named logic gate.

Solution - Part (a)(i) Identify the logic gates

Gate W

The roof motor is turned on when the Master Key is on (1) and the temperature is high (1), so gate W must be an AND gate.

Gate Y

The heater operates when the temperature is low (0). Therefore in order to have a positive (1) signal into gate Z, gate Y must invert the signal, so gate Y is a NOT gate.

Gate Z

The heater operates when the temperature is low (0), i.e. when the output of gate Y is 1, and the Master Key is switched on (1). Therefore gate Z is an AND gate.

Gate X

The flashing light alarm is on (1) when either the roof motor is operating or the heater is on. Therefore gate X must be an OR gate.

Worked example 5: Greenhouse control system

Summary of gates required

Gate	Type
W	AND
X	OR
Y	NOT
Z	AND

Solution – Part (a) (ii) Draw truth tables for gates X and Y
Since gates C and E are both AND gates, they each have the same truth table. This shown below.

Truth table for gates X (OR gate)

Input 1	Input 2	Output
1	1	1
1	0	1
0	1	1
0	0	0

Truth table for gates Y (NOT gate)

Input	Output
1	0
0	1

Solution – Part (a) (iii) Explain why limit switches are required
A limit switch is required to turn the motor off when the roof is fully opened. A second limit switch is required to turn the motor off when the roof is fully closed.

Solution - Part (a) (iv) Explain the term latch and outline how a latch can be constructed from a named logic gate
A latch is used to keep an output switched on, even after the input has been switched off. A latch can be made from an OR gate as shown in the diagram below.

When the input A goes to a 1, this causes output Y to become a 1 (because it is an OR gate). Because Y is 1, input B is also 1. If we take away input A (i.e. make it 0), output Y will stay at 1, because input B is 1.

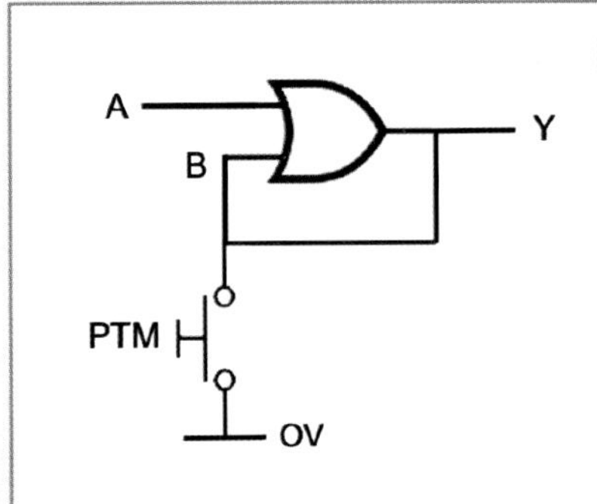

The latch can be reset using the PTM switch shown. Pressing the switch will reset input B to 0. This will cause output Y to become 0. When PTM switch is released, output Y stays at 0 because both inputs A and B are 0.

Worked example 5: Greenhouse control system

Part (b)

A second system is required to automatically water potted plants in the greenhouse. The system will pump water from a rainwater reservoir to a water trough under the potted plants if low water levels are detected.

(i) Identify the logic gates required at R, S and T.
(ii) Sketch a modification to the system shown which will activate an alarm if the reservoir and the water trough are dry. Sketch a truth table for your modification.

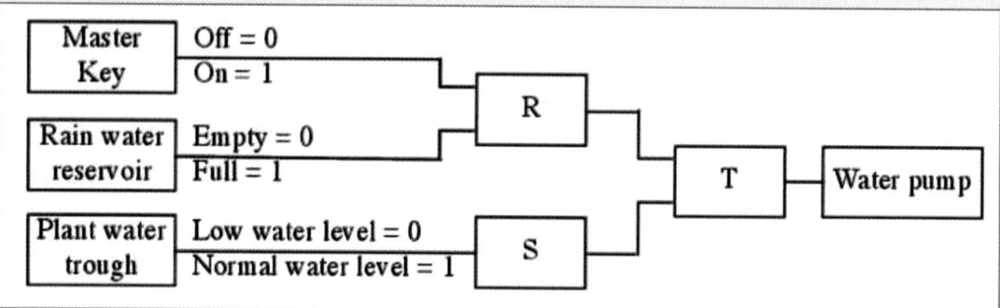

Solution - Part (b)(i) Identify the logic gates required at R,S and T

Gate R

The water pump operates when the master key is turned on (1) and the reservoir is full (1) so gate R must be an AND gate.

Gate S

The water pump operates only when there is a low water level signal (0). Therefore gate S is a NOT gate so that the output of S is 1 when the water level is low (0).

Gate T

We want the water pump to operate when the inputs of gate T are both 1. The pump operates when the master key is on, the rainwater reservoir is full and the water trough level is low. Therefore gate T needs to be an AND gate.

Worked example 5: Greenhouse control system

Solution - Part (b)(ii) Sketch a modification to activate an alarm if the rain water reservoir is empty and the plant water trough is empty). Sketch a truth table for your modification

The circuit below will activate an alarm (1) if the rain water reservoir is empty (0) and the plant water trough water level is low (0)

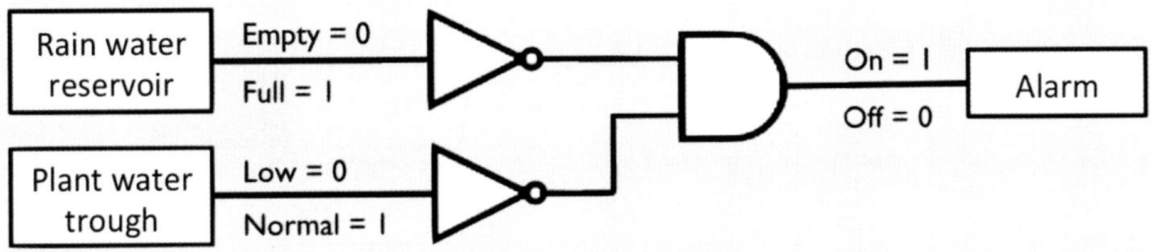

If the reservoir is empty and the water trough level is low then both signals are 0. Therefore the NOT gates make both of these signals into 1s. The AND gate turns on when both of its inputs are 1s so its output turns on when the reservoir is empty and the water trough level is low.

Truth table for the above system

Rain water reservoir	Plant water trough	Alarm
Full = 1	Normal = 1	Off = 0
Full = 1	Low = 0	Off = 0
Empty = 0	Normal = 1	Off = 0
Empty = 0	Low = 0	On = 1

Key points

1. A digital control system uses logic gates to set the value of its outputs, based on the value of its inputs.
2. If you are given the logic gates, and need to work out the value of outputs, just apply the truth tables of the logic gates, working your way from the inputs to the final outputs.
3. If you need to work out which logic gates are needed, take each output in turn, and analyse the description of the input conditions that should generate that output. Look for words that suggest AND and OR combinations of inputs.
4. Analyse any diagrams supplied in the question. These may show you further input conditions that are needed to set the outputs.
5. When you have chosen an AND or an OR gate correctly based on the logic required for the output, you may also need to use a NOT gate on one or more inputs, in order to achieve the correct operation.
6. Timers can be used to ensure that an output stays on for a particular length of time only.
7. Latches can be used to make sure an output stays on, even after the inputs that caused that output, change.

Past exam questions

1. To improve the safety of the machine shown, a control system, using logic gates, is required to prevent the operator starting the machine without the safety guard in place. A master key must also be in place and turned on before the machine will start. A flashing light operates whenever the safety guard is open.

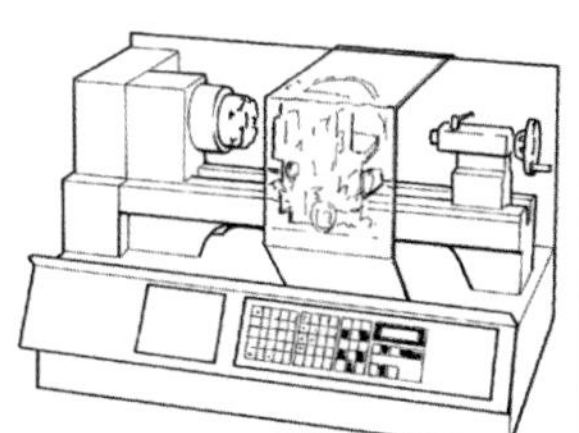

A block diagram of a possible system is shown.

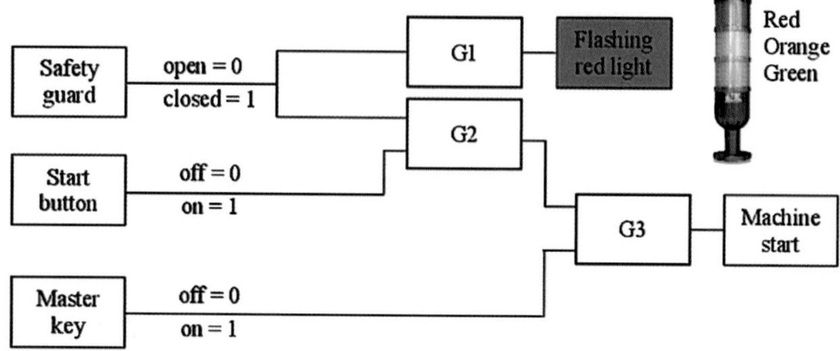

(i) Identify the logic gates required at G1, G2 and G3.
(ii) Sketch and complete a truth table for logic gates G1 and G3.
(iii) Indicate clearly how you would modify the system shown to display a green light, only when the machine is operating correctly, i.e. when the master key is turned on, the safety guard is in place and the start button is pushed.
(iv) Indicate clearly how you would further modify the system shown to display an orange flashing light if any one of the conditions in (iii) is not set correctly.

2. The graphic shows a tea and coffee dispensing machine. Drinks are dispensed if a coin is inserted in the machine and either coffee or tea is selected. The student-designed system shown below is intended to control the dispenser. A pump will add hot water to a paper cup containing tea or coffee only if the correct coin is inserted and the water is hot. A "Wait" sign is lit if the water is cold.

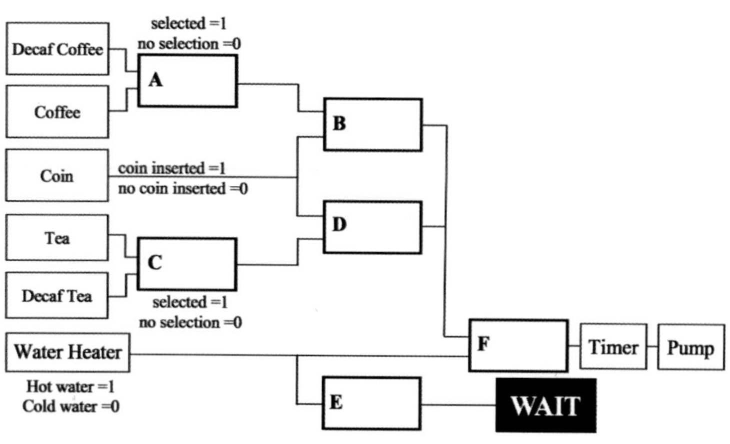

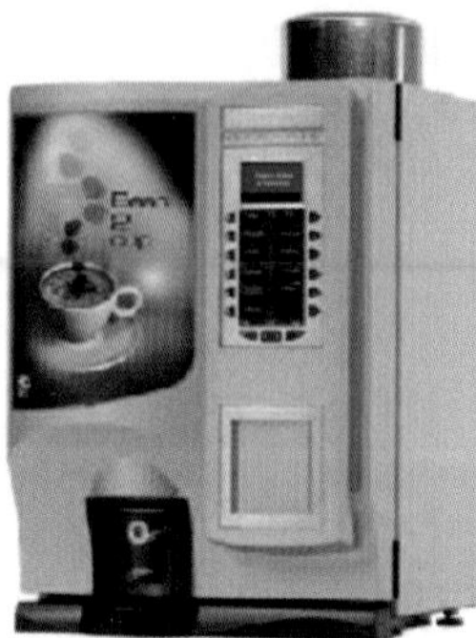

Part (a)
(i) Name the logic gates required at A, B, E and F.
(ii) Sketch truth tables for gates B and E.
(iii) Explain why a timer is required in the system.
(iii) Name the component required for detecting hot water.

Past exam questions

Part (b)

Outline how the system could be modified to illuminate a "Service required" sign if the dispenser has either: no stock of paper cups or no water to heat.

3. A block diagram for a motor car safety system is shown. The system will automatically switch on the car headlights when it is dark or when it rains. The system will operate only when the ignition key is turned on.

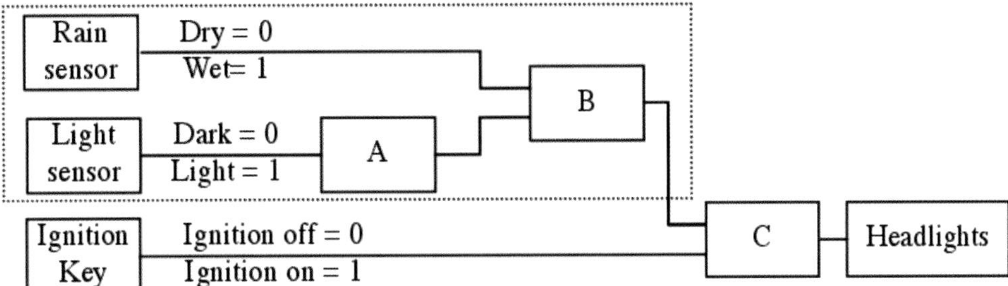

Part (a)

(i) Identify the logic gates required at A, B and C.

(ii) Sketch and complete a truth table for logic gates A and C.

(iii) The block diagram below shows a modification to this system to allow the driver switch on the lights when required. Name the gate required at "D" and explain why the system will work with the selected gate.

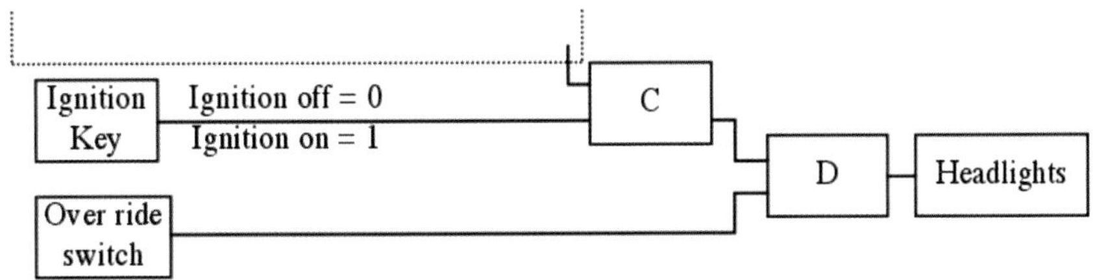

Part (b)

A second system is required to turn on the interior light at night, if either the driver door or the passenger door is opened. The interior light must turn off if the ignition key is turned on. Name the gates required at E, F, G, H and I for this system.

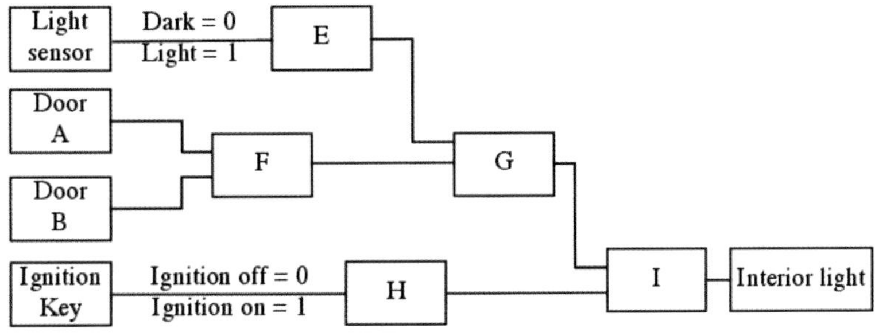

Past exam questions

4. The graphic shows a student design for a light-sensing buggy. The buggy contains the following parts:

- 3 light sensors (S1, S2 and S3).
- Two motor-driven wheels (W).
- One free turning rear wheel (R).
- A suitable control circuit (C).

The buggy is designed to move forward or turn towards a light source by running on one or both motors controlled by the system shown.

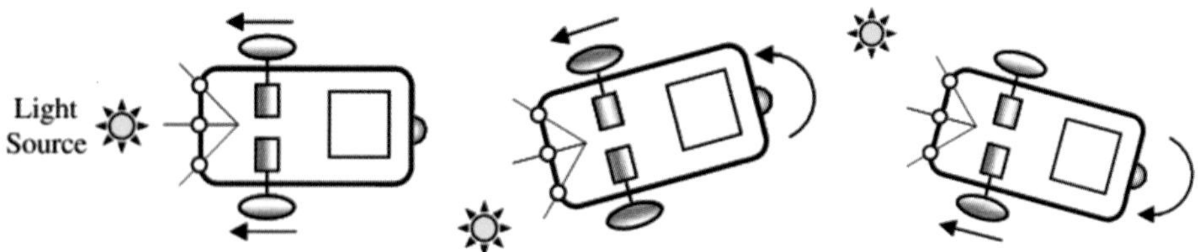

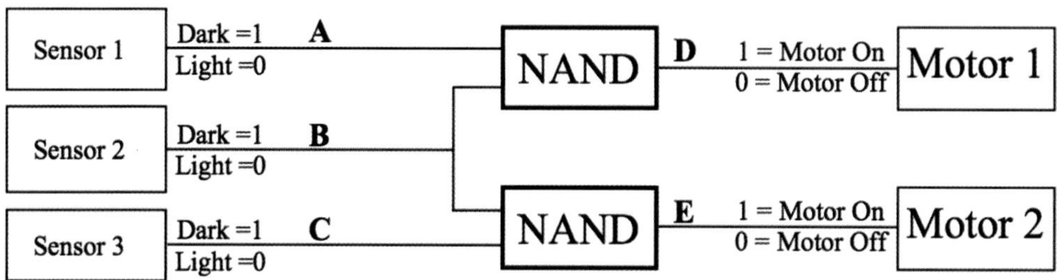

Part (a)

(i) Name a suitable component for use at S (light sensor).

(ii) What property of this component changes with changing light levels?

(iii) The light sensors will be placed in a "potential divider" in the circuit. Explain what is meant by a "potential divider" and outline why a potential divider is required.

Part (b)

(i) An incomplete truth table for the buggy control system is shown. The system uses NAND gates (AND followed by NOT). In your answer book, copy and complete the truth table for the system shown above.

A	B	C	D	E
1	1	1		
1	1	0		
1	0	0		
0	0	1		
0	0	0		

(ii) From the truth table identify the sensor states (light or dark) which will cause the buggy to turn left or right.

(iii) Outline a suitable modification to this system, which will turn on a flashing LED only when both motors are turned off.

Automation and robotics

Introduction

This chapter is about robots and automated machines. You should have studied the "Mechanisms", " Digital control systems" and "Information and communications technology" chapters before starting this one.

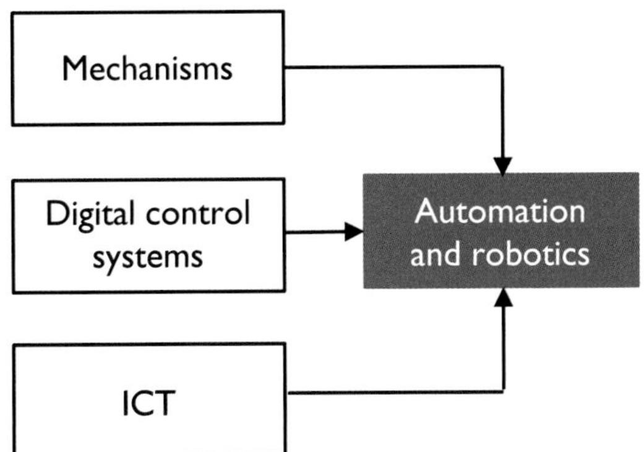

Automation and mechanisation

Mechanisation

Mechanisation means using machines to carry out work. The first machines were simple mechanisms like levers, wheels and pulleys, and these were operated by hand. Later, we developed more powerful machines that were powered by steam engines, petrol engines, and electric motors. Today, two of the most widely used technologies for powering machines are called hydraulics and pneumatics (silent "p"). These are explained below.

Hydraulic systems

Hydraulic systems use a liquid (usually oil) travelling through pipes to transfer movement from one place to another. You can see how this works below. If you press down on the left piston, the right hand piston will rise because the fluid cannot compress. If the left piston is, for example, 4 times smaller in diameter than the right piston, you can move a weight four times as heavy on the right hand side. However you will have to move the left hand piston four times as far. It works just like a lever.

Hydraulic systems are convenient because you can use flexible tubes to transport the power to moving parts. In a hydraulic system, an oil pump driven by an engine or motor usually replaces the left piston.

Hydraulic systems are very powerful and are widely used in large machinery like mechanical diggers and robots.

Machines powered by hydraulics are much more powerful than machines powered by electric motors. If you look at a mechanical digger, you will see the pistons that move the arms, and the pipes that carry the hydraulic fluid. The hydraulic pistons are like a digger's muscles and are sometimes called rams.

Pneumatic systems

Pneumatic systems use compressed air to transfer power and movement through pipes. Pneumatic systems are cleaner to use than hydraulic systems because they use air rather than oil, but they are not quite as powerful. Pneumatic systems are used in dusty or explosive environments instead of electric motors, which are hazardous in these situations.

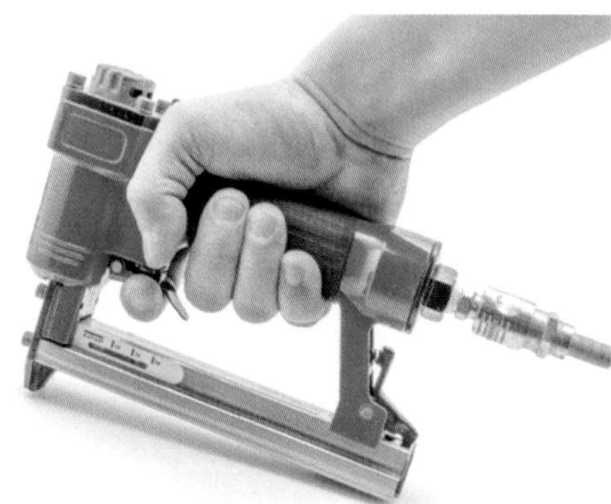

With pneumatics, the compressed air is allowed to escape into the atmosphere when you want to stop or reverse the movement. You will often hear the sound of air escaping when a bus stops, because the brakes and the doors are pneumatically operated. Fairground rides are often operated by pneumatics. Dentists use pneumatic drills in our mouths.

Pneumatic systems can produce very fast movements. Drills for digging up roads and industrial power tools, such as the stapler shown, are powered by pneumatics.

Automation

Automation means work that is carried out with little or no human involvement. Automation uses computers to control machines, and to carry out tasks like data collection, calculations and reporting.

When automating mechanical work, computers control machines like conveyor belts, robots and other tools. This is called CAM (computer-aided manufacturing). CAM and automation can build products faster, more accurately, with higher quality and more cheaply, than people. The picture shows robot arms at work on a car production line.

Robots

A robot is a machine that can perform actions normally carried out by a person. A robot may perform these actions automatically, or a person may control the robot directly. Robots often have arm-like parts and sometimes have wheels or tracks. Robots are controlled by computerised control systems.

Features of robots

Feature	Description
Moveable arms	• Moveable arms, called manipulators, are used to grip and move items. • They are usually powered by hydraulics or pneumatics. • An end effector or "hand" of a robot is connected to its arm. The end effector often contains sensors to detect when the object has been securely grasped.
Wheels or tracks	• Some robots need to move around (e.g. in bomb disposal or space exploration). If so, they will need wheels or tracks. • Tracks are suitable for rough ground. • Robots are often steered, not by pivoting the front wheels, but by making the wheel/s on one side go faster or more slowly than the wheel/s on the other side. • For example, if the wheel on the right side of the robot shown rotates faster than the left wheel, the robot will turn around in a circle to the left.
Sensors	• Sensors capture information in the environment of the robot. • A robot may use a camera, a proximity detector, or an ultrasonic device to "see" or measure distance. • A robot may use a microphone sensor to "hear". • A robot may use pressure-sensitive sensors to "touch" and "feel". • Sensors send their information to the control system software (see next page).
Operator control interface	Humans need to control robots, for example to stop and start them, select a different program, fix a problem or put the robot into service mode. Operators often use special wireless remote control devices to do this, as shown in the picture. With some robots, the operator directly controls the movement of the robot. This can be done using a joystick, or special gloves that fit over the operator's hands.

Feature	Description
Control system	A robot has an internal computer program (software) that acts as its "brain". This is shown as the "controller" in the diagram below. The controller software monitors (keeps reading and checking) the information coming in from the sensors, and controls the robot by sending signals to the various motors and hydraulic systems to move the arms and wheels of the robot. This monitor and control operation is an example of feedback. Feedback means that the value of the output is measured and used as an input in order to control the value of that output. For example, the sensors might tell the controller "the robot arm is too far to the left". The controller will then send a signal to move the arm to the right, until the input sensors tell it "you are now in the right position".
Controller hardware	The control system software runs on some "on-board" computer hardware inside the robot. This can be a special microprocessor board, or a PIC (programmable interface controller) as shown in the picture. The capability of the robot, i.e. what it can do, is determined by the power of the CPU in the on-board computer, and how complex the control software is. You can connect an external computer to the robot, to download and update the control software inside the robot. Note that if you load a different program into the same robot, it can carry out a different task.
Skills, maintenance and Servicing	Using robots means that you need specialised and skilled people to design, build, install, maintain and update them. These include engineers, designers and programmers to update the controller software, and skilled technicians to build and maintain all fixed and moving parts.

Applications and uses of robots

Robots are used across the following areas of society.

Manufacturing

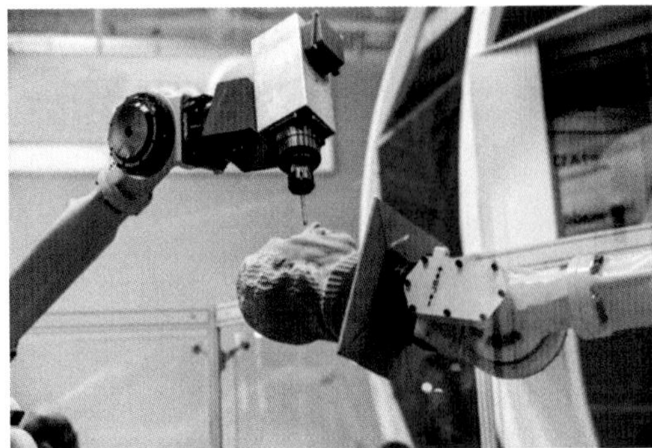

Robots are widely used in the manufacture of high-volume products such as cars or toys. High-volume (often called "mass-production") is where hundreds or thousands of the same product are made every day.

Robots are used in high-volume manufacturing because they are very accurate and can work for 24 hours a day, 7 days a week. Robots are cheaper and faster than humans at assembly tasks.

If a high-wage country is competing with a low-wage country making the same products, the high-wage country must use lots of robots and automation in order to keep the price of its products down.

Hazardous industrial environments

Robots are ideal for use in environments that are dangerous for humans, for example: handling toxic chemicals or nuclear materials, or cleaning up after chemical or nuclear accidents.

Bomb disposal and drones

A good example of using robots in hazardous environments is the bomb disposal robot.
Flying robots called drones are also used to carry out surveillance and fire weapons. The big advantage of robots in the military is that there is no danger to army personnel.

Space exploration

Space is a hazardous environment for humans. Robotic astronauts or "Robonauts", can be built to cope with this environment. They can explore and work in space, using the same tools as an astronaut.

Robots are also used in space as planetary rovers. A rover is a mobile robot that can travel over the surface of a planet and collect valuable data and transmit it back to Earth.

A main concern for rovers is how to power them over very long time periods. The main options are solar power and nuclear power. However, solar power is weak, and gets weaker the further the rover travels from the sun. When the robot lands on a planet or is in orbit around it, solar power is only available to it during the planet's day.
Nuclear power is a good option for rovers because it is powerful, does not take up much space, will last for a very long time, and does not rely on sunlight.

Healthcare and medicine

Robots have many beneficial uses in healthcare:

- Robots can be used in artificial limbs.
- Robots can be used in devices to help disabled people. These devices can be voice-activated.
- Doctors can use robots to perform remote surgery on patients. The doctor and patient can be in different countries.
- Robots are widely used in medical laboratories to carry out thousands of repetitive tests on blood samples for example, or in DNA testing.
- Robots are used in research to carry out repetitive tests on new drugs.

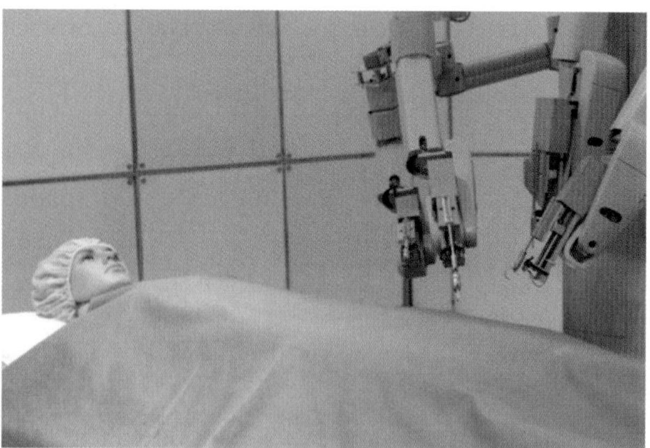

Robot performing test surgery on a human dummy

Education

Robot kits are available for schools and universities, so that students can learn to build and program their own robots. Lego Mindstorms is one such kit.

Secondary students can participate in robot building competitions such as the Irish Robotics Championships.

Domestic and home

Robot vacuum cleaners and robot lawn mowers, such as the one shown on the right, can travel around automatically and detect obstacles using sensors.

Entertainment

Robots are used in toys and games. Many such devices are voice-activated. In some toys and games, the software can be upgraded regularly in order to fix problems and provide new features.

Artificial intelligence (AI)

Artificial intelligence means that computer programs are able to learn and teach themselves, much like a human does. When coupled with artificial intelligence, robots will be become capable of doing complex tasks.

Robots that look like humans are called "humanoid" robots. Some people fear that many jobs will be lost to robots, because they will have become so intelligent, and they can work for long hours without having to be paid.

Impact of robots and automation

Advantages of robots and automation

- More products have become affordable because they can be made cheaply and consistently in high volumes, using robots and automation.
- Robots have improved our health and safety because we can use robots in hazardous environments, and to carry out surgery and assist the disabled.
- While there are now fewer jobs in manufacturing in developed countries, the jobs that are available are generally in more skilled and highly paid areas.

Disadvantages of robots and automation

- Because of robots and automation, fewer people are employed in manufacturing industries than decades ago.
- Many people fear that more jobs will be lost as robots become more intelligent and human-like.
- Automation and robots require large amounts of energy and power to operate.
- Automation systems and robots are costly to develop.

Test yourself

1. What is meant by automation?
2. What is a robot?
3. What is meant by CAM?
4. What is a hydraulic system?
5. Name two devices or machines that use hydraulic systems.
6. What is a pneumatic system?
7. Name two devices or machines that use pneumatics.
8. Which is the more powerful: hydraulics or electric motors?
9. What are the main components of a robot?
10. What is meant by feedback?
11. Name three areas of society where robots are used.
12. Give two advantages of robots.
13. Give two disadvantages of robots.
14. Provide two examples of where robots are used in healthcare.
15. What are sensors used for on robots?

Worked example: Robots in entertainment and industry

Past exam question

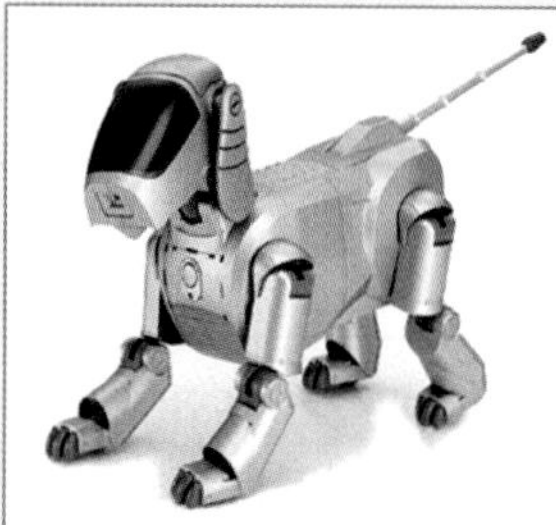

(a) Modern entertainment robots are designed to interact with humans.
   (i) Outline two ways in which data can be acquired by an entertainment robot.
   (ii) Explain why the robot response to data input is limited.
   (iii) Explain why software upgrades are made available for these robotic toys.

(b) Industrial robots require **control software**, a **computer interface** and **feedback sensors.**
   (i) Explain the meaning of each of the terms in bold above.
   (ii) State two advantages of using CAM in mass production.
   (iii) Explain why pneumatics or hydraulics are commonly used in place of electric motors to move industrial robotic arms.
   (iv) Explain why robotic industrial production lines are more likely to be found in first world countries. Give two reasons for your answer.

Valid answers

Part (a)

(i) Data can be acquired by a robot using sensors to react to light, sound and touch.
(ii) The robot response to data input may be limited because it may have a small (i.e. not powerful) CPU inside, and limited software program.
(iii) Software upgrades are made available for these robotic toys to provide new features for customers, and to fix any problems.

Part (b)

(i) **Control software** resides inside the robot and controls the actions of the robot.
A computer interface allows you to connect a computer to the robot to load the control software into the robot, and to change it as required.
Feedback sensors provide information to the control software to allow it to control the movements of the robot more accurately.

(ii) The advantages of using CAM in mass production are: low cost, high speed and high quality.

(iii) Pneumatics or hydraulics are commonly used in place of electric motors to move industrial robotic arms, because pneumatics and hydraulics are much more powerful than electric motors. Pneumatics and hydraulic systems are safer in explosive areas or where there is a danger of fire from flammable substances, e.g. fuels.

(iv) Robotic industrial production lines are more likely to be found in first world countries because labour costs would be too high without using automation. Also the use of robotics requires availability of skilled people to build, operate, maintain and manage automated factories. Funding for the high initial development costs is easier to obtain in more developed countries.

Worked example: Robots in space exploration and industry

Past exam question

Part (a)

The Mars Science Laboratory "Curiosity" is a mobile robot intended to explore the surface of Mars.

(i) Explain, giving two reasons, why a robot is required to explore the surface of Mars.

(ii) A nuclear power source will generate electricity for the robot. Explain briefly, why this is the most appropriate energy source for use on Mars.

(iii) An on-board computer will monitor and control the robot's operations. Explain briefly, how the robot could carry out each of these functions.

Part (b)

(i) Robots are commonly used in industry. Outline, using two examples, where robots are used in industry.

(ii) Outline two areas of expertise, required by operators, in order to service and maintain industrial robots.

(iii) Outline one example of the use of a robotic device in the home.

Valid answers

Part (a)

(i) A robot is required to explore Mars because Mars is a hazardous environment for humans. It would be much more expensive to send humans, it would take a long time, and it would be difficult to bring the humans safely back to Earth.

(ii) Nuclear is the most appropriate energy source for use on Mars because it is smaller and more powerful than a solar panel, and it also operates at night.

(iii) The on-board computer carries out the function of monitoring by reading information from sensors on the robot, e.g. to detect position. The on-board computer carries out the function of control by sending signals to the motors and hydraulic systems to move the robot components and to take related actions.

Part (b)

(i) Examples of robots used in industry are:
(a) Manufacturing products on automated production lines.
(b) Handling hazardous materials such as chemicals or nuclear materials.

(ii) Two areas of expertise required by operators to service and maintain industrial robots are:
(a) Computer programming – to design, build and maintain the control system software.
(b) Engineering – to design, build and maintain the physical parts of the robot.

(iii) One example of the use of a robotic device in the home is an automatic vacuum cleaner.

Past exam questions

1. The hydraulic rams in a digger are powered using: oil pressure, water pressure or air pressure?

2. Modern manufacturing industries commonly use industrial robots.

   (i) Suggest two advantages of using robots in industry.
   (ii) Suggest two disadvantages of using robots in industry.
   (iii) Outline two areas, other than manufacturing industry, where robots are used and explain their function.
   (iv) Explain why computers are necessary to operate robotic devices.

3. Modern commercial robotic machines can be classed as: domestic, industrial, research or military.

   (a) In the case of any two robotic machines:
      (i) Outline the function and operation of each robotic machine.
      (ii) Explain why each selected robot is a suitable replacement for a person.
   (b) Outline two ways in which the operation of a robot might be controlled or altered.
   (c) Explain why external sensors are required by robots and outline the importance of "feedback" in controlling the operation of a robot.
   (d) Explain, using suitable sketches, how robotic machines can move over uneven ground.
   (e) Outline two power sources that can be used to provide movement for robotic arms.

4. Robots are commonly used in industry and in planetary exploration.

   (i) Explain where and why robots are used in industry.
   (ii) Explain how the actions of industrial robots are controlled and modified.
   (iii) Outline two differences between robots used in industry and in planetary exploration.
   (iv) Outline two other applications of robotics.

Past exam questions

5. The graphics show a base platform for an educational robot.

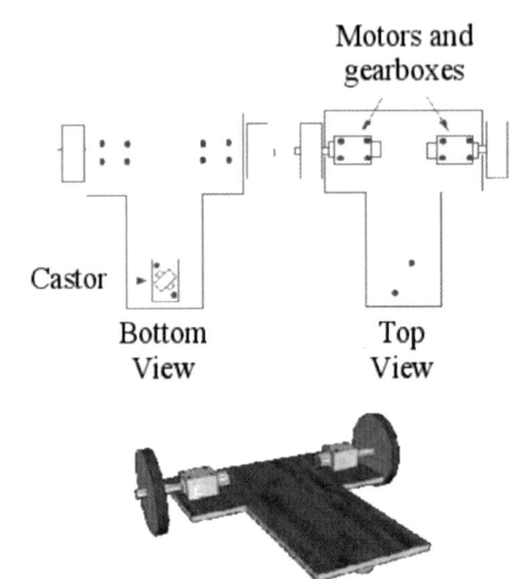

Part (a)

(i) Outline two reasons why the castor is required.

(ii) Explain why gearboxes are attached to the drive motors.

(iii) Outline two reasons why some robots use tracks instead of wheels.

(iv) Explain how, using the two motors, the robot can move forward in a straight line and then turn left.

(v) Outline how such a robot could detect and avoid an obstacle (e.g. a wall).

Part (b)

Robotic devices are commonly used in military operations and in space exploration. In each case, explain the advantages of using robotic devices for these operations.

17 CHAPTER

Technology and society

Introduction

This chapter is about how technology affects our lives.

What is meant by technology?

Technology means more than just computers, smartphones and the Internet. It also includes the invention and use of materials, tools, machines, structures, buildings, and chemicals and the use of different forms of energy like light and radio waves.

Technology in use at the Olympic Games

What is meant by society?

Society is how a country or a large group of people lives, works, interacts with, and takes care of each other. Society includes areas like health, education, employment, transport, entertainment, sport, and the environment.

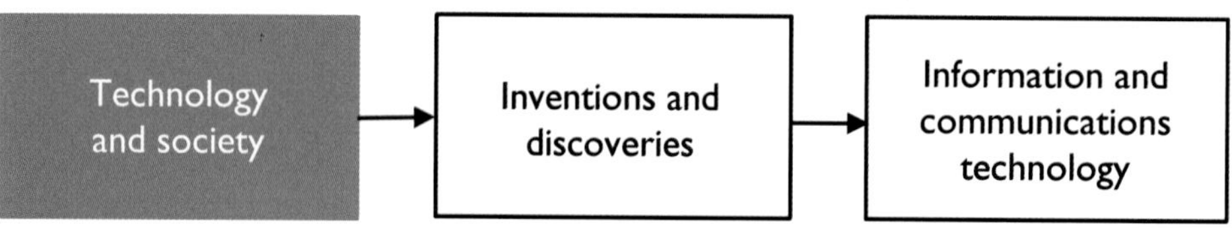

Activities

Before you read the next section, try to think of as many examples as possible of how technology is used in your home. After you have read the next section, try to think of some more.

Technology in the home

Overview

Our homes are full of technology. They are built using man-made materials such as concrete, steel, timber, glass and plastic. They can stay bright at night because of electricity and lighting. We can heat our homes using modern heating systems, and we can stay warm because of effective insulating materials. Water, electricity, gas, telephone, and internet connections are supplied to our homes.

Waste is taken away in pipes and collected from our bins. Electric machines help us with cleaning, food preparation, and gardening. Electronic devices provide entertainment and enable us to communicate with others.

Washing machines and dryers

For most of human history, the washing of clothes was carried out by hand. Even soap and washing powders are a relatively recent invention. The picture on the right shows an early electric washing machine. A wringer device is shown on top. Modern washing machines and dryers have many more features than this old machine.

Features of a modern washing machine

Features of a modern washing machine include:

- Automatic filling, heating of water, dispensing of washing powder, draining, spinning, and drying.
- A built-in computer that controls the motors, valves and heaters.
- A choice of programs for different types of fabric.
- Sensors to detect when the water is at the correct level, heated to the right temperature, drained, and when clothes are dry.
- A standard design to fit in kitchens and under worktops.

Vacuum cleaners

Vacuum cleaners use electric motors to suck up dust. They are often called hoovers because a company called Hoover made the first popular vacuum cleaners. Some vacuum cleaners (like the Dyson shown in the picture) don't have bags to empty. Some vacuum cleaners are robots, and can travel around your house on their own.

Food preparation

Most ovens are heated by electricity and have a fan to circulate the air around evenly. Some ovens are computer-controlled and have programs for different types of meals. Our kitchens contain other helpful machines such as electric cutting knives, food processors and blenders. We can look up recipes on our smartphones and computers before we start cooking.

Clothes

Technology has made it possible to produce large amounts of clothes very cheaply, using large factories, machines, and transport technologies. Technology has created new man-made materials like nylon, polyester and Kevlar, which are used to make strong, lightweight and waterproof clothes and shoes. Technology has also provided elastic materials and convenient clothes fasteners such as zips and Velcro.

Cosmetic products

Technology has led to the development of many products for looking after our bodies, such as scissors, razors, hair dryers, hair straighteners, jewellery, fragrances and cosmetics.

Home technologies in developing countries

Developing countries may not have access to all the comforts and time-saving devices of developed countries. This means that more time and work may be required to take care of the basic necessities of life, for example people may have to walk long distances to fetch water, or may have no access at all to clean water.

Mobile technologies and smartphones are becoming more widespread in developing countries. This is helping to spread information and knowledge, and to improve communication.

Advantages of technologies in the home

More time available

- Domestic appliances like washing machines and dishwashers save us large amounts of time. This saved time can be used for other things such as relaxing or working.
- Electric light in the home adds more hours to the day so we can do more things.
- Computers and internet connections allow people to work from home, so they can save time on travelling to work (commuting).

Increased comfort

- Modern houses keep us safe, warm and comfortable.
- Home entertainment technologies help us to relax and enjoy ourselves.

Disadvantages of technologies in the home

Damage to social relationships

If we spend too much time on computers and entertainment devices at home, our family and social relationships can suffer.

Poorer health

We can get less physical exercise than we should because of home entertainment devices and domestic appliances. This can damage our health.

Damage to the environment

Home technologies create large amounts of waste, as each old technology is thrown away in favour of new products. Packaging from food, kitchen and bathroom products, cosmetics and electronic devices also creates waste.

Activities

Choose an electric domestic appliance in your home. Write up a short history of it, i.e. find out what people used before it was available, and how it has improved people's lives. Write down two advantages and two disadvantages of the appliance.

Past exam questions

List three features of a modern washing machine, which would not have been available in older models.

Technology in communications and entertainment

Two hundred years ago communication was either done in person or by letter, which could take many months to reach its destination. Entertainment was limited to activities such as socialising, attending live events, or reading a book or newspaper. Nowadays we have a huge array of choices for communication, news, and entertainment.

Communication, information and news

- To communicate with others, wherever they may be, we have mobile phones and social media applications such as Facebook, Twitter, and Snapchat.
- We can make video calls and see each other on screen using internet software applications like Skype and Facetime.
- We can take pictures and make videos using smartphones and digital cameras, and send pictures and videos to friends, family and others over the Internet.
- Many people write and read blogs, which are information articles on websites.
- If we want to research something, we can do so instantly by searching for it on the Internet using a smartphone or computer. Before the Internet, we would have had to look up books and encyclopedias, or go to a library.

In the past, it took a long time for information to travel around the world, as it had to be passed from one person to another. Nowadays information travels around the globe instantly. People receive news and information from websites and social media as well as from newspapers, radio and TV.

Social media

Social media software applications like Facebook, Twitter and Snapchat, allow us to communicate with others via the Internet by "posting" messages, pictures and videos. Every social media user has a profile, which is often just a name and a picture. You can "follow" others and receive messages when they post them. There are lots of groups that you can join where people share information on common interests.

Entertainment

We have a huge range of entertainment options available in our homes, including radio, TV, video games, entertainment websites, social media channels, and internet-based film services such as Netflix.

Music

We can access a vast amount of free music and videos on websites such as YouTube. To listen to music in our home, we have sound systems and we can play vinyl records, CDs, or MP3 files or stream music over the Internet using software products such as Spotify. We can listen to music as we move around using portable devices such as smartphones.

Technology has totally changed the music industry because people no longer have to buy a physical product to listen to music. Music has become virtually free because people upload music to sharing websites like YouTube. This means that it has become more difficult for musicians to make money from sales of music.

Games

Before computers and the Internet, people played a lot of card and board games. Today, people play video games with others in different parts of the world. Virtual reality (VR) systems and headsets put players in a 3D virtual world.

Advantages of communications and entertainment technologies

Instant news

We can receive news from around the world, almost as soon as it happens.

Social contact

Communication technologies help us to keep in touch with friends and family, and to make new business contacts and friends.

Enjoyment

Communications and entertainment technologies help us to relax and enjoy ourselves.

Learning

Computers and the Internet give us the opportunity to learn more about the world and other cultures.

Disadvantages of communications and entertainment technologies

Information overload

- The abundance of information available can be overwhelming.
- People can become depressed because they are exposed to too much bad news.
- Information posted online by ordinary people is not checked to make sure that it is balanced or true.

Damage to social relationships and mental health

- If we spend too much time on smartphones, computers and social media, we can become disconnected from those around us.
- People can become addicted to online gambling, social media and video games.
- We can be exposed to bullying, extreme opinions, damaging material and fraud on the Internet.
- People online may not be who they say they are. They may have fake social media profiles.
- Communications technologies make it easier for workers to keep working in their free time. This can lead to over-work, stress, and spending insufficient time with family and friends.

Poorer physical health

Sitting in front of screens for long periods is not good for our eyes, back or posture. Lack of exercise reduces our levels of physical fitness and may cause us to gain too much weight.

Damage to the environment

Communications and entertainment technologies create a lot of waste, when old devices are disposed of.

Activities

1. Ask your parents and your grandparents what they did for entertainment when they were children.
2. Write down in your own words what you think the advantages and disadvantages are, of the Internet and social media.

Past exam questions

1. Explain, using two suitable examples, the positive impact which the Internet has had on society.

2. "Internet users continue to spend more time on social media sites than any other type of site".

   (a) Explain what is meant by "social media".

   (b) Outline one advantage of using these sites.

   (c) Outline one disadvantage of using these sites.

3. Web-based social networking sites have become an important part of the Internet.
   (i) Outline, using two examples, some of the services provided by these sites.
   (ii) Explain, using two examples, the impact that these services have had on society.
   (iii) In relation to these services, explain any two of the following terms:
   - Profile.
   - Blog.
   - Identity theft.
   - Privacy.

4. State two ways in which technology has changed the music industry in recent years.

Technology and food

The food industry is a major user of technology. The following sections describe how technology is used in the production, processing and distribution of food.

Technology in food production

Farms are highly mechanised. Mechanised means using lots of machines. Farmers use tractors and other large special machines to plant, spray and harvest crops, to milk cows and to feed animals.

Automated milking system

Farmers can use artificial fertilisers to grow plants, and may add growth additives to food for animals. They may use chemical pesticides on plants, and can give drugs to animals, to keep them free from disease.

Covered glasshouses, polytunnels, and automatic watering machines may be used to grow plants.

Some food crops are genetically modified (GM). This has been done for thousands of years by cross-breeding to produce better plants and animals. Nowadays this is done scientifically by modifying the genes of plant and animal cells so that they have different characteristics, such as resistance to disease or drought (periods of no water).

Some animals, such as chickens, are kept all their lives indoors in small cages in large industrial systems, where food and water are dispensed automatically.

Technology in food processing, preservation and packaging

In factories, food is processed, i.e. chopped up, changed, and put in containers, using large machines and robots. It is preserved, i.e. kept fresh for longer, using a number of techniques:

- Chemicals called preservatives are added to foods. Preservatives are often described by their "E numbers" on food packaging, e.g. E220.
- Food can be vacuum-packed. This means taking all the air out of the containers.
- Food can be pasteurised. This means heating the food for a short period to kill bacteria. This process is used on milk.
- UHT (ultra high temperature) treatment may be used. This is similar to pasteurisation but uses a higher temperature for longer. This is used to preserve milk for longer periods without the need for refrigeration.
- Food can be freeze-dried. This is done to make foods such as powdered sauces and custard.
- Additives may be added to food to make it look better, have the right colour or texture, or to taste better. These additives also have E numbers. Some of the biggest additives in food are sugar and salt. These are added to improve the flavour of the food.
- Food is packaged in containers, tins or bottles and labels are added, using large machines and robots.

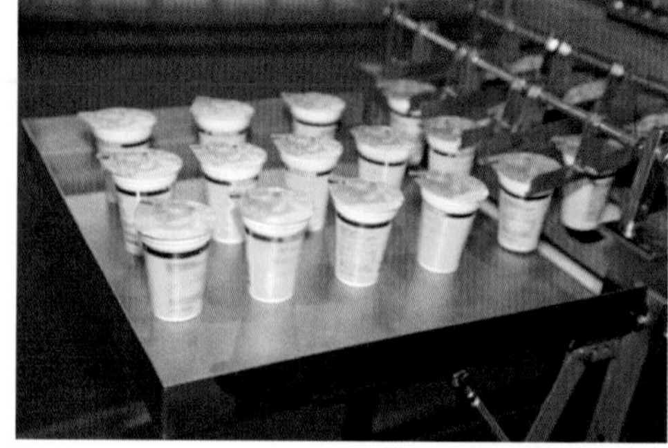
Filling yogurt pots in a factory

Food health and safety

Many people are worried about the health risks of the additives in our food. The EU and the Food Safety Authority of Ireland (FSAI), issue regulations about which additives are permitted, and how food must be labelled. They carry out inspections of factories and food to ensure that the rules are being followed, and that there are no diseases or harmful substances in our food.

Best before/use by dates

By law, most foods must be labelled with a "Best before" or "Use by" date. A product that is past its "Use by" date is not safe to eat. A product that is past its "Best before" date may possibly be safe to eat but it may not taste nice or be of good quality.

Organic food

Food that is produced without any artificial fertilisers, pesticides, additives or genetic modification is called organic. An organic animal product means that the animal is reared without growth hormones or antibiotics. There is a demand for organic food for these reasons.

Organic food generally costs more than non-organic food because it takes longer to produce and requires more labour.

Food transport and economics

Thousands of trucks, trains, ships and planes move large quantities food around the world every day. Some foods can only be produced in certain countries because of the weather. However, even if food can be produced in your own country, it can be cheaper to import food from other countries. This is because wages, currencies, farm sizes and government subsidies (financial support) vary in different countries.

Food production in developing countries

Poorer countries may have access to a smaller range of food, and be limited to food that is produced locally. However, people may be healthier because their food is less processed and there may be less environmental damage as a result of less mechanised food production and long distance transport.

Advantages of food technologies

Plentiful and cheap food

- The use of large farms, machines, fertilisers, refrigeration, factories and transport has made it possible to produce large amounts of food cheaply.
- Preservatives stop food going off too quickly. Food can be stored, transported and sold later. This makes the food cheaper too.
- Because food has become relatively cheap, more money is available to spend on other things.

Improved health

- We are healthier now than we were a hundred years ago, because food technology has given us access to a wide range of fresh, nutritious and affordable food in all seasons from around the world.
- GM technology has helped to create crops that are resistant to disease and can be grown in harsh environments. This has helped to feed more people than ever before, and reduce starvation. The use of GM crops can reduce the need for harmful artificial fertilisers and chemicals.

Disadvantages of food technologies

Poor health from processed food

- Many people are worried about the long-term health effects of additives in food.
- Processed food often has large amounts of added salt and sugar. High levels of salt can lead to high blood pressure and heart disease. High levels of sugar can lead to obesity and diabetes.
- Some people are worried about the health effects of GM crops, and that control of seeds and crop technology will be in the hands of multi-national companies.

Damage to the environment

- Over-production of food can create large amounts of food waste.
- The transport of food across the world every day burns huge amounts of fossils fuels (oil and gas). This causes air pollution and the emission of greenhouses gases, which contributes to global warming and climate change.

Test yourself

Name one way in which technology can be used to extend the shelf life of milk.

Activities

On your next few visits to the supermarket, do the following:

1. Look at the packaging or stickers on vegetables and fruit, and write down which countries they come from. Which country is the furthest away? How far away is that country roughly? How much of the fruit and vegetables on display comes from Ireland? Choose one fruit and one vegetable from other countries, and write down in each case why you think that fruit or vegetable comes from that country.
2. Look at the labels of common foods like milk, yogurts, rashers, and microwavable dinners. Write down the E numbers that you find. Write down the amount of sugar and salt, and the percentage that it is of your RDA (recommended daily allowance). Can you find products that don't have any additives or preservatives?
3. Can you find any products in the supermarket that don't have any packaging or stickers?

Past exam questions

1. "Many of the foods which are available in our supermarkets have benefited from modern technologies". Using one named example in each case, outline how new technologies have changed the following: Food production, food processing and food storage.

2. Describe two ways in which technology has extended the shelf life of food products.

3. Food production, processing and long term storage have all been changed by new technologies.
   (i) Using one named example in each case, outline how new technologies have changed food production, processing and storage.
   (ii) Explain briefly why a demand exists for "organic" food products.

4. Modern farming in Ireland is largely mechanised.
   (i) Outline two examples of this mechanisation.
   (ii) In relation to modern farming, explain the term "GM crops".

5. Name two modern methods of food preservation.

Technology and shopping

Technology has changed how we shop. The following sections outline some of the technologies involved in shopping.

Advertising

Technology is used to create advertising for billboards, buses, trains, TV, radio, websites and social media. On the Internet, computers track the websites and social media sites that you visit, and send you advertisements based on your clicks and interests.

Shopping centres

Decades ago most shops were small, family-owned and located in town centres. Nowadays, we have very large supermarkets and shopping centres (or malls) where many shops, restaurants and services are located together. Shopping centres are often located on the outskirts of towns, where there is enough space to construct large buildings and car parks.

Computer tracking of products

Computer technology is used to manage goods in stores and supermarkets. Most products have a barcode or an RFID (radio-frequency identification) device on them. Each type of product is given a price on the computer system, so that the right price will appear at the checkout. The computer system keeps track of which products are being sold, how many products are left in stock, and when it is time to re-order more goods.

Product display

Technology is used to design products and packaging that will appeal to customers, and to make attractive and well-lit displays. In-store sound systems are used to play music and to make customer announcements.

Checkout systems

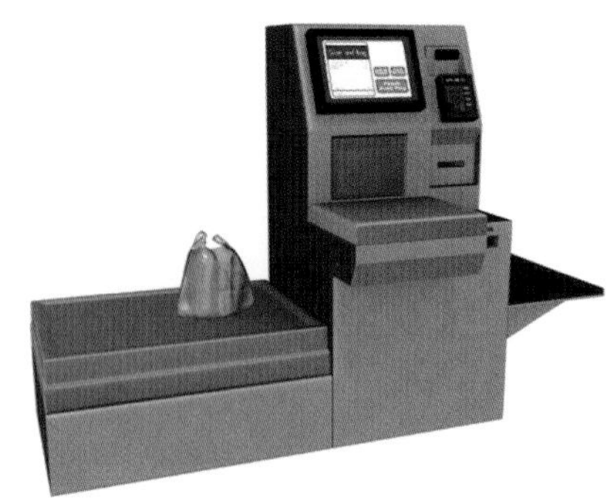

Checkouts have laser scanners and computer-based tills. When you scan the barcode on the product, the computer system looks up the price and adds it to your bill. Scanning is much faster and more reliable than having to type in a price. Many shops also have self-checkout areas, as shown on the right, which can speed up the checkout, and keep staff costs down.

Payment systems

You can pay for products by cash, bank cards or by smartphone. Card payment systems contact your bank over a telephone line or other connection, to check whether there is enough money in your account. Many shops have loyalty systems. A loyalty scheme gives customers discounts or special offers, depending on how much they spend. If you have a loyalty card with a barcode, the store computer system keeps track of what you are buying.

Store security

Digital CCTV cameras are used to monitor entrances and exits. Security personnel use radio phones ("walkie-talkies") to communicate with each other. Shops have security gates that will sound an alarm if a product passes through them that has an RF (radio-frequency) security tag attached.

Online shopping

The Internet has changed shopping greatly. Most items can be bought online from "virtual" stores, and delivered to your home. However, with some products, people prefer to see, feel, hear, or try them on before buying them.

Advantages of shopping technology

Choice

Large stores, supermarkets, shopping centres, and internet shopping provide us with a wide range of products to choose from.

Time saving

- It can take less time to shop in large shopping centres and supermarkets because they may have all the products you need in one location.
- Online shopping can save lots of time, as you don't have to leave your house.

Price

- Large stores can be cheaper than smaller stores because they can buy their goods in greater quantities and, as a result, more cheaply.
- Internet-only stores can be cheaper because they don't have to pay for retail premises and staff.

Disadvantages of shopping technology

Damage to smaller local producers and communities

- Smaller local shops can go out of business because they cannot compete with large stores or online stores.
- Town centres can become less vibrant with fewer shops and people, as a result of out of town shopping centres and internet shopping.
- If a local shop closes down, this removes a valuable source of convenience and social contact for many people, especially older people.
- Most large stores are owned by multi-national companies and much of their profit may leave the country.

Over-spending

- Advertising influences us to spend more than we might do otherwise.
- It is easy to over-spend and get in to money difficulties. Credit cards make it easier to spend too much.

Local markets

Due to some of the disadvantages of modern food production and shopping, old-style markets are making a comeback in developed countries, as many people wish to buy local products and to have a more personal shopping experience.

Shopping technologies in other societies

Poorer countries may not have large shopping centres, or computer-controlled stores, and the range of goods may be limited to local produce.

Past exam questions

1. Shopping in the supermarket is now a very different experience to what it was some years ago. Suggest three ways in which technology has improved the shopping experience.
2. Using two examples, explain how the Internet has changed the way we shop.

3. State two advantages in using laser scanners at supermarket checkouts.
4. "When examining the operation of a modern high tech shopping centre, the gap between developed and developing countries becomes very obvious". Explain, using two suitable examples, the meaning of this statement.

Technology in transport

Power used for transport

A hundred years ago, the horse was still an important means of transport. The invention of the internal combustion engine (now used in petrol and diesel cars) caused a transport revolution. Today, engine technology is moving to environmentally friendly electric motors. The table below the types of power used for transport.

Tranport power	Example	Advantages	Disadvantages
Human power	Walking or cycling.	• Healthy	• Slow
Horse power	Horses were the main method of personal transport until just over a hundred years ago, mainly pulling carriages and cabs.	• Much faster than humans	• Not good for long distances
Coal-powered steam engines	This type of engine powered factories, trains, and ships in the 19th century and created the Industrial Revolution.	• Enabled more trade and travel • Allowed more goods to be made	• Very dirty, caused a lot of air pollution • Mining coal is dangerous
Internal combustion engines: petrol, diesel, aviation fuel	This type of engine is used in cars, trucks, buses, planes, trains and ships.	• Created personal freedom in travel • Fast	• Causes air pollution • Releases CO_2 greenhouse gases which cause global warming
Electric motors	Many trains, trams, buses and cars are now powered by electricity. Electricity is either stored in a battery, or supplied via overhead wires.	• Environmentally friendly • No harmful emissions • Quiet	• Recharging can take a lot of time
Nuclear reactors	Used in military ships and submarines.	• Can stay at sea for years without re-fuelling	• Danger of radiation and explosion • Toxic waste products

Car technologies

Bodies and engines

Bodies are made from steel or aluminium, and are coated with advanced paints to resist rusting. Many types of plastic are used in the interior (inside).

Car safety technologies

Modern cars have a wide range of safety features:

- **Safety belts** – prevent drivers and passengers being thrown through the windscreen or against the body of the car if there is a crash.
- **Child seats** - small children are not secure in adult-size belts, so they are strapped into smaller seats.
- **Air bags** – when a crash is detected, these devices blow up into a soft cushion in front of the driver and passengers.
- **ABS (anti-lock brakes)** – prevent the wheels from stopping completely and causing a skid when the car is still moving.
- **Crumple zones** – the front and the back of the car are designed to crumple up on impact which takes some of the energy out of the impact.

Car enviromental technologies

- **Fuel-efficient engines** – modern cars use a lot less fuel than previous models.
- **Regulated emissions** – modern cars are only allowed to emit limited amounts of polluting substances.
- **Electric engines** – the most environmentally-friendly solution, with no harmful emissions.
- **Hybrid cars** – use a combination of an electric motor and a petrol engine. The car can switch automatically between electric and petrol operation.

Car convenience, comfort and security technologies

- **Alarms** – turned on and off by remote control.
- **Keyless entry** – open doors and control other features of the car using an electronic device.
- **Sat nav** – built-in devices tell the driver how to get to their destination.
- **Bluetooth connectivity** – enables you to use the phone in the car while driving safely.
- **Wifi** – enables passengers to connect to the Internet and other devices in the car.
- **Parking sensors** – produce different sounds depending on how close you are to the neighbouring car.
- **Cruise control** – the car computer keeps you at pre-set speed.
- **Self-drive cars** – the car computer will drive the car for you, using cameras and sensors to detect what is around the car.

Technologies in public transport

Public transport includes trains, buses, trams, planes, ships, and taxis.

Advantages of public transport

If it is available, it is better to take public transport than to drive your own car because:

- Public transport uses less fuel and energy per person than private cars.
- Public transport can be faster than cars, especially if it uses special lanes/tracks or goes underground.
- Public transport is much cheaper, especially considering the cost of buying and owning a car.
- You can relax, read a book or get some work done instead of driving.
- Public transport reduces traffic congestion in cities.
- Internet technology makes it easy to look up routes and times and to buy tickets online.

Technologies used with public transport

Public transport makes use of websites, smartphone apps and special displays to allow you to:

- View routes and timetables.
- Book, pay for and print tickets.
- View real time information on locations and arrival times.

Other technologies used by public transport systems include:

- Ticket machines to read your ticket and open the gate.
- Integrated ticketing so that one ticket works for different types of transport, e.g. trains and buses.
- WiFi connections on trains and buses.
- Automatic recorded announcements of the next station.
- Computer-controlled signalling to control trains and trams.
- Automatic road-crossing gates.
- Security X-rays and metal detectors at airports.

Underground trains/metros

Advantages

- **Extremely fast** – no need to stop for other traffic, as there is none. Different underground train lines operate at different depths so they don't need to cross tracks.
- **Ideal for large cities** – underground trains can transport millions of people every day.
- **Requires very little space over ground** – just entrances and exits.
- **Are operated by electricity** – no fumes or refuelling.

Disadvantages

- Very expensive to build the tunnels and underground stations initially.

Bicycles

Bicycles are an extremely healthy and cheap way to get around. Many cities and towns have built bicycle lanes to encourage bicycle use. Bicycles can be faster than cars in many cities.

Public bicycle schemes

Some cities have installed racks of public bicycles for hire at certain locations. For a small daily or yearly fee, you receive a ticket or card that enables you take a bike out of the lock, and return it to any other rack within a certain time.

Public bicycles have many advantages. They are:

- Cheap to hire.
- Fast and convenient for short city trips.
- Widespread.

If you have access to such a scheme, there is no need to buy or transport your own bike.

Test yourself

Give three advantages of public transport over private transport.

Past exam questions

1. Give three examples where technology has changed the way we travel.
2. Many cities, including Dublin, provide specially designed bicycles for hire and use. Suggest two advantages of this system of transport in cities.
3. Underground rail systems are used in many large cities. Suggest two reasons for this.
4. Name two safety features found in modern cars.
5. Services to customers of intercity rail travel have improved through technological advances. Outline, using two examples, new technologies now available to rail customers.
6. Describe two ways in which modern technologies have improved public transport. Give two reasons why public transport should be used in cities in place of cars.
7. Modern cars have changed dramatically since they were first introduced in the early 1900's.
   (i) Explain, using three examples, the environmentally friendly features available in modern cars.
   (ii) Outline the operation of any two of the following technologies in modern cars:
   - Air bags.
   - Bluetooth connectivity.
   - Keyless entry.

Technology in sport

Examples of technologies in sport

- **Equipment and clothing** – most sports use high-tech, strong and lightweight materials for equipment and clothing.
- **Electronic measuring devices** – athletes use electronic devices (often smartphones or smart watches) to measure times, distances, heart rates, sugar levels, breathing rates etc.
- **Goal line technology** – high-speed cameras and computers are used to record and analyse whether the ball crossed the line or the post.
- **Roving TV cameras and drones** – roving cameras can move along tracks at the side of the pitch, be suspended from cables, or fly over the pitch. Computers are used to control the movement of the cameras. Operators use a remote control to move and point the cameras, and to zoom the lenses for close-up shots. At a major event, there could be 20 or more cameras. In the control room, the editor decides which camera signal to broadcast.
- **Video replays and analysis** – computers can be used to replay the video from any point, slow it down, or draw extra lines on the screen. Replays are used in some sports, e.g. rugby to help the referee make a decision.

- **Electronic scoreboards and screens** – large electronic screens are used in stadiums to display the score, replays, pictures of the crowd, close-up shots, and other information such as match statistics.
- **Disability sports aids** – special wheelchairs and running devices help people with disabilities to enjoy and compete in sports.
- **Drugs and drug testing** – sophisticated technology devices are used to detect whether athletes have taken illegal performance enhancing substances.

Advantages of technologies in sport

- We have the opportunity to see a lot more sport because of cameras and TV technology.
- Goal-line and video replay technology help the referees to make decisions.
- Video technology helps coaches to improve their team's performance.

Disadvantages of technologies in sport

Some sports competitors have taken illegal drugs to try to enhance their performance. This means that everyone must get tested for drugs at important sports events.

Past exam questions

Electronic technology plays an ever-increasing role in sport. Describe three modern uses of technology in sport.

Technology in health and safety

Technology plays a major part in improving our health and keeping us safe.

Technologies in health

- **Drugs** – medicines, vaccines and antibiotics have saved countless lives.
- **Pacemakers** – these electrical devices are inserted into your chest to keep your heart beating regularly.
- **Artificial limbs** – are used to give movement back to people that are missing arms or legs.
- **Incubators** – keep babies safe that are born with illnesses, or too early (prematurely).
- **X-ray machines** – can take pictures of the bones in your body.
- **MRI scanners** – can take detailed pictures ("slices") of the muscles and organs in your body.
- **Computer information systems** – are used to track people's health records to make sure the correct treatment is given.
- **Radiotherapy** – is used to kill cancer cells.

Technologies in safety

- **Protective helmets and clothing** – workers on building sites wear hard helmets and boots to prevent injury.
- **Robots** – are used instead of people, when working conditions are very dangerous, e.g. handling nuclear and toxic materials, or bomb disposal.
- **Food testing** – machines are used to test food to ensure it doesn't contain dangerous substances.

Health and safety of older people

People become more vulnerable to injuries and sickness as they get older. As we age, our bones and our muscles get weaker. This means that it can be harder to get around. If older people fall, they are likely to break bones. If they live alone and fall or have a heart attack, nobody may know. Technology can help older people in many ways, as outlined below.

- **Wearable personal alarms** – if a button is pressed, the alarm contacts an operator who can call an ambulance or relatives/neighbours. The device can also use GPS so its location can be tracked.
- **Stair lifts** – fit on to normal stairs and use an electric motor to move a seat up and down from one floor to the next.
- **Mobility scooters** – these single-seat electric buggies can be driven slowly along the footpath.
- **Security cameras and alarms** – can help older people feel safer in their homes.

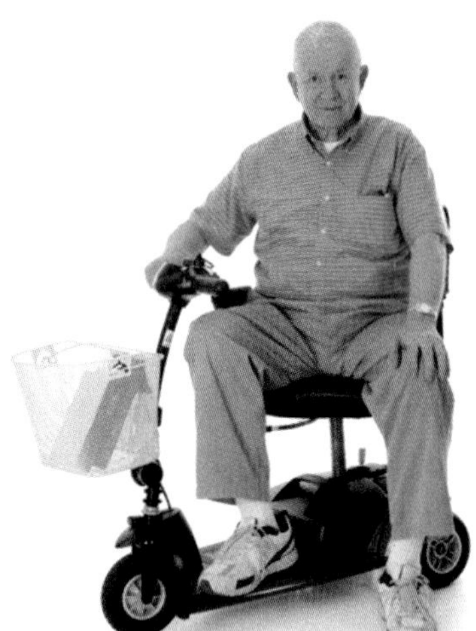

Advantages of health and safety technologies

People live longer, healthier and safer lives because of these technologies.

Disadvantages of health and safety technologies

The cost of medical treatments and use of medical technologies gets higher every year, as more people live longer. This cost is passed on to people in insurance premiums and government taxes.

Test yourself

Name three ways in which technology has improved healthcare.

Past exam questions

The personal safety of elderly people is an important issue in modern society.

(a) Describe two situations where elderly people may be particularly vulnerable and state why.

(b) In each case, suggest an application of technology, which could contribute, to making their environment safer.

Technology in education

Examples of technology in education

- **Interactive whiteboards** – teachers connect these screens to a computer and display documents and presentations. The screens can be drawn on, and a picture of the screen saved to a computer file.
- **E-books, computers and tablets** – many students use e-books rather than paper books.
- **Educational websites and videos** – students and adults can use educational websites and videos, and free educational websites such as Khan Academy and FutureLearn.
- **Computer software** – students can use software as part of class learning. For example, the software packages SolidWorks and Circuit Wizard are available in many schools to help with drawing, product design, and the understanding and building of electronic circuits.

Advantages of technology in education

- Students don't have to carry heavy books when using e-books.
- Learning can be improved by using videos and software in the classroom.

Disadvantages of technology in education

- Students can become distracted with personal computers and tablets in the classroom.
- Students can become weaker at working out or remembering solutions for themselves, if an answer can be looked up on the Internet.

Test yourself

Name two types of technologies used in education.

Past exam questions

State one advantage and one disadvantage of using electronic tablets in schools.

Technology in work and employment

Changes in work due to technology

The world of work has been completely changed by technology. Centuries ago, most people worked to produce food and products, in farming, trades and factories. Nowadays, most jobs in developed countries are office-based and require high levels of knowledge and skills.

More people are employed in providing services to others, for example in business, health, and education, than in making things, for example in manufacturing, construction, and farming.

This change has come about largely because of machines and computers. Machines and computers can do the work of many people so fewer people are needed to carry out many tasks. However, new jobs have been created in other areas, for example in industry making machines and computers, applying computers to work situations (information technology), and in leisure activities (hotels, restaurants, and fitness).

Examples of how technology impacts on work

- **Farming and fishing** – once employed the majority of people, but now only employ a small percentage of the workforce, because large machines can do the work of many people.
- **Banking and finance** – computers, internet banking and ATMs (automated teller machines) have replaced many people. However, more jobs have been created in providing financial services.
- **Manufacturing** – robots, machines and computers have replaced many people. More skilled jobs, e.g. maintaining and improving machines and processes, have replaced unskilled jobs.
- **Health** – more jobs have been created in health industries, as technology keeps people alive for longer, and there is demand for more technology.
- **Education** – more education is needed to prepare people for more skilled jobs, and a more complex society.
- **Tourism and leisure** – a lot of employment has been created in tourism, accommodation, catering and events, as people travel more around the world.

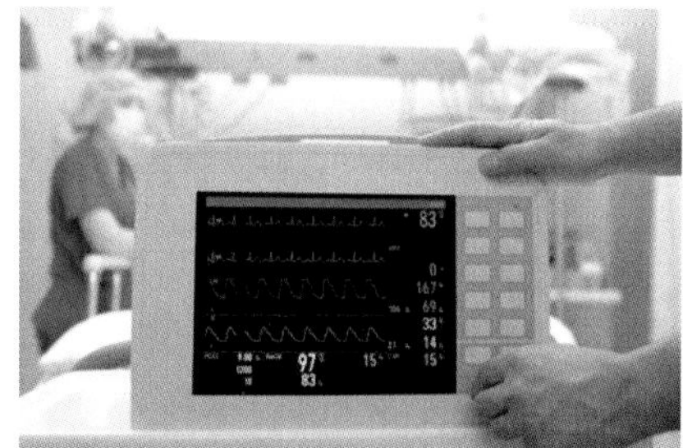

- **Military** – as superior technology can contribute to successful military outcomes, a lot of money is spent in many countries in producing and purchasing military software and equipment.

Developing countries and lower wages

Many jobs in manufacturing have moved from developed countries to developing countries. This is because wage costs are lower in developing countries. Developed countries cannot compete directly with developing countries by making the same products.

In order to maintain employment, developed countries need to invest in research and education to provide services, designs and ideas that require innovation and high skills. Some of the high-skilled areas that provide jobs today are in IT, such as software development, and in the design of sophisticated health products, such as drugs and medical devices.

Advantages of technology at work

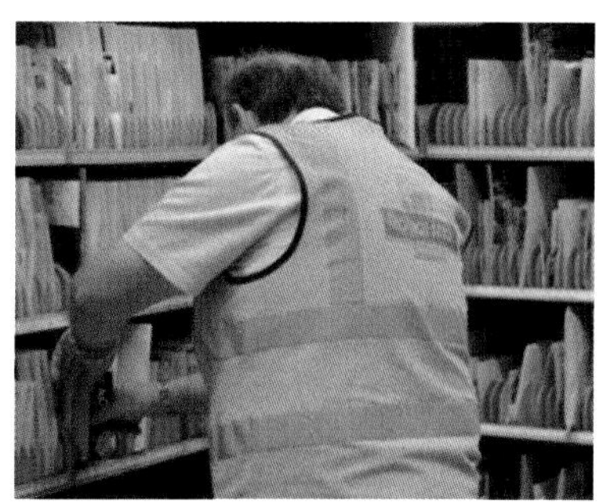

Productivity

Technology makes people and society more productive. More goods and services can be produced by the same amount of people. For example, automatic sorting systems mean that postal workers no longer have to sort all the post by hand.

More interesting work

Technology has made many jobs more skilled and interesting, as well as less tedious and physically demanding.

Safer work

Technology has made hazardous work environments safer by using machines and inventions.

Disadvantages of technology at work

Fewer unskilled workers are needed

- People with low levels of skill find it hard to obtain employment with good conditions that pays well.
- People in employment need to upgrade their skills on a regular basis (life-long learning).

Risks to physical and mental health

- Communications technologies can keep us connected to work in an unhealthy way.
- Sitting for long periods of time in front of computer screens is unhealthy and requires frequent breaks.

Test yourself

Give three examples of how technology has changed employment in Ireland.

Past exam questions

1. State two reasons why computers are used to control modern manufacturing.
2. Manufacturing jobs in Ireland are frequently lost to developing countries.
   (a) Explain why jobs are being transferred to other countries.
   (b) Outline the types of skills required by the Irish workforce to maintain employment in Ireland.

Environmental impacts of technology

Environmental problems caused by technology

Technology creates large amounts of waste and damages the environment. Reasons for this include:

- Technology changes quickly - people buy new products and discard the old ones.
- Many products are designed to be disposable, i.e. thrown away, usually after a short time.
- Discarded products and packaging often contain plastic, which is hazardous to the environment.
- Discarded electrical goods such as batteries, fridges and fluorescent bulbs contain harmful chemicals.
- A lot of energy is required to manufacture and transport technology products. Most of this energy comes from burning fossil fuels such as oil and gas. This pollutes the air, and releases carbon dioxide and other greenhouse gases that cause global warming and climate change.

Short product life cycles

Many products have short life cycles. A short product life cycle means that the product doesn't stay on the market for long before it is replaced by a new or improved version. Some products are designed to last for a short time only. An example of a short life cycle can be seen with smartphones. The problem with short product life cycles is that they create a lot of waste.

Disposable products

Disposable products are designed to be thrown away after a short time. Examples of disposable products are razors, nappies, plastic bags, and plastic pens.

Companies make disposable products because:

- Products can be made more cheaply if they don't have to last as long.
- It can be cheaper to make a new product than to repair an old one.
- People like the convenience of disposable products.
- Disposable products create sales for new products.

Managing and processing waste

Several techniques have arisen to manage the large amount of waste being generated.

Landfill

Landfill means dumping waste products and rubbish in a large hole in the ground, and when it is full, covering it over with earth. Landfill is damaging to the environment, as some waste products contains toxic chemicals that pollute the ground, rivers and seas. Landfill looks and smells bad, and attracts rats and birds. More land is needed for landfill as we generate more waste.

Sea

Some waste is dumped at sea. This causes pollution for fish and sea life. Fish can eat tiny pieces of plastic, which can kill them.

Recycling and separation of waste

The amount of waste sent to landfills can be greatly reduced by recycling. Recycling means separating out the different materials in waste products, and reusing those materials to make new products. Metals, glass, certain types of plastic, paper, batteries, and organic waste can be recycled. Organic waste means food or garden waste.

Recycling symbol

Reasons for recycling

It is important to recycle tins, bottles, plastics and paper because this reduces the amount of waste and pollution in the environment. Fewer natural resources and energy are used to make new materials, for example:

- Fewer trees are cut down to make more paper.
- Less oil is used to make more plastics.
- Less mining is needed to make metals.
- Less fossil fuel is burnt to create electricity to make new materials and products.

Processing of organic waste and biodegradable products

Organic waste is biodegradable. This means that bacteria will decompose organic waste into nutrients that are useful for the soil. Organic waste can be processed in several ways:

- It can be turned into compost and natural fertilisers for farms and gardens.
- Organic waste gives off gas that can be collected, sold and used.
- Burning this gas can generate electricity.

Biodegradable plastic

Biodegradable plastic, made from cornstarch, is now available. One use of this plastic is to make bio-bags, for holding organic waste prior to collection and recycling. Another valuable use is in product packaging.

Electrical waste and WEEE

Because technology generates a huge amount of waste, the EU has issued a law stating that countries must recycle electrical waste, and sellers of electrical goods must take back old electrical goods when people buy new ones.

This type of waste is called WEEE (waste from electrical and electronic equipment). You may have seen free WEEE collection points in your community.

WEEE waste includes old fridges, TVs, microwaves, washing machines, bulbs and batteries. WEEE products are broken up and separated into different types of materials like metals, glass, plastics, batteries and bulbs, which are sent off for recycling.

Activities

1. Try to find out what happens to waste in your local area. Where does organic waste go? Where does plastic and paper waste go?
2. Choose an area of technology or an area of our society that is causing damage to the environment. Write a short report on what is happening, and what could be done to improve the situation.

Past exam questions

1. Communication and entertainment products have benefited greatly from technological advances.
   (a) Many of these products have a short "life-cycle". Explain, using a suitable example, the meaning of product life-cycle.
   (b) Outline, giving two reasons, why many of the products are regarded as disposable.
2. Waste batteries should be disposed of in a: (a) landfill site? (b) recycling centre? (c) household bin?
3. Why should we recycle soft drink cans? State two reasons why plastic bottles should be recycled.
4. Explain the term "biodegradable" and name one common biodegradable household material.
5. State the meaning of the graphics shown.

6. Many "end of life" microelectronic devices (e-waste) find their way to landfill.
   (a) Outline two reasons why many electronic devices have a "short working life".
   (b) Outline two reasons why sending these products to landfill is not good practice environmentally.

CHAPTER 18

Inventions and discoveries

Introduction

Technology progresses by people continually improving what is available to them. This chapter lists some of the people that made discoveries or invented products that went on to become significant in society.

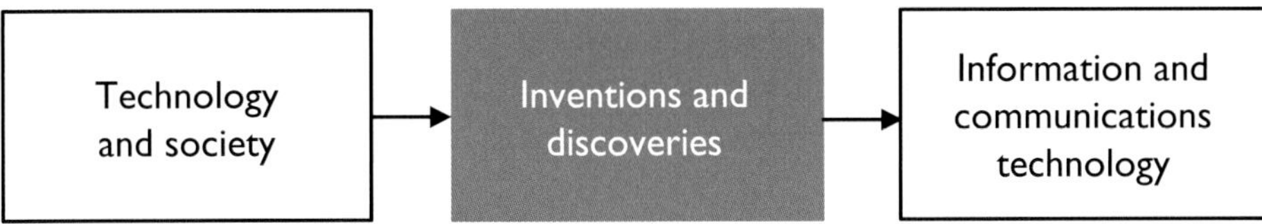

Inventions and discoveries

Transport

Name	Invention or discovery
John Kemp Starley	**Bicycle** Although Penny Farthings existed already, Starley invented the modern rear-wheel-drive cycle, with two similar-sized wheels.
George Stephenson	**The "Rocket" train, and passenger rail transport** Stephenson built the first commercial steam train, the "Rocket", and the first steam train engine railway.
James Watt	**Improved steam engine** Watt created a design for a steam engine that went on to power the Industrial Revolution. The unit of power (watt) is named after James Watt.
Nikolaus Otto	**Petrol engine** Otto developed an internal combustion engine using petrol as fuel. This type is widely used today in cars.
Rudolf Diesel	**Diesel engine** Diesel developed an internal combustion engine that uses diesel as fuel. Diesel engines are more fuel-efficient than petrol, but are noisier and heavier. They are used in buses, cars, trains, and ships.
Karl Benz	**Car** Benz built a petrol engine in 1878, and after a few years, he combined this engine with a 3-wheeled carriage, which was the first automobile.

Name	Invention or discovery
John Boyd Dunlop	**Pneumatic tyre** Dunlop developed inflatable tyres, which made journeys over bumpy roads more comfortable.
Henry Ford	**First mass-produced cars** Ford was responsible for the development of the assembly line technique of mass production, making cars affordable. The first car that he produced was called the "Model T".
Harry Ferguson	**Tractor** Ferguson developed the modern agricultural tractor. His name lives on in the name of the Massey Ferguson company.
John Philip Holland	**Submarine** Holland was an Irish engineer from Co. Clare. He realised that the best way to attack ships was from underneath. He developed the first modern submarine, commissioned by the U.S. Navy.
The Wright Brothers	**Aeroplane** The "Flyer" made just four short flights but the Wright Brothers went on to make more successful planes.

Domestic appliances

Name	Invention
Hoover and Spangler	**First production vacuum cleaner** Asthmatic James Spangler invented an electric suction machine. Boss Hoover bought the patent from Spangler and mass-produced "hoovers".
Josephine Cochrane	**Dishwasher** Cochrane said that she invented the dishwasher so that tired housewives would not have to wash up after meals. Her business Garis-Cochran, began production in 1897 but dishwashers did not become common household items until the late twentieth century.
James Dyson	**Bagless vacuum cleaner** Dyson has made sales of more than £3 billion from developing a bagless vacuum cleaner that would not lose suction as it picked up dirt.
Laszlo Biro	**Ball point pen** A biro is a pen that has a tiny ball rolling in a socket at the tip. As the pen is moved, the ball turns and picks up ink from a tube, and deposits the ink on the page.

Communications and entertainment

Name	Invention
Alexander Graham Bell	**Telephone** Bell's mother and wife were both deaf, which influenced his life's work. His research on hearing devices led to him inventing the telephone.
John Logie Baird	**Television** The first working television was a mechanical system, invented in 1925 by John Logie Baird. TVs are now electronic.
Guglielmo Marconi and Nicola Tesla	**Radio** Although the invention of radio was a complicated mix of inventions by both Marconi and Tesla, Marconi was the one who made radio communications profitable, and most people today think of him as the father of the radio.

Health

Name	Invention or discovery
Marie Curie	**Radioactivity** The word "radioactivity" was invented by Marie Curie, who was a famous scientist. She discovered that some materials give out (radioactive) rays. These are now used to kill cancerous cells.
Louis Pasteur	**Pasteurisation** Pasteurisation means the heating of drinks (such as milk, wine and beer) to a certain temperature for a period of time to kill bacteria.
Louis Braille	**The Braille language** Braille is a written language for blind people, where characters are represented by patterns of raised dots, which are "read" by fingertips.

Clothing

Name	Invention
Stephanie Kwolek	**Kevlar** Kwoelek was a chemist who worked for the DuPont chemical company. She invented Kevlar, a lightweight fibre that is stronger than steel. It is used in bulletproof vests, helmets and other protective clothing.
Whitcomb Judson	**Zip fastener** To "relieve the tedium of fastening high button boots", Judson developed the zip.

Electricity and electronics

Name	Invention
Thomas Edison	**Filament light bulb** Edison had over 1000 patents for devices, including the phonograph and the motion picture camera, but he is best remembered for the electric light bulb.
Michael Faraday	**Electric motor** Faraday studied electricity and magnetism. This led to his invention of the electric motor, which is used in many household devices.
Alessandro Volta	**Battery** Volta was the first to generate electricity chemically in a casing.

Computers

Name	Invention
Charles Babbage	**Computers (hardware)** Babbage is considered by many to be the "father of the computer", Babbage is credited with inventing the first mechanical computer.
Ada Lovelace	**Computer program** Lovelace was a brilliant mathematician who worked with Charles Babbage. She wrote what many consider to be the world's first computer program.
George Boole	**Computers (software)** Boole was professor of mathematics at UCC, and his logical and mathematical work, boolean logic, is the basis of digital computing and electronics.
Tim Berners-Lee	**The World Wide Web (WWW)** In 1989, Tim Berners-Lee came up with the idea of using hyperlinks across a computer network to link documents together. This made possible the enormous "web" of web pages that we have today.
Bill Gates	**First commercial successful personal computer** Bill Gates started the Microsoft company that produced software for the first IBM personal computer. Microsoft went on to become one of the largest computer software companies in the world.
Steve Jobs	**Apple products, the iPhone** Steve Jobs started the Apple computer company with a focus on design, and started the smartphone revolution with the iPhone.
Mark Zuckerberg	**Facebook** As a student, Mark Zuckerberg and some college friends, invented Facebook, the popular social networking website.

Past exam questions

1. The first car was invented in 1885 by: (a) Louis Pasteur (b) John Starley (c) Karl Benz?
2. From the history of technology, name any two inventors and describe their achievements.
3. The television was invented by: (a) Thomas Edison (b) John Logie Baird (c) Nikola Tesla?
4. State the contribution made by any two of the following to the development of modern transport. (a) Henry Ford (b) Wright brothers (c) George Stephenson.
5. The pneumatic bicycle tyre was invented by: (a) Garry Ferguson (b) John Boyd Dunlop (c) John Philip Holland?
6. The production of the Model T Ford in 1920 was one of the first examples of (a) one-off production (b) just-in-time production (c) mass production.
7. A method of reading for blind people was developed by: (a) Louis Pasteur (b) Louis Braille (c) Louis Vuitton?
8. Alessandro Volta invented the first: (a) motor (b) battery (c) light bulb?
9. The inventor of the zip fastener was Whitcomb L. Judson. (a) State one advantage of the zip fastener. (b) Name three other inventors and their inventions.
10. Name the inventors of: (a) the practical electric light bulb (b) the first modern automobile.
11. Name the modern inventor responsible for the invention of the bagless vacuum cleaner.
12. Name an invention credited to Alexander Graham Bell.
13. Describe briefly the contribution made to technology by one of the following: (a) Alexander Graham Bell (b) Charles Babbage (c) John Logie Baird (d) Guglielmo Marconi.
14. The steam engine was developed by (a) Thomas Edison? (b) George Stephenson? (c) Nicholas Otto?
15. Michael Faraday built the first (a) car? (b) motorcycle? (c) electric motor?
16. Name the inventors associated with the following inventions: (a) Rocket (b) Flyer.

17. From the following list of inventors, identify the inventor associated with each of the inventions listed below. Inventors: T. Edison, M. Faraday, G. Marconi, G. Stephenson, J. Dunlop

Invention	Inventor
Light bulb	
Steam train	
Electric motor	

Information and communications technology

Introduction

This chapter describes the technologies that have created the information age - computers and communications technologies. It looks at different types of computers, and the components that they are made from. It describes communications networks such as mobile phones, computer networks and the Internet. It also looks at video and music technologies, and common software applications.

Computers

Information processing

Computers are devices that process information. The use of computers to process information is called "information technology" or "IT".

> **Information technology (IT)** means the use of computers to process information.

The information processed by computers is stored in digital form. Digital means that information is stored as a set of numbers, using 1s and 0s. Digital information used by computers is called data. Data is saved as files. A file is a block of data saved on a computer.

Basic operation of a computer

Computers are composed of two main parts: hardware and software.

> **Computer hardware** means the physical parts of a computer.

A computer needs hardware in order to work. However, a computer cannot do anything useful with only hardware. A computer is a general-purpose machine, it needs to be "told" what to do by the software. Files containing these instructions are called computer programs.

> **Computer software** means the set of programs that run on a computer.

Software is stored as a set of files on the computer. The hardware runs the software. The software processes information, i.e. it reads input data and generates output data. You cannot see software - you can only see its effects, for example what it outputs to a screen.

Computer hardware

The diagram shows the main components of a computer.

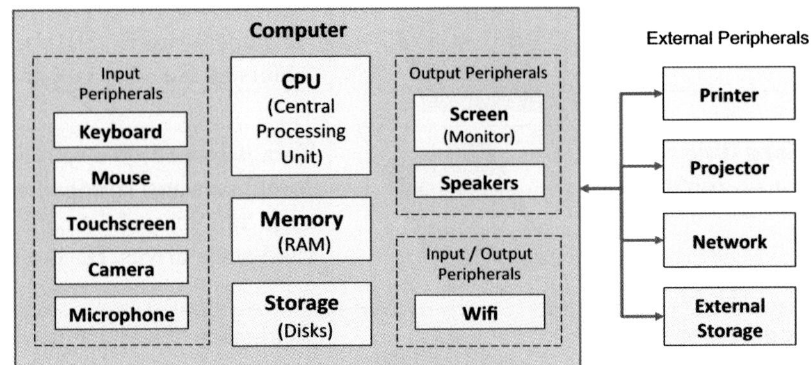

Main components of a computer

CPU

The CPU (central processing unit) is a large digital "chip". The CPU acts as the "brain" of the computer and carries out all the processing and calculations.

Memory

The CPU uses memory to store the data that it is currently working on. Memory is typically measured in gigabytes (GB). There are two types of computer memory:

- RAM (random-access memory). RAM is read-write memory. This means the CPU can write data to RAM as well as read data from it. However, RAM is not permanent memory, it loses its data when the power is switched off.
- ROM (read-only memory). Data can only be read from ROM. The CPU cannot write data into ROM. ROM is permanent memory, it retains its data when the power is switched off. A computer starts up by first running a program stored in ROM. Once the computer is up and running, it switches to RAM.

Peripherals

Peripherals are devices that supply data to, or receive data from the CPU and memory. Peripherals can be internal (built in to the computer) or external (outside the computer).

Input peripherals	Output peripherals	Input and output peripherals
• Keyboard • Mouse • Microphone • Scanner • Joystick • Touchscreen • Camera or webcam	• Screen (monitor) • Speaker • Printer • Projector • Network router	• External storage (hard drives) • SD card • Network router • Ethernet port • WiFi interface • USB port

Storage devices

Storage devices are used to store data permanently. Storage devices are read-write, which means that they can be written to as well as read from. A computer will contain at least one internal storage device. Further storage devices can be connected externally via cables or wirelessly. Data storage is usually measured in GB. Common types of computer storage devices are listed in the table on the next page.

Storage devices are commonly used for backup. Backing up means making a copy of your data in case the original data is deleted, changed or lost.

Type	Picture	Description
Flash memory		Flash memory is permanent storage on a chip that you can read and write to. Flash memory is used in mobile phones and tablets as it is very fast and has no moving parts.
Hard disk drives (HDD)		Data is stored on a spinning magnetic disk. Most desktop computers and laptops have a hard disk inside. They can store large amounts of data. They are slower than flash memory and solid-state drives. Portable hard drives are also available.
Solid-state drives (SSD)		Solid-state drives are made from flash memory. Even though they are more expensive, they are beginning to replace hard disk drives in computers, because they are faster, quieter and smaller.
USB memory stick (or key)		USB sticks provide additional or portable data storage. They are made from flash memory, and plug in to the computer's USB port.
SD memory card		SD cards are portable flash memory in a very small thin package. They are commonly used in cameras and tablets to store photos and videos. They can be inserted and removed from a small slot in the device.
CDs, DVDs and Blu-ray disks		Compact disc (CD) and DVD (digital versatile disk) are optical data disks that can be read from an internal or external drive. CD-R and DVD-R are read-only disks. CD-RW and DVD-RW are read-and-write disks. Optical disks are often used for longer-term backup of data.
Cloud storage		Cloud storage means storing data on computers on the Internet. An advantage of cloud storage is that the data is accessible from any location, and a certain amount of cloud storage is usually free of charge. A disadvantage is that it is slow because the data has to be transferred over the Internet. Also your data may not be as secure or private if it is accessible via the Internet.

Worked example 1: Data storage

Past exam question

Data storage has changed in recent years. (i) Name two portable data storage devices. (ii) Outline two uses of portable data storage devices. (iii) What are the units of data storage capacity? (iv) Suggest one possible disadvantage of using a portable data storage device.

Valid answers

(i) Portable data storage devices are: USB memory keys, CDs, and portable hard drives.
(ii) Uses of portable data storage devices are: to back up files and to transfer files from one computer to another.
(iii) Units of data storage capacity are gigabytes (GB).
(iv) A disadvantage of a portable storage device is that it could be lost or stolen.

Types of computers

Computers exist in many forms. Some of these forms are not obvious, for example your smartphone and your washing machine contain computers.

Computer type	Picture	Description
Desktop computers/ personal computers (PCs)		The first computers started out as large machines available only in big corporations. When electronics technology advanced, smaller personal computers (PCs) could be made. Desktop computers are widely used in businesses and in homes. Desktop computers usually have separate computer casings, large easy-to-read screens and keyboards. They are easy to use, but they are not portable.
Laptops		As computer and battery technology developed further, portable computers could be made. In a laptop computer, the keyboard is built-in to the case, and the screen folds over like a book. Laptops have a built-in WiFi connection. Programs that run on a desktop will also run on a laptop. Laptops are often not as powerful as desktop computers, and they have a smaller screen. However, they have the advantage of being portable.
Tablets		Tablets have no built-in keyboard, and are lighter and more portable than a laptop. They use a touchscreen instead of a keyboard and a mouse. They are fast to start up, and reliable. Many software applications for desktops and laptops also run on tablets.
Smartphones and smart watches		Smartphones contain a combination of a phone, a computer and a camera. They have a touchscreen and a built-in WiFi connection. Since they are portable, smartphones are suitable for running communications-related applications (apps). Smartphones are not suitable for detailed tasks like writing documents and creating technical drawings because of their small screen size.
Industrial computers and microcontrollers		Small powerful computer systems called microprocessors or microcontrollers have been built in to countless machines and devices. These include cars, planes, traffic light systems, supermarket tills, washing machines, televisions, cameras, robots and all kinds of machines used in manufacturing. The computer technology inside those devices enables those devices to do more complex things, and communicate with us and other devices more effectively.

The evolution of computers

Computers have improved enormously in terms of power, size and cost in the last few decades. The first computers took up a whole room and were made from valves (transistors that look like light bulbs). They required an enormous amount of electricity and weren't very powerful. Nowadays, computers are small, fast, incredibly powerful, and can be run from a battery.

Reasons for continual improvement in computers

Computers have continued to improve for the following reasons:

- **Miniaturisation (shrinking of electronic components)** – the enormous reduction in the size of components allows more complex processors to be made, which run faster, use less power, and are more affordable.
- **Improvements in screen technology** - technology has advanced to allow millions of pixels (light points) to fit on a flat and affordable liquid crystal display (LCD) screen. Also, the development of touchscreens has allowed us to use small devices without keyboards as computers, such as smartphones and tablets.
- **Improvements in battery technology** - laptops, tablets and smartphones would not have been possible without huge advances in battery technology, which has made batteries smaller, lighter, powerful and longer lasting.

Evolution in digital technologies

Improvements in the size and power of computer technology have had major impacts in other technology areas and industries. We look at some of these below.

Photography and video technologies

Cameras have undergone huge improvements in recent years, because of computer and digital technology.

Film cameras

Early cameras used film. Film is a roll of thin plastic that is coated with light-sensitive chemicals. When it is exposed to light briefly, it can capture an image. In order to see the image on the film, the film had to be "developed", using chemicals to make the image correct and stay fixed. It was a time-consuming process.

Digital cameras

Digital cameras have now almost completely replaced film cameras. Digital cameras work by splitting the image up into millions of tiny dots called pixels. The values of the colours and brightness of each pixel are recorded as numbers. This means that the entire image becomes recorded as a set of numbers.

Numbers are easy for computers to work with. There is a computer inside a digital camera that does all the processing and saving of images. It also allows you to see the image on screen, and to choose different functions to operate the camera.

Video

Video is generated by showing a series of images very quickly one after the other. This used to be done using rolls of film, and it now can be done using digital cameras, by recording all the moving images as sequences of numbers.

Storage of images and video

Digital images and video can be stored on any digital storage device. On a stand-alone digital camera, digital images and video are usually stored on an SD card. SD cards are small and light and can hold lots of data. You can transfer photos and videos from your digital camera to other devices.

Formats of images and video

Images and data are stored in a few common file formats. A file format is a specific way of saving information into a file. Common image formats are JPEG, GIF, PNG and TIFF. Common video formats are MP4, WMV and MOV.

Integrated cameras

Digital cameras are integrated into smartphones and tablets. The camera function can be implemented using the computer that is present inside the smartphone or tablet.

Webcams

Computers that do not have a built-in camera can use a webcam. This is an external camera that can plug in to the computer.

Webcam

Advantages of digital cameras over film cameras

- Digital cameras produce higher quality images.
- There is no need to buy costly film.
- There is no need to get film developed, which is costly and time-consuming.
- You can take as many photos or videos as you like at no additional cost.
- Digital cameras are not expensive.
- Digital cameras are built in to most phones.
- You can store lots of photos and videos on your computer, and back them up.
- You can easily share digital photos and videos with others via messaging, social media, and video and image sharing websites.

Disadvantages of digital images and video

Because it is easy to copy and distribute digital files, producers of digital media (photographs and video) are not paid properly for their work if their products are illegally copied and distributed.

Movies, DVDs and video streaming services

Movies used to be sold on VHS cassettes, which had magnetic tape inside. DVD technology then became available. This is an optical disc with the information recorded digitally. It offered a much higher picture and sound quality. A Blu-ray disc offers even higher quality video playback.

Old VHS recorder and cassettes

Video streaming technology is similar to downloading a file from the Internet, but with some differences. With streaming, you don't have to wait until the entire file is downloaded before you can play it. It will play as soon as the streaming starts. With streaming, a file is never stored on your device, so it doesn't take up lots of data storage space.

Companies such as Netflix offer video streaming services over the Internet for films (movies) for a monthly subscription. This means you don't have to buy or rent and return physical movies on a DVD or Blu-ray. You can stream video on your computer, or a smart TV which has a computer inside, with the right software.

Music and sound technologies

The recording, distribution and playback of music have undergone a revolution because of electronic, computer and digital technologies.

Vinyl records

The first successful commercial technology for music was vinyl records. Music is recorded as vibrations in circular grooves in plastic disks. To play it back, a needle is inserted into the groove, and the vibration of the needle as the disc spins, creates an electrical signal, which is amplified to drive the loudspeakers.

Vintage vinyl record player

Cassette tapes

Magnetic tape cartridges became popular after vinyl records. They had the advantage of being smaller and so could fit into portable wearable devices. The user could also record on to them.

Compact disc (CD)

CD (compact disc) was the first digital music technology. Music is coded as a sequence of numbers (1s and 0s) on to the disk. A laser reads the 1s and 0s back and converts them back into a music signal. The quality of CD recordings was higher than vinyl and the disc couldn't be damaged as easily as vinyl.

MP3 players

MP3 technology allowed digital music to fit into smaller computer files. Now music didn't need to be bought on physical discs or tape, it could be downloaded directly to computers. Also computer and battery technology had become so good, that portable computer devices could be made. One of the first portable MP3 players was the iPod. Now all smartphones and computers can play MP3 files.

Music streaming services

Instead of downloading files, music can be streamed. Streaming technology doesn't store any files on your computer. It just sends the data to your computer over the Internet in small pieces, and your computer puts the pieces back together again and plays them. Spotify and internet radio are streaming services.

Personal musical devices

Early electronic devices were large and music had to be listened to inside buildings. Now electronics and computers have become so small that we have portable and wearable music technology.

Advantages and disadvantages of internet-provided music

- People have access to virtually any music they want, and it is extremely cheap.
- Because music has become so accessible and inexpensive, many musicians and singers struggle to make an income by selling recordings of their music.

Book and print technologies

Computer and digital technology have also had an impact on print media. Books have become available as e-books. E-books can be read on tablets or smartphones or on special book-reading devices, such as a Kindle. Many e-books have become much cheaper than print books, and some have become free.

Many books are now also available as audio books, where they can be listened to, rather than read. The sales of newspapers and magazines are affected by the digital media revolution, as many people access news and opinions freely from the Internet.

Communications technologies

Communications technologies allow us to communicate with each other over long distances.

CT stands for communications technology.

Telegraph and telephone

The electric telegraph was a device for transmitting and receiving messages over long distances. It was the first long-distance fast communications technology invented. By the end of the nineteenth century it was followed by the telephone. The first telegraph and telephone networks needed electric wires to transport the electrical signals across long distances.

A **signal** is the transmission of some information from one place to another.

Radio

Radio has revolutionised communications because it doesn't require any wires. Radio waves can be transmitted through the air because they are electromagnetic (like light). The following technologies use radio waves to transmit information:

- Radio channels.
- Television (TV).
- WiFi.
- Bluetooth.
- Mobile phones.
- Satellite communications.

Mobile phones

Mobile phones use radio signals to transmit digital data to and from mobile network masts. GSM and LTE are two radio communication technologies used by mobile phones. A SIM card is needed in a mobile phone in order to connect to a mobile network.

Satellites

Satellites are radio communications devices that orbit (rotate around) the Earth in space. They are used to send telephone and internet data signals around the world.

GPS

GPS (global positioning system) is a technology, which uses a set of GPS satellites to continuously beam down radio signals to Earth. By analysing the signals coming from four different satellites, a GPS-enabled device can calculate where it is in the world, to within a few metres.

Computer networks

A computer network is a group of computers connected so that they can communicate with each other. Computer networks can be created using the technologies and devices described below.

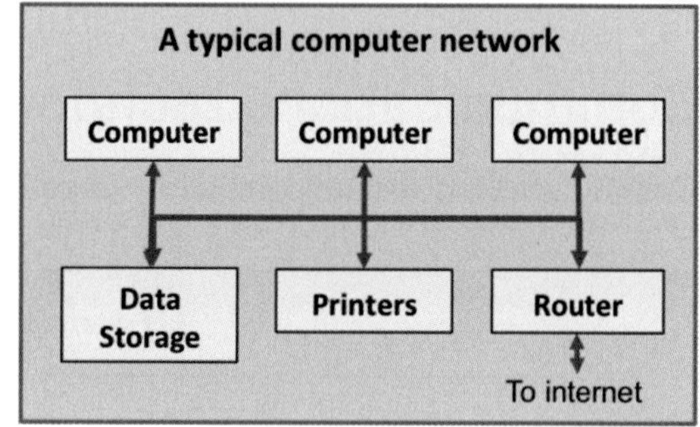

Ethernet

Ethernet is a type of cable and communication system that is used to connect computers to form computer networks.

WiFi

WiFi is a technology that allows computers and network devices to connect to each other without using wires or cables. It uses high frequency radio signals to transmit data. It only operates within a limited range. Public places where you can access WiFi are called "access points" or "WiFi hotspots".

Routers

A router connects one network to another. For example, a router will connect a WiFi network in your home or school, to the telephone network (which will connect you to the Internet).

Fibre-optic cables

Fibre-optic cables are extremely fast and are used for high-speed internet connections. Fibre-optic cables are fast because they transmit information as pulses of light through narrow flexible glass tubes.

USB

USB (universal serial bus) is a connection system used to connect peripherals to computers, e.g. mice, keyboards, and external storage devices. The USB system has two functions: it can be used to transfer data, and it can also be used to power the peripheral devices themselves. The USB symbol is shown on the right.

USB symbol

Bluetooth

Bluetooth is a short-range radio technology that is used to wirelessly connect peripherals (such as mice, keyboards and speakers) to computers. It can also connect phones together.

Bluetooth symbol

The Internet

The Internet is a giant computer network. It uses a combination of the different communications technologies above, such as telephone networks, satellites, Ethernet and fibre-optic cables - plus many millions of computers - to connect business and personal computers all over the world.

The Internet has enabled the sharing of information between people to an extent that has not been possible before. Documents and software programs can be downloaded from websites and computers that are connected to the Internet. This network of websites and documents is called the World Wide Web.

Computers and communication technologies

ICT stands for information and communications technology.

The diagram below shows an example of ICT. It shows a smartphone communicating with other phones and with other computers via the Internet. You don't have to memorise this diagram, it is just to show you how devices can connect to each other using different kinds of networks. Points related to the diagram are listed on the next page.

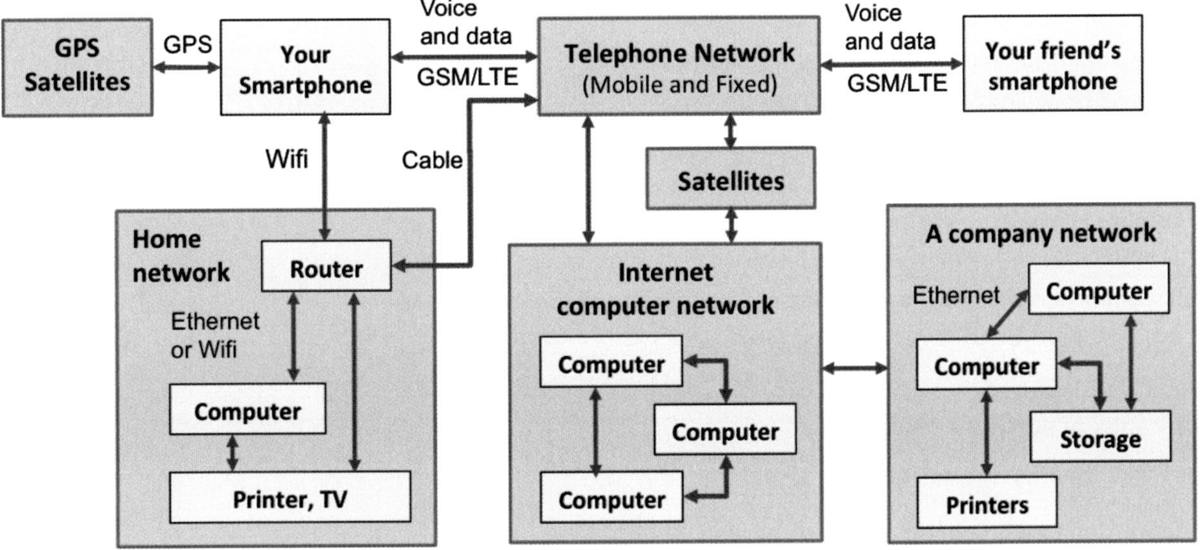

Diagram showing smartphones and computers communicating via ICT technologies

Points to note from the previous diagram

- The smartphone uses its GPS connection to locate where it is.
- The smartphone can "talk" to other phones by connecting to the mobile telephone network (via GSM or LTE).
- The smartphone can connect to a home network (and to the Internet) using its WiFi connection.
- The smartphone can also connect to the Internet through the telephone network.
- The telephone network uses satellites to connect across long distances.
- The Internet is made up of many computers connected to each other in different ways, e.g. via the telephone network, via satellites and via other computer networks.
- For example, the smartphone on the left could be communicating with one of the computers on the right, which could be in a different country.

Software applications

Software refers to the programs that run on a computer. Software allows the same computer to carry out many different tasks. A piece of software that is designed to carry out a specific set of tasks is called a software application. "Application" is often shortened to "app", especially on smartphones.

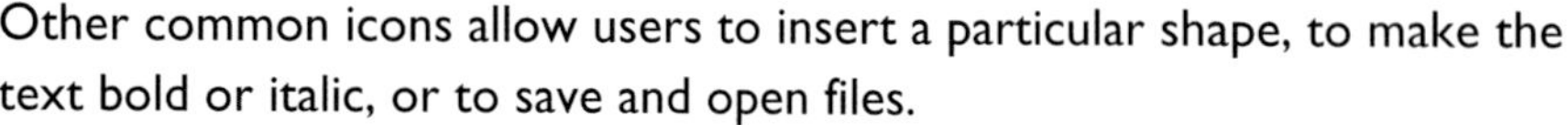
A **software application** (or **app**) is a program that runs on a computer.

Software design - toolbars and icons

Software icons are visual symbols on screen that make computer programs easier to use. Some examples of icons are shown on the left. Icons are often grouped together in what is known as a "toolbar".

Using the example toolbar shown on the right:

- When the user selects the pen icon (indicated by "X"), this will allow the user to draw lines on the screen.
- When the user chooses the paint bucket icon (indicated by "Y"), this will allow the user to fill in a selected area on the screen with a selected colour.

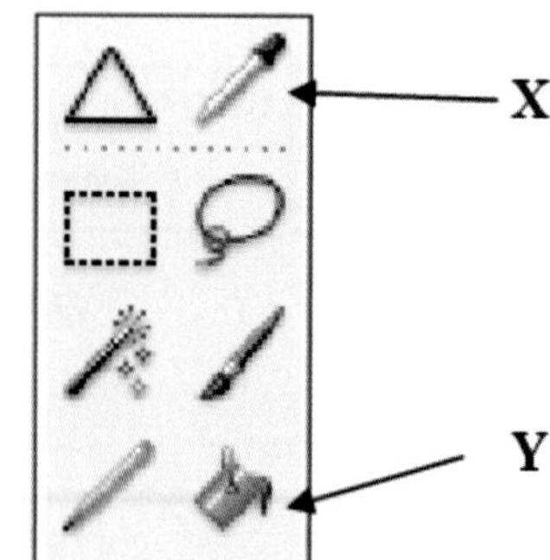

Other common icons allow users to insert a particular shape, to make the text bold or italic, or to save and open files.

Advantages of software icons

Icons make it easier to use software because:

- Icons don't take up much space on screen.
- The same icons are used across different computer programs. This means that you only have to learn what the icon means once.

The set of screens used by a computer program, and how they look and operate, is called the graphical user interface (GUI). The design of the GUI is important to make the software easy to use.

Operating systems software

Probably the most important piece of software on a computer is called the operating system. This software is necessary to control the computer hardware and to be able to allow other software applications to run. Common operating systems are listed below.

Operating system	Description
Microsoft Windows	Run on a majority of desktop computers and laptops. Also runs on some tablets and smartphones.
Mac OSX	Runs on Apple desktop and laptop computers.
IOS	Runs on Apple smartphones and tablets, such as the iPhone and iPad.
Android	A free operating system from Google that runs on many tablets and smartphones.
Linux	A free open-source operating system based on the Unix operating system.

Open-source software

Many software programs are "open-source". Open-source software is developed by many people working together. With open-source software you can change the software code yourself and upload a new version of it so that others can use it. Most open-source software is free to use, or costs a small support fee.

Communications and entertainment software

Email

Email was one of the first digital communications software applications to be developed. It is mostly used for business communications.

Internet browsers

An internet browser, or web browser, is a software program that allows you to read web pages online. "Online" means via the Internet. Web pages are written in a language called HTML. A collection of web pages is called a website. A website is identified by a URL – a web location name like "www.google.com". Web pages contain hyperlinks. If you click on a hyperlink, your browser will fetch and display the web page that the hyperlink points to. Internet browsers also have built-in video and music player software.

Websites are used to communicate news and information about businesses and services over the Internet. Websites can also run software so that you can search for and purchase products and services, using on-line shopping carts and checkouts.

Internet messaging and social media software

The wide availability of smartphones means that social media applications, such as Facebook, Twitter, Snapchat, Instagram and others, enjoy huge popularity. Social media applications allow you to connect with others over the Internet, to send messages, pictures and sound, and to "follow" and receive messages from other individuals or organisations.

Social media applications combine many computer and communications technologies: computers, mobile communications, internet communications, messaging technologies, digital video technologies and digital music technologies. The impact of social media applications is discussed in the "Technology and society" chapter.

Video software

Software applications are available to allow people to communicate via video, and to share videos. This has been made possible by internet communications and the digital video technologies we saw earlier.

The picture shows video-conferencing software being used to hold a meeting between people who are in different physical locations.

YouTube is a video sharing application with an enormous database of videos. It allows anyone to upload videos, and to have them seen by anyone in the world.

Skype and Facetime are free software applications that allow you to communicate via video over the Internet, with anyone else who has the same software application.

There are also software applications for creating and editing videos, such as: Final Cut Pro, Adobe Premier Pro, iMovie and Windows Movie Marker.

Music software

Software applications, such as Spotify, allow customers access to very large catalogue of digital music. Soundcloud allows sharing of music and sounds. Most radio stations also have an internet channel, where you can listen to broadcasts over the Internet using an internet browser or music player application.

Games software

Games are complex software applications. They combine computer, internet, video, and music technologies. Console games require high-speed computer hardware and usually special controllers to play them. Simpler games for smartphones are very popular. Players from different countries can play against and with each other over the Internet, and compete in competitions.

Business software

Computer software is highly important in business and most businesses cannot operate effectively without it. Most businesses also have their own websites and use social media for advertising.

Desktop publishing and document creation

Software such as Microsoft Word has been available for a long time for the creation of documents such as business letters, reports and CVs. Similar products are Apple Pages, and free products such as Google Docs and Open Office.

Desktop publishing is used to create more complex documents containing advanced layouts and images, e.g. books, posters and web pages. Examples of desktop publishing software include Microsoft Publisher and the Adobe range of products, which includes Illustrator, In Design, and Photoshop. Advantages of document creation and desktop publishing software include:

- You can mix text and images and lay them out as you like.
- It is easy to use – you can use software icons and drag-and-drop controls.
- You can see how it is going to look on screen before you print or publish it.
- You can collaborate with others by sending or sharing the document with them.
- It is easy to store documents and files on a computer as they don't take up any physical space.
- You can send the files to a printer or a printing company.

Financial and business software

Spreadsheet software is used to carry out calculations on data. A spreadsheet is a grid, where you can enter or load in data. You can also input formulas. The spreadsheet carries out calculations on the data and displays the answers in the grid. Spreadsheets can also draw graphs and charts based on the data. Microsoft Excel is an example of spreadsheet software. Other examples are Google Docs and Apple Numbers.

Accounting and payroll software is used by most businesses. This software is more advanced than spreadsheets. It can be used to track all your transactions, to generate receipts and bills, to pay your staff and suppliers, and to manage your bank accounts. Banks use a lot of computers and software to track customers' transactions, and to manage the investments and loans that the bank makes.

Managing customers

Managing customers is a very important area for businesses and there are software applications to help with this. CRM (customer relationship management) software is used to track contacts, customers and enquiries. It can be used in advertising to send emails and messages, to track sales and to manage after-sales support and service.

Staff in call centres use CRM and communications software to receive, route, record and track all incoming calls, and to record correspondence.

Staff in a call centre

CAD and manufacturing software

CAD (computer-aided design) software is used to design and draw products for manufacture. It can also be used to design electronic circuits. CAD software has a large library of parts, and can produce very accurate drawings and specifications. It allows you to test products and circuits to see how they work, without having to physically build them.

Manufacturing software in factories can use the information in the CAD files to control machines to make those products.

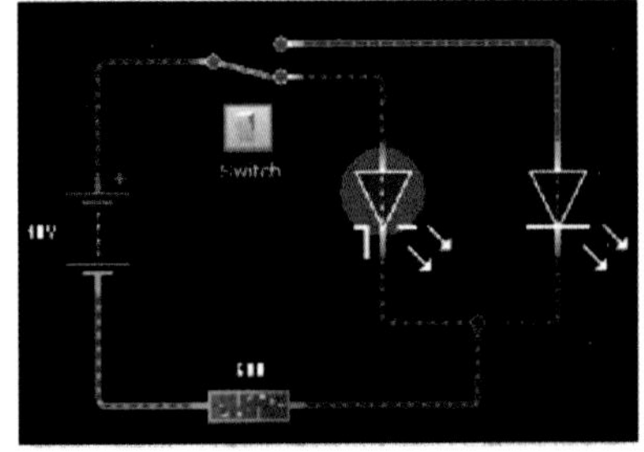

Circuit simulation software

Travel software

Navigation software (sat nav)

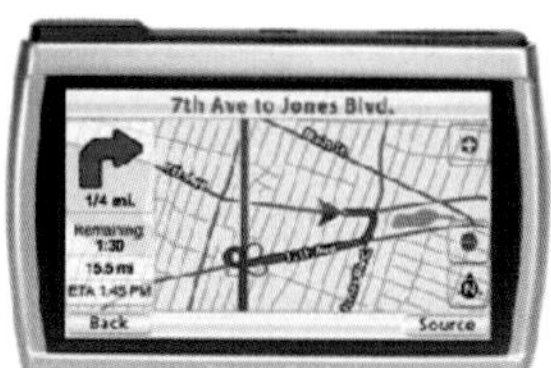

A sat nav device

Smartphones and special car devices can run sat nav (satellite navigation) software. This software uses the GPS communications technology that we saw earlier, combined with video and sound technologies, to tell you where you are in the world. It uses a large database of map information, which it can usually download over the Internet, to show you where you are on a map.

The sat nav software can plot a route from one point to another, and give you instructions on how to get there, i.e. tell you what turns to take and when.

Automatic car tolls and meter-reading

Car toll software uses video and radio technologies to detect when your car passes a toll point, and will send you a bill or apply a charge to your toll account. Software can be used to remotely read and process meters for electricity, gas, water, and industrial pipelines.

Software for cars and aeroplanes

Many cars have cruise control software, which is used to keep the speed of the car constant. Driverless cars are becoming available. These cars use lots of software to read information from cameras and sensors in the car, to control the car's speed and direction. Aeroplanes use auto-pilot software, which can fly the plane without humans.

A driverless car

Health software

This is a rapidly growing area for software applications, especially with the widespread availability of smartphones. Smartphones can monitor the amount of exercise a person is getting, measure the number of steps and distances walked or cycled, lap times, calories burned, heart and breathing rates, and sleep patterns. Using smartphones and health apps, groups can arrange to meet, collaborate or compete in health-related activities.

Educational software

Many school books are available as e-books which can be read using laptops and tablet devices. One advantage of this is that the student has to carry fewer heavy books. Some disadvantages include the cost of the device, the likelihood of it breaking if dropped, and the temptation to use other software on it during class.

There is a lot of educational software available for young children, which makes learning fun. There are lots of useful and interesting videos on technology subjects available on Youtube and educational websites.

Smartphone software

Because of its portability and because it has lots of communication technologies built in, a smartphone is particularly suited for certain types of software applications.

Software suitable for smartphones

Software that is suitable for smartphones includes:

- Navigation systems and maps.
- Health and fitness apps.
- Communications software such as email, internet browsing, messaging, social media, and photo sharing.
- Games.
- Podcasts (audio shows) and audio books (downloadable over the Internet).
- Audio recorder/dictation.
- Digital music players.
- Software for paying small amounts to shops.

Because of their small screen size, smartphones are not suitable for detailed tasks like creating documents, drawings and images.

Features of smartphones that support particular software applications

Smartphones are suitable for particular software applications because they are small, light, portable and battery-powered. They also have the following built-in features:

- Connections to mobile phone, WiFi and GPS networks.
- Bluetooth transmitter and receiver.
- Photo and video camera, and flash light.
- Powerful computer.
- Touchscreen.
- Speakers.
- Microphone.
- Tilt sensor.

QR codes

QR (quick response) codes are two-dimensional barcodes. They can be read by a camera and special software. A common use of QR barcodes is to place them on a product, and when you scan the barcode with your smartphone, it will bring you to the webpage of that product or company. They can also be used to track goods for delivery and within factories.

Security and privacy

Because so much valuable information is held on computer systems (such as our bank accounts), and because computers can be connected to each other via the Internet, security technologies have needed to be developed in order to protect this information.

Fraud and identity theft

Criminals use the Internet to steal. One of the ways they can do this is by identity theft. This means obtaining your bank account or credit details so that they can pretend to be you, and use your accounts. Two techniques used for this are called phishing and skimming.

Phishing

You may have received emails that pretend to be financial institutions or foreign princes in distress. These try to get you to reveal or type in your bank details or usernames and passwords. This is called phishing. These emails can bring you to websites that look like very like the real thing.

Skimming

Skimming involves using a fake card reader to try to capture your bank card details. The fake card reader can be inserted into ATM machines or used in restaurants.

Security techniques

The following techniques are used to make it difficult for people to gain access to private information.

Passwords

Most information is protected by passwords. We have to type in a certain code to access the information. However, passwords can sometimes be guessed or "cracked".

Smart cards

Computers systems can be designed so that you must scan a special card (with a electronic chip in it) before you will be allowed access. This system is used for accessing bank accounts, combined with a password.

Data encryption

Data can be encrypted, i.e. translated into an unreadable code. This means that even if it gets into the wrong hands, the data cannot be read without a special key to decrypt it (translate it back).

Firewalls

A firewall is a piece of software that checks the attempted access that is coming through a computer network. It will only allow connections from trusted computers.

Biometric data

Biometric technology is where a part of your body such as your fingerprint or your eye is must be scanned in order for you to be allowed access. Many smartphones now have fingerprint access technology.

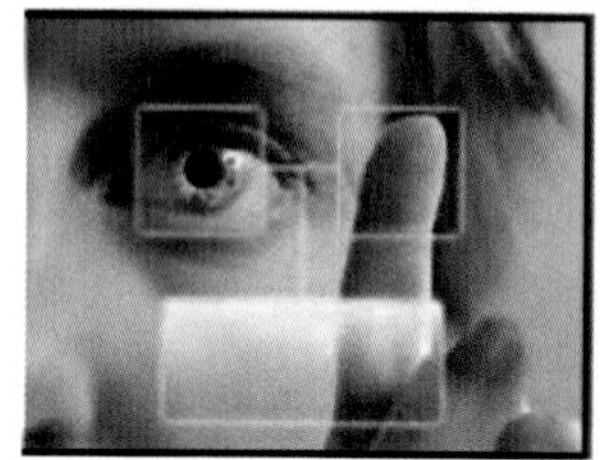

Jobs and roles in ICT

ICT is a large and growing industry employing lots of people. The types of roles that are needed include:

- **Management** – to organise and manage people, money, equipment and to keep projects on track.
- **Design** – to choose how products will look and operate.
- **Engineering** – to design, build and test the hardware components of products.
- **Programming** – to design, write and test the software that operates products.
- **Test and quality** – to independently ensure that products are high quality.
- **Sales and marketing** – to sell products, find out who will buy them, and to carry out promotion.
- **Support** – to look after customers who have bought your products.
- **Research** – to investigate what new technologies or products should be offered in the future.
- **Finance** – to manage the overall money that comes in and goes out of the company and to keep it safe.

Worked example 2: Software applications

Past exam question

Give an example of one activity that can be carried out using each of the following:

- Word processor.
- Desktop publisher.
- CAD.
- Spreadsheet.

Valid answers

- Activity using a word processor: Write a business letter or CV.
- Activity using desktop publisher: Create a newsletter with lots of images.
- Activity using CAD software: Create a design for a technology project, using technical drawings with dimensions.
- Activity using a spreadsheet: Calculate the cost of a technology project.

Worked example 3: Desktop publishing

Past exam question

Students use desktop publishing software to produce design folios for project work.

List four advantages of using this software.

Valid answers

1. You can combine both text and images.
2. You can save your project and make additions and changes at any time.
3. You can see what the printed copy will look like on screen.
4. You have easy-to-use toolbars and icons.

Worked example 4: ICT roles

Past exam question

Outline the role of designers, engineers and programmers in the development of mobile phones.

Valid answers

- **Designers choose the mobile phone's shape, style, colour, functions and technology.**
- **Engineers develop and test the mobile phone's components.**
- **Programmers write and test the software to implement the desired functions of the phone.**

Past exam questions

1. In computing, does IT stand for:
   - Information transmission?
   - Information technology?
   - Information terminal?

2. State the meaning of each of the abbreviations:
   - ROM.
   - USB.
   - CPU.

3. Identify two data storage devices that can be used with a computer.

4. Outline, using two examples, how technology has changed the way in which information is transmitted around the world.

5. Name two technological developments that have improved computer laptop design.

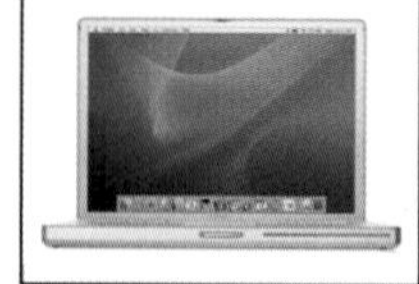

6. What does DVD stand for?

7. The design of modern mobile phones has changed dramatically since they were first introduced.
   (i) Describe one technological advance which made these design changes possible.
   (ii) Describe one additional function available only in modern mobile phones.

8. State two ways in which data on a computer can be protected from unauthorised access.

Past exam questions

9. In what units is the capacity of an external hard drive measured?

10. Communication and entertainment products have benefited greatly from technological advances. Outline two advanced technologies used in these products.

11. Identify this component.

12. Name the technology that allows "sat nav" devices to determine a location.

13. Explain the term "smartphone" in relation to modern mobile phones.

14. Name two new technologies found in handheld devices.

15. Describe two useful mobile phone "apps".

16. WiFi technology has become very common in recent years.
    (i) Explain what is meant by WiFi technology.
    (ii) In relation to WiFi explain the term "access point" (hotspot).
    (iii) Outline, using two examples, some of the benefits of WiFi technology.

17. Name two appliances found in homes that use wireless technology.

18. Outline the meaning of the term "Wi-Fi Hotspot" in relation to communication devices.

19. Home entertainment systems have improved greatly in recent years. Using at least two examples, discuss how home entertainment systems have changed and improved.

20. State two functions of a USB port on a computer.

21. Name two USB devices which can be used with a computer.

22. State two reasons why cassette tapes were replaced by CDs and digital files, for sound recording.

23. Name a software application that requires the use of a webcam.

Past exam questions

24. Electronics play a vital role in music technology. Identify two ways in which electronics enhance our experience of music.

25. State two reasons why digital cameras have become more popular than film cameras.

26. The technologies of GPS, GSM, sat nav, DVD, MP3 and USB are in common use.
    (i) Explain the meaning of any two of these technological terms.
    (ii) For each of the two selected terms, outline the advantages of these new technologies.

27. What does this symbol mean?

28. State the purpose of the QR symbol shown.

29. Mobile phone technology is changing rapidly in response to consumer demand. Describe three recent developments in mobile phone technology.

30. Outline the role of designers, engineers and programmers in the development of mobile phones

31. A software application used for 3D solid modeling is:
    - Microsoft Excel?
    - SolidWorks?
    - Adobe Reader?

32. Explain the term CAD.

33. Explain the function of the symbols X and Y shown, found in a graphics application menu.

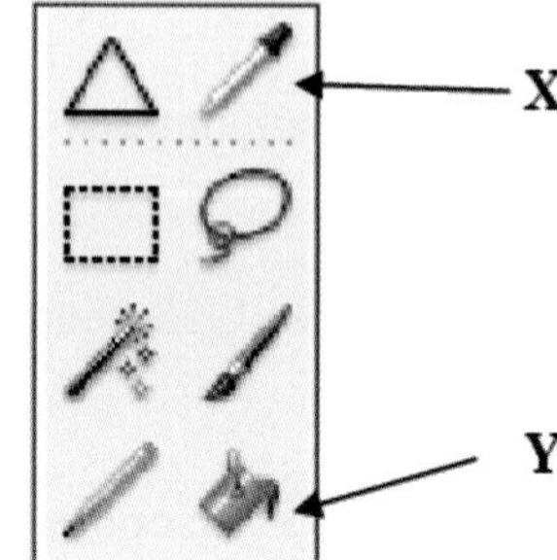

34. How has computer game technology changed in recent years?

35. Give an example of one activity that can be carried out using each of the following:
    - Word processor.
    - Desktop publisher.
    - CAD.
    - Spreadsheet.

Assembling projects

Introduction

This chapter provides a set of techniques and activities to help you to practice assembling working models from different types of structures, and mechanical and electronic components. This experience will be useful for designing and building your own projects, and for answering examination questions.

The following topics are covered in this chapter:

- Joining processes for materials of different types.
- Useful components for project assembly.
- Common project assembly techniques and design solutions.
- Project assembly exercises for you to complete.

Note, this chapter does not focus on the design aspects. This is covered in the following two chapters. The aim of this chapter is to help you to become familiar with assembling different components.

Previous knowledge

Before starting this chapter, you should have completed the "Manufacturing processes", "Mechanisms" and "Electronic circuits" chapters.

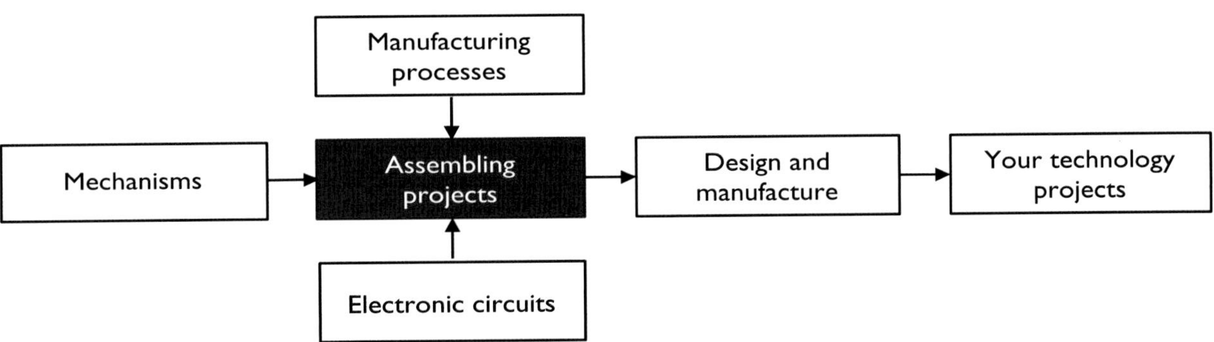

Design sketches

A design sketch is always needed to tell you how to assemble a model. Your teacher may give you a design sketch of a model to assemble, however you should try to make your own. Without a design sketch, you may have to repeat the manufacture and assembly operations because you may not know in advance how the parts are going to fit together. You may also make the parts the wrong size, or run out of space.

The skill of design sketching is also needed for your formal technology projects and to answer design examination questions.

Structures and casings

All models and projects will require a structure or casing to hold mechanical and/or electronic components. The structure may also need to support other moving parts.

Wood or plastic are good materials for these casings. Wood is easy to work with and components can be attached to wood easily using wood screws or glue.

Wooden casing for a technology project

Joining materials of different types

The table below lists some common ways of joining materials of different types together.

Materials to be joined	Possible joining methods
Plastic to wood	• Glueing: Glue with two-part epoxy glue or Super Glue (e.g. Mitre Bond). Note that Super Glue will cause acrylic to discolour. • Screwing: For thin plastic, drill holes through the plastic and screw the plastic to the wood using wood screws.
Metal to wood	• Glueing: Glue with two-part epoxy glue or Super Glue (e.g. Mitre Bond). • Screwing: Drill holes through the metal and screw the metal to the wood using wood screws.
Metal to plastic	• Glueing: Glue with two-part epoxy glue or Super Glue (e.g. Mitre Bond). • Bolting: Drill holes through both plastic and metal and tighten on to each other using nuts, bolts and washers.

Notes:

- "Plastic" above refers to the plastics used for technology projects such as acrylic, polystyrene/HIPS (high-impact polystyrene), ABS, polythene, or PET.
- Extreme care is required with Super Glue. Fingers can become stuck. Use under teacher supervision.

Activities

1. Glue a small piece of sheet plastic to a piece of cut MDF.
2. Drill two holes in a small piece of sheet plastic and screw the plastic to a piece of wood. Why is it best to drill more than one hole, and use more than one screw? Which makes a stronger bond, screws or glue?
3. Glue a small piece of flat metal to wood.
4. Use a metal bracket and screws to join two small pieces of wood together at 90°.

Useful components

Before assembling projects and models, it is a good idea to familiarize yourself again with the components, tools and materials you have available in your technology room. In previous chapters, you will likely have built wooden and plastic structures, simple mechanisms, and electronic circuits on their own but you may not have assembled these together into working models.

Can you identify the components in the pictures below?

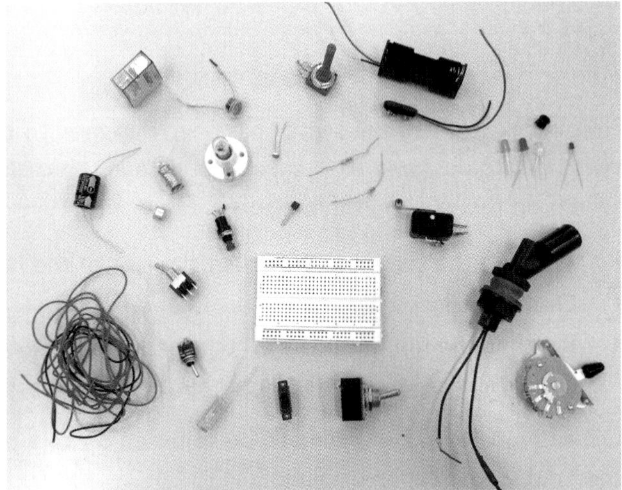

Common assembly techniques

This section describes some tasks that are frequently required when assembling models and projects. Note that when attaching electronic components such as switches, motors and PCBs to a casing, it is usually better to mount the components on to the casing first, and then connect them with wires and solder.

Assembling axles and wheels (or gears)

In your projects, you will very frequently need axles to allow wheels or gears to turn. Usually the axle is fixed to the gear or wheel, and the axle is held but allowed to turn, in a support of some kind which is attached to or part of a body/structure.

- Choose your wheels/gears first then choose a brass or steel rod for the axle that has the same diameter as the inner hole.
- Check where you need to fix the axle and how long the axle needs to be.
- To hold the axle, you can use a special axle support component like that shown in the picture. It is attached to the casing with screws, or you can drill holes in the casing to hold the axle.
- Measure and cut the axle to the length required.
- If you are using an axle holder like the one pictured, screw or glue it on to the structure.
- Thread the axle through the supports and the wheels or gears. If the wheels or gears have a grub screw on them, use that to tighten the wheel or gear on to the axle. Otherwise you can glue the wheel or gear on to the axle with epoxy or Super Glue.

Preventing an axle from moving from side to side

Use the following methods to prevent an axle from moving from side to side:

- If the casing is made of wood, partially drill through the wood so that the axle is held in place in the holes on each side.
- Create a thread on the ends of the axle using a die, and screw a nut (with a washer on the inside) to the ends of the axle.
- Use polymorph (quick-setting plastic) to create a mound of plastic on the axle that prevents it slipping sideways through the axle support.

Attaching switches to a casing

First check to see if the switch has been designed to be attached in a certain way. For example, many switches are designed to fit through a hole in the casing and come with a nut that is used to tighten the switch on the casing. In this case:

- Measure the switch to work out the size of the hole needed.
- Drill the correct size hole.
- Remove the nut, push the switch through the hole from the back/inside of the casing, and tighten the nut again on the front of the switch.

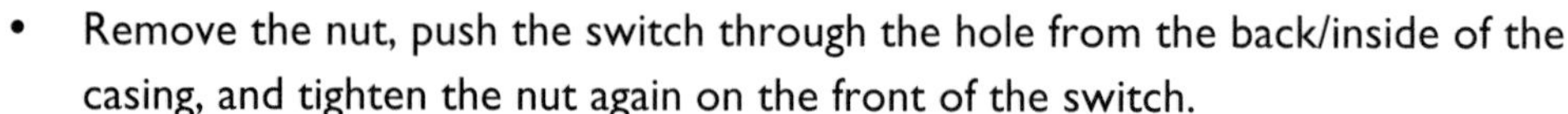

Other switches are designed to be soldered on to a printed circuit board. Limit switches can either be screwed to the casing or glued.

If your switch is already wired to your circuit, e.g. to test the circuit, and you want to mount the switch on the casing:

- Disconnect the power first.
- Disconnect/de-solder the switch from the circuit.
- Attach the switch to the casing.
- Reconnect re-solder the switch back in to the circuit.

Attaching LEDs to a casing

LEDs are often pushed through a small hole in the casing to give an attractive visual appearance. However, avoid pushing them through the casing on their own. LEDs come with a plastic holder designed for this purpose. It protects the LED and forms a tight and more secure fit.

- Drill a hole in the casing to the diameter of the LED holder.
- Insert the bulb part of the LED in the LED holder from the back.
- Insert the LED and holder in through the hole in the casing from the front.
- The LED holder will usually fit snugly in the hole as it compresses a little.

You can then solder connecting wires on to the LED legs.

Securing batteries

Use a plastic battery holder that will hold the right type and number of batteries to give you the voltage you need. The battery holder usually comes with screw holes so you can screw them to your casing, or you can glue them.

Attaching a circuit board to a casing

Spacer columns can be used to attach a circuit board to a casing. These are small plastic cylinders with holes in them (see right), or small wooden blocks, placed under the circuit board.

When attaching with screws

Some circuit boards already have holes for mounting. If not:

- Drill at least two small holes in the corners or in an available part of the circuit board.
- Place the spacers under the circuit board.
- Use a long screw through the spacers to screw the circuit board to the casing.

When attaching with glue

Use Super Glue to glue the spacers on to the circuit board, and to glue the spacers to the casing.

Attaching a motor to a casing

Motors need to be securely attached as they rotate and vibrate and could cause damage and even injury if they come loose.

Some motors come with mounting holes, so screws can be used to screw the motor to the casing.

If there are no mounting holes on the motor, you can glue a flat part of the motor to the casing. If your casing is made from wood, and your motor body is plastic, you may get a better bond if you first screw a piece of plastic to the wooden casing, and then glue the motor to the plastic.

Common design solutions for projects

This section lists some functions that you might need or want to implement in your projects, and describes the components and designs that you could use to implement those functions.

Project requirement	How to implement requirement
Create a repeating up and down movement	• Use a cam-and-follower mechanism driven by a motor. • Use a crank with a connecting rod.
Create a repeating sliding back and forth movement	• Use a cam-and-slider mechanism driven by a motor.
Create a waving oscillating movement	• Use a peg-and-slot mechanism driven by a motor.
Create a linear side to side or up and down movement	• Use a rack-and-pinion mechanism driven by a motor. • Use a pulley belt drive.
Stop linear movement	• Use a limit switch to detect the end of travel and to switch off the motor.

Project requirement	How to implement requirement
Create high rotation speeds	• Use compound gears (large gears turning the small gears), driven by a motor.
Create very low rotation speeds	• Use compound gears (small gears turning the large gears) and/or a worm drive, driven by a motor.
Lift heavy weights	• Use a screw mechanism driven by a motor that slides up and down in a groove or cylinder. • Use a worm drive to turn a winch that winds up a cable.
Open and close a sliding gate	• Use a rack-and-pinion mechanism with limit switches.
Open and close a hinged gate	• Use a worm drive or low speed gears to turn the axle of the gate, with limit switches to detect the end points.
Remove panels for access, viewing	• Use Velcro to hold a removable panel in place. • Use a hinge on one side of the panel.
Create flashing lights	• Use a timer circuit and LEDs.
React to light, temperature, wetness, or proximity	• Use a sensor circuit with the appropriate sensor (LDR, thermistor, probes, proximity sensor).
Detect water levels	• Use a float switch.
Detect an object tilting	• Use a mercury tilt switch.
Detect an object close by	• Use an infra-red proximity detector device.
Detect an object hitting another	• Use a limit switch.

Model assembly activities

This section provides some model assembly activities for you to try yourself. They should not take too long to carry out but you may need several classes to complete them.

The activities include ideas and options for building different kinds of assembly. You will need to sketch a design of your final assembly yourself before you make it. The activities become more complex as the activity number gets higher. Your teacher may have other designs that you can also assemble.

You may have built LED and motor circuits already, as part of the "Electronic circuits 1" chapter. If so, you can assemble those circuits into new casings.

Activity 1: Assemble a simple toy car with wheels

To make a simple model car with four wheels, so that the car can move freely across a surface:

- Note the available components, e.g. materials, wheels, rods for axles, axle supports, and tools and equipment.
- Body options: The body of the car could be shaped from a single piece of wood, or it could be made from number of pieces of wood joined together. The base of the body could be made from sheet metal that is bent over to form short sides to hold the axles. The body could be made entirely of plastic that is moulded in a vacuum former.
- Axle options: you could use special axle support components or brackets attached to the underside of the body or you could drill holes through the side parts of the body. If the wheels come with special screws for securing them to the axles, you can use these. If not, secure the wheels to the axles with glue.
- Make a sketch of how you plan to make your model, showing how the parts connect.
- Make your car body. Smooth the rough parts.
- Cut your axles to size and smooth the rough edges.
- Fit your axles and wheels to the body.
- Apply a surface finish.

Activity 2: Assemble a simple LED display

To make an acrylic display stand with a number of LEDs that light up:

- Decide what type of stand you wish to design, e.g. a model Christmas tree.
- Make a sketch of the LED circuit you will use. (See LED circuit diagrams in "Electronic circuits I".)
- Decide where you will place and hide the electronic components. You may need to attach the components to a wooden base.
- Make a sketch of what the fully assembled item will look like, also showing how it is wired.
- Cut acrylic to size, smooth edges, drill holes for LED holders and insert the LEDs into the holders.
- Bend acrylic using a strip heater to 90° to make the acrylic stand up.
- Attach acrylic stand to the larger base.
- Insert LEDs into holes in acrylic and wire up your resistors, switches and battery or power supply.

Activity 3: Assemble a manual belt drive

To make two pulley wheels connected by a belt or elastic, housed in a casing, and turned by hand:

- Note the available components.
- Decide what size pulleys or gears you want to use.
- Decide what material and shape you want to use for the casing.
- Decide where and how you want to mount the pulley/gears. You could have both visible on the outside, or one hidden inside, or both hidden inside the casing.
- You could have a propeller or similar on one of the axles, visible on the outside of the casing.
- If you have a crank handle of a suitable size, or you can make one, you could attach that to the first axle.
- Make a sketch of how you plan to make it, showing how the axles will be supported.
- Make the casing and attach the pulleys and belt.
- Turn one axle to cause the other to move.

Activity 4: Assemble a motor-driven gear train

In this activity the motor and gears are inside a casing, and there is a rotating part on the outside of the casing. To make a set of rotating gears turned on by a switch:

- Take note of the motor and gears you have available, and rods for axles.
- Decide whether you want to slow down the motor or to speed it up. You can make a compound gear by putting two gears on the same axle. You could use a worm gear on the output of your motor.
- Decide what kind of structure you will use to contain and support the gears and motor. You could use a wooden box that has access from the rear.
- To support the axles, you could make holes in the structure or you could use support pieces of material on the inside.
- Make sketches showing how it will look, and how the parts will fit together and be supported.
- Make your casing. Measure out where the axles will need to go, so that all the gears will inter-connect, and connect back to the motor shaft. Make a hole for an "on" switch if needed.
- Fit the motor, axles and gears inside the casing. Attach any outside display parts.
- Wire up the motor and switch.
- Connect a power supply from the workbench, and switch on.

Activity 5: Assemble a motor-driven cam-and-follower

To make a cam-and-follower mechanism, powered by a motor housed inside a casing:

- Note that the follower should stick out of the top of the casing and move up and down.
- Note the cams, gears and motors that available, and rods for axles. You may want to use an existing cam or build your own.
- You could use a slot in the top of a wooden or plastic box to allow the follower to move up and down. You will probably need to build a support or groove into the casing so that the follower can slide up and down without moving sideways.
- Do not make the follower too heavy. If the cam and follower are both made out of nylon they will slide well over each other.
- You may need to slow down your motor speed. You could use a worm gear or compound gear on the output of your motor. Note which way your motor turns and which way the cam will be turning.
- To support the axles, you could make holes in the structure or you could use support pieces of material on the inside.
- Make sketches showing how it will look, and showing how the parts will be supported and connected together inside.
- Make your casing. Measure out where the axles need to go, so that the cam will be right under the follower, and so that the gears will connect back to the motor. Make a hole for a switch if needed.
- Assemble the cam on its axle, and drop in the follower on top of the cam. Test that the follower will move up and down when you rotate the cam. You may need to use some grease or candle wax at the contact points to reduce friction.
- Fit the gear axles and gears, and then the motor.
- Wire up the motor and a switch.
- Connect the power supply and switch on.

Activity 6: Assemble a motorised rack-and-pinion with limit switches

To make a sliding mechanism, powered by a motor housed in a casing:

- Note that when the sliding part reaches either end, a limit switch should turn off the motor. You can reverse the direction of the sliding part by changing the direction of a switch.
- Find the circuit that you will need. You will need a SPDT switch for on/off, a DPDT switch for the motor direction, two limit switches, a motor, and a rack and pinion gear mechanism.
- You will need a slow-turning motor, or a motor with a worm drive, to turn the pinion gear, which will then slide the rack along.
- Using sketches, think about how you will make a sliding part and how you will keep the sliding part in position as it slides. Think about how you will connect the rack and pinion to the sliding part, support the axle for the pinion gear, and attach the motor. Think about where you can mount the limit switches so that they will be activated just before the sliding part gets to the end of its travel in both directions.
- You could use a flat piece of plastic that slides in two side support grooves, with the rack attached to the underside of the plastic, and the pinion and motor underneath.
- Sketch out your final design, showing how the parts fit together.
- Make the casing and assemble the rack and sliding part. Check that it slides properly in the casing. You may need to grease the contact areas.
- Take off the sliding part and mark out where the axles and motor will go, so that all the gears will connect back to the motor.
- Attach the motor, axles, gears, and replace the sliding part. Check that they are all connected to each other, and will move when the motor turns.
- Attach the limit switches, so that they will be activated when the sliding part gets to the end.
- Wire up the limit switches, on/off switch, DPDT switch and motor according to the circuit diagram.
- Connect the power supply and switch on. Be ready to switch off the power if the limit switches don't work properly initially.
- Adjust the position of the limit switches or other components if needed.

Activity 7: Assemble a manual chain drive

Repeat the steps in Activity 3 using two plastic gears and a light metal chain instead of pulley wheels.

Activity 8: Incorporate a sensor circuit with LED output into a casing

Take the "Darkness sensor with LED output" circuit that you built in "Electronic circuits 2" and incorporate it into a casing/small box, made of acrylic or wood:

- Make the casing.
- Drill small holes in the top to mount the on/off switch, the LDR and the LED.
- Mount the switch, LDR and LED on the top of the casing.
- Secure the rest of the electronics, and a battery as a power supply, inside.

Design and manufacture

Introduction

This chapter will give you practice at answering the "Design and manufacture" exam questions. It will also give you ideas and experience that will be very useful when designing and building your own technology projects.

In order to be able to follow this chapter, you should have completed the previous chapters as shown in the diagram below.

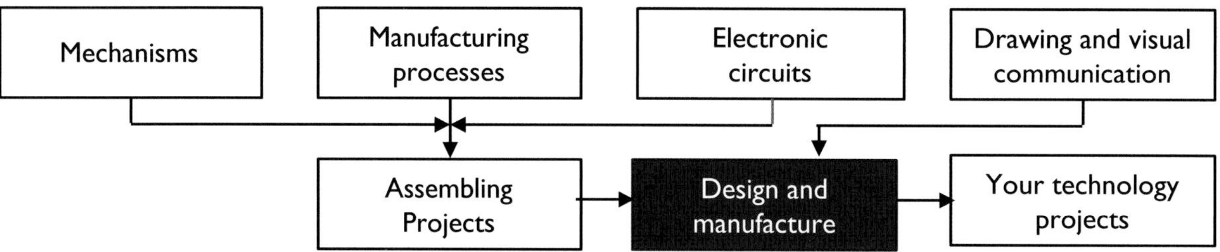

The examples and questions in this chapter begin with simple examples, and then become more challenging.

The design process is introduced first. After that, the chapter gives you practice at sketching your own designs. The chapter finishes with full examination questions.

Important notes regarding sketches in examination questions

- If an examination question asks for a sketch, you can draw free-hand (without a ruler) if you wish. This is what has been done in this chapter.
- If an examination question specifically asks for an orthographic drawing (a plan or elevation) or an isometric drawing, you should use a ruler (and the isometric grid, if provided with the question).

Also note that worked examples in this chapter often provide more information than you would need to write down in an exam situation. This is done for learning purposes.

A design and manufacture process

This section describes a method to carry out design and manufacture. It provides previous examination questions that relate to the design process. Some examination questions are completed for you as worked examples, and others are left for you to finish so that you gain practice.

Why is good design important?

Good design is essential to make products that are safe, work well, look well, and are not too expensive. Being good at design will help you answer design-related examination questions, and it will help you a great deal with your technology projects.

What is required to be good at design?

To be good at design you must be able to:

- Understand the brief, i.e. what you are being asked to do.
- Work out what users would like and need.
- Determine the requirements, i.e. the essential information that you need before you can design the product.
- Think about different ways of solving the problem.
- Have a good knowledge of different materials, tools, processes, mechanisms and electronics that could possibly be used to solve the problem.
- Be able to sketch and draw your design ideas.
- Evaluate your own design, and be able to change it to improve it.

What makes a good design?

A design is good if it solves the problem well. First of all, you need to know as much as possible about the problem that you are trying to solve. This means that you need to understand what the requirements are. To work out the requirements, you will need to consider factors like those listed in the table below.

Requirements areas	Further information
Who will use the design?	What age are the users? What do they like? What will help them? Where will it be used?
What does it need to do?	How does it need to move, measure or indicate things? What size and weight does it need to be? What other weights or sizes might it need to hold or contain? How would the user operate it?
What should it look like?	How important are the aesthetics, i.e. how it looks and feels? Consider the colours, shapes and surface finishes.
How easy would it be to make?	What components, materials, tools, and time are needed? Are these available? A design may need to be built using only the components available in the technology room.
How safe is it?	Could any part of it be dangerous to anyone? What changes or additions could make it less dangerous? (See "Design for safety" section later in this chapter.)
How about the environment?	How environmentally friendly is the design? Does it contain any materials that would be harmful to the environment? Could I solve this problem in more environmentally friendly ways? In what sort of environment will it be operated? What environmental factors must be taken into account?

Requirements areas	Further information
What would it cost to make?	There is always a limit on what it can cost.

Note that it may not be possible to meet all the desired requirements. For example, it might be desirable for a product to look well, carry out complicated functions, and cost less than 5 euro but this may not be possible. So you may need to rank and prioritise the requirements, i.e. to decide which requirements are more important than others, which are essential and which are just nice to have.

The design process

Design consists of a process that can be applied to any design task. The main steps of this process are shown in the diagram.

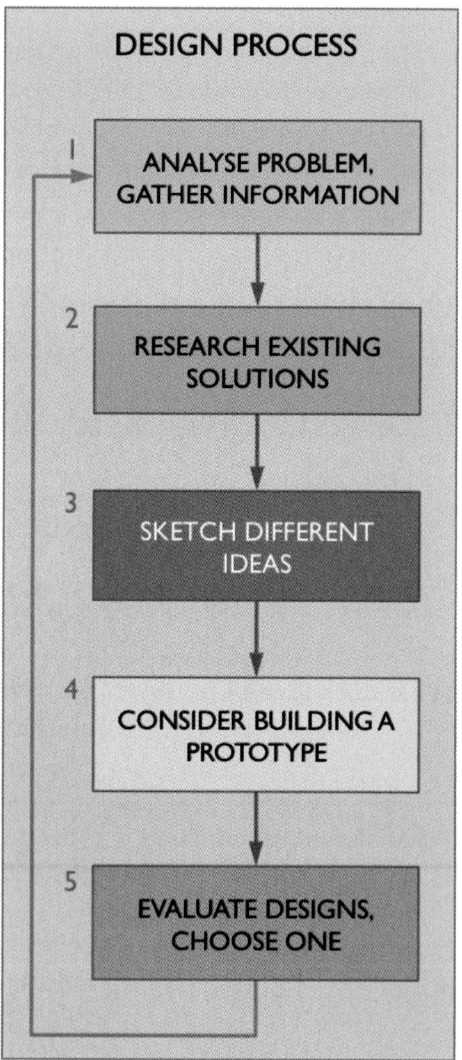

Step 1 - analyse problem, gather information

Analysing the problem means thinking more about how the product might be used. Make a list of all the requirements you can think of, before you start thinking about different designs. Ask others and users, if possible.

Step 2 - research existing solutions

Research where this kind of thing has been done before. Investigating possible solutions can help you to:

- Source design ideas.
- Evaluate existing solutions.
- Identify suitable components, materials, circuits and processes.

Step 3 - sketch different ideas

For each idea you have, draw out rough sketches of how it might look, and how different components might fit together. Draw it from different angles if you need to get a clearer view. This helps you to see how it might work, and to judge how hard or easy it might be to manufacture.

Step 4 - consider building a prototype

If you are designing a large and expensive item, it is a good idea to build a small model of it from cheaper materials. This will help you and other people visualize how the end product might look and function, without having to spend a lot of money on manufacturing.

Step 5 - evaluate your designs and pick one

Decide which of your designs best meets the requirements that you listed in Step 1. Consider how easy or expensive each design would be to build. You must have reasons for choosing a particular design.

Carry out the design process more than once if required

On the diagram on the previous page, your will notice an arrow at the bottom that goes back up to the top. This looping back is called iteration. This means that if you find your initial ideas are not working so well, you can and should go back to an earlier step in the design process. For example, you may have forgotten an important requirement about how the product might be used, or you may have discovered that the design will not work so well in practice, or that it may be too difficult or expensive to manufacture. Design is an iterative process.

The manufacture process

The manufacture process also consists of a series of steps. If you go on to build your design, you will need to use this process. The main steps are shown in the diagram. If you are carrying out a technology project, you will need to document each of these steps in your project folder. (See "Your technology projects" chapter.)

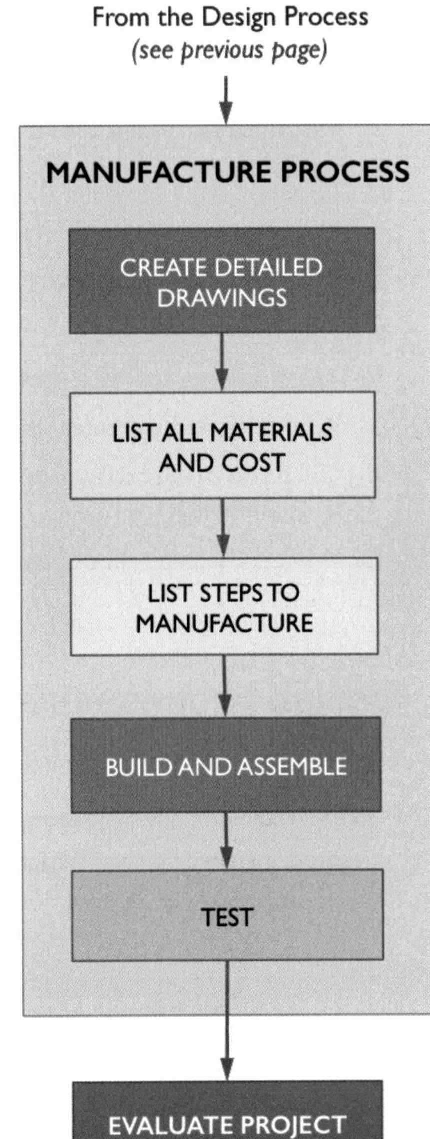

Create detailed drawings

Make sure that all of your drawings are accurate. They should include all the parts with the information needed on how to make and assemble them. For example, label each part with its name, and include the dimensions (lengths, widths, depths, diameters etc.) that you will need for cutting, shaping and assembling. You can also create drawings showing how to assemble the parts.

List all materials and cost

Make a list of all the materials needed, and what they cost.

List steps to manufacture

Write out detailed instructions as to how to make and assemble each part. List the tools and equipment needed.

Test

Test that the assembled product looks and functions as desired, according to the requirements you specified back in the design stage. If not, check that the manufacturing steps were correct and carried out properly. If the product is still not working as desired, go back to the design stage.

Evaluate project

For each project, it is important to understand what worked well, and what could be improved next time. Make a list of everything that worked well, and anything that you could have done differently to improve the outcomes. This helps you to learn how to deliver better designs and projects in the future.

Key points

1. First try to understand the problem and gather requirements for a solution.
2. Then investigate possible different solutions, and evaluate different designs.
3. Before you finish, evaluate the whole task or project.

Test yourself

1. What are the benefits of good design?
2. What does analysing mean?
3. What is meant by requirements?
4. Why is it a good idea to investigate or research different solutions?
5. When would you consider building a prototype? What are the advantages of a prototype?
6. What does evaluating a design mean?
7. What does evaluating a project mean?
8. Why is it good to sketch design ideas?
9. Once you have chosen a design, what steps would you need to carry out before you attempt to build and assemble it?
10. What is the difference between testing a product and evaluating a project?

Design process practice

The worked examples and questions below are taken from previous exam questions, and cover:

- Understanding different parts of the design process.
- Gathering specific requirements.
- Evaluating specific designs.

Worked example 1: Mobile phone holder design

Past exam question
List four important things that the designer had to know before designing the mobile phone holder shown.

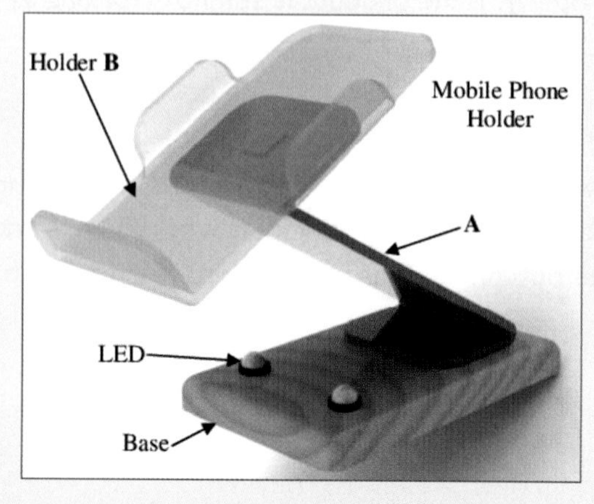

Valid answers
The designer would need to know the following before designing the mobile phone holder:

- Dimensions of the phones that it needs to support.
- Weight of the phones it needs to support.
- Location of the charger point on the phone.
- Location of audio port on the phone.

Worked example 2: Wheelbarrow design

Past exam question
State one advantage and one disadvantage of the two-wheel barrow design shown, as compared with a single-wheel barrow.

Valid advantages
The two-wheeled barrow would be:

- More stable and less likely to fall over.
- More suited to using on flat ground.

Valid disadvantages
The two-wheeled barrow would be:

- Harder to turn, harder to steer on rough ground.
- More expensive to make and buy.

Past exam questions

1. In relation to technology tasks, state two reasons why it is important to undertake an "Investigation of possible solutions".

2. State two reasons why a completed project should be evaluated.

3. Many car companies produce concept designs before introducing a new model. Suggest two reasons for this.

4. Designers commonly use cardboard to produce models of their ideas. State two advantages of using cardboard to make the model shown on the right.

5. A graphic of a wooden toy is shown on the right. Identify two features of good design in this toy.

   The choice of surface finish for children's toys is important. Why?

   List three possible objectives identified by the designer of this toy.

Past exam questions

6. Two different toast racks are shown below.

   For each toast rack:

   (i) Identify a design feature of the toast rack that you like, and give a reason why.

   (ii) Evaluate the design of the toast rack under the following headings: (a) appearance, (b) how well it works (functionality), (c) hygiene, (d) suitability of materials.

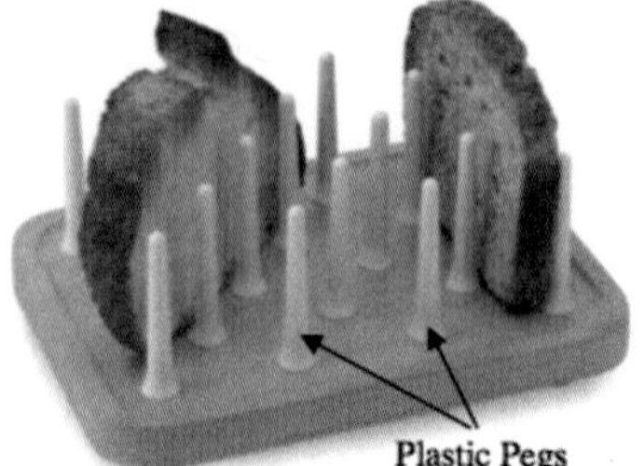

7. List three things that would need to be known before designing a toolbox.

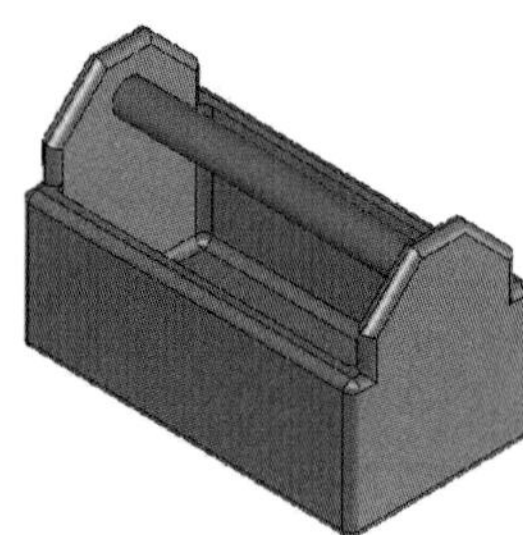

8. An image of an electronic "Steady Hand Game" is shown. Suggest two ways in which this game could be improved to make it more exciting to play.

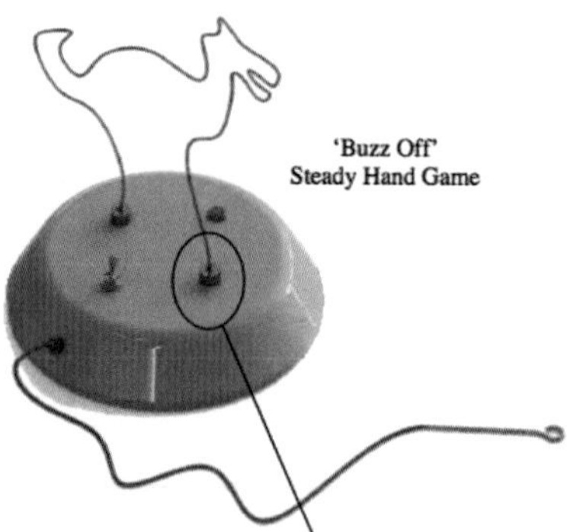

Designing for safety

Products need to be designed so that they are as safe as possible. A good way of designing for safety is to think about the possible risks there could be, and then think about ways in which the product could be designed to reduce those risks. Most products have been designed for safety, so you will find lots of ideas in existing products.

The following table lists safety risks and suggests possible design features to address each risk.

Safety risk	Design features to address safety risk
Cutting yourself	• Make sure there are no sharp edges or rough surfaces. • If any parts have to be sharp, design safety covers for them that are not easy to open.
Injury from moving parts	• Hide moving parts inside casings. • Build guards around moving parts. • Make sure moving parts are securely fastened and cannot come loose. • Design so that moving parts will stop if they meet too much resistance.
Poisoning or infection	• Use non-toxic paints and surface finishes. • Make sure the product is easy to clean. • Make sure there are no harmful chemicals on the surface, and no harmful chemicals can be emitted from the product.
Electric shock	• Use plastic casings for appliances. • Make appliances waterproof. • Operate equipment at low voltages. • Install fuses so that the current will be cut if there is an overload or short circuit.
Burns and fire	• Make sure there is a cooling system if temperatures can rise to unsafe levels. • If certain parts have to be hot, design protective casings or guards.
Injury in moving vehicles	• Seatbelts and airbags for drivers and passengers. • Headrest to avoid neck injuries. • ABS (Anti-lock Braking System). This prevents the wheels from locking (stopping completely), losing grip with the road and causing a skid, if you jam your foot on the brake. • Ensure driver can see 360° around the car using mirrors. • Rubber bumpers for small impacts. • Crumple zones - the body and doors of the vehicle crumple on impact, to reduce the effect on the driver and passengers. • Electronic detection systems for road obstacles. • Automatic parking systems.
Injury from tools	• Safety guards for dangerous components such as blades, drills, and hot areas. • Built-in clamps for work pieces. • Large easy-to-access emergency stop button. • Cordless operation (no electric wires). • Automatic cut-out if tool is overloaded. • Plastic casings. • See the "Tools" and the "Safety" chapters for more information.

Worked example 3: Safety in domestic appliances

Past exam question

Name two domestic appliances. In the case of one, outline one safety feature present in the appliance. Explain the purpose and operation of the safety feature.

Valid answers

1. **Toaster**
   Safety feature: fuse. Toasters and other electrical appliances are fitted with fuses, which are designed to "blow" (i.e. break) if more than a certain amount of current flows through them. This means that if there is an electrical fault with the appliance, or if water gets in, or if a person comes in contact with mains electricity via the appliance, the current will be cut immediately.
2. **Hand held blender**
   Safety feature: plastic casing. The plastic casing prevents electricity from inside the blender being conducted on to the person who is holding it.
3. **Microwave oven**
   Safety feature: safety on/off switch. Microwave ovens will only switch on if the door is closed.
4. **Oven**
   Safety feature: safety door. Some oven doors are equipped with a special lock on the outside so that children cannot open them.

Past exam questions

1. What precautions should be taken when designing a toy for a young child?
2. Name a safety feature that a manufacturer should include on a child's bike.
3. What safety features would need to be designed in to a rocking chair?
4. Name two safety features found in modern cars.
5. A bookend made from sheet metal is shown. Identify one safety hazard in this design.

6. Evaluate the safety of the design of the toast rack shown.

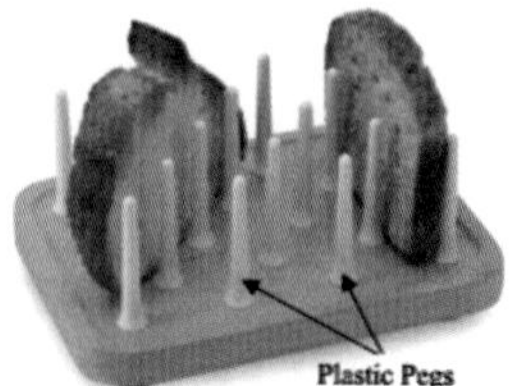

Past exam questions

7. State one safety feature that should be incorporated into the toy Ferris wheel design shown.

8. It is required to manufacture a lightweight show-jumping fence. Outline two safety features, which should be included in the design of the fence.

9. A student intends to manufacture a toy airboat based on the design shown. Outline two safety features that should be included in the design of the boat.

Design sketching practice

This section gives you an opportunity to practice sketching designs, using past examination questions as examples. Sketching by hand is a very valuable skill. If you practice doing this, it will help you to:

- Answer the many examination questions that require sketches.
- Come up with good designs for both examination questions and technology projects.
- Compile a high quality project folder for your technology projects. (See "Your technology projects" chapter.)

Worked example 4: Sketch a tape dispenser

Past exam question

The graphic shows a student design for a tape dispenser.

1. Sketch a development of the body of the tape dispenser.
2. Sketch a method to hold the roll of tape securely in the dispenser.
3. Sketch a design for an attachment to cut the tape.

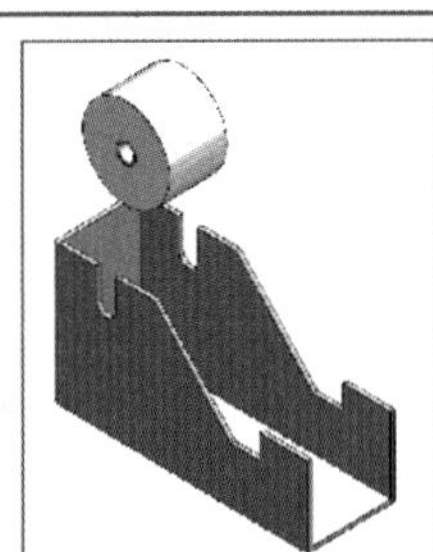

Worked example 4: Sketch a tape dispenser

Valid answers

1. The hand sketch shows a development of the body of the tape dispenser.

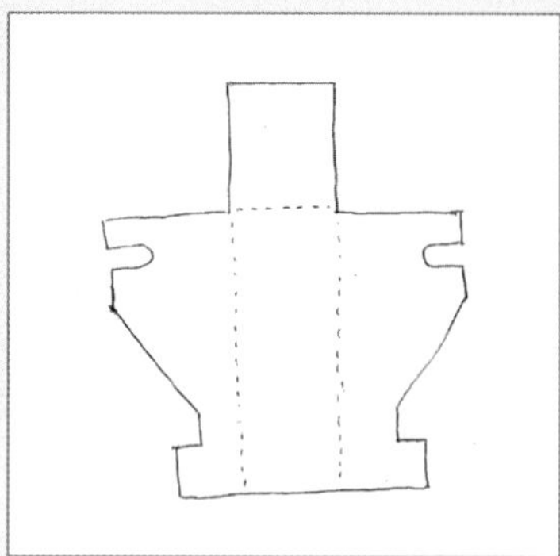

2. The hand sketch on the right shows one way of holding the roll of tape securely in the dispenser. A wooden dowel (wooden roller) fits through the hole in the tape roll, and drops in to the slots in the tape dispenser body. The ends of the dowel have a narrower diameter (e.g. made using a lathe) to prevent the dowel from slipping out of the slots.

   An alternative method would be to use a metal axle. Make a screw thread at the end of the axle using a die, and screw a lock nut on each end of the axle, allowing enough clearance for the axle to turn. Or use a tap to make a thread in two wide diameter metal discs to act as the ends of the axle.

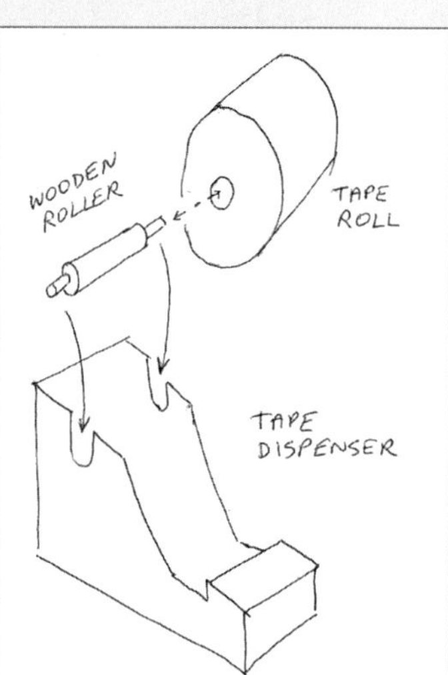

3. The sketch shows one way of fitting an attachment to the body of the dispenser to cut the tape. A metal strip with a serrated edge fits over the end of the tape dispenser body.

   It could be held in place with 2 self-tapping screws (drill a hole slightly smaller than the diameter of the screw). The metal strip could be bent over a straight edge, e.g. using a vice. The cutter strip could also be made from a hard plastic.

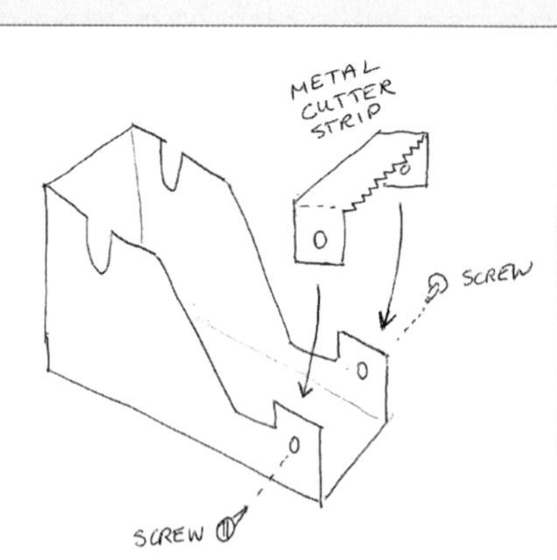

Past exam questions

1. The body of an MP3 player docking station is shown. The slots of the speaker on the MP3 docking station allow the sound to come through from the speakers behind (speakers not shown).

   (a) Make a drawing of your design for a different speaker grille pattern.

   (b) Suggest two pieces of information that the designer would need to know in order to design this product.

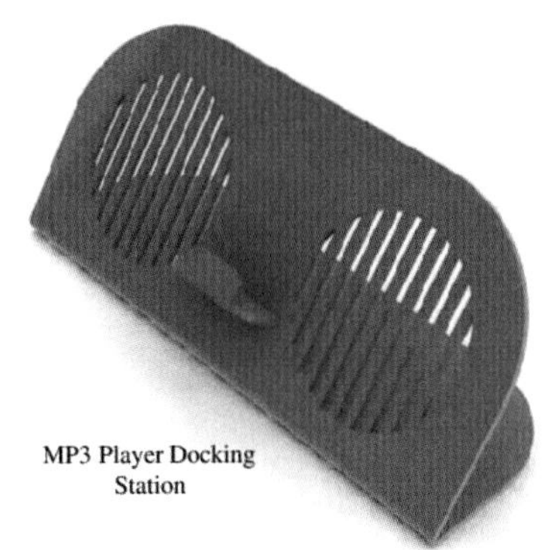

MP3 Player Docking Station

2. The diagram shows a student design of a desktop holder for an MP3 player.

   Sketch a suitable modification to prevent the MP3 player from falling from the supporting platform.

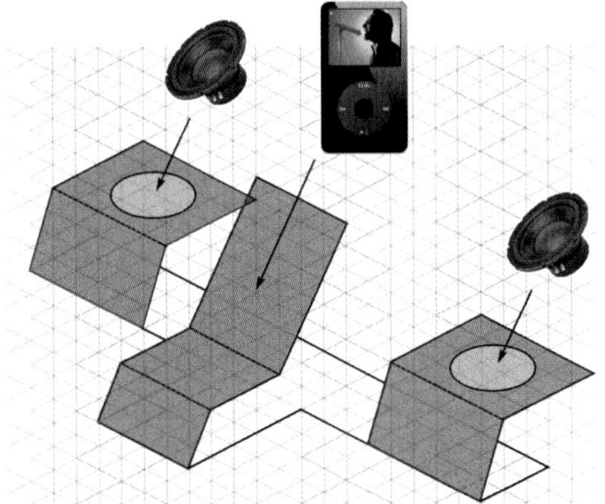

3. A lightweight frame bridge is to be constructed to span from A to B. Sketch your design for the bridge.

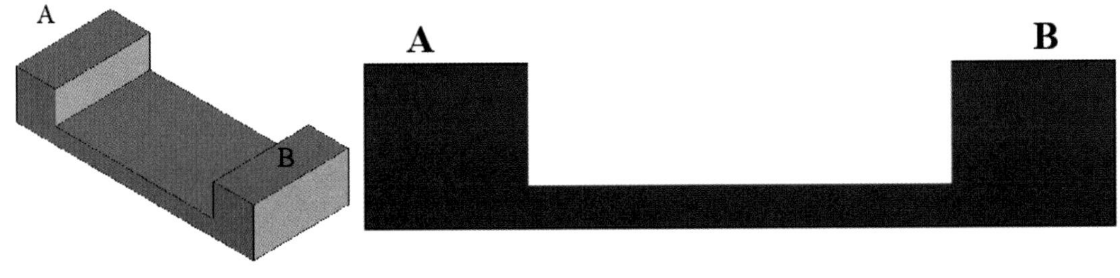

Past exam questions

4. The graphics show a student's unfinished design for a document (A4 page) stand. The stand is to be manufactured from a single sheet of 3 mm acrylic.

   (a) Sketch a design for a removable paper clip container to fit in the space labelled X.

   (b) When testing, it was found that A4 pages fell off the stand. Describe, using sketches, a design modification to solve this problem.

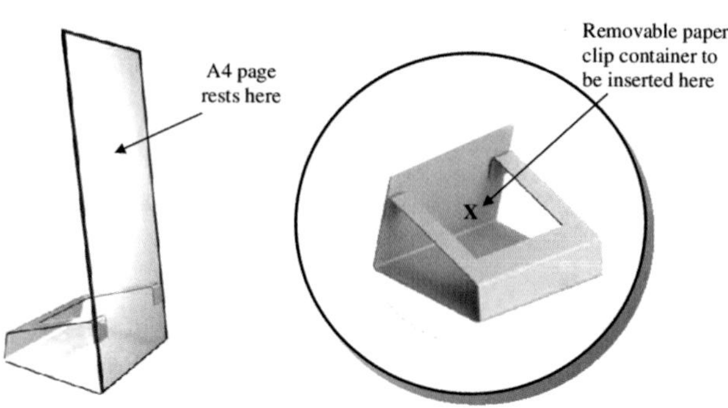

5. The uprights, platform and base of a model bridge structure are shown below. Cables are to be attached to the bridge to make it stronger. Sketch the cables needed to strengthen the bridge.

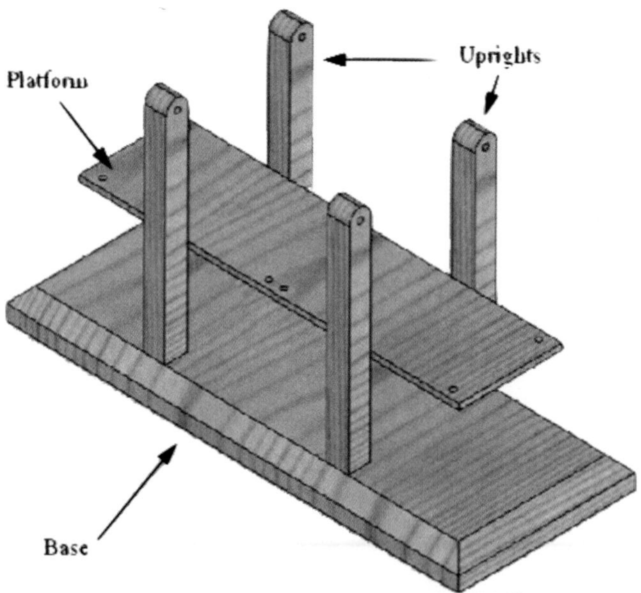

Designing for manufacture

This section will help you to create designs that can be manufactured easily. This involves deciding what materials to use, how to form them into shapes, what tools to use, how to join parts together, and how to create surface finishes. It gives you the opportunity to combine and apply your knowledge of materials, tools and processes.

As well as helping you with the design and manufacture examination questions, this section will also give you ideas and skills for your technology projects. All examples and questions in this section are taken from past examination questions.

Worked example 5: Manufacture a toy car

Past exam question
A design for a child's toy car is shown. The wheels have plastic centres with a rubber ring fitted.

1. Name a suitable metal for the axles.
2. Name a suitable plastic for the wheel centre giving a reason for your choice.
3. Describe a suitable method (other than glueing) of connecting the axles to the wheels. Name all the equipment used in your suggested method.

Valid answers

1. Suitable metals for the axles would be steel, brass, or aluminium.
2. Suitable plastics for the wheel centre would be acrylic because it has a good finish, or nylon because it is hard wearing.
3. Thread the ends of the axle using a stock and die. Place a nut and washer on each side of the wheel, when connected to the axle. Use a lock nut on the outside.

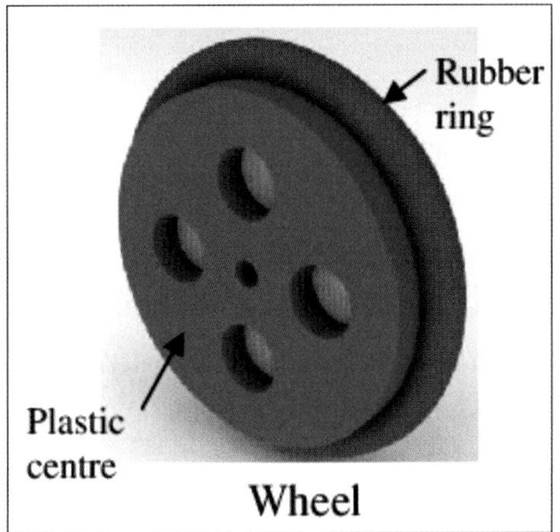

Worked example 6: Manufacture a desk tidy

Past exam question
The graphic shows the top panel of a desk tidy, made from plastic. Explain how the large slot could be made, describing the tools and processes used.

Valid answer

Drill four holes at the corners of the slot, use a scroll saw to cut out excess material, and then file the internal edges smooth with a file.

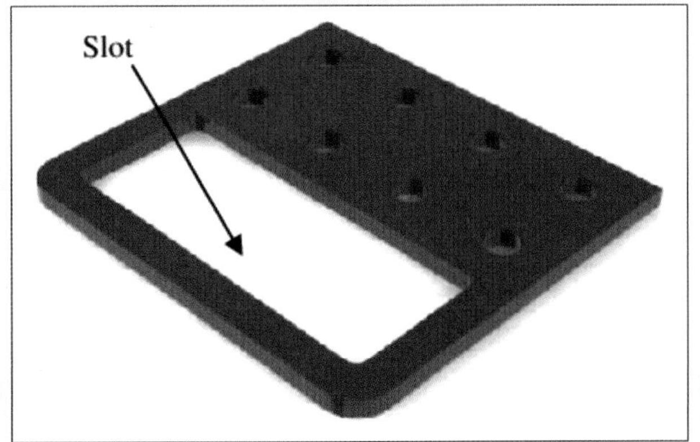

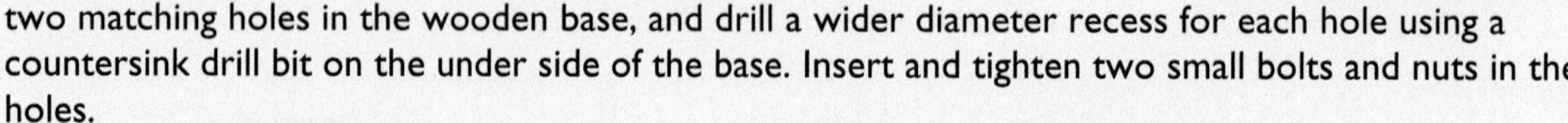

Worked example 7: Manufacture a mobile phone holder

Past exam question

The graphic shows a mobile phone holder.

1. Describe a method of attaching part A to holder B.
2. Describe a method of attaching part A to the base.

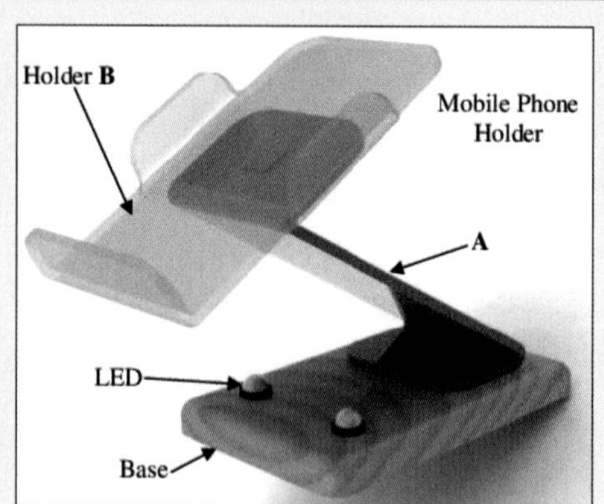

Valid answers

1. Use a suitable adhesive/glue to attach holder B to part A.
2. Drill two small holes in the bottom part of part A. If there is space to use a screwdriver, use screws to attach part A to the base. If there is no space to use a screwdriver, drill two matching holes in the wooden base, and drill a wider diameter recess for each hole using a countersink drill bit on the under side of the base. Insert and tighten two small bolts and nuts in the holes.

Past exam questions

1. Two lamp posts similar to that on the right are to be used to light up a bridge.

   (a) Suggest a suitable material for the lamp post.
   (b) Suggest a method of fixing part C to part D, and describe three steps in carrying out this process.

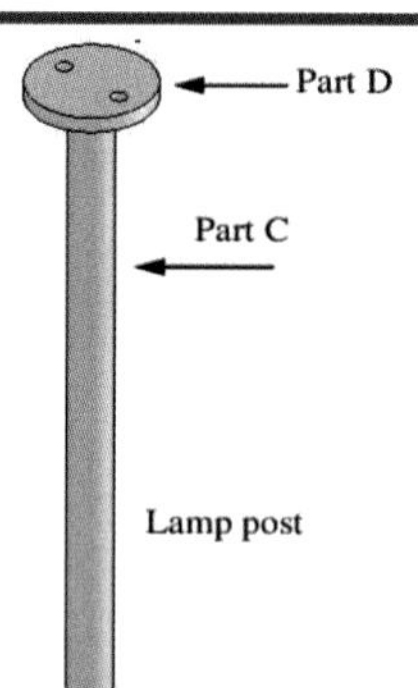

2. The graphic shows a design for a night light holder made from copper sheeting and tubing.

   (a) Give two reasons why copper is a good choice of material for this task.
   (b) Describe how you would bend the base into the required shape.
   (c) Other than copper suggest a suitable material.

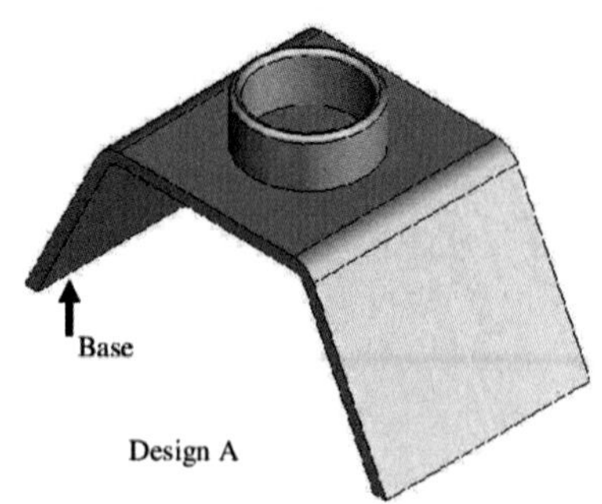

3. The chassis of a motorised toy buggy is shown.

   (a) Suggest two reasons why rubber is a suitable material for the wheels.
   (b) Using sketches, show how the wheels could be attached to the chassis.

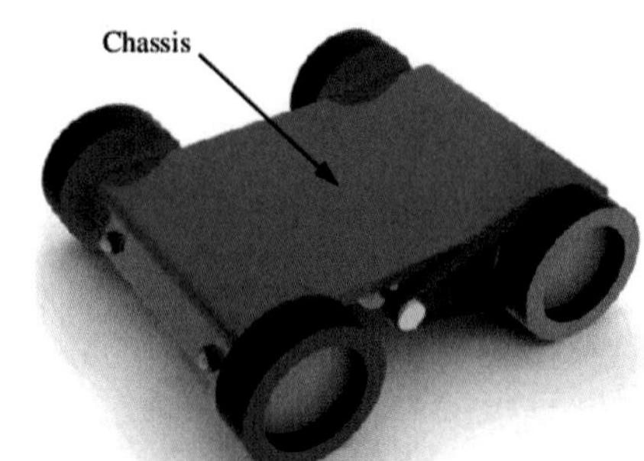

Past exam questions

4. A model of a rotating advertising sign is shown. The base and upright are to be made from hardwood.

   (a) Name a suitable hardwood for this purpose.
   (b) How would you join the uprights to the base?

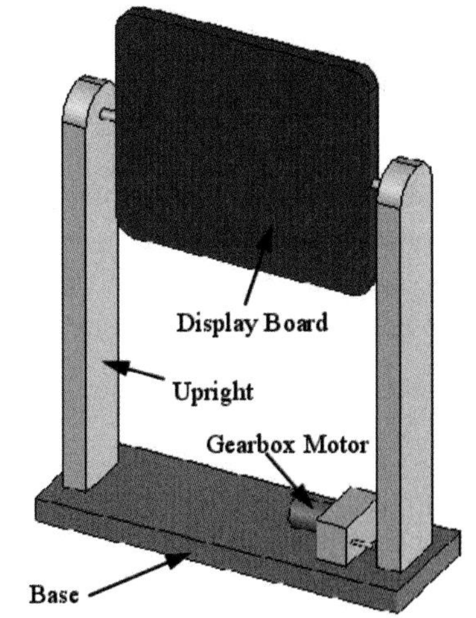

5. The graphic shows a toy car. The body is made from 160 x 50 x 30 mm red deal. The top is made from translucent acrylic and can be removed to allow access to a motor and battery.

   (a) A hollow space needs to be formed in the wooden body of the car to hold a battery and a motor. Describe, using suitable sketches, how this hollow space could be formed.
   (b) The acrylic top can be easily removed to replace the battery. Describe, using suitable sketches, how the top could be attached and detached from the car.
   (c) Name two processes that could be used to finish the wooden car body to a high standard similar to the graphic shown.

6. A student is required to manufacture a working model of a hovercraft using the vacuum forming mould shown.

   (a) Describe, with the aid of sketches, the steps required to manufacture the mould. Name the materials, tools and processes used.
   (b) Describe, with the aid of sketches, two modifications to improve the mould design.

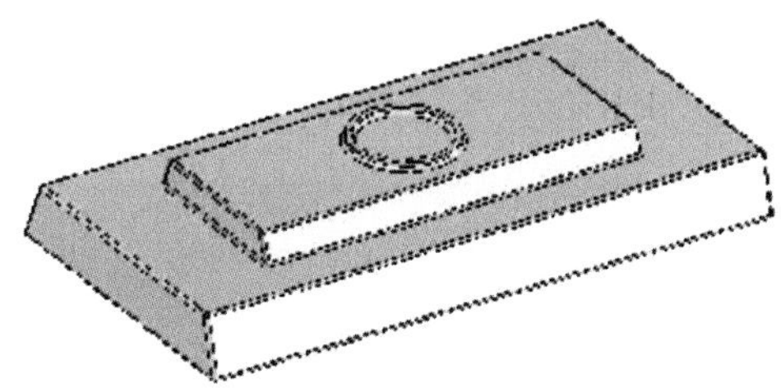

   (c) Describe, with the aid of sketches, the steps required to vacuum form the body of the hovercraft from a sheet of 3 mm acrylic.

Design practice

This section provides practice at designing more complex items. All examples and questions are taken from previous examination questions. This section requires knowledge of mechanisms and electronic circuits.

Worked example 8: Tipper truck design

Past exam question

Describe a suitable mechanical method of raising and lowering the body on the tipper truck shown below.

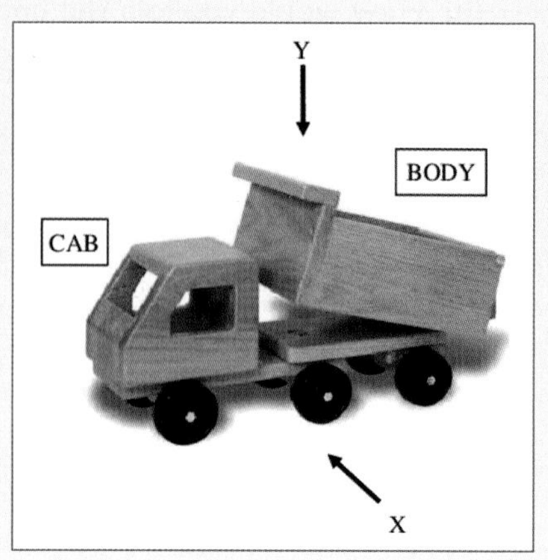

Valid answers

- A hydraulic piston could be used.
- A rack and pinion mechanism could be used (motor turns the pinion).
- A worm wheel could be used on the axle of the tipping body (motor turns the worm).

Worked example 9: Pulley-driven car design

Past exam question

A motorised pulley-driven toy car made from wood is shown.

1. Name two other mechanisms that could be used to drive the vehicle.
2. When in use it was found that the wheels did not grip well. Describe how you would solve this problem.

Valid answers

1. Other mechanisms that could be used to drive the vehicle would be: chain and sprocket, gears, toothed belt.
2. To improve the grip of the wheels, fit rubber tyres to the wheels.

Worked example 10: Lighthouse design

Past exam question

1. Describe, with the aid of suitable sketches, a motorized mechanical system to activate the flashing light in the lighthouse by opening and closing the micro-switch.
2. Explain how this mechanical system could be modified to change the number of light flashes per minute.
3. Describe how this motorized mechanical system could be activated automatically at nightfall.

Worked example 10: Lighthouse design

Valid answers

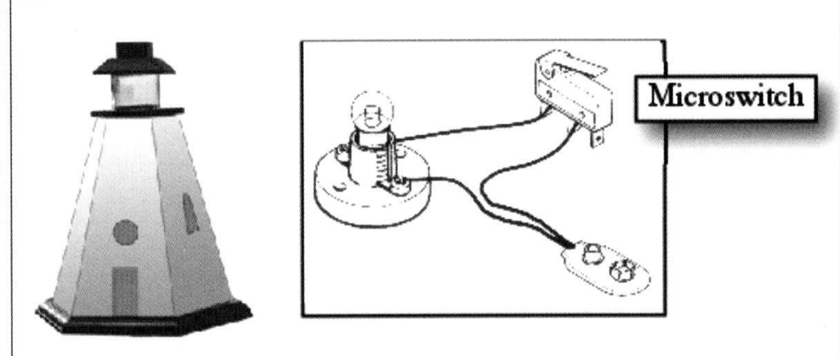

1. To activate the flashing light, a motor turning a cam could be used. When the cam is on its high point, it pushes the micro switch down to complete the electrical circuit and turn on the light. When the cam is at its low point, the micro-switch is not pushed down and closed, and so there is no power to the light.
2. To change the number of light flashes per minute, the shape of the cam could be changed so that there are more high points on the cam. This would open and close the switch more than once per rotation. Alternatively, a gear could be used to change the speed of rotation of the cam.
3. The system could be activated at nightfall by adding a darkness sensor circuit and a relay to the above circuit. The relay is in series with the micro-switch. The darkness sensor circuit uses an LDR (light-dependent resistor) to close the relay when darkness falls. The LDR could be mounted on the outside wall of the lighthouse.

Worked example 11: Car park barrier design

Past exam question

A student is required to manufacture a working model of a motorized car park barrier as shown in the diagram. The barrier will be opened by a security keycard.

1. Name and describe two suitable mechanisms to raise and lower the barrier.
2. Explain why a DPDT relay and limit switches are recommended in the design.
3. Explain briefly how a keycard system allows the barrier to open.
4. Explain one security limitation of this system.
5. Outline one other modern security system used to overcome the stated limitation.

Valid answers

1. (a) A set of compound gears powered by a motor could be used to rotate the axle of the barrier.
   (b) A rod attached to a crank or wheel could be used to pull down the barrier lever on the short side, causing the other side to go up. The crank wheel could be rotated by a motor via a set of gears.
2. A DPDT (double-pole, double-throw) switch is used to reverse the direction of the motor, to either raise or lower the barrier.
3. A sensor in the barrier casing would read the magnetic strip on the card. The sensor would activate a transistor or a relay to cause current to flow to the motor. Limit switches are needed to turn the motor off when the barrier reaches the top or bottom of its travel.

Worked example 11: Car park barrier design

4. A different person with a correct card could activate the barrier. The card could be stolen.
5. Modern security systems could have fingerprint detection, or voice detection, or a CCTV camera at the barrier.

Worked example 12: Show jumping fence design

Past exam question

It is required to manufacture a lightweight show-jumping fence. The fence should be both freestanding and height-adjustable.

1. Outline two safety features that should be included in the design of the fence.
2. Describe, with the aid of sketches, a proposed structure for the side supports of the show jumping fence.
3. Describe, with the aid of sketches, the features of your design that will allow the horizontal fence rails to fall if struck by a horse.
4. Outline with the aid of labelled sketches, a suitable mechanism to allow one person easily adjust the height of the fence.

Valid answers

1. Two safety features that should be included in the design of the fence are:
   - The fence should easily collapse if the horse or the rider hits it.
   - There should be no sharp edges on the fence in case of falls.

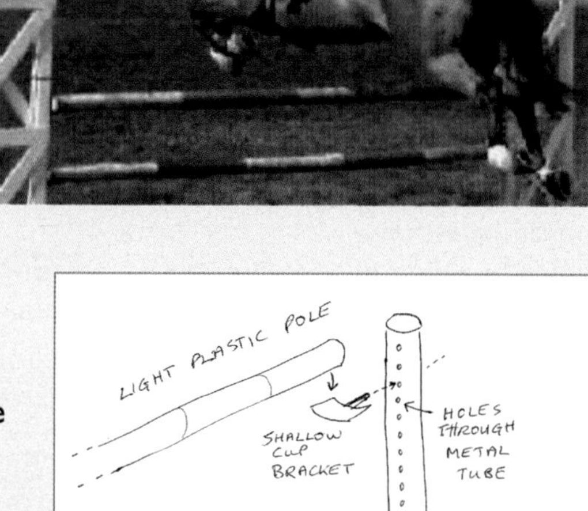

2. The sketch shows one possible design for the side supports:
   - The vertical support is a hollow metal tube, for strength and also for lightness of weight.
   - The vertical support tube fits over a solid metal stand, which has four wide splayed feet, to provide stability. The stand can be detached which makes it easier to transport. It can also be used with different lengths and colours of vertical poles. The stand could also be made from wood, but this would be less hard-wearing.
   - The vertical support tube has lots of holes in it in a vertical line (drilled through the front and back of the tube).
   - A shallow metal cup bracket fits into the holes in the vertical support tube.
   - The end of the pole sits on the shallow bracket.
   - The poles are made from plastic, which is much lighter than metal, easier to transport, and safer for horse and rider.

Worked example 12: Show jumping fence design

3. The features of the design that allow the poles to fall off if hit by a horse are the shallow cup brackets that hold the poles. This arrangement allows the poles to fall off the brackets if the horse or rider bumps into them.

4. As can be seen from the sketch, one person can easily adjust the height of the horizontal poles by:
   - Taking the pole off the brackets.
   - Sliding the bracket out from the holes in the vertical side support.
   - Inserting the bracket in a higher or lower hole in the side support.
   - Doing the same on the other vertical support.
   - Replacing the pole back on the brackets.

   The pole is now at a different height.

Option 2: Another design option for the horse jump fence is to use a very long vertical metal screw inside the vertical tube, turned by a crank handle at the top. The bracket for the pole threads on to the screw, and moves up and down in a slot in the side of the tube, as the screw/handle is turned.

Worked example 13: Wind direction indicator design

Past exam question

A student is required to manufacture a model of a wind speed and wind direction indicator based on the partial design shown. The completed model will be placed outdoors, and must turn freely around a supporting pole. *(Do not include the propeller in your answer.)*

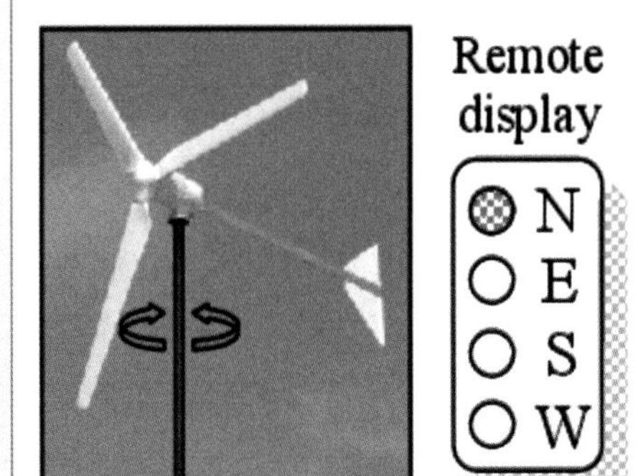

1. Describe, with the aid of sketches, how the model could turn freely about a supporting pole.
2. Describe, with the aid of suitable sketches, how the model and supporting pole will be supported to remain upright in strong winds.
3. Sketch a suitable 9 V circuit diagram, to be included in the model, which will display the wind direction by lighting LEDs on a remote display.
4. Identify any limitations in the circuit design sketched, and suggest a possible improvement.

Valid answers

1. An axle mechanism is required at the top of the supporting pole to allow the propeller unit to rotate. Some possible solutions are shown below. The solution can depend on the materials that the pole and the propeller unit are made from, and how much access there is to the inside of the propeller unit.

   Option A: A hollow tube with a flat bottom is attached to the bottom of the propeller unit (either via glueing or a nut and bolt). The hollow tube fits down over the pole and can rotate around it. Grease would be used between the parts to allow it to move more freely.

Worked example 13: Wind direction indicator design

Option B: A small hole is drilled through the bottom of the propeller unit. A wood screw is inserted through to a wooden pole underneath. The screw is not tightened fully. Metal washers are used between the propeller unit and the top of the pole, and between the screw head and the propeller unit. This provides more flat space, and allows it to rotate more freely. Oil or grease could also be used.

Option C: A wooden pole is hollowed out at the top using a drill and a ball-bearing mechanism is inserted and glued in place. A metal rod is attached to the propeller unit with a bolt (using a tap to create a thread in the rod). The rod will turn very freely in the ball bearing mechanism.

Option A

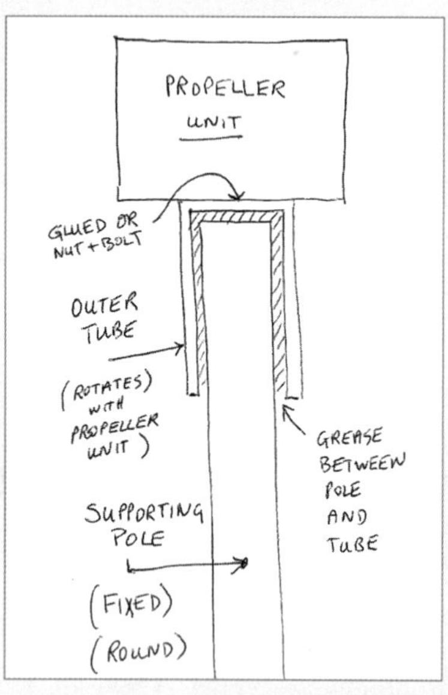

Option B

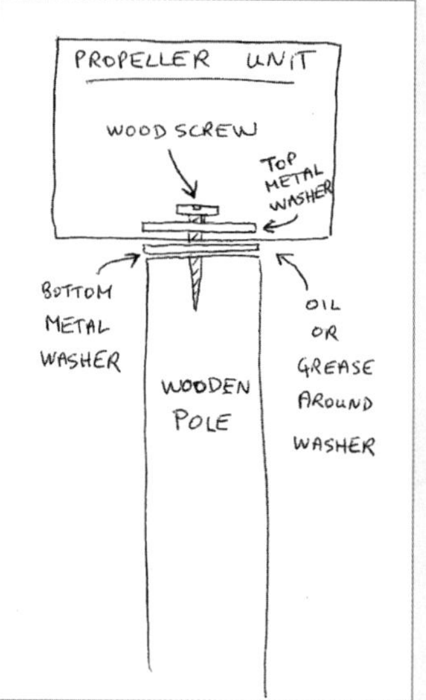

Option C

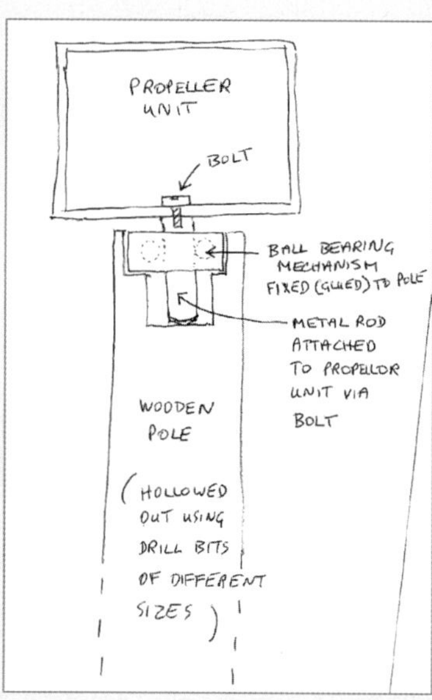

2. The model and supporting pole could be supported to stay upright in high winds in several ways.
   (a) The supporting pole could be attached to a building using a bracket.
   (b) The supporting pole could be inserted in a very heavy base made of concrete. If a base is used it should be as wide as possible. The supporting pole itself could be driven deep into the ground.
   (c) The pole could be secured to the ground using cable stays and pegs inserted into the ground.

These options are illustrated in the sketch on the right.

The sketch shows a combination of a flat heavy base and supporting cable stays attached to pegs driven into the ground.

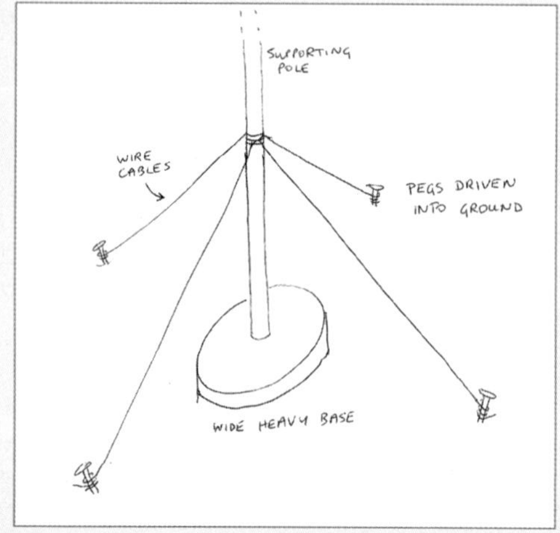

Worked example 13: Wind direction indicator design

3. A circuit diagram to turn on one of four LEDs, depending on which switch is closed, is shown below.

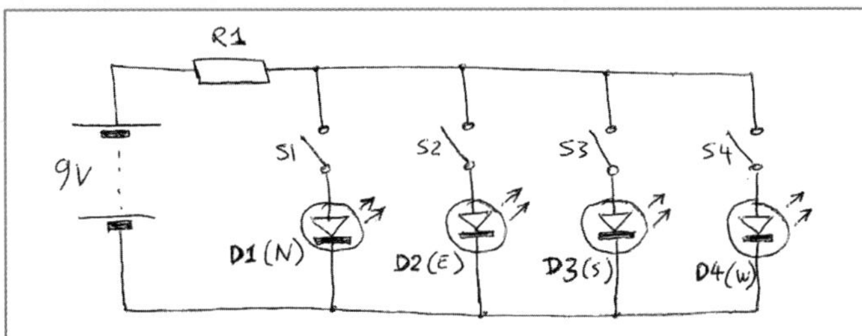

It is necessary to work out how to close the relevant switches as the propeller unit rotates. Because the display must be a remote display, the circuit cannot be mounted in the propeller unit itself. Also, wires cannot go in to the propeller unit from the supporting pole, as they would become twisted by the rotation of the propeller unit, and this would eventually prevent the propeller unit from rotating.

A means of activating the switches would need to be mounted in or outside the pole. A possible design for this is shown below.

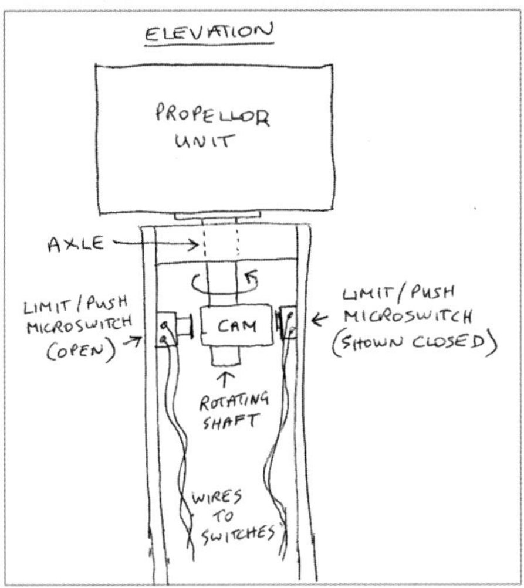

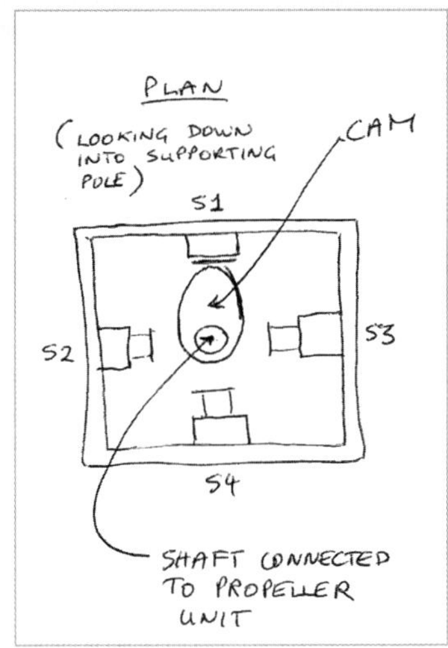

A shaft (cylindrical rod) is attached to the propeller unit, and fits down into an axle in the supporting pole. This could be a ball-bearing axle, or just a simple hole. A cam is fixed to the shaft. The four switches are mounted on the inside of the pole. As the propeller unit turns, the cam moves, and presses down on one of the switches. This connects power to the relevant LED and the LED lights up. The wires from the switches go back down to the circuit, which can be at the base of the pole or further away. For clarity, only two switches are shown in the elevation sketch. All four switches are shown in the plan sketch.

4. A limitation of the above circuit design is that the LED will only light when the cam/propeller unit is pointing very close to where the switch is located. If the cam/propeller unit is pointing in between the switches, e.g. pointing north-east, no LED will light. A better design would be to have 8 switches and 8 LEDs. Alternatively, a custom-made switch could be made, with power going to the metal cam in the centre (via brushes), so that the cam is always touching one of four sprung metal quadrants around the outside. Each metal quadrant is connected to separate LEDs.

Past exam questions

1. A working model of a "Mars Rover" is shown. This vehicle is designed to run on solar power and is also capable of taking panoramic photographs through 360°.

   (i) Explain why tracks are used on the Rover instead of wheels and tyres.
   (ii) The camera on the Rover must be capable of rotating through 360°. From the mechanisms below, choose the most suitable mechanism for this purpose, and explain the reason for your choice.

   (iii) When testing the Rover, it was found that corners A and B caused the Rover to get stuck when going over rough terrain. Suggest two changes to the design that could overcome this problem.

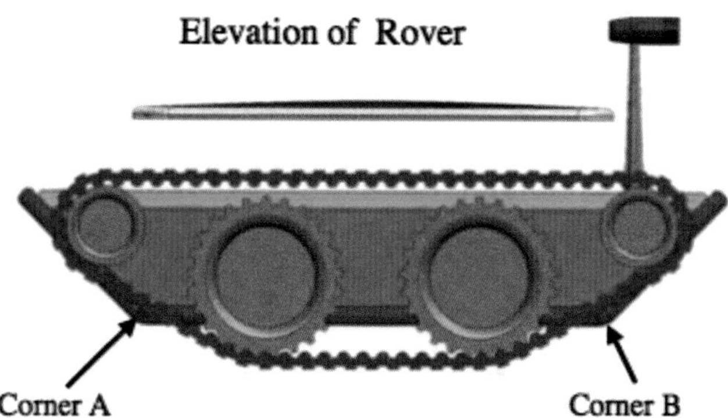

2. The graphics show a design for a model tank. Sketch and name a suitable mechanism which will allow the turret to rotate through 360°

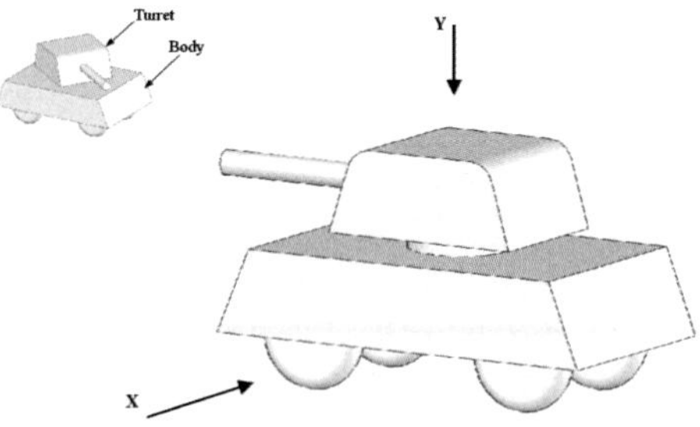

3. A student is working on a working model of a hovercraft shown on the right.
   (i) Describe the steps required to motorise the hovercraft for lift.
   (ii) Describe the steps required to motorise the hovercraft for forward motion.
   (iii) Sketch a suitable circuit diagram to operate the hovercraft's motors from a single power source.

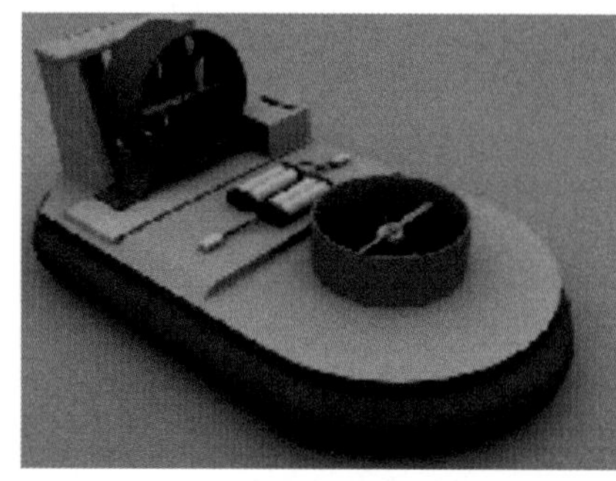

Past exam questions

4. The graphic shows a design for a toy plane. The body is made from 30 x 30 mm red deal. The wings are made from 30 mm wide strips of 6 mm acrylic. Design, using suitable sketches, a suitable undercarriage for the toy. Explain how the undercarriage will be attached to the body of the plane.

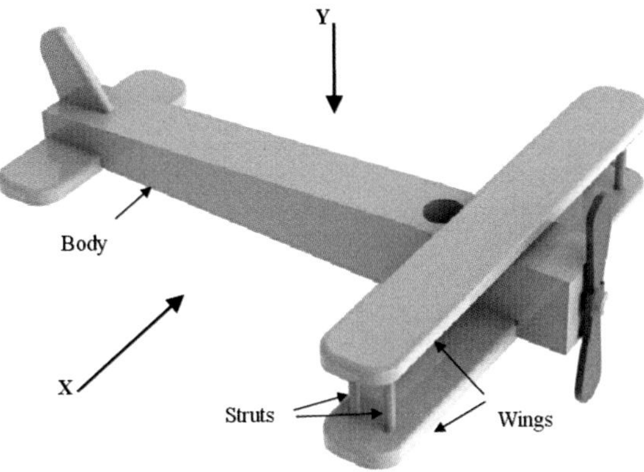

Design and manufacturing practice

This section provides practice at the full-length "Design and manufacture" questions as they have appeared in previous Junior Cycle examinations. A number of worked examples are provided as well as questions for you to complete. The examples and questions in this section require knowledge from the following chapters:

- Design and manufacture.
- Technical drawing.
- Materials.
- Tools and processes.
- Mechanisms.
- Electronic circuits.

Worked example 14: Toolbox

Past exam question

An injection-moulded plastic toolbox made in a factory is shown.

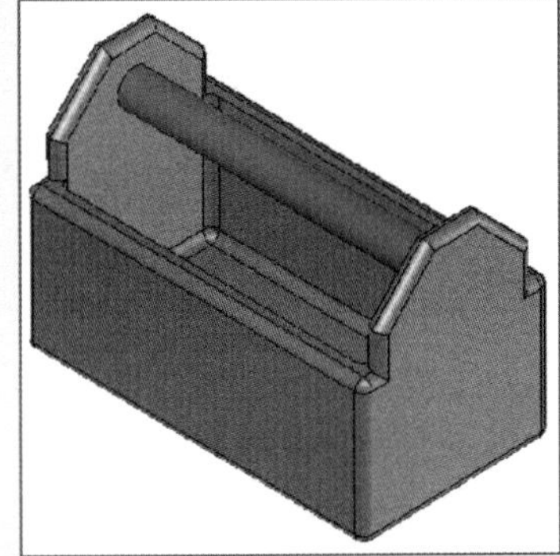

1. List three advantages of using plastic to make this toolbox.
2. The toolbox was found to slip easily when placed on a smooth surface. Explain how you would solve this problem.
3. The toolbox has rounded edges. Suggest two reasons for this.
4. List three things that you would need to know before designing a toolbox.

Valid answers

1. Advantages of using plastic include: low cost, nice finish, durability, soft edges, and easy to mass-produce.
2. The toolbox can be prevented from slipping by adding rubber feet to the base.

Worked example 14: Toolbox

3. Reasons for rounded edges include:
   - Safety, there are no sharp edges.
   - Aesthetics, it looks well.
   - Ease of manufacture, it is easier to mould with round edges.
4. Before designing the toolbox we would need to know:
   - What it will be used to carry.
   - The dimensions of the items to be carried.
   - The number of items to be carried.
   - The total weight of the items to be carried.
   - Who will carry the toolbox and whether it is to be used by adults or children.
   - The kind of environment that it will be used in, e.g. outdoors or indoors.
   - The environmental conditions that it will be exposed to, e.g. temperature, wetness, wind, chemicals.
   - The budget for manufacturing it.

Worked example 15: Airboat

Past exam question

A student intends to manufacture a toy airboat with a flat hull, based on the design shown.

1. Describe, with the aid of sketches, the steps required to manufacture the hull of the boat from a suitable material. Name any tools required and state the processes used.
2. Outline two safety features that should be included in the design of the airboat.
3. Describe, with the aid of sketches, how the fan and motor assembly could be attached to the hull of the boat.
4. Describe, with the aid of sketches, how you would construct a drive system (motor, gear train and propeller) to produce the highest possible output speed from the following components:

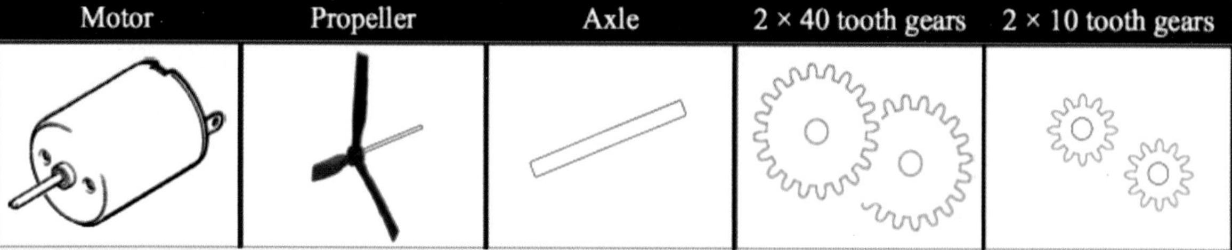

Motor	Propeller	Axle	2 × 40 tooth gears	2 × 10 tooth gears

5. If the motor turns at 100 RPM, calculate the speed of the propeller for the gear arrangement you have shown.

Worked example 15: Airboat

Valid answers

1. A suitable material to manufacture the hull from would be HIPS (high impact polystyrene) sheeting. This is because the hull is a complex shape and HIPS can be easily formed using vacuum forming (and this can be done in the technology room). It is also light, waterproof, durable and inexpensive. The steps required to manufacture the hull would be the following:
   a) Make a wooden mould of the shape of the hull.
   b) Place the mould in the vacuum former oven.
   c) Place the plastic sheet above the mould in the oven. Cut to size if necessary and hold in place with clamps.
   d) Switch on the vacuum forming heater. The plastic becomes soft.
   e) When the heater is at the right temperature (indicated by light), lift up the mould towards the plastic sheet using the lever.
   f) Turn on the vacuum pump. The plastic sheet is sucked into the shape of the mould.
   g) Turn off the vacuum pump and allow the plastic to cool. Remove the moulded plastic from the vacuum former and trim off any excess plastic.

2. Safety features that should be included in the design of the boat:
   - There should be a safety guard around the propeller to prevent injury.
   - There should be no sharp edges on the toy airboat.
   - The boat should be powered by a low-voltage battery, so that there is no risk of electrical shock to the user.
   - There could be a temperature sensor to prevent the motor overheating.

3. If both the hull and the fan and motor assembly are made from plastic, they can be attached using a special-purpose glue, such as liquid solvent cement (Tensol Cement). If the hull was made from wood, a metal bracket and screws could be used.

4. A drive system with the highest possible output speed can be constructed as follows:
   a) Make a compound gear by putting both a 10-tooth gear and a 40-tooth gear on the axle.
   b) Put the other 40-tooth gear on the motor spindle.
   c) Put the other 10-tooth gear on the propeller shaft.
   d) Turn the 10-tooth gear on the compound gear with the 40-tooth gear on the motor.
   e) Turn the 10-tooth gear on the propeller shaft with the 40-tooth gear of the compound gear.

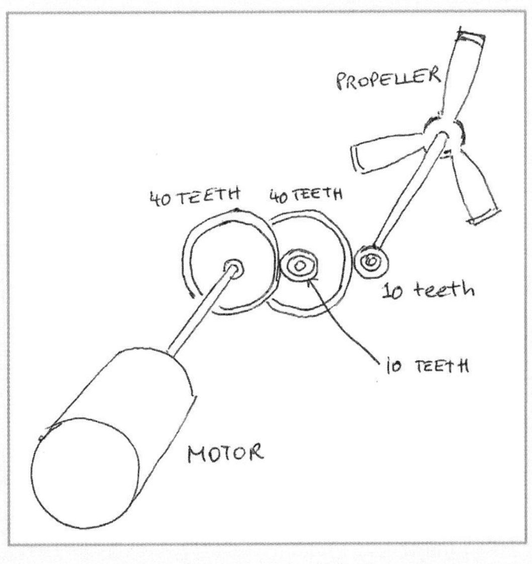

(The sketch shows the gear drive with the distances expanded out for clarity.)

Worked example 15: Airboat

5. With the compound gear described above, the output gear (propeller) turns 16 times faster than the input gear (motor).

   Explanation: The first gear combination of the compound gear multiplies the input speed by 4 (40 teeth driving 10 teeth), and the second gear combination of the compound gear multiplies the speed by 4 again (40 teeth driving 10 teeth), so the total output speed is 16 times the input speed. Since the input speed (speed of the motor) is 100 RPM, then the output speed (speed of the propeller) is 1600 RPM.

   Another way of calculating this is:

$$\text{Gear ratio of the first (input) gear combination} = \frac{\text{no of teeth of output gear}}{\text{no of teeth of input gear}} = \frac{10}{40} = \frac{1}{4} = 0.25$$

$$\text{Gear ratio of the second (output) gear combination} = \frac{\text{no of teeth of output gear}}{\text{no of teeth of input gear}} = \frac{10}{40} = \frac{1}{4} = 0.25$$

$$\text{Total gear ratio} = \text{first gear ratio} \times \text{second gear ratio} = 0.25 \times 0.25 = 0.0625$$

$$\text{Output speed} = \frac{\text{input speed}}{\text{gear ratio}} = \frac{100\text{ RPM}}{0.0625} = 1600\text{ RPM}$$

Worked example 16: Toy tipping-truck

Past exam question

A student is required to manufacture a toy tipping-truck based on the design shown.

1. Describe, with the aid of sketches, the steps required to manufacture a suitable tipping body. Name the materials, tools and processes used.
2. Outline two safety features, which should be included in the design of the toy.
3. Explain, giving two reasons, why plastics have almost completely replaced wood and metal in the manufacture of toys.
4. Outline, with the aid of sketches, a suitable motorized mechanism to raise and lower the tipping body.
5. Outline where limit switches could be included in your suggested mechanism.

Valid answers

1. A suitable material from which to manufacture the tipping body would be plastic, such as high-impact polystyrene (HIPS).

Worked example 16: Toy tipping-truck

A suitable method to manufacture the tipping body would be vacuum forming and the steps required to manufacture it are as follows:

a) Make a wooden mould in the shape of the tipping body.
b) Place the mould in the vacuum former oven.
c) Place the plastic sheet above the mould in the oven. Cut to size if necessary and hold in place with clamps.
d) Switch on the vacuum forming heater. The plastic becomes soft.
e) When the heater is at temperature (indicated by light), lift up the mould towards the plastic sheet using the lever.
f) Turn on the vacuum pump. The plastic sheet is sucked into the shape of the mould.
g) Turn off the vacuum pump and allow the plastic to cool. Remove the moulded plastic from the vacuum former and trim off any excess plastic.

2. The following safety features should be considered in the design of the toy:
   - No sharp edges.
   - Non-toxic materials.
   - Prevent the tipping body from tipping or closing further if it meets resistance.

3. Plastics have almost completely replaced wood in the manufacture of toys because they are:
   a) Cheap.
   b) Non-toxic.
   c) Easy to mould into different shapes.
   d) Easy to create in different bright colours for children.
   e) Easy to clean.

4. A suitable motorised mechanism to raise and lower the tipping body would be a worm drive and compound gear. The motor turns the worm, which turns the worm wheel. The worm wheel is a compound gear, which turns the output gear, which is connected to the axle of the tipping body.

   The combination of a worm drive and compound gear reduces the speed of the motor greatly, and increases the turning force available from a small motor to turn the tipping body. In addition, the worm drive prevents the tipping body from slipping back down, because the worm wheel cannot turn the worm.

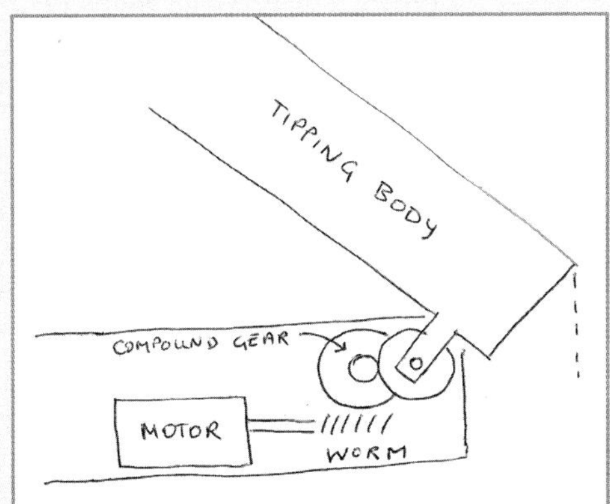

   Alternative suitable mechanisms include a hydraulic piston, a rack and pinion, or a long screw thread.

5. Limit switches will be needed in two places: (a) to detect when the tipping body is at its full height, so that the motor is turned off, and (b) to detect when the tipping body is back down at its rest position, so that the motor is turned off.

Past exam questions

1. The hull of a motorised propeller-driven airboat is shown. Holes for the motor, battery and switch are also shown.

   a) Name a suitable material for the hull, and list three steps in its manufacture.

   b) List two important design features that take into account the operation of the airboat on water.

   c) When the propeller shown was fitted to the motor, the airboat was found to be unsafe to operate. Sketch a guard for the propeller, which would make the airboat safe.

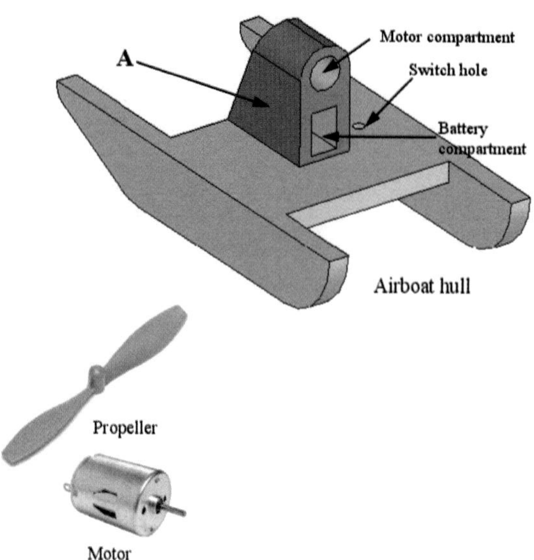

2. The graphic shows a design for a toy car. The body is made from 200 × 50 × 50 mm red deal. A hollow space is required under the body of the car, to hold a battery, motor and gear box.

   a) Describe, using suitable sketches, how this space could be formed.

   b) If the aerofoils were made from acrylic instead of wood, describe how smooth edges could be created on the acrylic.

   c) Outline two processes that might be used to finish the toy car to standard similar to that shown in the graphic.

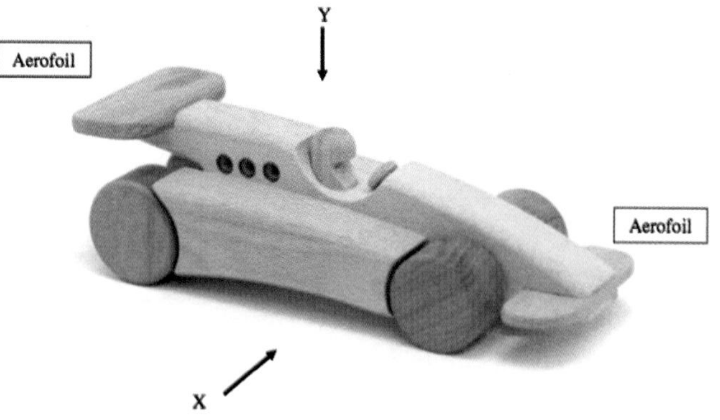

3. A student is required to manufacture a wall-mounted night light for a child's room, based on the design shown.

   a) Name a suitable material for the night light, and give two reasons for your choice.

   b) Describe, with the aid of suitable sketches, the steps required to manufacture the night light from the named material.

   c) Sketch a suitable 9 V circuit diagram, which will light a white LED in any four of the stars on the night light.

   d) Outline, with the aid of suitable sketches, a design for a novelty switch to turn the LED circuit on and off.

   e) Describe, with the aid of suitable sketches, the steps you would take to ensure the night light and circuit are safe for use by a child.

CHAPTER 22

Your technology projects

Introduction

This chapter helps you to implement your technology projects.
It provides information on:

- What a technology project is.
- How to design, build and document your technology project.
- Previous Junior Cycle projects.
- What you need to know before tackling your technology project.

Student project with coin operated chute and LED flashing eyes

What is a technology project?

A Junior Cycle technology project is a large task involving analysis, design, manufacture and evaluation. Each stage of the project must be documented and the documentation must be filed in a project folder.

A technology project may also be called a "design task". The project folder may also be known as a "design folder", or "design folio".

Your final Junior Cycle project accounts for 70% of your overall Junior Cycle technology mark .

What does a project consist of?

A project consists of a project folder, containing the documentation, and a working model (also called an artefact). The artefact will consist of multiple parts, usually a structural body made from wood and/or plastic components, and one or more mechanisms and/or electronic circuits working together to fulfill the project brief.

A project begins with a brief, which is a short statement of what the project is required to be or to do. Based on the brief, you will need to carry out some research, come up with one or more designs, choose a design, build and test it in the technology room, and document it all in the project folder.

What is the difference between a project and other practical work?

The differences between a project/design task, and other practical activities that you may be asked to carry out in the classroom, are:

- You must design a project yourself. You need to choose the materials, shapes and component parts, and design all the parts so that it all works together. The design work must be carried out by you.
- You must document all your design, manufacture, evaluation, and more steps in a project folder.

How do I prepare for my technology project?

You will need to build up your knowledge and practical skills during your Junior Cycle years so that you are well prepared to carry out your Junior Cycle project. The flowchart below shows one way of doing this.

The coloured boxes are chapters, the grey boxes are suggested tasks. Years are rough guidelines. In general, try to carry out lots of practical activities in first and second year. In second year, consider doing a fully designed and documented practice project. Your teacher will decide.

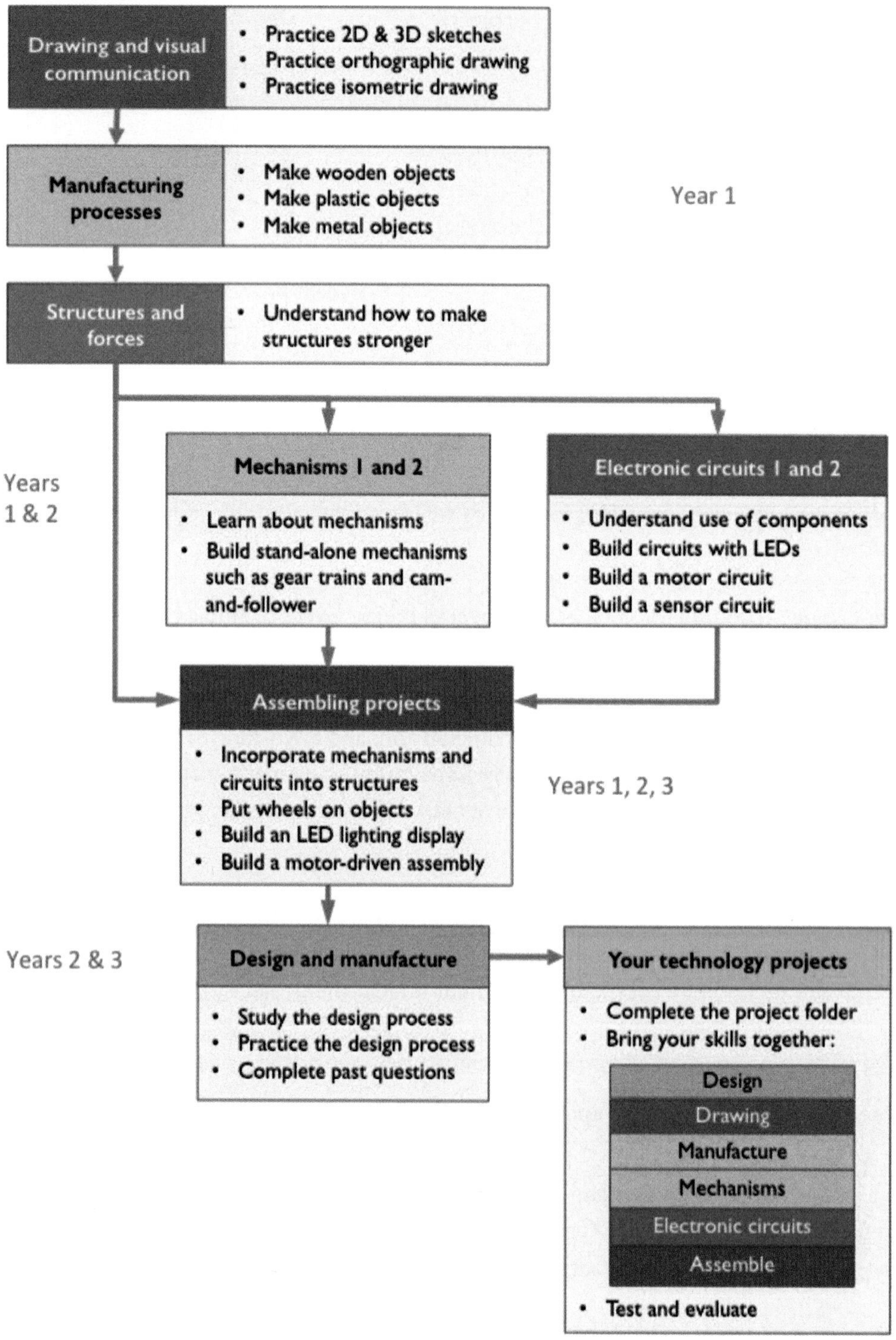

Year 1

Drawing and visual communication
- Practice 2D & 3D sketches
- Practice orthographic drawing
- Practice isometric drawing

Manufacturing processes
- Make wooden objects
- Make plastic objects
- Make metal objects

Structures and forces
- Understand how to make structures stronger

Years 1 & 2

Mechanisms I and 2
- Learn about mechanisms
- Build stand-alone mechanisms such as gear trains and cam-and-follower

Electronic circuits I and 2
- Understand use of components
- Build circuits with LEDs
- Build a motor circuit
- Build a sensor circuit

Years 1, 2, 3

Assembling projects
- Incorporate mechanisms and circuits into structures
- Put wheels on objects
- Build an LED lighting display
- Build a motor-driven assembly

Years 2 & 3

Design and manufacture
- Study the design process
- Practice the design process
- Complete past questions

Your technology projects
- Complete the project folder
- Bring your skills together:
  - Design
  - Drawing
  - Manufacture
  - Mechanisms
  - Electronic circuits
  - Assemble
- Test and evaluate

By carrying out lots of practical tasks as you work your way through the book, you will gain a good understanding of materials, tools, processes, mechanisms and electronics. This will help you in your exams.

1. Practice sketching of 2D and 3D objects.
2. Design and build objects from wood, plastics and metals.
3. Build a number of mechanisms and electronic circuits.
4. Build a number of assemblies, combining materials, mechanisms and electronic circuits.
5. Read the design process in the "Design and manufacture" chapter, follow the worked examples, and answer a number of past exam questions.
6. Try to carry out a documented practice project before your final Junior Cycle project.

Previous project briefs

Looking at previous Junior Cycle project briefs will give you a good idea of what is meant by a project, the different types of model that students build, and the kind of work that is involved. A full list of past Junior Cycle project briefs can be found in Appendix 3 at the back of this book.

Notes:

- When a project brief uses the term "electro-mechanical" it means movement caused by electricity, i.e. an electric motor.
- When a project brief refers to a large real-world object, you only need to design and build a scale model of it.
- The wording of the project briefs below has been shortened for space reasons.

Selection of previous Junior Cycle project briefs

Design and make a working model of:

- An animated Olympic Games display/diorama for a sports shop window.
- A working model of an electro-mechanically-controlled dumb waiter operating between two floors.
- A working model of a gate that automatically closes at nightfall.
- A flagstaff that raises a flag automatically in the morning and lowers it automatically at night.
- A pet-grooming table where the height of the table can be adjusted electro-mechanically.
- A working model of an environmentally-friendly garden shelter, that can be electro-mechanically rotated on its own axis as desired by the user, and which will illuminate automatically at nightfall.
- A domestic photovoltaic cell (PV) that can be rotated and tilted so that it faces the sun. One of these movements must be electro-mechanical and must include limit switching.
- A ventilation control system that opens or closes an air vent as the room temperature rises or falls.
- A chair/seat where the height can be adjusted electro-mechanically, but only when the user is seated.
- A wind vane with a remote electronic wind direction display (wireless display not required).
- A monorail transport system to move people from one airport terminal to another.
- A wind-powered whirligig that depicts a novelty scene that illuminates automatically at night.

Common project features

By scanning the list of previous Junior Cycle projects, you can see that projects have many characteristics in common. Common features of projects are described in more detail in the table below.

Feature	Description
Structural body	Typically made from wood, plastic, or metal, or a combination of those materials, assembled together. The shape and finish of the body are important. The body: • Sometimes needs to represent a real-life object. • Needs to act as a framework to support other objects, or motion and/or light or sound effects. • Should be attractively finished with surface finishes that are appropriate to the materials chosen, and consistent with the objectives of the brief.
Internal compart-ment	The body will usually need to have an internal compartment that can house and support an electrical circuit or motor, batteries, and possibly mechanisms to support movement. Internal components need to be visible to an assessor, for example, via a door in the body, or via an opening in the reverse side of the body.
Moving parts	Moving parts will usually be activated via one or more mechanisms connected to a small electric motor, and supported by the main body.
Internal limit switches	Limit switches in conjunction with an appropriate electronic circuit will be required to stop or reverse a movement when the movement reaches its desired end point.
Light or sound outputs	Projects often have bulbs or LEDs that light up under certain conditions, or a buzzer that sounds under certain conditions.
Sensor circuits	Projects often require an electronic circuit that will detect light/darkness, temperature, wetness, or the proximity (closeness) of an object, and activate an output, e.g. lights or buzzers, as a result.
Timer circuit	Sometimes there is a requirement to activate something (a light or a buzzer or a movement) after a certain amount of time has elapsed. This can be done using a timer circuit.
Switches	If the project is electrically powered, there should be at least one switch on the outside of the device to turn it on, or to activate certain parts of the functionality as required. The switches should be labelled as to their function.
DC input voltage	Projects that are electrically-powered should be powered by a DC voltage that is no higher than 12 volts. For stand-alone use, the project can be powered by a battery, which is held in a battery holder attached inside the body. When using and testing the project in the technology room, there should be a means to connect the project to an external DC power supply available in the technology room, e.g. via longer wires and crocodile clips. The voltage that is required to power the project should be labelled on the project itself, and noted in the project folder.

Choosing a project brief

For your Junior Cycle technology project, you will be given a choice of 5 or 6 project briefs. Discuss the choice of project brief with your teacher. Consider the different options carefully before choosing.

Your project folder

The best way to execute your project is to fill in your project folder as you go along. Do not leave the project folder until the end. The project folder is designed to help you. It has sections in it that are designed to guide you (along with this book) to include the information that you will need in order to design and build a good project.

Project folder structure

The diagram below shows the different sections in the project folder that you need to fill in. There are four design-related sections, and four manufacturing-related sections.

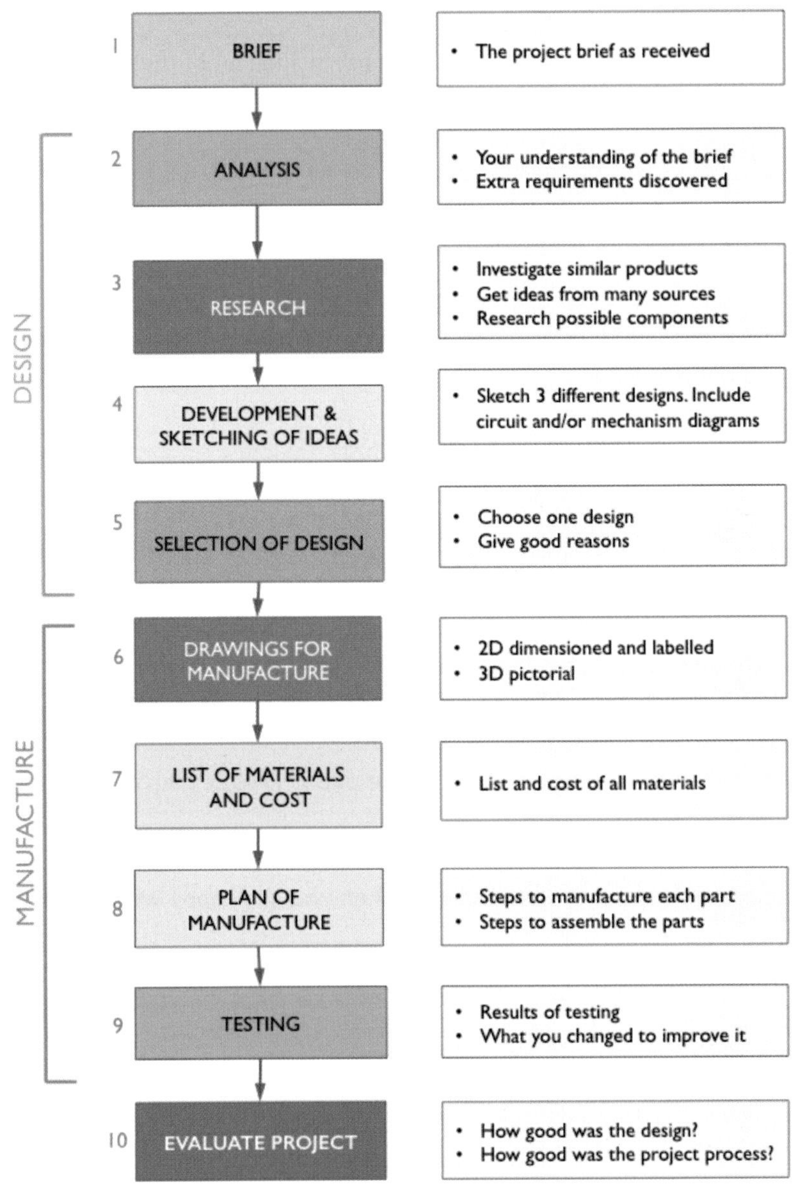

Project folder format and examples

Your project folder should be neatly typed and laid out in A4 format. It should contain plenty of pictures and be bound with a cover.

A Microsoft Word template of a Junior Cycle project folder is available to download on the website of the publisher of this book www.goldenkey.ie.

As well as the samples provided in this chapter, you should look at model project folders, i.e. those from previous projects that have been completed to a high standard. Your teacher will have some of these and will show them to you.

The sample design folios on the T4 website (Department of Education's support site for teachers of technical subjects) are also worth examining. These will give you a good idea of the type of content, layout, drawings and photos required.

Structure of project folder

The structure of the project folder consists of a number of sections. You must include all of these in the folder.

Note on the sample content provided

There is not enough space in this book to provide a complete project folder but this chapter contains examples of the sorts of information that you might include.

Your folder should contain information that is specific to your project, i.e. your research, designs, drawings, testing, and the challenges that you met and overcame, etc.

Note that your project folder should contain lots of drawings and photos, more than are shown here. You will get a good idea of the number and quality of images and drawings required by looking at model project folders.

Drafting material for each section

Draft all the material for each section. Continue until you are happy with the content and length of it. Make sure that you have enough material and that it is easy to read and understand.

Check that you are satisfied with your sketches and drawings, and select the photo images that you want to use.

Ask your teacher to review what you plan to put in your project folder. When you are happy with it, type it up and transfer it to the relevant section.

How to complete your project folder sections

Section 1 - Brief

For your Junior Cycle project, type in the full text of your chosen project brief as provided in the "Design task" document from the Department of Education. If your project is a practice project, write in the project brief that was provided by your teacher.

Olympic Games display: example of a "Brief" section

Design and make an animated display/diorama for the window of a sports shop to represent the activities of at least one event in the 2016 Rio Olympic Games. The display should be electro-mechanical in operation and should attract the attention of passers-by. *Note: A diorama is a model representing a scene.*

Section 2 - Analysis

Make sure to read the "Design process" section of the "Design and manufacture" chapter before completing this section.

Purpose of the analysis section

In this section, you are trying to gain a better understanding of what the project needs to be, or could be, before you start designing anything. If you carry out the analysis thoroughly, you will end up with better designs, and save time. Re-read the project brief and make sure you understand all the words in it.

Possible questions

The table below provides examples of the sorts of questions that you can ask yourself about the project brief. You can include more questions of your own. The answers to the questions will provide you with further information about your project. You should write down all of this and file it in your project folder.

Analysis area	Example questions
Users	Who will the users of the artefact be? What will they be using it for? What is their age group? What do they need from the artefact? What features would they like? What would help them?
Functionality and dimensions	What does the project need to do? How does the product need to move, measure or indicate things? Are there important dimensions to work out and write down? What size and weight does it need to be? What other weights or sizes might it need to hold or contain? How would the user operate it?
Appearance	How important are the aesthetics, i.e. how the artefact looks and feels? Consider the colours, the shapes, the surface finishes, and the feel of it. Does it need to look like other objects? Does it need to be a fun item, with shapes and colours? Does it need to advertise something and therefore have a logo or words on it? Are there any special requirements regarding the type of surface finishes that should be used?

Analysis area	Example questions
Safety	What kind of things could be dangerous with this type of project? What kinds of safety features may be needed to make it safer?
Environment	Where will the model be used? Will it be outdoors? Are there additional requirements arising from the location where it will be used? How can this product be made as environmentally friendly and sustainable as possible? What features might make it more environmentally friendly?
Manufacturing and cost constraints	Is it possible to make this kind of project with the resources available in the technology room? Might special items be needed? How much would this cost to build? How much money is available for you to spend on this?
Time constraints	How much time is available to carry out all the stages of this project? What is the deadline for completion of the project?

Filling out the analysis section in your project folder

Now that you have gained a greater understanding of, and further information about your project brief, it is time to fill out the analysis section of the project folder. Write out your understanding of the project brief in your own words, adding any extra information that you have uncovered. An example of a completed analysis section is given below.

Olympic Games display: example of an "Analysis" section

Include a short background description here if it helps to explain how you came up with the summary points below.

Analysis of the project brief: requirements and constraints for the Olympic Games display

- Dimensions: The Olympic Games display should fit in a shop window, e.g. either on the window ledge, or be supported by a stand behind the window. The display cannot be deep or it may not fit in a shop window. Also, the display cannot be very wide, because the store may want to have other items displayed in their shop window.
- The display should attract attention from people passing by the window outside.
- The display will need to have one or more moving parts. The moving parts will need to be operated by a motor powered by a battery or power supply.
- The display should not require a user to operate it. The user should just be able to turn it on and leave it running.
- The user should be able to turn the display on and off from the back.
- The parts should move continuously while it is turned on, to attract attention.
- Because it is in a shop window, the project primarily needs to function as a display when viewed from the front. It doesn't necessarily need to function as a display when viewed from the rear.
- Passers-by ideally shouldn't be able to see the motor and the internal mechanisms.
- The display should be sturdy and reliable, as it will need to operate for long periods.
- The display needs to highlight at least one of the Olympic sports. This means some parts of the display needs to be shaped like athletes engaged in that sport, and/or like some of the objects that are used in that sport.
- The display should probably have the Olympic logo on it, as it is a very recognizable symbol.

Olympic Games display: example of an "Analysis" section

- The parts of the display should move in a way that is typical for the chosen sport.
- The display should be safe, so ideally should have no sharp edges. Fast-moving parts should have guards around them.
- I don't think the body or base of the display should move, it should stay securely in one position in the window, for safety and stability. Only the parts on the display should move.
- The display should have an attractive surface finish, as it is for display.
- The display should be brightly and attractively coloured to attract attention.
- The display does not necessarily need to have built-in lights.
- The user should ideally be able to clean the device easily, as it will get dusty in the shop window.
- There are no particular requirements on what materials the display needs to be made out of, except that it needs to be strong and reliable, because it will be operating for long periods in the window.
- I need to be able to make this product from the materials available in the technology room.
- I need to complete this project in 5 months.

Project plan

As part of your analysis, you should also produce a project plan. Estimate how much time it will take you to complete each stage of the project and each section of the project folder. Ask your teacher for help with this. As you work on your project each week, check to see how you are progressing against your plan, and update the plan as needed. This will help you get your project completed on time.

Section 3 – Research and investigation of existing solutions

In this stage, you are trying to get more ideas and information about where your kind of project has been done before.

Research process

Sources of information include: the Internet, libraries, books and magazines. You could visit shops and other places where similar items can be found. Speaking to, or carrying out a survey of people with experience in this area, especially users (or those who will benefit from your project), can be very valuable.

Find similar products, and evaluate how well they work. Take similar products apart to see how they are designed and put together.

Note that you are researching all aspects of the project, e.g. materials, features, surface finishes, movements, mechanisms and electrical circuits that could be used.

Recording the results of the research

Write down the types of research you carried out, and most importantly what you learned from it. Write down how your research affected your thinking about how the project should be designed. For example: what new ideas did you get from your research? Did your research steer you towards particular designs, and why? Did your research steer you away from other designs, and why?

For each research area, include pictures of the items that influenced you.

Olympic Games display: example of a "Research" section

Research for the Olympic Games display

For this project I carried out the following research and learned the following things.

Customer research: visits to sports shops

I visited my local sports shop and two major sports stores. I talked to the store managers about what they would like to see in an Olympic Games display, if it were displaying in their shop window. From these visits, I learned:

- The display should ideally be no more than 20 cm deep to fit in the window, and should have a flat base.
- Any movement by the display is limited by the amount of space in the window area. The movement should be mostly be parallel to the window, and not so much from front-to-back.
- The shop owners would like to see athletic events featured, as they think they are typical of the Olympic Games and these events are in keeping with common running products that they sell in their shops.
- They think the display should have the Olympic logo.
- They think that lighting on the display is unnecessary as the unit will be displayed in summer, and would not be left plugged in overnight.

Design research: searches on the Internet

- Most Olympic displays that I found contain the Olympic symbol.
- I couldn't find much on the Internet about student Olympic Games displays.

Design research: survey

I spoke to my parents and friends and they suggested different events like running, basketball, high jump, long jump, javelin throwing, boxing and sailing. I didn't think swimming was a good idea, as working with water would be difficult, and not so safe. One person suggested highlighting one of the sports that Ireland was competing in, which I thought was a good idea.

Materials research

As the project needs to be sturdy, I thought it might be a good idea to make most of the project out of wood. My technology teacher said we would have plenty of resources to manufacture the display from wood and/or plastics, and a good design could be made from either or both of those materials. He also thought that it would be sufficient to have one Olympic event displayed, i.e. just one action figure.

Mechanisms research

The unit will need to be powered by an electric motor. I researched the kind of mechanisms that I could connect to an electric motor to make different kinds of continuous movements.

Olympic Games display: example of a "Research" section

As a result of this, I would consider using the following:

- Cam-and-follower – to change the rotary motion of the motor into a reciprocating motion.
- Crank-and-slider – to create reciprocating motion.
- Peg-and-slot – to create oscillating motion.
- Belt drive - to create a rotary motion at a distance from the motor.
- Worm drive - to reduce the speed of the motor, and to create greater output torque to move the display arm, which could be heavy if made from wood.

I could use other mechanisms like a rack and pinion, but then I would have to continuously reverse the direction of the motor using limit switches and this might not be reliable if the display was running for a long time.

(In your project folder, insert photos of these mechanisms and a small electric motor.)

Section 4 - Development and sketching of ideas

This is where you sketch three different possible designs for your project brief.

Design process

Design ideas should be guided by the information that you gathered in the analysis and research stages. Try out many different design ideas. Use rough hand sketches to begin with. Don't put design sketches in your project folder yet. Once you start sketching, other ideas will come to you. Think about the shape of the body, the type of movement, mechanisms and electrical functions that could satisfy the requirements that you wrote down in the analysis section.

Try brainstorming with your friends to get more ideas. Look at the "Mechanisms", "Electronic circuits", "Assembling projects" and "Design and manufacture" chapters in this book. Discuss your ideas with your teacher. If a particular design idea doesn't seem to be working out, try a different idea.

Speed and gear calculations

If you are planning to use a motor to create motion, you will probably need to calculate the type, number and size of gears that you will need in order to reduce the speed of the motor. Ask your teacher for help on the speed of the motor.

Prototypes/mock-ups

It can be helpful to make a cardboard model of a design or part of it and/or to build some of the main mechanisms, which you can operate by hand. If you do this, take photos and include this information in this section. It is also useful to ask others what they think of your design ideas at this stage.

Document your designs in the project folder

When you have three design ideas that you are happy with, you should document these in your project folder.

Provide a brief description of each design, and provide a good (ideally 3D) labelled sketch. You may need more than one 3D or 2D drawing to show the design idea fully. Cut-away drawings can be very useful to show internal mechanisms. You don't need to show dimensions or developments at this stage. The sample below shows one design idea for the Olympic Display. Each design idea must include a circuit or mechanism, or both, that could be used as part of the design. You will lose marks if you leave these out.

Olympic Games display: example of a "Development and sketching of ideas" section

Design idea A: Javelin thrower

The sketch shows design idea A for the Olympic Games display – a javelin thrower. The javelin will move back and forward to attract attention. The Olympic Games logo will be shown on the front of the back panel. The display will be brightly painted, and the Olympic Games logo will be painted in the Olympic logo colours.

The base, back panel and javelin thrower body will be made from wood. The javelin will be made from light brightly-coloured plastic and it will not have any sharp points for safety reasons.

There will be space within the base for the mechanisms and motor, which can be attached to the underside of the base. The motor and mechanisms can be seen from the rear of the display. There will be a switch mounted on the rear of the unit to turn on the display.

The thrower's arm rotates around a swivel pin. The throwing arm is connected via a rod through a slot in the base to a crank axle, which is connected via a set of gears to a small electric motor. As the motor turns, the crank moves the arm up and down in a reciprocating motion, which makes it look like the model athlete is throwing the javelin.

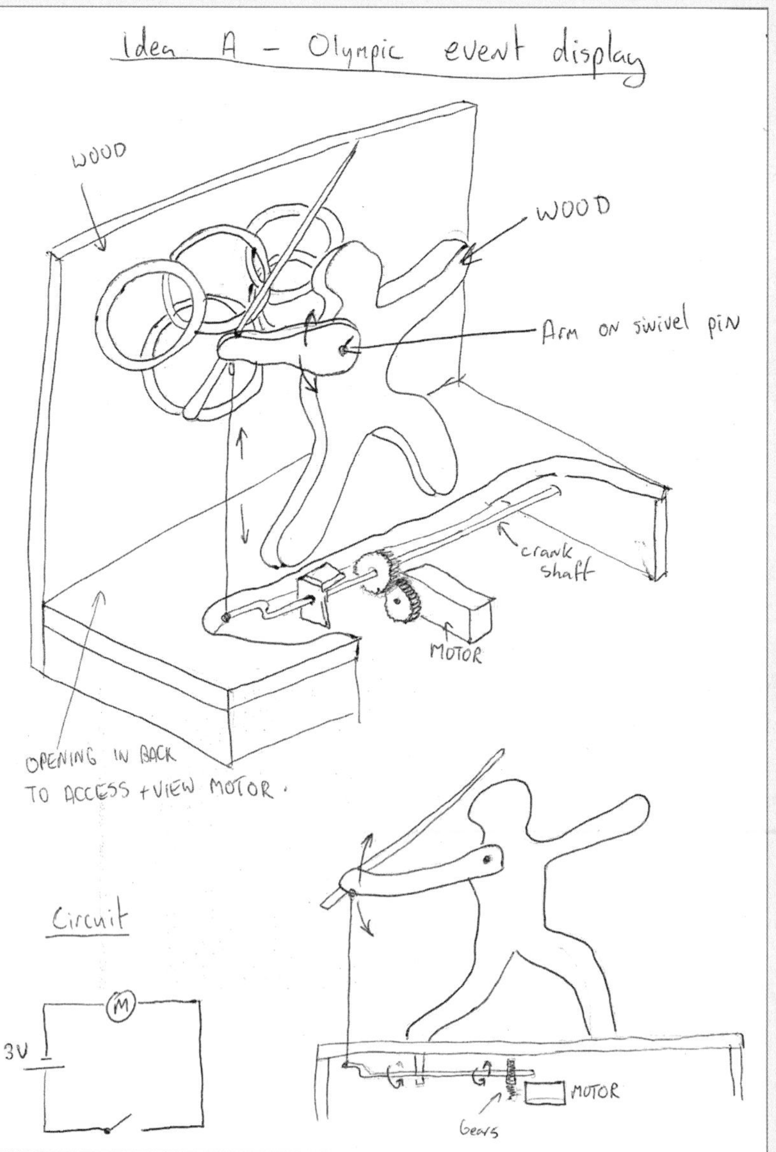

(Include two additional design ideas in this section, e.g. a rower or a runner.)

Section 5 - Selection and justification of solution

At this stage of the project you must decide which of your three designs is going to go forward to the manufacturing stage. However, you will need to justify your choice and explain why your chosen design is the most suitable. To justify your choice, you will need to refer back to the requirements for the project that you wrote out in the analysis section, and show that your chosen design is the one that best meets those requirements.

To help you decide which design is the best, and before you fill in the project folder, make out a list of the advantages and disadvantages of each design, in terms of how well each one meets the requirements. When you are happy with your choice and reasons, write up this section in the project folder.

Olympic Games display: example of a "Selection of solution" section

Selection of solution for Olympic Games display

I compared each of my three designs to the project brief and to the requirements in the analysis section.

I chose design idea A, the javelin thrower, for the following reasons:

- The javelin thrower meets the project brief and all the requirements listed in the analysis section.
- It has a solid base, limited movement, no sudden movements, and will be sturdy.
- It has a simple way of making continuous motion, which will be reliable and attract attention.
- The javelin-throwing action won't be very realistic but it will be effective and eye-catching.
- I can manufacture it from components, materials and tools that are available in the technology room.
- I can give it a smooth surface finish and paint it to provide an attractive finish for a display.
- I could make the Olympic rings from overlapping rings of acrylic so it will look even better.

If the javelin is found to be a little unsafe after manufacture, it can easily be shielded with a transparent perpex/acrylic shield.

I ruled out the other two designs, the runner and the rower, for the following reasons:

- The runner design requires more complex mechanisms to create the running action, and it needs the body of the runner to be suspended while the legs move. It would be more difficult to get to work, and it might not be possible to achieve a good-looking running action. This means that this design might not function well as a display for a sports shop. As there are more risks with this design, I decided not to go forward with it.
- The rower design came in second place. It could look very well and be impressive. It could use similar mechanisms to make the back-and-forth reciprocating motion of the rowing.

  However, the body of the rower is more complex and would take longer to make and to get functioning correctly with movable joints etc. Also, to show a more realistic rowing action, the rowing seat would need to slide back-and-forth with the rower, and this would require further mechanisms, such as linkages or another cam and slider.

  More of the internal mechanisms might be visible to passers-by. As the rower is a sliding design, it would require lubrication to work properly. The rower would probably not be able to operate for long periods like the simpler javelin thrower design.

From this process, I learned that simpler designs are often better than more complicated ones.

Section 6 - Drawings for manufacture

Now that you have chosen your design, it is time to specify in detail how to manufacture it. The first part of this process is to draw up accurate drawings for manufacture. This section should include the types of drawings described in the table below.

Drawing type	Description
Body component drawings	2D drawings (orthographic projections) or developments of the component parts that you will need to cut out and shape in order to make the various parts of the body structure. Each part should be drawn to scale and the required dimensions for each length and curve should be shown. The locations and dimensions of any cut-outs are required. Drawings should be labelled and include dimensions. Specify the material that the part is made from, and show any bend lines required.
Assembly drawings	2D or 3D drawings to show how the different parts of the body and the various mechanisms and electrical components all fit together. To do this, you may need to show drawings from different angles, or with one of the body panels removed, or use a cut-away drawing. You may need to show positions of joining components like dowels, screws, brackets and nails. Include labels and dimensions on these drawings too.
Circuit diagrams	Electronic circuit diagrams for the electric circuits in the project. Also if the wiring is complex, wiring diagrams, showing how to physically connect the physical devices together with wire, should be included.
Final product sketch	A 3D pictorial drawing of how the finished product should look. This drawing should be in colour.

First carry out some practice drawings, so that you can get them right, and then select which drawings to transfer to your project folder.

Section 7 – List of materials and costs

In this section you must list all the component parts that you will need to manufacture and assemble your project, and their costs. Include all the main parts, electrical and mechanical components, and parts used for joining and finishing. Include dimensions for main parts.

For prices, look up reference catalogues and ask your teacher for help.

Calculate a total cost for the:

- Body components.
- Assembly components.
- Project as a whole.

Tables are a good way to present this information.

Olympic Games display: example of a "List of materials and costs"

Body components

Part name	Material	Height	Width	Thickness	Number	Cost
Back panel	Plywood	30 cm	40 cm	9 mm	1	€1.00
Base panel	Plywood	20 cm	40 cm	9 mm	1	€0.80
Side panel	Plywood	5 cm	20 cm	15 mm	2	€0.40
Front panel	Plywood	5 cm	40 cm	15 mm	1	€0.20
Athlete	Plywood	30 cm	20 cm	9 mm	1	€0.80
Olympic Rings	Acrylic	Outer diameter 10 cm, inner 8.5 cm		3 mm	5	€3.00
Javelin	Nylon rod		20 cm	2 mm	1	€0.50
				Total body cost		**€6.70**

Assembly components (mechanical, electrical, joining, finishing)

Item	Cost
Electric motor	€3.00
Nylon gears	€1.00
Axles, rods	€0.50
Joining pins	€0.50
Glue	€0.50
Screws	€0.10
Brackets	€0.50
Paint	€0.50
Total	**€6.60**

Total project materials cost	**€12.90**

Section 8 - Plan of manufacture

In this section, list all the steps required to manufacture each part, and the steps to assemble and finish all of the components. Group the steps into sections to make it clear. List the tools needed.

Olympic Games display: example of a "Plan of manufacture" section

Tools and materials needed: Bandsaw, drill, coping saw, file, bradawl, sandpaper, hammer, screwdriver, rivet gun, soldering iron, nails, pop rivets, gear grub screw, solder, wire, wood glue, Tensol cement, Super Glue, clamps, and paintbrush.

Steps to manufacture and assemble the body parts

1. Mark out the dimensions required, and cut the wooden base and back panel to size, using a bandsaw.
2. Sand with sandpaper to provide smooth surfaces.
3. Mark out the location of the slot on the base unit. Choose a drill bit that is the diameter of the slot and drill a hole at either end of the slot. Unhook the blade of the coping saw and pass through the hole, re-attach the blade, and cut out the slot using the coping saw.
4. Smooth out the slot with a straight file and a round file.
5. Assemble the base and side supports using wood glue and nails. Leave to set.
6. Assemble the back panel to the base unit using glue and wood screws. Create holes for the screws first using a bradawl. Leave to set.
7. Cut out the shape of the athlete's body and arm from the rectangle of plywood using a fretsaw. Sand smooth.
8. Attach the athlete's body to the base of the unit in the correct position relative to the slot, using the two small metal brackets and wood screws.
9. Drill an appropriately-sized hole in the athlete's shoulder and arm.
10. Apply a wood primer to the wooden base and athlete's body, and to the athlete's arm, and allow to dry.
11. Sand with a fine sandpaper.
12. Paint the assembled unit and athlete's body and arm in attractive colours. Leave to dry.
13. Attach the athlete's arm to the athlete's body and allow it to pivot using a pop rivet. Add additional space using cardboard and then remove the cardboard.
14. Glue the acrylic rings to each other to form the Olympic logo using Tensol cement. Leave to set.
15. Glue the Olympic logo to the back panel using Super Glue. Hold in place by turning the unit on its back.

Steps to assemble the mechanical and electrical components

1. Drill holes through the blocks of wood used as the axle/crank supports.
2. Bend the axle at one end using a vice and pliers to create a crank. Keep the remainder of the axle straight.
3. Thread the axle and gear through the axle supports. Tighten the gear on the axle using the gear grub screw.

Olympic Games display: example of a "Plan of manufacture" section

4. Attach the axle supports to the underside of the base using small brackets and small woodscrews, so that the crank is underneath the slot. Test that the crank can rotate underneath the slot.
5. Connect the crank to the athlete's arm using the connecting wire rod, with loops at either end.
6. Prevent the wire loop falling off the crank by using quick-setting cement on either side.
7. Test that the athlete's arm moves by turning the gear underneath the base. Adjust as required.
8. Line up the motor so that its output worm gear engages with the axle gear, and secure the motor to the underside of the base using wood screws through the holes in the motor holder.
9. Mount the battery holder to the underside of the base using screws.
10. Mount the on/off switch to the underside of the base so that the switch lever protrudes out of the rear of the unit.
11. Connect the motor to the switch and to the connection points on the battery holder using wire and solder.
12. Solder long wires to the connection points on the battery holder so that the display can be connected to a remote power supply.
13. Write 6 V on a label and stick it on the rear of the unit near the power switch.
14. Label the switch to show which way is on, and which way is off.
15. Connect the power supply at the correct voltage and turn on the switch.

Section 9 - Testing

In this section, write down the tests that you carried out on your project, what the results of those tests were, and what you did to improve things. It is normal for some things to go wrong and to require improvement. The important thing is to write down what you tested, noticed, and improved.

To test your project fully, look back at the list of requirements that you wrote in the analysis section and check that your completed project satisfies them.

As part of testing, you will often need to create or simulate the environment that your project needs to work in. For example, if your project is supposed to do something when it gets dark, you must test this by making the room dark or by covering the sensor. If it needs to measure water levels, you must create different water levels. If it needs to measure wind, you'll need to supply wind etc. If your project is supposed to work outdoors, you should check that it tolerates getting wet. Take photos of any testing environments that you set up and add them to your folder.

Test as soon as you can, i.e. test each part or sub-assembly as you go along. Don't wait until the end. Also, ask other people to test your product. Their feedback will be useful.

Olympic Games display: example of a "Testing" section

Testing the Olympic Games display

When testing functionality (moving the javelin):

- I attached the arm to the javelin throwers body and tested it to see if it could rotate freely. It was a bit stiff, so I applied some Vaseline between the moving parts, which freed it.
- I turned the crank initially, it was too large, and hit off the base of the unit. I took it out again and made it smaller.
- I connected the crank to the arm and tested that turning the crank would cause the arm to move in a reciprocating way. It didn't work initially. It got stuck at the bottom and top. I had to change the way that the rod connected to the arm so that it would work more freely. I also had to make the rod longer so that the javelin looked more realistic.
- I tested turning on the motor. The gear slipped a little so I had to move the motor closer. Also the javelin was moving too fast so I had to use a larger gear to reduce the speed more.
- The switch at the back worked well, as designed.

When testing aesthetics and other requirements:

- I tested the look of the display myself, by asking my friends, and also by showing photos of the display to the sports store managers that I spoke to during the research phase.

The results were as follows:

- The coloured acrylic rings looked very striking and professional.
- The athlete didn't stand out as well as it could against the background, so I painted him in different colours. I also added some red hair.
- The display would fit well in a display window. It was quite eye-catching, even though the range of movement was quite small.
- People felt that if it were taller it would be more eye-catching as it would come up to the line of sight of passers-by.
- The testers felt that the unit was safe, and easy to operate.

Evaluate project

In this section, evaluate your design and the overall process that you used to carry out your project. Write down what worked well, and what you would do differently if you were to do the project again.

Olympic Games display: example of an "Evaluate project" section

Design evaluation

What worked well:

- The design satisfied the project brief and all the analysis requirements.
- It was eye-catching.
- It functioned well, and it could operate reliably for a long time in a shop window.
- The sports store managers liked it.

Olympic Games display: example of an "Evaluate project" section

What could be improved:

- The display would be more eye-catching if it were larger and especially if it were taller.
- The display moved too quickly. I could have built in a variable resistor to allow the speed of the motor to be adjusted.
- It was a bit noisy and a little jerky. A smoother mechanism could be used to move the arm.

Manufacture evaluation

What worked well:

- The wooden painted body was a good choice because it was easy to manufacture using very common materials and tools. It made a strong and solid structure, and it looked good.
- Purchasing acrylic rings and assembling the Olympic logo from them, was a good idea. The material looked great, and also it would have been difficult to manufacture perfect circles. It was a good compromise between bought components and made components.

What could be improved:

- Assembling the mechanical parts was very time consuming and I had to move things and do things several times to get the dimensions and connections right so that it would work. More research on mechanisms and more detailed manufacturing drawings would have helped.

Evaluation of the process I used for the project

What worked well:

- Overall the project was completed on time, it fulfilled the brief, and I got my project folder completed nicely, so I am pleased.
- It was well worth spending quite a bit of time on the analysis and research stages of the project. I got a lot of ideas from that, and it led to a good design. I was glad that I didn't rush into trying to design something quickly.

What could be improved next time:

- The manufacturing and assembly tasks took a lot more time than I had planned. I should have allocated more time to these tasks.
- The completion of the project folder also took a lot more time than I had intended. I should have completed more of the project folder as I went along, and allocated more time at the end of the project for tidying up the folder.
- I should have discussed the progress of my project with my technology teacher more often, so that I could get more advice on what I had done already, what I should do next, and how long I should spend on each stage of the project.

Project checklists

Project folder checklist

Review the following key points to ensure you have the main items covered in your project folder.

Key points for project folder

1. Is the folder attractively presented, typed, with neat layout, good use of diagrams, sketches and photographs?
2. Have you analysed the brief to understand what is required? Did you ask yourself questions about the project brief, and write out a list of the requirements and constraints?
3. Did you research existing solutions and materials and components that you could use? Have you written up what you learned?
4. Have you included 2D and 3D sketches of three design ideas?
5. Did you explain why you chose your final design? Did you give good reasons for choosing one design over the other possible designs?
6. Have you included good-quality sketches and drawings for manufacturing and assembling, including circuit diagrams?
7. Did you produce a comprehensive list of the parts needed and their cost?
8. Did you list all the steps required to manufacture all the components, assemble the components, and finish off the surfaces?
9. Have you described how you tested the project, and what you found? Have you described what you changed to improve things?
10. Did you evaluate the design and manufactured item against the brief and the requirements for the project? Did you evaluate the overall process you used for the project? Did you write down what worked well, and what you would do differently if you did it again?

Design and manufacture checklist

Review the key points below to check the quality of your design and your built item.

Key points for design and manufacture

1. Do the design and the built item satisfy the brief?
2. Are the design and the built item attractive and well-presented?
3. Is there good use of shape and colour?
4. Were appropriate materials chosen?
5. Does it function as required? How well does it function?
6. How inventive is the design?
7. How well was safety considered?
8. Are internal components visible?
9. Is there appropriate use of electrical and mechanical components?
10. Were appropriate processes used for manufacturing and assembling the product?
11. Is there a high quality of manufacture, including the standard of finishes?
12. Does it demonstrate an appropriate level and range of skills and technical competency?
13. Is there an appropriate use of commercially available components or sub-assemblies (i.e. not too many)?

Test yourself

1. What is the purpose of the analysis section of the project folder? What should you write in it?
2. How many different design ideas should you sketch in your project folder?
3. What kind of information should be in the research section of your project folder?
4. What is the difference between testing your product, and evaluating your project?

Photos from previous Junior Cycle technology projects

Model of a frog on a lily pond

In this project, the frog's mouth moves up and down via a cam-and-follower mechanism. The fly moves from side-to-side using a peg-and-slot mechanism. The wooden frog sits on a shiny green water lily made from acrylic. The body is painted blue to suggest water.

Pet grooming table

A screw mechanism raises and lowers the table. Limit switches stop the motor when the table gets to the top and bottom of its travel.

Olympic cyclist

A chain and sprocket mechanism is used to make sure the front wheel, back wheel and pedals all turn in the same direction. The cyclist's legs are hinged and its feet are hinged to an acrylic disk to make them go around.

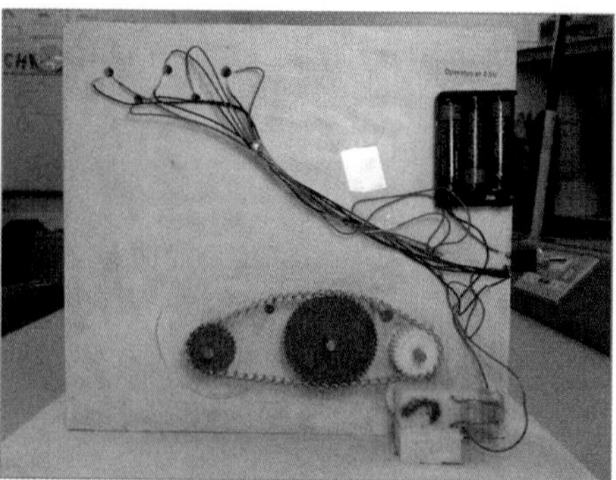

Model house with garden gate

The photo shows a project under construction with a gear mechanism to turn the gate. Limit switches will detect the fully-open and fully-closed positions and stop the motor.

A removable wooden front cover for the base unit attaches with Velcro.

Olympic Games display with tennis player

In this project, an electrically-turned crank mechanism moves a tennis player's arm up and down.

Project subassemblies

A rotating vertical shaft with gears and motor

Belt/pulley drive for hoisting a flag

	Chapter	Image title	Source
1	Technology and society	WEEE Ireland logo	Weee.ie
2	Inventions and discoveries	USS Holland	Chief of US Naval Operations, Wikipedia
		Stephanie Kwolek	Invention.si.edu
4	Drawing and visual communication	Javelin thrower	Paul McCarthy, Loreto Balbriggan
5	Materials	Red deal; white deal	Tree Council of Ireland
		Sheets of acrylic	Choudhary Plastics
6	Safety	Safety visor	Plmg.tradeindia.com
		Fume mask	Images.lowes.com
7	Tools	Scriber	Toolstop.co.uk
		Inside calipers	Toolstop.co.uk
		Marking knife	Toolstop.co.uk
		Bench stop	Gianteaglessupply.com
		Bench hook	Axminster.co.uk
		Bending machine	Bulldog-uk.com
		Vacuum forming	Grupoimpacto.ind.br
8	Manufacturing processes	Vacuum forming	Grupoimpacto.ind.br
		Bending metal in a vice	BBC Bitesize
9	Structures and forces	Diagram of beam	Spindustrious, Wikimediacommons
11	Mechanisms 2	Worm gear winch	Sens.com
12	Energy	Sellafield nuclear power station	Greenpeace, Nick Cobbing
14	Electronic components	Tilt switch	Oakbluffclassifieds.com
19	Automation and robotics	Basic hydraulic system	Defensivedriving.com
		Using a teach pendant with a robot	Mfgnewseb.com
20	Assembling projects	Wooden casing for technology project	Alexandra Chircu, Loreto Secondary School, Balbriggan
		Plastic spacers	Aliexpress.com
22	Your technology projects	Javelin thrower	Paul McCarthy, Loreto Balbriggan
		Frog on a lily pond	Alexandra Chircu, Loreto Balbriggan
		Pet grooming table	Naomi Rodgers, Loreto Balbriggan
		Model house with garden gate	Róisín Flynn, Loreto Balbriggan
		Olympic cyclist	Sophie Weldon
		Olympic Games display with tennis player	Méibh O'Sullivan, Loreto Balbriggan
		Project subassembly with gears and motor	Róisín Flynn, Loreto Balbriggan
		Project subassembly with belt and pulley drive	Leianisha Behal

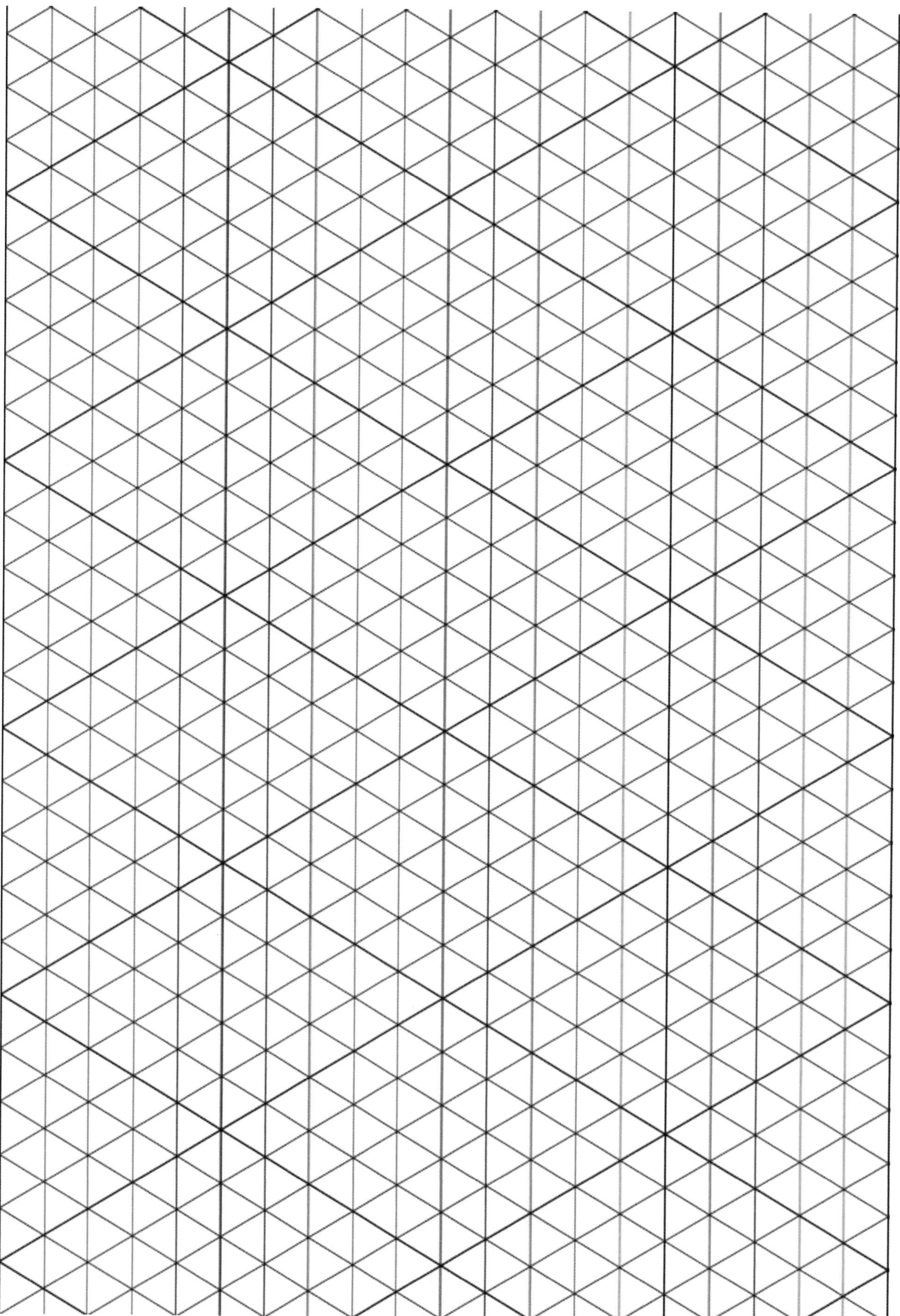

1. A working model of an electro-mechanically-controlled dumb waiter operating between two floors.
2. A working model of a gate that automatically closes at nightfall.
3. A flagstaff that raises a flag automatically in the morning and lowers it automatically at night.
4. A pet-grooming table where the height of the table can be adjusted electro-mechanically.
5. A working model of an environmentally-friendly garden shelter, that can be electro-mechanically rotated on its own axis as desired by the user, and which will illuminate automatically at nightfall.
6. A domestic photovoltaic cell (PV) that can be rotated and tilted so that it faces the sun. One of these movements must be electro-mechanical and must include limit switching.
7. A ventilation control system that opens or closes an air vent as the room temperature rises or falls.
8. A chair/seat where the height can be adjusted electro-mechanically, but only when the user is seated.
9. A wind vane with a remote electronic wind direction display (wireless display not required).
10. A monorail transport system to move people from one airport terminal to another.
11. A wind-powered whirligig that depicts a novelty scene that illuminates automatically at night.
12. A walking aid for the elderly or infirm, which has a compartment to hold items and a lighting system for night use.
13. A novelty cooling fan for a wind turbine company, which switches on and off automatically in response to the surrounding temperature.
14. An all-weather wild bird feeding station that indicates electronically that a bird is feeding.
15. A model of a basketball hoop where the height of the hoop can be adjusted electro-mechanically.
16. An animated window display to advertise an upcoming rock festival or concert.
17. An electro-mechanical canopy that will cover plants when the temperature drops and retract when the temperature rises.
18. A revolving jewellery tree with a built-in lighting system that switches on automatically in darkness.
19. An electro-mechanical paper towel dispenser, which allows for refilling of the dispenser.
20. A lightweight structure/enclosure that could be used to host an event at the Olympic Games, which incorporates an automatic lighting system to enhance the appearance of the structure at night.
21. A novelty toothbrush holder, which incorporates a timer and suitable output, to indicate that a child has brushed his/her teeth for a sufficient period of time.
22. An electro-mechanical golf trolley with a means of controlling the speed of the trolley.
23. A model of a show-jumping fence where the height of the fence can be adjusted electro-mechanically.
24. An electronic high-visibility unit that can be attached to a bicycle to make it safer at night.
25. A novelty water fountain for a playschool. The pump should only activate when the water level in the reservoir is sufficiently high, and should switch off if the water drops to a low level.
26. A working model of a swing bridge to allow boats to travel up and down a river. The bridge should stop automatically when it reaches its open and its closed limits.
27. A motorised toy vehicle capable of travelling over rough terrain, which can be controlled electro-mechanically by the operator.
28. A motorised mobile suitable for a child's playroom which incorporates either:
    - A light that switches on automatically at night or
    - A timer circuit that controls the period for which the motor operates.
29. A hand-held game to amuse children and/or adults on long journeys.
30. A working model of an electro-mechanically controlled data projector screen, which stops automatically at its top and bottom limits.
31. A bedside tidy, which incorporates a mobile phone holder, a clock, and a small light that activates automatically in darkness.

32. A working model of a vehicle warning system that alerts a driver if his vehicle is too high to pass under a bridge. The system should be mounted on a gantry and be highly visible to the driver.
33. An electro-mechanical hand nail dryer. The device must switch on automatically when a hand is placed in position and switch off when the hand is removed.
34. An electronic water level gauge that will indicate at least two different levels of water in a tank. All electronics must be suitably housed and the design should include a means of attachment to the tank.
35. A turnstile that counts the number of people that have passed through it. The counter must be capable of being reset. The counting may be either decimal or binary.
36. An electro-mechanically-controlled security bollard that can be raised and lowered to prevent illegal parking in a restricted zone.
37. An animated scaled-down display for a movie of your choice for the foyer of a cinema.
38. A model of a motorised display of a car manufacturer's logo, which illuminates automatically at night.
39. A door for a chicken coop that will automatically open in the morning and close at night.
40. A working model of a wind generator that powers a small electrical system.
41. A working model of a buggy that automatically executes an avoidance routine when it comes close to, or bumps into, an object.
42. A water-traversing vehicle which will automatically propel itself when it is placed in water.
43. A model of a car trailer and a system which can tip the trailer without removing it from the car.
44. A working model of a road vehicle which can be both solar-powered and also powered by a battery.
45. A game which has an integrated electronic feature.
46. A lightweight bridge structure that spans a distance of 400 mm, and automatically illuminates at night.
47. A computer-controlled card-punching device that will automatically pierce a hole in a piece of card when it is inserted into a slot. The device must pierce the card only once each time the card is inserted.

Notes